DATE DUE

DE 1 2'00			
FE 2'02			
MY 2 0'03			

DEMCO 38-296

Understanding Sport Organizations

The Application of Organization Theory

Trevor Slack, PhD
Professor and Head of School
School of Physical Education, Sport, and Leisure
De Montfort University

Human Kinetics

Library of Congress Cataloging-in-Publication Data

Slack, Trevor, 1948-
    Understanding sport organizations : the application of
organization theory / Trevor Slack.
        p.   cm.
    Includes bibliographical references and index.
    ISBN 0-87322-948-7
    1. Sports administration--Handbooks, manuals, etc.
2. Organizational sociology--Handbooks, manuals, etc.   I. Title.
    GV713.S576   1997
    796'.09'9--dc20   96-26111
                                                         CIP

ISBN: 0-87322-948-7

Copyright © 1997 by Trevor Slack

Acquisitions Editor: Rick Frey, PhD; **Developmental Editor**: Holly Gilly; **Assistant Editor**: Chad Johnson; **Editorial Assistant**: Amy Carnes; **Copyeditor**: Tom Taylor; **Proofreader**: Erin Cler; **Indexer**: Theresa Schaefer; **Graphic Artist**: Sandra Meier; **Graphic Designer**: Judy Henderson; **Photo Editor**: Boyd LaFoon; **Cover Designer**: Jack Davis; **Illustrator**: Studio 2-D; **Printer**: Braun-Brumfield

Printed in the United States of America

10 9 8 7 6 5 4 3 2 1

Human Kinetics
Web site: http://www.humankinetics.com/

United States: Human Kinetics, P.O. Box 5076, Champaign, IL 61825-5076
1-800-747-4457
e-mail: humank@hkusa.com

Canada: Human Kinetics, Box 24040, Windsor, ON N8Y 4Y9
1-800-465-7301 (in Canada only)
e-mail: humank@hkcanada.com

Europe: Human Kinetics, P.O. Box IW14, Leeds LS16 6TR, United Kingdom
(44) 1132 781708
e-mail: humank@hkeurope.com

Australia: Human Kinetics, 57A Price Avenue, Lower Mitcham, South Australia 5062
(08) 277 1555
e-mail: humank@hkaustralia.com

New Zealand: Human Kinetics, P.O. Box 105-231, Auckland 1
(09) 523 3462
e-mail: humank@hknewz.com

Contents

CHAPTER 15   Leadership and Sport Organizations   287

Preface

In the early 1980s, when I began my doctoral studies in the area of sport management, I started to read the books that were being written about this relatively new area of study. Although there were only a few sport management texts at this time, I became increasingly frustrated with those that did exist because, with very few exceptions, they failed to take account of the vast body of literature available in the broader field of management studies. Why, I wondered, did scholars in the field of sport management fail to utilize work from such areas as organizational theory, organizational behavior, strategic management, marketing, the sociology of organizations, finance, and accounting? Don't sport organizations have cultures? Are they not expected to formulate strategies? Are their operations not influenced by technological and contextual changes? And do they not exhibit the same political and decision making processes as other types of organizations? The answer to each of these questions is, obviously, "Yes!".

Over the last 10 to 15 years, however, a number of researchers in our field *have* become increasingly aware of the contribution that the literature from the areas just cited can make to understanding the structure and operations of sport organizations. The formation of the North American Society for Sport Management and the creation of the *Journal of Sport Management* have helped tremendously in this regard. However, despite these advances, a significant amount of the literature in sport management still shows little evidence of being informed by work in the broader field of management studies. *Understanding Sport Organizations: The Application of Organization Theory* is a modest attempt to try to correct this situation.

The particular focus of this text is on the area of organizational theory (and to a lesser extent organizational behavior). It demonstrates how concepts and theories from these fields can be used to inform our understanding of sport organizations and their management. Some of the basic concepts of organizational theory and the way this field of study differs from organizational behavior are outlined in chapter 1. There I also describe some different ways of looking at organizations and how the view sport

managers adopt will influence what they see. In chapter 2 the focus is on the concept of effectiveness, which in many ways is the central problem of the sport manager. I review the major theoretical approaches to understanding effectiveness and show how the concept of effectiveness is paradoxical. Chapters 3 and 4 are devoted to the issues of structure and design. Different types of sport organizations will adopt different structural elements and, hence, different designs. Some designs are more effective for certain types of sport organizations than for others, so I describe how structural elements are patterned into the various design types available. Certain determinants, such as strategy, size, environment, and technology, greatly influence the choice of an organization's design, and those are the topics of chapters 5 through 8. In chapter 9, I take a less deterministic approach and look at power and politics in sport organizations and the role each may play in shaping a sport organization's structure and operations.

Chapters 10 through 13 focus on some of the processes that take place in sport organizations, including managing conflict, implementing change, dealing with human resource issues, and making decisions. For many organizational theorists, issues of culture and leadership are what hold an organization together and provide it with its direction, and they are the topics of the last two chapters of the book.

I've provided numerous examples throughout the book to illustrate the concepts and ideas being discussed. The examples are taken from the wide variety of organizations that collectively make up the sport industry. All examples are from real organizations; in just a few cases the names of the organization or individuals involved have been changed to maintain confidentiality. As of the time of writing, all information about the organizations cited in the text is accurate. However, organizations change over time, and in the future their structure and operations may be different from what I've described.

I've provided several elements in each chapter that will help students bring the theoretical information into the practical realm. In addition, instructors may use the cases that appear at the end of each chapter for class discussion, and may develop questions other than those that accompany the case studies. The utility of several of the cases as topics for discussion is not necessarily limited to the focus of the chapter in which they appear. For example, the case on the Calgary Olympics appears at the end of chapter 2 to raise issues about the effectiveness of organizations, but it also draws attention to issues of power and politics, which are the topics of chapter 9. Similarly, the case at the end of chapter 11 about change at Cannondale also raises questions about the relationship between the size and structure of an organization, the focus of chapter 6. In addition to the cases, the Time Outs that appear throughout the chapters may be used for discussion about how the concepts in the chapters are used in the real world. The questions at the end of the chapters provide students a self-check of their understanding of the material.

Understanding Sport Organizations: The Application of Organization Theory contains a very detailed bibliography that includes citations from articles from the field of sport management as well as references to the organizational/management literature. Citations include articles that have appeared in such major journals as *Organization Studies, Administrative Science Quarterly, Journal of Management Studies, Academy of Management Journal*, and *Academy of Management Review*. References to the seminal works in the field are outlined in each chapter as are more recent articles that have built on these earlier concepts and frameworks. Students and faculty members interested in a particular topic are advised to not rely solely on the summaries found in this text. Return to the original works and search the journals cited and others for more information. The suggestions for further reading at the end of each chapter are merely illustrative and should by no means be considered a definitive listing. I've cited only material that would be available in any reasonably sized university library. I've included very few references to the many unpublished theses that have focused on managerial issues in sport organizations because they are not readily accessible to students and instructors.

I have tried to be conscious of maintaining a gender balance. However, when using quotes I retained the original pronouns. At all other times I have alternately used she and he, him and her. Where possible, I've used examples involving women managers; however, these are not as widely available as examples with male managers. That is something I hope the readers of this text will strive to rectify.

Sport management is an exciting, new, and rapidly growing area of study. It is my hope that this text will assist with this growth and will spotlight for students and instructors the idea that if we are going to realize the potential our field holds, our work must be informed by the ideas and theories found in the broader field of management/organization studies. I welcome any comments on the appropriateness of this text in helping achieve this goal.

Acknowledgments

Anyone who has ever written a book will know that there are many people who make a contribution to the final product. This book is no exception and there are a number of people whom I would like to acknowledge for their help and support. First, I owe a tremendous intellectual debt to my friend and colleague Bob Hinings. Much of what I have learned about organization theory I have learned from Bob. I am also grateful for the support that my colleagues Ann Hall, Tim Burton, and Dave Whitson have given me over the years. Each in their own way has contributed to my intellectual growth and I have enjoyed working with them. I have also been fortunate in attracting an outstanding group of doctoral students to work with—Rob Pitter, Lisa Kikulis, Lucie Thibault, Tim Berrett, John Amis, Laura Cousens, Lloyd Bentz, Dan Mason, Julie Stevens, and Rob Schinke have all been a pleasure to work with, and I hope they have learned as much from me as I have from them. I was fortunate while writing this book to secure a McCalla Research Professorship from the University of Alberta and I thank the Support for the Advancement of Scholarship fund at the university for this award. Writing was also completed while I was a visiting Scholar at the Centre for Corporate Strategy and Change at Warwick Business School. The Centre's Director Andrew Pettigrew and his staff made my stay at Warwick both a highly enjoyable and intellectually stimulating experience. The people at Human Kinetics have been great to work with and particular thanks go to Rainer who first encouraged me to proceed with the book and to Rick, Holly, Amy, and Chad who have all helped in its preparation. Terry Haggerty and Carol Barr reviewed the book for Human Kinetics and I am grateful for their comments. In addition, I received suggestions on different aspects of the book from Sue Inglis, Jim Weese, Wendy Frisby, and Donna Pastore. Their help is much appreciated. I would also like to thank those individuals and companies who supplied me with material for the book and those who gave permission to reproduce their work, particularly those that didn't charge a fee! Finally, my greatest debt is to my wife Janet and my two daughters Chelsea and Meghan. Janet has supported my academic work for the last twenty-one years, often placing her own goals secondary so that I could achieve my ambitions. Chelsea and Meghan are still not sure writing about sport is a real job and have had the good sense to drag me away from my computer at frequent intervals to engage in more serious activities! To all these people I am grateful.

Photo Credits

Philip Knight, *Nike President and CEO*

Organization Theory and the Management of Sport Organizations

You should be able to

1. explain why it is important for sport managers to understand about organizations;
2. define what we mean when we talk about a sport organization;
3. explain the terms organizational structure, design, and context;
4. distinguish between organizational theory and organizational behavior;
5. explain the different ways of looking at sport organizations; and
6. discuss the types of research studies dominating the field of sport management.

The Nike Story

Most of you have probably walked through your local sporting goods store and seen the wide variety of athletic shoes lining the shelves and display units—shoes for football, running, tennis, golf, basketball, aerobics, cycling, windsurfing, cheerleading, and a whole range of other sporting activities. The shoes, each with their own distinctive logo, come in bright colors, with added high-tech attractions such as HydroFlow, gel, and the Energy Return System.

One of the major producers of athletic footwear, with 1994 revenues of nearly $4 billion (US), is a company called Nike, with corporate headquarters in Beaverton, Oregon. *Forbes* magazine identified Nike's president and chief executive officer, Philip Knight, as one of the four hundred richest Americans. But Nike has not always been a large multimillion-dollar organization. In fact, Knight started the company by selling shoes from the back of his station wagon at track meets.

In the late 1950s Philip Knight was a middle distance runner on the University of Oregon's track team, coached by Bill Bowerman. One of the top track coaches in the United States, Bowerman was also known for experimenting with the design of running shoes in an attempt to make them lighter and more shock-absorbent. After attending Oregon, Knight moved on to do graduate work at Stanford University; his MBA thesis was on marketing athletic shoes. Once he had received his degree, he traveled to Japan where he contacted the Onitsuka Tiger Company, a manufacturer of athletic shoes. Knight convinced the company's officials of the potential for its product in the United States. In 1963 he received his first shipment of Tiger shoes, 200 in total.

In 1964, Knight and Bowerman contributed $500 each to form Blue Ribbon Sports, the small company that later became Nike. In the first few years, Knight worked for an accounting firm and later as an assistant professor of business administration at Portland State University. He distributed shoes from his father's basement and out of his car at local and regional track meets. The first employees hired by Knight were former college athletes, mainly from the University of Oregon. The company did not have the money to hire "experts"; even if they had there was no established athletic footwear industry in North America from which these people could have been recruited. In its early years the organization operated in a freewheeling, unconventional manner that characterized its innovative and entrepreneurial approach to the industry. Communication was informal; people discussed ideas and issues in the hallways, on a run, or over a beer. There was little task differentiation and some people moved from one job in the organization to another; what coordination was required was done informally by the senior managers. There were no job descriptions, rigid reporting systems, or detailed rules and regulations. The team spirit and shared values that were developed as athletes on Bowerman's teams carried over, and provided the basis for the collegial style of management that characterized the early years of Nike.

When in the late 1960s and 1970s running became fashionable, Oregon became the running capital of the world. As a result, Blue Ribbon Sports grew: Revenues increased from $8,000 in 1964 to nearly $300,000 in 1969, and $3.2 million in 1973. As the organization grew, its nature started to change. In 1965 its first full-time employee was hired; by 1969 it had 20 employees and several retail outlets. In 1971 it started to manufacture its own shoe line; the swoosh logo and new company name "Nike" were created. In 1972, Nike introduced the famous waffle sole, which had been developed by Bowerman pouring rubber into a kitchen waffle iron. During the 1970s manufacturing facilities were opened in the United States, Korea, and Taiwan; top athletes signed contracts to wear Nike products and the number of employees rose to nearly 3,000. By 1980, Nike controlled nearly 50 percent of the athletic footwear market.

Today, Nike's structure and the way it operates are considerably different from the organization Knight originated from the back of his car and his father's basement. As the company grew and more people were hired, jobs became more specialized. The organization now has 37 units, 24 of which deal with footwear. With increased size and complexity, the informal style of operating was no longer as efficient as it was in the past. More formalized management systems had to be introduced: Meetings at all levels of management were held with relative frequency, the coordinating roles of managers were more formally established, planning systems were used to integrate related job functions, and policies and procedures were introduced to standardize operating practices.

Not surprisingly, Nike lost some of the team spirit that characterized its early operations. Units became compartmentalized and some managers expressed concern over the lack of communication among the different levels of the organization. Professionally trained managers now head departments concerned with areas such as international marketing, sales, finance, and advertising and promotion. The company is no longer solely concerned with footwear; it has expanded into athletic apparel and accessories.

Based on information in Davies, P. (1990, May). Hot Shoes. *Report on Business Magazine*; Harvard Business School. (1984). Nike (B). (Case No. 9-385-027). Boston: HBS Case Services; Magnet, M. (1982, November). Nike starts on the second mile. *Fortune*; Timelines. (mimeographed) distributed by Nike; Eales, R. (1986). Is Nike a long distance runner? *Multinational Business*, *1*, 9-14.

What Philip Knight created was a sport organization. As the organization grew, he found that the original informal operating structure and style of management were no longer efficient for producing 300 models of athletic shoes in 900 different styles for a worldwide market. This kind of volume requires a different type of organizational design, one with specialized units, complex coordinating mechanisms, and a hierarchical management structure. The success that Knight has achieved is, in large part, a result of the changes made to the structure of Nike as it has grown and faced new and different contextual pressures. To be able to compete in the athletic footwear industry, Knight set up offshore manufacturing plants to ensure minimal production costs, hired specialist designers to keep ahead of changing trends, and established computerized warehouses to ensure that products are shipped on time to the right retail outlets.

Nike's situation is not unique. To operate effectively and efficiently, any sport organization needs to adapt its structure and management processes to meet the demands of its contextual situation. As we will show in this book, a knowledge of organization theory can help the sport manager in this task.

Why Sport Managers Need to Understand About Organizations and Organization Theory

In North America, Europe, and throughout many countries of the world, sport is a rapidly growing and increasingly diverse industry. Increased amounts of discretionary income, a heightened awareness of the relationship between an active lifestyle and good health, and a greater number of opportunities to participate in sport have all contributed to this growth. In Great Britain, the journal *Retail Business* described the sport industry as "one of the most buoyant consumer markets of the 1980s" (Economic Intelligence Unit, 1990, p. 61) and predicted real-term growth into the 1990s. In the United States the magazine *Sports Inc.* predicted that the "gross national sport product" would be $85 billion in 1995, growing to $121 billion by the year 2000. In Canada it was estimated that Canadians spent close to $4.5 billion on sporting goods alone in 1989. Although it is difficult to exactly measure the size of the sport industry, figure 1.1 provides some indication of its magnitude.

A large number of different types of organizations make up the sport industry, that wide array of

1. In 1992 teenagers spent $3 billion (US) on athletic shoes.
2. Four of the top 75 "hot growth companies" identified by *Business Week* in 1994 had interest in the golf industry.
3. In 1993 Americans spent $6 billion (US) on spectator sports.
4. Sport in Britain generates earnings of more than £8 billion per year and jobs in the industry increased from 100,000 in 1985 to 467,000 in 1990.
5. Estimates placed the 1991 value of the New York Yankees at $225 million (US).
6. Over 80,000 buyers visit the annual Sporting Goods Manufacturers Association show.
7. Canadians spend $11.7 billion (Cdn) on fitness related and basic sport expenditures.
8. Corporate sponsorship of the 1996 Olympic Games in Atlanta will total $628 million (US).

Figure 1.1   Indicators of the size of the sport industry.
1. Teens. (1994, April 11). *Business Week*, p. 39. 2. Hot growth companies. (1994, May 23). *Business Week*, pp. 101-103. 3. The entertainment economy. (1994, March 14). *Business Week*, p. 60. 4. Sport makes £8 billion to defeat the recession. (1992, September 16). *International Express*, p. 10. 5. Secrets of the front office. (1991, July 9). *Financial World*, p. 42. 6. Ballard, S. (1989, February 20). A show that has all the goods. *Sports Illustrated*, p. 37. 7. *Sport the way ahead*. (1992). Ottawa: Ministry of Supply and Services, p. 244. 8. Rozin, P. (1995, July 24). Olympic partnership. *Sports Illustrated*, n.p.

public, private, and voluntary organizations involved in the provision of sport products and services. Some, like Brunswick Corporation, heavily involved in bowling centers and marine equipment, and the Forzani Group, a large sporting goods retailer, have sales in the millions of dollars and employ thousands of people. Others, such as Holland Cycle, a custom bike-frame builder in Spring Valley, California, and the Derbyshire Skeet and Trap Club, a gun club operated by former Olympic skeet shooter Joe Neville, operate on a considerably smaller scale. A large number of the organizations we will look at in this book are designed to make a profit for their owner(s); others, such as Recreational Equipment Inc. (REI) of Seattle, operate on a cooperative basis and turn a large percentage of their profits back to their members—the people who buy their products. Many sport organizations operate as voluntary or nonprofit organizations; the funds they generate are used to further activities which benefit their membership and/or the communities where they are based. Some sport organizations, particularly those from the public sector, have as their primary function to aid and assist other organizations in the delivery of sport. For example, the Sport, Recreation, and Culture Division of the Government of the Province of New Brunswick has as its primary goal "to provide support and direction to provincial sport organizations. . . ." (Beaulieu, 1990, p. 18). Many sport organizations are linked to educational institutions and provide recreational and competitive sport opportunities as a part of the educational process. The sport industry also includes professional sport organizations, which contract with athletes and pay them to compete in their particular sport; the event is then sold to live audiences and to TV companies for its entertainment value.

Organizations are, then, an integral and pervasive part of the sport industry. For those of you who hope to work in this industry, a knowledge of organization theory will help you to understand the organizations with which you will interact (and by which you may be employed), and why they are structured and operated in a particular way. For students specializing in sport management presumably one of the reasons for studying organizations is that someday you hope to work in or eventually manage one. A knowledge of organization theory, that is to say a knowledge of organizations that has been systematically and scientifically derived, can help you to better understand the problems you will face as a manager. It can help you design an appropriate structure, manage the changes that need to be made in your organization's structure as changes take place in its contextual situation, provide appropriate leadership, adopt appropriate technologies, resolve conflicts, manage human resources, and achieve the goals of your organization. *It can, in short, help **you** become a better manager.*

Some Definitions

We have already seen that there are many different types of sport organizations. The terms structure, design, and context have been used to describe aspects of these organizations; and it has been suggested that organization theory can help in the task of managing these organizations. But what exactly is meant by these terms? In this section of the book some definitions are provided to help facilitate an understanding of these concepts; more detailed explanations can be found in later chapters. Although some management theorists (cf. March & Simon, 1958) suggest that definitions are of limited use because they do not clearly delimit the object being examined, Hall (1982, p. 28) argues that definitions help to "provide a basis for understanding the phenomena to be studied." While we acknowledge that sport organizations (and their context, structure, and design) are not unitary entities that can be exactly defined, but rather are complex processes and sets of socially and historically constituted relationships, the approach taken here is consistent with Hall's argument that defining concepts can provide a basis for their understanding.

What Is a Sport Organization?

While Nike and agencies like the Atlanta Falcons, the Amateur Athletic Association, the Ladies Professional Golf Association, Creative Health Products, the British Columbia Lions Football Club, the Alberta Cricket Association, and Manchester United Soccer Club can all be classified as sport organizations, what is it that makes them sport organizations? Certainly it's not size (Creative Health Products makes a variety of fitness testing products and yet has only seven employees). It's not the amount of money they make (a number of professional sport teams such as those in the Canadian Football League consistently lose money), nor is it the existence of employees (the Alberta Cricket Association has no paid staff). The definition of a sport organization used in this book is based on definitions of an organization provided by Daft (1989) and Robbins (1990) and is as follows: **A sport organization is a social entity involved in the sport industry; it is goal-directed, with a consciously structured activity system and a relatively identifiable boundary.**

There are five key elements in this definition and each warrants further explanation:

- *Social entity.* All sport organizations are composed of people or groups of people who interact with each other to perform those functions essential to the organization.
- *Involvement in the sport industry.* What differentiates sport organizations from other organizations such as banks, pharmaceutical companies, and car dealerships is the former's direct involvement in one or more aspects of the sport industry, for example, through the production of sport-related products or services. While agencies like banks, pharmaceutical companies, and car dealerships can be and have been involved in sport (primarily through sponsorship), they are not usually directly involved with the phenomenon and hence are not included in this book. The aim of the book is, however, to be inclusive rather than exclusive in explaining the nature of sport organizations. Hence, examples will be drawn from companies such as W.L. Gore & Associates, Inc., the manufacturer of Gore-Tex, a product used to make a wide range of sportswear and equipment; the various national and state park and recreation agencies that support many natural resources in which sport activities are often practiced; and organizations such as Yamaha and the Minnesota Mining and Manufacturing Corporation (3M), which, while they do not have sport products or services as their central focus, still have substantive involvement in the sport industry.
- *Goal-directed focus.* All sport organizations exist for a purpose, be it making a profit, encouraging participation in a given sport, or winning Olympic medals. The goals of a sport organization are not usually as easily obtainable by an individual as they are by members working together. Sport organizations may have more than one goal, and individual members may have different goals from those of the organization.
- *Consciously structured activity system.* The interaction of people or groups of people in sport organizations does not occur through random chance; rather, there is a conscious structuring of activity systems such as marketing, product/service development, financial management, and human resource development. The main functions of the sport organization are broken down into smaller tasks or groups of tasks; the mechanisms used to coordinate and control these tasks help ensure that the goals of the sport organization are achieved.
- *Identifiable boundary.* Sport organizations need to have a relatively identifiable boundary that distinguishes members from nonmembers. Members of a sport organization usually have an explicit or implicit agreement with the organization, through which they receive money, status, or some other benefit for their involvement. For some sport organizations, particularly those in the voluntary/nonprofit sector, the boundaries may not be as easily identified as in those sport organizations concerned

with making a profit or those in the public sector. Nevertheless, every sport organization must have a boundary that helps distinguish members from nonmembers, but these boundaries are not fixed and may change over time.

The elements of our definition are evident in Nike, the sport organization that Philip Knight and Bill Bowerman created. The goals of the company are to produce athletic footwear and to sell it at a profit. As Nike has grown and more people have been hired, activity systems have been consciously structured to effectively and efficiently achieve the goals of the organization. The people hired identified themselves as employees and managers of Nike, which creates for them an identifiable boundary to differentiate their company from its competitors in the athletic footwear industry.

Organizational Structure of a Sport Organization

The term *organizational structure* is used here to define the manner in which the tasks of a sport organization are broken down and allocated to employees or volunteers, the reporting relationships among these role holders, and the coordinating and controlling mechanisms used within the sport organization. A typical organizational chart outlines, in part, the structure of an organization (see figure 1.2).

Identifying the dimensions that constitute the structure of any organization is, at best, a difficult exercise and one that has yielded inconsistency across studies. Yet organizational structure is an important concept to study because, as Miller (1987a) suggests, it "importantly influences the flow of interaction and the context and nature of human interactions. It channels collaboration, specifies modes of coordination, allocates power and responsibility, and prescribes levels of formality and complexity" (p. 7). Hall (1982), Miller and Dröge (1986), and Van de Ven (1976) all suggest that structure should be examined using three dimensions: complexity, formalization, and centralization. We look at each of these structural dimensions in more detail in chapter 3.

Organizational Design

The concept of organizational design refers to the patterning of the structural elements of an organization. All managers seek to produce a design that will enhance their ability to achieve the goals of their organization. Miller (1981) argued that organizations must be constructed so as to ensure that there is complementary alignment among their structural variables. In what is probably the best known attempt to identify organizational designs, Mintzberg (1979) proposes five "design configurations": the simple structure, the machine bureaucracy, the divisionalized form, the professional bureaucracy, and the adhocracy. Sport organizations can be found in each of these categories; we discuss them more specifically in chapter 4.

The Context of a Sport Organization

The structure of a sport organization is closely related to the particular context in which the organization operates. The term *context* merely refers to "the organizational setting which influences the structural dimensions" (Daft, 1989, p. 17). We find variation in the structures of sport organizations mainly because they operate with different contextual situations. As was the case with organizational structure, different studies have identified different dimensions as characterizing an organization's context. Contextual dimensions are often referred to in the literature as determinants, imperatives, or, most frequently, contingencies. Supporters of this school of thought (i.e., contingency theory) argue that changes in an organization's structure are contingent on changes in its contextual situation. We look at the four main contextual factors identified as influencing structure—strategy, size, environment, and technology—in chapters 5, 6, 7, and 8.

Organizational Theory

Organizational theory, a disciplinary area within the broader field of business/management studies, is concerned with the structure and design of organizations. Scholars in this field seek to identify commonly occurring patterns and regularities in organizations, and understand their causes and consequences. While organizational theorists are concerned with theoretical issues, that is, pushing back the frontiers of knowledge about organizations, sport management students should not be concerned that the subject area has no practical application. On the contrary, scholars in this area frequently work with the practicing manager; the central focus of a large percentage of the research they undertake is to discover ways to help the manager in her job. For sport managers, organizational theory can

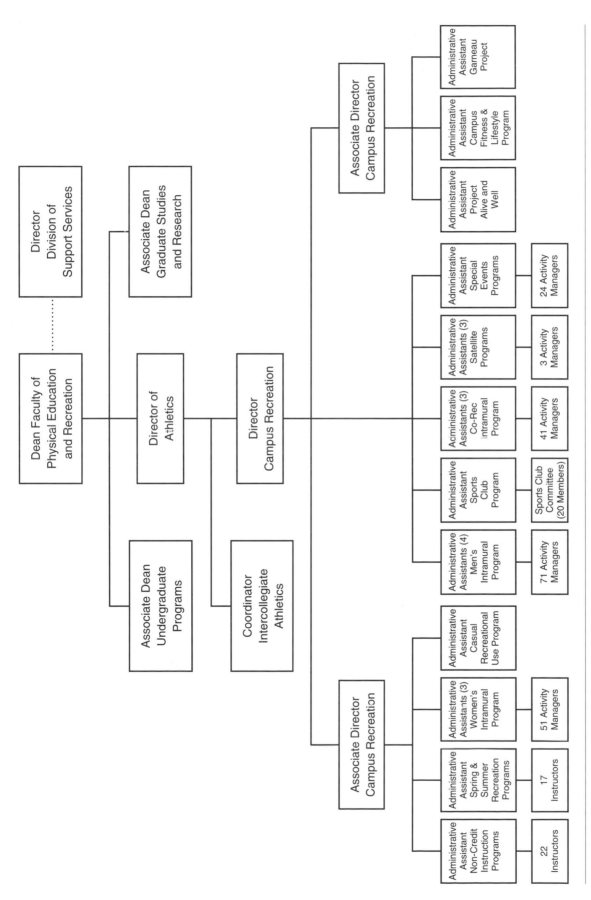

Figure 1.2 Organizational chart: University of Alberta campus recreation unit.

help provide a better understanding of the way sport organizations are structured and designed, how they operate, and why some are effective when others are not. This understanding can help sport managers analyze and diagnose more effectively the problems they face, and enable them to respond with appropriate solutions.

The Distinction Between Organizational Theory and Organizational Behavior

All organizations can be studied at different levels and in different ways; sport organizations are no exception. Within the field of sport management students should understand what is often referred to as the *macro/micro distinction*, or the distinction between organizational theory (OT) and organizational behavior (OB). Organizational theory, the macro perspective, focuses on the organization (or its primary subunits) as its unit of analysis. To explain a sport organization from this perspective, it is necessary to "look not only at its characteristics, but also at the characteristics of the environment and the departments and groups that make up the organization" (Daft 1989, p. 25). Organizational theorists are concerned with the total organization's ability to achieve its goals effectively; thus, they must not only consider how it is structured but also how it is situated in a broader sociopolitical and economic context. Organizational behavior, the micro perspective, focuses on individuals and small groups within the organization, and the characteristics of the environment in which they work.

Organizational theorists usually study topics related to the structure and design of organizations; the impact of contextual factors such as strategy, size, and technology on structure and design; and such issues as the role of power in organizations and how such processes as decision making and change are managed. Researchers in OB are more concerned with individually based issues such as job satisfaction, leadership style, communication, team-building, and motivation. Organizational theory draws strongly from sociology, while OB draws predominantly from social psychology. This distinction between OB and OT is an important one for sport management students to understand because, with some exceptions, the dominant trend of the empirical work in our field has been concerned with OB topics, such as the level of job satisfaction of sport managers, their leadership traits, and their motivations.

The OT/OB distinction is certainly not a clear one; both approaches are important to a full understanding of sport management. For example, the lack of women in senior positions in management (and sport management in particular) has often been explained by looking at the individual and her motivation, leadership ability, and skills—an OB approach. While this approach can provide useful material to start to correct some of the inequalities we see in sport organizations, it fails to address the structural conditions that constrain women's progress in these organizations, something an OT approach would consider. Studies from both perspectives would provide a fuller understanding of the gendered nature of sport organizations and many other important issues in management. (See Kanter [1977] for work of this nature and Hall, Cullen, and Slack [1989] for an overview of the gender and management literature as it applies to sport.)

The approach taken in this book draws predominantly on work from OT to help explain how to better manage sport organizations. However, some chapters, such as those on leadership and human resource management, utilize some work traditionally more closely aligned with the perspective of OB. Sport management students should not view OB and OT as opposing or conflicting perspectives. Rather, each perspective emphasizes different levels of analysis and as such should complement each other in providing a fuller understanding of sport management.

Ways to Look at Sport Organizations

In contrasting OT with OB it is important to point out that OT is not monolithic in its approach to understanding organizations and their management. There are many ways that researchers in OT have looked at organizations; some of these approaches are complementary, some overlap, and some are conflicting, but all can be applied to the study of sport organizations and their management. The approach termed *systems theory*, which has tended to dominate OT-based studies in sport management, grew out of the work of the theoretical biologist Ludwig von Bertalanffy (1950, 1968) and is best exemplified in its application to organizations by the work of Katz and Kahn (1978). As we will see later, however, there are a number of problems with systems theory and a number of other equally viable ways to look at sport organizations. One of the best and most recent works to categorize the different ways of looking at organizations is Gareth Morgan's *Images of organization* (1986). Morgan's basic argument is that different "theories and explanations of organizational life are based on metaphors that lead us to see and understand organizations in distinctive yet partial ways" (p. 12). By looking at these different perspectives on organizations we come to better understand them and their management. These metaphors are explained in more detail in the passages to follow, and where available examples from the literature on sport organizations are provided.*

Organizations as Machines

One of the most pervasive images we have of organizations is as machines. Originating with the classical theorists, such as Fayol, Gulick, and Urwick, and in particular Frederick Taylor with his notions of scientific management, organizations are seen from this perspective as a series of interrelated parts, each performing a narrowly defined set of activities to achieve a particular end product. Like a machine, the organization is expected to operate in a rigid, repetitive, and impersonal manner.

Although heavily criticized for their impersonal nature (cf. Braverman, 1974), ideas grounded in "Taylorism" still pervade the way in which many organizations, including some in the sport industry, operate. Sport organizations most likely to employ elements of this approach are those involved in the assembly-line production of commodities such as athletic shoes, baseball bats, hockey sticks, and bicycles. Mechanistic approaches to organization are also promoted in some elements of the sport management literature. Several textbooks in the area are constructed around Henri Fayol's concepts of planning, organizing, coordinating, commanding, and controlling. In addition, many public-sector documents on the management of sport, and some sport management texts (cf. Horine, 1985; VanderZwaag, 1984), stress the usefulness and importance of the more modern mechanistic approaches to management such as management by objectives (MBO) and planning, programming, budgeting systems (PPBS). Sports teams have also often been described as machine-like in their operation (cf. Castaing, 1970; Terkel, 1972).

Organizations as Organisms

In large part as a reaction to the technical emphasis of scientific management, scholars like Herzberg, Mausner, and Snyderman (1959), Maslow (1943), and McGregor (1960) started to focus on the "needs" of the individual, the group, and the organization. This focus, by necessity, drew attention to the environment in which the organization existed as a source of satisfaction for these needs. Thus, organizations were likened to organisms which come in a variety of different forms and which rely on their environment in order to survive. Also, like organisms, organizations were seen to exhibit different systems (usually termed the input, throughput, and output systems) which interacted with each other and their environment. Figure 1.3 shows these systems as they would apply to a sport equipment manufacturer. In each of the three systems there is a reliance on the environment for certain organizational "needs."

The "systems" approach to the study of organizations has frequently been used in sport management. Chelladurai, Szyszlo, and Haggerty (1987a), for example, used a systems-based approach to examine the effectiveness of Canadian national sport organizations. Friend (1991) suggests a systems approach to deal with personnel issues.

Within the broader field of management, a logical extension to systems theory and a more dominant approach to the study of organizations is contingency theory. In keeping with the metaphor of organizations as organisms, the structure of an organization is seen as being contingent on contextual factors (size, strategy, etc.). Effectiveness is seen as being dependent on there being "a fit" between structure and context. For example, a large sport organization such as Rossignol, the ski manufacturer, will require a different structure from a small retail sporting goods store. The structure of each organization must "fit" with the demands that their size produces. While work on sport organizations has often implicitly acknowledged the importance of context to structure and effectiveness, there have been few studies specifically focused on these relationships. The idea that organizations are products of their context and the realization that these contexts vary gave rise to the notion of variation in organizational design. Like organisms, some organizational forms are more suited to certain contextual conditions than to others. This idea has led

*Parts of this section were published in Slack, T. (1993). Morgan and the metaphors: Implication for sport management. *Journal of Sport Management, 7,* 189-193.

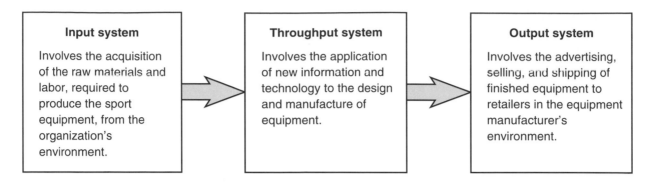

Figure 1.3   Systems of a sport equipment manufacturer.

researchers to attempt to classify different types of organization and the conditions under which they will be most effective (cf. Mintzberg, 1979). In the field of sport management there have been attempts to use existing typologies to classify sport organizations (cf. Chelladurai, 1985). However, Kikulis, Slack, Hinings, and Zimmermann (1989) have taken the idea of classification further. Building on the ideas of scholars like Carper and Snizek (1980), McKelvey (1975, 1978, 1982), and Miller and Friesen (1984), they developed an empirical taxonomy of organizational design for voluntary sport organizations. The taxonomy illustrates the different types of organizational design with which these organizations can operate.

The biological metaphor of organizations as organisms has also been adopted by researchers who approach the study of organizations from what is termed the life cycle perspective (Kimberly & Miles, 1980). Here, organizations, like organisms, are seen to go through distinctive life stages, their management requirements reflecting the stage of their development. Yet a further extension of the biological metaphor has given rise to an approach to studying organizations termed "population ecology." Unlike many other approaches, population ecology focuses not on individual organizations but on populations of organizations. The idea is that "organizations, like organisms in nature, depend for survival on their ability to acquire an adequate supply of the resources necessary to sustain existence. In this effort they have to face competition from other organizations, and since there is usually a resource scarcity, only the fittest survive" (Morgan, 1986, p. 66). By plotting birth-and-death rates and patterns of growth and decline in organizations, population ecologists have provided important insights into organizations and their management. Although this approach has not been used by sport management scholars to date, sport organizations

that come and go very rapidly, such as fitness centers, aerobic studios, and sporting goods stores, would provide a highly appropriate population of organizations for this type of work.

Organizations as Brains

The image of organizations as brains draws attention to the information-processing capacity of organizations. While the mechanistic type of organizations advocated by Frederick Taylor may work well for performing regularized tasks in a stable environment, organizations that operate under changing conditions have to be able to monitor these conditions, question the appropriateness of their actions, and if necessary make modifications. This necessity requires that organizations, like brains, have to exhibit information-processing capabilities and communication and decision making systems. As such they may also have to develop the capacity to learn in a brain-like way and eventually engage in self-management and self-organization.

This way of thinking about organizations owes much to Herbert Simon's (1945) work on decision making and his concept of bounded rationality (see chapter 13). For Simon, organizational actors have limited information-processing capabilities which become institutionalized in the structure and ways of operating of organizations. Thus, organizations become understood "as kinds of institutionalized brains that fragment, routinize, and bound the decision process in order to make it manageable" (Morgan, 1986, p. 81). New ways of thinking about organizations and their design and operation have developed from this emphasis on decision making. Galbraith (1974, 1977) and Thompson (1967), for example, have focused on the relationship between the information-processing capabilities of an organization and organizational design.

This interest in information processing has led organizational researchers to cybernetics, a field of study concerned with "the behavior, organization, and design of mechanisms, organisms, and organizations that receive, generate, and respond to information in order to attain a desired result" (Haggerty, 1988, pp. 54-55). Applied to organizations, the field of cybernetics has been concerned with designing systems that can learn, much like a brain learns, and thus can regulate themselves. A further extension of this approach is to view organizations as holographic systems where each part of the organization has a picture of the whole, thus allowing learning and self-renewal. Given the rapid expansion of information processing in organizations, we may see cybernetic and holographic approaches, while still developing as ways to understand organizations, as providing the direction for future changes that will accompany these developments. In the field of sport management only Terry Haggerty (1988) has completed work using this approach. Haggerty suggests that cybernetic strategies can be used for improving the control and information systems of sport organizations.

Organizations as Cultures

With the success of Japanese management and the globalization of many industries has come an increased interest in the relationship of culture to organizational life. While organizational theorists acknowledge that the culture of the society in which an organization exists will influence its modes of operation, there has been growing interest in what is often termed "corporate culture." Growing out of the idea that organizations are themselves minisocieties, culture in this sense is concerned with the shared values and meanings that create the reality of organizational life. Scholars who study organizations as cultures are concerned with issues such as the way these shared values and meanings are created and maintained, the role of leadership in this process, the existence of competing cultures, and the manifestation of an organization's culture in its design and operation.

Corporate culture reveals itself in such areas of the organization as its ceremonies, stories, myths, symbols, language, and physical layout. Sport organizations are rich in these areas. Ceremonies to initiate rookie football players, stories about coaches and managers, the symbols of athletic goods companies (the Nike swoosh, Adidas's three stripes), and the specialized language that characterizes many sports can all be examined to gain an understanding of the shared values and meanings that underpin the design and operation of sport organizations. Despite the potential of the culture approach to understanding sport organizations, there has been virtually no work of this nature in sport management. Many popular books on sport organizations (cf. Prouty, 1988; Williams, 1995) provide implicit accounts of the type of values that shape their operation, yet by their nature offer little or no scholarly analysis. Hall, Cullen, and Slack (1989) briefly examine the potential of a cultural approach to understanding gender issues in sport organizations but warn that it is frequently men's accounts of organizational reality, not women's, that usually dominate most analyses of an organization's culture. The work that comes closest to a systematic analysis of the culture of a sport organization and its effects on structure and design is Fine's (1987) work on Little League Baseball.

Organizations as Political Systems

All organizations are political. The image of organizations as political systems challenges the view that they are rational entities that work for a common end. Rather, the view is one of individuals and groups loosely coupled together in order to more efficiently realize their own ambitions and self-interests. Scholars who work with this perspective are interested in the political activity that manifests itself in the power plays and conflicts pervading all organizations. Some would suggest this approach is particularly applicable to those organizations concerned with sport!

Few studies in sport management have specifically examined sport organizations as systems of political activity. Stern's (1979) analysis of the development of the National Collegiate Athletic Association (NCAA) is probably one of the best examples. However, there are other studies that, although it was not their primary focus, provide examples of the type of political struggles that shape sport organizations. Sack and Kidd (1985) and Kidd (1988) have discussed the political struggles of athletes to gain representation in the sport organizations that control their athletic destinies. Macintosh and Whitson (1990) examined struggles between professional staff and volunteers to determine the program focus of national sport organizations in Canada. Much of the work on gender and organizations is about political struggles between men and women (cf. Hall, Cullen, & Slack, 1989; Hult, 1989; Lovett & Lowry, 1994; White & Brackenridge, 1985).

Organizations as Instruments of Domination

In describing organizations as instruments of domination, Morgan (1986) suggests that we are usually encouraged to think of organizations as positive entities created to benefit the interests of all who come into contact with them. Certainly sport organizations are often portrayed in this manner; however, Morgan points out a critique of this perspective. Here organizations are seen as instruments designed to benefit the interests of a privileged few at the expense of the masses; sport organizations have not been immune from this critique. From this more critical perspective, organizations (or more accurately their dominant coalitions) are seen as exploiting their workers, their host communities, and often the environment, for their own ends. Unions, work-related stresses, industrial accidents, drug and alcohol abuse, and alienation are all products of this exploitation. While researchers who see themselves as working primarily in the field of sport management have, for the most part, failed to place these issues on their research agendas, they are no less important than any others for a comprehensive understanding of sport organizations and their successful management.

While neglected by sport management scholars per se, this approach to organizations has been used by a number of writers from both the popular and academic literature on sport. Several authors have written in the popular press about the manner in which professional sport organizations (most notably football teams) and some colleges dominate and exploit their athletes (cf. Huizenga, 1994; Manley & Friend, 1992; Telander, 1989). Government organizations have also been seen as exploiting the talents of their international athletes to meet their own ideological and policy aims (cf. Harvey and Proulx, 1988; Kidd, 1988; Macintosh & Whitson, 1990), and strong arguments have been made for class-, race-, and gender-based exploitation in sport organizations (cf. Cashmore, 1990; Gruneau, 1983; Whitson & Macintosh, 1989). Finally, companies like Nike have been criticized for exploitative labor practices in their Third World production plants (Ballinger, 1993; Clifford, 1992).

State of the Art in Sport Management and Suggestions for Future Directions

As we have just seen, there are a number of ways we can look at sport organizations. The central premise of Morgan's approach to understanding organizations is that they cannot be adequately described, understood, or explained using just one approach. By looking at different images of organizations, we are better able to understand their complex and paradoxical nature, and thus become better managers. As the few previous examples illustrate, sport management scholars have tended to be relatively narrow in the way they look at sport organizations. The two dominant perspectives within the literature have been to look at organizations from a mechanistic point of view or to utilize the systems theory approach. While work of this nature is not without value, it is somewhat problematic in terms of its ability to provide a holistic understanding of sport organizations and their management. (A large number of studies in the field of sport management fail to use any type of theoretical framework; as such, while some of them provide useful descriptive material, they do little to enhance our overall understanding of sport organizations and their management.)

Mechanistic approaches to the study of sport organizations, as noted earlier, have generally focused on some variant of Henri Fayol's five basic managerial functions. A number of textbooks in our field have been constructed around these concepts. However, such approaches are problematic; because, as Mintzberg (1973a, p. 10) notes, "these words do not in fact describe the actual work of managers at all, they describe certain vague objectives of managerial work. As such they have long served to block our search for a deeper understanding of the work of the manager." Such an approach is also limited in that it fails to recognize the ability of organizations to change as their contextual situation changes. It can also be dehumanizing for employees; because it promotes an image of workers as cheerful robots unquestioningly going about their daily tasks, it can promote bureaucratic pathologies such as goal displacement and alienation. Finally, this approach to organizations fails to recognize the importance of power and politics in creating the reality of organizational life.

While studies based on systems theory have been more useful in providing interesting and relevant information, this approach is also limited in its explanatory abilities. Studies based on systems theory tend to be overly deterministic, ignoring the role of strategic choice in the construction of organizations. That is to say, far too much emphasis is placed on context as a determinant of structure and design and far too little attention is given to the creative actions of individuals within the organization. Such an emphasis also presents a view of organizations as functionally unified where all the component parts work together to a common end. Consequently, as with mechanistic approaches, issues of power and politics are ignored and conflict is dismissed as merely being "dysfunctional."

It is important that students of sport management realize the strengths and limitations of the dominant approaches to the study of sport organizations. While the findings that emanate from the most prevelant type of studies in our field are useful and informative, they frequently present only a partial view of sport organizations and their management. Studies based on the approaches of contingency theory and population ecology, for example, while not without their shortcomings, would certainly enhance our understanding of the impact of contextual pressures on the structure and design of sport organizations. It is also important to conduct studies to determine the nature and extent of variation in the design of sport organizations. As McKelvey (1975) has suggested, such classifications are in many ways one of the fundamental elements in the development of a comprehensive understanding of organizations. The increasing importance of information processing and communication in organizations, and the interest generated by such popular literature as Peters and Waterman's (1982) *In search of excellence* and Kanter's (1983) *The change masters,* have respectively prompted an interest in cybernetics and organizational culture. These approaches would provide useful insights if applied to sport organizations. Work that looks at sport organizations as "political systems" and "instruments of domination" would help free us from the highly functional view of these organizations that has long characterized our field. These approaches would also bring issues of power and politics, something that has been missing from previous studies, to a more central position in the study of sport management.

However, the adoption of some of these perspectives will require us to employ different theoretical approaches from those currently found in the sport management literature. For example, very few published studies on sport organizations have used either the theoretical approach of resource dependence or that of institutional theory (see chapter 7), both extensions of the contingency approach. Yet each offers considerable potential for the development of a more in-depth understanding of the operation and management of sport organizations. Any of the approaches that comprise critical theory have not only been absent from the study of sport

organizations, but their use has been implicitly if not explicitly frowned upon. For example, studies underpinned by Marxist theory in any of its variant forms are noticeably absent from our literature; yet organizational scholars such as Thompson and McHugh (1990) and Clegg (1989), to name but a few, have employed elements of western Marxist thought to make a major contribution to our understanding of organizations and their management. Marx himself wrote considerably about one organization, the state, which in many western liberal democratic countries has a considerable impact on the way sport is managed.

While feminist theory has been used more frequently in the sport management literature, most of the completed work in this area has adopted a liberal feminist approach that emphasizes how women need to change to better fit into the existing male-stream system. Such work does little to challenge or change the hegemonic conditions that have long constrained women's mobility in organizations, but a body of work is emerging in the organizational literature that critically analyzes the role of gender in organizations. This work (Burrell, 1984; Hearn & Parkin, 1983, 1987; Hearn, Sheppard, Tancred-Sheriff & Burrell, 1989; Mills & Tancred, 1992), with its emphasis on sexuality, has considerable scope for work on sport organizations (cf. Hall, Cullen, & Slack, 1989).

The adoption of any of these approaches will, of course, require somewhat different research techniques from those previously found in sport management. As Olafson (1990) demonstrated, survey-type studies have dominated the sport management literature. While there is still considerable scope for this type of work, new and different theoretical approaches will require us to employ research designs and modes of analysis not commonly used to study sport organizations. Those who engage in quantitative studies will need to become more sophisticated in terms of the statistical procedures they employ and the manner in which their data are integrated into or used to extend existing theoretical frameworks. Qualitative approaches, which have been noticeably absent from the academic sport management literature, will also have to be more frequently employed. Techniques such as participant observation, in-depth interviews, and semiotic analysis, when applied appropriately, could all yield new insights to help the sport manager.

The essential point here is not that one theoretical approach or research technique is better than another, but that different approaches explain different parts of the reality of organizational life. In sport management, we have tended to use only one or two perspectives and a limited range of research methodologies; consequently, our view of sport organizations is very narrow. As Morgan (1986) points out, organizations are complex and paradoxical; by using different approaches to understand their complex and paradoxical nature, we will be better able to design and manage them.

It is impossible in one book to deal, even in a minor way, with all the different approaches to sport organizations mentioned here. In fact, some of them are only in their infancy in the broader field of management. The point of discussing the state of the art in our field is to alert readers to the potential these approaches have to enhance our understanding of sport organizations and their management. This text has been written in an effort to tap some of this potential. By focusing on a number of the central ideas in organizational theory and their application to our field, it is hoped that the book will provide students with a better understanding of sport organizations, and that this increased understanding will ultimately make them better managers.

Format of the Book

Like a successful sport organization, a good text book needs an appropriate structure. The fifteen chapters in this book are arranged to provide a logical progression to understanding the structure, context, and processes of sport organizations. As you have seen, chapter 1 explains what organization theory is and how it can help the sport manager to understand sport organizations. In chapter 2, we discuss the central problem with which sport managers must be concerned: the issue of organizational effectiveness. Effectiveness is strongly linked to an appropriate organizational structure and design. Consequently, in chapter 3 we look at the different structural elements of sport organizations and how they are related. In chapter 4, we look at the patterning of structural variables and how they combine to produce particular organizational designs. We focus specifically on Mintzberg's five design configurations—simple structure, machine bureaucracy, divisionalized form, professional bureaucracy, and adhocracy—and show that we can find examples of each of these in the sport industry. Because of the importance attached to an appropriate organizational design, considerable attention is given to those factors seen as influencing this aspect of organization. Consequently, in chapters 5 through 8 we focus on strategy, size, environment, and technology. In chapter 9 we move away from the contextual situation of the organization, and focus on the way in which dominant individuals and coalitions exercise power in an organization to create a design that will maximize their control. In the final six chapters we focus on some of the processes with which managers are involved, specifically conflict, the management of change, human resources, decision making, organizational culture, and leadership.

Format of Each Chapter

Although each chapter varies slightly depending on the topic being covered, the format throughout the book is fairly consistent: Each chapter begins with a vignette from an actual sport organization, illustrating the topic to be covered. The major theoretical ideas about the particular topic are then introduced and related specifically to sport organizations. Appropriate figures and tables are used to help explain the points being made. At several places in each chapter you will find Time Outs, which illustrate the issues being discussed by providing accounts taken from actual situations concerning sport organizations or from research findings. Each chapter has a summary and a list of the key concepts discussed. A set of review questions is provided to stimulate discussion about central issues in the chapter. A section containing suggestions for further readings at the end of each chapter includes readings from the general management literature and the sport management literature. Finally, each chapter (except chapter 1) has a case for analysis, taken from an actual situation in a sport organization (in some instances the names of the people and organizations involved have been changed for reasons of confidentiality). Questions about the case are provided for class discussion.

Key Concepts

Sport organization

Organizational structure

Organizational design

Organizational context

Organizational theory

Organizational behavior

Systems theory

Scientific management

Life cycle perspective

Population ecology

Cybernetics

Organizational culture

Systems of political activity

Instruments of domination

Review Questions

1. Is a group of friends playing basketball a sport organization? Why or why not?

2. Why is an understanding of organization theory important for the sport manager?

3. What factors do you feel have contributed to the growth of the sport industry?

4. Select a sport organization with which you are familiar. Briefly explain how each part of the definition of a sport organization applies to the organization you selected.

5. Compare organizational structure and organizational design.

6. Select a sport organization with which you are familiar. Explain the context in which it exists.

7. Contrast organizational theory with organizational behavior.

8. How can the approaches of OT and OB complement each other?

9. Pick a sport organization with which you are familiar and, using two or more of the ways to look at organizations described in the text,

explain how your impression of this sport organization would vary depending on the perspective you picked.

10. Contrast the image of organizations as machines with the one which sees them as political systems.

11. What problems can you see in an approach to understanding sport organizations that likens them to organisms?

12. Select a research article on sport organizations. Which perspective on organizations do you think it uses?

13. Why do you think sport management scholars have not focused to any great extent on issues of power and politics in sport organizations?

14. Which of the ways of looking at sport organizations do you personally feel most comfortable with? Why?

15. Using the vignette at the start of the chapter, explain how Nike's structure and context have changed over the years.

Suggestions for Further Reading

The first edition of the *Journal of Sport Management* (Vol. 1, No. 1) contains an interesting article by Zeigler (1987) about the past, present, and future status of sport management. Also noteworthy in this edition is Paton's (1987) article on the progress that has been made in sport management research. Olafson's (1990) article in the *Journal of Sport Man-*

agement (Vol. 4, No. 2) provides some interesting and relevant ideas on research needs in sport management. My own work (Slack, 1991a) on future directions for our field (*Journal of Sport Management*, Vol. 5, No. 2) relates to some of the ideas found in this first chapter. Students are of course referred to Gareth Morgan's (1986) *Images of organization* as probably the best source of information about the different ways researchers have looked at organizations. Also see my article (Slack, 1993) "Morgan and the metaphors: Implications for sport management," which appeared in the *Journal of Sport Management* (Vol. 7, No. 3). Finally, although more

sociologically than managerially oriented, students may also find useful ideas in Rob Beamish's (1985) "Sport executives and voluntary associations: A review of the literature and introduction to some theoretical issues" in *Sociology of Sport Journal* (Vol. 2, No. 3, pp. 218-232).

2

Goals and Effectiveness in Sport Organizations

When You Have Read This Chapter

You should be able to

1. explain why goals are important in a sport organization,

2. identify the different types of goals that may be found in a sport organization,

3. explain the difference between organizational effectiveness and efficiency,

4. understand the different approaches that have been used to study organizational effectiveness, and

5. compare and contrast the benefits of each approach.

Swimming Canada: An Effective Organization?

At the 1978 British Commonwealth Games held in Edmonton, Alberta, Canadian swimmers won 15 gold medals. Graham Smith, the world record holder in the individual medley, won six of those golds. Members of the Canadian Amateur Swimming Association (now Swimming Canada) were understandably elated and felt that there were even greater achievements to come. At their 1978 annual general meeting, delegates demonstrated their optimism about the future when they adopted as their organization's goal to be number one in the world rankings by the end of the 1980s. They even adopted a catchy motto, "Go for 1t" where the "i" in "it" was replaced by a number "1."

Canada, along with most Western nations, boycotted the 1980 Olympic Games in Moscow but by the 1984 Games, Swimming Canada appeared to be on their way to achieving their goal. Canadian swimmers won 10 medals, 4 of which were gold. Even the absence of Eastern Bloc athletes did little to detract from the Canadian performances; three of the four gold medals were won with world record times. During the 1980s, Canadian swimmers also won two world championship gold medals; athletes like Anne Ottenbrite, Peter Szmidt, Victor Davis, Alex Baumann, Tom Ponting, and Allison Higson produced world class times.

However, in 1988 in the Olympic Games at Seoul, Canadian swimmers won only two medals, one silver and one bronze; both were won in relay events. Some members started to suggest that Swimming Canada had promoted its goal, to be number one, at the expense of other components of the national program. The organization was seen as not having the necessary infrastructure to meet the high performance requirements of the sport: It had no adequate talent identification system, coaching education was lagging behind other countries, and for many the needs of the grassroots members were not being met. As a result, in April 1989, a provincial executive directors' meeting proposed a new organizational goal: "To provide the opportunity for every individual involved in the sport of swimming to reach his or her maximum potential in fitness and excellence."

Based on information in Stubbs, D. (1989). Swimming Canada charts a new course for the future. *Champion, 13,* 20-23.

All organizations exist to achieve a particular goal or set of goals. For Swimming Canada, that goal was to be number one in the world by 1990. Despite the successes of many individual athletes, the organization did not achieve its goal. Does this mean that Swimming Canada was not an effective organization? Effectiveness, as we will see, is a difficult concept to define and measure. Researchers over the years have had considerable difficulty deciding exactly what the term means. In fact, some researchers (Goodman, Atkin, & Schoorman, 1983; Hannan & Freeman, 1977a) have even suggested abandoning "effectiveness" as a scientific concept. In a similar vein, Connolly, Conlon, and Deutsch (1980, p. 211) criticized the research literature on effectiveness for being in a state of "conceptual disarray"; Nord (1983, p. 95) suggested the area is in a "chaotic state of affairs";

and Quinn and Cameron (1983) describe effectiveness as a paradoxical concept.

Robbins (1990) notes that a review of the organizational effectiveness studies that proliferated in the 1960s and 1970s identified 30 different criteria, all claiming to measure effectiveness (see Campbell, 1977; Steers, 1975). Included were such concepts as productivity, profit, growth, goal consensus, and stability. In a study of effectiveness in intercollegiate athletic programs, Chelladurai, Haggerty, Campbell, and Wall (1981) identified 11 criteria of effectiveness:

- Achieved excellence
- Spectator interest
- Adequacy of facilities
- Career opportunities
- Student recruitment potential

- Competitive opportunities
- Sharing of costs by team
- Operating costs
- Activity as a life sport
- Satisfaction of athletes
- Sport characteristics (promotes fitness)

Despite the problems associated with the idea of organizational effectiveness, creating an effective organization is in many ways the central task of the sport manager. As Cameron (1986, p. 540) notes, "all theories of organization rely on some conception of the difference between high-quality (effective) performance and poor-quality (ineffective) performance. Hence, effectiveness is inherently tied to all *theory* on organizations" (emphasis in original). Benson (1977) makes a similar argument when he suggests that, within the field of organizational analysis, a great deal of attention has been given to studies of organizational effectiveness, and that even studies which do not focus on effectiveness "deal with it implicitly, as a background orientation" (p. 4).

In this chapter we examine the idea of goals and effectiveness. We look specifically at the importance of goals for a sport organization, the different types of goals a sport organization may have, the contrast between effectiveness and efficiency, and the different approaches used to study organizational effectiveness. The chapter also presents some of the concerns that have been expressed about the concepts of goals and effectiveness.

Importance of Understanding About Organizational Goals and Effectiveness for Sport Managers

Sport organizations are goal-seeking entities, structured to achieve a particular purpose (or purposes). The goals of a sport organization are extremely important for communicating its purpose and identity, to both employees and to external constituents. For some sport organizations, such as a professional hockey team or a college basketball team, it is often assumed that effectiveness is simply measured by the number of games the team wins. If this were the case, we may ask, why in 1988 did Edmonton Oiler's owner Peter Pocklington trade away the NHL's all-time leading goal scorer Wayne Gretzky at the height of his career? Did Mr. Pocklington not want an effective organization? The answer is ob-

viously yes! But, for a businessman like Mr. Pocklington, effectiveness was not measured solely by the number of games the Oilers won, but also by the amount of money they made.

For an organization such as the Commonwealth of Virginia's state Department of Conservation and Recreation, effectiveness may be determined by its ability to provide opportunities for participation in outdoor sports and recreation and, at the same time, conserve natural and recreational resources—two goals which at times may prove conflicting. For the many voluntary organizations involved in sport delivery, as new executive members are elected goals may change. Some amateur sport organizations may in fact have conflicting goals: Some members may see its purpose as increasing the numbers participating in the sport, while others may see its most important goal as producing medal-winning athletes. The *primary* goal of some women's athletic programs at major universities may be to secure a more equitable share of resources, so that they can achieve *other* program goals.

As these brief examples illustrate, effectiveness is not a simple concept. Some organizational goals are not always readily apparent; different constituents of a sport organization, for example, the athletes, coaches, owners, and spectators, may view effectiveness in different ways. Some sport organizations may have goals that conflict, and others may change their goals as their elected representatives change. In some sport organizations the achievement of financial goals may be necessary before other important goals can be attained. To manage this type of complexity, sport managers need a clear understanding of organizational goals and the relationship of these goals to measures of organizational effectiveness.

Organizational Goals

In this section, we look at the importance of goals for a sport organization, and examine the different types of goals a sport organization may set.

Importance of Organizational Goals

There are two main reasons why goals are important in sport organizations. First, as pointed out in chapter 1, all sport organizations exist for a purpose; if a sport organization does not have a purpose then there is no need for it to exist. Goals are statements that summarize and articulate the purpose of a sport

TIME OUT

At Eastern Michigan University Is Winning the Only Thing?

A policy developed at Eastern Michigan University was designed to tie a coach's salary increases to the team's win/loss record, game attendance, and student grades. Kathleen D. Tinney, the director of information services and publications at Eastern Michigan, was quoted as saying the "goal is to provide an incentive for coaches to improve their programs to the level of those who consistently win." The formula for rewarding coaches was to be based on goals set before the season. Salary raises would be determined by whether or not the coach exceeded, met, or fell short of her/his goal. Tinney noted that "It is an objective system but there is room for subjectivity."

Several athletic directors from other institutions criticized the system and suggested that it could lead to such abuses as cheating and coaches being pressured to play athletes with injuries. Charles McClendon, former Louisiana State football coach commented, "I just hope the football coach gets to set his own schedule. A couple of toughies against someone out of your class could blow your raise for the entire season."

Based on information from Macnow, G. (1985, July 17). Eastern Michigan's plan to tie coaches' pay to performance derided on other campuses. *Chronicle of Higher Education*, pp. 27-28.

organization. Second, as outlined in more detail in this chapter, goals provide guidelines for managers and other employees in such areas as decision making, performance appraisal, the reduction of uncertainty, the direction and motivation of employees, and organizational legitimacy (Daft, 1989).

Decision Making

All sport managers are required to make decisions that influence the operation of their organization and its employees. Goals provide sport managers with an understanding of the direction in which their organization is to proceed. With this understanding, sport managers can then more easily make decisions about such areas as structure, product expansion, and personnel recruitment, all of which move a sport organization toward achieving its goals. For example, in September 1985 when Jack Murray purchased Wilson Sporting Goods from PepsiCo Inc., Wilson's financial position was poor. In 1984 Wilson had suffered an operating loss of $17.3 million (Oneal, 1988). Murray's primary goal when he took over the company was to return it to its former profitability. This goal served to guide Murray in a number of the decisions he made, including focusing on research and development, reducing inventory, reestablishing links with private clubs and sporting goods retailers, and simplifying his product's pricing structure (Helm, 1986).

Performance Appraisal

At certain intervals, the performances of both individuals and subunits within a sport organization have to be assessed. The guidelines or criteria that provide a standard for this assessment are the goals of the organization. Those individuals or subunits seen as contributing the most to organizational goals are usually given the biggest rewards. Often in performance appraisals, suggestions are made as to how individuals or subunits can better contribute to organizational goals. In sport, we frequently base the performance appraisals of professional athletes on their contribution to the organizational goal of winning: The players who score the most goals or points are often given the highest salaries. For example, for the 1991-1992 season, Edmonton Oilers' star Esa Tikkanen, who had in the previous year scored 27 goals and 42 assists to lead his team in points, received a base salary of $800,000. In contrast, Kevin Lowe, a stalwart for the Oilers and holder of five Stanley Cup rings but a player who only had 3 goals and 13 assists in the 1990-1991 season, received a base remuneration of $350,000. However, in some types of sport organizations, such as those in the voluntary sector or a retail sporting goods store, it is not as easy to measure objectively an employee or subunit's performance. More details of performance appraisal techniques are provided in chapter 12.

Reducing Uncertainty

Uncertainty can be defined as "a lack of information about future events, so that alternatives and their outcomes are unpredictable" (Hickson, Hinings, Lee, Schneck, & Pennings, 1971, p. 219). Sport organizations, like all organizations, seek ways to reduce uncertainties; one of the ways to do this is through the setting of goals. The process of goal-setting is designed to allow the various constituents of a sport organization to discuss alternative goals, to reach consensus, and to decide on the goal(s) that are most important for the organization. Once goals are established, uncertainty within the organization is reduced. As Michael (1973, p. 149) notes, "goal-setting is attempted as a psychological means for reducing uncertainties and when participants succeed in stating and agreeing on goals; it symbolizes a reduction in uncertainty."

Directing and Motivating Employees

Goals describe a desired end or future state for a sport organization, and as such they give direction to employees. They can also motivate, if employees are a part of the process of goal-setting. For example, Ski Kananaskis Inc., the company that operates Nakiska, the ski site of the 1988 winter Olympic Games, sets its goals at a yearly meeting (traditionally away from the work site) where employees also take part in recreational activities such as horseback riding and whitewater canoeing. Mark Faubert, general manager at Nakiska, suggests that this type of involvement in goal-setting helps in the "team-building process," and as a result employees become more committed to goals (personal communication, May 29, 1990).

Establishing Legitimacy

Sport organizations gain legitimacy through legal means such as incorporation or affiliation with some accredited body. However, they can also gain legitimacy through the goals they establish. Goals are a statement of the sport organization's purpose; as such, they communicate what the organization stands for, and they provide a rationale for people to accept it as a legitimate entity. Goals legitimize a sport organization to both its employees or members and to external constituents such as funding bodies, alumni, and clients. Slack and Hinings (1992), for example, describe how Canadian national sport organizations that adopted the goal of producing high-performance athletes as their central focus increased their legitimacy in the eyes of the government funding agency, Sport Canada.

Types of Organizational Goals

Sport organizations usually have several different types of goals; each type performs a particular function within the organization. Some types of goals may overlap; for example, official goals are usually nonoperative, while short-term goals are usually operative. Table 2.1 summarizes those types of goals most frequently found in sport organizations, and provides an example of each as it could relate to a professional football team. Each type is then explained in more detail in the text that follows.

Official Goals

Charles Perrow (1961, p. 855) suggests that official goals are "the general purposes of the organization as put forth in the charter, annual reports, public statements by key executives, and other authoritative pronouncements." For example, the official goal

Table 2.1   Classification of Goals: Examples From a Professional Football Team

TYPE OF GOAL	EXAMPLE
Official goal	To provide a high quality football program that is both entertaining and of benefit to the community.
Operative goal	To make money.
Operational goal	To sell over 50,000 tickets for each home game.
Nonoperational goal	To provide a fair return on investment to shareholders.
Short-term goal	To win two of the first three away games of the season.
Long-term goal	To win the Super Bowl.
Department/subunit goal	To generate at least 350 yards of offense each game.

(or mission statement, as it is often called) of the Canadian Figure Skating Association is expressed as follows: "The Canadian Figure Skating Association is an association dedicated to the principles of enabling every Canadian to participate in skating throughout their lifetime for fun, fitness, and/or achievement" (Canadian Figure Skating Association, National Championship Program, 1994). Official goals, often subjective and usually not measurable, express the values of the organization and give it legitimacy with external constituents; they describe the reason(s) for the organization's existence, and serve as a means by which employees/members identify with the organization.

Operative Goals

While official goals exemplify what a sport organization says it wants to achieve, operative goals "designate the ends sought through the actual operat-

ing policies of the organization; they tell us what the organization actually is trying to do, regardless of what the official goals say are the aims" (Perrow, 1961, p. 855). An indication of the operative goals of an organization, which are usually not explicitly stated, may often be obtained by examining the way resources are allocated. The late owner of the Toronto Maple Leafs, Harold Ballard, gave a good indication of his operative goals for "the Leafs" when shareholders at the 1985 annual general meeting inquired about the team's dismal performance on the ice. He told them "our shares are all right and we're making money so what the hell do we care?" (Mills, 1991, p. 11).

Operational Goals

Operational goals are goals that can be measured objectively; they may be official but are most likely to be operative. One of the main ways operating

---

TIME OUT

The Operative Goals of Intercollegiate Athletics

Chelladurai and Danylchuk (1984) conducted a survey of athletic administrators to investigate their perceptions of the operative goals of intercollegiate athletics. They surveyed administrators at each of the 44 member institutions of the Canadian Intercollegiate Athletic Union. To determine the operative goals, the researchers asked respondents to rate statements about each of nine possible goals:

1. Entertainment—to provide a source of entertainment for the student body, faculty/staff, alumni, and community.
2. National sport development—to contribute to the national sport development.
3. Financial—to generate revenue for the university.
4. Transmission of culture—to transmit the culture and tradition of the university and society.
5. Career opportunities—to provide those athletic experiences that will increase career opportunities for the athletes.
6. Public relations—to enhance university/community relations.
7. Athlete's personal growth—to promote the athlete's personal growth and health (physical, mental, and emotional).
8. Prestige—to enhance the prestige of the university, students, faculty/staff, alumni, and community.
9. Achieved excellence—to support those athletes performing at a high level of excellence (relative to athletes in other universities).

Athletic administrators were consistent in ranking transmission of culture, athlete's personal growth, public relations, and prestige as the most important operative goals of their program. Administrators from small and medium-sized universities also ranked entertainment as an important goal.

Based on information in Chelladurai, P., & Danylchuk, K.E. (1984). Operative goals of intercollegiate athletics: Perceptions of athletic administrators. *Canadian Journal of Applied Sport Sciences, 9*, 33-41.

goals can be developed in sport organizations is through a process known as Management by Objectives (MBO). Growing out of the work of classical management theorists such as Fayol and Urwick, MBO is probably most often associated with the work of Peter Drucker (1954). Although it promotes the type of mechanistic approach to organizations that was outlined in chapter 1 and fails to consider many of the human and political aspects of organizations, MBO has frequently been suggested as a means of goal-setting for sport organizations (cf. Jensen, 1983; Kelly, 1991; VanderZwaag, 1984).

Nonoperational Goals

A nonoperational goal is one that cannot be measured objectively. Official goals, or mission statements, are usually nonoperational. For example, Huffy Corporation, one of the leading U.S. producers of bicycles, has the following as a part of its mission statement: "Our mission is to increase the value of our shareholders' investment through growth in both equity and dividends. To accomplish this, we must achieve sufficient levels of profit to fund the needs of our existing businesses, to finance future expansion opportunities, and contribute toward the development of employees and the communities in which they live." (Huffy Corporation, Annual Report, 1989). As can be seen, the statement is for the most part subjective, and hence nonoperational.

Long-Term Goals

Long-term goals are those the sport organization would like to achieve over a relatively lengthy period of time—maybe a season or a period of years. For example, in its 1989 Annual Report, Johnson Worldwide Associates, Inc., a major U.S. manufacturer and marketer of recreational products such as camping equipment, canoes, diving, and snorkeling products, set the following as long-term goals:

- Annual growth of 10%-15% from continuing operations with net income rising faster than sales.
- Acquisitions contributing one-fourth to one-third of sales growth.
- Return on shareholders' equity of over 20% (Johnson Worldwide Associates, Inc. Annual Report, 1989).

Short-Term Goals

Short-term goals are those which are set for a relatively brief period of time. For example, the general manager of a baseball team will often set short-term goals for the team, such as winning 50 percent of their games on their next road trip.

Department/Subunit Goals Versus Overall Goals

As we have seen, sport organizations formulate overall goals. They may be official or operative, operational or nonoperational, long-term or short-term. However, departments or subunits within a sport organization may also formulate their own goals. For example, the sales department of a company that produces sport equipment may set as its goal to sell a certain amount of their product, or the defensive unit of a college football team may set as its goal to hold opponents to under a certain yardage. It is important that subunits or department goals do not work counter to overall organizational goals. Department/subunit goals should not be seen as ends in themselves but as a means of achieving the sport organization's desired end state.

Effectiveness or Efficiency

As Hannan and Freeman (1977a) point out, within the tradition that emphasizes the importance of organizational goals, an important distinction needs to be made between the concepts of organizational effectiveness and organizational efficiency. Effectiveness refers to the extent to which an organization achieves its goal or goals. Efficiency, on the other hand, takes into account the amount of resources used to produce the desired output (cf. Pennings & Goodman, 1977; Sandefur, 1983). It is often measured in economic terms, usually the ratio of inputs to outputs. However, as Mintzberg (1982, p. 104) notes, "because economic costs can usually be more easily measured than social costs, efficiency often produces an escalation in social costs. . . ." Macintosh and Whitson (1990) illustrate the occurrence of such a situation in sport when they suggest that Sport Canada's push for international sporting success has been achieved at the expense of some of the other more socially oriented goals of sport such as gender equity and regional access.

While efficiency is a goal of all sport organizations, an efficient organization is not necessarily effective. For example, a sport organization may be efficient in the way that it makes its product but, like Puma athletic shoes in the mid-1980s (cf. Roth, 1987), if there is a reduction in the number of people buying the product, the organization will not be effective in meeting its goals. Likewise, an organization may be effective in that it achieves its goal(s) but it may not be efficient. For example, a professional soccer team that wins a championship but does so by spending large sums of money to buy established players would fall into this category.

Approaches to Studying Organizational Effectiveness

As would be expected, the varying opinions of what constitutes organizational effectiveness have led to several different approaches to studying the concept. Cameron (1980) identified four major approaches to evaluating effectiveness: the goal attainment approach, the systems resource approach, the internal process approach, and the strategic constituencies approach. We now look at each of these approaches, and the more recently developed competing values approach (Quinn & Rohrbaugh, 1981, 1983). The main principles of each approach are examined, and strengths and weaknesses discussed.

The Goal Attainment Approach

As we saw earlier in this chapter and in our definition in chapter 1, all sport organizations exist to achieve one or more goals. The goal attainment approach to organizational effectiveness is based on the identification of these goals, and how well the sport organization attains or makes progress toward them. Effectiveness is based on the achievement of ends, not means. The most important goals to focus on when using this approach to organizational effectiveness are operative goals (Hall & Clark, 1980; Price, 1972; Steers, 1975). For the goal attainment model to be workable, the sport organization being studied must have goals that are clearly identifiable, consensual, measurable, and time-bounded (Cameron, 1984). There must be general consensus or agreement on the goals and there must be a small enough number of them to be manageable. Campbell (1977, p. 26) suggests that MBO "represents the ultimate in a goal-oriented model of effectiveness."

In studies of sport organizations the goal attainment approach has been the most frequently used method of evaluating effectiveness. The goals "most often measured in a sport context reflect an emphasis on performance outcomes and have been operationalized in terms of win/loss records or performance rankings in comparison to other teams" (Frisby, 1986a, p. 95). For example, Chelladurai, Szyszlo, and Haggerty (1987) in their study of national sport organizations used the number of medals won at major competitions and the number of victories at dual international events as indicators of effectiveness. They suggest that the goal model may be useful for evaluating the effectiveness of elite sport programs, but they reject the use of this approach for mass sport programs, since goal attainment is not as easily measured in the latter. Former Dallas Cowboy's owner H.R. "Bum" Bright shows how, in evaluating effectiveness, it is possible to reject one measure of goal effectiveness in favor of another. He noted "the actual success or failure of our investment in the Cowboys will not be measured by the profit/loss bottom line, but will be measured by their success in their competition on the football field" (Hampton, 1984, p. 24).

Despite its popularity, the goal attainment approach to organizational effectiveness has a number of problems. The first and, according to Hannan and Freeman (1977a, p. 111), the most substantive of these problems arises because of "the likely multiplicity of organizational goals." While some sport organizations will only have one goal, others have more; the faculty of Physical Education and Recreation at the University of Alberta, for example, has goals that relate to teaching, research, and service. This multiplicity is compounded in organizations when operative goals are added, and when subunits have their own goals, as is so often the case.

The multiplicity of organizational goals can also be problematic in that, as was pointed out earlier in the chapter, some goals may be competing or even incompatible. For example, the editors of the British soccer fanzine *When Saturday Comes* (a magazine produced by the fans of a particular soccer team for other fans) had as one of their goals to change their circulation from monthly to weekly (Arthur, 1989). The infusion of capital to change their circulation could probably have been obtained by increasing the percentage of advertising in the fanzine or getting support from a larger publisher, but such a move would have subverted the original goal of an independent magazine produced by fans for fans. The presence of such multiple and conflicting goals means that effectiveness cannot be solely determined by one single indicator.

A second problem with the goal attainment approach is how to identify goals and actually measure the extent to which they have been achieved. As we pointed out earlier in the chapter, official goals are usually vague and operative goals are often not written down. While it is relatively easy

TIME OUT

Win/Loss Record and the Setting of Organizational Objectives: A Study of the NFL

One of the indicators of effectiveness frequently used in conjunction with professional sport teams is the win/loss record. Latham and Stewart (1981) were interested in determining if the setting of organizational objectives was related to a sport organization's win/loss record. In a study involving interviews with 40 representatives from 10 NFL teams, each representative completed a Likert scale designed to ascertain the importance that his/her organization attached to particular objectives, such as whether the organization needed to improve its image, produce a winning team, make the playoffs, satisfy the needs of the local community, and so on. The teams were then categorized as winning, moderate, or losing teams, based on a three year win/loss record. Comparing the setting of objectives and win/loss record, Latham and Stewart (1981) found that the setting of objectives was related to a team's success on the playing field. Whether the setting of objectives led to success or vice versa was not clear. They concluded that "winning teams seem to place somewhat less emphasis on entertainment and winning objectives relative to moderate and losing teams, but place more emphasis on certain other objectives, for example, survival" (p. 408). It is suggested that those teams that have done well in terms of win/loss record "have adopted a more balanced multi-objective position for their organization [and that] less successful teams may not have that luxury but must respond to the more immediate pressures of bringing fans to the stadium" (p. 408).

Based on information in Latham, D.R., & Stewart, D.W. (1981). Organizational objectives and winning: An examination of the NFL. *Academy of Management Journal, 24*, 403-408.

to argue that for sport organizations like the Los Angeles Lakers and the Chicago White Sox the number of games won is a measure of goal effectiveness, it is harder to both identify and measure the goals of a high school physical education department. Likewise, profit-making sport organizations and professional sport teams may also have goals that relate to such areas as job satisfaction and player development. These goals can usually only be measured qualitatively and progress toward them is difficult to assess, further complicating the use of the goal attainment approach to effectiveness. Price (1972) suggests that one way to overcome the problem of goal clarity is to focus on the organizational decision makers, because their statements and actions regarding the organization's operations reveal its priorities. However, as Chelladurai (1985) points out, although Price's suggestion has merit, it tends to ignore the fact that there may not be consensus among decision makers as to what the sport organization's goals are; in addition, their goals may change inasmuch as their power to influence decisions changes.

A third problem with the goal attainment approach relates to the temporal dimension of goals. As Hannan and Freeman (1977a, p. 113) ask, "Should we consider the short run or the long run or both?" They go on to suggest that most published empirical studies employing cross-sectional data focus on the short run, but whether this focus is appropriate depends on "the nature of the goals function for each organization." For organizations that stress a quick return on investment, as some profit-making sport organizations do, short-run goals should be considered; for organizations oriented toward continued production, however, such as a university faculty of physical education producing graduates, research, and so on, "year-to-year fluctuations in performance should be discounted and the average performance over longer periods emphasized" (Hannan & Freeman, 1977a, p. 113). In addition, different sport organizations operating in the same environment and with the same structure may have similar goals but may place a different emphasis on their rate of return on investment.

A final problem with the goal attainment approach concerns whose goals count. Even within the senior management levels of a sport organization, there will be variation in beliefs about what are appropriate organizational goals. In some sport organizations the people with power may actually be outside the senior management levels. This condition is not uncommon in voluntary sport organizations, where individuals who may have held a power position (e.g., president) in the organization remain after their tenure, as a member of the rank and file. Such individuals, despite not holding an official position, may still exert considerable influence on organizational goals. The goals usually attributed to the organization are actually those of the dominant coalition. It is also possible that the goals of an organization may be considerably influenced by the contextual situation in which the sport organization exists. Macintosh and Whitson (1990), for example, have suggested that Sport Canada strongly influenced the high-performance goals of Canadian national sport organizations.

Where then, we may ask, does all this leave us? How useful is the goal attainment approach to organizational effectiveness? While it is hard to question the fact that one of the main functions of sport organizations is to achieve their goals, the problems are identifying these goals, deciding which are important (or more important than others), and measuring whether or not they are achieved. Robbins (1990, p. 57) suggests five ways to increase the validity of the identified goals:

1. Ensure that input is received from all those having a major influence on formulating the official goals, even if they are not part of the senior management.
2. Include actual goals obtained by observing the behavior of organization members.
3. Recognize that organizations pursue both short- and long-term goals.
4. Insist on tangible, verifiable, and measurable goals rather than relying on vague statements that merely mirror societal expectations.
5. View goals as dynamic entities that change over time rather than as rigid or fixed statements of purpose.

Notwithstanding these suggestions and the fact that the goal attainment model of effectiveness has been used in several studies of sport organizations, those who choose to use this approach may be wise to consider Warriner's (1965, p. 140) caution, that goals should be thought of "as fiction produced by an organization to account for, explain, or rationalize its existence to particular audiences rather than as valid and reliable indications of purpose."

The Systems Resource Approach

While the goal attainment approach to effectiveness focuses on organizational outputs, the systems resource approach focuses on inputs. This particular approach to organizational effectiveness is based on open systems theory. Organizations develop exchange relationships with their environment in order to obtain resources. Consequently, effectiveness is defined as "the ability of the organization in either absolute or relative terms to exploit its environment in the acquisition of scarce and valued resources" (Yuchtman & Seashore, 1967, p. 898). The organizations seen as being most effective "are those that receive greater resource inputs from their environments" (Molnar & Rogers, 1976, p. 403).

From a systems resource perspective, a sport organization like the New York Yankees which increased their attendance every year between 1984 and 1988, would be considered effective on this criterion for this time period. Similarly, an organization like the Canadian Hockey Association, which has over 400,000 members, would from a systems resource perspective be considered more effective than the Canadian Weightlifting Federation, which has just over 1,200 members. It is important, however, to note that Yuchtman and Seashore (1967, p. 900) do not "limit the concept of resources to physical or economic objects or states" but follow Gamson's (1966) argument "that the 'reputation' of individuals or groups as 'influentials' in their community political affairs is itself a resource." Macintosh and Whitson (1990) exemplify the use of this type of resource when they point out that national sport organizations in Canada have actively sought out board members with "corporate credentials." Obviously those organizations who succeeded in placing senior management individuals on their board would, from a systems resource perspective, be seen as effective.

As Chelladurai (1985, p. 176) points out, it may "appear at first glance that the goals model and the system resource approach are significantly different—the former emphasizes the outputs of the organization while the latter emphasizes the inputs." But as he goes on to point out, an organization can only secure inputs from its environment on a continuous basis "when its outputs are acceptable to the environment." The acquisition of resources, as Hall (1982, p. 277) notes, "does not just happen but is based on what the organization is attempting to achieve, namely its goals." For example, when Virginia Tech's basketball team won the National Invitational Tournament in 1973, its president,

T. Marshall Hahn, noted that considerable sums of money were pledged to the university. He also added that he felt alumni, corporations, and the state legislature would look more favorably on the university as a result of its success (Creamer, 1973). Clearly, here is a case where the output of the organization affected its sources of input. Frisby (1986a), in her study of Canadian national sport organizations, did in fact find significant correlations between measures of goal attainment and resource acquisition.

The strengths of the systems resource approach to effectiveness are threefold. First, unlike the goal attainment approach, which considers goals as cultural entities arising outside of the organization, the systems resource approach treats the organization itself as its frame of reference. Second, it takes into account the organization's relationship to its environment. Third, it can be used to compare organizations that have differing goals (Daft, 1989). For example, because all sport organizations have to obtain human, physical, and financial resources to survive (survival being the most basic measure of effectiveness), they can be compared on their ability to obtain these resources from their environment. The local baseball association able to attract a large number of members, for example, will probably be seen by the municipal council as more effective than an orienteering group with just a few members.

Despite the fact that it does possess some appealing qualities, the systems resource approach also exhibits several problems as a means of assessing effectiveness. First, and in many ways the foremost, of these problems is the fact that although this approach to organizational effectiveness is widely quoted in the management literature and even within the relatively sparse literature on the effectiveness of sport organizations, it has produced "no coherent line of research" (Goodman & Pennings, 1977, p. 4). A second problem is semantic; it concerns the question of what is an input and what is an output. By way of illustration, consider the example of attendance at New York Yankees games just cited; is this in fact one form of resource acquisition or is it actually a goal of the organization to increase attendance?

The systems resource approach is also problematic in its applicability to public-sector organizations concerned with sport, and to some voluntary sport organizations. The problem arises because often, for these types of organizations, a percentage of their funding is guaranteed, or at least highly certain, because it comes from a higher-level organization. For example, unlike the U.S. equivalents, many na-

tional sport organizations in Canada and Great Britain obtain a fairly large percentage of their financial resources from the government. Thus, using financial resources as an indicator of effectiveness is not particularly appropriate. It would, however, be legitimate to measure the effectiveness of these sport organizations by the amount of funding they obtain from other sources, such as membership fees or corporate sponsorship, because these funds are not guaranteed.

A final problem with the systems resource approach is that, as Cameron (1980, p. 68) points out, "an organization can be effective even when it doesn't possess a competitive advantage in the marketplace or when the most desirable resources aren't obtained." As an example, he uses the "no-name" Seattle Supersonics, who "did not succeed in attracting superstars to their basketball team in 1977 and 1978, (i.e., they did not secure a competitive advantage), yet even with a rookie coach and no standout stars the team reached the National Basketball Association finals in 1978 and won in 1979."

The systems resource approach does present an alternative perspective to assessing organizational effectiveness. It is most applicable to understanding the following types of sport organizations: those whose outputs cannot be objectively measured; those where there is a clear connection between the resources (inputs) obtained and what is produced (outputs) (cf. Cameron, 1980); and those whose supply of resources is not guaranteed by some formalized arrangement with another organization.

The Internal Process Approach

A third approach to determining organizational effectiveness is called the internal process approach. From this perspective, "effective organizations are those with an absence of internal strain, whose members are highly integrated into the system, whose internal functioning is smooth and typified by trust and benevolence toward individuals, where information flows smoothly both vertically and horizontally and so on" (Cameron, 1980, p. 67). While the goal attainment approach focuses on organizational outputs and the systems resource approach focuses on inputs, this approach focuses on the throughputs or transformation processes found in an organization. These relationships are illustrated in figure 2.1. Throughputs are the internal activities and processes of the organization by which inputs are converted into outputs.

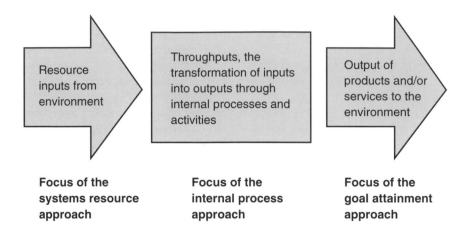

Focus of the systems resource approach

Focus of the internal process approach

Focus of the goal attainment approach

Figure 2.1   Approaches to the measurement of organizational effectiveness.

The basis for this approach can be found in the work of writers such as Argyris (1964) and Likert (1967), who have all suggested that human resources practices are linked to organizational effectiveness. Daft (1989) suggests that, from this perspective, indicators of an effective organization would include such things as the supervisors' interest and concern for their workers; a feeling of team spirit, group loyalty, and teamwork; good communications; and a compensation system that rewards managers for performance growth, the development of subordinates, and the creation of an effective working group. In a study of national sport organizations, Chelladurai and Haggerty (1991) used items such as the meaningful organization of work, information sharing among members, and concern over employee welfare and happiness, as indicators of internal process effectiveness.

In contrast to an emphasis on human resources, some writers have suggested that economic efficiency should be the focus when evaluating the internal processes of an organization. Martindell (1962), for example, developed a management audit of organizations, which appraises performance on such criteria as health of earnings, fiscal policies, research and development, production efficiency, and sales. There are ten areas in total in Martindell's audit and each is assigned a weight in terms of its perceived contribution to the organization's overall performance. Although many of the criteria are related to organizations of a profit-making nature, it is possible to modify the approach for use in voluntary organizations. In a similar vein to the management audit, Evan (1976) developed a quantitative method of looking at the economic efficiency of an organization. He suggested that it was possible to examine the inputs (I), throughputs (T), and

outputs (O) of an organization; these variables could then be examined as ratios to evaluate the performance of the organization. Table 2.2 shows some of the ratios that could be used in a profit-making sport organization, a local basketball association, and a faculty of kinesiology. For example, if we use the ratio of throughput to input for the local basketball association or the faculty of kinesiology as an indicator of economic effectiveness, we could get three possible results. If the cost of operations is higher than the annual budget the ratio would be X:1 where X>1. In this situation the organization would probably be seen to be ineffective because it has gone over budget. If the cost of operations and the annual budget were the same the ratio would be 1:1. If the costs of operations were less than the annual budget the ratio would be Y:1 where Y<1. In these last two situations the organization would probably be seen as effective because it has stayed within its budget.

The major advantage of the internal process approach is that it can be used to compare organizations that have different outputs, different inputs, or little control over their environment. However, the first of a number of problems with this approach relates to the measurement of human resource variables. For example, in their study of Canadian national sport organizations, Chelladurai, Szyszlo, and Haggerty (1987) used such throughput (transformation) variables as "morale among staff members and volunteers involved in community based programs" and "the working relationship between the NSGB [national sport governing body] and its provincial branches on elite programs." While important aspects of the internal processes of these organizations, they are extremely difficult concepts to measure in any valid or reliable way.

Table 2.2   Effectiveness Measures of Systems in Selected Sport Organizations

SYSTEMS VARIABLES	PROFIT-MAKING SPORT ORGANIZATION	LOCAL BASKETBALL ASSOCIATION	FACULTY OF KINESIOLOGY
O/I	Return on investment	Number of games *played*; annual budget	Number of students *graduated*; annual budget
I/I	Change in working capital	Change in number of players	Change in number of students
T/I	Inventory turnover	*Cost of operations*; annual budget	*Cost of operations*; annual budget

O = Outputs
I = Inputs
T = Throughputs

Adapted, by permission, from W.M. Evan, 1976, Organizational theory and organizational effectiveness: An exploratory analysis. In *Organizational effectiveness: Theory, research, utilization*, edited by S.L. Spray (Kent, Ohio: Kent State University Press), 22-23.

Also, because it does not focus on organizational outputs or an organization's relationship with its environment, the internal process approach offers only a very limited view of organizational effectiveness. As Das (1990, p. 146) notes, "organization success may be attributable to the simultaneous presence of a number of factors and conditions, and a change in even some of these contributing factors could lead to a totally different organizational outcome."

The internal process model also takes no account of the notion of equifinality—the ability of organizations to achieve similar ends through different means (Hrebiniak & Joyce, 1985). Two organizations with different internal processes may produce the same outputs and "conversely two organizations that have similar internal processes may produce differing outcomes" (Das, 1990, p. 146).

Finally, the internal process model is lacking in that an organization may have internal problems such as low morale, poor communication, and conflict, yet still be successful. Cameron (1980, p. 69) provides a classic example, the New York Yankees of 1977 and 1978: "Lack of team discipline, fights among players and between players and coaches, threatened firings, turnover in key personnel, and lack of cohesion seemed to be the defining characteristics of that organization during the 1977 and 1978 baseball seasons. Yet the Yankees were the most effective team in baseball in terms of goal accomplishment; they won the World Series both years."

The Strategic Constituencies Approach

A fourth, and more integrative, approach to organizational effectiveness is the strategic constituen-cies approach which emanates from the work of Connolly, Conlon, and Deutsch (1980). (It may also be beneficial to look at Keeley's [1978] treatment of effectiveness for information on the origins of this perspective.) Fans, the media, sponsors, and owners are all examples of groups that could be considered the strategic constituents or stakeholders of a professional basketball organization. Each has a different interest in the performance of the organization and, in turn, the organization relies on these groups for resources and support. The extent to which the team is able to satisfy the criteria used by each group to evaluate it will determine its effectiveness. Table 2.3 provides examples of the type of effectiveness criteria that might be used by selected strategic constituents of a professional basketball organization. It is important to note that constituents may be internal (e.g., players) or external (e.g., sponsors) to the organization.

The strategic constituency approach is similar to the systems resource approach, yet with a different emphasis. While the systems resource approach is concerned with acquiring critical resources from the environment, the strategic constituents approach is also concerned with the actions of its stakeholders. For example, a professional baseball team like the Montreal Expos does not acquire resources from members of the print media, so from a systems resource perspective they would not be considered particularly important. However, the print media are stakeholders, in that they have an interest in the team and are able to exert considerable influence on its success. Therefore, from a strategic constituents perspective they are a significant group that can influence the team's effectiveness.

The strategic constituencies approach takes into account the fact that managers have to work toward

Table 2.3 Effectiveness Criteria of Selected Strategic Constituents of a Professional Basketball Team

CONSTITUENCY OR STAKEHOLDER	TYPICAL CRITERIA OF EFFECTIVENESS
Owners	Profit; increased value of franchise.
Players	Adequate salary and benefits; good working conditions.
Fans	Entertaining games; reasonably priced tickets; concessions, etc.
Community	Visibility through team activities; economic benefits for local businesses.
Media	Newsworthy coaches and players.
National Basketball Association	Compliance with rules; efforts to promote a positive image of the game.
Sponsors	Media exposure; high attendance.

several goals simultaneously. Typically, they have to satisfy the interests of a number of constituents who influence the organization's ability to achieve success. Consequently, the goals selected are not value-free; each favors one constituent over another. As a result, organizations are political; they have to respond to the vested interests of their various constituents. This is a very important point for sport managers, since much of the literature in our field has presented a view of sport organizations as apolitical (Slack, 1991a).

A strength of the strategic constituents approach is that effectiveness is seen as a complex, multidimensional construct. It also considers factors internal and external to the organization. In addition, the issue of corporate social responsibility is taken into account (something that is not a consideration in any of the other approaches to effectiveness that we have examined so far), that is, what moral and ethical obligations the organization has to the community within which it operates. Another strength of this approach is that it forces sport managers to be cognizant of groups whose power could have an adverse effect on their operations. The Time Out on page 31 provides a graphic example of the importance of this point. By knowing whose support it needs to maintain its operations, an organization can modify its goals to meet the demands of those particular constituents.

It is not always easy, however, to identify an organization's constituents and their relative importance. For example, in the case of the professional sport team, who is more important to success: the fans or the media? Another difficulty is that different people in the organization will see different constituents as being important; the finance officer of a university athletic department, for example, is unlikely to see the constituents of the organization in the same way as the head basketball coach. Also

problematic is the fact that the relative importance of the different constituents will change over time. For example, in the founding stages of a fitness center, financial institutions will be important constituents; the center will need access to capital for startup costs and will look to these institutions to provide this money. In later years when the center is well established and has an established clientele, lending institutions will be less important as a strategic constituent. Finally, even if the constituents can be identified, how do sport managers identify their expectations for the organization, and correctly measure this type of information?

Despite these difficulties, this approach to organizational effectiveness is gaining popularity (cf. Cameron, 1984; Kanter & Brinkerhoff, 1981). It offers a more holistic approach than previous models and, as mentioned earlier, emphasizes the political nature of organizations. Along with the competing values approach, which we will discuss next, it provides one of the better ways of determining organizational effectiveness.

The Competing Values Approach

Like the strategic constituents perspective, the competing values approach is based on the premise that there is no single best criterion of organizational effectiveness; rather, effectiveness is a subjective concept and the criteria used to assess it depend on the evaluator's value preferences. For example, in an athletic shoe manufacturing company like Reebok, we would expect to find that the finance and accounting managers would define effectiveness in terms of profitability and a balanced budget; marketing managers would look at percentage of market share; production managers would be concerned with the number and quality of shoes manufactured. Finally, the council at Stoughton,

TIME OUT

Responding to Strategic Constituents: The Athletic Footwear Industry

Rudolf and Adolf Dassler first started making shoes in the German town of Herzogenaurach in 1920. Their business grew slowly; in 1936 they made the shoes in which Jessie Owens won four gold medals at the 1936 Olympic Games. However, in 1949 the brothers quarreled and each went his own way; Rudolf left and formed the Puma company, while Adolf, renaming the business adidas, stayed on at the old factory. Throughout the 1950s, 1960s, and most of the 1970s, adidas and Puma dominated the athletic footwear market. In the 1970s the industry started to change; jogging became a major recreational activity, athletic shoes became fashion wear, and the aerobics boom started to take off. Companies like Nike and Reebok started to cater to these changing customer demands by developing a broad range of brightly colored fashionable shoes. Adidas and Puma, slow to respond to these consumer demands, continued to make the type of shoes they had in the past; their market share dropped considerably, and the companies lost their preeminent position in the market. Adidas and Puma had failed to respond to the needs of one of their most important strategic constituents—their customers.

Based on information in Hartley, R.F. (1989). *Marketing mistakes* (4th. ed.). New York: Wiley. Chapter 10 The Crest Riders of the Running Boom; Bruce, P. (1985, October 14). Two Barvarian companies battle for citizens soles. *The Toronto Globe and Mail*, p. B4; Roth, T. (1987, February 6). Puma hopes superstar will help end U.S. slump, narrow gap with adidas. *Wall Street Journal*, p. 24.

Massachusetts, where Reebok is headquartered, would define effectiveness in terms of the growth of the company's workforce.

The competing values approach was developed by Quinn and Rohrbaugh (1981), who used a list of criteria that Campbell (1977) claimed were indicators of organizational effectiveness. The list was analyzed using multidimensional scaling. It produced three dimensions of organizational effectiveness seen as representing competing values. The first set of values concerns organizational focus; these values range from those that emphasize the well-being and development of the people in the organization (an internal focus on the organization's socio-technical system) to a concern with the well-being and development of the organization itself (an external focus on its competitive position) (Quinn & Rohrbaugh, 1983). The second set of values concerns the structure of the organization, from a structure that emphasizes flexibility (i.e., a decentralized, differentiated structure with the ability to adapt, innovate, and change) to a structure that favors control (i.e., centralized, integrated and

exhibiting stability, predictability, and order). The third set of values concerns means and ends. A focus on means stresses internal processes such as planning; a focus on ends emphasizes final outcomes such as profitability or win/loss record. As Quinn and Rohrbaugh (1981, p. 132) note, "these three sets of competing values are recognized dilemmas in the organizational literature."*

The three sets of values can be combined as shown in figure 2.2. The two axes of flexibility/control and internal/external focus produce four quadrants. Quinn (1988) suggests that each one of the quadrants represents one of the four major models in organization theory—human relations, open systems, internal process, or rational goal. He goes on to suggest that the two sets of criteria in each of the quadrants relate to the implicit means/ends theory that is associated with each of the models. Thus, in the human relations model, a focus on means would see effectiveness being represented by a cohesive workforce where morale is high; a focus on ends would emphasize human resources development. Table 2.4 shows the four models and

*For more information on the competing values approach refer to Vol. 5, No. 2 (June 1981) of *Public Productivity Review* which contains five articles (including Quinn & Rohrbaugh's work) which focus on this particular approach to organizational effectiveness.

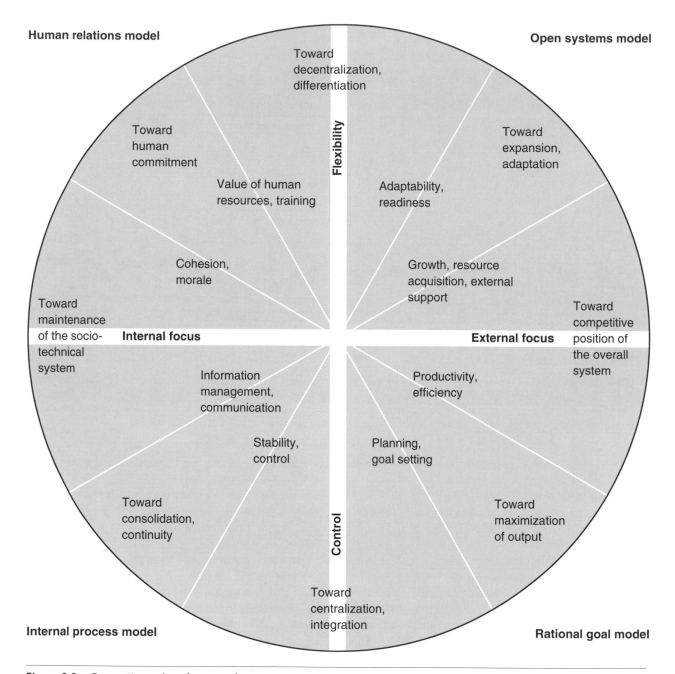

Figure 2.2   Competing values framework.

Quinn, R.E. *Beyond rational management: Mastering the paradoxes and competing demands of high performance*, p. 48 (Figure 5). © 1988 by Jossey-Bass Inc., Publishers.

how effectiveness would be defined in each, depending on whether the focus is on means or ends. It is important to note that each model has a polar opposite. As Quinn (1988, pp. 47-48) points out, "the human relations model, which emphasizes flexibility and internal focus, stands in stark contrast to the rational goal model which stresses control and external focus. The open systems model, which is characterized by flexibility and external focus, runs counter to the internal process model, which emphasizes control and internal focus."

Quinn goes on to point out parallels between the models. Both the human relations and open systems models emphasize flexibility; the open systems and rational goal models are focused on external issues such as responding to change. Control is a value emphasized in the rational goal and internal process models; the human relations and internal process models both have an internal focus that

Table 2.4   Criteria of Effectiveness for Competing Values Models

MODEL	CRITERIA OF EFFECTIVENESS
Human relations	
Means	A cohesive work force where morale is high; employees work well together.
Ends	An emphasis on the training and development of human resources to perform tasks in a proper manner.
Open systems	
Means	A flexible work force able to respond well to changes in external conditions and demands.
Ends	A focus on growth and the ability to acquire external resources.
Internal process	
Means	A focus on communication and information management; people being well informed about issues that influence their work.
Ends	A focus on stability, order, and control; operations run smoothly.
Rational goal	
Means	An emphasis on planning and the setting of identifiable goals.
Ends	High productivity; efficiency in terms of outputs to inputs.

emphasizes such things as the organization's human and technical systems. Managers are faced with decisions about which of these values will direct their organization.

The competing values perspective, unlike other approaches, takes into account the paradoxical nature of effectiveness. For example, the Indiana University basketball team coached by Bobby Knight is generally seen as a very successful organization, at least in terms of win/loss record. Using the competing values perspective, most people would score the team high in terms of productivity (i.e., the rational goal model). However, as Feinstein (1986) indicates in his book on Knight and the Hoosier's basketball team, some of this success has been achieved at the expense of a concern with human resources. The competing values approach does not suggest that these opposing values cannot mutually exist; rather, it helps us understand the trade-offs necessary in evaluating the effectiveness of an organization.

To operationalize the competing values approach, it is first necessary for a sport manager to identify those constituents that are seen as necessary for the organization's survival. The next step is to determine the importance those constituents place on the various values. This task can be done by the sport managers themselves, who have to try to determine what the various constituents value in the organization; alternatively, the constituents themselves may be surveyed.

Table 2.5 provides an example of an instrument from a research project that used the competing values approach. The purpose of this project was to examine the outcomes of employee fitness and health programs, which were valued in major corporations (cf. Wolfe, Slack, & Rose-Hearn, 1993). The instrument was administered to fitness and health professionals and to the corporation's senior management, to determine the type of outcomes they valued in an effective employee fitness and health program. By plotting the cumulative scores from an instrument like this, it is possible to get a picture of how different organizations, or different groups within an organization, determine effectiveness.

Figure 2.3 shows how two sport organizations could be plotted in terms of the four models of effectiveness (see also Quinn, 1988, chapter 9). Sport organization A could be a relatively large organization that has been in business for a number of years. It is quite likely to be structured along bureaucratic lines. Its primary emphasis is on productivity and efficiency. Planning and goal-setting are emphasized within this organization. There is little concern with flexibility, nor is there a great deal of concern with human resources development issues. In contrast, Sport organization B could be a relatively new organization seeking to establish itself in its particular market. Consequently, adaptability and the acquisition of external resources are highly valued in this organization. There is some concern with human resource issues and with productivity and planning, but there is little value placed on stability and information management.

The type of diagram shown in figure 2.3 can help determine the organization's effectiveness. If cumulative scores from the different constituents are used to plot the diagram, it tells managers in

Table 2.5   Measuring Competing Values: An Example of Employee Fitness and Health Programs

The following items relate to values you may attribute to your company's employee fitness and health program. Please use the following scale to indicate the extent to which each of the following is a value you attribute to this program.

MINOR
REASON   1   2   3   4   5   6   7   MAJOR
                                                                               REASON

(Please write the appropriate number in the space provided.)

1. _____ To improve employee morale (HR)*
2. _____ To contribute to a more stable work force (IP)
3. _____ To contribute to organizational profit (RG)
4. _____ To contribute to the organization's external competitiveness (OS)
5. _____ To improve employee cohesion (HR)
6. _____ To contribute to the continuity of the work force (IP)
7. _____ To create a more flexible and adaptable work force (OS)
8. _____ To contribute to achieving organizational goals (RG)
9. _____ To decrease employee conflict (HR)
10. _____ To increase cross-functional and cross-level interaction (IP)
11. _____ To contribute to organizational efficiency (RG)
12. _____ To ensure that our work force will be ready to meet its challenges (OS)
13. _____ To positively influence employee communication (IP)
14. _____ To contribute to individual productivity (RG)
15. _____ To positively affect the value of human resources (HR)
16. _____ To positively influence our external image (OS)

*The letters in parentheses indicate to which of the four models the statements relate. They were not included on the actual instrument.

what particular areas they are strong and where they may improve. If plots are made for each of the constituent groups, the diagram shows the type of values each constituent expects from the organization. For example, in a company that produces some type of sports equipment the workers would probably see the organization as being effective if it emphasized values related to human resources development; shareholders' values would more likely relate to productivity. Plotting how the organization scores in these areas can help managers determine how effectively constituents believe it is performing its tasks. This information can then be used to determine the relative trade-offs that have to be made to maintain overall effectiveness.

It is important to note that different values may be emphasized at different stages of the organization's life cycle (cf. Cameron & Whetten, 1981; Quinn & Cameron, 1983). For example, in a relatively new organization like Sport organization B in figure 2.3, flexibility, creativity, and the ability to acquire resources from external sources are most likely to be the most valued as indicative of effectiveness. Later on in the life cycle, in what Quinn and Cameron (1983) call the formalization and control stage, the sport organization is more established, and constituents will likely value stability and productivity as measures of effectiveness.

The strength of the competing values approach is that it takes into account the paradoxical nature of organizational effectiveness. It also acknowledges that different constituents use different types of criteria in their assessment of an organization, that some of these criteria may be conflicting, and that some may change over time. The biggest problems with the competing values approach are determining which constituents are important to an organization, and then measuring the criteria they value and use in determining the effectiveness of their organization.

Summary and Conclusions

This chapter has examined the concepts of organizational goals and effectiveness. Goals serve a

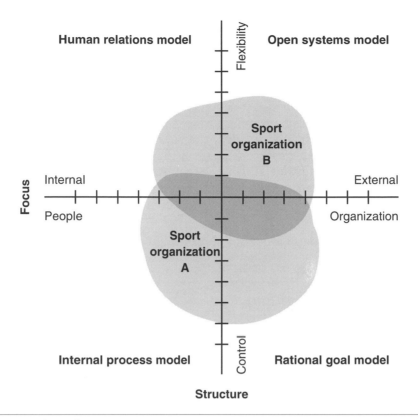

Figure 2.3 Effectiveness values of two sport organizations.
Based on information in Rohrbaugh, J. (1981). Operationalizing the competing values approach. *Public Productivity Review*, 2, pp. 141-159.

number of purposes in a sport organization: They provide a direction for the organization, guide managers in decision making and performance appraisal, reduce uncertainty, and help the sport organization establish legitimacy both with its own personnel and with external agencies. Sport organizations usually have several different types of goals; some are formally stated, others are more implicit in the activities of the organization; some are objective, others are purposely vague and general.

If a sport organization achieves its goals, it is often considered as being effective. However, as we saw, there are problems with this approach, and researchers have proposed several other methods of determining organizational effectiveness. As opposed to focusing on the organization's goals or outputs, the systems resource approach focuses on the organization's ability to obtain resources from its environment. The internal process approach focuses on internal climate and efficiency as the appropriate criteria for determining effectiveness. Two more contemporary approaches take a broader view of effectiveness. The strategic constituents approach focuses on the extent to which an organiza-

tion satisfies the requirements of its stakeholders. The competing values approach emphasizes that different constituents value different organizational outcomes. Effectiveness is determined by the extent to which an organization is able to meet these often differing value preferences.

Which of these approaches is the best? Each one in its own way is useful. Some writers have even suggested that effectiveness is better measured by integrating different approaches. Chelladurai (1987, p. 39), for example, suggests:

When organizations are viewed as open systems inputs affect throughputs which affect outputs, which are exchanged with the environment for a return of inputs for the organization. From this perspective of an organization the goals model, system resource model, and process model focus, respectively, on the output, input, and throughput sectors of an organization. The multiple constituencies approach emphasizes the organization's dependence on its environment represented by the various interest groups and the need to satisfy their expectations. Since all of the models deal with specific elements of the system . . . they are interrelated.

Hall (1982) extracts key elements from the systems resource and goal attainment approaches to produce what he calls a contradiction model of effectiveness. He argues that, because organizations have multiple and conflicting environmental constraints, goals, external and internal constituents, and time frames, no organization is effective. Rather, organizations are effective (or ineffective) to the extent in which they are able to reconcile these contradictions. In a similar vein, Cameron (1986, pp. 544-545) suggests that "organizational effectiveness is inherently paradoxical," and approaches to assessing effectiveness must consider the relationship among paradoxical criteria.

Because of the paradoxical nature of the concept of effectiveness, one of the best ways to summarize the various approaches that have been presented is to suggest that each is useful under different circumstances. Table 2.6 summarizes each of the approaches presented in this chapter, how it defines effectiveness, and when it is most useful.

Table 2.6   A Comparison Among Major Models of Organizational Effectiveness

MODEL	DEFINITION	WHEN USEFUL
	An organization is effective to the extent that . . .	*The model is preferred when . . .*
Goal attainment model	it accomplishes its stated goals.	goals are clear, time-bound, and measurable.
Systems resource model	it acquires needed resources.	a clear connection exists between inputs and outputs.
Internal process model	it has an absence of internal strain, with smooth, internal functioning.	a clear connection exists between organizational processes and the primary task.
Strategic constituencies model	all strategic constituencies are at least minimally satisfied.	constituencies have powerful influence on the organization (as in times of little organizational slack), and it must respond to demands.
Competing values model	the emphasis of the organization in four major areas matches constituent preferences.	the organization is unclear about its own emphases, or changes in criteria over time are of interest.

Adapted, by permission, from K.S. Cameron, 1984, The effectiveness of ineffectiveness. In *Research in organizational behavior: An annual series of analytical essays and critical reviews*, edited by B.M. Straw and L.L. Cummings (Greenwich, CT: JAI Press), 276.

Key Concepts

Official goals	Effectiveness
Operative goals	Efficiency
Operational goals	Goal attainment approach
Management by Objectives	Systems resource approach
Nonoperational goals	Internal process approach
Long-term goals	Strategic constituencies approach
Short-term goals	Competing values approach
Department/subunit goals	Contradiction model

Review Questions

1. How do an organization's goals influence managerial action?

2. Pick a sport organization with which you are familiar and find out what its official goals are. How do you think these might differ from its operative goals?

3. How do the operative goals of a college football team differ from those of a professional football team?

4. Who should set the goals for a women's sport advocacy organization such as the Women's Sport Foundation or the Canadian Association for the Advancement of Women and Sport?

5. In the Time Out "At Eastern Michigan University Is Winning the Only Thing?" what approach to assessing effectiveness was being used? Why was it criticized?

6. Why is effectiveness such a difficult concept to measure?

7. What is the difference between effectiveness and efficiency? Can an organization be efficient without being effective and vice versa?

8. "For an organization that produces sport equipment or sport clothing the only measure of effectiveness is profit." Discuss.

9. You are the athletic director of a small junior college whose basketball team has just finished a season in which they won just under half of their games. Attendance at games was, however, the highest it has been for ten seasons, and two players made the conference all-star team. How would you assess the team's effectiveness?

10. In what way are the systems resource model and the goal attainment model of effectiveness related?

11. Identify the strategic constituents of a community gymnastics club.

12. Select a sport organization you are familiar with and discuss how your assessment of its effectiveness would vary depending on the approach you used.

13. What are the major advantages and disadvantages of the internal process approach to organizational effectiveness?

14. Discuss the ways in which the competing values approach to organizational effectiveness differs from the goal attainment approach.

15. How will the stages of a sport organization's life cycle affect the way effectiveness is assessed?

Suggestions for Further Reading

The most significant work on the effectiveness of sport organizations is that of Chelladurai and his associates. Chelladurai's (1987) article in the *Journal of Sport Management* presents an interesting perspective on integrating approaches to effectiveness into a comprehensive framework. His work with Szyszlo and Haggerty (Chelladurai, Szyszlo, & Haggerty, 1987) produced a psychometric scale for determining effectiveness in national sport organizations; his work with Haggerty (1991) focuses primarily on differences between professionals and volunteers in their perceptions of process effectiveness. In the broader field of management, the most comprehensive examinations of effectiveness are found in Goodman, Pennings, and Associates' edited book (1977) *New perspectives on organizational effectiveness*, and Kim Cameron and David Whetten's (1983b)

Organizational effectiveness: A comparison of multiple models. Both are collections of essays containing interesting and useful analyses of effectiveness. In the Goodman and Pennings book, students are referred in particular to the chapter by Campbell (1977), which presents a major review of the different theories of effectiveness, and to the Hannan and Freeman (1977) chapter, which presents a more critical examination of the concept and deals with some of the methodological problems in studying effectiveness. The Cameron and Whetten book is useful in that the various contributors, when presenting their approach to effectiveness, compare it to other perspectives, "in order to highlight the basic assumptions of each approach, the trade-offs necessary in using one approach versus another, and the strengths and weaknesses of each approach" (p. xi).

A useful and unique addition to this text is that each chapter concludes with nine questions—three related to theoretical issues, three to research issues, and three to practice. Each author addresses the questions in these areas from the perspective of his or her approach to studying effectiveness.

Case for Analysis

The 1988 Calgary Olympic Games: Success or Failure?

In 1981 the city of Calgary, Alberta was awarded the 1988 Winter Olympic Games. Armed with strong public support and unbridled enthusiasm, the members of OCO '88 (Olympiques Calgary Olympics '88), the Olympic Winter Games organizing committee, promised to stage the best Games ever. Handling the complex task of overseeing the organization of the Games required someone with strong managerial skills. David Leighton, an author and director of a number of large companies, with a doctorate in business from Harvard, was selected for the job in March 1982, and began full-time work in September. At the same time that Leighton was appointed, four paid vice presidents were added to the Games staff.

The committee that had developed the original bid for the Games had selected locations for the various sports events, but 9 of the 10 identified sites were changed within two years of Calgary's being awarded the Games. Particularly controversial was the decision to move the alpine events to Mount Allan in Kananaskis country, a Rocky Mountain tourist resort that the provincial government was trying to develop. The site was described as windswept, barren of snow, and environmentally fragile; conservationists claimed irreparable damage would be done to a herd of bighorn sheep that grazed on the mountain. In addition, individual skiers and ski groups criticized the hill as being too easy for Olympic competition.

Controversy was not, however, restricted to site selection. In January 1983 David Leighton resigned from the job he had just taken up. While the official line on Leighton's resignation was "differences in management philosophy" (Leighton wanted to rely on professional help while the organizing committee wanted to use volunteers), insiders suggest Leighton was forced out because of personality differences with key organizing committee members.

Bill Pratt took over from Leighton. One of his first tasks was to secure financial commitments for the Games from the three levels of government. Pratt and his team were successful in gaining a $200 million commitment from the federal government, $130 million from the province, and $43 million from the City of Calgary, to build facilities and operate the Games. In addition to securing funding Pratt also worked at creating a structure to run the Games; by September 1983, 300 volunteers had been appointed, 1,100 had committed to future positions, and 30 staff had been hired.

In fall 1983 the first Olympic facility was opened. The Olympic Saddledome was to be used for the figure-skating and hockey competitions, but its long-term purpose was as a home for the NHL's Calgary Flames. The euphoria over the opening of the Saddledome was somewhat tempered by a cost overrun of some $16.5 million. The local taxpayers, a number of whom had formed an association called HALT (Human Action to Limit Taxes), were outraged that public money was being spent on "entertainment" items such as a professional hockey facility. This concern over the public expenditure on the Games would dog the organizing committee throughout its tenure.

On January 25, 1984 the organizing committee received something of a financial windfall. ABC-TV bid a record $309 million (US) to broadcast the Games. The IOC would receive $82.4 million, the Olympic Organizing Committee the rest. In anticipation of the TV contract, curling, short-track speed skating, and freestyle skiing were added to the program as demonstration sports. By the end of 1984 OCO '88's paid staff had grown to 51, and 500 volunteers worked on over 50 committees. When he visited Calgary in 1985 IOC President Juan Antonio Samaranch declared OCO '88 the best organizing committee he had seen. A decision had been made to build a world-class speed-skating oval at the University of Calgary, marketing agreements were in place with the Canadian Olympic Association, and a committee to develop educational materials had been created. The Games organizers were pleased with their progress. While there was some degree of public and media criticism about the use of public funds to build facilities and operate the Games, most Calgarians felt they were a good idea.

Early in 1986 a public information facility called the Calgary Olympic Centre was opened to give local residents and visitors an appreciation of the Games. By the time the Games closed, over 500,000 people from all over the world had visited the Centre. In May 1986 it was announced that a record number of 1.6 million tickets would go on sale in September. The educational program was also launched in May; resource kits were distributed to nearly 500,000 students in 1,700 schools across the province.

One week after tickets went on sale, irregularities were found in the ticketing process. The ticketing manager was charged with theft and fraud, and ultimately convicted. The ticketing department was thrown into chaos. There was public displeasure at the lack of availability of tickets; local residents felt too many tickets were going to "the Olympic family" and other alleged VIPs. Although the public eventually received 79 percent of an increased number of 1.9 million tickets, many were left disgruntled.

Despite ticket problems and a management review conducted out of concern over the Games operation, more facilities opened as the Games neared. Preview events were staged in ski jumping and nordic combined, although both were poorly attended. By the end of 1986, some 4,000 volunteers were actively working on the Games, and over 15,000 had expressed an interest. By June 1987, 59 countries (a Winter Games record) had confirmed they would attend. The number of volunteers increased to 9,000 by September 1987, with 460 paid staff.

When the Games opened on February 13, 1988, over 60,000 spectators watched the event live; two billion saw it on TV. A legacy fund of over $30 million was left after the Games, to support long-term training and competition at the Olympic venues.

Based on information in XV Olympic Winter Games Organizing Committee. (1988). *Official report*. Edmonton, Alberta: Jasper; and Reasons, C. (1984). It's just a game?: The 1988 Winter Olympics. In C. Reasons (Ed.), *Stampede city: Power and politics in the west* (pp. 122-145). Toronto: Between the Lines and various newspaper clippings.

Questions

1. How would you evaluate the effectiveness of the Olympic Winter Games Organizing Committee?

2. How would your perception vary depending on which of the approaches you took to measuring effectiveness?

3. What other type of information about the 1988 Olympic Winter Games would help you make a better assessment of the effectiveness of the Organizing Committee?

4. What elements of this case demonstrate the political nature of organizational effectiveness?

3

Dimensions of Structure in Sport Organizations

When You Have Read This Chapter

You should be able to

1. explain the three most commonly cited elements of organizational structure;
2. describe the different ways in which a sport organization exhibits complexity;
3. discuss the advantages and disadvantages of formalization;
4. understand the factors that influence whether or not a sport organization is considered centralized or decentralized; and
5. explain the interrelationship of complexity, formalization, and centralization.

Brunswick Restructures

In the early 1980s Brunswick, one of the oldest companies in the U.S. involved in the sport industry, was a highly diversified organization with interests in bowling, billiards, recreational boats, defense, and medical equipment. Financial analysts were critical of the company and were pessimistic about its future suggesting that its only valuable asset was its medical equipment business. Chief executive officer Jack Reichert was annoyed by what he heard. Going against popularly held views he sold off the medical equipment business, a subsidiary that had generated Brunswick approximately one fifth of its net earnings, and set out to restructure the rest of his organization.

The steps Reichert took were drastic. Four hundred white collar jobs and layers of middle management were eliminated. Corporate staff was reduced by nearly 60 percent and there were only five layers of management between Reichert and the lowest level of employee. Two thirds of the 600,000 square foot company headquarters was subleased saving the company $2 million. Computer systems were introduced, a just-in-time management program was created and staff were given incentive pay. Two of three corporate jets were sold off and the executive dining room was eliminated. While the latter move did not save the company large amounts of money it was symbolic of Reichert's efforts to cut costs. Approximately $20 million was saved in salaries and other operating costs. Eleven divisions were consolidated into eight. Reichert was quoted as saying "The pyramid was too tall." The company started to focus on what it did best—involvement in the sports industry, with some continued work in aerospace and defense. Bowling alleys, which were spread throughout the country, were consolidated. At Brunswick's Mercury Marine Division, which produced outboard motors for boats, a product line structure and four divisions were changed to a functional structure.

Reichert's restructuring worked. In 1984 Brunswick's debt fell to 26.6 percent of capital as compared to 39.4 percent in 1981. By 1987 sales had risen from a 1982 figure of $1 billion to $3 billion. Managers at the operating level no longer had to go through numerous hierarchical levels to get approval for projects. The general managers of each of the divisions now reported directly to Reichert and the turnaround time for decisions was reduced from months to days or even hours.

Based on information in A slimmed-down Brunswick is proving Wall Street wrong (1984, May 28). *Business Week*, pp. 90, 94, 98. Reichert, J. (1988, January). Reichert bowls a perfect game; Keeping up with the Joneses. *Management Review, 77*, 15-17. Bettner, J. (1988, September 12). Bowling for dollars. *Forbes*, p. 138.

What Jack Reichert did at Brunswick was change the structure of the organization so that it could more effectively achieve its goals. But what exactly do we mean when we talk about structure? For many people, organizational structure is something represented by the patterns of differentiation and the reporting relationships found on an organizational chart, and to a certain extent this view is correct. For Thompson (1967, p. 51), structure referred to the departments of an organization and the connections "established within and between departments." He suggested that "by delimiting responsibilities, control over resources and other matters," structure was the means by which an organization was able to set limits and boundaries for efficient performance. The term structure has in fact been used by different theorists to encompass a wide variety of organizational dimensions and their interrelationships.

In this chapter we focus in detail on only the three most commonly used dimensions. However, we show how the terms complexity, formalization, and centralization may actually encompass some of the other terms used to describe organizational structure. We also look at the interrelationships among these three primary dimensions.

Complexity

Complexity is, in many ways, one of the most readily apparent features of any sport organization. Anytime we look at an organization we cannot help but be aware of such things as the different job titles individuals hold, the way in which the organization is departmentalized or divided into subunits, and the hierarchy of authority. Even a cursory look at a sport organization such as a university's faculty of health, physical education, and recreation will verify this observation. Individuals have job titles such as dean, chair, professor, research associate, graduate student, and secretary. Faculties may also be divided up into departments or subunits, with names such as Leisure Studies, Health, and Sport Sciences. Even sport organizations such as a local judo club, which may at first glance appear relatively "noncomplex," will probably have job titles, a committee structure, and a simple hierarchy of authority. In some sport organizations the level of complexity may actually vary among departments that are perceived as equally important. A large sports equipment manufacturing company, for example, may have a research-and-development department with little in the way of a hierarchy of authority, no clearly defined division of labor, and a relatively wide span of control. In contrast, the production department is quite likely to have a clear chain of command, high levels of task differentiation, and a narrow span of control.

As we can see from these brief examples, complexity is concerned with the extent to which a sport organization is differentiated. This differentiation may occur in three ways: horizontally, vertically, or spatially (geographically).

Horizontal Differentiation

Horizontal differentiation occurs in two separate yet interrelated ways, specialization and departmentalization. Specialization, in many ways one of the central tenets of organizational theory, has its foundations in such works as Adam Smith's *The wealth of nations* (1776/1937) and Emile Durkheim's *The division of labor in society* (1893/1933). There are two ways in which specialization occurs in sport organizations: first, through the division of an organization's work into simple and repetitive tasks, and second, through employing trained specialists to perform a range of organizational activities. The more a sport organization is divided up in these ways, the more complex it becomes. Complexity

occurs because task differentiation (or functional specialization, as it is often called), the dividing up of work into narrow routine tasks, means there are more jobs to manage, and a need to establish relationships among these jobs. The specialization of individuals rather than their work, what Robbins (1990) calls social specialization, also increases organizational complexity. The different training and knowledge that specialists, such as professionals (e.g., a sport lawyer) and craft workers (e.g., a custom-skate maker), possess create different approaches to work, and thus make the coordination of their activities more difficult. They may have different ideological positions, different goals for the organization, and even different terminology for the work they do. All of these differences make interaction among these people more complex. Slack and Hinings (1992), for example, report that as a result of their training and background, the professional staff of national sport organizations in Canada showed greater commitment to changes being brought about by a government-initiated rational planning system than did the volunteers who had traditionally operated these organizations.

The task differentiation that occurs when work is broken down into simple and repetitive tasks is most often found in sport organizations where large quantities of a commodity are produced in the same way. For example, when Hillerich and Bradsby build one of their Power Bilt golf woods, the production process is broken down into 77 operations; an iron requires 36 operations. Since these processes are routine and uniform, this type of division of labor creates jobs that are relatively unskilled; hence, there is usually high substitutability in this type of work, and management can usually replace workers easily. On the other hand, when the type of work to be performed is nonroutine and varied, specialization is usually based on education and training. Professionals or craft workers are employed because their skills cannot be easily routinized. In sport we find this type of specialization in organizations such as architectural firms specializing in sport facilities, custom-bike manufacturers, and university physical education departments. For example, Daniel F. Tully Associates Inc., an architectural firm with a specialization in sport and recreation facility planning, not only utilizes a core project team but also has in-house professionals with such specialist titles as architect, engineer, designer, graphic artist, cost estimator, interior designer, and construction manager.

While specialization creates increased complexity within a sport organization, which must be managed through processes of coordination and integration, there are several advantages to specialization. While these advantages pertain primarily to functional specialization, some are relevant to social specialization. Specialization means that the time required to learn a job is relatively short, the chances of making errors when learning the job are reduced, and (because the task is frequently repeated) the person becomes more skillful in its execution. Specialization also means that time is not lost switching from one task to another; the chance of developing techniques to improve the way the task is carried out is improved, and individual skills are used in the most efficient manner. The dehumanizing aspects of specialization (primarily functional specialization) have been well documented by human relations theorists such as Argyris (1964) and Likert (1967). In an attempt to counter these dehumanizing aspects, many organizations employ techniques such as job rotation, job enlargement, job enrichment, and (more recently) quality circles (see Crocker, Chiu, & Charney, 1984; Lawler & Mohrman, 1985).

The specialization of individuals and their work gives rise to the second form of horizontal differentiation, that of departmentalization. Departmentalization refers to the way in which management groups differentiate activities into subunits (divisions, work groups, etc.) in order to achieve the organization's goals most effectively. As figure 3.1 shows, departmentalization may occur on the basis of product or service, function, or geographic location.

Reebok is departmentalized along product lines; Human Kinetics, the publisher of sporting books (including this one!) is departmentalized by function; and Basketball Canada is departmentalized by geographic location.

Researchers in both sport management and the broader field have defined these forms of horizontal complexity in different ways. Hage and Aiken (1967b) focused on levels of occupational specialization and professionalization. They suggested (p. 79) that complexity includes three components: the number of occupational specialties, professional

---

TIME OUT

Using Quality Circles in Intercollegiate Athletic Departments

In recent years intercollegiate athletic departments have experienced considerable change. Increasing pressure resulting from shifts in client attitudes, changing societal needs, and increased public and private competition have resulted in these organizations becoming more complex in terms of their structural arrangements. Such complexity can result in communication problems, employee feelings of inferiority, and loyalty to a subunit rather than to the department. Hunnicutt suggests that, by introducing quality circles into athletic departments, these type of problems can be eased and team spirit can be created.

Quality circles, which originated in Japan but in recent years have been introduced into a number of North American businesses, are designed to bring small groups of employees together to solve problems relating to their work. Hunnicutt suggests three steps to making quality circles work in athletic departments. First, he suggests it is necessary to establish who participates in the circle. Membership should be voluntary and the size of the unit should be somewhere from six to ten people, who meet approximately four times per month for about an hour, usually during business time, to work on problems which they select. Problems discussed may range from issues such as academic advisement to facility maintenance. Second, the quality circle should have a facilitator, who helps the members of the circle in case of difficulty and acts as a liaison with other circles. Finally, quality circle evaluation should be undertaken in a constructive manner. Hunnicutt believes that integrating participative management techniques such as quality circles can improve teamwork in an athletic department, increase productivity, and help solve the communication problems that may result from increasing complexity.

Based on information in Hunnicutt, D. (1988). Integrating quality circles into college athletic departments. *Journal of Sport Management, 2,* 140-145.

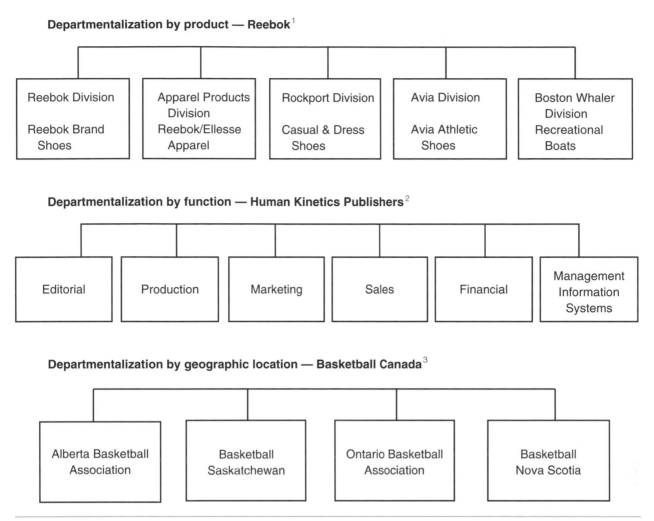

Figure 3.1   Three types of departmentalization.
[1]Based on Reebok's 1989 Annual Report. [2]Based on material provided by Human Kinetics. [3]Based on material provided by Basketball Canada.

activity, and professional training. They then classified individuals as to their occupational specialty (e.g., teacher, coach, athletic therapist) based on their major duties. Professional activity was measured by the number of professional associations in which an individual was a member, number of meetings attended, and so on, and the variable professional training was measured by the amount of education and other professional training an individual had experienced (see also Hage & Aiken, 1967a; Hage & Aiken, 1970). For Hage and Aiken (1967a, p. 507), "the greater the length of training required by each occupation, and the greater the degree of professional activity, the more complex the organizational structure." Basically, Hage and Aiken's argument is that the more training people have in their different specialties, the more differentiated they are, and hence the greater the level of organi-

zational complexity. In many ways Hage and Aiken's treatment of complexity (i.e., horizontal differentiation) is similar to that of Price (1968, p. 26), who notes that "complexity may be defined as the degree of knowledge required to produce the output of a system. The degree of complexity of an organization can be measured by the degree of education of its members. The higher the education the higher the complexity of the organization is likely to be."

In later work Price (1972) adopts a somewhat different definition of horizontal differentiation but one similar to that used by Peter Blau and his colleagues in some of their work. Blau and Schoenherr (1971), for example, define horizontal differentiation as the number of major subdivisions in an organization and the number of sections per division. Hall, Haas, and Johnson (1967) and the Aston group (Pugh,

Hickson, Hinings, & Turner, 1968) use similar measures to those of Blau. Hall et al. (1967) focus on the number of major divisions or departments in an organization and the way they are subdivided. The Aston group focus on functional specialization and the extent to which there are specialized roles within these functions.

In the sport literature both Frisby (1986b) and Kikulis et al. (1989) have used aspects of the work of the Aston group to examine horizontal complexity. Frisby, in her study of the organizational structure and the effectiveness of voluntary sport organizations, used measures of professionalism and specialization. Professionalism was defined as the level of education attained by both volunteers and paid staff; specialization measures were based on the number of roles for board members, executive committee members, paid staff, and support staff, as well as the number of committees in the organization. Kikulis et al. (1989) used the concept of specialization in their work. It was a composite variable defined as "the extent and pattern of differentiated tasks, units, and roles allocated to different organizational segments" (p. 132). Table 3.1 shows the items that Kikulis et al. include in their measure of specialization.

Vertical Differentiation

Vertical differentiation refers to the number of levels in a sport organization. The more levels there are, the greater the problems of communication, coordination, and supervision, hence the more complex the sport organization. The number of levels in an organization is usually related to the size of an organization and also to the extent to which it is horizontally differentiated. A small custom-bike builder like H H Racing Group of Philadelphia has virtually no vertical differentiation and very little horizontal differentiation. In contrast, a large producer of sporting goods like Huffy has several vertical levels and shows a high level of horizontal differentiation. Although research findings vary, horizontal differentiation is generally seen as being related to vertical differentiation, because, as Mintzberg (1979, p. 72) notes, "when a job is highly specialized in the horizontal dimension, the worker's perspective is narrowed, making it difficult for him to relate his work to that of others. So control of the work is often passed to a manager. . . . Thus, jobs must often be specialized vertically because they are specialized horizontally."

The pattern of vertical differentiation is often assumed to represent the hierarchy of authority in an organization and, as Hall (1982) notes, in the vast majority of cases it does. There are, nevertheless, situations in some sport organizations where this assumption may not be valid, for example, when professionals work in bureaucracies. In professional service firms in the sport industry (e.g., companies that specialize in sport law, sport medicine clinics, and architectural companies that specialize in sport facilities), professionals, because of their specialist training, are central to the firm's operations. Because the professionals require a relatively high degree of autonomy to do their job, management has to

Table 3.1   Measures of Specialization in Voluntary Sport Organizations

MEASURE OF SPECIALIZATION	OPERATIONALIZATION
Program specialization	The number of programs operated by the sport organization, e.g., national team, coaching certification.
Coaching specialization	The number of coaching roles within the sport organization, e.g., men's head coach, women's head coach, junior coach, etc.
Specialization of professional staff	The number of professional staff roles, e.g., managing director, coach, technical director.
Specialization of volunteer administrative roles	The number of administrative roles held by volunteers on the sport organization's board of directors, e.g., vice president administration, treasurer.
Specialization of volunteer technical roles	The number of technical roles held by volunteers on the sport organization's board of directors, e.g., vice president coaching, director of officials.
Vertical differentiation	The number of levels in the sport organization's hierarchy.

Based on information in Kikulis, L., Slack, T., Hinings, C.R., Zimmermann, A. (1989). A structural taxonomy of amateur sport organizations. *Journal of Sport Management, 3*, p. 135.

delegate to them a considerable amount of authority, responsibility, and, subsequently, control. Heightened by their voluntary nature, this type of situation has been increasingly prevalent in national sport organizations in Canada. Volunteers who have traditionally managed these organizations have in recent years lost much of their control to professionally trained sport managers who are actually positioned at a lower vertical level in the organization (cf. Macintosh & Whitson, 1990; Thibault, Slack, & Hinings, 1991). Thompson (1961) suggests that one way to deal with such a situation is to create a dual hierarchy. However, Schriesheim, Von Glinow, and Kerr (1977) raise a number of questions about the use of dual hierarchies. A more recent development to address this situation, and one used by a number of Canadian national sport organizations, is an organizational design known as the professional bureaucracy. Whereas the traditional bureaucracy "relies on authority of a hierarchical nature . . . the Professional Bureaucracy emphasizes authority of a professional nature—the power of expertise" (Mintzberg, 1979, p. 351). We discuss this type of organizational design more fully in chapter 4.

As we have discussed, size influences the number of levels in an organization. It is nevertheless quite possible for two sport organizations with a similar number of nonmanagerial employees to have a different number of vertical levels. As figure 3.2 shows, some organizations like Organization A can have what is usually referred to as a flat structure. In contrast, Organization B has a relatively tall structure. The difference, as figure 3.3 shows, relates to what is termed the span of control (sometimes called the span of management). The span of control in an organiza-

tion refers to the number of people directly supervised by a manager. In figure 3.3, although Organization X has just over 200 more first-level employees than organization Y, it has a span of control of seven, and consequently fewer managers and a flatter structure. Organization Y, which has a span of control of three, has a tall structure and more managers.

Opinions vary as to what is an appropriate span of control. Classical theorists such as Urwick (1938, p. 8) suggest that "No superior can supervise directly the work of more than five or, at the most, six subordinates whose work interlocks." Human relations theorists favor a broader span of control that gives more autonomy to workers. A wider span of control can also enhance communication in an organization. As Simon (1945, p. 26) notes, "Administrative efficiency is enhanced by keeping at a minimum the number of organizational levels through which a matter must pass before it is acted upon."

Employees may feel more secure in a taller structure because they are easily able to obtain help from a supervisor. However, tall structures with a narrow span of control may result in closer supervision than employees see as necessary. Cummings and Berger (1976) suggest that senior managers prefer tall structures whereas lower-level managers are more comfortable with a flatter structure. The nature of the work being performed also affects the size of the span of control. Some jobs require close supervision; others, particularly professional jobs, do not.

Spatial Differentiation

Spatial differentiation can occur as a form of either vertical or horizontal differentiation. That is to say,

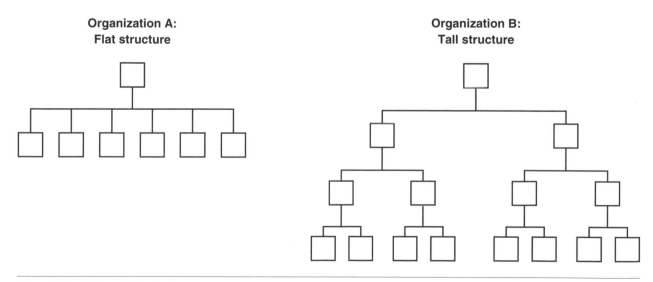

Organization A:
Flat structure

Organization B:
Tall structure

Figure 3.2   Flat and tall structures.

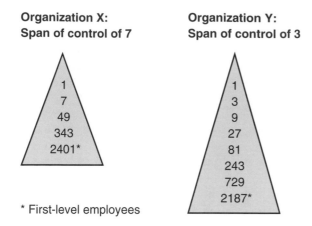

Organization X:
Span of control of 7

1
7
49
343
2401*

Organization Y:
Span of control of 3

1
3
9
27
81
243
729
2187*

* First-level employees

Figure 3.3   Comparing the span of control.

both levels of power and tasks can be separated geographically. For example in the province of Saskatchewan, the department responsible for sport, the Department of Culture, Multiculturalism, and Recreation, has a number of zone offices throughout the province that help facilitate the provision of opportunities for participation in sport. Power is differentiated between these zone offices and the central government offices in the provincial capital, Regina. Because senior managers are housed in the provincial capital and lower-level zone managers are placed throughout the province, complexity is increased more than if they were all in one location.

Horizontally differentiated functions can also be dispersed spatially. Muddy Fox, a UK-based mountain bike company, has offices and a warehouse just outside London, but buys Japanese components, has them assembled in Taiwan, and sells them through the approximately 600 approved Muddy Fox dealers dispersed throughout the UK (and a growing number in the United States) (Ferguson, 1988). The location of the organization's central office, production source, and assembly plant in different parts of the world, and the use of 600 sales outlets, obviously increase organizational complexity.

The physical separation of an organization's operations increases its complexity, which can be further increased as a result of distance (cf. Hall et al., 1967). For example, a sporting goods company with several retail outlets throughout London would be considered less complex than the same type of company with a similar number of like outlets dispersed throughout the U.S.

Interrelationship Among Elements of Complexity

Although we have treated each of the three elements of complexity separately, you may be tempted to

ask if there are interrelationships among the three. The most obvious interrelationships are in very big and very small sport organizations. Companies like Cooper Canada Ltd., a major manufacturer of hockey skates; Bally Manufacturing Corporation, a leading owner of health and fitness centers; and L.A. Gear, an athletic footwear manufacturer (and at one time one of North America's fastest-growing companies), all exhibit high levels of horizontal, vertical, and spatial differentiation. In contrast, companies such as Ed Milner Consulting Services, a small company that provides advice on sport surfaces and facilities; Yeti Cycles Inc. of Agoura Hills, California, a small custom-bike manufacturer; and the Double G Card Shop, a sports card store in Spruce Grove, Alberta, are low in all three areas.

Beyond these extremes of size it is hard to generalize. Universities, for example, often have high levels of horizontal differentiation in terms of the number of departments that exist, a relatively low level of vertical differentiation, and usually no spatial differentiation. Football teams have high horizontal differentiation, with roles such as running back, wide receiver, and linebacker, but usually only have two levels of vertical differentiation, coaches and players (Hall, 1982).

The Managerial Consequences of Complexity

As sport organizations grow, which most aim to do, they generally become more differentiated. People occupying different roles, working in different departments, and having different levels of training exhibit different attitudes and behaviors; they also have different goals and expectations for the organization. This complexity leads to problems of communication, coordination, and control. Consequently, as a sport organization becomes more complex increasing pressures are placed on managers to ensure that the organization progresses smoothly and efficiently toward achieving its goal(s). In short, managers have to manage complexity, so they introduce such things as committees, rules, procedures, and management information systems. The more complex the sport organization becomes, the more time and effort managers have to spend dealing with issues of communication, coordination, and control.

Hall (1982, p. 90) describes this phenomenon as "an interesting paradox in the analysis of organizations." He notes that, although complexity is increased to help organizations economically and to improve their efficiency, it also creates pressures to

TIME OUT

The Emergence of Elements of Complexity in a Voluntary Sport Organization

The Alberta Section of the Canadian Amateur Swimming Association [CASA(AS)] was founded in the 1920s by the members of three Edmonton swimming clubs. In its early years the organization operated with a relatively loose and informal structure; there was little in the way of any type of role specialization, as all members at various times had to assume the responsibilities of coach, meet organizer, timer, starter, and so on. The members of the organization, with little in the way of any professional qualifications, attained their position in the organization because of their enthusiasm, not through any type of specialist training or credential.

As the organization grew, clubs from other parts of the province began to join the provincial association; hence, the organization became more geographically dispersed. Increased size also meant that members began to take on specialist roles; some started to concentrate on being coaches, others focused on organizing meets or being a timekeeper. As more and more clubs joined the association, zones were created, with the effect of introducing another level into the hierarchy of the organization, because these zone associations acted as a link between the clubs in their area and the provincial association. Eventually as the association grew relatively complex, one of the unstated qualifications for getting elected to the provincial executive was some type of professional qualification. It was felt that, by having people on the board with specialist training in areas such as accounting and business management, the association would be run more effectively. Ultimately the workload of the organization became so great that it could no longer be handled by volunteers, and a staff person with a professional background in sport management was hired.

Based on information in Slack, T. (1985). The bureaucratization of a voluntary sport organization. *International Review for the Sociology of Sport*, 20, 145-166.

add managers to maintain communication, coordination, and control, and to reduce conflict. Consequently the economies and efficiencies realized by increased complexity have to be counterbalanced by the added burden placed on managers to keep the organization together.

Formalization

The second structural dimension with which we deal is formalization, a key dimension because it strongly influences the way individuals are able to behave in an organization. Just as the rules of a sport limit the way an individual can behave in the playing area, formalization in organizations works to control the amount of discretion individuals or groups are allowed to exercise when performing their job. As Hall (1982, p. 95) notes, the focus on the way formalization controls individual behavior does not mean a move away from "the organizational level of analysis. Formalization has important consequences for

the organization and its subunits in terms of such processes as communication and innovation."

What Is Formalization?

Formalization refers to the extent to which mechanisms such as rules and regulations, job descriptions, and policies and procedures govern the operation of a sport organization. If a sport organization is highly formalized it will have lots of rules and regulations, comprehensive policies and procedures, and detailed job descriptions to guide its operations. In this type of sport organization, employees have little discretion over how and when they do their work. In sport organizations where formalization is low, however, employees are given the freedom to exercise discretion about their work and how and when it is carried out. In this sense, formalization is not just a structural component of organization but a control mechanism that has political and ethical ramifications (cf. Braverman, 1974; Clegg & Dunkerley, 1980).

Different types of sport organizations exhibit different levels of formalization. W.L. Gore & Associates, Inc., the manufacturer of Gore-Tex, a product used in sports equipment such as ski clothing, tents, and sleeping bags, prides itself on low levels of formalization. In contrast, other companies that mass-produce sports equipment usually have relatively large numbers of unskilled jobs, which are likely to be highly formalized. Even sport organizations that require employees to use some degree of discretion in their work will formalize aspects of their operations. U.S. Athletics, a specialty athletic footwear store, for example, has "compiled a 50-page training manual, [for staff] which includes everything from store policies, to the anatomy of a shoe, to information about features and quality in athletic footwear" (Gill, 1987, p. 47). The more professionals there are in a sport organization, the less likely it will have high levels of formalization. Doctors who specialize in sport medicine, university professors who teach sport management, and architects who design sport facilities are all professionals found in different types of sport organizations that would demonstrate relatively low levels of formalization.

The extent of formalization differs not only from organization to organization but also among the hierarchical levels of an organization and among departments. At the higher levels of a sport organization, jobs are generally broad and nonrepetitive, and allow more discretion over how they are carried out than at the lower levels; consequently, the managers who perform these jobs are less likely to be required to follow formalized procedures than those individuals at the lower levels of the organization. As we have already noted, production departments tend to be highly formalized; in contrast, a research-and-development department, because of the nature of the work it involves (i.e., being creative), and the fact that it is likely to be staffed by professionals, will not have high levels of formalization.

There is some question as to whether or not rules, procedures, and so on have to be stated in writing in order for an organization to be considered "formalized." Pugh et al. (1968) used the terms "formalization" and "standardization" in their work. The two concepts are in fact highly correlated. Formalization refers to "the extent to which rules, procedures, instructions, and communication are written" (Pugh et al., 1968, p. 75). In the research by Pugh et al. (1968) the concept was operationalized by measuring the extent to which an organization had such written documentation as policies and procedures, job descriptions, organizational charts, and employee handbooks. Standardization, on the other hand, referred to events that occurred regularly and were legitimated by the organization but not committed to written form. Pugh et al. (1968) rated activities such as stock-taking, materials ordering, and interviewing, for their degree of standardization. Hage and Aiken (1970) used the term "formalization" to include both written and unwritten rules, by breaking formalization down into two elements: job codification (i.e., how many rules a person is asked to follow) and rule observation (how closely individuals must adhere to these rules). For their work they used both official documents and the perceptions of employees as measures of formalization. As Hall (1982) notes, the use of perceptual measures recognizes the existence of informal procedures in an organization, something that cannot be obtained if only official records are used. Despite the fact that both approaches purport to measure the same concept, they have been shown to produce different results (cf. Pennings, 1973; Walton, 1981).

Studies carried out on sport organizations have tended to focus on the existence of written documentation as an indicator of formalization. Frisby (1986b) in her study of organization structure and effectiveness used three indicators: publication formalization, the total number of publications produced by the sport organization; constitution formalization, an estimate of the number of words in the sport organization's constitution; and job description formalization, an estimate of the number of words in volunteer and paid staff job descriptions. Slack and Hinings (1987b) used the term "standardization" but note that standardized procedures are often committed to writing. Thibault et al. (1991), in their study of the impact that professional staff have on the structural arrangements of voluntary sport organizations, operationalize the concept "formalization" by measuring the existence of written documentation across a range of organizational activities such as personnel training, planning, marketing, and promotion.

Reasons for Formalization

Of the reasons for formalizing the operations of a sport organization, the most central are to replace direct supervision, which would be unduly expensive, and to provide a consistent way of dealing with recurring problems. In small organizations such as a local sport equipment store, a manager can supervise employees directly, because they are in close contact and there are few employees. In larger sport organizations this type of direct supervision is not possible. Although a narrow span of control can help supervision issues, it can be time-consuming if a problem has to go through several hierarchical levels before a decision can be made. Formalizing procedures so that recurring problems are handled in a consistent way can alleviate supervision problems.

Formalization also helps monitor employee behavior. In many sport organizations employees are required to submit reports about what they accomplish in their job on a weekly, monthly, and/or yearly basis. These reports help managers ensure employees are contributing to achieving the goals of the sport organization. Companies like Tottenham Hotspur Football Club, Reebok, and Huffy, because they are publicly held, all file formalized annual reports for their shareholders, who in essence own the company, thereby keeping them informed of its accomplishments. As well as helping to monitor the behavior of employees, formalized procedures can help also to ensure that employees behave in a consistent manner. Professors who teach sport management courses, for example, are often provided with guidelines by their university, about how to mark student papers and what to do if students miss assignments because of illness. Such procedures help ensure that students are dealt with fairly and in a consistent manner. In a somewhat different way, procedures for the hiring of temporary staff at a local sport center provide another example of how formalization can be used to produce consistency.

Economic aspects of formalization are also important to consider. Formalizing jobs generally means that they require less discretion, and in turn can be filled by less qualified, and hence cheaper, workers. Formalization also helps ensure efficiencies, because organizations often spend considerable time, effort, and money to determine the best way to conduct a particular operation; once the best way is arrived at, formalizing the procedure helps ensure that other people who perform the operation do so in the most cost-efficient manner.

Formalization clarifies what employees are expected to do in their jobs. At Louisiana State University, student football managers are given an 87-page handbook that outlines their job responsibilities and how they should be performed (Equipment Handbook, 1988). Formalizing procedures is also beneficial when employees become sick or leave the organization. Prouty (1988) describes the problems the U.S. Cycling Federation ran into when one of its employees became ill. He notes she was an extremely valuable employee but there were no operating and procedures manuals for the computer she used for the bookkeeping and financial data; she kept all the codes in her head.

No organization can develop formalized rules and procedures for every possible situation that can arise, but there are ways in which formalization can help. Many professional organizations develop a written code of ethics, which provides generally

TIME OUT

Policies and Procedures Manuals: Making Life Easier for Athletic Department Administrators

Milton E. Richards and George Edberg-Olson suggest that the management of college athletic departments has changed considerably over the last decade. In many ways athletic directors have become more like business people. In order to help the athletic director in her/his work Richards and Edberg-Olson suggest the development of a policies and procedures manual that formalizes many of the athletic department's operations. The format for the policies and procedures manual which they suggest is based on an analysis of the manuals of 31 Division 1A schools. Table 3.2 provides a sample outline of the areas Richards and Edberg-Olson suggest should be contained in the manual.

The authors acknowledge that it is not possible or maybe even desirable to cover all aspects of an athletic department's operations in a policies and procedures manual. However, they suggest that "for handling routine operations and normal, daily activities, many athletic administrators believe a manual of policies and procedures is an invaluable aid" (p. 40).

Based on information in Richards, M.E., & Edberg-Olson, G. (1987, August). A manual for all seasons. *Athletic Business*, pp. 38-40.

Table 3.2   A Sample Outline for a Manual of Policies and Procedures

1. General preface or introduction
2. Purpose (and short history) of the department of intercollegiate athletics
3. Department personnel
    A. Organizational chart
    B. Job description and duties: relationships between department members as well as outside administration
    C. General policies and procedures
    D. Policy and professional organizations and meetings, scholarships, and publishing
4. Financial policies
    A. Budgeting
    B. Accounting and budget control
    C. Business office policies and procedures
    D. Athletic ticket priorities and privileges
    E. Funding, fund-raising, foundations, booster and pep clubs, cash donations, gifts, gifts-in-kind (trade outs)
5. Travel policies—team and individual
    A. Travel request policy
    B. Expense vouchers
    C. Accommodations: air travel, bus, personal automobiles, van, hotel, other
6. Purchasing
    A. General
    B. Equipment
    C. Capital expenditures
    D. Emergency requests
7. Facility operations
    A. Scheduling
    B. General maintenance
    C. Maintenance of records and files
    D. Events management
8. Scheduling/contracts
    A. Philosophy and mechanics of scheduling
    B. Revenue sports
    C. Non-revenue sports
9. Student-athletes
    A. Recruiting
    B. Admissions
    C. Financial aid
    D. Housing
    E. Academic advising (eligibility)
    F. Rules and regulations governing athletes
    G. Training and medical services
    H. Strength and fitness center
    I. Letter awards, academic honors, dean's list, etc.
    J. Sports banquets
10. Public affairs
    A. Sports information and publicity/media relations
    B. Marketing/promotions
11. Sports camps and clinics, lectures and demonstrations
12. Miscellaneous

Reprinted by permission, copyright 1987, M.E. Richards and G. Edberg-Olson, and *Athletic Business* magazine.

accepted principles based on professional values, and which can be followed when unfamiliar situations are encountered. Earle Zeigler has proposed such a code of professional ethics for the North American Society for Sport Management (see Zeigler, 1989). Included in Zeigler's proposal are a commitment to a high level of professional practice and service, the availability of such services to clients of all ages and conditions, and professional conduct based on sound management theory.

Finally, formalizing procedures provides an indication to employees as to the purpose of the organization, its overall goals, and what they as employees can expect from their involvement. Formalization can strengthen an employee's identification with the organization and provide a safe-guard, because the organization's commitment to its employees is formally documented. Formalized commitments can help morale because employees have a tangible indication of their rights and responsibilities.

Methods of Formalization

There are a number of ways in which managers can formalize the operations of a sport organization. In this section we examine the methods most frequently used.

Hiring the Right Employee

As we saw earlier, sport organizations with high numbers of professionals tend to score relatively low on the extent to which their operations are formalized. The reason is that in many ways professional training is a surrogate for formalization, and may be considered a means of standardizing behavior prior to a job. Through their training, individuals not only learn technical skills but also the standards, norms, and accepted modes of behavior of their profession. Consequently, in staffing, organizations face what Robbins (1990) calls "the make or buy decision": The organization can either control employee behavior directly through their own formalized rules and procedures, or control can be achieved indirectly by hiring trained professionals (Perrow, 1972).

Regardless of whether an organization is hiring professional staff or unskilled workers, candidates are often subject to a battery of application forms, tests, reference letters, and interviews before they are given a job, to ensure that the "right" person is hired. The right person is someone who it is perceived will perform the job well and is willing to follow rules and regulations, one of the measures of formalization used by Hage and Aiken (1970). Coaches often use this type of logic in team selection. Because they want players who are willing to conform to rules and show consistent behavior patterns, they do not always select talented players unless they "fit in" with the team. Selecting the right person is then a method of formalization; it helps ensure consistency in employee behavior.

On-the-Job Training

Even though they go to considerable lengths to hire the right people, some sport organizations still provide on-the-job training for their employees. Training activities may be influenced by a number of factors and can include such activities as workshops, films, lectures, demonstrations, and supervised practice sessions (cf. Slack, 1991b). The idea behind all of these methods is to instill in new employees the norms and accepted patterns of behavior of the organization. Mecca Leisure, a British organization involved with ice skating and billiard and snooker halls, could not find the type of staff it needed from higher education, so it developed its own in-house training program (Brown, 1990). The Universiade '83 Corporation, which staged the World University Games in Edmonton in 1983, developed a training program for volunteer employees. The program provided volunteers not only with information about the history, philosophy, and operation of the Games, but also with some knowledge of the protocols that had to be followed when dealing with visiting dignitaries, members of competing teams,

and spectators. Again the idea behind the training was to standardize employee behavior.

Policies

Policies are general statements of organizational intent. They provide employees with a certain amount of discretion in making decisions in the areas covered by the policy. Policies may be internally focused; for example, Human Kinetics Publishers has policies which cover such areas as the advancement of employees and attendance at work. Policies may also be externally focused. A small sporting goods store, for example, may use them to cover situations such as returning merchandise and cashing personal checks. Policies are generally written to provide some leeway in their interpretation. The City of Winnipeg's Parks and Recreation Department Sport Services policy (1990) states: "The Department will cooperate with other agencies and organizations to ensure a base level of sport programs and opportunities and encourage advanced levels of participation." The policy does not specifically state how the department will cooperate; consequently, staff are given the discretion to determine whether cooperation will merely mean endorsing a program or providing funding and other resources.

Procedures

Procedures, developed to ensure the standardization of particular organizational activities, are different from policies in that they provide written instructions as to *how* an employee should carry out an activity. These instructions, usually based on what has been determined as "the one best way" of operation, contribute to the efficiency of a sport organization by standardizing inputs and outputs, and ensuring the optimal use of time and resources in the transformation process. While procedures can facilitate the smooth running of a sport organization, too many procedures, like other methods of formalization, can create difficulties for both employees and customers/clients. Good sport managers establish procedures only when they are necessary to help achieve organizational goals.

Rules

Rules are specific statements that tell an employee what he or she may and may not do: "No smoking in the building"; "Employees are allowed an hour lunch break"; "All accidents must be reported immediately." Rules, unlike procedures, do not leave any leeway for employee discretion. Some sport organizations have rules for clients as well as employees. Snow Valley Ski Club in Edmonton, Alberta has the following rules for skiers:

- Place skis in rack when not in use.
- Skis must have safety straps or brakes.
- Ski poles must have baskets (Snow Valley Ski Club, 1992).

Rules such as these perform a public-relations function; they signal to people using the ski hill that the management is concerned about their safety. They also serve a legal function in that they set limits on clients to reduce the chances of injury.

Job Descriptions

Each individual in a sport organization has a particular job to perform. Job descriptions provide written details of what a job entails. As such they regulate employee behavior by making sure that job requirements are carried out and individuals do not impinge on other people's responsibilities. Job descriptions vary in terms of detail; some are very explicit as to responsibilities, while others are far more loosely defined. In general the farther up the organizational hierarchy one moves, the less specific the job description. The areas usually covered in a job description are to whom the individual is responsible, what staff the incumbent is responsible for, and the specific duties of the job. The job description for the vice president of public relations of the Pittsburgh Pirates Baseball Club lists several such responsibilities:

- Manage and direct the staff of professionals in the Public Relations department.
- Direct and coordinate the strategic placement of all items of public information in the appropriate media.
- Direct all media and community activities which enhance the Pirates image in the Tri-state marketing area, and nationally.
- Counsel Pirate officials in terms of statements made to the media, and in public speaking engagements.
- Coordinate all press conferences and the identification of Pirate personnel to represent the Club in outside engagements (Pittsburgh Pirates, 1990).

Committee Terms of Reference

Many sport organizations, particularly those that are volunteer-based, operate with a committee structure. Much as job descriptions provide individuals with direction to perform their job, so terms of reference provide committees with direction as to the areas for which they are responsible. For example, the Olympic and International Committee of the Canadian Canoe Association has as part of its terms of reference the following responsibilities:

- Recommend to the Council [the Sprint Racing Council] criteria and procedures governing the selection of members to the National Sprint Racing Canoe Teams, to be used by the National Team Head Coach.
- Recommend to the Council, criteria and procedures governing the selection of sprint racing canoeists, who in turn are recommended to Sport Canada for "C", "C-1", "D" card status following nomination by the National Team Coach (Canadian Canoe Association, 1988).

The Dangers of Excessive Formalization

As we have seen, there can be considerable advantages to formalizing the operation of a sport organization. Nevertheless, excessive amounts of formalization can produce a number of dysfunctional consequences.

Goal Displacement

In some sport organizations adherence to rules and regulations becomes so important to members of the organization that the rules and regulations themselves become more important than the goals which they were designed to help achieve. As Merton (1957, p. 199) explains, "Adherence to the rules, originally conceived as a means, becomes transformed into an end-in-itself." This condition results in what he calls goal displacement.

Minimal Adherence to Rules

The purpose of rules and regulations is to indicate to employees what is considered unacceptable behavior. But as Gouldner (1954, p. 174) points out, they can also serve "as a specification of a minimum level of acceptable performance." If employees are not motivated by their work, the existence of rules can encourage apathy; they come to define minimum standards of behavior rather than unacceptable behavior. When employees perform at the minimum acceptable level, management attempts to control behavior even more.

Bureaupathic Behavior

As a result of the growing gap between managers who have the right to make rules and regulations and the specialists (i.e., the skilled workers who operate at lower levels of the organization but have the ability to solve specialized problems), superiors come to depend on subordinates. This dependence creates anxieties and insecurities in superiors, who then react with excessive controls, over-reliance on rules, and insistence on the rights of their position. This tendency to over-emphasize rules and follow them for their own sake is what Thompson (1961) refers to as bureaupathic behavior.

Formalization and Complexity

A number of researchers have identified a strong positive correlation between formalization and complexity. In a study by Pugh et al. (1968), overall role specialization correlated highly with overall standardization (0.80) and with overall formalization (0.68). Other studies have produced similar findings (cf. Child, 1972a; Donaldson & Warner, 1974), but they apply primarily to situations where employees are performing simple and routine tasks in a repetitive manner. Here standardized rules are used to control employee behavior. In sport organizations this type

---

TIME OUT

John Tarrant, the Ghost Runner: The Tragic Consequences of Goal Displacement

John Tarrant was born in London in 1932. Due to the death of his mother and his father being away in the army, John spent much of his early life in a children's home. In his last two years of school John developed an interest in running, but when he left school at age 15 to work as a plumber's mate, he found little interest in running in the town where he lived. He did, however, meet former RAF boxing champion Tom Burton, who was keen to promote boxing. Burton approached several local young men in the town to see if they would be interested in earning a little money in a boxing tournament. In 1950 Burton promoted his first tournament; 18-year-old John Tarrant fought four two-minute rounds, for which he was paid £1.00 (about $1.50 US). In just under two years John fought eight bouts in unlicensed rings and won a total of £17.00 (about $25 US), his largest "purse" being £4.00. In his eighth fight John was knocked out in 55 seconds; that convinced him that boxing wasn't his sport and he decided to return to his first love, running.

But when John applied to the Amateur Athletic Association (AAA) he was told that because he had boxed for money he would have to first be reinstated by the Amateur Boxing Association (ABA). John tried, but because he had broken the amateur rules he was turned down by the ABA. Despite repeated letters to both associations, John was unsuccessful in his efforts. But John's desire to run was not easily quashed; on August 12, 1956 he ran his first marathon as an unofficial competitor. Over the next year John gate-crashed several races, and in August 1957 actually received an invitation to gate-crash a 7 1/2 mile race. When he arrived at the race, instead of a number John was given a piece of cardboard with the word "GHOST" on it. John ran many races as the ghost runner. In 1958, after considerable pressure from the media and fellow runners, John was reinstated by the AAA, but under the rules of the International Amateur Athletic Federation (IAAF). The fact that John had broken amateur rules and boxed for money meant that he could not compete internationally for his country. Despite this ruling John continued to run in England and "ghosted" other races in different parts of the world. He set world records for the 40- and 100-mile distances, and won a number of marathons and many of the classic long-distance races. But because he had won £17.00 boxing, John had broken the rules; rigid adherence to those rules meant that he was never allowed to realize his ambition of competing for his country.

Based on information in Watman, M. (Ed.). (1979). *The ghost runner*. Kent, UK: Athletics Weekly.

TIME OUT

The Impact of Hiring Professional Staff on the Levels of Formalization in Voluntary Sport Organizations

While the presence of professionally trained employees is usually associated with lower levels of formalization, Thibault et al. (1991) found in a study of voluntary sport organizations that when professionals were hired in these organizations, formalization increased. They provide two possible explanations for this unexpected phenomenon. First, when the professionals entered the organizations being studied, formalization was low; consequently the professionals created written rules, procedures, and guidelines in order to clarify their roles. A second explanation was that increased formalization was initiated by volunteers as a method of retaining control of the organization. Because they were not willing to give up the power they had previously held to these newly hired professionals, the volunteers imposed formalized behavior controls on them. By instituting formalized policies and guidelines, the volunteer executives were able to help ensure that the consistency they had established was maintained in the accomplishment of tasks, that standards were kept uniform throughout the organization, and (most important for them) that they maintained the control of the organization.

Based on information in Thibault, L., Slack, T., & Hinings, C.R. (1991). Professionalism, structures and systems: The impact of professional staff on voluntary sport organizations. *International Review for the Sociology of Sport, 26*, 83-99.

of work situation is most frequently found where a particular product, such as a hockey stick, is mass-produced.

In situations where work is less narrowly defined and professionals or craft type workers are used, the relationship does not hold true (cf. Hage, 1965), because, as we noted earlier, professional training is a surrogate for formalization. Consequently, in situations where relatively unskilled workers perform narrow and repetitive tasks, formalization will be high, but where professional or craft workers are used, formalization will generally be low. However, as the Time Out below shows, this general trend may not hold in some situations, such as this one involving voluntary sport organizations.

Centralization

All sport managers make decisions. The question is: Which managers get to make which decisions and how do they make them? For example, it is unlikely that Paul Fireman, the CEO of Reebok, makes decisions about the purchase of paper clips and staples for his office staff; these decisions are delegated to lower-level managers. But in 1987 when Reebok acquired Avia, another athletic footwear company, Fireman and other members of the board of directors of Reebok were intimately involved in the acquisition decision. Questions about the authority to make decisions and how they are made are the issues addressed when we look at our third element of organizational structure, centralization.

What Is Centralization?

Of all the three elements of organizational structure centralization is by far the most difficult to explain. It is generally accepted that if decision making takes place at the top of the organization, it is centralized; when decisions are delegated to lower levels, the organization is decentralized. But consider the following:

• In a large sports equipment manufacturing company the authority to make decisions has been delegated to department managers. However, the CEO of the company closely monitors these people; because she can considerably influence their career prospects, the department managers make their decisions based on what they think the CEO wants.

• In a chain of retail sporting goods stores managers have been told they "can run their own show." But policy manuals and frequent memos from head office detail how inventory must be displayed, how sales people should deal with clients, and what type of sales promotions the store should be using. In addition, a computer information system provides corporate headquarters with up-to-the-minute information in areas such as staff costs, inventory, and sales figures.

- In a national sport organization the coach of the team has the authority to select the players he thinks are the best. However, final ratification of his decisions has to be undertaken by the members of the organization's board of directors, many of whom have never seen the players perform together.

- Judy Smith served four terms as president of a state high school athletic association; she then stepped down as president but still remains a member of the organization. Despite the fact that she is no longer on the board, many directors still consult Judy about the decisions they have to make.

These few hypothetical examples should serve to illustrate the difficulties of determining the extent to which a sport organization is centralized or decentralized. Researchers who have studied this aspect of organizational structure have had similar difficulties in their work and as a result have produced conflicting results; probably the most notable debate in the literature concerns the question of whether or not bureaucracies are centralized (stu-

dents are referred to Aldrich, 1975; Blau & Schoenherr, 1971; Child, 1972a; Child, 1975a; Donaldson, 1975; Greenwood & Hinings, 1976; Holdaway et al., 1975; Pugh et al., 1968). Researchers have also defined the concept of centralization in a number of different ways. Pugh et al. (1968, p. 76) suggest that centralization has to do with the locus of authority to make decisions affecting the organization. This point in the hierarchy was ascertained by asking "Who was the last person whose assent must be obtained before legitimate action is taken—even if others have subsequently confirmed the decision?" This approach to centralization has been used in several studies of sport organizations (cf. Kikulis et al., 1989; Slack & Hinings, 1987; Thibault et al., 1991). Van de Ven and Ferry (1980) also use locus of decision making authority as a central premise of their definition. They suggest (p. 399) "when most decisions are made hierarchically, an organizational unit is considered to be centralized; a decentralized unit generally implies that the major source of decision making has been delegated by line managers to subordinate personnel." Van de Ven and Ferry further suggest that any consideration of centralization must take account of the substance of the decision. In a study of Canadian voluntary sport

---

TIME OUT

Centralized Functions at Synchro Canada

In a study of Synchro Canada, Canada's governing body of synchronized swimming, Morrow and Chelladurai (1992) found that three primary organizational functions were centralized at the top of the organization's hierarchy with its board of directors. The three areas over which the board had ultimate control were budgeting, policy development, and personnel selection. The first stage in the preparation of the organization's budget was undertaken at the vice-presidential level. The various vice presidents in the organization forwarded their budget request to the finance committee (a group consisting of the president, the vice president of finance, the treasurer, and the executive director). The finance committee was responsible for preparing an overall budget for revision and review. The final budget was approved by the board of directors, the highest level of the organizational hierarchy, and submitted to the annual general meeting for ratification.

Policy proposals were also ultimately approved or rejected by the board of directors. While standing committees and professional staff could recommend and offer input into the policy process, the ultimate power for policy lay with the board. In terms of personnel decisions, a personnel committee was responsible for developing policy for employees. However, the hiring and firing of professional staff was the responsibility of an executive committee of the board of directors.

Based on information in Morrow, W.W., & Chelladurai, P. (1992). The structure and processes of Synchro Canada. *Journal of Sport Management, 6*, 133-152.

organizations Kikulis, Slack, and Hinings (1995a) extend this idea and suggest that decisions of less strategic importance are more likely to be decentralized.

Mintzberg (1979) focuses his definition primarily on the issues of who has the power to make decisions and the extent to which this power is concentrated. He notes (1979, p. 181) that "when all power for decision making rests at a single point in the organization—ultimately in the hands of a single individual—we shall call the structure centralized; to the extent that the power is dispersed among many individuals we shall call the structure decentralized." Hage and Aiken (1970, p. 38) propose a similar definition:

> Centralization refers to the way in which power is distributed in any organization. By power we mean the capacity of one actor to move another (or other) actors to action. The smaller the proportion of jobs and occupations that participate in decision making and the fewer the decision making areas in which they are involved the more centralized the organization.

This approach was used by Frisby (1986b) in her study of the organizational structure and effectiveness of national sport governing bodies.

Brooke has examined the way the terms "centralization" and "decentralization" have been used in a number of empirical studies, and summarizes the differences in the connotations attached to the two concepts, as shown in table 3.3.

Issues of Centralization

The question of determining the extent to which an organization is centralized is complicated by several issues; some have already been alluded to in the examples in the preceding section of this chapter. In this section we explore these issues more fully.

What Role Do Policies and Procedures Play?

While many managers will delegate decisions to the lower levels of a sport organization, the amount of discretion an individual is allowed in making a decision may be severely constrained by the existence of policies and procedures. A sport manager can use them to limit the choices available to lower-level decision makers. Consequently, while the organization gives the appearance of being decentralized, decisions are actually programmed by the policies and procedures, and a high degree of centralization remains (Hall, 1982). For example, if a lifeguard at a swimming pool sees someone in the pool not following the established procedures, the person concerned may be asked to leave the pool. While it may appear that the lifeguard is making the decision to remove this individual, the procedure and steps to follow in this situation have been established by management; consequently, the lifeguard has little choice in this situation.

What About Informal Authority?

As we saw in the preceding section the definitions of centralization used by both Pugh et al. (1968) and Van de Ven and Ferry (1980) focused on the authority to make decisions. While not explicit in their definitions, both are referring to the formal authority vested in managerial positions. But what about our example involving Judy Smith? Although Judy no longer had any formal authority, she was still able to influence the decision making process of her state athletic association through informal channels.

Table 3.3   Characteristics of Centralized and Decentralized Structures

CENTRALIZED	DECENTRALIZED
Decisions made at the top of the organization.	Decisions made at the lower levels of the organization.
Limited participation by lower level staff in decision making.	Lower level staff actively participate in decision making.
Lower level staff have restricted choice of decision making alternatives.	Lower level staff given choices when making decisions.
Top down decision making	Participative decision making
Senior managers control	Senior managers coordinate
Autocratic structure	Democratic structure

Based on information in Michael Z. Brooke (1984) *Centralization and Autonomy*. London, Holt, Reinhart and Winston.

While most definitions of centralization focus only on formal authority, informal influences on the decision making process should not be discounted.

Do Management Information Systems Help Maintain Control?

In many sport organizations advanced computer technology has become an accepted means by which managers obtain information about their organization's operations. Management information systems (MISs) are used to "collect, organize, and distribute data to managers for use in performing their management functions" (Daft, 1992, p. 288). Like policies and procedures, MIS's act as a mechanism to control decision making. Even if decision making is delegated to the lower levels of the sport organization, using an MIS allows managers to closely monitor these decisions. If lower-level managerial decisions are not in line with the expectations of senior managers, corrective action can quickly be taken. In these situations, although there is an appearance of decentralization, the sport organization remains centralized.

What Effects Do Professionals Have on Centralization?

The presence of professionally trained staff results in a more decentralized organization (Hage, 1980). The work of a professional is generally too complex to be supervised directly by a manager or to be standardized through the use of rules and procedures (Mintzberg, 1979). Consequently, professionals usually get to make many of the decisions concerning their work. In fact, Lincoln and Zeitz (1980) note that professionals seek participation in decision making, and as the number of professionals in an organization increases, all employees experience increased influence.

Centralized or Decentralized: Which Way Is Best?

The decision to centralize or decentralize the operations of a sport organization is a difficult one that involves a number of tradeoffs. There are advantages and disadvantages to both types of structure; the advantages claimed for one approach are often the limitations attributed to the other.

The most commonly presented argument for a centralized structure is that it is the best means of achieving coordination and control in a sport organization. It is also argued that top managers should control decision making because they typically have the most experience. They may also own the sport organization or have a large amount of their own capital invested in it. From their position at the top of an organization, senior managers get a broader perspective on its operations and thus can make decisions based on the best interest of the entire organization. They can also see the relative balance between organizational activities and are therefore in the best position to make decisions to maintain this balance.

A centralized structure is also economically advantageous. It avoids some of the duplication of effort or resources that can occur in decentralized organizations. Economic benefits are also realized by centralizing certain activities, such as planning, personnel, and finance, which are common to a number of organizational subunits. If responsibility for these activities were dispersed to subunits, it would be difficult for them to justify such costs from their own budgets.

Given all these advantages, why do organizations decentralize? First, it is often physically impossible for one person to understand and deal with all the issues about which decisions have to be made in a sport organization. How can the CEO of a chain of retail sporting goods stores with its corporate headquarters in Chicago make day-to-day decisions about store operations in California? Even with sophisticated computer technology, one person simply does not have the time or capacity to absorb all the necessary information to make informed decisions. By decentralizing operations, individuals who best understand the specifics of the situation are given the power to make decisions. Senior managers are then given more freedom to devote their time to broader policy issues that may have longer-term consequences for the sport organization.

Decentralization also allows an organization to respond quickly to changes in local conditions (Mintzberg, 1979). Information does not have to pass through the various hierarchical levels of a sport organization before a decision can be made. Those people closest to the changing situation, because they are seen as having direct access to necessary information, can respond immediately.

A third argument for decentralization is that it can help motivate employees. As human relations theorist Rensis Likert (1961, p. 103) noted, "to be highly motivated, each member of the organization must feel that the organization's objectives are of significance and that his own particular task contributes in an indispensable manner to the organization's achievement of its objectives." Involving employees in decisions about their work can help them see the importance of what they are doing to overall organizational goals. This involvement is particularly important in sport organizations staffed by professionals but governed by volunteers. As we noted earlier, professionals expect to be involved in decision making. Only by allowing these people the power to make decisions about their own work can the sport organization expect to retain their services. A decentralized decision making system can also motivate lower-level employees because by being involved in decisions about their work they come to understand the rationale behind decisions that affect them. Such involvement can also improve communication among the different hierarchical levels of the sport organization and engender a greater feeling of commitment to the organization. Filley, House, and Kerr (1976), in an examination of 38 studies on participative management, noted that such an approach to decision making is almost always related to improved employee satisfaction, productivity, or both. Miller and Monge (1986) report similar findings.

Where a sport organization consists of relatively independent subunits, for example, franchised retail sporting goods stores, decentralizing decision making to the managers of these units can result in a more effective system of control. The responsibilities of each subunit can be identified, input costs are readily determined, and the consequences of managerial action, as evidenced in performance outcomes, can be easily assessed. The use of profit centers and strategic business units are just two methods of decentralizing authority underpinned by this logic of control.

A final reason for decentralization is that it can act as an aid in management development. Involving lower-level managers in decision making can provide a good training ground for these people, if they wish to progress to the more senior levels of the sport organization.

Carlisle (1974, p. 15) identifies 13 factors of importance when "determining the need for a centralized or decentralized structure." These are listed below and followed by a brief explanation.

1. **The basic purpose and goals of the organization.** Some organizations, for example a research-and-development company like Gore-Tex, because they seek to develop innovative new products, find it necessary to operate with a decentralized structure. In contrast, a football team requires the control that comes with centralized decision making.

2. **The knowledge and experience of top level managers.** If senior managers have more knowledge and experience than lower-level employees, the sport organization is likely to be centralized.

3. **The skill, knowledge, and attitudes of subordinates.** If lower-level employees have specialized skills and knowledge (i.e., they are professionally trained), and are seen as being committed to the goals of the sport organization, decision making is likely to be decentralized.

4. **The scale or size of the organizational structure.** As the size of a sport organization increases so does the number and complexity of decisions that have to be made. Consequently, there is a tendency to decentralize.

5. **The geographical dispersion of the structure.** The more geographically dispersed a sport organization, the harder it is to have a centralized structure.

6. **The scientific content or the technology of the tasks being performed.** As organizational tasks have become more specialized and sophisticated, decision making responsibility for these tasks is delegated to the specialists responsible for their execution.

7. **The time frame of the decisions to be made.** Decisions that need to be made quickly are usually decentralized.

8. **The significance of the decisions to be made.** Decisions that are of less strategic importance to a sport organization are more likely to be decentralized.

9. **The degree to which subordinates will accept, and are motivated by, the decisions to be made.** Involving subordinates in decision making has been shown to increase their acceptance of that decision. Consequently, when it is beneficial to get subordinates' acceptance of a decision because they will be responsible for its implementation, a decentralized system should be used.

10. **Status of the organization's planning and control systems.** If decision making is highly structured as a result of organizational planning and control systems, sport managers may decentralize because they are able to determine with relative accuracy what the outcome of a particular decision will be.

11. **The status of the organization's information systems.** Decisions are often decentralized if the sport organization has a good management information system, because errors can be quickly spotted and corrective action taken.

TIME OUT

Decentralizing Club Corporation of America

Club Corporation of America is described as the world's largest manager of private clubs. It owns or manages over 200 facilities, including a number of golf and racquet clubs. In 1988 Club Corp. had 400,000 members, an annual revenue of over $600 million, and a staff of 18,000. Much of the growth that Club Corp. has experienced has been attributed to a 1985 decision to decentralize its club operations. Management at Club Corp. determined that it could not realize the aggressive growth goals it had set for itself, nor could it continue to provide the necessary attention to employees and members, if it maintained its centralized power structure. Control of operations was concentrated at the top of a pyramid-shaped organization. President Bob Johnson felt that with this type of structure they were unable to keep in touch with what was going on at the club level. He felt they could better serve their members by delegating responsibility for decision making down the organization and having those managers who dealt with them on a daily basis involved in the management process. Consequently, as part of an overall restructuring, the company was divided into several smaller companies. The club operations were then divided into six regions, each staffed with experts in the areas of management, finance, food and beverage services, human resources, and recreation. Because these regional officers and managers were closer to their customers, they were better able to meet the demands of each club.

Based on information in Tobin, D. (1989, March). Selling by serving. *Club Industry*; and Symonds, W.G. (1989, June). Driving to become the IBM of golf. *Business Week*, pp. 100-101.

12. **The conformity and coordination required in the tasks of the organization.** Organizational tasks requiring precise integration are best accomplished using a centralized system.

13. **External factors.** If a sport organization deals with several external organizations it is best to centralize the point of contact for each organization.

As Carlisle (1974, p. 15) notes, not all factors are "present in all situations, and their significance will vary from situation to situation." He also stresses that it is the "composite interrelationships of the variables" that a manager must consider. All 13 factors will not necessarily always point to the same type of structure; they do, however, provide guidelines for managers in determining the need for a particular type of structure.

Centralization, Formalization, and Complexity

Several studies have examined the relationship of centralization to the other two structural variables. The findings of these studies are summarized here.

Centralization and Formalization

Research examining the relationship between centralization and formalization has produced conflicting results. Hage (1965, p. 297) in his "axiomatic theory" proposed that "the higher the centralization, the higher the formalization." The Aston group (Pugh et al., 1968), however, found no strong relationship between formalization and centralization; Hinings and Lee (1971) supported this conclusion. Child (1972a) replicated the Aston studies using a national sample rather than following the Aston approach of drawing a sample from just a single region of the country. He also focused on autonomous organizations, whereas the Aston studies included subsidiaries and branch units. Child found a strong negative correlation between formalization and centralization; that is, where formalization is high the organization will be decentralized. Donaldson (1975) reran the Aston data removing the nonautonomous organizations and concluded it made no difference to the original Aston correlations. Child (1975a) responded that it may be beneficial to look at the difference between the governmental and nongovernmental organizations in the Aston study. Aldrich (1975) then removed the government organizations from the Aston sample and also found that it made little difference to the original correlations. Holdaway, Newberry, Hickson, and Heron (1975) complicated the issue even more with their study of educational organizations, where they found a positive relationship between centralization and formalization. In response to these differing results, Greenwood and Hinings (1976) looked at the Aston measures of centralization once again, and suggested that rather than treating centralization as a single scale it should have been viewed as three subscales. In the most recent attempt to solve this problem, Grinyer and Yasai-Ardekani (1980) used a different set of organizations from the Aston study and found support for the relationship between formalization and decentralized decision making.

Within the sport management literature there has been no attempt to examine the relationship between formalization and centralization. Intuitively it would seem logical to suggest that in sport organizations such as an equipment manufacturing plant, where work is relatively narrowly defined and mainly filled by unskilled workers, we would find high levels of formalization and also centralized decision making. In sport organizations where there are a large number of professionals, such as a faculty of kinesiology, there would be decentralized decision making and little formalization, at least in those areas directly related to the professionals' work. However, as the Time Out detailing the work of Thibault et al. (1991) (p. 56) shows, there are exceptions to this general trend. Given the diversity of organizations in the sport industry and the lack of research on this relationship in these organizations, it is hard to draw conclusions beyond general trends. As with many other aspects of organizational structure, there is considerable scope for work of this nature on sport organizations.

Centralization and Complexity

As with centralization and formalization, there have been no studies within the sport management literature explicitly examining the relationship between complexity and centralization. The literature from the broader field of management indicates a strong relationship between high complexity and decentralization of decision making (cf. Hage & Aiken, 1967b; Pugh et al., 1968). We could assume a similar relationship in sport organizations; that is, as the complexity of a sport organization increases either through the addition of professionals or the dividing up of work into more narrowly defined tasks, we could expect decision making to

become decentralized. Once again, however, research on this relationship in a variety of sport organizations could move us beyond these intuitive suggestions.

Summary and Conclusions

In this chapter we looked at the three most common dimensions of organizational structure: complexity, formalization, and centralization.

Complexity is concerned with the way in which an organization is differentiated. Three types of differentiation are found in a sport organization: horizontal, vertical, and spatial (geographic). Sport organizations are horizontally differentiated when work is broken down into narrow tasks, when professionals or craft workers are employed, and when the organization is departmentalized. Vertical differentiation refers to the number of levels in the organizational hierarchy. A sport organization is spatially differentiated when tasks are separated geographically. Spatial differentiation occurs vertically when different levels of the organization are dispersed geographically, and horizontally when the functions of the organization take place in different locations. The greater the horizontal, vertical, and spatial differentiation, the more complex the sport organization.

One of the ways used to manage complexity is formalization, the second dimension of organizational structure which we examined. Formalization refers to the existence of mechanisms, such as rules and procedures, that govern the operation of a sport organization. Formalization, whose purpose is to regulate employee behavior, takes place in two ways: through the existence of written documentation such as job descriptions, and through professional training. The former approach is most common where work is narrowly defined, the latter when jobs are broader and require greater discretion.

Centralization, the last dimension of structure and the most problematic of the three, is concerned with who makes decisions in a sport organization. When decisions are made at the top of an organization it is considered centralized; when decisions are made at the lower levels it is decentralized. However, several factors can complicate this general trend: the decisions to be made, the existence of policies and procedures, the use of a management information system, and the presence of professionals.

The structural elements of a sport organization provide a means of describing and comparing these types of organizations. They show how the work of the sport organization is broken down and the means used to integrate the different tasks. To manage a sport organization effectively and efficiently, it is essential that sport managers understand the various elements of structure and their interrelationships.

Key Concepts

Complexity	Horizontal differentiation
Task differentiation	Functional specialization
Social specialization	Departmentalization
Division of labor	Vertical differentiation
Hierarchy of authority	Span of control
Tall structure	Flat structure
Spatial differentiation	Formalization
Standardization	Goal displacement
Minimal adherence to rules	Bureaupathic behavior
Centralization	Decentralization

Review Questions

1. How do levels of complexity vary within and among sport organizations?

2. Why has functional specialization been criticized as dehumanizing, and what steps can be taken to counter its dehumanizing qualities?

3. How does the span of control affect an organization?

4. Do employees prefer working in an organization with a tall or a flat structure?

5. Why does increasing complexity create a paradox for managers?

6. Select a sport organization with which you are familiar. How has it formalized its operations?

7. How does your training in sport management relate to formalization? Discuss.

8. What are the advantages and disadvantages of formalization for employees?

9. If you were studying a group of sport organizations, how would you measure formalization?

10. As the manager of a group of professionals, what areas of their work do you think it would be feasible to formalize?

11. What is it about centralization that makes it a difficult concept to study?

12. Select a sport organization with which you are familiar. How are decisions made in this organization? What influences the way they are made?

13. If you were the manager of a small racquet club, which decisions would you centralize and which would you decentralize?

14. What are the trade-offs involved in the decision to centralize or decentralize the operations of an organization?

15. How would you expect the relationship between centralization and formalization to vary among different types of sport organizations?

Suggestions for Further Reading

Much of the key work on organizational structure was carried out in the 1960s and early 1970s. Of particular importance are the works of Hage and Aiken (see especially Hage, 1965; Hage & Aiken, 1967b, 1970), the Aston group (Hinings & Lee, 1971; Pugh et al., 1968) and Child (1972a). Other related and important early works that shaped much of the future work on organizational structure are Lawrence and Lorsch's (1967) *Organization and environment* and Thompson's (1967) *Organizations in action*.

Given the nexus between writings on bureaucracy and organizational structure, it is useful for students to read Weber's writing on bureaucracy (Gerth & Mills, 1946, chapter 8). Also important is Richard Hall's work in this area (Hall, 1963, 1968; Hall & Tittle, 1966).

More recent works that deal with organizational structure are Henry Mintzberg's (1979) *The structuring of organizations*, particularly part II, and Richard Hall's (1982) *Organizations: structure and process*, chapters 3, 4, 5, and 6. Both provide a comprehensive treatment of the issues along with extensive referencing. Mintzberg's approach is managerial; Hall's is more sociologically informed.

Both Slack and Hinings (1987) and Frisby (1985) have developed frameworks specific to sport, based on the Aston approach to organizational structure. Frisby (1986b) uses her framework to examine the relationship of structure to organizational effectiveness in Canadian national sport organizations.

Case for Analysis

Restructuring the Oakland A's

In 1980 Walter Haas Jr. bought the Oakland Athletics baseball club from Charles Finley for the bargain price of $12.75 million. Despite the fact that they had won three consecutive World Series championships in the 1970s, Finley was disillusioned with the A's. In the 1979 season they had drawn only 306,853 fans, an average of 3,788 per game.

Haas didn't really want to buy the club but felt something of a civic duty. To run the team he appointed his son Wally and son-in-law Ray Eisenhardt. Both were lawyers; Wally had worked as director of community affairs for his father's Levi Strauss Company; Eisenhardt was a partner in a San Francisco law firm. Neither the younger Haas or Eisenhardt had any experience in professional sport.

What they found when they took over the A's offices in the Oakland Coliseum was something of a shock: The front office had a staff of six, including secretaries; there was no receptionist to greet visitors; a black telephone had been placed on a desk with handwritten instructions to anyone entering the offices to ring for help. When Haas and Eisenhardt asked for a computer list of season ticketholders they got a shoebox with the names of all 75 listed on index cards. Files were stacked among the three World Series trophies. The A's four-team minor league farm system was described as a joke. There was nothing in the way of market research, and the stadium in which the A's played was a drab lackluster facility.

What Haas and Eisenhardt tried to do was apply the same type of principles that had made Levi Strauss successful to the A's. Despite the fact that previous owner Finley had tried to liquidate a number of his players through trades, the team itself wasn't that bad. So Haas and Eisenhardt's first task was to reestablish the front office. Sandy Alderson, a colleague of Eisenhardt's, was hired to undertake legal and contract work. Andrew Dolich was hired to become vice president of business operations. Dolich had previously worked for the Madison Square Garden Corporation; his first job was to sell season tickets. In December 1981 he hired 35 sales people to go door to door in the Bay Area selling tickets. He also worked with local media outlets to improve the image of the A's by promoting controversial manager Billy Martin. "Billy Ball" became a catchphrase. Marketing surveys showed fans wanted a more pleasant stadium, one appealing to families. Concessions areas, some with children's attractions, were increased and made more attractive, sky boxes were built, and advanced electronic sound and TV systems were installed. To meet the needs of young families, change tables and diapers with the A's logo were made available by Procter & Gamble; a 40-member cleanup crew kept the facility clean.

Eisenhardt and Alderson expanded the A's farm system to six teams, put a detailed scouting system into place, and recruited the best coaches they could for the farm teams, rather than using the positions as perks for ex-players. A number of aggressive marketing strategies were pursued to promote the team. In 1986 Tony LaRussa, also a lawyer, was hired to manage the team. LaRussa was described as a businessman who was an ideal partner for Alderson.

Based on information in Schlender, B.R. (1990, August 13). Take me out to the gold mine. *Fortune*, pp. 93-94, 96, 98, 100; and Stuller, J. (1982, June). For Roy Eisenhardt, business is a ball. *Inc.*, pp. 31-36.

Questions

1. What steps were taken to restructure the Oakland A's organization when Haas and Eisenhardt took over?

2. What impact would the hiring of more staff have on the structure of the organization?

3. What other structural changes not described in the case would you expect that Haas and Eisenhardt made?

4. What problems do you think Haas and Eisenhardt encountered in the restructuring process? In what way do you think these were dealt with?

Henry Mintzberg, *organization theorist*

Design Options
in Sport Organizations

You should be able to

1. understand the difference between a typology and a taxonomy,

2. explain the five parts of an organization,

3. describe each of the five basic design types,

4. explain the advantages and disadvantages of each design type, and

5. know under what conditions each design type would be found.

Bicycle Manufacturers With a Difference

Huffy Corporation is a publicly held company described as the United States' largest domestic supplier of bicycles. In 1989 Huffy had a 30 percent market share of the U.S. cycle industry, twice as much as its nearest competitor, Murray Ohio Manufacturing Co. At its 820,000-square-foot manufacturing plant in Celina, Ohio, "the world's largest bicycle manufacturing facility," Huffy's 1,700 employees turn out 15,000 bicycles per day. The plant is highly automated as a result of a 1987 $15 million upgrading program: Each bike takes just over 40 minutes to make; much of the production is carried out by computer-controlled equipment; and, when completed, bikes are painted by electronically controlled machines. Companies that supply Huffy must certify that their parts and materials meet required specifications. Quality control is achieved by statistical processes that make sure all steps in the production process are correctly executed and requirements such as the tension level of spokes fall within a certain range of prescribed measurements. If you want to buy a Huffy bike you would find them in stores such as K-mart, Toys 'R' Us, Wal-Mart, Target, and Child World.

Bill Holland also makes bicycles, but you won't find them in these type of stores. Holland Cycle Inc. operates from a much smaller facility than Huffy, in Spring Valley, California. They make about 125 bikes per year, and also do repaints on frames. In 1990 Holland Cycle had six employees, including owner/manager Bill Holland and a part-time caretaker. Holland Cycle produces a bike frame in approximately two to two and one-half months from the date of order; the actual hands-on time is less—about 10 hours to make the frame and three to five hours for painting, depending on the design required. When customers order a frame from Holland Cycle they fill out a detailed form about their current cycle, what they want their new bike for, and their special requirements. A lot of customers actually come to the shop with their old bike; Bill Holland watches them ride and suggests modifications to the frame. In the production process five people work on the bike. Bill takes the order and makes the frame; his assistant brazes the small parts such as bridges and water bottle fittings, then files the frame. The "prep man" prepares the frame for painting by priming it, doing the spot puttying and hand-sanding. The painter finishes it off with the selected color scheme and design. A fifth worker completes the process by cleaning threads and attaching bolts and screws. The atmosphere in the shop is described as relaxed. The day I called to obtain information on the organization, everyone but the assistant frame-maker was out riding bikes.

Based on information in Winter, R.E. (1987, November 30). Upgrading factories replaces concept of total automation. *The Wall Street Journal*, pp. 1, 8; Smith Barney (1989, September 15). *Consumer products research: Huffy Corporation*; and information supplied by Damon Rinard, Manager Holland Cycle, Inc., and Jason Lilley, Holland Cycle, Inc.

Despite the fact that they both make bicycles, Huffy Corporation and Holland Cycle are structured very differently. In fact, no two organizations within the sport industry are exactly alike, even though they may operate within the same market. The Chicago Bulls management structure is different from that of the New York Knicks. Likewise, the athletic department at the University of Massachusetts has a different mode of operation from that used at the University of Tennessee.

Although no two sport organizations are exactly alike, they do have commonly occurring attributes that allow us to classify and compare them. Take, for example, Holland Cycle, Inc. and the Double G Card shop; one makes bikes, the other buys and trades sports cards. But if we look closely at their structures we find they have at least two common features: Each is low in complexity and formalization. By identifying commonly occurring features of sport organizations we can classify them into what are termed design types or configurations. In many ways classification is one of the central tasks of organizational theorists (cf. McKelvey, 1982; Miller & Friesen, 1984; Mintzberg, 1979). Once commonalties are identified and sport organizations are classified, it is possible to use the resultant design types for the generation of hypotheses, models, and theories. As Mills and Margulies (1980, p. 255) point out, "Typologies play an important role in theory development because valid typologies provide a general set of principles for scientifically classifying things or events. What one attempts to do in such endeavors is to generate an analytical tool or instrument, not only as a way of reducing data, but more significantly to stimulate thinking."

This point is further underscored by McKelvey (1975, p. 523):

> Organization science, and especially the application of its findings to the problems of organizations and managers, is not likely to emerge with viable laws and principles until substantial progress is made toward an acceptable taxonomy and classification of organizations. The basic inductive-deductive process of science does not work without the phenomena under investigation being divided into sufficiently homogeneous classes. Managers cannot use the fruits of science unless they first can discover which of all the scientific findings apply to their situation.

In this chapter we look first of all at the methods used to classify organizations and produce design types. We then discuss the typology of organizational designs developed by Mintzberg (1979). We look in depth at each of Mintzberg's designs and show how examples of each can be found within the sport industry. We also explain the advantages and disadvantages of each design, and describe the conditions under which it is most likely to be found.

Typologies and Taxonomies

Two main approaches can be used to uncover design types (configurations). The first of these is the creation of typologies; the second is the development of taxonomies.

> Typologies are, in a sense, of an *a priori* nature; they are generated mentally, *not* by any replicable empirical analysis. . . . Taxonomies . . . are derived from multivariate analyses of empirical data on organizations. Typically organizations or aspects of their structure, strategies, environments, and processes are described along a number of variables. Attempts

are then made to identify natural clusters in the data, and these clusters, rather than any *a priori* conceptions, serve as the basis for the configurations. (Miller & Friesen, 1984, pp. 31-32) (emphasis in original)

In the next few pages we look briefly at the main typologies and taxonomies found in the management literature, and those schema that have been developed for classifying sport organizations.

Typologies

The first attempt to classify organizations into types can be found in Weber's (1947) writings on social domination and the attendant patrimonial, feudal, and bureaucratic forms of organization. Weber demonstrated how each type of organization "could be characterized by a number of mutually complementary or at least simultaneously occurring attributes" (Miller & Friesen, 1984, p. 32). In the 1950s, Parsons (1956) followed Weber and created a typology based on the goals or functions of the organization. He identified organizations that had economic goals, political goals, integrative functions, or pattern maintenance functions. As Carper and Snizek (1980, p. 66) note "Parsons' approach represents an early and limited form of systems theory thinking in that it attempts to tie the organization to the environment through the activities that the former performs for the latter."

Burns and Stalker (1961) suggested two types of organizational design, organic and mechanistic. The organic type of organization was found in changing conditions where new and unfamiliar problems had to be dealt with; it contained no rigid control systems, and employees showed high levels of commitment to the organization. In contrast, mechanistic organizations were found in stable conditions; tasks were narrowly defined, and there was a clear hierarchy of control, insistence on loyalty to the organization, and obedience to superiors. This form of organization is very much like Weber's legal-rational bureaucracy. These two types of design were viewed as polar opposites, with organizations described according to their position on a continuum between them. Shortly after Burns and Stalker, Blau and Scott (1962) produced a typology based on the principle of *cui bono* or "who benefits" from the organization. Four types of structure were identified: mutual benefit organizations, where the prime beneficiary is the membership; business concerns, where the prime beneficiary is the owner(s) of the business; service organizations, where the clients benefit; and commonweal organizations, whose prime beneficiary is the public at large. Chelladurai (1987) has suggested that the prime beneficiary approach could be used in conjunction with the strategic constituents approach to evaluate the effectiveness of sport organizations.

Several typologies have focused on the organization's technology as the criterion variable for classification. Woodward (1958; 1965) distinguished organizations as to whether they used unit/small batch, large batch/mass or continuous-process types of technology. Perrow (1967; 1970) focused on whether technology was craft, routine, non-routine, or engineering; Thompson (1967) used core technologies, which he described as either long-linked, mediated, or intensive, as his basis for classification (see chapter 8 for more details of the work of Woodward, Perrow, and Thompson).

Another typology is Gordon and Babchuk's (1959) tripartite classification: instrumental, expressive, instrumental-expressive. Specifically developed to classify voluntary organizations, it has been used to examine voluntary sport organizations. Instrumental organizations are designed "to maintain or create some normative condition or change" (Gordon & Babchuk, 1959, p. 25). Expressive organizations are designed to satisfy the interests of their members. Instrumental-expressive organizations show elements of both functions. In a study of the members of badminton and judo clubs, Jacoby

(1965) found a very high expressive and very low instrumental orientation.

The only attempts to create typologies specifically related to sport organizations are those developed by Chelladurai (1985; 1992). In his 1985 book *Sport management: Macro perspectives*, he proposes a 12-cell classification system for sport and physical activity organizations. As shown in figure 4.1 the classification was based on three dimensions: (1) whether the organization was profit-oriented or not-for-profit; (2) whether it provided professional or consumer services; and (3) whether it was part of the public, private, or third sector. "Third sector" indicates an organization, for example, some universities, "partly or wholly funded by tax moneys and managed privately" (Chelladurai, 1992, p. 39).

Chelladurai (1985) makes no attempt to categorize sport organizations into the various cells of his model; some of the cells may actually describe few if any sport organizations. For example, it may be difficult to find public-sector sport organizations that explicitly aim to make a profit and offer consumer services. Public-sector organizations are generally not concerned with making a profit per se, and usually provide professional (not consumer) services. Notwithstanding these shortcomings, which Chelladurai (1985) acknowledges when he suggests his framework requires extensive research, this classification scheme does provide a useful starting point for further discussion.

	Consumer service		Professional service	
	Profit	Nonprofit	Profit	Nonprofit
Private sector				
Public sector				
Third sector				

Figure 4.1 Framework for classifying sport organizations.
Reprinted, by permission, from P. Chelladurai, 1985, *Sport management: Macro perspectives* (London, Ontario: Sports Dynamics).

In extending his work on classification Chelladurai (1992) does not focus on sport organizations per se but on the services they provide. Using two dimensions, "the type and extent of employee involvement in the production of services" and "client motives for participation in sport and physical activity," he produces six classes of sport and physical activity services: consumer pleasure, consumer health/fitness, human skills, human excellence, human sustenance, and human curative. Chelladurai (1992) goes on to describe each of these classes and discuss their managerial implications.

We see, then, that we can classify organizations, including sport organizations, in a number of ways. Although fewer typologies have been created in the sport literature than in the general management literature, sport organizations can obviously be typed in many of the more general classification schema. We could, for example, categorize sport organizations on the organic/mechanistic continuum or on the basis of "who benefits."

Carper and Snizek (1980, p. 70) have criticized the large number of typologies produced, suggesting that "there are virtually as many different ways to classify organizations as there are people who want to classify them." They suggest that the diversity of conceptual schemas which have been developed indicates a lack of agreement as to which variables should be used in constructing a typology. Most existing typologies have limited explanatory power because they are based on only one or two variables. Miller and Friesen (1984) support the need to focus on a broad array of variables when constructing typologies. They argue (1984, p. 33) that narrowly focused typologies "are not sufficiently encompassing to serve as a basis for reliable prediction or prescription." One typology which uses a large number and wide range of variables is that developed by Mintzberg (1979). Based on an extensive survey of the literature, Mintzberg's classification scheme attempts to synthesize many of the research findings of the past two decades to produce five design types (Miller and Friesen, 1984) We examine these design types in detail a little later in this chapter, and show how they apply to sport organizations.

Taxonomies

Taxonomies are empirically constructed classifications that identify "clustering among organizational variables that is statistically significant and predictively useful and that reduces the variety of organizations to a small number of richly defined types"

(Miller & Friesen, 1984, p. 34). McKelvey (1978; 1982) has advocated the development of taxonomies to understand a number of organizational phenomena such as environmental adaptation, structural design, and change. Nevertheless, there have been considerably fewer attempts to construct taxonomies than to construct typologies. The first empirical taxonomy of organizations was developed by Haas, Hall, and Johnson (1966). Using a sample of 75 organizations they produced 10 design types; the number of organizations found in each design type ranged from 2 to 30. Much of their work deals with the methods they used to generate their taxonomy; there is no attempt to elaborate on the nature of the design types they established, or to replicate their approach on a different set of organizations to see if the same type of designs emerge.

Pugh, Hickson, and Hinings, the Aston group, (1969a) developed a taxonomy based on structural data obtained from 52 relatively large (over 250 employees) organizations. Their analysis produced seven different types of bureaucratic structure, which led them to conclude (1969a, p. 115) that the Weberian notion of a single bureaucratic type "is no longer useful, since bureaucracy takes different forms in different settings."

In other taxonomic studies Goronzy (1969) used a specifically designed computer program to produce a fourfold classification of organizations based on their size and level of technology. Like the Aston group, Samuel and Mannheim (1970) focused on organizational structure and used a multidimensional scalogram analysis method to produce six bureaucratic types from a sample of 30 organizations.

The most sophisticated use of taxonomy is found in the work of Miller and Friesen (1984). Using a sample of 81 organizations described along 31 variables of strategy, structure, information processing, and environment, they produced 10 common organizational design types, or what they term "archetypes." Identifying six of these types as successful, four as unsuccessful, Miller and Friesen argue that the notion of taxonomy can be extended to study organizational transitions between these archetypes. Using historical data on changes in organizational strategy, structure, and information-processing methods, they produce 135 intervals of transition from a sample of 36 organizations. Based on 24 variables that described changes in such areas as strategy-making, structure, and environment for each transition, nine "transition archetypes" were produced. Thus they argue that the taxonomic approach can identify common paths in organizational evolution.

Within the sport literature there have been only two instances of using a taxonomic approach to identify organizational design types. Both of these emanate from the work of Slack and Hinings and their students. Using data on the structural arrangements of 36 Canadian national level sport organizations Hinings and Slack (1987) developed 11 scales that addressed three aspects of organizational structure: specialization, standardization, and centralization of decision making. After factor analysis two factors were produced, one concerned with the extent of professional structuring in these organizations, and the other with volunteer structuring. By dividing the scores of the 36 organizations at the mean on each factor Hinings and Slack produced nine organizational design types, and were thus able to demonstrate the extent to which these national sport organizations exhibited characteristics of professional bureaucratic structuring. Sport Canada, the federal government agency that provided a large portion of their funding, has been pushing them toward such a design.

In a somewhat similar study Kikulis et al. (1989) created a taxonomy using data from 59 provincial-level sport organizations. Using Ward's method of hierarchical agglomerative clustering, Kikulis et al. produced eight structural design types, ranging from sport organizations that were "implicitly structured" to those that, within this institutional sphere, showed high levels of professional bureaucratic structuring. Kikulis et al. argue the merits of their study in demonstrating the variation in structural design in these sport organizations and as a basis for understanding a range of organizational phenomena. They note (1989, p. 148) that, once structural designs are identified, it is possible "to conduct in-depth studies of representative organizations and develop qualitative data bases to provide us with richer insights into the internal dynamics, formative processes, and performance implications of each structural design."

Mintzberg's Approach

One of the most sophisticated and frequently used of all organizational typologies is the one developed by Henry Mintzberg (1979). Mintzberg uses "design parameters"—specialization, formalization of positions, training of members, and the nature of decentralization—along with contingency factors—age, size, and environment—to produce five design types, or what he terms **configurations**: the simple

structure, the machine bureaucracy, the professional bureaucracy, the divisionalized form, and the adhocracy. Essentially, Mintzberg argues that there are five parts of an organization and five methods by which coordination is achieved. The five parts of the organization are shown graphically in figure 4.2, and explained here.

Parts of the Organization

• **The Operating Core:** This is where we find those employees responsible for the basic work necessary for producing the organization's products or services. At Huffy Corporation this is where we find the people who are involved in assembling the bikes. In a sport medicine clinic, the doctors and physiotherapists who treat the patients constitute the operating core.

• **The Strategic Apex:** This is where we find the senior managers of the sport organization.

• **The Middle Line:** These are the managers who join the operating core to the strategic apex. In a government agency concerned with sport, for example, these people would be the middle managers who provide the link between staff and the senior bureaucrats.

• **The Technostructure:** This is where we find the analysts responsible for designing the systems that standardize work processes and outputs in a sport organization. In an organization that produces sports equipment, the technostructure would be made up of people such as the industrial engineers, who standardize the work process, and the planners and accountants, who standardize the organization's output.

• **The Support Staff:** These are the people who provide support to the sport organization. For example, in a competitive gymnastics club, the support staff includes everyone from the athletic therapists and sport psychologists to the staff who take care of the equipment.

Methods of Coordination

Mintzberg (1979, p. 3) describes the five ways in which coordination can be achieved in an organization—direct supervision, standardization of work processes, standardization of outputs, standardization of skills, and mutual adjustment—as "the most basic elements of structure, the glue that holds the organization together." Each is explained here as they may apply to a sport organization.

- **Direct Supervision:** Here one individual in the sport organization gives orders to the others, to coordinate their work.

- **Standardization of Work Processes:** This method is used when the way in which work is to be carried out is determined by someone else. For example, the way ski jackets are produced in a company like Sun Ice is determined by the people who control the computerized design and pattern-making systems, not by the people who actually produce the jackets.

- **Standardization of Outputs:** This method is used when the results of the work, that is the type of product or performance to be achieved, are specified. For example, output is standardized when the corporate headquarters of a sporting goods company specifies to its divisions that it wants them to increase sales by 10 percent in the upcoming year, but leaves the method of achieving this increase up to the divisional managers.

- **Standardization of Skills:** Skills are standardized through programs designed to ensure the coordination and control of the work processes.

Sport medicine clinics employ doctors just for this purpose. When an injured athlete enters the clinic, the doctor has been trained to deal with the situation and assess the injury and the treatment required.

- **Mutual Adjustment:** Here the coordination of work is achieved through informal communication. A group of sport management professors who plan a training workshop for local entrepreneurs in the sport industry would probably adopt this approach to coordination.

Design Types

In each of the design types (configurations) one part of the organization and one method of coordination dominates. Mintzberg (1984, p. 75) explains:

> The natural tendency of a *strategic apex* concerned with tight control is to coordinate by *direct supervision*; when that is what the organization needs vertical and horizontal centralization results, and the organization tends to use what we call the *Simple Structure*. The

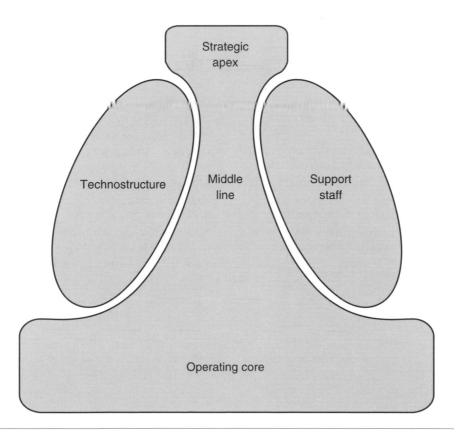

Figure 4.2   Five basic parts of organizations.
The structuring of organizations by Mintzberg, © 1979. Adapted by permission of Prentice-Hall, Inc., Upper Saddle River, NJ.

technostructure encourages coordination by *standardization* (especially of *work process*, the tightest form), since it designs the systems of standards; when that is what the organization needs, it accepts limited horizontal decentralization to the technostructure, and a configuration called *Machine Bureaucracy* results. The workers of the *operating core* prefer autonomy above all, which they come closest to achieving when coordination of their work is effected mainly by the *standardization of skills*; organizations that must rely on this form of coordination accept vertical and horizontal decentralization to their highly skilled operators and use the *Professional Bureaucracy* configuration. The managers of the *middle line* try to balkanize the structure, to encourage limited vertical decentralization to their level so that their units can operate as semiautonomous entities, controlled from above only by performance control systems based on *standardization of outputs*; when this is what the organization needs, the *Divisionalized Form* results. And when the *support staff* (and sometimes the operators as well) favor collaboration—the working together in groups whose tasks are coordinated by *mutual adjustment*—and this is what the organization needs, selective vertical and horizontal decentralization results and the structure takes on the form of what we call an *Adhocracy* (emphasis in original).

We find examples of each of these design types or configurations in the sports industry. Each has strengths and weaknesses and works best under certain conditions. In the remainder of this chapter we look in detail at each design type, discuss its advantages and disadvantages, and discuss when it is the most appropriate design for sport managers to use.

The Simple Structure

What do sport organizations such as Holland Cycle, Inc., a ski rental shop, the local water polo club, and a small voluntary group such as the Canadian Luge Association all have in common? They all exhibit the characteristics of a simple structure.

As its name implies, the most evident characteristic of this design type is its simplicity. Typically the simple structure has little or no technostructure, few support staff, no real middle line (hence no lengthy managerial hierarchy), and a loose division of labor (Mintzberg, 1979). The organization has low levels of formalization and is unlikely to rely heavily on planning and training devices. As figure 4.3 shows, the most important parts of this organizational design are the strategic apex and the operating core. The structure is a relatively flat one and everyone reports to the strategic apex, which is usually one individual in whom power is concentrated. Coordination is achieved through direct supervision. Decision making is informal, with all important decisions being made by the CEO who, because of proximity to the operating core, is easily able to obtain any necessary information and act accordingly.

Advantages and Disadvantages

The main advantage of the simple structure is its flexibility. Because the person at the strategic apex is in direct contact with the operating core, communication is easily achieved. Information flows directly to the person in charge, so decisions can be made quickly. The goals of the sport organization are easily communicated to employees and they are able to see how their efforts contribute to achieving these goals. Since everyone reports to the strategic apex, lines of accountability are clear and straightforward. Many people enjoy working in a simple structure because they are unencumbered by

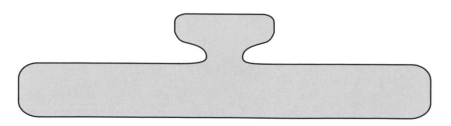

Figure 4.3   The simple structure.
The structuring of organizations by Mintzberg, © 1979. Adapted by permission of Prentice-Hall, Inc., Upper Saddle River, NJ.

TIME OUT

Sun Ice: From Simple Structure to the Top of the World

Born in Germany in 1936, Sylvia Rempel came to Canada in the early 1950s and worked in the sugarbeet fields of Southern Alberta to pay back her fare from Europe. Her husband Victor was born in the Ukraine and came to Canada in 1948. They met while both were in their teens and married in 1956. Sylvia, who had worked as a seamstress in Europe, started to sew clothes for her husband and children. While Vic was pursuing his academic training Sylvia took garment manufacturing and pattern-making at the Southern Alberta Institute of Technology.

When her four children started skiing Rempel started to sew their ski outfits. In 1975 she sewed a number of outfits for her children's friends and the technical school she had attended asked her to teach a course specifically on ski clothing. By this time Rempel had an idea that local ski shops would sell her product. By 1978 half a dozen Calgary retailers were carrying her designs; sales totaled about $35,000. Rempel hired another seamstress to help her, working from the basement of the Rempel's home. In 1979 she moved out of the basement, rented an old pool hall, and bought used sewing machines from Montreal. The number of seamstresses grew to 12 and Rempel's daughter Angel joined the business.

From these relatively humble beginnings Sun Ice, the company started by Sylvia Rempel, has grown rapidly to become "Canada's largest outwear and sportswear manufacturer." The organization is no longer the simple structure of its beginnings; growth has meant that a new, more appropriate, organizational form has emerged, and the organization now operates very much like a machine bureaucracy. With offices in the United States and Hong Kong, Sun Ice sells products throughout North America and in selected European and Japanese ski and sporting goods retail stores. In 1982 Sun Ice supplied members of the Canadian expedition that successfully scaled the world's highest peak, Mount Everest; in 1988 they were official suppliers to the XV Olympic Winter Games. In 1990 sales totaled just under $30 million.

Based on information in Gould, A. (1989). *The new entrepreneurs*. Toronto: Seal Books; I was brought up for work. (1987, December 28). *Maclean's*, pp. 24-25; and Sun Ice (1990). *Annual Report*.

bureaucratic controls; a sense of mission often pervades this type of sport organization.

The main disadvantage of the simple structure is that it is only really useful for smaller sport organizations. As a sport organization grows and/or its environment becomes more complex, the simple structure design type is no longer appropriate. The complexities of a large sport organization cannot be handled by a simple structure There is also the possibility that the person who has the power to make changes, the CEO, may resist growth because it will mean increased formalization and possibly a reduction of this individual's power. The centralization of power at the top of the simple structure is in fact a double-edged sword. While it facilitates decision making, it can lead to the CEO's being unwilling to give up responsibility to others and a resentment on the part of employees that one person "calls all the shots." Mintzberg (1979, p. 331)

also notes that centralization is advantageous in that it ensures that a "strategic response reflects full knowledge of the operating core" but disadvantageous because CEOs who get too involved in operating concerns may lose sight of the strategic issues. Finally, a simple structure is a risky design type in that, as Mintzberg (1979, p. 312) puts it, "one heart attack can literally wipe out the organization's prime coordinating mechanism."

Where Do We Find the Simple Structure?

The most common place to find a simple structure is in a small sport organization, a sport organization in its formative years, or one that is entrepreneurial in nature. Simple structures are also used when a sport organization's environment is simple and dynamic, when larger sport organizations face a hostile environment, and when CEOs have a high need for power or power is thrust upon them.

In a small sport organization coordination is achieved through direct supervision, so there is no need for high levels of formalization or any type of technostructure. It is relatively easy for one person to oversee the organization's operations and to communicate informally with employees. Many different types of smaller organizations within the sport industry have adopted the simple structure for these reasons. Figure 4.4 shows the structure of Mike's Bike and Sport store, a small retail sporting goods store that operates with a simple structure.

A sport organization's stage of development, as well as its size, can influence its design. Most organizations exhibit characteristics of a simple structure in their formative years, but some may maintain this design type beyond this stage of their development (Mintzberg, 1979). The Time Out earlier in this chapter illustrates how, in its early days, Sun Ice operated with a simple structure.

Entrepreneurial organizations within the sport industry often adopt the simple structure design. Mintzberg (1979, p. 310) suggests "the entrepreneurial firm seems to be the best overall illustration of the Simple Structure." Because the entrepreneurial firm is aggressive and innovative, because it seeks environments that are simple and dynamic, and because the entrepreneurs themselves "often tend to be autocratic and sometimes charismatic" (Mintzberg, 1979, p. 310), the simple structure is ideal for this type of operation. Successful entrepreneurial companies often do not maintain the simple structure type of design for any lengthy period of time; as they grow, the design is replaced with a different set of structural arrangements. Gould (1989) describes how successful entrepreneurial sport organizations such as the Fitness Group of Vancouver, Sun Ice, and Bloor Cycle all operated with a simple structure in their early years.

Even for nonentrepreneurial companies a simple and dynamic environment is best served by a simple structure. The simple environment is easily scanned by the person at the strategic apex and the organic operating core found in a simple structure means a quick reaction to changes in the environment.

A crisis situation may force larger sport organizations to adopt the characteristics of a simple structure. When a sport organization's environment is hostile, the CEO may tend to centralize power and reduce bureaucratic controls to respond to the crisis situation. In 1984, for example, when Nike was experiencing financial problems and a serious challenge from Reebok, Philip Knight took back the presidency of Nike, which just over a year earlier he had turned over to Bob Woodell.

Finally, the need for power may also precipitate the adoption of a simple structure. Given the concentration of power at the strategic apex and the lack of formalization or any type of technostructure, this type of design is ideal for those CEOs who seek to maintain power. Alternatively, this design may be found when CEOs do not necessarily seek power but members bestow it on them. Mintzberg (1979) refers respectively to these variants of the simple structure as *autocratic* and *charismatic* organizations.

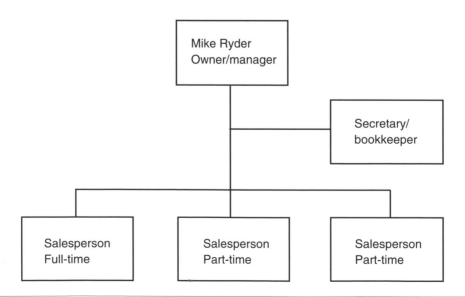

Figure 4.4   Mike's Bike and Sport store: a simple structure.

The Machine Bureaucracy

When a sport organization produces a standard output such as a hockey stick, when there is a requirement for fairness and public accountability such as we find in a government agency, and when consistency is required in performing relatively simple tasks such as on a football team, the most appropriate structure to use is a machine bureaucracy. Like Weber's legal-rational bureaucracy, the machine bureaucracy is characterized by high levels of standardization, formalized communication procedures, the functional grouping of tasks, routine operating procedures, a clear delineation between line and staff relationships, and a centralized hierarchy of authority. Figure 4.5 shows Mintzberg's depiction of a machine bureaucracy. In this type of design the technostructure is the key part of the organization, where we find the analysts, such as the quality control engineers, planners, and designers who standardize the work to be performed. Although their role is primarily advisory, they exercise considerable informal power because they structure everyone else's work (Mintzberg, 1979).

Advantages and Disadvantages

The main advantage of the machine bureaucracy is its efficiency. As Mintzberg (1979, p. 333) notes, "when an integrated set of simple, repetitive tasks must be performed precisely and consistently by human beings, the machine bureaucracy is the most efficient structure, indeed the only conceivable one." The grouping of specialist tasks in a machine bureaucracy results in certain economies of scale and less duplication of activities. In some cases, particularly those sport organizations involved in mass production, the high levels of standardization found in a machine bureaucracy mean less qualified and hence cheaper employees can be used. In government agencies that use what Mintzberg (1979) calls a public machine bureaucracy design, the use of low-cost labor is less pronounced. Because the lines of authority are clearly outlined in a machine bureaucracy, everyone knows his or her responsibilities. And, centralized control means that outside of the strategic apex, and to a certain extent the technostructure where work is standardized, there is little need for creative thinking.

The three disadvantages of a machine bureaucracy identified by Mintzberg (1979) are human problems, coordinating problems, and adaptation problems at the strategic apex. Many of the human problems emanate from the narrow specialization of work found in this design type; often dehumanizing for employees, it stifles any creative talents they may have, and produces feelings of alienation.

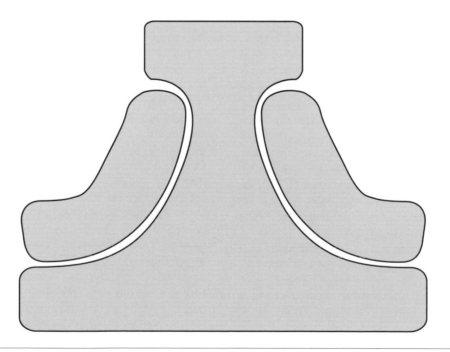

Figure 4.5   The machine bureaucracy.
The structuring of organizations by Mintzberg, © 1979. Adapted by permission of Prentice-Hall, Inc., Upper Saddle River, NJ.

The grouping of tasks into narrow functional areas means that employees work in relative isolation from other parts of the sport organization and hence coordination is made difficult. Such divisions can also promote "empire building" within the functional areas, which in turn creates conflicts that impede communication and coordination.

Finally, while the machine bureaucracy works well in stable environments it does not respond well to change. As Mintzberg (1979, p. 342) points out, change generates nonroutine problems. When these become frequent "managers at the strategic apex quickly become overloaded" because these problems are passed up the hierarchy. Quick responses are difficult since managers are not in direct contact with the problem areas.

Where Do We Find the Machine Bureaucracy?

The machine bureaucracy is found in simple and stable environments. Sport organizations that adopt this design type are usually relatively large, with routine technologies in which work is easily standardized. In the sport industry companies like Head, Bolle, and Dunlop, which mass-produce equipment, would probably operate with this type of design. So, too, would government agencies concerned with sport and related activities, such as the Oregon Parks and Recreation Department; the Province of Newfoundland Department of Culture, Youth, and Recreation; and Vermont's Department of Forests, Parks, and Recreation. In these organizations the treatment of clients and the hiring and promotion of employees must be seen to be fair. The machine bureaucracy, with its highly regulated systems, achieves this perception best. Guttmann (1978) suggests that many of the major governing bodies of sport such as the Marylebone Cricket Club (MCC), the International Amateur Athletic Federation (IAAF), and the Federation Internationale de Football Association (FIFA) exhibit a number of the characteristics of a machine bureaucracy.

Even sport teams such as a baseball team or a football team may operate as machine bureaucracies. George Allen, the former general manager of the Washington Redskins, exemplified this type of thinking when he suggested this analogy:

> A football team is a lot like a machine. It's made up of parts. I like to think of it as a Cadillac. A Cadillac's a pretty good car. All the refined parts working together make the team. If one

part doesn't work, one player pulling against you and not doing his job, the whole machine fails. (Terkel, 1972, p. 508)

The owner of the team represents the strategic apex, the players the operating core, and the general manager the middle line. The support staff is made up of team doctors, athletic therapists, strength coaches, and equipment personnel. The technostructure consists of coaches, assistant coaches, and scouts who standardize the work processes of the players in the operating core.

The Divisionalized Form

Sport organizations such as Johnson Worldwide Associates, Inc., Brunswick Corporation, Coleman Company, Inc., and Wembley Group PLC all use some type of divisionalized form, essentially a set of relatively autonomous organizations coordinated by a central corporate headquarters. In some of the examples used here, not all of the company's divisions operate in the sport industry. Brunswick Corporation, for example, as well as being a major manufacturer of power boats and heavily involved in bowling centers, also produces defense materials, aerospace components, and industrial products. Wembley Group PLC, in addition to staging sports events, has interests in areas such as catering and the entertainment industry. One of the characteristics of a divisionalized form is, in fact, that it operates in a diversified market. Figure 4.6 shows Mintzberg's depiction of the divisionalized form.

The key part of the design is the middle line—the managers who head the various divisions and are usually given control over the strategic and operating decisions of their respective divisions. Corporate headquarters provide centralized support in areas such as finance, personnel, and legal matters. They also exercise some degree of control over divisions by monitoring and evaluating outcomes such as profit, market share, and sales growth. Essentially, division managers are allowed to operate as they see best provided they conform to corporate guidelines. The divisions that constitute the overall structure may exhibit a variety of designs. But the fact that corporate headquarters retains control by monitoring performance, a procedure that requires clearly defined standards, means that "the Divisionalized Form works best with machine bureaucratic structures in its divisions (Mintzberg, 1979, p. 385).

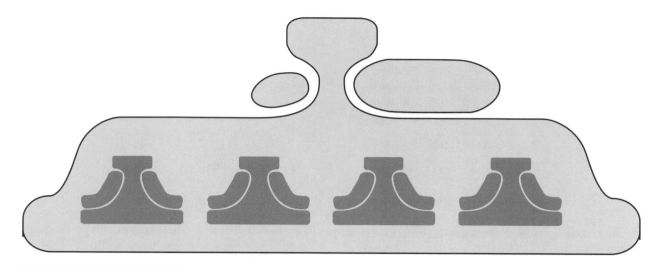

Figure 4.6   The divisionalized form.
The structuring of organizations by Mintzberg, © 1979. Adapted by permission of Prentice-Hall, Inc., Upper Saddle River, NJ.

Advantages and Disadvantages

One of the main advantages of the divisionalized form is that its divisions are relatively autonomous. Their managers "control the operations and determine the strategies for the markets that fall under their responsibility" (Mintzberg, 1979, p. 388). This means that corporate staff do not have to concern themselves with day-to-day operational issues and thus can pay more attention to long-term strategic planning for the entire organization. Using a divisionalized form means that corporate headquarters can allocate its financial resources more efficiently. If needed, capital can be extracted from one division and allocated to another. This type of structure has also been seen as a good training ground for senior managers. Since division managers essentially run a business within a business, they are able to gain experience in all areas. The divisionalized form is advantageous in that it allows a company to spread its risk (Mintzberg, 1979). Since it operates in diversified markets economic fluctuations are dealt with more easily; so much so that if one part of the organization does not perform up to required expectations it can be closed down or sold off with relatively little impact on other operations.

As might be expected, the divisionalized form is not without its faults. Some of its main disadvantages revolve around the relationship among divisions and between divisions and corporate headquarters. Conflict may occur among divisions when they compete in similar product markets or when they vie for corporate resources. Conflict is also created when a division's goals run counter to corporate goals or when the constraints the corporation imposes on a division are seen as overly restrictive.

The existence of several divisions within the overall structure can lead to problems of coordination and control. Control in this type of design is usually achieved through quantitative performance measures, which can in turn lead to an emphasis on economic indicators and a tendency to ignore the social consequences of the division's operations.

Where Do We Find the Divisionalized Form?

The divisionalized form is most frequently found in organizations operating in diversified markets. As Mintzberg (1979, p. 393) points out, this type of structure "enables the organization to manage its strategic portfolio centrally, while giving each component of the portfolio the undivided attention of one unit." For our purposes it is important to note that in most cases not every division of the overall organization will be operating within the sport industry. Some companies such as Brunswick have a majority of their operations in sport and sport related products while for others, sport may be just another product market in a company that also produces musical instruments and motorcycles.

Because it usually consists of integrated machine bureaucracies, the environment where the divisionalized form works best is relatively simple and stable, the same conditions that favor the machine bureaucracy. Size and age are also associated with the divisionalized form. As organizations grow they tend to diversify in order to protect themselves from market fluctuations; such diversification leads to divisionalization. Likewise, with time, a company's existing product markets may face challenges from new competitors; thus they are forced to look for new markets. Success in these markets leads to an increased number of divisions.

The Professional Bureaucracy

The last three decades have seen the emergence of many new professions (Larson, 1977; Johnson, 1972). Sport, like other areas of social life, has not gone untouched by these developments (cf. Lawson, 1984; Macintosh & Whitson, 1990). Sports psychologists, athletic therapists, coaches, and sport managers have all laid claim to professional status. The rise of professionalism has led to the creation of a new organizational form. The professional bureaucracy combines the standardization of the machine bureaucracy with the decentralization that results from a professional's need for autonomy. The professional bureaucracy is found in a number of different areas of the sport industry; faculties of kinesiology often adopt this type of design, as do sport medicine clinics, sport marketing companies, and some voluntary sport organizations (cf. Hinings and Slack, 1987; Kikulis et al., 1989).

As figure 4.7 shows, the key part of the professional bureaucracy is the operating core. This is where we find the specialists, the professionals who operate relatively autonomously in this decentralized structure. The skills of the professionals are standardized through their training and their involvement in their professional association and related activities, but discretion is granted in the application of skills. So, for example, in a sport marketing company an individual client services manager, like most of her colleagues, will be expected to have some standard skills in the different areas of marketing but at the same time will be given relative discretion as to how to go about obtaining accounts. Unlike the machine bureaucracy, where work standards are developed by analysts in the technostructure and enforced by managers, the standards of the professional emanate from their training and their involvement in their professional association. In addition to the operating core, the only other part of the professional bureaucracy developed to any extent is the support staff who assist the professionals. Because work is too complex to be supervised by a manager or standardized by analysts, there is usually only a small strategic apex and middle line, for example, the senior partner of the sport marketing company and perhaps some managers who have a coordinating function. There is also little need for any type of technostructure.

Advantages and Disadvantages

In chapter 3 we saw how some elements of bureaucratic structuring, such as formalization and centralization, conflicted with professional values for autonomy. The advantage of the professional bureaucracy is that it minimizes these conflicts by combining the professional's need for autonomy with standardization. However, standardization is not achieved with detailed rules and procedures, but through training and other forms of professional practice (social specialization). The autonomy the professionals achieve is only acquired after lengthy education and often on-the-job training, so when an orthopedic surgeon working in a sports medicine clinic operates on the knee of an athlete, the athlete knows any chance of a mistake has been

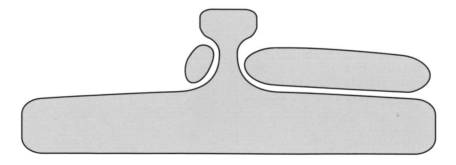

Figure 4.7   The professional bureaucracy.
The structuring of organizations by Mintzberg, © 1979. Adapted by permission of Prentice-Hall, Inc., Upper Saddle River, NJ.

minimized because the surgeon has trained for the procedure in medical school. She has also watched and helped colleagues perform the surgery many times before she attempts it on her own.

The autonomy that a professionally trained person experiences from working in a professional bureaucracy is the major advantage of this type of design. It does, however, have disadvantages in that it can create coordination problems. Professionals such as sport management professors, who work in a department that operates as a professional bureaucracy, may for example have little in common with colleagues in exercise physiology. They have different training, different research agendas, and even a different terminology for their work. While each may prefer to be left alone "to do his own thing," it is necessary for them to get along with colleagues from other areas and coordinate their efforts to produce a well-balanced physical education and sport studies program.

A further disadvantage of this type of design is that, as Mintzberg (1979, p. 373) notes, it is "appropriate for professionals who are competent and conscientious. Unfortunately not all of them are, and the professional bureaucratic structure cannot easily deal with professionals who are either incompetent or unconscientious." This type of structure is also problematic in that allowing professionals a high level of autonomy can work against the development of any type of team approach to the problems and issues confronting the sport organization.

Where Do We Find the Professional Bureaucracy?

We find professional bureaucracies in environments that are both complex and stable. Environmental complexity means that the skills to be learned require extensive periods of training but the stability of the environment means these skills can be well defined, in essence standardized. Age and size do not play a major role in influencing the choice of a professional bureaucratic design. We find small professional bureaucracies; for example, a law firm that specializes in contract work for professional athletes

---

TIME OUT

A Structural Taxonomy of Amateur Sport Organizations: The Professional Bureaucracy

In a study of provincial-level sport organizations Kikulis et al. (1989) produce a structural taxonomy of organizational design types. Five of the organizations in the study—figure skating, ice hockey, soccer, swimming, and volleyball—exhibited the characteristics of a professional bureaucracy. These organizations had high levels of professional specialization and an extensive range of programs. Volunteer specialization, in both technical and administrative roles, was not as high as in many other organizations, thus indicating that program operation and management were in the hands of professionals assisted by volunteers. Coordination of programs and staff was achieved through a large number of meetings. There was, however, a relatively high level of standardization, a structural characteristic not usually found in professional bureaucracies but, for these organizations, a reflection of their strong ties to government.

Decision making was centralized at the volunteer board level. While in an ideal professional bureaucracy the decision making is decentralized to the professional levels, Kikulis et al. point out that in voluntary sport organizations, the situation is somewhat more complex. In these type of organizations, decisions are actually *made* by professionals but *ratified* by the board. Although decisions must go to the board level for approval, the professionals in these organizations are able to structure the flow of information to the board in order to get the response they want. Consequently, while there is an appearance of board control, decision making is controlled by the professional staff, as we would expect in a professional bureaucracy.

Based on information in Kikulis, L., Slack, T., Hinings, C.R., and Zimmermann, A. (1989). A structural taxonomy of amateur sport organizations. *Journal of Sport Management, 3*, 129-150.

may operate with three or four lawyers, an office manager, and support staff; we also find the professional bureaucratic design used in relatively new sport organizations. Unlike the machine bureaucracy, which often starts out as a simple structure, the professional bureaucracy requires little startup time.

The technology of the professional bureaucracy is, as Mintzberg (1979, p. 367) notes, important for what it is not, that is, "highly regulating, sophisticated, nor automated." The presence of any of these characteristics in the organization's technology mitigates against the autonomy of the professional who requires discretion to carry out her work.

Adhocracy

Adhocracy is a highly flexible and responsive form of sport organization, what Burns and Stalker refer to as an organic structure. Used when a high level of innovation is required in the work processes, it may be a permanent or temporary design. The adhocracy has low levels of formalization, no structured hierarchy of authority, and high levels of horizontal differentiation, with specialists grouped into functional units for organizational purposes but often deployed to project teams to do their work. There are high levels of decentralization, little if anything in the way of standardized operating pro-

cedures, and coordination achieved through mutual adjustment, as teams containing managers, operators, and support staff work together to solve unique problems. In sport we find the adhocracy being used in television companies covering major sporting events, in research-and-development companies such as W.L. Gore & Associates, Inc., and in some university research labs.

As figure 4.8 shows, the adhocracy has little or no technostructure because its work cannot be standardized or formalized. The middle-line managers, the operating core, and the support staff are all professionals, so there is no clear demarcation between line and staff. Decisions are made by those who possess the expertise. The managers in the strategic apex spend their time monitoring projects, resolving the conflicts that inevitably arise in this type of free-flowing structure, and (probably most importantly) liaising with the external environment.

It is difficult to produce an organizational chart for an adhocracy because the internal structure of these organizations changes frequently as new problems require new project teams. Unlike the professional bureaucracy, the experts who work in adhocracies cannot rely on standardized skills to achieve coordination, as this leads "to standardization instead of innovation" (Mintzberg, 1979, p. 434). Rather, in the adhocracy, groups of professionals combine their efforts to build on their existing knowledge and skills to produce innovative solutions to new and different problems. For example,

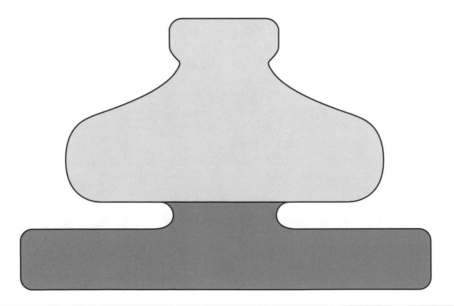

Figure 4.8 The adhocracy.
The structuring of organizations by Mintzberg, © 1979. Adapted by permission of Prentice-Hall, Inc., Upper Saddle River, NJ.

TIME OUT

Televising the Olympic Games

NBC paid $300 million for the American rights to televise the 1988 Summer Olympic Games from Seoul, South Korea. It's not an assignment that happens regularly at NBC. In fact, the last time the network televised an Olympics was the 1972 Games from Sapporo, Japan.

NBC spent three years planning the two-week extravaganza. What made the project uniquely challenging was its complexity. First, all preparations had to be made in addition to NBC's normal broadcasting operations. None of the planning effort for the Olympics could interfere with the day-to-day broadcasting of NBC's regular programs. If it was necessary to take people off their normal jobs to work on the Olympics, someone had to be found to fill in for them. Second, the project was immense. The physical distance of Seoul from NBC's New York headquarters, plus language and cultural differences, made the job particularly challenging. A 60,000-square-foot broadcast center had to be erected in Seoul. Sixty million dollars in state-of-the-art technical equipment had to be shipped to South Korea and set up. More than 1,100 NBC employees—500 in engineering, 300 in production, and 300 in management and clerical positions—were needed to run the 100 monitor control rooms, 15 edit rooms, 150 tape machines, 100 NBC cameras, 17 mobile units, and to coordinate operations. Third, televising the Olympic Games demands high flexibility because unexpected, world-class performances can occur at almost any time. There were 220 events taking place at 23 different locations throughout Seoul. In many cases a half-dozen or more events were going on simultaneously, and NBC had to be able to switch from one site to another instantly if something noteworthy was occurring. Finally, NBC had a lot at stake in the Games. It was competing against ABC's successful record of televising past summer and winter Olympics. Moreover, it had sold some 1,750 minutes of advertising time at an average of $660,000 per minute in prime time. Sponsors were expecting high ratings; if they didn't materialize there was the possibility that NBC would have to return part of the money to the advertisers. If ratings slacked, the estimated $50 to $75 million in profits that NBC was estimating from the Games could quickly turn to a loss. Of course, a successful performance in the ratings would have a positive effect, giving the network's fall schedule a strong boost.

How did NBC organize the task of broadcasting the Games? They utilized an adhocracy. While NBC is essentially a machine bureaucracy, the structure used to plan and operate the Olympics had few formal rules and regulations. Decision making was decentralized, although carefully coordinated by NBC's executive producer for Olympic operations. The need to bring together more than a thousand technical specialists, who could apply their skills on a temporary project in a dynamic environment requiring the ability to respond rapidly to change, led NBC to use an adhocracy. To have used any other design would have lessened the company's effectiveness in achieving its objectives.

Organization theory; Structure, design, and applications, 3/E by Robbins, © 1990. Reprinted by permission of Prentice-Hall, Inc., Upper Saddle River, NJ.

in order to conduct research on the contribution that sport and other forms of physical activity make to increasing an individual's well-being, a department of health, physical education, and recreation may create a research unit that houses physiologists, psychologists, and sociologists. While these people do not normally work together, they could all combine their knowledge and skills to produce innovative solutions to this type of problem. A similar type of adhocratic structure may be created by a municipal council developing a plan to build a new multi-use sport facility; experts would be needed from departments concerned with land-use planning, sport programming, environment, transportation, and so on.

Advantages and Disadvantages

The main advantage of the adhocracy is that it can respond rapidly to change. It promotes creativity by bringing diverse groups of professionals together to work on specific projects. Adhocracies may be permanent structures, such as the lattice type of organizational design used at W.L. Gore & Associates, Inc. (Rhodes, 1982), or they may be set up on a temporary basis. For example, in 1993 the Government of Canada created a task force, which is a type of adhocracy, to investigate the funding of amateur sport. The task force filed its report with the Minister of Canadian Heritage in late 1993 and was then disbanded. This type of temporary setup is not as easily achieved with other organizational design types.

The flexibility of the adhocracy is a weakness as well as a strength. High levels of flexibility mean that the adhocracy is the most politicized of the design types we have examined. There are no clear lines of authority and no formalized rules; consequently, employees may be involved in "political games" to achieve their goals, more so than in other organizational designs. The political nature of the adhocracy means a potential for high levels of conflict, which can create stress for employees and for those who do not like rapid change, but prefer stability in their job. These stresses are compounded by the flexibility of the adhocracy.

Inefficiency is also a weakness of the adhocracy. The flexibility required in this structure means high levels of face-to-face communication, frequent discussions and meetings, all costly in time and money. Also, as Mintzberg (1979, p. 464) notes, "a further source of inefficiency in the Adhocracy is the unbalanced workloads." Not all of the specialists can be kept busy all of the time; there will be slow periods and periods of intense activity, an inefficient use of this type of resource.

Where Do We Find the Adhocracy?

The innovative nature of the work performed in an adhocracy means that it is found in environments that are both dynamic and complex. As Mintzberg (1979, p. 449) notes, "in effect, innovative work, being unpredictable, is associated with a dynamic environment; and the fact that the innovation must

be sophisticated means that it is difficult to comprehend, in other words associated with a complex environment." For these reasons, research units such as those found in a faculty of physical education and sport studies may choose to adopt this organizational design. So, too, may the organizing committee for a temporary event such as a road race or a basketball tournament.

Technology will also influence the decision to structure as an adhocracy. An organization with a sophisticated technical system requires "specialists who have the knowledge, power, and flexible work arrangements to cope with it" (Mintzberg, 1979, p. 458). This requirement creates a decentralized structure and considerable integration of the analysts in the technostructure, the operators, and the support staff, an integration best achieved with an adhocracy.

Other factors influencing the choice of an adhocracy are age or, as Mintzberg notes, more specifically, youth and fashion. Youth is a factor because a number of young organizations seek to be innovative with new products and markets; adhocracy facilitates this quest for innovation. Fashion is a factor because much of the "pop management" literature has critiqued notions of hierarchy and centralization in organizations, and has suggested the need for more organic structures and innovations such as project teams and task forces. Again, the adhocracy is designed to meet these kinds of requirements.

Organizational Designs as Ideal Types

It is important to note that the five design types described here are, in fact, ideal types. As such, it is quite possible that no sport organization will be exactly like one of these designs. For example, when we look at a set of sport organizations we may find that a number of them may be in transition between designs. In the late 1950s Coleman Co., a major producer of equipment for outdoor sports, had been operating with a machine bureaucracy design; management, realizing it had grown too big and diverse for this type of structure, started a process of divisionalization. Such changes take time to achieve; anyone studying this organization in its transition period would not find a neatly laid-out design type as described here. Kikulis et al. (1989) show evidence of transitional designs. In their research they found a number of amateur sport organizations that

TIME OUT

W.L. Gore & Associates: The Lattice Organization

W.L. Gore & Associates is a manufacturing and research company worth over a billion dollars. Gore-Tex fabrics are used to make skiwear, running suits, golfwear, tents, and clothing for hunting and fishing. The company promotes innovation through a unique organizational design, the lattice, a type of adhocracy in which the guiding principle is described as "un-management." Within the lattice organization every "associate" (as employees are called) must deal with other associates one-on-one. There are no hierarchies, no job titles, no bosses, and no authoritative commands. When they join the organization, new associates are sponsored by an established associate. New associates pick the area to work where they think they can make the best contribution. They are then challenged to do their best in this area. Associates are given the freedom to experiment with new ideas and to follow through on those that are potentially profitable. They must, however, consult with associates before taking any action that the company terms as being "below the waterline" and thus having the potential to cause serious damage to the organization.

Based on information in Simmons, J. (1987). People managing themselves. *Journal for Quality and Participation, 10*, pp. 14-19; and Rhodes, L. (1982, August). The un-manager. *Inc.*, pp. 34-43.

were moving toward a professional bureaucratic structure but, at the time of the study, had not reached this design; they called these organizations nascent professional bureaucracies.

As well as finding organizations in transitional states, it is also possible that we will find a number exhibiting what is referred to as a hybrid structure. That is to say, they exhibit the characteristics of more than one design type. It may be, for example, that a company producing sports equipment and operating with a machine bureaucracy design may wish to develop new products and enter new markets; it may create a small adhocracy as an appendage to its existing machine bureaucracy design. Brunswick took this type of initiative when it established venture capital groups within its divisions in order to nurture new products.

What does all this mean, then? Does the fact that we may not find the exact type of organizational design we have described mean that they are not useful? Of course not. As we pointed out at the start of this chapter, scholars who study organizations of all types have long considered a means of classification as one of the basic requirements of the field. As table 4.1 shows, the five designs developed by Mintzberg enable us to compare and contrast sport organizations on a number of dimensions. They also provide us with a basis for studying a wide variety of other organizational phenomena. For example, how does a sport organization change from a simple structure to a machine bureaucracy to a divisional-

ized form? Do machine bureaucracies and professional bureaucracies formulate strategy in different ways? Are decisions made differently in a professional bureaucracy from how they are made in an adhocracy? And, how is power exercised in each of these different designs? All of these questions, and many more, are valid topics of investigation for sport management students. The design types outlined can provide a useful basis for investigation into these areas.

Summary and Conclusions

Although no two sport organizations are exactly alike, they do exhibit commonly occurring features that can be used as a basis for classifying them into design types, or configurations. Classification has been identified as one of the most important tasks for organizational theorists, because it provides a basis for the generation of hypotheses, models, and theories. There are two main ways of classifying organizations: Conceptually-based schema are called typologies; those that are empirically based are referred to as taxonomies.

One of the most commonly used organizational typologies is the one developed by Mintzberg (1979), who identifies five parts of an organization. Depending on the part that dominates, we get one of five organizational designs: the simple structure,

Table 4.1   Dimensions of the Five Organizational Design Types

DIMENSIONS	SIMPLE STRUCTURE	MACHINE BUREAUCRACY	PROFESSIONAL BUREAUCRACY	DIVISIONALIZED FORM	ADHOCRACY
Horizontal complexity	Low	High-functional	High-social	High-functional	High-social
Vertical complexity	Low	High	Medium	High within divisions	Low
Formalization	Low	High	Low	High within divisions	Low
Centralization	High	High	Low	High within divisions	Low
Technology	Simple	Regulating/ not automated/ not sophisticated	Not regulating or sophisticated	Divisable like machine bureaucracy	Sophisticated/ often automated
Size	Small	Large	Varies	Large	Varies
Environment	Simple/ dynamic	Simple/stable	Complex/stable	Simple/stable diversified markets	Complex and dynamic
Strategy	Intuitive and opportunistic	To maintain performance in chosen markets	Developed by individuals controlled by professional association	Portfolio	Seeks new products and new markets

The structuring of organizations by Mintzberg, © 1979. Adapted by permission of Prentice-Hall, Inc., Upper Saddle River, NJ.

the machine bureaucracy, the divisionalized form, the professional bureaucracy, or the adhocracy. We can find sport organizations representative of each of these design types.

The simple structure, most commonly found in small sport organizations and those in the early stages of their development, usually shows low levels of specialization and formalization. The key part of a simple structure is the strategic apex, where we find the individual who runs the sport organization and with whom power is centralized. Simple structures work best in environments that are simple and dynamic.

The machine bureaucracy is usually found in sport organizations that produce a standard output, government agencies concerned with sport, and organizations that need relatively simple tasks performed in a consistent manner. Its main attribute is its efficiency. The key part of the machine bureaucracy is the technostructure where work is standardized. We find the machine bureaucracy in simple and stable environments.

The divisionalized form is actually a group of organizations, usually machine bureaucracies, coordinated by a central headquarters. The divisions, not all of which are always involved in sport,

provide product and market diversity. The key part of this organization is the middle-line managers, those individuals who control the divisions. The divisionalized form is found in large organizations that have either product and/or market diversity; it operates in simple and stable environments.

The professional bureaucracy caters to the needs of the professional by providing the standardization of the bureaucracy but at the same time allowing professionals control of their own work. Faculties of physical education and sport studies often operate with a professional bureaucratic structure, as do sport medicine clinics and architectural firms specializing in sports facilities. The key part of the professional bureaucracy is the operating core, which contains the professionals. We find this type of design in sport organizations with complex and stable environments.

The final design is the adhocracy. NBC used this form of organization when they televised the Seoul Olympics. We also find it in research units and specialized structures such as a task force. Its strength is its flexibility and hence its ability to respond to change. The key part of this sport organization is the support staff, where we find the experts on which the organization is dependent. We find this type of structure in complex and dynamic environments.

Each of the designs discussed is an ideal type, so we seldom find sport organizations that fit the pattern exactly as described. Some sport organizations may approximate one of the main designs, some may be in transitional states between design, and others may exhibit a hybrid structure, that is, a structure that exhibits the characteristics of more than one design.

Key Concepts

Typology

Operating core

Middle line

Support staff

Machine bureaucracy

Professional bureaucracy

Ideal types

Taxonomy

Strategic apex

Technostructure

Simple structure

Divisionalized form

Adhocracy

Hybrid structure

Review Questions

1. How does a typology differ from a taxonomy?

2. What does Mintzberg suggest are the five parts of an organization?

3. What type of organizational design would you expect a small entrepreneurial organization within the sport industry to use? Why?

4. Describe the characteristics of the machine bureaucracy. What are the advantages and disadvantages of this design?

5. Pick some sport organizations that you are familiar with. What type of design do they have?

6. What type of design would you expect to find in a faculty of physical education and sport studies?

7. Discuss how the method of coordination varies in each of the five designs.

8. Describe the divisonalized form and explain where you might find this type of organiza-

tion in the sport industry. What are its advantages and disadvantages?

9. What are the characteristics of an adhocracy? Where would you expect to find this type of design in the sport industry?

10. In what type of sport organizations would you expect to find the professional bureaucracy?

11. What type of design did Nike use in its early years (see chapter 1)? What type of design do you think it uses now?

12. How does an adhocracy differ from a professional bureaucracy?

13. Discuss how the role of the strategic apex varies in each of the five designs.

14. Adhocracies have been described as fashionable. Why do you think this is?

15. In which of the design types is formalization likely to be low? Why?

Suggestions for Further Reading

For further reading, students are obviously referred to Henry Mintzberg's work on organizational design. The most comprehensive treatment is found in his book (1979) *The structuring of organizations*. While part 4 of his book deals specifically with design, the earlier chapters lay much of the foundation for his work in this area and should have relevance for students interested in this topic. More condensed versions of Mintzberg's work on design can be found in his chapter, "A typology of organizational structure," in Miller and Friesen's (1984) text *Organizations: A quantum view* and his articles (1981) "Organizational design: Fashion or fit?" in *Harvard Business Review*, and (1980) "Structure in 5's: A synthesis of the research on organizational design" in *Management Science*. Information on typologies and taxonomies can be found in Miller and Friesen's (1984) *Organizations: A quantum view*. While this is the most sophisticated work on these topics, some of it is difficult reading, particularly chapter 2, which deals with methods of developing taxonomies. Students should also see Carper and Snizek's (1980) "The nature and types of organizational taxonomies: An overview," in the *Academy of Management Review*.

Within the sport literature, Chelladurai's work (1985) on typologies in *Sport management: Macro perspectives* is a useful starting point for discussions on this topic. Also interesting is his 1992 article "A classification of sport and physical activity services: Implications for sport management," in the *Journal of Sport Management*. In regard to taxonomies of organizations, students should see Hinings and Slack's (1987) chapter "The dynamics of quadrennial plan implementation in national sport organizations" in their (Slack & Hinings, 1987a) edited book *The organization and administration of sport*. A more methodologically sophisticated taxonomy is developed and discussed in an extension of this work in Kikulis et al.'s (1989) article, "A structural taxonomy of amateur sport organizations," in the *Journal of Sport Management*.

Case for Analysis

Reshaping National Sport Organizations

Sitting in her home in the suburbs of Toronto, Susan Collinson, the volunteer president of a small Canadian sport organization, reread the material she had just received from the federal government agency, Sport Canada.* Susan had been the president of her organization for two years and had frequently expressed her concern about the increased involvement the government was taking in its operation. The material she just received had Susan worried.

For the past 15 to 20 years Sport Canada had provided many of the national-level amateur sport organizations with funds to operate their programs. The funds were not large and they were given with few strings attached. Susan's organization had been fairly successful and had used their funds well, building a very strong volunteer base within the various clubs that existed throughout the country. Their provincial associations were also well organized. The national organization's board of directors were an enthusiastic group of volunteers, many of whom held managerial positions with local and national companies. Using the funds they received from Sport Canada, and other moneys from membership fees and fund-raising ventures, this group of volunteers had established a wide range of developmental programs to encourage people to

get involved in their sport. They had also been reasonably successful in international competition, because Jim Kramer, one of the top club coaches in the country, had worked with the national team as a volunteer coach.

The organization operated in a collegial manner. Although there were the occasional disputes, members worked well together. They had no detailed policies and procedures they had to follow; they basically "got on with the job." About three years ago the board had hired Katrina Torkildson, a former athlete who understood the sport, to be their executive director. While she had no formal management training she was regarded as bright, enthusiastic, and well organized. Katrina worked for the board and essentially helped do the things they needed doing to make the organization run smoothly. As Susan read the material from the federal government, she wondered if all this was going to change.

Essentially, what the government was proposing was to increase significantly the amount of money they were providing to the national sport organizations. In large part their rationale was that this new funding would increase Canada's chances of doing well in the Olympic Games and other major

---

*Although the situation in this case is based on actual events the names are fictitious.

international sporting events. Although no definitive figures were given, Susan roughly estimated that the funds her organization was receiving could quadruple.

However, there was a catch. To receive the funds, national sport organizations had to prepare a "plan." The plan should outline the type of changes the sport organization would make in order to operate in a more efficient and business-like manner. This efficiency, Sport Canada felt, was what was needed to increase Canada's medal count at major games. The plan should also contain detailed policies and procedures that documented how the organization conducted its business. One of the other changes the government appeared to be promoting was the hiring of an increased number of professionally trained staff to run the affairs of the organization, enhance its developmental programs, and coach its national teams. Funds were to be provided, up to 75 percent of their salary, to hire these people; Sport Canada would, however, have a voice in who was hired. Although it was not stated as such, implicit in the material Susan received was the idea that volunteers would play a considerably smaller role in the organization's operation, which would be turned over to the new professional staff. As Susan pondered the material, she wondered what impact all this would have on her organization and how she should deal with the information she had received.

Questions

1. What would you do if you were Susan and you had just received the material from the federal government?

2. What is the potential impact of the government's proposed initiatives on the design of this national sport organization?

3. How do you think Jim and Katrina will feel about the government's proposals?

4. Is there any way that Susan could take advantage of the increased funding offered by the government, yet at the same time maintain the type of organizational design that currently exists?

5

Strategy in Sport Organizations

When You Have Read This Chapter

You should be able to

1. explain what we mean by the term *organizational strategy*,

2. explain the different corporate-level and business-level strategies that a sport organization can adopt,

3. describe how strategy is formulated and implemented,

4. explain Mintzberg's three modes of strategy formulation,

5. describe the strategy-structure relationship, and

6. compare Miles and Snow's four strategic types.

Reebok's Strategy Takes It to the Front of the Athletic Footwear Race

In 1979 while attending a sporting goods trade fair in Chicago, Paul Fireman, who at the time was operating his family's fishing and hunting equipment business, came across an interesting-looking running shoe, produced by a small company from the north of England called Reebok. Fireman acquired the license to sell Reeboks in North America. Over the next few years his organization did a modest business but lagged behind the leading athletic footwear companies like Adidas and Nike. However, in the early 1980s the aerobics boom hit North America, Jane Fonda released her first video, and women besieged shoe dealers with requests for aerobic shoes. Despite reservations from Pentland Industries, a British conglomerate that had joined with Fireman in 1982 and bought Reebok and its worldwide licensing rights, the company entered the aerobics market. Their strategy was to produce a comfortable, colorful, and stylish shoe with a ballet-slipper type of top and a durable rubber sole; the shoe was called the Freestyle. Fireman and partner Jim Barclay promoted the shoe by discounting or giving them away to aerobics instructors. Their strategy worked; sales boomed. Between 1984 and 1985 Reebok's profits rose from $6.2 million to $39 million. Their aerobics shoes were not only used for exercise classes but were adopted as casual wear by the fashion-conscious.

Unlike Reebok, Nike, the industry leader at that time, did not adjust its strategy to respond to the changing environment precipitated by the growth of the aerobics phenomenon; its marketers saw aerobics as a flash in the pan and the company continued to produce the same type of running shoe that had made it so successful throughout the 1970s. Their inventory increased and by mid-1983 Nike had 22 million pairs of unsold running shoes on its hands. By 1986 it had lost its position as the industry leader as Reebok's turnover rose to $850 million.

Based on information in Sedgwick, J. (1989, January). Treading on air. *Business Month*, pp. 28-34; Benoit, E. (1988, September). Reebok's lost youth. *Financial World*, pp. 28-31; Dodds, L.S. (1985, August/September). Heading back on the fast track. *Financial World*, pp. 90-91.

Reebok changed its strategy to respond to changes in its environment. It created a fashionable shoe that appealed to the increasing number of people, especially women, participating in aerobics. Nike, on the other hand, failed to make a strategic response to the changing environmental conditions and consequently its market position suffered. A number of research studies (Miles, Snow, Meyer, & Coleman, 1978; Miller, 1987b) have suggested that, in order to be successful, organizations must respond to changes in their environment with appropriate strategies, which will in turn require structural change. In fact, when organizational theory first started to develop as a distinct area of study, there was a belief that strategy was the only variable to determine structure. To be effective there had to be an appropriate "fit" between an organization's strategy and its structure (Robbins, 1990).

Now we know that strategy is in fact just one variable that can influence the structure of an organization. In the next four chapters we look at these contingencies, determinants, imperatives, or contextual factors (as they are variously called). In this chapter we focus on the concept of organizational strategy. We look at what we mean when we talk about strategy and we discuss the differences between corporate-level strategies and business-level strategies. We also examine how strategy is formulated and implemented, and the relationship between strategy and structure. In the following three chapters we look at the influence of size, environment, and technology on the structure of a sport organization. We then look at how power, a non-contingent factor, can be used to influence structure.

What Is Organizational Strategy?

Das (1990, p. 294) likens an organization's strategy to the game plan developed by a sports team:

> [B]efore a team enters the field, an effective coach looks at the team's strengths and weaknesses and also those of its competitors. The coach carefully studies the two teams' past successes, failures, and behaviors on the field. The obvious objective is to win the game with minimal risk and personal injuries to the players. Thus, a coach may not use all the team's best players if it is not warranted (they may be kept in reserve for future games or to maintain an element of surprise). The key goal is to win the game and the game plan itself might be modified to recognize the emerging realities.

Das goes on, however, to point out that while a football or volleyball team has a game plan for each game and each opponent, an organization's strategy is more long-term and must deal with a number of issues, internal and external to the organization. Thus, he suggests, a strategy can be thought of as "a comprehensive and integrated plan with relatively long-term implications designed to achieve the basic objectives of the organization. It incorporates the strengths and weaknesses of the organization and takes into account the environmental realities and trends. [It] include[s] decisions to compete in specific product-market segments, to diversify, to expand, to reduce or even close down specific operations or subunits" (Das 1990, p. 294). Alfred Chandler, one of the first to carry out research on organizational strategy, provided a similar explanation. He suggested (1962, p. 13) that "strategy can be defined as the determination of the basic long-term goals and objectives of an enterprise and the adoption of courses of action and the allocation of resources necessary for carrying out these goals." Sometimes the term "strategy" is used synonymously with the terms "goals" and "objectives." But, as both Das and Chandler's explanations make clear, strategy is more than goals and objectives; it also involves the means by which goals are to be achieved.

All sport organizations formulate strategies; they may be deliberate or emergent. Deliberate strategies are intended courses of action that become realized. In contrast, emergent strategies are those that are realized but not necessarily intended (Mintzberg, 1978). The 1990 acquisition of Cooper Canada by Canstar Sports, Inc. is an example of a deliberate strategy. As Canstar president Gerald Wasserman noted, Cooper was "a natural fit" for his company. The acquisition made Canstar, already the world's biggest manufacturer and distributor of skates, one of the largest makers of protective hockey equipment ("Cooper 'natural fit'," 1990). An example of a more emergent type of strategy was the one displayed by Wilson Sporting Goods. Originally in the meat business, Wilson diversified into sporting goods because gut, a byproduct of the meat industry, was used in the stringing of tennis racquets (Aris, 1990). In a somewhat similar vein, Walvin (1975) describes how the strategy of some churches to use soccer as a means to combat urban degeneration among the working classes led to the formation of soccer clubs. Aston Villa, Birmingham City, Bolton Wanderers, and Fulham are all notable examples. It is, of course, possible that deliberate strategies, as they become realized, may become in part emergent, and emergent strategies in time get formalized as deliberate (Mintzberg, 1978).

In summary, strategy may then be planned and deliberate, it may emerge as a stream of significant decisions, or it may be some combination of both. In any of these situations organizational decision makers base their choice of strategy on their perceptions of the opportunities and threats in the environment, and the internal strengths and weaknesses of their organization. Then, as a result of the strategy they choose, they institute an appropriate organizational structure. This sequence is shown graphically in figure 5.1.

Levels of Strategy

Sport organizations can formulate strategy at two levels, the corporate level and the business level. Corporate-level strategies, which are followed by the organization as a whole, are required when a sport organization competes in a number of different industries. They answer the question "What businesses should we be involved in?" For example, John Labatt Ltd. followed a corporate strategy that involved it not only in the brewing industry but also in major league baseball, through its ownership of the Toronto Blue Jays. Obviously there are benefits, if corporate-level strategies involve "synergies among the business units and with the corporation" (Yavitz & Newman, 1982, p. 60). The Labatt/Blue Jay relationship accomplished this synergy; ownership of the Blue Jays gave Labatt access to the television coverage and advertising vital to the brewing industry.

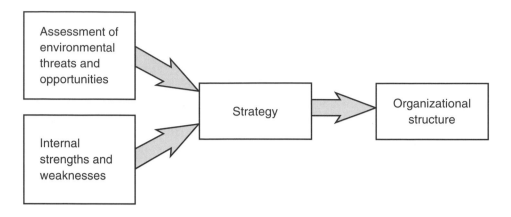

Figure 5.1   Strategy-structure relationship.

While some degree of synergy among the different businesses in a corporation can be beneficial, some organizations adopt a strategy of operating in diversified markets. We have previously mentioned Brunswick (powerboats and defense) and Wembley Group PLC (hosting sport events and catering). Other examples involving sport are Wight, Collins, Rutherford, and Scott, a major UK communications company which up until 1993 had as part of its portfolio Alan Pascoe Associates (APA), a sport sponsorship company; Yamaha, which produces musical instruments and motorcycles, as well as a variety of other sports and recreational goods; and Provigo, a consumer-goods distributor that up until early 1994 owned Sports Experts Inc., a chain of sporting goods stores.

Business-level strategies address questions about how to compete within a particular industry; when a sport organization only competes in one industry, its business-level strategy and its corporate-level strategy will be the same. But for sport organizations competing in a number of industries, each division will formulate its own strategy. For example, a corporation like Huffy will in all likelihood formulate strategies for its cycle division, its sport division (which produces basketball accessories), and its juvenile products division (which markets car seats, strollers, and other products for children). Figure 5.2 shows the relationship between corporate-level and business-level strategy.

A corporate strategy "typically incorporates the results of a business-level analysis through a technique referred to as portfolio analysis" (Bates & Eldredge, 1984, pp. 24-25). We discuss this topic more fully in the next section of this chapter, where we examine corporate strategies in more detail.

Corporate-Level Strategies

There are four different types of corporate strategy in which an organization can engage. Hodge and Anthony (1991) term them growth strategies, stability strategies, defensive strategies, and combination strategies.

Growth Strategies

Almost all sport organizations seek growth as one of their goals. A growth strategy may be pursued in two major ways at the corporate level: diversification and integration. Diversification helps a company grow while at the same time spreading its risk. Diversification strategies may be related or unrelated. A related diversification strategy "calls for the acquired investment to have some relation to the existing businesses such as technology, product group, managerial knowledge, or distribution channels. [It] permits a firm to spread its risk while at the same time capitalizing on its strengths" (Bates & Eldredge, 1984, p. 137). The acquisition of Cooper Canada by Canstar Sports, Inc., mentioned earlier in this chapter, is an example of a related diversification. An unrelated diversification strategy means that a corporation is pursuing acquisitions in areas not necessarily related to its existing business units. The decisions of successful business people such as Tom Monaghan (Domino's Pizza), Jerry Jones (oil) and Victor Kiam (Remington) to acquire professional sport franchises (respectively the Detroit Tigers, the Dallas Cowboys, and the New England Patriots), are all examples of an unrelated diversification strategy; Ted Turner's involvement in the Atlanta Hawks and the Atlanta Braves, however, could be seen as a related diversification, since both teams provide programming for his TV station.

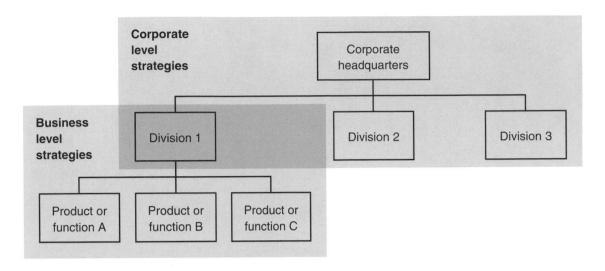

Figure 5.2 Levels of strategy.

In addition to diversification, growth can also be achieved through integration. Integration may be achieved horizontally or vertically. Horizontal integration involves adding another product, often a competitor in the same business, by buying an organization. AstroTurf manufacturer Balsam's acquisition of smaller artificial turf producers such as All Pro, Omni Turf, and Super Turf is an example of horizontal integration. Vertical integration occurs either when a sport organization acquires its distributors (forward integration) or its suppliers (backward integration). The former strategy may be pursued "to reduce duplicate marketing costs, ensure availability of product, or to acquire the higher margins that typically occur close to the final sale. The latter is followed when increased raw material costs cannot be passed on or when a firm operates with a continuous production process" (Bates & Eldredge, 1984, p. 138). Nike, for example, in 1991 purchased Tetra Plastics Ltd., the company that produces the plastic film used in the production of Air Sole Cushioning—an example of backward integration. In the early 1990s it also bought out many of its distribution operations, an example, of forward integration ("Can Nike just do it?", 1994).

A sport organization can use a number of techniques when it adopts a growth strategy. For example, diversification may be achieved through mergers, acquisitions, takeovers, or joint ventures. A merger occurs when two or more companies combine to produce one. For example, in Canada in 1989, the Canadian Women's Field Hockey Association and the Canadian Field Hockey Association, previously two separate entities, merged to form Field Hockey Canada. An acquisition involves one company buying another and absorbing it into its operations. Such was the case in 1983 when Bally Manufacturing, best known for its association with slot machines, acquired Health & Tennis Corp. of America, the world's largest chain of health clubs. A takeover involves one company attempting to obtain control of another against the wishes of shareholders and management. Irwin L. Jacobs' 1985 acquisition of AMF Inc., a sport and leisure products company, is an example of a takeover (cf. Ehrlich, 1985; Ross, 1985). Joint ventures occur when one company joins with another to work on a specific project. The joining of Ellerman Lines and Greenall Whitley to develop The Belfry golf complex, described in the Time Out on p. 97, was essentially a joint venture. So, too, was Nike's 1980 agreement with Nissho Iwai, the Japanese trading company, which linked Nike's trademark license for Japan with a credit agreement from Nissho to finance Nike's growth (Strasser & Becklund, 1991).

Internal growth can also occur when a sport organization is able to expand its market share. This growth may be acheived by saturating existing markets with current products or services. Alternatively, a company may take an existing product or service, which has been successful in one market, into a new market.

Stability Strategies

Hodge and Anthony (1991) suggest that an organization may engage in two types of stability strategies. A neutral strategy means that the organization

TIME OUT

Reebok Diversifies With Acquisitions

Following Reebok's tremendous success in the first part of the 1980s, chairman and cofounder Paul Fireman faced a problem of what to do with a company that had grown from virtually nothing to over $1 billion in sales. Fireman's answer: a diversification strategy that involved a series of acquisitions. In making acquisitions Fireman looked for established products, geared to the trendsetting 18-to-45 age group, that could be built into major national brands and sold in upscale specialty, sporting goods and department stores. Upscale retailing was important to Fireman. "I believe the consumer judges the quality of the brand today by the quality of its distribution," he said. "A department store can sell a Reebok product for 25 percent off and it won't do any damage to the cachet. But if a mass merchandiser sold it for 25 percent above retail it would be considered cheap."

Accordingly, in spring 1987 Reebok shelled out $180 million to acquire Avia, the Portland, Oregon-based maker of high-priced aerobic, running, tennis, and basketball shoes. (Along with Avia came Donner Mountain, a hiking boot manufacturer.) Obviously looming large in Fireman's thinking was that Avia, with $70.3 million in sales in 1986, was emerging as a major competitor to Reebok in aerobic shoes. "Sometimes there's a cult following that develops among a group of core consumers who want to believe they are ahead of everyone else," Fireman said. Avia was, in fact, close to becoming the next hot fad product.

Fireman believed that walking shoes would be the next big craze. Playing this hunch he paid $118 million in 1986 for the Rockport Co. of Marlboro, Massachusetts, a fast-growing maker of walking, casual, and dress shoes. Statistics bore him out. In 1987, according to American Sports Data, Inc., about 25 million Americans were fitness walkers, and one in four took the sport seriously enough to average about 700 miles per year.

Reebok also picked up (for practically nothing, Fireman said) Marlboro's Frye Boot Co., which was drowning in debt but had a good management and nationwide recognition. He merged Frye with Rockport and put Frye president Stanley Kravetz in charge. Reebok's intent was to develop the Frye label into a line of men's and women's classic hand-sewn shoes with the look and price tag of Ralph Lauren shoes.

Jessica J. Reif, footwear analyst at Arnhold & Bleichroeder, Inc., said Fireman's acquisitions were brilliant: "Avia is a great fit and captures a segment where Reebok potentially could have had some competition. And Rockport's demand is so high, they can't fill the backlog; with Frye they are getting the production capability and management they need."

From A.L. Stern, 1987, "Reebok in for the distance," *Business Month*, 22-25.

continues to do what it has done in the past with no intent to grow. A harvesting or milking strategy is used when a product is becoming obsolete or if a business unit lacks potential and there is little chance to turn the situation around. This type of strategy involves management in an attempt to increase its cash flow from the product or business unit by severely reducing or eliminating the capital it puts into areas such as facility maintenance, advertising, and research (Harrigan & Porter, 1983).

There are two possible consequences of a harvesting strategy. First, the product or business unit may justify its existence by continuing to be successful enough, with little or no investiture, to generate cash flow that can be diverted to other units. Alternately, it may lose market share but generate an initial, albeit short-term increase in capital that can be directed elsewhere. When the cash flow from the product or business unit starts to decline, liquidation usually follows.

TIME OUT

The Belfry

In the early 1970s PA Management Consultants was retained by Ellerman Lines, one of Britain's major shipping companies, to help identify growth opportunities through diversification. At the same time as they were working for Ellerman, PA was doing work for Greenall Whitley, a brewing company that also owned a number of hotels, including one called the Belfry. In the early 1970s the hotel industry in Britain had become increasingly competitive; although Greenall wanted to modernize and expand its hotels, its major capital expenditure was directed toward its brewing interests. One of Greenall's ideas for the Belfry was to turn it into a major golf complex, but they needed a large amount of capital. Greenall's board had just spent £10 million on a brewery and consequently were not willing to put large sums of money into the Belfry. The PA consultant had the idea of getting Ellerman and Greenall together. Ellerman was looking for diversification opportunities and Greenall was looking for capital to create its golf complex. The two parties met and agreed: Ellerman would have 86.7 percent of the complex and Greenall would hold 13.3 percent. Ellerman provided the capital to purchase the necessary surrounding land and convert it into two golf courses; Greenall for its part provided the Belfry and its grounds. The Belfry, which is used for Ryder Cup play, is now one of Britain's premier golf complexes.

Based on information in Pugh, P. (1989). *The Belfry: The making of a dream.* Trowbridge, Wilts, UK: Cambridge Business.

Defensive Strategies

Defensive strategies, or what are sometimes termed decline strategies, are used when the demand for a sport organization's product or service starts to decrease. Defensive strategies try to reverse this situation or overcome a particular problem. There are three principle types of defensive strategy: turnaround, divestiture, and liquidation.

Turnaround strategies are used to counter increased costs and falling revenues, and to increase cash flow and liquidity. They involve actions such as a reduction or change in the products or markets served, layoffs, replacing senior management, and cost cutting (Schendel, Patton, & Riggs, 1976). Nike, in an attempt to compete with Reebok's success in the aerobics shoe business, moved into the women's casual shoe market in the early 1980s. As Strasser and Becklund (1991, p. 506) point out, they "struggled to compete in an area in which [they] had no experience, no reputation, poor styling, and no price advantage." As their fortunes continued to decline, founder Philip Knight adopted the elements of a turnaround strategy. He stepped back into the presidency of Nike, a position he had relinquished just over a year earlier, and told his staff he wanted to lower factory costs, control inventories, improve time lines, and increase profit margins. He also laid off 400 employees, about 10 percent of his workforce.

If a turnaround is not possible a company has the option of divestiture or liquidation. Divestiture involves selling off a business or some portion of the ownership of a business. For example, in 1987 Bally Manufacturing Corp. tried to divest itself of Health & Tennis Corp. of America, the nation's largest chain of health clubs. As McCarthy (1987, p. 14) noted, divesting itself of Health & Tennis Corp. "would help Bally concentrate on its growing hotel and casino businesses, and allay persistent Wall Street concerns that Bally's long-term earnings could be hurt if the fitness boom fizzle[d]." A similar example from the public sector is the decision by the City of Saskatoon to divest itself of the operation of softball and baseball fields by turning responsibility over to local volunteers. The move is expected to save the city over $100,000 (Robinson, 1994).

Liquidation involves closing down a business and selling off its assets. Major (1990, p. 71), for example, describes how in 1986 Golden Bear International, solely owned by golfer Jack Nicklaus, was so fragmented that its executive committee felt it had "to consolidate and refocus on core (golf-related) businesses and reduce the mountain of debt." A number of the company's operations were liquidated, while others were merged.

Topps' Turnaround Strategy

Between 1980 and 1992 the sports card business grew from a market value of $50 million to $1.5 billion. Throughout the 1980s interest in sports cards increased and the value of individual cards rose significantly. Topps Co., the leader in the business, was anxious to take advantage of the growing demand for their product. They saturated the market with a wide variety of cards, but collectors were confused and unwilling to speculate that the newer cards would increase in value. Topps' profits fell 65 percent to $19 million in the fiscal year ending in February 1992; sales fell 13 percent. Topps' shareholders were so irate they sued the company, alleging that it had not accurately reported the value of its sports card business.

To counteract the declining interest in sports cards, Topps is deemphasizing this aspect of its business and shifting to a more broad-based entertainment focus. Its new emphasis will be on superhero comics and card sets that relate to children's TV shows and popular movies such as *Jurassic Park*.

Based on information in Lesly, E. (1993, August 23). A burst bubble at Topps. *Business Week*, p. 74.

Combination Strategies

The fourth type of corporate strategy involves a diversified sport organization using the different strategies outlined above in combination. As Hodge and Anthony (1991, p. 237) point out, "next to growth strategies, this strategy is the most common one." Rarely will a diversified sport organization have only one strategy; it may seek to expand certain parts of its operation while at the same time reducing or totally eliminating its involvement in other areas. William Blair and Company's (1988, p. 8) report on Johnson Worldwide Associates Inc., a major publicly held company involved with sporting goods, exemplifies the use of a combination strategy:

> Since July 1985, Johnson Worldwide has acquired eight companies with sales volumes in the $1 to $10 million range for a total cost of $12 million. We expect future acquisitions to be relatively small, fold-in companies, particularly in light of Johnson Worldwide's current financial leverage and of management's philosophy of restricting its experience to businesses it knows. Also in the vein of redeploying assets, we expect Johnson Worldwide to divest any operations which they deem no longer meet the company's strategic and financial objectives.

Portfolio Analysis

In large diversified companies that use combination strategies, one popular technique for analyzing the relative merits and cash flow requirements of their product and/or service offerings is that developed by the Boston Consulting Group (BCG). The BCG approach requires that a company identify Strategic Business Units (SBUs) for each of the business areas in which it competes. The SBUs are then assessed along two dimensions: relative market share and growth rate. In assessing the first dimension, the ratio of the SBU's market share to that of its nearest competitor is used. For example, an SBU with a market share of 20 percent in an industry where its largest rival has 30 percent would have a relative market share of 20/30 (.66). A relative market share score over 1 (i.e., it is an industry leader) is seen as high; a score below 1 is low. Growth rate is determined according to whether the SBU's industry is growing faster than the economy as a whole. Growth rates above average are high; those below are low (Hill & Jones, 1989). Using the dimensions of market share and growth rate, a 2 × 2 matrix can be constructed as shown in figure 5.3. Each SBU can then be placed into one of the four cells. The SBUs in cell 1 are referred to as "stars"; they have high growth rates and high market share. Whether or not they are self-sufficient depends on if they can generate enough cash flow to support their rapid growth. Established stars are likely to be able to support themselves, while emergent stars will need cash support. Stars offer long-term profit potential when the growth rate of their market decreases; that is, they become "cash cows." The SBUs in cell 2 are question marks, sometimes referred to as "problem children." They are weak in

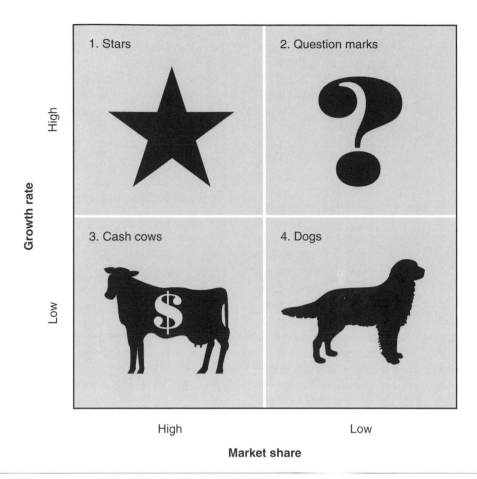

Figure 5.3 The BCG matrix.

that they have a low market share, but because they are in high growth industries they could become stars. To transform question marks into stars often requires a large infusion of cash. Strategists have to weigh the relative benefits of an increase in capital expenditure against the benefits of selling off this type of unit.

Cash cows, in cell 3, have a high market share and low growth rate; as such, they generate more profit than they need investment. Cash cows are to be "milked" and the profits they generate used for other corporate functions such as research and development and debt reduction. They can also be used to finance other SBUs such as those classified as question marks or emergent stars. In cell 4 we find "dogs." Dogs, in low-growth industries with low market share, do not generate large amounts of cash, nor do they require large amounts. Some companies may keep these SBUs active to offer customers an entire product line; others choose to divest themselves of dogs, which offer little potential for growth.

The strategic implications of the BCG portfolio analysis involve maximizing the profitability and growth potential of an organization. The BCG recommends that managers financially support selected question marks and emerging stars, often with capital extracted from cash cows. Managers must also make decisions about selling off those question marks they don't think have potential, to avoid excessive demands on company cash. They must also consider the relative merits of retaining dogs. The manager aims to obtain a suitable balance of cash cows, stars, and question marks. If this balance is not present, the company must look at acquisitions and/or divestments as a means of producing a balanced portfolio.

All diversified sport organizations, whether or not they use the BCG matrix, use some form of portfolio analysis. Strasser and Becklund (1991), for example, describe how in 1979 over half of Nike's business was in running shoes, 22 percent in basketball, and 16 percent in tennis. Their market share in those areas had risen 22 percent in running, 77 percent in basketball, and 37 percent in tennis. But Philip Knight felt that tennis had already peaked, the market for running shoes was approaching saturation, and basketball was getting expensive. He "didn't like the dependence on such a narrow range of products. . . . Like a good portfolio manager, Knight was always searching to minimize risk and maximize gain by balancing the sources of revenue" (Strasser & Becklund, 1991, p. 398). Knight made a number of financial decisions to consolidate cash flow and eventually diversify more than before, into product areas such as apparel and soccer boots.

The strength of the BCG matrix for diversified companies is that it forces them to focus on their cash flow requirements and plan their corporate strategy accordingly. It alerts managers to the need for acquisitions and divestitures. There are, however, as Hill and Jones (1989) point out, several problems with the BCG approach (see also Seeger, 1984). While the simplicity of the matrix is appealing, market share and growth are not the only two factors to consider when assessing portfolios. A company may have a low market share but establish a strong market position through differentiating its product line to serve the needs of a particular section of the market. Berrett, Burton, and Slack (1993) suggest that a number of entrepreneurs in the sport industry have established such a position by focusing on quality products and service. Hill and Jones (1989) also suggest that the relationship between market share and cost saving is not as straightforward as presented in the BCG matrix, and that a high market share in a low-growth industry does not always produce a high cash yield.

Given the BCG's focus on large diversified companies, it may appear to be of limited use to some sport organizations, particularly those such as collegiate athletic departments or campus intramural departments. However, in an interesting adaptation of portfolio analysis Graham (1983) uses criteria such as cost-per-participation unit, user/community support, or level of participation compared to maximum capacity, as opposed to market share, to show how the BCG matrix could be used by sport managers to develop strategies in these types of organizations.

Business-Level Strategies

Business-level strategies are those used by a sport organization to gain a competitive edge for its particular product or service. The most influential work on this topic is that of Harvard's Michael Porter. Porter (1980) identifies three basic strategies a business-level manager can choose: cost leadership, differentiation, and focus. These strategies can be used in manufacturing, service, or voluntary sport organizations. Sport managers can gain a competitive advantage for their organization by selecting a strategy appropriate both for the industry in which they are involved and the type of competitive position they seek to establish. Each of Porter's three strategic types are explained in more detail here.

Cost Leadership Strategy

A sport organization that adopts a cost leadership strategy prices its product or service lower than that of its competition, by using cheaper labor power (often developing countries), efficient manufacturing processes, economies of scale, technological innovation, and low levels of product differentiation. Sport organizations that follow a cost leadership strategy do not spend large amounts on new product or service development; rather, they follow market trends and provide the product feature or service when there is an established demand. The idea is that, by providing goods or services at a lower cost, a sport organization can capture a large share of the market or maintain higher profit margins.

Gore-Tex imitators such as Sympatex and Helly-Hansen follow a cost leadership strategy. Dan Hansen, marketing coordinator at Helly-Hansen said of his company's product, "our best seller was a basic warm-up suit that retailed at about $120; a Gore product would cost $150 or more. By eliminating the middlemen, we can offer a comparable product at a more competitive price" ("Give them stormy weather," 1986). Many public-sector providers of sport services also follow a cost leadership strategy, in large part because of their mandate of catering to a broad client base.

The main strength of this type of strategy is that a cost advantage protects a sport organization from the fluctuations of the marketplace caused by such factors as changing input costs and imitators. Problems do arise, however, when a competitor does find a way to produce the same product at a lower cost. Cost leaders have to strive constantly to maintain their cost advantage.

There are several structural implications to using this type of strategy. As Miller (1988, p. 303) notes, cost leadership goes "hand in hand with the use of controls [as] . . . tight controls can slash costs. . . ." This control, combined with the need for economies of scale and efficient manufacturing processes, means that sport organizations that adopt a cost leadership strategy are likely to be centralized, high in complexity, and high in formalization.

Differentiation Strategy

Sport organizations that pursue a differentiation strategy attempt to gain a competitive advantage by presenting an image of their product or service as unique. Because the product or service is seen as unique, the sport organization is able to charge a premium price. Reebok followed a differentiation strategy in the athletic footwear industry with The Pump; golf complexes like the Broadmoor did it with luxury and prestige in their service provision; and Karsten, the maker of Ping golf clubs, did it with square grooves. L.L. Bean, the mail-order house specializing in outdoor sports equipment, does it in customer service with its unconditional guarantee: "you can send back a Bean product for any reason at any time, and get a replacement or your money back. Wear it a year, decide that it is not holding up, and send it back; the guarantee still holds" (Skow, 1985, p. 92). The main strength of a differentiation strategy is that it develops product or service loyalty, a relatively enduring phenomenon. The weaknesses of this approach are maintaining the aura of uniqueness for the product or service in a changing market, and ensuring that pricing is in accordance with what the market will bear.

Because it requires creativity to produce unique products or services, sport organizations that adopt a differentiation strategy employee "technocrats—well trained experts such as scientists and engineers—to design innovations" (Miller, 1988, p. 282). Because these people work most efficiently in flexible structures, a sport organization that adopts a differentiation strategy will most likely exhibit low levels of complexity, low levels of formalization, and decentralized decision making.

Focus Strategy

This strategy is directed toward serving the needs of a particular market, one defined by such criteria as geographic area, age, sex, or segment of a product or service line. Once the particular market has been chosen, the sport organization decides on a cost leadership or differentiation strategy within that market. L.A. Gear, for example, entered the athletic footwear industry by initially focusing on "the valley girl" set, 12- to 25-year-olds who wanted fashionable athletic shoes (L.A. Gear, 1988). Concentrating on this market, the company differentiated it-

self from other manufacturers by producing shoes with fringes, colored cutouts, brightly colored laces, and rhinestones. Human Kinetics has adopted a focus strategy: while some publishers produce books on a wide range of subject areas, Human Kinetics has focused on physical education and exercise/sport science publications. Another example of a focus strategy is the decision by F.W. Woolworth and Company to complement its Foot Locker stores by opening Lady Foot Locker specifically for women. So, too, is Sumac Ridge Golf Club's decision to offer a women-only club (Kelowna Golf Club, 1994). In the public sector, the decision made by federal government officials to focus the efforts of Sport Canada solely on elite sports could also be seen as a focus strategy.

The strengths of a focus strategy are that the company develops the ability to provide products/services that others cannot and, because of a focused market, the company can stay closer to its customers and more easily respond to their changing needs. The main disadvantage is that costs may be higher because of a generally smaller product volume. Also, there is the possibility that the market niche the company occupies, for example L.A. Gear's fashion footwear focus, may disappear or experience a decline in popularity. The type of structure adopted by a sport organization that follows a focus strategy will depend on whether or not it decides to focus either through differentiation or through a low cost approach.

Stuck in the Middle

Not all sport organizations are able to gain a competitive advantage; some don't make the right choices about their product or service and the markets in which they wish to operate. Porter (1980) describes these organizations as "stuck in the middle."

Sport organizations get stuck in the middle for a variety of reasons. The low-cost company may decide to use some of its profits to diversify into product markets where it has less experience, or to invest in research and development that management thinks may bolster the prestige of the organization. Such actions are expensive and have no guarantee of success. "Consequently, bad strategic decisions can quickly erode the cost leader's above-average profitability" (Hill & Jones, 1989, p. 137).

Differentiators may get undercut by imitators who produce a cheaper or more specialized product. Those who adopt a focus strategy may not keep abreast of market trends and thus lose their market

TIME OUT

Bill Nelson, Focusing on Pins

Bill Nelson, a former marketing professor and entrepreneur, first became aware of the growing interest in decorative and collectible lapel pins during the 1984 Los Angeles Olympic Games. Seeing an opportunity to capitalize on the interest being generated, Nelson and his wife set up business in their home in Tucson, Arizona. While some retailers sell pins as one item in a wide array of sporting goods and memorabilia, Nelson focuses exclusively on pins. In 1988 he was described as the largest U.S. distributor of Olympic pins. He held the exclusive marketing rights to the Olympic pins of Time Inc., Visa, Adidas, Maxwell House, Federal Express, and Blue Cross/Blue Shield. Nelson's strategy for his business involved not only the distribution of pins but also the creation of an eight-page publication entitled *The Bill Nelson Newsletter*, which provided information about pins and pin buying, and served as a marketing tool for Nelson's business. The first newsletter was distributed locally to about 200 "pinheads." In 1988 the newsletter, termed "the pinhead's bible," was mailed to over 100, 000 collectors.

Nelson's rapid success was helped by his decision to focus on a particular market. To cater to the needs of this market he provided information through his newsletter, which also promoted his business. His strategy also involved staying in close contact with his clients. He personalizes all correspondence and developed a camaraderie with these people. He responded immediately to collectors who answered ads he placed in consumer and trade sports publications. To facilitate the ordering of pins Nelson makes extensive use of the fax machine; when he heard that some Japanese taxi cabs had faxes he offered free Olympic pins to the first person to place an order from one. "We not only got the order, but we increased the visibility of the fax ordering process," Nelson noted.

Based on information in Going for gold. (1988, October). *Target Marketing*, pp. 72, 74.

niche. Retaining a competitive advantage requires constant managerial action and attention to possible tactics: monitoring the environment for changing trends, filing patents to prevent imitations, lobbying to restrict foreign competition, establishing contracts with suppliers to limit their ability to supply competitors, and even acquiring competitors.

Strategy Formulation and Implementation

Formulating and implementing a strategic plan involves a series of interrelated steps. These steps include formulating a mission statement for the sport organization, conducting an analysis of the organization's external environment and internal operations (sometimes called a SWOT analysis—Strengths, Weaknesses, Opportunities, and Threats), making choices about appropriate corporate and/or business level strategies, and selecting the cor-

rect organizational structure and integration and control systems to ensure that the strategy is effective. The first three steps are primarily about strategy formulation; the fourth step is the implementation stage. The process is shown graphically in figure 5.4

Although the process of formulating and implementing strategy is shown as a linear progression, it was noted earlier in this chapter that strategy formulation could be either deliberate or emergent. The traditional point of view has been to see strategy formulation as a deliberate process following a series of sequential steps. Emergent strategies are less likely to follow this clearly defined sequence. Sport managers must evaluate the merits of emergent strategies against the organization's mission, its operating strengths, its environmental opportunities, and so on. Only by undertaking this type of comparison is a manager able to determine the "fit" of that strategy for the sport organization. Each of the stages of strategy formulation and implementation are outlined in more detail here.

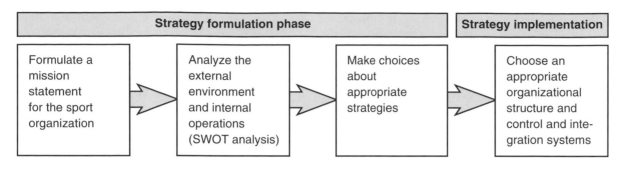

Figure 5.4 Steps in the formulation and implementation of strategy.

Defining a Mission Statement

The senior managers' first step in the formulation of a strategic plan involves defining a mission statement for the sport organization. They may invite representatives from other subunits, for example, unions, support staff, or students, to be involved in the process. The mission statement or official goal (see chapter 2) defines the purpose of the sport organization, what business(es) it is in, and who its principal customers, users, or clients are. The mission statement serves as a foundation for the strategic planning process by prescribing direction for the future. As Hill and Jones (1989, p. 9) point out, it provides "the context within which intended strategies are formulated and the criteria against which emergent strategies are evaluated."

Internal and External Analysis

Once the sport organization's strategic planning group has established a mission statement, the next step in the process of strategy formulation is an analysis of the organization's external environment and internal operations. This step involves what is commonly called a SWOT analysis—an examination of opportunities and threats in the external environment of the organization, and the determination of its internal strengths and weaknesses. When analyzing the external environment, strategic planners must consider both the industry or industries within which they are competing—current and potential competitors, cost structures and margins, levels of product differentiation, existing brand loyalties, and so on. Strategic planners must also consider the broader socioeconomic and political environment—political issues, economic trends, globalization, demographic shifts, and the like. All have the potential to impact a sport organization and hence must be considered. From an analysis of these environments, strategic planners can identify

opportunities and threats facing the sport organization.

The internal analysis assesses strengths and weaknesses in the sport organization's operations, by evaluating the available expertise and resources in areas such as research and development, manufacturing, marketing, human resources management, and new product development. In a sport organization that operates in more than one industry, the internal analysis should include an evaluation of the company's business portfolio using a technique such as the BCG matrix.

Selecting an Appropriate Strategy

The final stage in the strategy formulation phase involves making choices about the appropriate strategy or strategies for the sport organization. The choice of strategy will depend on the sport organization's mission and the match between its internal strengths/weaknesses and the external threats/opportunities. As Hill and Jones (1989, p. 12) point out, "For the single business organization, the objective is to match a company's strength to environmental opportunities in order to gain a competitive advantage and thus increase profits. For the multibusiness organization, the goal is to choose strategies for its portfolio of business that align the strengths and weaknesses of the portfolio with environmental opportunities and threats."

For example, for many years Converse was one of the strongest companies in the athletic footwear market; their black high-tops were standard wear on the basketball court. But the athletic footwear boom that started in the 1970s caught Converse off guard. Their black high-tops were not as appealing as the colorful and high-tech Nikes and Reeboks. Seeing the opportunities in athletic footwear, Converse president J.P. O' Neil and chief executive R.B. Loynd decided to focus on this market. "Our strategy," said O' Neil, "was to continue to gain in basketball while introducing strong performance shoes in all product categories." The company decided to change its internal operations by consolidating its strengths; it dumped product lines such as hockey pucks and fishing boots to concentrate on athletic footwear. To promote its athletic footwear a strong marketing campaign was developed that included purchasing the title of "Official Athletic Shoe of the 1984 Olympics."

Mintzberg's Three Modes of Strategy Formulation

In each stage of the process of formulating strategy, sport organizations make a number of important decisions. Mintzberg (1973b) suggests that the most popular approach is what he refers to as the planning mode, a highly rational approach to strategy formulation, controlled by an analyst or planner who works with senior management and uses "scientific techniques to develop formal comprehensive plans" (Mintzberg, 1973b, p. 47). The highly structured process subjects all decision choices to systematic cost benefit analysis. In the planning mode the "organization's strategy is designed at essentially one point in time in a comprehensive process (all major decisions are interrelated). Because of this, planning forces the organization to think of global strategies and to develop an explicit sense of strategic direction" (Mintzberg, 1973b, p. 48). The planning mode of strategy formulation is most frequently used in large established sport organizations looking for both efficiency and growth.

Although the planning mode has been the most popular method of strategy formulation, Mintzberg also identifies two other approaches: the entrepreneurial mode and the adaptive mode. In the entrepreneurial mode, the owner/entrepreneur makes decisions using her intuition and experience to seek out growth opportunities for the organization. The early years of sport organizations such as Nike (cf. Strasser & Becklund, 1991) and Coleman, the outdoor sport outfitters (cf. Coleman & Jones, 1976) were characterized by this approach to strategy formulation. The entrepreneur makes bold decisions about "where his organization can make dramatic gains" (Mintzberg, 1973b, p. 45). This mode of strategy formulation is most frequently found in small and relatively new sport organizations. The process of strategy formulation involves only the owner/ entrepreneur (and perhaps some close associates); it is informal in operation, and decisions are rarely committed to paper.

The main characteristic of the adaptive mode of strategy formulation is, as its name implies, a continual adjustment of organizational goals and the means by which they are to be achieved. The process of formulating strategy is a reactive one "rather than the proactive search for new opportunities" (Mintzberg, 1973b, p. 46). Decisions are made in an incremental and relatively disjointed manner. This approach to strategy formulation is used in established sport organizations where power is dispersed and there is no simple organizational goal. For example, we may find this approach to strategy formulation in a faculty of health, physical education and recreation where power is dispersed among faculty and where research, teaching, and service are all seen as important goals. Mintzberg suggests that Lindblom's (1959) term "the science of muddling through" is a good description of the adaptive approach to strategy formulation. Certain organizational conditions such as size, leadership, and the degree of competition and stability within the environment favor one mode of strategy formulation over another. It is, however, quite possible that an organization will operate with some combination of these three modes that reflects its particular needs.

Designing an Appropriate Organizational Structure and Selecting Control and Integration Systems

To implement the selected strategy or strategies, an appropriate organizational structure and the necessary control and integration systems need to be put into place. As we saw in chapters 3 and 4, a sport organization can be structured in a number of different ways. An appropriate structure is selected, based on decisions about how to distribute authority within a sport organization, and what subunits are required to carry out its functions. Systems must be developed to integrate and control the actions of these various subunits. We discuss the relationship between strategy and structure next.

Strategy and Structure

As we saw in the preceding section of this chapter, an important aspect of implementing a strategic plan is the selection of an appropriate organizational structure along with the necessary integration and control systems. Different types of structure and systems "provide strategic planners with alternative means of pursuing different strategies because they lead the company and the people within it to act in different ways" (Hill & Jones, 1989, p. 222). In this section we look in more detail at the strategy-structure relationship. We start by focusing on the landmark contribution of Alfred Chandler that has influenced much subsequent work on this relationship. We then look at the best known of the contemporary work on this issue, the writings of Miles and Snow. Finally, we conclude the section by looking at the question, "Could structure determine strategy?"

Chandler's Work on the Strategy-Structure Relationship

Published in 1962 Chandler's book *Strategy and structure*, the first substantive work to examine the strategy-structure relationship, was based on a study of large American companies such as General Motors, Du Pont, and Sears. Chandler looked at changes in these organizations over a period of approximately 50 years. The companies began by offering a limited number of product lines and exhibited a centralized structure. As they grew they followed a diversification strategy; consequently, if they were to continue to function effectively, they needed a different type of structure. The new structure was more complex because units were added and, over time, decisions were decentralized. Chandler's (1962, p. 15) main conclusion was that a new organizational strategy "required a new or at least refashioned structure if the enlarged enterprise was to be operated efficiently." That is, structure had to follow strategy.

Chandler's research suffered from his limited conceptualization of strategy and structure. In his study, strategy was limited to growth through diversification, and structure was limited to divisionalization. Also, his results are not generalizable because the organizations in his study were large corporations; there was no attempt to include other types and sizes of organizations. Nevertheless, despite its shortcomings, Chandler's work has been replicated by a number of other scholars (cf. Channon, 1973; Rumelt, 1974), who have all used similar types of organizations to confirm his general findings. It would appear, at least in certain cases, strategy does indeed influence structure. However, the concept of strategy is very broad, and recent work has extended and elaborated ideas about the strategy-structure relationship.

Miles and Snow's Strategic Typology

The best known of the more recent work on strategy and structure is Miles and Snow's four-part classification of organizations as Defenders, Prospectors, Analyzers, and Reactors.

Defenders

Organizations that adopt this type of strategy attempt to limit themselves to a narrow range of products or services offered to only "a limited segment of the total potential market, and the segment chosen is frequently one of the healthiest of the entire market" (Miles & Snow, 1978, p. 37). Organizations operating with this type of strategy carve out a niche for themselves and then work very hard to protect it. They strive for internal efficiencies while at the same time seeking to improve the quality and/or price of their product or service. Because they are inwardly focused, Defenders tend not to pay a lot of attention to changes outside of their immediate domain. The type of structure associated with a Defender strategy is centralized, with a high level of task specialization and a relatively high level of formalization. The centralized structure means control is in the hands of senior managers; integration is achieved through formalized policies and procedures. An example of a sport organization that has successfully adopted a Defender strategy is the Running Room, a specialty store for running equipment, founded in Edmonton in 1984, with branches in Edmonton, Calgary, Vancouver, Toronto, and Ottawa. The owner of the store quickly carved out a niche in local markets by providing quality running equipment and knowledgeable staff. Although the company experimented with aerobics and walking gear, it found it was more successful just focusing on running. The owner felt that in trying to service a wider market, the company sacrificed focus. He noted (as quoted in a course paper by Lizz Zahary at the University of Alberta), "the more we do [stick to our core market] the more successful we've been; then at least you're known for something." In a similar vein, a college or university athletic department that traditionally offers (and is successful in) a limited number of intercollegiate sports, instead of offering a wide range of activities, could be seen as operating with a Defender strategy.

Prospectors

In contrast to Defenders, who stick to established products and markets, Prospectors actively seek new products and new market opportunities. These companies establish their reputation by being the first on the market with new products. Because their success depends on innovation, Prospectors must scan their environments constantly for new trends and opportunities. The need for Prospectors to respond rapidly to environmental changes means they must adopt a flexible structure. Employees require the type of skills that enable them to be moved from one project to another; consequently, task specialization is low, as is formalization; decision making is decentralized but there are complex integration systems. Control is achieved largely through the professional status of the Prospector's employees. W.L. Gore & Associates, Inc. is an example of a company operating with a Prospector strategy. Constantly looking for new applications for its products—which are used for running suits, skiwear, and camping equipment—the company has adopted a very informal operating structure referred to as a "lattice" organization (cf. Rhodes, 1982).

Analyzers

Analyzers lie somewhere between Defenders and Prospectors. "A true Analyzer is an organization that minimizes risk while maximizing the opportunity for profit . . . [it] combines the strength of both the Prospector and the Defender into a single system" (Miles & Snow, 1978, p. 68). The Analyzer operates with a mix of products and markets, some of which will exhibit stability while others will be more dynamic. In the stable product market areas Analyzers operate as routinely and efficiently as they possibly can. In the changing environment Analyzers watch their competitors and, once one of their products gains acceptance, move quickly into the area, trying to copy the idea so that their product arrives on the market on the heels of the developer. The idea is to maintain a base of traditional products while at the same time locating and exploiting the opportunities available in new markets and products.

The sport organization adopting an Analyzer strategy will have to develop a structure that allows them to exercise tight controls over the stable product and market areas, and looser controls over the areas in which new products are being developed. The organization adopts a more formalized and centralized structure in the former product/market areas and a more decentralized and flexible structure in the latter. Because of the presence of different types of subunits, control involves a delicate balance between systems that are "centralized

and budget-oriented to encourage cost-efficient production of standard products [and systems that are] . . . decentralized and results-oriented so as to enhance the effectiveness with which new products can be adapted" (Miles & Snow, 1978, p. 77). The Analyzer label has been ascribed to companies that mass-produce fashionwear imitations of popular brands such as Sun Ice and the major athletic footwear companies (cf. "U.S. dollar decline," 1988). However, it has also been attached to larger and better known companies such as Digital Equipment Corporation and IBM (cf. Robbins, 1990), both tangentially involved in the sports industry, the former through its involvement as the official computer vendor of the NFL ("Digital scores with the NFL," 1986) and the latter through its sponsorship of the Olympic Games.

Reactors

Reactors are organizations that do not respond appropriately to their environment. Organizations find themselves operating with a Reactor strategy when "(1) management fails to articulate a viable organizational strategy; (2) a strategy is articulated but technology, structure, and process are not linked to it in an appropriate manner; or (3) management adheres to a particular strategy-structure relationship even though it is no longer relevant to environmental conditions" (Miles & Snow, 1978, p. 82). Because a Reactor strategy is an inappropriate strategy, there are no clear linkages between this type of strategy and structure.

The first three of these strategic positions are each appropriate under different environmental conditions and each requires a different type of structure. It is, of course, possible that two managers in different sport organizations within the same industry may scan their environment and respond with a different strategy. The vignette at the start of this chapter illustrates this point. Paul Fireman of Reebok saw a changing environment for the athletic footwear industry because of the aerobics boom. Consequently, he adopted a Prospector strategy and his company aggressively pursued the aerobics market. Philip Knight and the people at Nike saw aerobics as a passing fad and as such adopted a Defender strategy, concentrating on their already successful running shoe business.

Managers who pursue a Prospector strategy need to adopt an organizational structure that can respond quickly to changing environmental conditions. Consequently, they cannot be encumbered by highly formalized procedures and formal

Coke and Pepsi Follow an Analyzer Strategy in the Sport Beverage Market

Since it first purchased Gatorade in the mid-1980s, Quaker Oats Co. has turned the sport beverage into an operation with sales of approximately $1 billion. Quaker's success has not gone unnoticed by soft-drink industry giants Coca-Cola and PepsiCo. After some years of watching Gatorade grow, Coca-Cola has introduced PowerAde and PepsiCo is marketing All Sport, to challenge the Quaker company's preeminent position. As well as using the force of their distribution operation to promote their new sport drinks, Coca-Cola and PepsiCo have started to use their marketing departments to lure away Gatorade drinkers. Basketball star Shaquille O' Neal has been recruited by PepsiCo; Coca-Cola has signed football/baseball player Deion Sanders. Both companies are also starting to promote their new drink through sponsorship of sporting events. Already Coca-Cola and PepsiCo have started to impact on Gatorade's market. The 86.5 percent share held by Gatorade at the beginning of March 1983 was down by 3.6 points in March 1994. Some analysts say it may go as low as 70 percent. To fight back, Quaker is trying to expand its distribution channels beyond grocery stores into fountains and vending machines, and has doubled its advertising spending to over $50 million.

Based on information in Gatorade is starting to pant. (1994, April 18). *Business Week*, p. 98.

hierarchies where control is centralized with senior managers. Defenders can function with this type of structure because their environment is stable, or changing very slowly, and the highly formalized and bureaucratic structure allows them to capitalize on the efficiencies it provides. Sport organizations that choose an Analyzer strategy must balance the quest for efficiency with the need to be able to respond rapidly to change.

Could Structure Determine Strategy?

Much of the literature on the strategy-structure relationship has followed Chandler and worked from the premise that the selection of an appropriate structure comes after the selection of a strategy. However, a number of writers (cf. Bourgeois & Astley, 1979; Burgelman, 1983; Fahey, 1981) suggest that it is quite possible that structure determines the choice of strategy, or that they evolve simultaneously.

Scott (1973), for example, suggests that in a small entrepreneurial company with little or no formal structure operated by one individual, the decisions made about strategy will reflect the needs of the owner rather than those of the company. In a large multi-product company operating in different markets, strategic choices about entering and exiting

from markets, and the allocation of resources to these markets, will dominate. In both cases structure determines the choice of strategy. Fredrickson (1986) looked at the effect that structural dimensions of centralization, formalization, and complexity could have on strategic choice. His ideas are summarized in table 5.1.

For Mintzberg (1990, p. 183) the relationship between strategy and structure is a coordinated one:

No organization ever wipes the slate clean when it changes its strategy. The past counts, just as the environment does, and the structure is a significant part of that past. . . . We conclude, therefore, that structure follows strategy as the left foot follows the right in walking. In effect strategy and structure both support the organization. None takes precedence: each always precedes the other and follows it.

What the work of these writers suggests is that, as is the case in many areas of organization/ management theory, there is no definitive answer to the question "Does structure follow strategy or vice versa?" Not only can strong arguments be made for both positions (and for the position that they evolve together), but other factors, which we briefly mention here, can impact on this relationship.

Table 5.1　Propositions Regarding the Effects of Three Dimensions of Structure

Centralization

As the level of centralization increases, so does the probability that

- the strategic decision process will be initiated only by the dominant few, and that it will be the result of proactive, opportunity-seeking behavior;
- the decision process will be oriented toward achieving "positive" goals (i.e., intended future domains) that will persist in spite of significant changes in means;
- strategic action will be the result of intendedly rational "strategic choice," and moves will be major departures from the existing strategy;
- top management's cognitive limitations will be the primary constraint on the comprehensiveness of the strategic process; the integration of decisions will be relatively high.

Formalization

As the level of formalization increases, so does the probability that

- the strategic decision process will be initiated only in response to problems or crises that appear in variables that are monitored by the formal system;
- decisions will be made to achieve precise, yet remedial goals, and that means will displace ends (goals);
- strategic action will be the result of standardized organizational processes, and moves will be incremental;
- the level of detail that is achieved in the standardized organizational processes will be the primary constraint on the comprehensiveness of the strategic decision process; the integration of decisions will be intermediate.

Complexity

As the level of complexity increases, so does the probability that

- members initially exposed to the decision stimulus will not recognize it as being strategic, or will ignore it because of parochial preferences;
- a decision must satisfy a large constraint set, which decreases the likelihood that decisions will be made to achieve organization-level goals;
- strategic action will be the result of an internal process of political bargaining, and moves will be incremental;
- biases induced by members' parochial perceptions will be the primary constraint on the comprehensiveness of the strategic decision process; in general, the integration of decisions will be low.

Adapted, by permission, from J.W. Fredereckson, 1986, "The strategic decision process and organizational structure," *Academy of Management Review* 11: 280-297.

The first of these is the question of lag. That is, if structure follows strategy, how much lag time is there between the adoption of a new strategy and the adoption of a new structure? Chandler (1962) suggested that a lag could result in inefficiencies. But, we may ask, is this lag time the same for all organizations or does it vary by industry or industry sector? For example, will the lag time be the same for a collegiate athletic department as it is for a sporting goods retailer? A second factor influencing the strategy-structure relationship is the organization's stage of development. In newer organizations managerial choice is likely to be far less constrained than in older organizations where structures and modes of operation are well established and hence more likely to constrain choice on strategy issues.

The point here is that many questions need to be answered about the strategy-structure relationship and strategy in general. It is a burgeoning area of study in organization/management theory; some

business schools offer specific courses on business strategy (or "policy" as it is called when related to private-sector organizations). However, very few studies focus specifically on strategy in sport organizations. Since sport organizations, like all other organizations, implicitly or explicitly formulate strategy, which in turn influences many other aspects of management, more work needs to be undertaken on this topic in sport management.

Strategy in Voluntary Sport Organizations

Of the small amount of research carried out on the strategies employed by sport organizations, much has focused on the voluntary sector. In a study of Canadian national sport organizations Thibault,

Slack, and Hinings (1993) developed a theoretical framework to identify four types of strategy that could be pursued by these organizations. Using work by MacMillan (1983) on nonprofit organizations, Thibault et al. (1993) identified six strategic imperatives that must be considered when developing strategies: fundability, the ability of the sport organization to secure financial resources from external sources; size of client base, the number of clients the sport organization serves; volunteer appeal, the organization's ability to attract human resources; support group appeal, the extent to which the sport organization's programs are visible and appealing to those groups capable of providing current or future support; equipment costs, the amount of money required for equipment at the introductory levels of the sport; and affiliation fees, the costs associated with participating in a sport.

The first four of these imperatives were seen to constitute the organization's level of program attractiveness, that is, its ability to provide services and programs to its members while at the same time securing the necessary resources for these programs. The last two imperatives made up the sport organization's competitive position, that is, its potential to attract and retain members. By dividing the dimensions of program attractiveness and competitive position into high and low components, Thibault et al. (1993) were able to construct a 2 × 2 matrix as shown in figure 5.5. The four quadrants within the matrix represent the types of

strategy that national sport organizations can pursue.

Enhancers were those national sport organizations that scored high on both dimensions. These sport organizations already had well-developed strategies in place and an existing network through which to operationalize new initiatives. The sports in this category were generally popular and inexpensive to pursue; this position gave them the opportunity to experiment with new programs at little risk, thereby enhancing their already well-established strategic position. *Innovators* had a strong competitive position but low program attractiveness. That is, they were relatively cheap to pursue but had little in the way of existing programs and members, so the strategic focus of these organizations was a need to adopt innovative initiatives to get people involved. The strong competitive position of innovators helped these organizations because there were few cost barriers to participation in their sport. *Refiners* already had well-established strategies but their weak competitive position, that is, the high costs associated with their sport, made expanding these programs difficult. These sport organizations were expected to follow a strategy of refining existing programs. *Explorers* were in the worst strategic position, since they had low levels of program attractiveness and their sport was costly. It was expected that these organizations would explore a number of strategies to create programs to enhance their sport's position. Later, Thibault, Slack, and

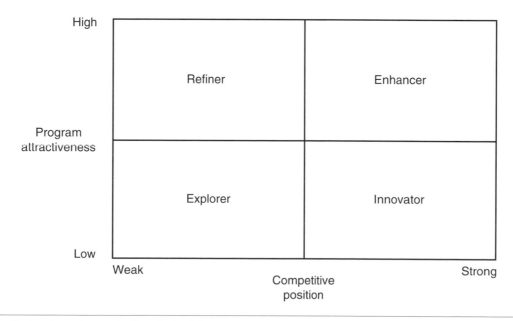

Figure 5.5 National sport organization strategic types.
Reprinted, by permission, from L. Thibault, T. Slack, and C.R. Hinings, 1993, "A framework for the analysis of strategy in non-profit sport organizations," *Journal of Sport Management* 7: 36.

Hinings (1994) empirically verified the dimensions of their framework and located a sample of national sport organizations according to the type of strategy they were following.

Summary and Conclusions

Organizational strategy is concerned with the long-term goals and objectives of a sport organization. Strategy, one of the major determinants of organizational structure, can be deliberate or emergent. Strategy can be formulated at two levels, the corporate level and the business level. Corporate-level strategies may focus on growth, stability, or decline (defensive strategies); companies may also adopt these strategies in combination. One technique used to determine the strategic needs of a corporation is portfolio analysis. Business-level strategies are used by individual business units to gain a competitive advantage. The most commonly used business-level strategies are cost leadership, product differentiation, and focus.

Strategy formulation and implementation involve a series of steps, including formulating a mission statement, conducting an assessment of external threats/opportunities and internal strengths/weaknesses, selecting the appropriate strategy or strategies, and designing the necessary organizational structure and control and integration systems. Mintzberg suggests three modes of strategy formulation: the planning mode, the entrepreneurial mode, and the adaptive mode.

The relationship between strategy and structure has been a topic of considerable debate. Alfred Chandler, one of the first writers in this area, suggested that structure follows strategy; a number of other researchers replicated Chandler's work and produced similar results. Recent research, however, has suggested that strategy may follow structure or that the two evolve simultaneously. Work by Miles and Snow identified four strategic types: Defenders, Prospectors, Analyzers, and Reactors. Each strategic type is associated with a particular set of structural arrangements. Two other factors seen as influencing the strategy-structure relationship are the concept of lag and the organization's stage of development.

Key Concepts

Deliberate strategy

Corporate-level strategy

Diversification

Horizontal integration

Acquisition

Joint venture

Turnaround

Liquidation

Portfolio analysis

Stars

Cash cows

Cost leadership

Focus strategy

Mission statement

Planning mode

Adaptive mode

Innovators

Explorers

Emergent strategy

Business-level strategy

Vertical integration

Merger

Takeover

Harvesting strategy (milking)

Divestiture

Combination strategy

Strategic business unit

Question marks

Dogs

Differentiation strategy

Stuck in the middle

SWOT analysis

Entrepreneurial mode

Enhancers

Refiners

Review Questions

1. Strategy is more than just setting goals and objectives. What else does it involve?

2. What is the difference between a sport organization with a deliberate strategy and one with an emergent strategy?

3. How does the concept of corporate strategy apply to a university athletic department?

4. Why would a sport organization engage in (a) forward integration, (b) backward integration? Give examples.

5. When would a company within the sport industry use a harvesting strategy? What are its benefits?

6. What are the benefits of a liquidation strategy to a sport organization?

7. A strategic business unit that moves from "a question mark" to "a star" to "a cash cow" has followed a success sequence. Why? What type of movement might be labeled a disaster sequence?

8. What type of structure do you associate with each of Porter's strategic types?

9. If you were formulating strategy for a university athletic department, what factors do you think you would have to consider in your external analysis?

10. What type of sport organization would you expect to find using the planning mode of strategy formulation? the entrepreneurial mode? the adaptive mode?

11. Why did Chandler conclude that structure followed strategy? Do you think his conclusions would have been different had he used a different sample of organizations?

12. In what type of business-level strategies would you expect a Prospector sport organization to engage?

13. What type of structure would you expect to find associated with each of Miles and Snow's strategic types?

14. Develop an argument that strategy follows structure.

15. How might the stage of a sport organization's development affect the choice of a strategy?

Suggestions for Further Reading

A fairly large body of literature within the broader field of management focuses on the topic of organizational strategy. In fact, a major publication, the *Strategic Management Journal*, deals exclusively with research on organizational strategy. Of the available literature, probably the best-known work on strategy is the Porter trilogy *Competitive strategy: Techniques for analyzing industries and competitors* (1980), *Competitive advantage: Creating and sustaining superior performance* (1985), and *The competitive advantage of nations and their firms* (1989). Of less popular appeal but equally substantive is the work of Danny Miller. Examples of his work on strategy include his (1986) "Configurations of strategy and structure" and (1987b) "The structural and environmental correlates of business strategy," both in *Strategic Management Journal*; (1987a) "Strategy making and structure: Analysis and implications for performance" and (1988) "Relating Porter's business strategies to environment and structure: Analysis and performance implications" appear in the *Academy of Management Journal*. Students may also wish to read Miller's (1990) book *The Icarus paradox*.

Students are also recommended to read Miles and Snow's (1978) book *Organizational strategy, structure, and process*; and Quinn, Mintzberg, and James' *The strategy process: Concepts, contexts, and cases* (1988), a large collection of readings about various aspects of organizational strategy.

Within the sport management literature there is a large void when it comes to strategy. However, some indication of the types of strategies pursued by sport organizations can be gained from books such as Strasser and Becklund's (1991) *Swoosh: The story of Nike and the men who played there*, and from the articles on sport organizations found in business magazines such as *Fortune*, *Forbes*, and *Business Week*.

Case for Analysis

Is There Life After Snowboards?

Chip Wilson has fashioned a radical success story by sensing what young people will want to wear. Right now, he's riding the crest of the snowboard craze sweeping winter resorts around the world. But the former beach boy faces a question that dogs every youth-clothing entrepreneur: What will be cool next? At the moment, he hasn't a clue. "It probably won't matter to us anyway for the next three or four years," insists the founder and design guru of Westbeach Snowboarding Canada Ltd. of Vancouver. "We see snowboarding growth as being exponential before it levels out." In some adult eyes, Wilson's baggy snowboard garb seems anti-fashion. Not that the 38-year-old designer cares much. He and his three partners project sales of $7.5 million this year, double the level of three years ago. Half of this revenue comes from snowboarding clothes and accessories so essential for "the look."

But the partners are grappling with a 15-year plan in an industry where today's maximum cool is tomorrow's carwash rags. The snowboard market should start to mature within five years, and Westbeach needs to anticipate the next new craze. Tracking that vision, while coping with fast growth, is forcing the four owners to shed the technical, hands-on roles they love. "Chip can't be the designer. The partners have to step out and provide direction and leadership," says Guyle Tippe, the consultant helping with the transition. Still, it's been a fun ride so far. The Westbeach group has built a successful youth-oriented business on Wilson's simple dictum: "There's always that thing about doing something different and looking different from your parents." They first applied that formula in 1985 as Endless Summer entrepreneurs, selling California beachwear from a store in Vancouver's beachfront Kitsilano area. Then the surfer crowd took to skateboards, and Westbeach led the switch to the baggy-pants look.

But the company's biggest break came in the late 1980s, when teenage trendsetters took the wheels off their skateboards and gate-crashed their parents' downhill ski domains. A renegade culture needs its own signature style, and Westbeach caught that wave. In two years, it went from 80 percent summer to 80 percent winter sales. The $40 pair of beach shorts became the $260 waterproof, insulated mountain jacket. Although banned at first from many ski

runs, snowboarding is moving mainstream fast. "It's a great new radical sport with lots of attitude. It has a real look to it and even its own music," says Chris Carter, marketing director at North Vancouver's Mount Seymour ski hill. Snowboarders account for 15 percent of Seymour's traffic, up from 1 percent three years ago.

This scene is, however, a long way from Wilson's first humble entrepreneurial stirrings. In 1980, on one of his frequent visits to California, he bought a pair of beach shorts for a girlfriend. Back home in Calgary he hired home sewers to stitch 400 pairs of his own design. His girlfriend hawked the shorts from a street stall, while he labored as a drilling-rights negotiator at Dome Petroleum. Peddling a line of reversible Bermuda shorts at a Vancouver boat show in 1982, Wilson parked a rack beside Scott Sibley, a former Dome coworker, and his Montreal partner Richard Mellen, who were selling sailboats. Showgoers went crazy over the shorts. "We said to hell with this—no one's interested in sailboats any more," Mellen says. They began buying clothes from Wilson on consignment for a store they owned in Vancouver.

From this start, Westbeach Surf Co. Ltd. (as it was known then) was born in 1985. It allowed Wilson to meet his goal of owning his own business by age 30—with three hours to spare. Today he is in charge of Westbeach's design, marketing, and future direction; Sibley is president and sales manager; Mellen is in charge of finances; and a fourth partner, Marco Allinott, heads U.S. operations.

One of Westbeach's strengths is Wilson's trend antenna. He bought his first snowboard in 1983—and waited. "In 1988 a kid came to us and said, 'Why aren't you guys making snowboard clothing?'" After testing the water further, Westbeach in 1989 launched the first of its "fat" snowboard pants and shirts in dark winter fabrics.

Growth has not been painless, however. Westbeach first spent its marketing budget trying to persuade middle-aged retailers to carry its youth clothing. Only when Westbeach poured money into awareness advertising—and kids started demanding the product—did stores begin to bite. The company put its own stores into Calgary, Edmonton, Toronto, and Victoria. But profits lagged badly behind those of the Vancouver store, to which the partners could devote personal attention. The stores were sold in 1989. In hindsight, Mr. Wilson says he should have enlisted active retail partners for Alberta and Ontario. Since then, the company has opened four West Coast stores.

The partners also lost their shirts on their first foray into Europe, when they budgeted their production costs around a $4-million order from a German distributor. But they did not get a securing letter of credit. The German company had imitations made in Turkey with counterfeit Westbeach labels, but before these products could flood Europe they were blocked by a last-minute court injunction. It was a costly delay in a promising market; Europe now accounts for 17 percent of the company's wholesale sales and snowboarding is about to take off there.

There are also banking headaches. Westbeach has to ship like crazy at the end of each month because its bank lends twice as much against receivables as against inventory. Last year the partners took bonuses out of the company, a move that ran down its equity. The Hong Kong Bank of Canada refused a working line of credit. It cost Westbeach $32,000 to have B.C. Trade Development Corp. guarantee letters of credit so the company could meet export orders.

But as they age, the owners are outgrowing a laid-back approach to finances. "They're a classic case of a company that got so far merely on quality product and image," says Mr. Tippe, a senior manager with Peat Marwick Thorne. "But they've simply hit the rails." Tippe is working with Westbeach to set goals, and identify strengths and weaknesses. He is helping deemphasize short-term profits to establish a structure that can respond to changing markets. Employees are being involved in planning for life after snowboards. "You have to create an environment where almost everybody is an entrepreneur," Tippe says. "It's not easy." For Wilson, it means sniffing the winds of fashion while wrestling with the discipline of a business strategy that ensures long-range survival.

Reprinted, by permission, from R. Williamson, 1993, "Chairman of the boards," *The Globe and Mail*, B6.

Questions

1. How would you describe the strategy that Westbeach has followed to date?

2. How will the company's strategy have to change in the future, and what factors are influencing this change?

3. If you conduct a SWOT analysis of Westbeach, what factors would be identified as strengths, weaknesses, opportunities, and threats?

4. Given that snowboarding is about to become big in Europe, and Westbeach currently has a 17 percent share of the market, what advice would you give to Wilson if he wants to expand his European operation?

Robert W. Gore, President; Genevieve W. Gore, Co-Founder; Wilbert L. Gore, Co-Founder; *W.L. Gore & Associates, Inc.*

The Impact of Size on Sport Organizations

When You Have Read This Chapter

You should be able to

1. describe the characteristics of large and small sport organizations;

2. understand the different ways in which the size of a sport organization can be measured;

3. explain the debates over the impact of size on organizational structure;

4. describe how size affects complexity, formalization, and centralization;

5. understand the impact of size on the ratio of managers to employees; and

6. explain the need for research on small-business enterprise in the sport industry.

At W.L. Gore & Associates, Inc., Small is Beautiful

Many sport managers subscribe to the adage that, for their organization, bigger is better. Large organizations are often equated with greater market share, a higher return on investment, and increased prestige for owners and managers. But Bill Gore, whose company produces Gore-Tex fabric, a material used for sports equipment such as running suits, golf, fishing, and skiwear, believed there are many benefits to keeping organizations small. In 1965 Gore was walking through his Newark, Delaware plant talking to staff when he began to realize that he didn't know a number of the people in his company. The company had grown and "associates" (as employees are called) were talking about the organization in terms of "they" rather than "we." The sense of camaraderie and togetherness that had characterized the development of W.L. Gore & Associates, and that Bill Gore had worked to maintain, was being lost. It was at that point that Gore decided to limit the size of the work force in each plant to approximately 150 associates. The opening of a second plant in Flagstaff, Arizona established a Western Gore presence and tested his reasoning. The workforce at the Newark plant was reduced to 150 and, according to Gore, that was the key to success. "People started smiling more," he said. "You could tell they felt better even by the way they said 'hello'." As the company grew, Gore stuck to his belief about the appropriate size for an organization. Anything over 150, he felt, resulted in a reduction in cooperation and an over-reliance on rules, regulations, and procedures to determine how people should work together. Today W.L. Gore & Associates, Inc. has over 40 plants and offices around the world.

Based on information in Milne, M.J. (1985, March). The Gorey details. *Management Review, 74,* 16-17; Rhodes, L. (1982, August). The un-manager. *Inc.,* pp. 34-43; Simmons, J. (1987). People managing themselves. *Journal for Quality and Participation, 10,* pp. 14-19; and Gore, W.L. (n.d.). *The lattice organization: A philosophy of enterprise* distributed by W.L. Gore & Associates, Inc.

Intuitively we know that large sport organizations such as Stride Rite (the manufacturer of Keds) and the Football Association operate differently from small companies such as the local sporting goods store or a community soccer league. But exactly how does size affect a sport organization? As sport organizations grow (for many an implicit if not explicit goal), they benefit from certain economies of scale. Growth is also important for recruiting and retaining top quality managers and for maintaining a sport organization's economic well-being. However, for people like Bill Gore these factors were not enough to outweigh the benefits that came from a smaller organization (see table 6.1).

Size, like strategy, is a factor many organizational theorists believe influences the structure and processes of an organization; for some it is the most important factor. In this chapter we look at the concept of organizational size. We first look at what we mean when we talk about the size of a sport organization. We then discuss the debates over the effect that size has on structure, and how size is believed to influence the dimensions of complexity, formalization, and centralization. We also look at how organizational size impacts the administrative component of an organization. We examine the phenomenon of small-business enterprise in the sport industry and finally briefly touch on the issue of organizational decline.

How Do We Measure Organizational Size?

There are a number of possible ways to measure the size of a sport organization. Total assets, return on investment, market share, sales volume, number of clients, number of employees, number of members, and net profits are all possible indicators. In what is probably the most comprehensive examination of studies on organizational size, Kimberly (1976) suggests that four important aspects of the

Table 6.1 Characteristics of Large and Small Sport Organizations

LARGE ORGANIZATIONS	SMALL ORGANIZATIONS
Stable	Responsive
Global	Innovative
Economics of scale	Flexible
Complex	Simple
Impersonal	Collegial
Diversified	Entrepreneurial
Access to greater resources	Niche oriented
Slow	Interdependent
Vertically integrated	Focused
Hierarchial	Flat structure

Table 6.2 The Relative Size of American League Baseball Stadiums

TEAM	SEATING CAPACITY	LEFTFIELD DISTANCE	CENTERFIELD DISTANCE	RIGHTFIELD DISTANCE
Baltimore Orioles	54,017	309	405	309
Boston Red Sox	38,182	315	390	302
California Angels	64,593	333	404	370
Chicago White Sox	43,931	347	409	347
Cleveland Indians	74,483	320	400	320
Detroit Tigers	52,416	340	440	325
Kansas City Royals	40,625	330	410	330
Milwaukee Brewers	53,192	315	402	315
Minnesota Twins	55,883	343	408	327
New York Yankees	57,545	399	408	385
Oakland Athletics	49,210	330	400	330
Seattle Mariners	58,150	324	415	313
Texas Rangers	43,508	330	400	330
Toronto Blue Jays	53,000	330	400	330

Based on information in New York Yankees 1990 Information Guide.

concept can be derived from the operational definitions found in the literature.

The first of these is the physical capacity of the organization. For example, the size of the University of Alberta's summer basketball camps is limited by the amount of available gym space, and the New York Road Runners Club limits the number of runners in its annual marathon because it can't handle more entries (Lebow, 1984). When determining size, it is "relatively easy to use other measures of the physical aspect of the size of an organization . . . in that they would provide a reasonably compa-

rable standard for measurement"(Kimberly, 1976, p. 587). In fact, measures such as available parking, seating capacity, number of tennis courts, and pool dimensions are often used to compare the relative size of organizations such as stadiums and sports clubs (see table 6.2).

Kimberly's second aspect of size is "the personnel available to an organization." This most common measure of size, used in over 80 percent of studies on this topic (Kimberly, 1976), is not without its problems. Many sport organizations are seasonal and employ part-time staff. The Broadmoor

Golf Resort, for example, employs approximately 1,100 people in winter but 1,500 in summer. The Edmonton Eskimos Football Club employs more people on game days than on other days and for obvious reasons ski resorts employ more staff in winter than in summer. It is also difficult to apply the available personnel criteria of size to many non-profit sport organizations. Is the number of personnel available determined by the number of active participants in the sport, the size of the membership, or the number of paid staff? Some sport organizations may have their size limited by external regulatory bodies. The NCAA and the Canadian Interuniversity Athletic Union both restrict the size of a college football team (a type of organization) by placing a limit on the number of players that can be carried on the roster. The goal for some organizations, such as sports clubs, may be to increase their size; others, such as a sporting goods retail store, will want to keep staff numbers low to reduce costs. Nevertheless, as Child (1973b) argues, despite the problems with using available personnel as a mea-

sure of size, it is *people* who have to be managed in an organization; as such, available personnel is one of the best and most frequently used measures of size. Table 6.3 shows the type of variation that may occur in sport organizations in the number of personnel employed.

The third aspect of size cited by Kimberly (1976, p. 588) is "the volume of organizational input or, occasionally, the volume of its output." The former could be represented by the number of athletes a sport marketing company such as Mark McCormack's International Management Group (IMG) represents, or the number of students enrolling in a sport management program. Outputs, which Kimberly notes are often conceptualized as indicators of performance rather than size, could include such measures as sales volume for a sporting goods store or the number of players going on to the professional levels from a college football team. Measures of organizational inputs and outputs are best suited for use with similar types of sport organizations.

Table 6.3   Number of Personnel Employed in Selected Sport Organizations

COMPANY	AREA OF BUSINESS	SALES	NUMBER OF PERSONNEL EMPLOYED
Sea Sport and Scuba, Inc.	Skindiving, scuba equipment and supplies	$250 thousand	6
Royal Canadian Golf Association	Public golf courses	$8.15 million	50
Seattle Mariners	Baseball club, professional and semiprofessional	$35 million	50
Calgary Olympic Development Association	Recreation & culture administration, municipal, local	$10.25 million	85
Toronto Blue Jays Baseball Ltd.	Professional baseball	Not Available	120
Athletic Wearhouse, Inc.	Sports apparel, specialty sport supplies	$5 million	125
Balsam Corp.	Grasses, artificial and preserved; synthetic rubber; athletic and recreation facilities construction	$81 million	260
Sporting Life, Inc.	Retail sporting goods and bicycles	$20 million	300
Schwinn Bicycle Co.	Bicycle and related parts; bicycle inner tubes; bicycle tires, pneumatic, exercise equipment	$205 million	500
Reebok Intl. Ltd.	Athletic shoes, except rubber or plastic; dress shoes, men's; dress shoes, women's; athletic (warm-up, sweat & jogging) suits: men's & boys'; athletic clothing: women's, misses', & juniors'; motorboats, inboard or outboard: building & repairing	$2.16 billion	3,000

Based on information in 1992 Dun & Bradstreet Publications.

The fourth and final aspect of size cited by Kimberly is the discretionary resources available to an organization, including measures such as organizational wealth and net assets. Although Kimberly (1976) acknowledges that these four aspects of size may be intercorrelated, he argues that they are conceptually distinct and should be considered not as interchangeable but as separate measures. Other writers suggest that, since number of personnel is highly related to other measures of size (cf. Pugh, Hickson, Hinings, & Turner, 1969b), "it should be a fairly accurate measure across organizations" (Robbins, 1990, p. 151). While many organizational theorists have taken this approach, it is nevertheless important to note that, when assessing size, industry sector will have an effect. For example, a sports medicine clinic with 50 staff may be considered quite large, whereas a sports shoe manufacturing company with 200 employees would be seen as small.

Also, as Robbins (1990, p. 151) points out, using available personnel has the effect of mixing size with efficiency: "If one organization requires 100 people to carry out the same activities performed by 50 people in another organization, is the first twice as large or merely half as efficient?" Robbins goes on to note these are not easy questions to answer.

Does Size Influence Structure?

At the beginning of this section we noted that a number of factors (imperatives) are thought to influence the structure of an organization; size was one of them. There have been more debates and written discussion about the impact of size on structure than about any of the other imperatives. Early studies of the size/structure relationship concluded that size had no significant impact on structure. Woodward (1965), in her research on manufacturing firms, found that it was technology rather than size that influenced structure. Hall (1963) suggested that size was not a major factor influencing the degree to which an organization was bureaucratized. However, Slack (1985), in his study of a voluntary sport organization, noted that as the organization grew its level of bureaucratization increased. Hall, Haas, and Johnson (1967), in a study of 75 organizations ranging in size from 6 to over 9,000 members, found only a weak relationship between size and organizational structure.

The first work to suggest a strong relationship between size and organizational structure was that of the Aston group (Pugh et al., 1969b). These researchers looked at 46 organizations and concluded that size was strongly related to increased specialization, formalization, and standardization. Using

TIME OUT

Boat Builders From the Prairies

Dave Steele and Phil Carroll first became friends on a plane returning to Calgary from a student youth conference in Montreal. In 1982 while traveling to Vernon, British Columbia to ski, they drove through the town of Sicamous. Steele and Carroll were struck by the number of houseboats they saw on the Shuswap Lake and thought these boats would be a good idea for a vacation. When they stopped and checked out the houseboats, they were surprised to see how run down they were, but even more surprised to learn they were all booked for the holiday season. In the next 48 hours Steele and Carroll entered the boat business, renting a farmer's barn to build boats and putting down a deposit on a marina. This was the start of Three Buoys Houseboats Charters Ltd. From these humble beginnings the company has grown rapidly. The company moved to a plant in Airdrie, Alberta in 1983 and then a 70,000-square-foot facility in Kelowna, British Columbia in 1985. Booking revenues grew: $30,000 in 1982; $280,000 in 1983; $800,000 in 1984; $2.3 million in 1985; and $10 million in 1986. Revenues from boat sales paralleled this growth. Starting from scratch in 1982 the company made $800,000 in 1983; by 1984 the figure was $2.7 million; by 1985 it was $8.75 million; and in 1986 sales reached $25 million. As revenues grew, so did the size of their organization. From a single employee in 1982 the figures rose to 15 in 1983; 60 in 1984; 250 in 1985; and 350 in 1986.

Based on information in Gould, A. (1989). *The new entrepreneurs*. Toronto: Seal Books.

similar measures, a number of researchers (cf. Hickson, Hinings, McMillan, & Schwetter, 1974; Tracy & Azumi, 1978) conducted cross-national studies and found general support for the Aston findings.

Following close behind the findings of the Aston group was the work of Peter Blau and his colleagues at the University of Chicago. Looking at over 1,500 state, local, and divisional agencies, Blau found that size led to an increase in differentiation—more spatial dispersion of work, increased specialization, new departments and divisions, and an increase in the number of levels in the organizational hierarchy—but that this differentiation occurred at a declining rate. That is, the same increase in size would be more likely to result in increased differentiation in a small organization than it would in a big organization. As a result of their work at the University of Chicago, Blau and Schoenherr (1971) suggested that size was the most important condition affecting the structure of organizations.

Child and Mansfield (1972) used the Aston measures to test the technology/size/structure relationship and, as a result, suggested that size showed a positive relationship with specialization, standardization, formalization, and vertical span. Centralization, however, was negatively related to size. That is, applying Child and Mansfield's findings to a sport equipment manufacturing organization, we would expect to find that as the organization got larger it would become more decentralized; decisions would be passed down the organizational hierarchy. Child also compared his findings to those of Blau and concluded (1973b, p. 171) that "larger organizations are more specialized, have more rules, more documentation, more extended hierarchies, and a greater decentralization of decision making further down such hierarchies." Slack (1985) found somewhat similar trends in his study of a voluntary swimming association.

Much of this work had proposed that size causes structural change in organizations, but the data used were cross-sectional in nature and therefore not indicative of causality. In an interesting and important study Meyer (1972), looking at changes in size and structure over a period of five years, found that size was related to the number of subunits in an organization, the levels of hierarchy, and the number of supervisors. While studies such as those by Blau and the Aston researchers prompted replications and extensions, they were not without their critics. Argyris (1972) analyzed Blau's data and criticized his findings, suggesting that Blau's use of official descriptions of structure were often inaccurate. He also pointed out that the civil-service type of

organizations that Blau used for his study often have budget limitations, distinct geographic limits, and predetermined staff sizes, which could influence the size/structure relationship. Finally, Argyris argued that managerial choice could influence the size/structure relationship because managers in public-sector agencies expect increases in size to be accompanied by increased differentiation.

Aldrich (1972b) took the Aston data and reanalyzed it using path analysis. His findings suggested that size may actually be a dependent rather than an independent variable, because organizations that are more highly structured and have a "greater degree of specialization, formalization, and monitoring of role performance simply need to employ a larger workforce than less structured firms" (p. 38). Aldrich's work also stresses the importance of technology as a major determinant of structure (also see Hilton, 1972; Aldrich, 1972a; & Heise, 1972 for further comments on Aldrich's approach).

Research by Geeraerts (1984) suggests that the status of an organization's management, that is, whether it is owner-managed or professionally managed, may well mediate the size/structure relationship. Increases in size in owner-managed organizations were less likely to result in increased differentiation, formalization, or a decentralized decision making system than increases in size in professionally managed organizations. Geeraerts (1984) suggests that this phenomenon may well be because professional managers are more likely to be socialized toward bureaucratic practices than owner-managers. It may also be a product of owner-managers' desires to keep control of their organization through a narrow span of control and centralized decision making.

Despite the large amount of research on the size/structure relationship, none has included any type of sport organization. There has also been no attempt within the sport management literature to look at the impact of size on the structure of different types of sport organizations. As the Time Out on the next page shows, isolated studies have looked at entrepreneurial sport organizations, which are usually small, but the specific focus of this research has not been to examine the size/structure relationship. Given the importance attached to size as a major determinant of structure, this type of research is an unfortunate omission from the sport management literature. Replications and extensions of such work could provide a useful addition to our understanding of sport organizations and at the same time extend theoretical knowledge in the broader field of management.

TIME OUT

For Entrepreneurs in the Sport and Leisure Industry Smaller Is Better

In a study of small-business entrepreneurs in the sport and leisure industry, Berrett, Burton, and Slack (1993) found that increasing the size of their operations was not a high priority. Many of the entrepreneurs had set up their companies because they themselves were extensively involved in the particular sport or leisure activity that was the focus of their business. Success for them was not measured by increased size but by being their own boss, by working in an area in which they were interested, and by owning their own company. For many, an increase in size would mean a resultant loss of control over their operations; the collegial atmosphere that many of them had been able to establish in their businesses would be replaced by more formal operating procedures. They were not willing to make these concessions to increased size.

Based on information in Berrett, T., Burton, T.L., and Slack, T. (1993). Quality products, quality service: Factors leading to entrepreneurial success in the sport and leisure industry. *Leisure Studies, 12,* 93-106.

The Impact of Size on Elements of Organizational Structure

As we saw in the previous section, and as table 6.4 shows, although there has been some debate over the impact that the size of an organization has on structure, the majority of studies acknowledge that the two concepts are related. As Child (1984, p. 10) notes, "the overall size of an organization has been shown in many research surveys to be closely associated with the type of structure adopted. . . ." In this section we look more closely at the relationship of size to each of the three main structural variables.

The Relationship Between Size and Complexity

Researchers (Blau, Falbe, McKinley, & Tracy, 1976; Khandwalla, 1977; Pugh et al., 1968) have all suggested that large organizations have higher levels of task specialization, increased differentiation, and a more developed administrative component (cf. Mintzberg, 1979). As organizations grow they tend to add more specialist functions because, as Child (1984, p. 11) notes, "size makes it economically possible to utilize specialist support." Also, large size results in the tendency for organizations to diversify into different fields or different geographic areas, to protect themselves from sudden changes in market conditions. In 1990, for example, Gatorade controlled over 90 percent of the U.S. sport beverage market, yet as a result of the introduction of sport beverages by companies such as Coca-Cola,

PepsiCo, and H.J. Heinz, it decided to protect itself by moving into a number of foreign markets (Smith, Arnold, & Bizzell, 1991).

The increased complexity resulting from the addition of specialists' functions and/or market and product diversification has to be managed. One way is to introduce new levels of management, a choice that increases the vertical complexity of the organization. Slack (1985) notes the occurrence of this type of phenomenon in his study of the Alberta Section of the Canadian Amateur Swimming Association. One of the first characteristics Slack observed in this organization as it increased its size was the emergence of a functional division of labor. As the organization grew, zones were introduced to help manage the growing complexity, with the effect of introducing another level into the vertical hierarchy of the organization. More research is needed to determine if these kinds of changes occur in other types of sport organizations.

The Relationship Between Size and Formalization

As we saw in chapter 3 formalization is highly correlated with complexity. Consequently we can expect that if size influences complexity it is also likely to have an impact on formalization. A number of studies support a strong positive relationship between size and formalization (cf. Miller, G., 1987), for two reasons. First, large organizations are often involved in repetitive tasks. To control product or service quality, tasks are standardized through formalized procedures. Parsley (1987), for example, describes how, with increasing usage, the services

Table 6.4 Summary of Studies on the Impact of Size on Structural Elements

STUDY	SAMPLE SIZE	ORGANI-ZATION TYPE	COUNTRY	REPORTED CORRELATION BETWEEN SIZE AND		
				SPECIALIZATION*	FORMALIZATION	CENTRALIZATION
Ayoubi 1981	34	Manuf.	Jordan	.78	.73	−.33
Azumi & McMillan 1981	50	Manuf.	Japan	.43	.53	.01
Badran & Hinings 1981	31	Mixed	Egypt	.53	.49	−.45
Birnbaum & Wong 1985	20	Banks	Hong Kong	.22	.21	−.28
Blau et al. 1976	110	Manuf.	U.S.	.25	n.a.	n.a.
Bryman et al. 1983	71	Mixed	G.B.	.77	n.a.	n.a.
Child 1972a	82	Mixed	G.B.	.61	.58	−.58
Child & Kieser 1979	51	Manuf.	W. Germany	.83	n.a.	−.35
Conaty et al. 1983	64	Mixed	Iran	.47	.37	.08
Conaty et al. 1983	65	Mixed	U.S.	.36	.57	-.49
Donaldson & Warner 1974	7	Unions	G.B.	.73	.70	−.62
Hickson et al. 1974	21	Manuf.	U.S.	.82	.48	−.37
Hickson et al. 1974	24	Manuf.	Canada	.49	.49	.38
Hickson et al. 1974	25	Manuf.	G.B.	.80	.45	−.01
Hinings 1979	81	Govt.	G.B.	.59	.13	−.06
Hinings 1979	9	Church	G.B.	.57	−.16	−.21
Hinings & Lee 1971	9	Manuf.	G.B.	.84	.83	−.64
Holdway et al. 1975	23	College	Canada	.43	.43	.47
Horvath et al. 1976	12	Manuf.	Sweden	.28	.69	.24
Kuc et al. 1980	11	Manuf.	Poland	.67	.26	−.35
Lincoln et al. 1978	54	Mixed	Japan	.69	.16	−.26
Marsh and Mannari 1981	50	Manuf.	Japan	.51	.40	−.07
Payne & Mansfield 1973	14	Manuf.	G.B.	.34	.53	−.63
Pugh et al. 1968	46	Mixed	G.B.	.67	.55	−.39
Shenoy 1981	35	Manuf.	India	.29	.28	−.31

*Miller uses the Aston concept of specialization, not complexity.

Reprinted, by permission, from G.A. Miller, 1987, "Meta-analysis and the culture-free analysis," Organization Studies 8: 316.

of an athletic facility he administers at the College of St. Thomas in St. Paul, Minnesota have benefited from detailed line and staff outlines, job descriptions, and a formalized employee schedule. Second, with the increased complexity that comes with large size, there is a greater need for control. This control can be achieved either through direct surveillance or through the introduction of formalized proce-dures such as rules and regulations. Slack and Hinings (1992) document this type of change in Canadian national sport organizations through the 1984-1988 period. As the organizations expanded their programs, more formalized operating proce-dures were also introduced. In large organizations direct surveillance is costly, so formalization is used as a means of control (cf. Rushing, 1980).

It is important to note, nevertheless, that the nature of the organization may also affect the size/formalization relationship. Organizations with large numbers of professionals, such as a sport medicine clinic, may be less likely to formalize procedures as they get bigger, because the professional training that sport medicine physicians and athletic therapists receive is actually designed to do the same thing as formalization, that is, "organize and regularize the behavior of the members of the organization" (Hall, 1982, p. 111). Robbins (1990) also suggests that an organization's status as a subsidiary of a larger company will influence its level of formalization because "parent firms often impose rules and regulations to maintain financial and reporting consistencies that would be unnecessary if the small firm were independent" (p. 160). For example, the golf clubs controlled by Club Corporation of America are subject to extensive reporting procedures required by the parent organization (O'Reilly, 1984). Such detailed procedures would be less likely in a smaller, independent club.

The Relationship Between Size and Centralization

The relationship between size and centralization is a somewhat difficult one. As Blau and Schoenherr (1971, p. 130) note, "the large size of an agency produces conflicting pressures on top management, as it heightens the importance of managerial decisions, which discourages delegating them, and simultaneously expands the volume of managerial responsibilities, which exerts pressure to delegate some of them." However, despite this dilemma, the general thrust of the research literature on size and centralization is that large size leads to decentralized decision making (Child, 1973a). Large sport organizations have to push decisions down the hierarchy to avoid overloading senior managers. Club Corporation of America, for example, decentralized its decision making as it grew because it realized it was limiting its capabilities by keeping power concentrated at the top of the organization. Small sport organizations do not have this problem; in this type of organization managers can more easily handle the volume of decisions.

The actual process of decentralization may be related to the increased use of rules that accompanies large size. With increased formalization decisions can be delegated to lower levels but there is no loss of control for the organization (cf. Mansfield, 1973). As with formalization, the use of professional staff may complicate the size/centralization relationship. As Hall (1982, p. 116) notes, it is "impossible to determine if increased size leads to pressures to delegate and thus to utilize experts, or if the hiring of experts leads to pressures to delegate, with size not really being a factor." Finally, the issue of whether a sport organization is owner-managed or professionally managed may also affect the relationship. Even with increased size, owner-managers will be reluctant to give up their control by delegating decision making; but professional managers will not experience this same reluctance.

The Impact of Size on the Administrative Component of an Organization

Within the field of organization studies, probably more work has been done on the impact of size on the administrative component of an organization than on any other aspect of the size/structure relationship. Much of the impetus for this work came from C. Northcote Parkinson's 1957 book *Parkinson's law*. Essentially, Parkinson's law suggests that work expands to fill the time available for its completion. It also suggests that there is no relationship between work and the number of people assigned to carry it out. Using data from the British Navy to support his arguments, Parkinson showed that despite a 68-percent decline in the number of warships commissioned between 1914 and 1928 and a 32-percent decline in the total number of personnel, the British Navy's officer corps rose by 78 percent and the onshore officials and clerks by 40 percent.

From Parkinson's somewhat tongue-in-cheek conclusions have emanated a number of studies attempting to extend and elaborate our knowledge about the size/administrative component relationship. Although there have been no studies of this relationship in sport organizations per se, the conclusions drawn from the work completed can inform our understanding of organizations in our field.

Two major findings come out of the work on the size/administrative component ratio. First, as size increases, the relative proportion of staff in the administrative component also gets larger. The basic idea here is that, as an organization (for example, a sports equipment producer) gets larger, it has more and more people involved in tasks such as production, design, marketing, and sales; managing this increased complexity requires a proportionately larger number of administrative staff. Several studies have supported this position. Terrien and Mills (1955) studied over 400 California school districts and concluded that as the size of the school district increased, so did the number of superintendents, business managers, and other administrative staff. Child (1973a) in a study of manufacturing organizations found a positive correlation between total employment and the total number of managers.

The second conclusion from research on the size/administrative component is contradictory to the first and suggests a negative correlation between the two dimensions. That is, the relative number of administrative personnel declines as size increases. The idea is that as organizations get bigger they benefit from economies of scale. Therefore, an organization that employs 100 people to manufacture tennis racquets may have 10 staff as its administrative component. An increase of 50 employees would not require a proportional increase in the number of managers. Likewise, a summer sports camp could increase its number of participants by 15 percent without any particular increase in camp counselors or administrators. Research by Indik (1964) supports this idea; he found that as the size of an organization increased the proportionate size of the administrative component decreased.

Factors Influencing the Size/Administrative Component Relationship

To understand the contradictory findings on the size/administrative component ratio it is necessary to look at several factors that researchers have suggested influence this relationship. Briefly examined here, these factors include whether an organization is owner-managed or professionally managed, whether an organization is in a period of growth or decline, the way in which the administrative component is measured, and the influence of contextual factors such as environment and technology.

Type of Management

As with the size/centralization relationship, the type of management in an organization can affect the size/administrative component relationship. Pondy (1969) studied 45 manufacturing industries and found that administrative intensity (the number of administrative personnel per 100 production workers) correlated negatively with organizational size. However, with the increased separation of ownership from management, the relative size of the administrative component increased. Pondy (1969, p. 57) explains his findings by suggesting that "owner-managers are unwilling to dilute their personal power and control over the organization by adding professional, nonfamily personnel, even if it means accepting a lower profit." Berrett, Burton, and Slack's (1993) work on entrepreneurial companies in the sport industry, although it did not specifically address this issue, provides indications that a similar situation exists in this type of organization.

Growth or Decline

Several researchers have suggested that the size/administrative component relationship is influenced by whether or not an organization is growing in size or declining. Tsouderos (1955) studied voluntary organizations and found that the size of the administrative staff component grew as organizational size increased, but when there was a decline in the number of members there was no similar decline in administrative staff; in fact, the size of the administrative component continued to increase albeit at a declining rate. The rationale that Tsouderos (1955, p. 206) presents for this continued increase is that "with a declining membership, efforts are made to control drop by introducing new incentives, added services, [and] professional and administrative staff in order to discharge and supervise such services."

In a study of nearly 300 school districts Hendershott and James (1972) found that there was a negative relationship between size and the administrative component; in addition, the rate of organizational growth was negatively related to the administrative component, independent of size. Also studying school districts, Freeman and Hannan (1975) found that as school size increased so too did the size of the administrative (supportive) component and what they call the direct component (the number of teachers employed). They did, however, qualify their findings by noting that "when demand [changes in enrollment] is increasing, the size of the direct component increases, as does the supportive component. But when demand declines, the loss in direct component is not matched by loss in the supportive component; that is, the supportive component tends to increase on upswings but decrease less on the downswings" (p. 227).

Findings such as those of Freeman and Hannan (1975) may be a result of the fact that, because management sees administrative employees as more difficult to recruit and costly to train, it is reluctant to lay them off. Production workers, in contrast, are usually less skilled, and therefore not as difficult to recruit and train. Findings such as these may also be a result of whether or not the decline is expected to be over the long or short term. If the decline is long-term and an organization is not experiencing a demand for its products or services, they are more likely to reduce their administrative component than if the decline is short-term. In the latter case they are more likely to reduce the number of employees directly involved in making the product or providing the service. No work in the sport management area has looked at this phenomenon. Studies of university sport studies departments, manufacturing companies in the sport industry, and public-sector agencies involved in sport could all provide useful information on the impact that growth and/or decline has on sport organizations.

Measures of the Administrative Component

One of the cautions, when comparing the results of work on the size/administrative component ratio and trying to extend this work to various types of sport organizations, is that different researchers used different measures of the administrative component. For example, Tsouderos (1955) in his work on voluntary organizations used as his measure the number of "administrative office workers," that is, clerical staff. By contrast, Indik (1964, p. 302) used individuals "whose functional role involved mainly direct interpersonal supervision or key organizational administrative decision making [and excluded] those non-rank-and-file personnel higher in the organization who were serving mainly clerical functions."

Some researchers have actually desegregated the administrative component. Holdaway and Blowers (1971, pp. 280-281) used three definitions of the administrative component in their study of school districts. The first was central office administrative personnel, "staff not directly involved with pupils but concerned more with planning, organizing, coordinating, etc." The second was central office professional personnel, "university trained, non-administrative staff such as psychologists, social workers, and teaching consultants." The final category was "central office personnel plus school principals." Rushing (1967), in his study of manufacturing organizations, broke the administrative component down into several subcomponents, including managerial personnel, professional person-

nel, and clerical personnel; each was negatively related to changes in size as measured by the number of production personnel. Child (1973a, pp. 336-337) used the Aston approach (what the Aston group called "nonworkflow employment") to identify the administrative component. That is, he used for his measure of the administrative component the total number of employees minus the combination of all direct employees and all managers of direct employees. He also looked at the relationship between 16 nonworkflow functions and the total number of employees, and found considerable differences in these functions, suggesting that what may be true for the administrative component as a whole may not be true for each of its different parts.

Environment and Technology

Both Freeman (1973) and Child (1973a) found that contextual variables may influence the size/administrative component relationship. Based on a study of manufacturing organizations, Freeman (1973) suggested that organizations with a more mechanized production technology and a more diverse environment will have a higher administrative component. In organizations where environmental constraints are stronger (for example, a subsidiary that has its autonomy limited by a parent organization), the administrative component will be lower. Child (1973a) showed that the influence of contextual factors will vary for different subcomponents of an organization, thus strengthening the argument that size is not the only factor influencing the administrative component.

There is no work within the sport management literature that has looked at the size/administrative component relationship, and scholars in our field may find this a potentially fruitful research area. However, as studies such as those cited above demonstrate, in conducting research of this type there is a need for care in determining how the size of the administrative component of a sport organization is measured. Also, size may not be the only factor that influences the administrative component; the effects of other variables must be taken into account.

Small Businesses in the Sport Industry

While a large sport organization such as Mark McCormack's International Management Group has about 1,000 employees, $800 million in turnover, and 46 offices worldwide ("A survey of the sports business," 1992), much of the activity within the sport industry takes place in relatively small organizations. Although there are no figures readily available on the number of small businesses in the sport industry, they represent a significant number of the over 600,000 new business incorporations that occur yearly in the United States. It would also seem logical to conclude that in Canada, Britain, and other Western European countries there is considerable small-business activity in the sport industry (cf. Berrett, Burton, & Slack, 1993; Collins & Randolph, 1991). Studies of these organizations, however, are relatively rare.

One of the obvious questions to ask about small-business enterprise in sport is whether the concepts of organizational theory apply to these kinds of organizations. The answer is undoubtedly yes. While we must be wary of unquestioningly applying any findings from one set of organizations directly to another, there is a great deal that organizational theory can help us understand about the structure and operations of small businesses in the sport industry. In fact, there is a growing literature on entrepreneurship that builds on ideas from organizational theory to specifically address issues relating to small business.

To date studies conducted on small businesses in the sport (and leisure) industries have looked only at business and entrepreneurial characteristics, internal and exogenous factors affecting success (Berrett, Burton, & Slack, 1993), and the commitment level of entrepreneurs (Jamieson, 1988). Several "how-to" articles on entrepreneurship in the sport and leisure industry have also appeared (cf. Bullaro, 1987; Crossley & Ellis, 1988; Pestolesi, 1987; Sheffield, 1988). The paucity of literature on this topic suggests an area of considerable scope for work by sport management scholars. The economic impact of sport (cf. Comte and Stogel, 1990; Economic Intelligence Unit, 1990) and the contribution of these types of organizations to economic activity also serve to underscore the need for work of this nature.

Organizational Decline

Often when we think about the concept of organizational size we think of organizations growing. However, not all sport organizations, nor organizations of any type, continually grow; some experience periods of decline, maybe even failure (cf. Meyer & Zucker, 1989). When we look at the concept of size we must consider the issue of decline as well as growth. The notion of organizational decline is, as Cameron, Sutton, and Whetten (1988, p. 5) note, "emerging as one of the most important topics addressed by organizational research." They add, however, that there are definitional problems with the concept of decline and a number of "practical and psychological roadblocks" to research on decline.

In looking at work that has been conducted on decline, Cameron, Sutton, and Whetten (1988) suggest four types of studies: those that look at the variables that precede or cause decline, those that are concerned with the processes that lead to decline, those that identify the consequences of decline for both the organization and the individual, and those concerned with the processes that come about as a result of decline. Within this research no studies have looked specifically at the process of decline in sport organizations. There are, of course, popular accounts of sport organizations going through difficult times— Crick and Smith (1989) on Manchester United and Harris (1987) on the NFL—and also sociological and historical accounts of organizations that have ceased to exist (Hult, 1989; Metcalfe, 1983) but these are not included in Cameron, Sutton, and Whetten's categorization, nor do they make use of the organizational literature on decline. Given the relatively fleeting existence of some sport organizations such as fitness centers and racquet clubs and also the decline (and in some cases the disappearance) of sport organizations such as the American Basketball Association, the World Football League, the United States Football League, the World Hockey Association, the Central Council for Physical Recreation, and the Association of Intercollegiate Athletics for Women, there is considerable potential for work on decline within the organizations that constitute the sports industry.

Summary and Conclusions

The topic of organizational size has received considerable attention in the management literature. However, virtually no studies within the field of sport management have looked at the impact of size on the structure and processes of sport organizations. The most commonly used measure of organizational size is available personnel. Although it is possible to use this measure in sport management studies, caution should be exercised in applying this approach to some sport organizations.

While the general consensus has been that size influences organizational structure, this position has

TIME OUT

Four Entrepreneurial Ideas

1. Ten years ago the manager of a sporting goods store in Texas carried a small line of ski equipment, mainly as a convenience to some of the regular customers. Over the years, ski equipment sales increased, but the manager did not really notice the change or expand this product line. Meanwhile, another store manager monitored sales very carefully. "Why would ski sales in Texas increase?" this manager asked. From customers it was learned that discount fares had made it easy for Texans to reach Colorado. The second manager expanded the store's line of ski equipment each year until it became the "ski center" for miles around. The unexpected success of this product line eventually contributed to a huge increase in profitability.

2. An eastern U.S. city recreation department had behavior and control problems in its adult men's basketball league. As problems continued for two years, participation dropped. Then the county recreation department (a competitor of sorts) initiated a "slow-break" league, which lowered the physical intensity of the game . Many older and former players of the city league signed up teams for the slow-break leagues. Within two years the slow-break league had three times more teams than the city program.

3. Gart Brothers, a Denver-based sports organization, realized that one problem in the retail sports business was the inability of customers to try a product before a purchase is made. To combat this problem they now provide customers with a variety of facilities where they can try out equipment. Their "Sports Castles" have a basketball court, tennis court, golf putting green, flycasting area, archery range, and a huge treadmill "ski machine" for testing equipment and learning skills. They also have a multipurpose classroom where they teach fly tying, hunter safety, and other classes related to the equipment sold. In addition, Gart Brothers offers a full-service travel agency, sells tickets to concerts and ski areas, and sponsors a variety of community sports events.

4. Steve Garside of Salt Lake City recognized that there is very little to distinguish the appearance of downhill skis. Any cosmetic difference had little to do with the performance of the ski, so he wondered why ski tops couldn't be personalized. Garside decided that his company, Evolution USA, would specialize in uniquely customized skis. For $400 customers got a good pair of skis and were allowed to design their own ski top.

This excerpt is adapted with permission from the *Journal of Physical Education, Recreation & Dance*, 1988, vol. 59, 35-38. *JOPERD* is a publication of the American Alliance for Health, Physical Education, Recreation and Dance, 1900 Association Drive, Reston, VA 22091.

its critics. Factors such as technology and ownership have been seen as influencing the size/structure relationship. One researcher even went so far as to suggest that size may in fact be a dependent rather than an independent variable. Those researchers who supported a relationship between size and structural elements have, for the most part, found increased size to result in increased complexity, increased formalization, and a decentralized decision making structure.

There have probably been more studies on the impact of size on the administrative component of an organization than in any other area. While research results are mixed, more studies suggest a negative than a positive relationship. Factors such as type of management, whether the organization is in a period of growth or decline, how the administrative component is measured, and contextual factors have been shown to influence the size/administrative component ratio.

The issue of small-business enterprise in the sport industry was recognized as an important area of further study. Finally, also relevant to the concept of size was the issue of organizational decline. While we often see changes in size as being related to growth many sport organizations go through periods of decline and there are important managerial issues relating to this topic.

The Decline of the World Football League

In October 1973, California lawyer Gary Davidson announced the establishment of the World Football League (WFL). Designed to compete with the NFL, which Davidson suggested had "grown arrogant and complacent," the league opened in July 1974 with 12 teams. Franchises were located in smaller cities with no professional sport teams, or in cities where the NFL team had a poor record. The teams themselves were given catchy names such as the Chicago Fire and the Portland Storm. Although the league secured a contract with the TVS Television Network and early season attendance figures were good, it soon ran into difficulty. First, it was discovered that many who attended the opening games were in fact allowed in free. Second, as the season progressed attendance dropped off rapidly; teams were playing in poor quality stadiums, and eventually a number began to experience cash-flow problems. The Jacksonville and Detroit franchises folded. Portland and Orlando suffered financial difficulties, the Houston Texans became the Shreveport Steamers, and the New York Stars moved to Charlotte, North Carolina and became the Hornets. Under pressure from team owners, Gary Davidson resigned as the league's commissioner on October 29. He was replaced by Chris Hemmeter, co-president of the Hawaii franchise. Hemmeter devised a plan to run the league on a break-even basis but the loss of the television contract and low attendance caused the league to close 12 weeks into its 1975 season.

Hartley (1983) suggests a number of major factors that contributed to the decline of the WFL. First, there was a lack of fan support; as a result, teams fell short of their financial break-even point. Second, TV coverage was lacking, particularly in the second year of the league's existence. Third, a lack of star players meant the caliber of play was not as good as the NFL. Finally, owners could not or would not put extra capital into their team or the league.

Based on information in Hartley, R.F. (1983). *Management mistakes*. Columbus, OH: Grid Publishing.

Key Concepts

Available personnel	Small business
Administrative component	Organizational decline
Economies of scale	Entrepreneurship
Organizational growth	

Review Questions

1. What different criteria could you use to measure the size of a professional baseball organization?

2. Is available personnel a useful way to measure the size of a sport organization? Explain.

3. How does the industry in which a sport organization operates influence its size?

4. What are the relative merits of large and small sport organizations?

5. What are the arguments for and against size as a major determinant of the structure of a sport organization?

6. When is size likely to have the greatest impact on the structure of a sport organization?

7. How does ownership mediate the size/structure relationship?

8. Explain how size influences complexity.

9. Explain how size influences formalization.

10. Explain how size influences centralization.

11. How does size affect the administrative component of a sport organization?

12. How might the effect of size on the administrative component of a sport organization be influenced by whether the organization is in a period of growth or decline?

13. What sort of problems is a small retail sporting goods business likely to face in the first few years of its existence?

14. What are the important issues that have been examined in work on organizational decline?

15. Pick a sport organization with which you are familiar. How has it been affected by changes in its size?

Suggestions for Further Reading

As we have noted at several points throughout this chapter, there is no work that specifically looks at the size/structure relationship in sport organizations. From work within the broader field of management students should see Kimberly's (1976) article, "Organizational size and the structuralist perspective: A review, critique, and proposal," which overviews a number of conceptual and empirical problems related to issues of size. Also useful as an overview of studies in this area is G.A. Miller's (1987) article, "Meta-analysis and the culture free hypothesis." Students are of course encouraged to read some of the articles cited throughout the chapter, particularly the work of Blau and his colleagues, Child, and the Aston group.

Although there is no work on the size/structure relationship in sport organizations, there are a few articles that deal with small businesses in the sport industry. The most comprehensive of these is Berrett, Burton, and Slack's (1993) article "Quality products, quality service: Factors leading to entrepreneurial success in the sport and leisure industry." Several descriptive articles on entrepreneurship appeared in the February 1987 and October 1988 editions of the *Journal of Physical Education, Recreation, and Dance*. Finally, the section on "Fitness, Sports, and Outdoor Recreation" in Allan Gould's (1989) book *The new entrepreneurs* is highly readable and informative.

Case for Analysis

Images Dance School

The Images Dance School was opened in 1963 by Mary Jamieson and Greta Brodeur, two sisters who both had extensive experience as dance teachers. The original school was started as a place where neighborhood children who were interested in dance could receive instruction and have an opportunity to perform. Neither Mary nor Greta started the school with the intention that it would make money; it was essentially a hobby and a means of providing some type of organized activity for their own children and those of their friends in the community. In the first year that formally organized classes were offered, 30 children registered. However, word of the school spread, and within a couple of years registrations were up over 200. Each year more and more registrations were received and the school expanded to offer an increasingly wide range of dance forms, including jazz, tap, highland, Ukrainian, and ballet. As the number of different classes offered increased, so too did the number of instructors required. The school now has over 18 staff, two full-time and sixteen part-time, in addition to Mary and Greta.

For the first 14 years of its existence Images was run out of rented facilities. Because numbers grew fairly rapidly the school constantly had to relocate to a larger facility to keep up with the demand for programs. When in the middle of their season the landlord of the facility they were renting decided to terminate their lease, Mary and Greta decided it was time for them to get their own facility. For most of their existence the registration fees from the dance classes had covered most of the expenses they had incurred and allowed them to pay themselves a small amount. With the decision to build their own facility, Mary and Greta had to remortgage their own family homes to generate the necessary capital. They also received financial assistance from a federal business development bank.

Using the capital they had available the two sisters decided that not only would they build a dance school but they would also incorporate into the facility a fitness and court club. The present facility has four racquetball courts and two squash courts, an exercise room, massage clinic, whirlpool, sauna, and a rental suite; there is also a small pro shop. In addition to the wide range of dance classes offered in the facilities, there are also programs for aerobic dance and gymnastics. The facilities and classes are available either through a membership system or on a pay-as-you-play basis.

Before its expansion the strength of Images lay in its relatively low overhead and in the dedication and quality of its instructors. About seven years ago its position was challenged when the city recreation department started to offer dance classes at a lower cost than Images could handle. The entry of the city into this market initially created problems for Images; there was an abundance of programs available and they could not compete with the city's offerings. As a result of this decline in demand for their programs, Mary and Greta had to have the mortgage on their facility restructured. In the last few years Images has, however, gained back its market share, in large part because its programs are generally perceived to be better organized and of a superior quality to those offered by the city. Staff loyalty to Images is also very strong.

The opening of the fitness and court facility was unfamiliar ground for Mary and Greta and although they employed a succession of managers for this part of their operation, early results were not good. Nevertheless, they have recently hired a new manager, who had helped develop an excellent facility in a neighboring city, and has been given considerable autonomy to promote the fitness and court side of Images operation.

Mary and Greta have developed a considerable reputation in their community for their work in dance; that part of their business is now on a relatively firm footing. They have kept abreast of changing dance trends and offered appropriate classes. They have also started to offer summer camps, helping fill a void in the summer months when the demand for children's classes is traditionally low. They have also started to see second-generation dancers in their facility—the students they taught are now bringing their children to classes. Images does, however, still face some competition from the city, which pays higher rates to its instructors and does not have to pay for facility rental. This problem is exacerbated because taxes on the facility that Mary and Greta own are based on square footage and, despite the fact that the dance studio portion of their operation is little more than four walls, a roof, and a floor, they still pay the going rate.

While the fitness and court part of their operations is getting better, Mary and Greta have been frustrated by the competition from the city, by the fact that they have been unable to secure financial help from a government-operated small-business debt reduction program, and by the city's tax policy, something they have lobbied their local council to change, so far without success. With the changes they have experienced in their business, Mary and Greta have also found there is less time for them to actually teach dance, which for both of them is their "first love."

This case is based on research on entrepreneurs conducted by Dr. Tim Burton from the University of Alberta. Although the situation is based on fact, for reasons of confidentiality the names are fictitious.

Questions

1. How has the change in the size of Images affected the structure of the organization?
2. How has the changing size of Images influenced its effectiveness?
3. Was the growth of Images a result of external demands for programs or a result of strategic decisions made by Mary and Greta?
4. If you were Mary or Greta, what type of changes would you make to Images to ensure it has a viable future?

Sport Organizations and Their Environments

When You Have Read This Chapter

You should be able to

1. describe the different aspects of a sport organization's environment;

2. discuss the major research studies that have been carried out on the influence of the environment on organizations;

3. explain the techniques that can be used to manage environmental uncertainty;

4. explain the major principles of institutional theory, resource dependence theory, and population ecology; and

5. explain the impact of environmental uncertainty on an organization's structure.

Adidas Makes Friends
and Then Strikes Deals That Move Sneakers

In the small German town of Herzogenaurach the only tourist attraction is the one-room museum devoted to the history of athletic shoes. There, neatly displayed in glass cases are some 200 pairs of the most famous shoes in sport, including the ones Jessie Owens wore in the 1936 Olympics. But the shoe museum alone doesn't explain the procession of Olympic-class athletes and sports officials who used to come to visit Herzogenaurach from all over the world. They came to enjoy the hospitality of the Sport Hotel, a cozy 32-room inn with an indoor swimming pool, tennis courts, soccer fields, saunas, coaches, trainers, and a chef who would do any hotel proud. Best of all, at checkout time there was rarely a bill to be paid by the guest.

The tab was picked up by the Sport Hotel's owner: Adidas, the German shoe and sporting goods maker (officially and legally, its name is not capitalized). Through such largesse its aim was to turn the world's top athletes into walking, running, vaulting, and kicking billboards for its logo. Adidas believed in making friends, then making deals. From the cash it once secretly gave to Olympic athletes to the free plane tickets it passed out to leaders of sport organizations, Adidas made itself the sugar daddy of international amateur sports.

Marketing through patronage made Adidas the largest sporting goods company in the world and its chairman, the late Adi Dassler, one of sport's most important power brokers. Many believe it was Dassler who was behind Juan Antonio Samaranch's rise to the presidency of the IOC and Dassler who was the key player in choosing Seoul (not favorite Nagoya) for the 1988 Summer Olympics. "He is the real boss of sport," said the former director of the IOC, Monique Berlioux.

Other companies, of course, saw sport as an attractive marketing vehicle but what set Adidas apart was its emphasis on amateur sport. Like its competitors, it paid professional athletes to wear its products but it also went to unusual lengths to associate its three-stripe logo and trefoil insignia with the five interlocking rings of the Olympics. Besides paying more than its competitors to outfit Olympic teams, Adidas mingled in Olympic politics with the diligence of a Washington lobbyist. An Adidas dinner or reception was commonplace at almost any IOC meeting, and an Adidas representative—usually Mr. Dassler himself—would spend the day mixing with delegates.

Adidas and its chairman worked themselves into almost every corner of sport politics. Their main vehicles were their contracts with national teams. For example, in 1985 Adidas gave out $30 million in cash and equipment to these teams. Like the best of politicians, Mr. Dassler listened more than he spoke, and asked more questions than he answered. A small army of Adidas representatives, stationed in many of the countries where the company did business, kept Dassler abreast of local sport politics. Dassler also employed operatives like Hassine Hamouda, a Paris-based former Tunisian military colonel, to influence sport leaders in Arab countries and in French-speaking Africa.

Adidas representatives sat on important Olympic advisory committees. Hamouda, for example, sat on the IOC press commission. Thomas Bach, also hired by Adidas, sat as a member of the athletes' advisory committee, and Richard Pound, a Montreal lawyer and former IOC vice president, did legal work for the company. Mr. Dassler acknowledged that his hospitality and other acts of friendship toward national Olympic committee and federation officials directly benefited Adidas as it competed to sponsor teams. "A lot of federations get higher offers than ours but refuse them because of what we have done over the last 10 years," Dassler said.

Dassler's Olympic connections came in handy at the IOC congress in Baden-Baden, Germany in 1985, when the marketing rights to the 1988 Olympic Games were awarded to ISL Marketing AG, a Swiss company run by former Adidas executives. Dassler and his four sisters owned 51 percent of the shares of ISL. Although sport marketing companies in the United States and Europe were more experienced, ISL—then only two years old—was assigned by the IOC in 1983 to develop a marketing plan for the 1988 games. Other bidders weren't invited, thus making a virtual certainty of the final approval in May 1985 of ISL's contract. Despite initial opposition by the U.S. Olympic Committee, the contract was approved by the majority of the Olympic committees of about 160 nations (including the United States).

A dominant theme in the study of organizations is that the environment in which an organization operates influences its structure and processes. To be effective, an organization must adapt to the demands of its environment. One way is to monitor changes in the environment and then take the necessary steps to respond to or control these changes. Adi Dassler did this better than anyone in sport. By creating links with many of the key figures in the world of amateur sport Dassler was able to keep informed of changes that could influence Adidas. By using his contacts to capitalize on opportunities in the environment, he developed Adidas into the number one sporting goods company in the world.

In this chapter we look at what we mean when we talk about the "environment" of a sport organization. We examine the main research findings on the environment of organizations and the methods that can be used to manage the environment. We also look at some of the major theoretical approaches that take an environmental perspective. Finally, we look at the relationship between a sport organization's environment and its structure.

The Nature of the Organizational Environment

What exactly do we mean when we talk about the environment of an organization? Certainly the term has been used in a wide variety of ways (cf. Starbuck, 1976). In one sense everything outside of the organization being studied is a part of the environment, but such a broad definition has little practical or theoretical use. Most researchers use a more focused approach to understanding the concept, and suggest, as shown in figure 7.1, that organizations have two types of environment: a general environment and a task environment.

General Environment

The general environment of an organization includes those sectors which, although they may not have a direct impact on the operations of a sport organization, can influence the industry in general ways that ultimately have an impact on the organization (Daft, 1992). The general environment of a sport organization can be divided up into a number of different sectors. Here we look briefly at the impact of each.

Economic

The general economic conditions in which a sport organization operates (whether publicly or privately owned), the system of banking in the country in which the organization operates, fiscal policies, and patterns of consumption are all components of the economic sector of a sport organization's general environment. Pugh (1989), for example, describes how austere economic conditions influenced the development of the Belfry golf complex; and Johnson (1986) describes how Brunswick's acquisition of Bayliner Marine was influenced by lower interest rates, which helped the boat market.

Figure 7.1   The sport organization's general and task environment.

Political

The prevailing political situation, the extent to which political power is concentrated, and the ideology of the party in power are all factors which can influence a sport organization. Geehern (1991), for example, describes how the dropping of trade barriers as part of the 1992 European Community reforms, and the opening up of the former Soviet Bloc, created considerable market potential for golf ball manufacturers such as Spalding and Acushnet. In a somewhat similar vein, bicycle manufacturers benefited considerably from the Mideast crisis of the early 1970s, when the fear of an oil embargo pushed bike sales to record levels (Charm, 1986). The political climate has also had a considerable effect on a number of Olympic Games organizing committees, most notably in 1980 and 1984 when, because of politically motivated rationales, a number of countries did not attend the Games (cf. Hill, 1992).

Sociocultural

Sociocultural factors that can influence a sport organization include the class structure of the social system, the culture in which the sport organization

exists, trends in consumer tastes, and the sporting traditions of the area in which the organization is situated. We see the impact of sociocultural conditions in the attempts to set up professional soccer leagues in North America. Despite being the most popular sport in the world, the sporting culture of the United States and Canada has mitigated against the survival of leagues such as the North American Soccer League. It is also well established (cf. Beamish, 1985; Macintosh & Whitson, 1990) that the administrative structures of many sport organizations reflect the inequalities of social life in terms of their class, race, and gender composition.

Legal

An important part of an organization's general environment, but one which Hall (1982, p. 228) suggests is often overlooked, "is the legal conditions that are part of the organization's surroundings." The type of legal system within the country in which the sport organization operates, the jurisdictions overseen by various levels of government, and the existence of laws covering such areas as taxation, unionization, and the regulation of organizations, all constitute the legal conditions affecting a sport organization. In the United States, antitrust

Blade Runners

In 1985 John Egart and his golfing partner David Soderquist sold sports equipment. As they visited retailers they noticed a new kind of skate with wheels mounted in line on a blade like an ice skate. Manufactured by Rollerblade, Inc. of Minneapolis, the new type of skates were becoming increasingly popular. However, as they talked to sporting goods buyers, Egart and Soderquist heard stories about problems with Rollerblade's pricing and distribution system. The two decided to leave their sales jobs and set up in competition with Rollerblade. With just under $400,000 in capital, Egart and Soderquist secured a manufacturing facility in Taiwan. By 1987, selling their product for about 15 percent less than Rollerblade, First Team Sports (as Egart and Soderquist had called their company) was doing about $65,000 worth of business per month. But even with this type of turnover it was still losing about $20,000 per month.

To help Egart and Soderquist out, their banker put them in touch with Minneapolis businessman Carey Schumacher. Schumacher in turn introduced them to a local underwriter, who agreed to make a public offering of First Team for $2.6 million. Egart and Soderquist received their check for the deal on October 19, the day the market crashed. Although the economic climate was not good, the underwriter let the deal go through. However, taking advantage of the poor economic conditions, he proposed that First Team merge with an insolvent gun and fishing-tackle distributor. Sensing a takeover, Egart and Soderquist said no to the deal. In 1988 Schumacher and the underwriter started a proxy fight to push the merger offer through. After an expensive legal battle Egart and Soderquist won their case. Now, having overcome the economic downturn and the proposed merger, First Team commands approximately 20 percent of the U.S. market. Their Ultra-Wheels skates are endorsed by stars such as Wayne Gretzky, Bret Hull, and Katarina Witt.

Based on information in Comte, E. (1992, October 12). Blade runner. *Forbes*, pp. 115, 117.

legislations (Freedman, 1987); in Canada, the Competition Act (Barnes, 1988); and in the United Kingdom, the Local Government Act of 1988 (Houlihan, 1991) all provide evidence of the ways legal conditions affect sport organizations.

Demographic

The type of people to whom a sport organization directs its products and/or services, changes in population distributions, and the age, gender, racial, ethnic, and class composition of the population, can all influence the organization. Sparks (1992) shows, for example, how directing its programming to a primarily male audience affects TSN's (The Sports Network's) operations. Richards (1986) demonstrates the influence of changing population cohorts. He suggests that Brunswick's purchase of Ray Industries, Inc., makers of Sea Ray boats, was in part inspired by the company's market research indications that the baby boomers were taking an increased interest in pleasure boats.

Ecological

Because a number of sport organizations depend on their physical surroundings for success, ecological factors are an important part of their general environment. Weather conditions can affect the staging of sports events and the operation of facilities such as ski hills. Hisrich and Peters (1992), for example, describe how in 1980 and 1981 poor snow conditions severely reduced the number of skiers, with a corresponding drop in ski equipment sales. Growing concerns about the total ecological system have encouraged sport organizations to pay attention to how their activities influence the natural environment. For example, companies like Recreational Equipment Inc. (REI), a Seattle-based retailer of outdoor gear and clothing, have created a number of environmental conservation programs and funded many more (Horwich, 1989). It is also this type of thinking that led Nike to include Earth Share, an environmental group, as an option in its 1992 payroll-deduction program, as well as the United Way.

Technological

All sport organizations are affected by technological developments that may improve production and/or service. They must monitor constantly any technological developments that could change the nature of the industry in which the sport organization is involved. Technological developments may also lead the sport organization to engage in new activities or approach existing activities in different ways. An example of the impact of technology on the operations of a sport organization is Huffy's decision to use robotics and computer-integrated manufacturing techniques in producing cycles. This initiative meant Huffy was able to reduce the size of its workforce while at the same time increasing its daily output of cycles (Slakter, 1988).

Task Environment

A sport organization's task environment is made up of those aspects of its general environment that can impact upon its ability to achieve its goals. Typically included in a sport organization's task environment are such groups as customers/members/fans, staff, suppliers, competitors, and regulatory agencies (cf. Thompson, 1967). In contrast to the general environment, which is more removed from the sport organization, the task environment is of more immediate concern to the sport manager, because it contains those constituents that can strongly impact the success of the organization. Each sport organization's task environment is unique and the constituents making up this environment may change over time.

Although they are conceptually distinct, a sport organization's general environment and its task environment are related. Consider for example, the effect of the increasing societal awareness of the inequalities of gender that exist in all types of managerial positions, including those in sport organizations—an aspect of the general environment. Legislative changes are made as more people become aware of and are actively involved in trying to eliminate such inequalities. These changes impact on hiring practices in sport organizations and, consequently, on its human-resources practices—aspects of the sport organization's task environment.

Domain

A sport organization's task environment will vary according to the domain in which it chooses to operate. Domain refers to the territory that a sport organization stakes out for itself, in regard to the services and/or products it delivers and the markets in which it operates. Different sport organizations even within the same sector of the sports industry can have different domains and therefore different task environments. Huffy Corporation and Holland Cycle, which we highlighted in chapter 4, both make bicycles but they have identified different domains in which to operate: Huffy primarily mass-produces bikes for ordinary consumers; Holland Cycle makes custom bikes for cycling aficionados. Consequently, they come into contact with different suppliers, customers, and competitors.

Perceived Environment

In discussing the concept of environment it is important to distinguish between actual environment and perceived environment. The actual environmental conditions surrounding a sport organization may be perceived differently by different managers at the same level (Leifer & Huber, 1977). For example, the same environmental conditions may be perceived as dynamic (providing opportunities for growth) by one sport manager and in a quite different way by the manager of another sport organization operating within the same sector of the industry. Take, for example, the situation of Reebok and Nike in the early 1980s. Reebok's senior managers, watching the aerobics boom, saw a rapidly changing environment for the athletic footwear industry. Nike's managers, however, did not perceive the aerobics boom as any sort of enduring change in their environment; they did not respond immediately to this opportunity and as a result their market share declined. The point here is that, while the actual environment affects the sport organization, it is the perceived environment to which managers respond. As Starbuck (1976) suggests, based on managerial perceptions organizations select those aspects of their environment to which they are going to respond.

Research on Organizational Environments

Many research studies that have contributed to our understanding of organizational environments can be applied to organizations in the sport industry.

Here we focus on three of the most important of these contributions: the work of Burns and Stalker, Lawrence and Lorsch, and Duncan.

Burns and Stalker

Burns and Stalker's (1961) study of 20 British manufacturing firms was the first research to try to identify what types of organizational structures and managerial processes were most appropriate under different types of environmental conditions. Burns and Stalker examined changes in scientific technology and product markets—changes in the organization's task environment. Their research identified two types of structure and managerial practice, each occurring under different environmental conditions. These were labeled organic and mechanistic. Mechanistic structures work best in stable environments; organic structures work best in rapidly changing environments. In the sports industry we would expect to find mechanistic structures in companies like Victoriaville, producers of hockey sticks, and in government agencies such as the Saskatchewan Department of Parks, Recreation, and Culture or the Manitoba Sports Directorate. These sport organizations have relatively stable environments and hence use designs such as the machine bureaucracy. These structures are what Burns and Stalker refer to as mechanistic. In contrast, organic structures are more like Mintzberg's professional bureaucracies or adhocracies, and are found in rapidly changing environments. The structure used by NBC to televise the Olympic Games (see chapter 4) was an organic structure. We would also find organic structures in sport physiology research labs, and where short-term groups are formed to stage a particular sporting event such as a basketball tournament or a road race. Table 7.1 shows the environmental, structural, and managerial characteristics associated with mechanistic and organic sport organizations.

In the most effective sport organizations there is "a fit" between the demands of the environment and the type of structure and managerial practice employed. Burns and Stalker recognized that organic and mechanistic structures are ideal types representing the ends of a continuum. Few if any sport organizations would be purely mechanistic or purely organic; rather, the majority show varying characteristics of each type. Burns and Stalker also did not see one type of structure as superior to the other; the environmental conditions determined which was the most appropriate.

Lawrence and Lorsch

Extending the work of Burns and Stalker (1961), Lawrence and Lorsch (1967) examined companies in three industries—plastics, packaged food, and standardized containers—that were seen as having considerably different degrees of environmental diversity and uncertainty. The plastics industry was chosen because its environment was uncertain and characterized by rapid changes in technology and customer needs. In contrast, the environment of the container industry was seen as stable and predictable; growth was steady and product innovation was low. The environment of organizations in the food industry was seen as somewhere in between plastics and containers.

Essentially, Lawrence and Lorsch (1967) argued that the more complex and uncertain an organization's task environment, the more differentiated the organization would have to be to handle the uncertainty, that is, the more subunits there would be, each dealing with a particular aspect of the environment. However, to meet the demands of their environment successfully, each subunit would require specialists with different attitudes and with different behaviors to meet their particular subunit's goals. As a result, "differentiation" referred not only to the existence of structural differences in functionally specialized subunits within the organization, but also to "differences in ways of thinking and working that develop among managers in these . . . units" (Lawrence and Lorsch, 1967, p. 9). These differences manifest themselves in variations in managerial goals, time orientation, and interpersonal orientation among the subunits. For example, applying Lawrence and Lorsch's ideas to an athletic footwear company, the goals of managers in the sales department would be different from those of production managers: Sales would be concerned with increasing volume and customer satisfaction; production managers would be concerned with reducing manufacturing costs and time. Similarly, production managers would more likely be concerned with the immediate problems of production, whereas the time orientation of the designers in the research-and-development department would focus on longer-term issues. Table 7.2 shows the type of variation that Lawrence and Lorsch found in the production, research-and-development, and sales departments of the organizations in their study. The greater this variation among the different organizational subunits, the more complex the organization and thus the greater need for integration through such mechanisms as rules and regulations, policies, and plans.

Table 7.1   Comparison of Mechanistic and Organic Systems of Organization

MECHANISTIC	ORGANIC
1. Tasks are highly fractionated and specialized; little regard paid to clarifying relationship between tasks and organizational objectives.	1. Tasks are more independent; emphasis on relevance of tasks and organizational objectives.
2. Tasks tend to remain rigidly defined unless altered formally by top management.	2. Tasks are continually adjusted and redefined through interaction of organizational members.
3. Specific role definition (rights, obligations, and technical methods prescribed for each member).	3. Generalized role definition (members accept general responsibility for task accomplishment beyond individual role definition).
4. Hierarchic structure of control, authority, and communication; sanctions derive from employment contract between employee and organization.	4. Network structure of control, authority, and communication; sanctions derive more from community of interest than from contractual relationship.
5. Information relevant to situation and operations of the organization formally assumed to rest with chief executive.	5. Leader not assumed to be omniscient; knowledge centers identified were located throughout organization.
6. Communication is primarily vertical between superior and subordinate.	6. Communication is both vertical and horizontal depending upon where needed information resides.
7. Communications primarily take form of instructions and decisions issued by superiors, information and requests for decisions supplied by inferiors.	7. Communications primarily take form of information and advice.
8. Insistence on loyalty to organization and obedience to superiors.	8. Commitment to organization's tasks and goals more highly valued than loyalty or obedience.
9. Importance and prestige attached to identification with organization and its members.	9. Importance and prestige attached to affiliations and expertise in external environment.

Reprinted, by permission, from R. Steers, 1977, *Organizational effectiveness: A behavioral view* (Santa Monica, CA: Goodyear Publishing Company).

Table 7.2   Differences in Formality of Structure and Orientation Between Departments

CHARACTERISTIC	PRODUCTION	RESEARCH AND DEVELOPMENT	SALES
Formality of structure	High	Low	Medium/high
Goal orientation	Cost reduction Process efficiency	Development of new knowledge Technological improvements	Customer problems Competitive activities
Time orientation	Short	Long	Short
Interpersonal orientation	Task oriented	Varied depending on type of research	Social oriented

Based on Lawrence, P.R., and Lorsch, J.W. (1967). *Organization and Environment*, Boston, Graduate School of Business Administration, pp. 30-39.

Lawrence and Lorsch's work was different from previous studies because they did not see the organization's environment as a unitary entity. They suggested that there were *parts* to the environment, just like there were parts (departments or other similar subunits) to an organization. Essentially, they believed that the ways different departments of an organization varied would reflect the variation in the subenvironment with which they interacted. Consequently, if the external environment of an organization was complex and diverse (i.e., there were a lot of parts to deal with), to be effective the internal structure of the organization would also have to be highly differentiated, leading in turn to the need for sophisticated integration mechanisms to coordinate the differentiated subunits. If an organization's environment was simple and stable, it would be less differentiated and consequently require fewer integrating mechanisms.

To test their ideas Lawrence and Lorsch (1967) identified three organizational subenvironments: technoeconomic, market, and scientific. These subenvironments corresponded to the production, sales, and research-and-development functions of the organization. Focusing on these areas, Lawrence and Lorsch (1967) found that the production, sales, and research-and-development subunits showed higher levels of differentiation in those organizations that had the most diverse and uncertain environments. That is, those organizations in the plastics industry were the most differentiated, followed by organizations in the food industry, and finally those in the container industry.

However, not only did Lawrence and Lorsch look at levels of differentiation, but they also looked at a number of effectiveness criteria and the use of integration mechanisms in these organizations. They found that, with one exception, the most effective organizations had a higher level of integration. It was not enough for an organization simply to have an appropriate level of internal differentiation to deal with the diversity and complexity of its environment; it also had to have the necessary integrating mechanisms if it was to ensure optimal performance.

What lessons, then, can the sport manager learn from Lawrence and Lorsch's (1967) work? First, it is important to understand that sport organizations, like other organizations, have a number of parts to their environment, each of which presents a varying level of uncertainty. For example, a collegiate football organization has as part of its environment the local and national media. While there may be a number of media organizations with which the football program has to interact, there is a level of certainty about this aspect of the environment. The number of media organizations covering the team will not usually change rapidly from one year to the next and their demands are fairly consistent— they want information on players, coaches, future opponents, and so on. This subenvironment, because of its relative stability, can probably be handled by one or two people. On the other hand, in addition to the media, a college football organization also has as a part of its environment a number of high school football programs, a source of input in that they provide the players for the college program. Because the football program is likely to deal with far more high schools than media agencies, and because there is a higher level of uncertainty here ("blue chip" players come from different programs each year and are also recruited by other colleges), there is more diversity and uncertainty within this subenvironment, and a higher level of differentiation within the organization is needed to deal with it. That is in general why the football organization will have more staff to deal with high school liaisons, scouting, and recruiting than it will have to deal with the media. This illustration highlights the second lesson sport managers can learn from Lawrence and Lorsch's work: A sport organization must have an appropriate level of internal differentiation to meet the demands of its various subenvironments.

However, a third point which Lawrence and Lorsch's work should alert sport managers to is that it is not enough merely to have appropriately differentiated subunits to deal with its subenvironments. Because different managerial goals, time orientations, and interpersonal orientations exist in these subunits, there must also be the necessary level of *integration* to ensure that these subunits are working toward a common goal. More complex sport organizations (those in the more diverse and uncertain environments) will accomplish integration through formal means such as policies, cross-functional teams, and systematic planning. In sport organizations operating in simpler environments, integration will be accomplished through more informal mechanisms such as direct supervision by managers.

Duncan

Concerned, like Lawrence and Lorsch, about environmental uncertainty and its impact on organizations, Duncan (1972) saw that the uncertainty of an organization's environment was influenced by two factors: the extent to which the environment was simple or complex, and the extent to which it was stable or dynamic (cf. also Dess & Beard, 1984; Tung, 1979).

The complexity of a sport organization's environment is determined by the number and heterogeneity of external elements influencing the organization's operations. A complex environment is characterized by a large number of diverse elements interacting with or influencing the sport organization. In contrast, a simple environment has only a small number of elements, which are for the most part relatively homogeneous, influencing the organization. The Toronto Raptors, the U.S. Olympic Committee, the athletic department at Ohio State

University, and SMG, a facility management group based in Philadelphia, all have complex environments. For example, a sport organization like the Raptors must deal with dozens of external elements: the media agencies that cover games, the NBA, the players' union, individual player's agents, companies that merchandise the team's logo, food and beverage companies that supply the concessions, equipment manufacturers, the airline companies that transport the team, and the hotels where the team stays while on the road. In contrast, a small sporting goods store, a local bowling alley, and a recreational soccer team all have, for the most part, a relatively simple environment. They do not interact with a large number of external elements and those they do interact with will be quite similar.

The extent to which a sport organization's environment is stable or dynamic refers to the amount of change in those elements constituting its environment. If a sport organization "faces a regular set of demands from the same environment, such as producing the same product or the same service for the same or very similar clients, the organization faces stable conditions" (Litterer, 1973, pp. 335-336). A faculty of kinesiology, a publicly owned golf course, and a state high school athletic association, for example, all face relatively stable environments. That is, they face very similar demands on a year-to-year basis and provide the same service to similar client groups. Dynamic environments, on the other hand, are characterized by rapid change, caused by any number of factors, such as competitors' developing a new product line, increased imports, or a declining market. Athletic footwear companies, such as L.A. Gear, and athletic clothing manufacturers, such as Body Glove and Speedo, all operate in dynamic environments, constantly facing new demands because they continually have to come up with product innovations and try to capture new market segments.

Duncan (1972) used the simple/complex, stable/dynamic dimensions to construct a 2 × 2 matrix as shown in figure 7.2. Each of the cells in the matrix represents a different level of environmental uncertainty. Sport organizations in cell 1, showing the lowest levels of uncertainty, have few elements in their environment, which basically remain the same over time. In contrast, sport organizations in cell 4 have to deal with a large number of highly unpredictable environmental elements.

The degree of uncertainty facing a sport organization strongly influences its structure and processes. We now discuss the ways sport managers can control the environmental uncertainty facing their organizations.

Controlling Environmental Uncertainty

All sport organizations face some degree of environmental uncertainty. As Daft (1992, p. 79) points out, "environmental uncertainty represents an important contingency for organizational structure and behaviors." To control these uncertainties, sport organizations can either respond to the demands of their external environment (by making changes to their internal structure, processes, and behaviors) or they can attempt to change the nature of the external environment. We look now at some of the techniques sport organizations commonly use to respond to environmental pressure, focusing first on internal changes and then on actions that are externally directed. It is important to note that internal and external initiatives are not mutually exclusive; often several different actions are used at one time. Some techniques are, however, more appropriate to production companies, others to service organizations.

Internally Directed Actions

A sport organization can take internally directed actions to control environmental uncertainty by making changes to the structure and processes of the organization. Details of some of the more popular actions employed by sport organizations are outlined below.

Buffering

The idea of buffering emanates from the work of J.D. Thompson (1967). The term essentially refers to attempts to protect the technical core, that part of the organization primarily responsible for production, from fluctuations in the environment. Buffering can occur on the input side by stockpiling raw materials and supplies so the organization is not affected by sudden market shortages, and on the output side by warehousing sufficient amounts of its product to allow its distribution department to meet unexpected increases in demand. Maintenance departments help buffer the technical core by ensuring that machinery is regularly serviced; personnel departments do it by ensuring the required amount of trained labor is available. Some

		Complexity of environment	
		Simple	Complex
Amount of change in the environment	Stable	Low perceived uncertainty. Small number of factors and components in the environment. Factors and components are somewhat similar to one another. Factors and components remain basically the same and are not changing. *Example:* A local sporting goods store	Moderately low perceived uncertainty. Large number of factors and components in the environment. Factors and components remain basically the same. Factors and components are not similar to one another. *Example:* A faculty of physical and health education
	Dynamic	Moderately high perceived uncertainty. Small number of factors and components in the environment. Factors and components are somewhat similar to one another. Factors and components of the environment are in a continual process of change. *Example:* A producer of athletic footwear	High perceived uncertainty. Large number of factors and components in the environment. Factors and components are not similar to one another. Factors and components of the environment are in a continual process of change. *Example:* The organizing committee of a major sport festival such as the Olympic Games

Figure 7.2   Characteristics of environmental states.
Adapted from "Characteristics of perceived environments and perceived environmental uncertainty" by R.B. Duncan published in *Administrative Science Quarterly*, volume 17, no. 3 by permission of *Administrative Science Quarterly*.

buffering activities, such as stockpiling raw materials and warehousing inventory, involve tying up large amounts of capital and may not be cost effective for some smaller sport organizations. Also, these techniques are not applicable to service-oriented sport organizations, since services cannot be kept in warehouses for use when needed. Buffering may occur, however, in service-orientated sport organizations, through ensuring the ready availability of trained personnel to provide appropriate services when needed.

Boundary Spanners

Boundary spanners are established to obtain information about environmental changes that can affect a sport organization, and to disseminate favorable information about the organization to other agencies in its environment (cf. Aldrich & Herker, 1977; Jemison, 1984; Tushman & Scanlan, 1981a; Tushman & Scanlan, 1981b). Boundary spanners can be thought of as links between the sport organization and its environment. The more diverse the environment, the more boundary-spanning roles or units the sport organization is likely to have. Public relations, sales, market research, advertising, and personnel departments can all serve a boundary-spanning role. Staff in these departments scan the environment for information important to the company (cf. Lenz & Engledow, 1986)

In the mid-1980s, when walking was becoming a popular fitness activity for people of many ages, the market research departments of a number of athletic footwear companies saw a potential demand

Meeting the Demands of the Athletic Footwear Market

When the athletic footwear business started to boom, industry leader Reebok could not make shoes fast enough. Over a three-year period sales jumped from $13 million to $60 million to $308 million. Orders were being shipped from six separate warehouses within a 30-mile radius of each other. Basketball shoes went from one warehouse, tennis shoes from another, and running shoes from yet another. "Each order was shipped from a different location, at a different time, all on separate bills," said Peter McQuaid, Reebok's maintenance engineering manager. "The customer was lucky if he got all of the parts of his order within three months of each order. . . . Often a customer received a backorder notice, not because we didn't have the product, but because we just could not find it."

To reduce its problems Reebok acquired a new 308,000 square-feet facility and consolidated its distribution. The new facility used bar codes and computers to help with shipping and billing. As a result, fluctuations in customer demand were more easily handled and environmental uncertainty was reduced.

Based on information in Witt, C.E. (1989, March). Reebok's distribution on fast track. *Material Handling Engineering*, pp. 43-45, 48; Better customer service justifies new center (1989, March). *Modern Material Handling*, pp. 14-15.

for walking shoes. As a result, Nike, Converse, and Reebok all entered the walking-shoe market. By scanning their environment the market research units of these companies, acting as boundary spanners, were able to keep management informed about important new trends.

Smoothing

Smoothing is very much like buffering but it takes place only on the demand side of an organization. Smoothing attempts to reduce fluctuations in the demand for a product or service (Thompson, 1967). Sport managers who operate a facility such as a swimming pool or a hockey rink often offer lower rental or admission prices at off-peak times to encourage people to use their facilities at these times. Another example of smoothing, from Berrett et al.'s (1993) study of entrepreneurs, involves the managers of two retail sporting goods stores, primarily retailers of hockey equipment. They found that, not surprisingly, their sales dropped off in the summer months. Consequently, they expanded their product line to include summer sports equipment, to help reduce seasonal fluctuations in the amount of product they were able to sell.

Rationing

If buffering, boundary spanning, or smoothing does not work, a sport organization can try rationing, the practice of allocating resources on the basis of some preestablished criteria. Doctors at a university sport medicine clinic, for example, may ration their services by establishing a priority system for non-varsity athletes. In a similar vein, many university sport studies departments ration certain classes by only allowing enrollment to students with necessary prerequisites, or only accepting those from certain faculties. Rationing, however, as Thompson (1967) notes, is not only limited to service organizations; when supplies are scarce many manufacturers ration allotments of their product to wholesalers or dealers. Rationing in any form is, nevertheless, an unsatisfactory technique because, while this practice may protect the technical core of the sport organization, there are customers in the task environment whose needs are not being met—a problem resulting in lost revenue and the customers' loss of faith in the organization.

Planning and Forecasting

All organizations, including those in the sport industry, control environmental uncertainties by developing plans and attempting to forecast future trends (Boulton, Franklin, Lindsay, & Rue, 1982). The more turbulent the sport organization's environment, the more difficult planning and forecasting become, but the more important it is for sport organizations to engage in these activities to identify future directions. Slack,

Bentz, and Wood (1985) describe a planning process that can be used by amateur sport organizations, and Macintosh and Whitson (1990) discuss some of the problems of the rational planning program in which all Canadian sport organizations were required to participate in preparation for the 1988 Olympic Games. Slack, Berrett, and Mistry (1994) also show that, in some cases, planning can actually bring about conflict in a sport organization.

Forecasting is related to planning and involves trying to predict future environmental trends. There are a variety of forecasting techniques, such as surveys, decision-tree analysis, and stochastic modeling. Matthew Levine, president of the Levine Management Group, a San Francisco-based sport and entertainment marketing firm, used in-depth fan surveys (one forecasting technique) to help the Golden State Warrior's organization increase attendance ("Improving your marketing game," 1987).

Externally Directed Actions

To obtain resources from other organizations, gain legitimacy, and sell its product or service, a sport organization must depend on certain elements within its general environment. This dependence creates uncertainty for the sport organization. To reduce this uncertainty an organization can use a number of techniques; the most common are outlined below.

Contractual Agreements

Sport organizations can reduce environmental uncertainty by entering into long-term contractual agreements with firms that supply their input, or those involved with the distribution and sale of their outputs. These contracts come in two forms. The first type involves one organization contracting to sell its product to another. For example, in 1984, when L.L. Bean was concerned about falling sales and losing its image as a sporting goods dealer, it entered into a contract with Cannondale, which agreed to supply it with private-label bikes (Charm, 1986; Skow, 1985).

A second form of contractual relationship, termed a licensing agreement, involves one organization buying the rights to use an asset owned by another organization. The most common form of licensing agreement found in the sport industry involves a company buying the right to use a logo, such as the Olympic rings or a professional sport team's emblem, on its product. As figure 7.3 shows, retail sales of licensed sport merchandise have risen considerably over the last five years as a result of this type of contractual agreement. The benefits of contracts and licensing agreements are that they reduce environmental uncertainty for a sport organization because they establish formalized links between

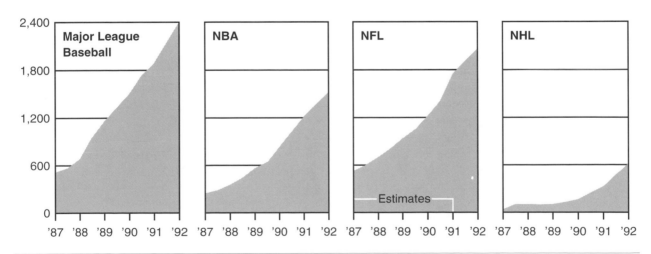

Beyond Baseball Caps
Retail sales of licensed sports merchandise
(Millions of dollars)
Data: Major League Baseball, NBA, NFL, NHL, *Sporting Goods Dealer*

Figure 7.3 Licensing agreements help boost retail sales of licensed sport merchandise.
Reprinted, by permission, from E. Lesley, November 30, 1992, What's next, Raider's deodorant?, *Business Week*, 65.

suppliers and their customers. These links serve as a protection against any change in the relationship between the two organizations for a specified time period.

Joint Ventures

By entering into a joint venture (two or more companies forming a separate corporate entity), the organizations involved can achieve objectives they could not attain on their own. For example, a joint venture might be used by a sport equipment manufacturer wanting to do business in a foreign country. By getting involved with a distributor in that country the manufacturer is more easily able to deal with local regulations and modes of operation. Thus environmental uncertainty is reduced.

Co-Optation

Co-optation occurs when a sport organization recruits influential people from important parts of its environment to be involved in the organization. Macintosh and Whitson (1990), for example, note how many national sport organizations in Canada have co-opted onto their boards people with busi-

ness backgrounds so they could "open corporate doors" and thus increase the sport organizations' chances of acquiring sponsorships.

Interlocking Directorates

An interlocking directorate involves an individual from one company sitting on the board of directors of another. The interlock allows the individual to act as a communication channel between the two companies and to essentially represent one company on the other's board. Such representation means that policy and financial decisions can be influenced. Gruneau (1983) provides evidence of these types of links occurring between Canadian professional sport teams and organizations in both the television and food and beverage industries. Mizruchi and Stearns (1988) suggest that such interlocks are more likely when companies are facing financial uncertainty. Certainly links between professional sport teams and television companies can help ensure that the team has a better chance of securing a television contract, and thus greater financial stability and less environmental uncertainty. Stern (1979) also provides evidence of the utility of

TIME OUT

Joint Venturing: The Medical Fitness Center

The Los Angeles Athletic Club was already established as an elite sports and fitness club in the middle of downtown, but it was finding difficulty in reaching the potentially lucrative market for executive physicals and fitness evaluations. A solution was found in a joint venture partnership with the California Hospital Medical Center to cofinance and operate the Medical Fitness Center, which functions independently of its parent organizations. The combination of a top-flight athletic club and a well-respected medical institution seemed to appeal to both parties as a natural draw for corporate executives in the downtown area.

"The relationship has worked very well," says David L. Geyer, marketing director of the Athletic Club and executive director of the Fitness Center. "We're very blessed to have the partner we do, a respected medical institution with a strong marketing orientation." The Medical Fitness Center venture came together fairly easily, says Geyer, because the corporate presidents—Charles Hathaway of the Athletic Club and Richard Norling of the Medical Center—served together on the Central City Association, a coalition of downtown business people. Still, says Geyer, the real key to a successful relationship is not how well the partners know each other but how they complement each other's needs. "What someone entering a relationship like this needs to think about is not who would be the best psychological partner for me, but who would be the most attractive to the market I'm interested in."

Reprinted by permission, copyright 1986, *Athletic Business* magazine.

interorganizational linkages in understanding the evolution of the NCAA.

Executive Recruitment

Several studies have examined the effect that replacing a coach or manager has on a professional sport team's performance (cf. Allen, Panian, & Lotz, 1979; Brown, 1982; Eitzen & Yetman, 1972; Gamson & Scotch, 1964; Grusky, 1963; Pfeffer & Davis-Blake, 1986). Although the general idea behind recruiting a new executive into the senior ranks of a sport organization is that the individual brings new contacts and ideas that can reduce environmental uncertainty and improve performance, the actual results of these studies yield mixed results. Essentially, one theory suggests that the recruitment of a new executive can improve performance, a second suggests it disrupts performance, and a third maintains that it has no effect (Allen, Panian, & Lotz, 1979). Despite these mixed findings, professional sport organizations in particular, and sport organizations in general, still continue to use executive recruitment as one means of controlling environmental uncertainty.

Public Relations and Advertising

Sport organizations try to influence key individuals and organizations through public relations programs and advertising. Such programs are especially important in highly competitive markets and in industrial sectors where there is variation in the demand for product. The athletic footwear industry is a case in point: Reebok's decision to underwrite Amnesty International's Human Rights Now concert tour in 1988 is an example of the type of public relations program that both enhanced the company's image and helped it sell shoes. As Graham (1988) points out, the program helped Reebok deal with its competition, because the publicity surrounding the tour helped upstage rival Nike's "Just Do It" campaign.

Mergers and Acquisitions

If a sport organization is unable to reduce environmental uncertainty by techniques such as contractual agreements, establishing interlocking directorates, and developing public relations programs, it may choose to purchase controlling interest in an organization or acquire ownership. While, as we outlined in chapter 5, mergers and acquisitions can be a type of growth strategy, they can also be a means of reducing environmental uncertainty by helping the sport organization obtain control over necessary resources or counteract competition. Reebok's purchase of Avia (See Time Out p. 96) is an example of the latter tactic (see also Sedgwick, 1989).

Changing Domains

Sport organizations, through their senior managers or owners, select the domain in which they wish to operate. Many factors, such as government regulations, a highly competitive market place, the increasing cost of supplies, or a declining consumer demand, can create enough uncertainty for a sport organization that it may choose to change or modify its domain. Acquiring new businesses or divesting parts of its existing business are the most frequent ways a sport organization will change its domain; another way is by adding new products or services. For example, Herman's World of Sporting Goods, a chain of sporting goods stores, expanded its offering in the area of water sports in the 1980s. H. George Walker, a vice president of the company, noted that "the water sport category is growing. More people do things at the water. No matter where you are, you find a river, a lake, or a pond. We've expanded the line to give it better presence" (Adams, 1987, p. 28). While Herman's and other sporting goods stores were moving into the water sports domain, the increased competition led to some mass merchandisers divesting themselves of any involvement in this area and focusing on their more traditional markets (Adams, 1987).

Trade and Professional Associations

Some sport organizations will attempt to influence their environment by joining together to form trade or professional associations. By acting collectively these associations can influence environmental issues such as government policy issues or trade regulations. The British organization ILAM (the Institute of Leisure and Amenity Managers) is an example of this type of organization; its objectives include "to act as an effective lobby whenever proposed legislation is likely to affect the industry" and "to offer advisory services in careers and technical matters" (Elvin, 1990, pp. 59-60). Examples of similar associations operating in North America include the American Society of Golf Course Architects, the International Association of Auditorium Managers, the National Sporting Goods

Association, and the United Ski Industries Association. All have either a direct or indirect mandate to work to control environmental uncertainty for their members.

Political Lobbying

Many sport organizations lobby various levels of government in order to influence decisions about issues such as tax regulations, grant programs, and labor questions. The lobbying may occur through a trade or professional association such as those discussed above, or a sport organization may engage in lobbying or other forms of political activity on its own behalf. Macintosh, Bedecki, and Franks (1987) illustrate how a number of Canadian sport organizations, such as the Canadian Sports Advisory Council, CAHPER (the Canadian Association for Health, Physical Education and Recreation), and the Sports Federation of Canada, have lobbied the Canadian government at different times in order to seek support in reaching program objectives. Reich (1986) provides many examples of the political activity that took place to ensure the smooth operation of the 1984 Los Angeles Olympics.

Illegal Activities

In some cases sport organizations will engage in unethical or illegal activities in order to control environmental uncertainty. These activities may include price fixing, monopoly, franchise violation, and illegal mergers and acquisitions (Staw & Szwajkowski, 1975). Also particularly relevant for university sport organizations are recruiting violations, which are becoming almost commonplace in U.S. collegiate athletics. By engaging in illegal recruiting activity the sport team is able to secure the services of a top-quality player; the team performs better, gate receipts go up, and alumni giving and television coverage increase. The net effect of these changes is that the level of environmental uncertainty facing the team is reduced.

Other Perspectives on the Organization-Environment Relationship

In addition to the work of researchers like Burns and Stalker, Lawrence and Lorsch, and Duncan, there are other ways of examining the relationship between a sport organization and its environment. Here we look briefly at the approaches of institutional theory, the resource dependence perspective, and population ecology.

Institutional Theory

The utility of institutional approaches to understanding the organization-environment relationship was first articulated by John Meyer and Brian Rowan in their 1977 article "Institutionalized organizations: Formal structure as myth and ceremony." Following Meyer and Rowan's article a number of researchers have examined the impact of the institutional environment on an organization's structure (cf. DiMaggio & Powell, 1983; Oliver, 1988, 1991; Tolbert, 1985; Tolbert & Zucker, 1983; Zucker, 1983, 1987). The institutional environment of an organization "is conceptualized in terms of understandings and expectations of appropriate organizational form and behavior that are shared by members of society" (Tolbert, 1985, p. 1). By changing its structure to conform to the expectations of the institutional environment, "an organization demonstrates that it is acting on a collectively valued purpose in a proper and adequate manner" (Meyer & Rowan, 1977, p. 349). This conformity helps to establish the organization as a legitimate entity and in turn to ensure its long-term effectiveness.

Organizations subjected to the same institutional pressures exhibit isomorphism, that is, they tend to become structurally alike. Slack and Hinings (1994), in the only work on sport organizations to employ an institutional perspective, show how the environmental pressures that Sport Canada placed on national sport organizations brought about increases in the structural homogeneity of these organizations, as institutional pressures moved them to a more professional and bureaucratic type of organizational design.

Resource Dependence

No sport organization exists in isolation from the other organizations in its environment, the source of the material and financial resources a sport organization needs to survive. To obtain these resources a sport organization engages in transactions with the appropriate organizations in its environment. Pfeffer and Salancik (1978), in their book *The external control of organizations: A resource-dependence perspective*, discuss the nature of these transactions.

They focus specifically on the ways organizations depend on their environment for resources, the resulting uncertainty, and the techniques managers use to reduce this uncertainty.

When a sport organization engages in a resource transaction with another organization, it reduces its vulnerability to environmental fluctuations, but at the same time increases its dependence on the organization supplying the resource, thus reducing its own autonomy and ability to act independently. The extent to which a sport organization depends on another organization for resources is determined by three factors: (1) the importance of the resource (i.e., the extent to which the sport organization requires the resource for its continued operation and survival), (2) the extent to which the organization providing the resource has discretion over its allocation and use, and (3) the extent to which there are alternative sources from which the dependent organization can obtain the resource. Slack and Hinings (1992) have shown how national sport organizations in Canada are dependent for their financial resources on the federal government, and how this dependence has allowed the government to control many of the actions of these organizations, in particular the emphasis they were required to place on high-performance sport.

However, while the organization supplying the resource can wield considerable control over the dependent organization, it is not the dependence per se that creates problems but the uncertainty surrounding the availability of resources. Pfeffer and Salancik (1978, p. 3) explain:

> The fact that organizations are dependent for survival and success on their environments does not, in itself, make their existence problematic. If stable supplies were assured from the sources of needed resources, there would be no problem. If the resources needed by the organization were continually available, even if outside their control, there would be no problem. Problems arise not merely because organizations are dependent on their environment, but because this environment is not dependable. Environments can change, new organizations enter and exit, and the supply of resources becomes more or less scarce. When environments change, organizations face the prospect of either not surviving or of changing their activities in response to these environmental factors.

In order to control the uncertainties created by resource supplies, dependent organizations attempt to "enact" their environment. That is, managers use techniques such as interlocking directorates, joint ventures, and executive succession to reduce the uncertainty surrounding their supply of resources. The resource-dependence perspective has considerable potential for understanding the impact of the environment on the structure and processes of different types of sport organizations, yet there has been virtually no published work in sport management employing this theoretical perspective.

Population Ecology

Originating with the work of Michael Hannan and John Freeman (1977b), the population ecology, or natural selection, approach to organization-environment relations is heavily influenced by the biological literature, in particular the notion of the survival of the fittest (cf. Ulrich, 1987a; Ulrich & Barney, 1984; Wholey & Brittain, 1986). The idea is that organizations, like living things, survive if they are able to exploit their environment for resources. Those that are unable to do so adequately, perish. Unlike other environmental approaches, the focus of population ecology is not on individual organizations but on populations of organizations; a population ecologist would not focus on individual sporting goods stores but on the population of these types of stores which exists in a particular community, for example, the state of California.

Researchers who adopt this theoretical position look closely at the birth and death rates of particular types of organizations. New organizations attempt to establish a niche for themselves, that is, an area of the market where they can obtain the resources necessary to survive. The idea is that, like living creatures, organizations must make use of the resources in their niche. If the niche is narrow, a specialist organization such as Peconic Paddler, a canoe rental and sales organization, is most likely to survive. If the niche is wider, a generalist organization is more likely. For example, narrow niches are represented by competitive cyclists' support of custom bike manufacturers such as Terry Precision Bikes for Women, whereas broad-based recreational cyclists who require a wider range of goods and services support the more general cycle manufacturers such as Huffy. Specialists are often more efficient than generalists but, because of their specialization, are more likely to suffer if the environment changes. Generalists, on the other hand, are buffered from environmental changes by the breadth of their operations. If an organization cannot locate itself in a niche, it will ultimately perish.

Each niche has a certain carrying capacity. Just as a forest can only support so many deer or similar animals, so a community can only support so many sports equipment stores or aerobics studios. The competition among these similar organizations for the limited resources means that some will be successful but others will fail (Aldrich, McKelvey, & Ulrich, 1984). In the language of population ecology, they will be selected out, just like weak animals are destined to perish. As well as niches, population ecologists are also interested in the concept of population density (Hannan & Freeman, 1988): The extent to which the population of organizations within a niche is able to exploit the resources available.

By using concepts like niche width, carrying capacity, and population density, scholars using the population ecology approach have been able to study the possibilities of success for new organizations entering a specific market, and why entry into the niche becomes less attractive as the number of organizations in a niche grows (i.e., as population density increases). They have also been able to show how organizations pursuing "a leader strategy" (Miles and Snow's Prospectors) may be successful if they are the first to establish themselves in a niche, but how, as population density increases, organizations pursuing "a follow-the-leader strategy," (Miles and Snow's Analyzers) are likely to be more successful. These findings have had a significant impact on our understanding of the way organizations operate.

Despite its utility in helping us understand many issues about organization-environment relation, population ecology has a number of limitations (cf. Hawley, 1981). First, it is highly deterministic, in that the environment is seen as the sole factor determining organizational effectiveness. Second (and related to the first limitation), population ecology takes no account of managerial action. For example, population ecologists believe that if you are the owner/manager of an aerobics studio and interest in aerobics as a form of exercise booms, then you will be successful, but if interest wanes then you will not survive, regardless of what action you take; the environment has determined success or failure, not the manager. A third limitation of population ecology is that survival is the only measure

of organizational effectiveness. If an organization survives, it is effective; if it perishes, it is not effective. Fourth, population ecology is not well suited to the study of certain types of sport organizations, because agencies like the U.S. Olympic Committee, the Amateur Athletic Association, and Alberta Basketball Association are unlikely to be put out of existence; no other organization can challenge what they do because they operate under monopoly conditions. Finally, population ecologists look at changes in organizational populations over relatively long periods of time. Short-term changes are seen as aberrations, which are inconsequential to understanding change in any significant way.

Notwithstanding its limitations, the population ecology approach has considerable potential to increase our understanding of the structure and processes of sport organizations. However, to date no work within the field of sport management has employed the theoretical ideas contained within this approach. Given the significant body of literature on population ecology in the broader field of management, there is considerable potential to apply these ideas to sport organizations.

The Relationship Between an Organization's Environment and Its Structure

As we have seen, all sport organizations are to some extent dependent on their environment. The more dependent an organization is on its environment the more vulnerable it is to changes in the environment. Here we look briefly at the effect of the environment on the structural attributes of complexity, formalization, and centralization.

Environmental Conditions and Complexity

Under conditions of environmental uncertainty, a successful sport organization will exhibit a relatively high level of complexity. To respond to uncertainty, the organization has "to employ specialist staff in boundary or interface roles—in positions where they form a link with the outside world, securing and evaluating relevant information" (Child, 1984, p. 219). Consequently, an uncertain environment will require an increase in both the number of departments and in the specialist personnel required to buffer the sport organization from environmental fluctuation. Also, there may be an increase in the level of vertical differentiation within an organization (thus increasing complexity) because, under conditions of environmental uncertainty, there is a need to delegate decision making to people who understand the local conditions and can make quick decisions.

Environmental Conditions and Formalization

The increased levels of organizational complexity found under conditions of environmental uncertainty require an appropriate means of integration. Successful organizations are more likely to use "flexible rather than highly formalized or hierarchical methods of coordination and information sharing..." (Child, 1984, p. 219), including face-to-face communication, the use of project teams, and the appointment of staff to liaison and negotiating roles. Under stable environmental conditions, sport organizations will tend to adopt formalized operating procedures; there is little need for rapid changes within the organization, so it can capitalize on the economies that result from the use of these formalized procedures.

Environmental Conditions and Centralization

Mintzberg (1979, p. 273) suggests that the more complex an organization's environment, "the more decentralized the structure." The complexity of the environment means that one person can't comprehend all the information needed to make appropriate decisions; consequently, the decisions are decentralized to specialists who make the decisions concerning the particular aspect of the environment for which they are responsible. There is, however, evidence (cf. Mintzberg, 1979) to suggest that under conditions of extreme hostility in the environment (i.e., a threat to an organization such as the advent of a new competitor), an organization will move to centralize its structure temporarily. While this temporary centralization may pose a dilemma for those organizations that operate in complex environments, given the choice the senior managers tend to opt for a centralized structure where everyone knows who is in control and decisions can be made quickly.

Summary and Conclusions

The environment, a source of uncertainty for the organization, has a major impact on the structure and processes of a sport organization. Managers must attempt to eliminate or minimize the impact of this uncertainty. While the environment can be broadly conceptualized as anything outside the organization, people managing sport organizations have to be concerned with those sectors of the general environment that can influence their operations and their organization's task environment. The task environment is composed of groups such as customers, suppliers, competitors, and related regulatory agencies. Also important for our understanding of the sport organization-environment relationship are domain, the area to which the sport organization directs its products or services, and the perceived environment, the manager's perception of the environment, which may be different from the actual environment.

We looked at three of the classic studies on the organization-environment relationship and what they mean for the managers of sport organizations. Burns and Stalker's work suggests that under conditions of environmental uncertainty an organic type of structure is most effective; when the environment is stable a more mechanistic type of structure works best. Lawrence and Lorsch conceptualized an organization's environment as made up of various subenvironments. Organizational subunits are required to meet the demands of these subenvironments if the organization is to be successful. Duncan saw environmental uncertainty as influenced by the complexity of the environment and the extent to which elements within the environment are stable or dynamic. To control environmental uncertainty the managers of sport organizations can use a number of techniques, some involving changes to the organization's internal structure and processes, others are directed toward changing the external environment.

We also looked at three of the more recent approaches to understanding the organization-environment relationship: resource dependence theory, institutional theory, and population ecology. The latter two in particular have generated a considerable amount of literature which has contributed considerably to our understanding of the organization-environment relationship.

Key Concepts

General environment	Task environment
Sectors	Domain
Perceived environment	Mechanistic
Organic	Environmental complexity
Environmental stability	Environmental uncertainty
Subenvironments	Buffering
Boundary spanners	Smoothing
Rationing	Planning and forecasting
Contractual agreements	Joint ventures
Co-optation	Interlocking directorates
Executive recruitment	Public relations/advertising
Mergers and acquisitions	Trade/professional associations
Political lobbying	Illegal activities
Institutional theory	Resource dependence
Population ecology	Niche
Carrying capacity	Population density

Review Questions

1. Pick a sport organization with which you are familiar. How do the different sectors of the general environment influence this organization?

2. What elements would make up the task environment of a private tennis club? Explain how these various elements influence club operations.

3. In understanding managerial action, is it the actual environment or the perceived environment that is most important? Why?

4. Why are organic structures more appropriate for a sport organization operating in a dynamic environment?

5. Pick a sport organization with which you are familiar. What can Lawrence and Lorsch's work tell us about the relationship of this organization to its environment?

6. What is the relationship between differentiation and integration? How do sport organizations achieve integration?

7. How do the simple/complex and stable/dynamic environment continuums influence a sport organization?

8. How do you think a sport equipment company like Nike or Prince buffers its technical core?

9. Who acts as boundary spanners for your university's athletic department?

10. What would be the advantage of a joint venture with a local distributor for a sport equipment manufacturer trying to enter a new Eastern European market?

11. There have been mixed findings about the relative merits of hiring a new manager or coach in professional sport. What do you think are the advantages and disadvantages of this means of controlling environmental uncertainty?

12. For what type of reasons would an athletic footwear manufacturer engage in political lobbying?

13. Institutional theory suggests that understandings and expectations about appropriate organizational form and behavior are shared by members of society. What are these understandings and expectations? Do they differ for the various types of sport organizations? How do managers deal with them?

14. How do amateur sport organizations and clubs control resource uncertainty?

15. How could population ecology help our understanding of the rapid growth of fitness clubs?

Suggestions for Further Reading

Students interested in finding out more about the relationship between organizations and their environment should begin by looking at the work of Burns and Stalker (1961), Lawrence and Lorsch (1967), and Duncan (1972) because, as we noted earlier in the chapter, these studies outline some of the more important findings on the organization-environment relationship and provide the basis for much of the subsequent work in this area. For those students who find the resource-dependence theory an appealing approach, Pfeffer and Salancik's (1978) book *The external control of organizations: A resource-dependence perspective* is a must. However, one of the shortcomings of the resource-dependence approach is that, despite its inherent appeal, there has been little in the way of any extension of Pfeffer and Salancik's original ideas.

Anyone interested in institutional theory should start off with Meyer and Rowan's (1977) article "Institutionalized organizations: Formal structure as myth and ceremony." Also useful and interesting is Lynne Zucker's (1988) book *Institutional patterns and organizations*, a collection of papers by scholars who employ the institutional perspective. For an understanding of population ecology it is useful to start with Hannan and Freeman's (1977b) "The population ecology of organizations." A number of books

have extended this earlier work. Howard Aldrich's (1979) *Organizations and environments* is probably the most comprehensive treatment of the organization-environment relationship using the population ecology approach. Also useful is Jitendra Singh's (1990) edited book *Organizational evolution: New directions*, a collection of papers written by many of the leading population ecologists. Further work on the two latter perspectives can be found by looking through any of the major organization or sociology journals (*Administrative Science Quarterly, Organization Studies, Academy of Management Review, Academy of Management Journal, Journal of Management Studies, American Journal of Sociology*, and *American Sociological Review*).

If we look specifically at research on sport organizations, there has been little theoretical or empirical work on the organization-environment relationship. Slack and Hinings, in their (1992) article "Understanding change in national sport organizations: An integration of theoretical perspectives," use resource-dependence theory and institutional theory to explain different aspects of the change process. Also their (1994) *Organization Studies* article, based on the arguments of institutional theory, empirically demonstrates the impact of institutional pressures on national sport organizations.

Case for Analysis

In-Line Skate Manufacturers Work to Control Environmental Uncertainties

Like psychedelic space-aged comic book heroes propelled by jet boots, they zip past at speeds reaching 30 miles per hour, becoming only a flash of neon or pink reef or electric lime or maybe endless wave. In-line skaters have become the hottest thing on eight wheels—for now. The challenge facing the companies making these skates is to turn a hip happening into a sport with staying power. The skates, which come in a bevy of styles and colors, feature a single row of four polyurethane wheels (three on children's models; five on the racer's) attached to a

metal "blade" connected to a molded or stitched boot. A rubber stopper on the back of one skate serves as a brake.

In-line skating first gained popularity in 1980 with ice hockey players seeking a summer training tool. It quickly found favor among other athletes, such as skiers. Despite its Midwestern roots, the Minneapolis-based original manufacturer Rollerblade knew if the product caught fire in trendsetting California, it would spark interest across America. The company gave away hundreds of skates to rental shops along the beach boardwalk, already considered Nirvana by rollerskaters, cyclists, and skateboarders. The scheme paid off. "Rollerblading" is now a term used generically to describe all in-line skating, and Rollerblade, a $3 million operation in 1987 had by 1990 commanded more than 50 percent of the $150-million U.S. market and its $15-million Canadian counterpart. Now all family members from young children to grandmothers are out hunting for greased turf (flat pavement). Nate Otis, product manager/product development for Vermont-based Canstar Sports, famous for its Bauer ice skates, said the sport attracts equal participation from both sexes. Canstar has made Bauer Precision In-Line Skates for the past four years, and Otis predicts the in-line business could eclipse the (Canstar) hockey business relatively soon.

Paolina Fasula, Rollerblade's Canadian marketing manager, credits the sport's popularity to "the underlying motivation of fun." But now comes the hard part for the manufacturers: how to keep the popularity of in-line skating rolling steadily into the future, and how to control the environmental uncertainty facing the industry. Fasula says Rollerblade's long-term aim is to develop in-line skating into a whole new sport, including sponsored in-line races under the jurisdiction of the recently created Rollerblade In-Line Skate Association, an organization created to cultivate new skaters and challenge experts. Several other in-line skating opportunities are being pursued: rollerhockey leagues and tournaments; in-line stunt competitions; Club Rollerblade, in which members get discounts and a newsletter; Team Rollerblade, a touring group of professional skaters who combine skating, choreography, and music; and demo vans that tour North America providing free skate test-rides.

Canstar also has demo vans on the road, and is involved in some organized demonstration/race events. Otis says a lack of person-power had kept the Bauer brand in the shadow of Rollerblade but a 1991 national print and transit campaign, "Kick some Asphalt," promoted in Canada by Canstar was designed to counter this trend. Otis also says Canstar has its eye on a current crop of loyal consumers: professional and amateur hockey players. Along with skates, manufacturers are looking at promoting accessories such as shirts, jackets, sweat pants, shorts, and hats, as well as a full line of protective gear. One of the problems the industry faces in maintaining its momentum is the image of the sport as a dangerous activity. The press has frequently focused on the injuries and law suits associated with the sport, and the places where skaters are banned. The manufacturers are currently working together to develop a Skate Smart campaign, which they hope will contribute to the legitimacy of the sport.

Adapted, by permission, from L. Medcalf, July 1, 1991, Rolling in dough, *Marketing*, 1, 3.

Questions

1. What actions have the in-line skate manufacturers taken so far to control some of the environmental uncertainty their organizations face?

2. What other types of actions could you suggest that they may wish to engage in to further reduce the uncertainty they face?

3. What type of changes do you think the programs started by Rollerblade and the other in-line skate manufacturers have had on their respective organization's structure?

4. Why do you think the manufacturers decided to work together on the Skate Smart campaign? What are the advantages and disadvantages of this type of joint initiative?

Sport Organizations and Technology

When You Have Read This Chapter

You should be able to

1. explain what we mean by technology;

2. describe how the work of Woodward, Perrow, and Thompson has contributed to our understanding of technology;

3. discuss the major critiques of the technology imperative and the important factors to consider when studying technology;

4. explain the principal types of microelectronic technology being used in sport organizations; and

5. describe how technology impacts on the structure of a sport organization.

The Changing Nature of Technology: Manufacturing Golf Balls

Dunlop Maxfli Sports Corporation is one of the leading manufacturers of golf equipment. In the 1920s when the company first started making golf balls much of the work was done by hand. A former worker recalls:

> In those days after the two halves of the golf balls were joined together and the core inserted . . . they were put into very hot water for about 30 minutes. Then they were put into cold water to cool off for 10 minutes. Next the balls were taken out and the girls used "trimmers"—a little instrument with a wedge—to take off the thin rubber [where the two halves were joined]. After that the paint went on. Girls put the paint in the palms of their hands [they never touched the ball with their fingers] and rolled the ball around, finally dropping it on the tray. They trimmed and painted all day. After the ball had been hardened other girls stenciled.

Back then, the only machines that were used were for core winding. Forty years later, production methods had altered drastically; practically everything was mechanized. Now refrigeration played an important part in the manufacture of a golf ball. The core of rubber-covered paste on which the ball started was frozen solid for the first winding—five feet of rubber tape. For the second winding, 21 yards of rubber thread were wound on at full tension by an ingenious machine. It held the ball between two oscillating rollers subjected to a jet of compressed air, the combination of forces turning the ball in all directions, ensured even winding. The gutta-percha shells were fitted around the core, followed by a molding process that left a seam, and then more freezing took place, rendering it brittle and easier to cut off. A brushing machine brushed the ball clean of dust (no more hands!). Next came a full-scale examination for all types of defects. Then came painting (automatic, of course) and a further series of five tests for resilience, weight, and so on.

Today the production of golf balls is a meta-science. A requirement of any good golf ball surface pattern is to provide uniform aerodynamics: The ball must fly accurately and consistently no matter how it is aligned to the club face. The surface pattern of Dunlop's DDH (dodecahedron) ball has been designed for greater accuracy, but the unique use of four different computer-established dimple sizes has produced a ball that has been shown in tests to go further than any other leading ball. The 12-pentagon format allows the manufacturer to get more seams on the ball. If you can construct a ball with a lot of seams on it, you will decrease its movement in the air. Some golf balls have only one seam but the dimple formation of the DDH gives it 10 seams; intensive testing has proved that this feature makes the ball the most accurate ever produced.

Adapted, by permission, from J. McMillan, 1989, *The Dunlop story* (London: Weidenfeld and Nicolson), 116-117.

As the Dunlop example illustrates, the manufacturing process involved in making golf balls has changed considerably over the past 70 years. Originally the balls were made by hand, the process was then mechanized, and today computer technology is used extensively in both the design and manufacturing of golf balls. These changes in the manufacturing process are largely a result of technological advances and their application to the sporting goods industry. Technology has changed the way virtually all sport organizations operate. Companies like Huffy use robotics in their manufacturing process, Sun Ice uses computer-assisted design and pattern-making technology to develop its sportswear, and coaches everywhere make extensive use of video analysis. Even the local sports club probably has a personal computer and a fax machine.

Technology, like size, is a major imperative that impacts on the structure and processes of a sport organization. In this chapter we look at what is meant when we talk about technology. We review some of the major research studies that have examined the impact of technology on organizational structure. We then look at some of the critiques of these studies and of the technology imperative. We briefly discuss the impact that the new micro-electronic technologies like computer-aided design (CAD) can have on a sport organization. Finally we draw some conclusions about the relationship between technology and the structure of a sport organization.

What Is Technology?

While there has been considerable variation in the way researchers have defined technology it is generally seen as being concerned with the means by which an organization transforms inputs into outputs. More specifically, it includes the materials, knowledge, equipment, and processes required to produce a desired good or service (cf. Perrow, 1967). All sport organizations, whether involved in manufacturing tennis racquets, designing swimming pools, or staging sports events for young children, use some type of technology.

The technology employed in a sport organization can be examined at three different levels. First, we can look at what is commonly referred to as organizational-level technology. Second, we can look at the work-group or department-level technology. Finally, we can look at individual-level technology. Organizational-level technology uses the total organization as its unit of analysis and focuses primarily on the technology required to produce the particular product or service. In a sport organization like Hillerich and Bradsby, a manufacturer of baseball bats, the primary type of organizational technology used is referred to as "mass production."

Studies of work-group or department-level technology recognize that different units making up an organization employ different types of technology (Grimes & Klein, 1973; Van de Ven & Delbecq, 1974). For example, Karsten Manufacturing, the makers of Ping golf clubs, will employ a different technology in its research-and-development department from that used in marketing. Studies of individual-level technology are primarily concerned with the nature of individual jobs and, in particular, job design (Hrebiniak, 1974).

Research on Technology and Organizations

Concern over the impact of technology on organizational structure and processes can be traced back to the work of Adam Smith. However, the 1950s and 1960s saw a heightened interest in the concept and since this time it has been an important variable in

---

TIME OUT

Checking Out the Pitcher's Arm

A player who can consistently throw good pitches is an extremely valuable asset to a baseball team. Yet it is very difficult to determine the actions that go into making a good pitch, because the movement of the player's arm, wrist, and fingers is so fast that it is hard to analyze. In an effort to remedy this problem, Greenleaf Medical Systems and VPL Research Inc. have joined together and developed a Lycra glove attached to fiber-optic cables. The glove relays movement signals through the cables to a computer, which is then able to quantify the motion. This new technology records up to 16,000 data points for every three-second pitch. Greenleaf has tested a number of major league pitchers and reported that they have been able to see subtle relationships among various aspects of the pitching motion. It is hoped the technology can be used to train pitchers, to help players in a slump, and to rehabilitate those coming off an injury.

Based on information in Virtual reality. (1992, October 5). *Business Week*, pp. 96-100, 102, 104-105.

the study of organizations. In this section we review the work of three authors whose research has had a major influence on our understanding of the relationship between technology and organizational structure, and provided the basis for much of the subsequent work in this area. We focus specifically on the work of Woodward, Perrow, and Thompson. We then examine some of the criticisms leveled at this work, and also look at some of the related issues to be considered when studying organizational technology.

Woodward: Technological Complexity

In the 1950s Joan Woodward and her research team in the Human Relations Research Unit at South East Essex Technical College studied 100 manufacturing organizations operating in the south of England. The organizations ranged in size from 100 employees to over 1,000. Woodward was interested in finding out which of their managers followed classical management principles, and whether they were more effective than those who didn't. Her research team collected data and established measures for a number of different aspects of organization, including span of control, levels of management, extent of formalization, economic performance, and technology.

Woodward's initial findings (1958; 1965) were that classical management principles were not consistently used in the organizations she studied and that, when they were, the application of these principles did not relate to effectiveness as measured by economic performance. However, Woodward

questioned her own findings and started to look for other factors that might be influencing performance. Using the criterion "type of production technology employed," she classified the organizations into 10 groups. Based on their level of technical complexity, these groups were further reduced into three major categories: unit or small-batch production, mass or large-batch production, and continuous-process production. Unit production was seen as exhibiting the least amount of technological complexity, and continuous-process production the most. When they were grouped according to the level of technological complexity, Woodward found that she could identify a typical type of organizational structure for the group, in essence a "correct" way to organize (see table 8.1). The organizations that came closest to this structure were the most effective, in terms of economic performance. Those organizations involved in unit production were less structured than those involved in mass production or continuous-process production. They tended to have a small number of managerial levels in their hierarchy, they were relatively low in formalization, and decision making was decentralized. The focus in these organizations was essentially on custom manufacturing. Examples of organizations within the sport industry that employ unit production would include Ernie's, a custom-bike shop in Brentwood, California, and Faulkner Brown, a British architectural company that designed Ponds Forge International and Community Sport Centre, the aquatic facility for the 1991 World University Games.

Table 8.1   The Relationship Between Technical Complexity and the Structural Characteristics of Effective Organizations

	TECHNOLOGY		
STRUCTURAL CHARACTERISTICS	UNIT PRODUCTION	MASS PRODUCTION	CONTINUOUS-PROCESS PRODUCTION
Number of levels of management	Low	Low to medium	High
Number of skilled workers	High	Low	High
Supervisor's span of control	Low to medium	High	Low
Manager/supervisor to total personnel ratio	Low	Medium	High
Centralization of decision making	Low	High	Low
Amount of formalization	Low	High	Low
Type of communication			
Verbal	High	Low	High
Written	Low	High	Low

Based on information in Woodward, J. (1965). *Industrial organization: Theory and practice*. London: Oxford University Press.

Mass-production organizations manufacture large quantities of the same product, often using assembly lines. The processes employed are repetitive and routine, hence the span of control is high, the number of skilled workers is low, and formalization is relatively high. Examples of organizations within the sport industry involved in mass production would include Huffy, which can make 16,000 bikes a day, and Fleer, a baseball card manufacturer.

Organizations that use continuous-process production are highly mechanized and their production process does not stop. This type of production is not found within the sport industry; it is generally used by organizations such as oil refineries, chemical plants, and breweries.

Woodward's work demonstrated that, within each of these three categories, those organizations whose scores came closest to the typical structure for the type of technology they exhibited were the most effective. She concluded that technology was the primary determinant of organizational structure.

Perrow: Task Variability and Analyzability

While Woodward's approach to understanding the impact of technology on organizations was limited to manufacturing firms, Perrow's work (1967; 1968) is more generalizable and can be applied to both manufacturing and service firms. It is also more applicable than Woodward's schema to understanding departmental or work-group technology (Daft, 1992). For Perrow (1967, p. 195) technology can be described as "the actions that an individual performs upon an object, with or without the aid of tools or mechanical devices, in order to make some changes in that object. The object or 'raw material' may be a living being, human or otherwise, a symbol, or an inanimate object."

To classify technology Perrow uses two dimensions. The first of these concerns the amount of variation in the tasks being performed, and refers specifically to the number of exceptions encountered in the work situation. When the work being performed is routine, there will be few exceptions.

TIME OUT

The Player's Agent: High Levels of Task Variability

Mark McCormack was described by *Sports Illustrated* as "the most powerful man in sports." He is a player agent, the founder and CEO of the International Management Group (IMG), the largest company of its kind in the world. In his job McCormack constantly encounters new and exceptional situations for which there is no readily available set of procedures to follow. McCormack discusses his work:

In more than 20 years . . . I have encountered every type of business situation and every type of business personality imaginable. I have had to cipher the complex egos of superstar athletes—and of their spouses, parents, lovers, neighbors, and camp followers. I have dealt with heads of state and heads of corporations, with international bankers and small-town advisers, with bureaucratic governing sports bodies and autocratic empire-builders. I have come into contact with every phase and facet of the entertainment, communication, and leisure-time industries. And at one time or another I have done business with practically every nationality on the face of the earth. What I haven't experienced myself I have observed. Because of our affiliations with major companies throughout the world I have been in countless executive suites and boardrooms, where I have witnessed a lot of companies in action. . . . I have seen every conceivable corporate style, culture, theory, and philosophy put to work. . . .

To deal with these situations, McCormack uses his experience and knowledge, what he refers to as street smarts, "the ability to make active, positive, use of your instincts, insights, and perceptions."

Based on information in McCormack, M.H. (1984). *What they don't teach you at Harvard Business School*. Glasgow, Scotland: Fontana.

For example, people assembling bikes or running shoes in factories will experience few exceptions in their work. Their jobs involve considerable repetition and few requirements for creativity. In contrast, people working in sport physiology research labs, or individuals working as player agents, will find a number of exceptions in their day-to-day jobs. They frequently encounter new situations and face problems they have not dealt with before.

Perrow's second dimension concerns the degree to which the exceptions encountered are analyzable. For example, if a problem occurs in some jobs, it is possible to follow a logical sequence of mechanical steps to seek a solution to the problem. The work of a sport lawyer is much like this. Although the problems sport lawyers face are complex, there is usually a fairly well established body of literature, in the form of previous court rulings and legal precedents, that the lawyer can call on to solve the problems. In contrast, a group of architects commissioned to design a new aquatic facility with both recreational and competitive pools, along with a water-slide facility, will probably not have encountered this situation before and will find little in the way of related literature to help solve the problems. Withey, Daft, and Cooper (1983) have developed a series of questions to determine the extent of task variability and problem analyzability in a department or work group (see table 8.2).

Using the two dimensions of task variability and problem analyzability, Perrow was able to construct a 2 × 2 matrix (see figure 8.1). The four types of technology found in this matrix are explained below. Perrow also suggests a simplification of the construction: Because task variability and problem analyzability are often highly correlated (if a task is low in variety it is usually easily analyzable, and if a task is high in variety it is not easily analyzable), it may be possible to have a single dimension of technology. This simplification is also shown in figure 8.1 as the routine/nonroutine continuum.

Perrow's routine technology has few exceptions, and those that do occur are easily analyzable. A salesclerk working in a sports equipment store and a person on the assembly line making golf carts are both engaged in routine technology. Craft technologies have very few exceptions, but those that do occur are not easily analyzable; skill and experience are needed to deal with them. Someone making custom bikes, a dance instructor, or a person choreographing a routine for a figure skater or gymnast would be involved with a craft technology.

Engineering technologies have a high number of exceptions but they are usually handled with relative ease because of established procedures. Sport lawyers usually find a number of exceptions in their work but, as noted, because they can call on previous decisions for indications of how to proceed,

Table 8.2   Questions to Determine the Extent of Task Variability and Problem Analyzability in a Department or Work Group

TASK VARIABILITY
How many of these tasks are the same from day-to-day?
To what extent would you say your work is routine?
Do people in this unit do about the same job in the same way most of the time?
Basically, do unit members perform repetitive activities in doing their jobs?
How repetitious are your duties?

PROBLEM ANALYZABILITY
To what extent is there a clearly known way to do the major types of work you normally encounter?
To what extent is there a clearly defined body of knowledge of subject matter which can guide you in doing your work?
To what extent is there an understandable sequence of steps that can be followed in doing your work?
To do your work, to what extent can you actually rely on established procedures and practices?
To what extent is there an understandable sequence of steps that can be followed in carrying out your work?

Adapted, by permission, from M. Withey, R.L. Daft, and W.H. Cooper, 1983, "Measures of Perrow's work unit technology: An empirical assessment and a new scale," *Academy of Management Journal* 26: 59.

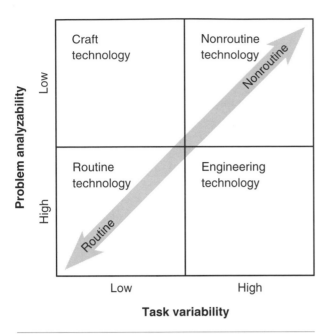

Low / High (Problem analyzability axis)

Low .... High (Task variability axis)

Craft technology | Nonroutine technology

Routine technology | Engineering technology

Nonroutine (arrow)
Routine (arrow)

Task variability

Figure 8.1 Perrow's technology classification. Based on Perrow, C. (1967). A framework for the comparative analysis of organizations. *American Sociological Review*, 32, p. 196.

these problems can be handled fairly easily. Architects who design and build traditional swimming pools and running tracks would also employ routine engineering technology. However, those who design more custom-built facilities will use nonroutine technology. Here the problems in design and construction are likely to be many, and systematic ways of solving these problems will be hard to find; the architect must count on experience and intuition. Researchers in a department of sport studies, and sport administrators who do management consulting, also exhibit nonroutine technologies.

Each of the four main technologies identified by Perrow is associated with a different type of organizational structure. Routine technology is found in bureaucratic type organizations; control is achieved through high levels of formalization and centralized decision making. Workers engaged in this type of technology are generally unskilled. Craft technologies require a more organic structure; consequently, there is less formalization and centralization. Coordination is achieved through mutual adjustment and the past experience of the staff. Engineering technologies require a structure somewhat like Mintzberg's professional bureaucracy; there is a moderate level of formalization and centralization but the people in the operating core are often professionally trained and hence have a certain amount of discretion in the decisions that are

made. Nonroutine technology requires a very flexible structure; formalization is low, and decisions are made collectively by mutual adjustment. The staff in these organizations are usually professionally trained. Finally, an important point is that quite possibly more than one type of technology will exist in an organization. For example, Reebok's production department will employ a routine technology but its research-and-development unit will use nonroutine technology. When a structure is used that does not fit with the technology employed, the unit tends to be less effective (Gresov, 1989).

Thompson: Task Interdependence

Thompson's (1967) approach to understanding the different types of technology used in organizations is based on the concept of interdependence, a term referring to the extent to which different units or departments within an organization depend on each other for the materials or resources they need to perform their particular tasks. When departments operate independently of each other, interdependence is low; when there is a need for substantive levels of communication and/or a frequent exchange of materials or resources among departments, interdependence is high. Thompson suggests that different types of interdependence require different technologies. These technologies are associated with different types of organizational uncertainty, and this uncertainty is managed using different types of strategies. We outline here the types of interdependence Thompson identified and the technologies associated with each. We also briefly discuss the structural implications of each type of technology and the way managers cope with the associated environmental uncertainty.

Sequential Interdependence

Sequential interdependence involves a series of steps in which task A must be performed before task B, which in turn must be performed before task C, and so on (see figure 8.2).

In essence the output from one worker or department becomes the input for the next. The steps involved are relatively routine but must be performed in the correct sequence. This type of interdependence, which requires what Thompson (1967) calls long-linked technology, is most frequently found in assembly-line production where "a single kind of standard product [is produced] repetitively and at a constant rate" (Thompson, 1967, p. 16). Within the sport industry we find long-linked technology in

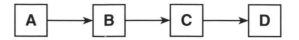

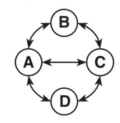

Figure 8.2   Thompson's categories of technology.

companies producing sport equipment such as baseball bats or hockey sticks.

Sequential interdependence requires high levels of coordination. There is a need to coordinate the various units involved in the different stages of the production process. The requirement that the product flow from one stage to the next necessitates that the organization emphasize planning and scheduling.

Structurally, organizations that employ long-linked technology to mass-produce large quantities of a product show relatively high levels of complexity, high levels of formalization, and a centralized decision making structure. Uncertainty is usually controlled through a process of vertical integration, either forward, backward, or both. In this way, sources of input and the means of dealing with output are controlled by the manufacturing organization. Nike's purchase of Tetra Plastics Ltd. (see chapter 5) demonstrates vertical integration.

Pooled Interdependence

As shown in figure 8.2, pooled interdependence involves linking together two independent customers or clients, using mediating technology. This process involves the organization acting as a go-between for customers and clients. Mediating technology is found mainly in service organizations. Within the sport industry, sport marketing compa-

nies like Britain's APA use a mediating technology to link sponsors with the promoters of sporting events. We also see a mediating technology used in chains of retail sporting goods stores such as Sport Experts and Jersey City, which link companies that manufacture sports equipment with those that want to buy it. Each Sport Experts store operates independently but is part of the overall Sport Experts operation. If each store performs well the total organization is strengthened, but stores in different parts of the country do not necessarily have to communicate with each other directly.

Structurally, mediating technology involves low levels of complexity, because few units are involved. Coordination is achieved through rules and procedures. Retail stores, for example, use rules and procedures to lay out how business should be conducted; sport marketing companies use contracts to ensure that each party understands its rights and obligations. Given this type of coordinating mechanism, formalization is relatively high. To control uncertainty, sport organizations that use a mediating technology try to increase the number of customers or clients served.

Reciprocal Interdependence

Reciprocal interdependence, the highest form of interdependence, is associated with what Thompson (1967) calls an intensive technology. This form of interdependence is found when people or units within an organization influence each other in a reciprocal manner (see figure 8.2). For example, the University of Alberta's Glen Sather Sports Medicine Clinic employs doctors, an X-ray technician, and physiotherapists. A patient who comes to the clinic will first visit a doctor, who may then refer the patient for an X-ray. The technician gives the X-ray to the doctor and, based on the results of the X-ray, the doctor may refer the patient to a physiotherapist for treatment. After the treatment the patient returns to the doctor, who may consult with the physiotherapists and possibly instruct the patient to get X-rayed again or to return for more physiotherapy. This is reciprocal interdependence: Doctors, X-ray technicians, and physiotherapists work together; the actions of one influence the behavior of the others. There is no predetermined sequence of events as in long-linked technology; the mix and order in which the skills are used to produce the product or service are in large part a result of feedback from the person or object on which work is being performed. We would also find reciprocal interdependence and an intensive technology in some sport physiology research labs and in some types of health spas, where dietitians, fitness appraisers, and masseurs may all work together with a client. Voluntary sport organizations also often exhibit reciprocal interdependence when a group of people work together cooperatively to stage a sports event.

Structurally, sport organizations that employ intensive technology are relatively organic. Coordination is achieved through frequent communication among the parties involved and by mutual adjustment on their part. Teamwork is an important aspect of this technology; decisions are often made collectively. Uncertainty arises out of the nature of the problem itself; while planning can help managers, it cannot possibly cover all the situations that arise in this type of organization. The people who work with this kind of technology are usually highly skilled, and hence able to call on their training and experience to make situations more predictable.

Critiques of the Technology Imperative

The contributions of Woodward, Perrow, and Thompson, as significant as they are, have generated considerable debate within the organizational literature about technology and its impact on orga-

nizational structure. In this section we look at some of the research that has sought to critique and extend these initial studies. We then look briefly at some general problems and issues relating to work in organizational technology.

The most notable critique and extension of Woodward's work is that of the Aston group members Hickson, Pugh, and Pheysey (1969). Essentially, what Hickson et al. (1969) suggested was that there were three types of technology: operations technology, materials technology, and workflow technology. However, their work focused only on operations technology, which they define as "the techniques that [an organization] uses in its workflow activities" (1969, p. 380). Operations technology was assessed using a measure called workflow integration, a composite measure applicable to both manufacturing and service organizations, examining such factors as the extent to which workflow equipment was automated, the rigidity of the workflow, the level of interdependence in the workflow, and the specificity of quality evaluation of operations. Organizations scoring high on workflow integration were seen to have a complex technology; a low score meant a simple technology. Using the workflow integration measure, Hickson et al. (1969) found only a weak relationship between technology and various measures of organizational structure. What their results did show, however, was that size could explain far more variation in structure than technology. Technology did, nevertheless, have an influence on structure in smaller organizations.

One of the first to criticize the Aston findings was Aldrich (1972b) (see also Kmetz, 1977/1978; Starbuck, 1981). Aldrich reexamined the Aston data using path analysis and suggested a different causal sequence, with technology influencing size. He (1972b, p. 40) suggested the Aston group's rejection of the technological imperative "to be ill-advised and premature."

At the same time that Aldrich was critiquing the Aston data, Child was replicating their work in what is known as the national study (see chapter 3). Child and Mansfield (1972) reexamined the technology/size/structure relationship using the Aston workflow integration measure of technology. Their work essentially confirms the Aston findings (see also Child, 1973a; 1973b; 1975b). Although role specialization, functional specialization, and standardization showed a reasonable correlation with technology, the correlation with size was higher, leading Child and Mansfield (1972, p. 383) to reject the technological imperative, concluding that "size has a much closer relationship to the aspects of structure

TIME OUT

Sport Teams: Variations in Levels of Interdependence

Robert Keidel suggests that business managers can learn from the way sport is organized. One of his articles on this topic focuses on the different types of interdependence exhibited by teams in three of the major North American professional sports: baseball, football, and basketball. Although Keidel acknowledges that to some extent each sport can exhibit every form of interdependence, each has a dominant form.

He suggests that of the three sports professional baseball exhibits the greatest degree of pooled interdependence. Team-member contributions are made relatively independent of each other. Where interaction does occur, it is usually between no more than two or three players (on the same team), for example, pitcher-catcher, batter-baserunner, infielder-infielder. Rarely are more than a few of the players on the field involved directly in making a play, outside of making adjustments in fielding positions in anticipation of a play (or to back up a play). The basic unit in baseball is the individual. More so than in either football or basketball, overall performance approximates the sum of team member's performances. This idea is vividly demonstrated by the way offense works: Players come up to bat one at a time. Of course, scoring typically requires a sequence of actions such as walks, hits, and sacrifices. But individual contributions remain rather discrete.

Professional football exhibits sequential interdependence in two ways. First, on offense, the line leads ("feeds") the backfield by providing the blocking necessary for running and passing. Second, in a more fundamental sense, the flow of plays usually required to score—a linear series of "first downs" across a "gridiron"—could not be more sequential. The basic units in football are the large group or platoon (offense, defense, and transition) and to a lesser degree, the small group (linemen, linebackers, backfield, and so forth). Overall performance is basically the sum of the platoon's performances. Each platoon's challenge is to be as machine-like as possible—a metaphor that is especially apt for this sport. It is instructive to picture the football field as a factory with the moving line of scrimmage representing product flow through the factory.

Professional basketball exhibits a high degree of reciprocal interdependence, as demonstrated by the back-and-forth flow of the ball among players. The reciprocal character of the sport is also shown in the often frenetic movement up and down the court— a far cry from the deliberate, measured advance of a classic football scoring drive. If offense and defense are "linked" in football, they are overlapping or "intersecting" in basketball. Offense and defense turn into each other instantaneously. The transition game is not a separate piece with separate players, as it is in football; it is continuous, part of the flow. The basic unit in basketball is the team. With only five players on the court, an intermediate grouping between the team and the individual is unrealistic. Unit performance, therefore, is a function of player interaction, where each player may be involved with every other player on the court.

measured than does technology." However, a more recent study by Reimann (1980) used a measure of technology based on Woodward's work and found significant correlations with several structural variables.

Like Woodward's work, Perrow's ideas have also been critiqued and extended. A number of studies have tested Perrow's conceptualization of technology; some have been concerned with the routine/ nonroutine continuum emanating from his model, while others have focused on his fourfold classification scheme.

Van de Ven and Delbecq (1974) used measures of task difficulty, a concept similar to Perrow's problem analyzability, and task variability to examine structural variability within work units. Their results also support Perrow's predictions: Those organizations involved with routine type work were more highly formalized than those involved with nonroutine activities.

Grimes and Klein (1973) used a slight variant of Perrow's four-cell matrix to examine the relationship of technology to the autonomy of management, something Perrow (1967) had alluded to in his original article. They found (1973, p. 596) "a direct although modest relationship" between technology and managerial autonomy. The influence of technology as a determinant of managerial autonomy was greatest at the work-group level; its influence became more diffuse as one moved further from this level.

Although Thompson's (1967) typology of technology is generally considered to be conceptually the richest of the three seminal works (cf. Bedeian & Zammuto, 1991; Das, 1990), it has probably led to the least amount of subsequent research. Mahoney and Frost (1974) examined the relationship of Thompson's three types of technology to measures of organizational effectiveness. Their results support Thompson's ideas; they found that, in organizations that used long-linked technology, the predominant criteria of effectiveness were smoothness of operations, output performance, and reliability of performance. In organizations using mediating technology, flexibility, smoothness of operations, output performance, supervisory control, and staff development were all cited as indicators of effectiveness. For those using intensive technologies, performance was once again important but so too were cooperation and staff quality; planning was not seen to be as important. Van de Ven, Delbecq, and Koenig (1976) used both task uncertainty (the difficulty and variability of the work undertaken), a concept from Perrow's framework, and Thompson's notion of workflow interdependence, to look at the modes of coordination at the work-unit level. They added to Thompson's types of interdependence a fourth category, "a team arrangement." As figure 8.3 shows, their results generally support Thompson's idea that the use of coordinating devices would increase as interdependence increased. They also show the relative use of the different coordinating mechanisms for the different types of technology.

In addition to the findings of studies that have sought to critique and extend the work of Woodward, Perrow, and Thompson, a number of other important issues should be mentioned in any consideration of technology as a structural imperative. The first concerns the definition of what exactly we mean when we talk about "technology." As we have seen, different studies have used the term in different ways. As Rousseau (1983, p. 230) notes, researchers have used the term "to refer to anything from job routineness to the hardness of raw materials." She goes on to suggest that "there is disagreement as to whether technology is an object, such as an assembly line or a computer, or a process, such as the flow of throughput within an organization." This lack of agreement as to exactly what technology *is* may well be a major reason for the different findings about its impact on organizational structure.

Another issue relates to the focus of the studies carried out on the technological imperative. Again, as Rousseau (1983) points out, the vast majority of work in this area has been conducted at the organizational level, and considerably less work at the work-group, department, and individual levels. Studies carried out at the work-group level have generally produced stronger support for the technological imperative than research conducted at the organizational level, possibly because technology is more directly related to the work group. As Robbins (1990, p. 193) notes, when we look at the overall impact of technology we must consider the size of the organization because "the smaller the organization the more likely it is that the whole organization will be impinged upon by the production workflow or operating core."

Another point raised by Robbins (1990), which indirectly relates to the size issue, is the fact that the industry and the niche within that industry will affect its technology. In our example at the beginning of chapter 4 we saw this issue in action: Huffy Corporation and Holland Cycle Inc. both make bicycles but the technology they employ is very different. In Perrow's terms, Huffy's technology is routine, while Holland Cycle uses a craft technology, a difference in technology determined in large part by the niche these sport organizations have selected for their operations. It would not be efficient for a large mass-production company like Huffy to have their customers come to their production plant and make modifications to their bike frame, as they do at Holland Cycle.

A final concern about technology is the issue of manufacturing versus service technologies. The bulk of the research on organizational technology

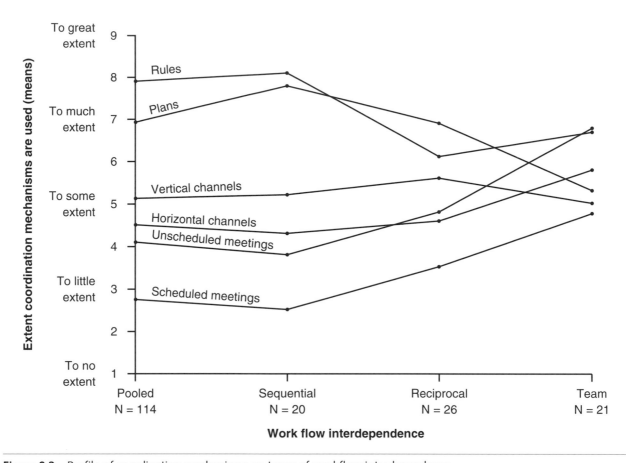

Figure 8.3   Profile of coordination mechanisms on types of workflow interdependence.
Reprinted, by permission, from A. Van de Ven, A. Delbecq, and R. Koenig, 1976, "Determinants of coordination modes within organizations," *American Sociological Review*, 4: 322-338.

has been carried out on manufacturing organizations, but many of the organizations in the sport industry are service oriented. Consequently, in any study of a service organization, sport related or otherwise, it becomes important to take account of differences in the two types of organizations (see table 8.3) and to employ a framework that takes account of these differences.

What then is the relevance, for people involved in sport management, of the studies that have sought to critique and extend the work of Woodward, Perrow, and Thompson and the related issues they have raised? Given the importance of technology and the paucity of work on technology and sport organizations, the studies reviewed here should provide an initial basis for some thoughts and subsequent studies of the impact of technology on the organizations within our field. Regardless of the diversity of findings, technology is an important factor that influences the structure and operation of *all* organizations.

It should also be apparent, notwithstanding some conflicting results, that technology can influence the

structuring of an organization, particularly at the work-group or department level. Consequently, it becomes important for managers in sport organizations to understand the impact of technology, in particular changing technology, on their organization. Understanding the "fit" between structure and variables such as technology and size is also important, because it can influence the effectiveness of an organization. Finally, it is important that sport managers, if they are to create effective organizations, understand the difference between manufacturing and service technologies, and the relationship between these technologies and factors such as the size of a sport organization and the industrial niche in which it operates.

Microelectronic Technologies

In the last decade or so, many traditional manufacturing and service technologies have been replaced or augmented with microelectronic technologies,

Table 8.3   A Comparison of the Characteristics of Service and Manufacturing Organizations Within the Sport Industry

Service organizations	Manufacturing organizations
Intangible output	Tangible output
Customized output	Standardized output
Customer participation	Technical core buffered from the customer
Simultaneous production and consumption	Goods consumed at a later point in time
Labor intensive	Capital intensive
Examples of service organizations within the sport industry	Examples of manufacturing organizations within the sport industry
Department of sport studies	Athletic footwear companies
Sport medicine clinics	Baseball card companies
Sport marketing companies	Golf club manufacturers
Municipal government sport departments	Sportswear companies
Fitness clubs	Tennis racquet manufacturers

Based on information in Bowen, D.E., Siehl, C., and Schneider, B. (1989). A framework for analyzing customer service orientations in manufacturing. *Academy of Management Review, 14*, pp. 75-95.

most of which are computer related. Athletic footwear manufacturers like Nike and Reebok, for example, use advanced computer technologies to help design their shoes; at Spalding Sports World, sales reps use laptop computers to check the availability of goods and to place orders (Radding, 1989). As Child (1984, p. 245) notes "this new form of technology has emerged as a major contingency which organizational designers have to take into account." In this section we look briefly at the types of microelectronic technology that may be used in a sport organization, the rationale for using these technologies, the impact they can have on organizational structure and operations, and their impact on job design.

Types of Microelectronic Technology

Two major facets of microelectronic technology are impacting upon the structure and operations of sport organizations: computer-integrated manufacturing (CIM) and advanced information technologies (AIT).

Computer-Integrated Manufacturing (CIM)

Computer-integrated manufacturing is the term used to refer to the linking together by computers of the different parts of the manufacturing process: the ordering and inventory of raw materials; the sequencing and control of the production process;

and the warehousing, shipping, and servicing of the finished product (Pennings, 1987). The different components of computer-integrated manufacturing may include an automated materials-handling system, computer-assisted engineering, and (the two most common elements of CIM) computer-assisted design (CAD) and computer-aided manufacturing (CAM). Computer-assisted design, used to help in the design and drafting of new products, speeds up these processes by allowing designers to easily make modifications to products using the available computer technology. In this way alternative designs can be developed and tested to meet changing customer needs. Because of the ease with which changes are made, CAD is more cost effective than traditional methods of product design.

Computer-aided design is used within the sport industry to produce a wide variety of sports equipment, from running shoes to tennis racquets. Heery Architects and Engineers Inc. Sports Facilities group, one of the leading builders of sports facilities, uses CAD in its design process. It is also a leader in the development of computer-aided design drafting software and the utilization of this software to produce construction documents.

Computer-assisted manufacturing (CAM) utilizes machines controlled by a computer to fabricate and assemble a product. This technology, because it requires fewer people to operate, can save a manufacturer money; it is also much quicker than conventional manufacturing technology. Using

CAM, a manufacturer can easily change from one product to another by merely changing software. This flexibility enables the manufacturer to respond more quickly to changing customer orders and the changing demands of the marketplace. Huffy Corporation, the cycle manufacturer, switched to computer-assisted manufacturing, a move that allowed it to undersell Taiwanese importers and keep its manufacturing plant in Ohio. "Computer-aided manufacturing means creating a factory of the future," according to Huffy chairman Harry A. Shaw (Sator, n.d.).

Advanced Information Technology (AIT)

Advanced information technology is a result of the merging of computer and telecommunications technology. By linking computers together via telephone systems, AIT allows virtually anyone with a microcomputer to send and receive information.

This type of technology can be used to manage geographically dispersed operations, to place orders and control inventory, to facilitate group decision making without everyone being in the same room, and simply to enhance communications. Quicker than traditional methods of sending and receiving information, it allows for better identification of problems and facilitates broader participation in decision making. Many sport organizations make use of AIT. Coleman, the sporting goods manufacturer, has recently increased its reliance on personal computers as a means of communication and as noted earlier, Spalding Sports Worldwide now uses personal computers to place client orders and check on inventory (Radding, 1989). Many university de-

partments of sport studies use local area network (LAN) systems so interdepartmental memos and announcements are no longer typed, photocopied, and placed in mail boxes; they are sent via computer. Using a related system, they are also able to send and receive messages from colleagues in different parts of the world.

Benefits of Advanced Technologies

We have already briefly alluded to some of the benefits of advanced technologies. Here we elaborate on the reason why an increasing number of sport organizations are utilizing these types of manufacturing and information systems. We focus specifically on four reasons identified by Child (1984): reduced operating costs, increased flexibility, better quality products and services, and increased control and integration.

Reduced Operating Costs

The introduction of advanced technologies like CAD and CAM is often accompanied by a reduction in the size of the organization's workforce. Huffy, for example, was able to reduce overtime by 65 percent as a result of the changes to its manufacturing process (Smith Barney, 1989). While there are obviously significant social consequences of laying off employees and/or reducing their workload, there is little doubt that, despite the fact that an initial large outlay of capital may be required, switching to CIM can ultimately reduce workforce costs. Such a move can also lower costs through "the reduction of wasted material and time [which is]

TIME OUT

Computer-Integrated Manufacturing at Sun Ice

The slogan "solutions through technology" has been the ongoing corporate motto at the sportswear manufacturing company Sun Ice. Today management at Sun Ice can say with pride that their production facility represents one of the most modern plants in North America. The application of CAD/CAM—computer-assisted design and computer-assisted manufacturing—in pattern-making, grading, and marker generation has speeded up the slow manual process. Fabric is spread by electronically driven automatic spreading machines; cutting is accomplished by both computer-driven robotic equipment and manual methods. The production flow is fully engineered, employing an automatic Unit Production System, which moves the garment from operator to operator. Production planning, scheduling, and ticketing are achieved through a sophisticated computer information retrieval and data processing software application.

Based on information in Sun Ice (1990) *Annual Report*.

made possible by the greater precision and lack of fatigue of programmed electronic devices"(Child, 1984, p. 249). Huffy's waste was reduced 45 percent when CAM was introduced (Smith Barney, 1989). Costs can also be reduced because information on available inventory can easily be accessed and hence orders can be quickly filled, reducing wasted search time and the costs of back ordering products not in stock. Reebok's director of distribution, Don Petersen, estimated that when they installed computers to operate their distribution center, output per hour doubled, thus generating a large saving for the company.

Increased Flexibility

Using microelectronic technologies like CAM allows a manufacturer to produce a range of different products using the same equipment. Different software systems can be used to reprogram design and manufacturing equipment so modifications are easily made. With traditional methods these changes were often difficult, time-consuming, and costly. Sun Ice's 1989 Annual Report (p. 7), for example, notes how using a computer-aided design system "designers can change styles, colors, and coordinates in minutes, [resulting in] efficient turnaround time, greater accuracy, and increased production readiness." Advanced information technologies also provide increased flexibility; equipment like cellular phones, fax machines, laptop computers, and modems mean that people do not have to be in a fixed location to send or receive information.

Better Quality Products and Services

Microelectronic technologies also improve the quality of products and services produced. The quality of manufactured products is improved with CIM because more design options can be considered, human errors in production are eliminated, and the completed product is more easily and rigorously tested. Sport organizations in the service sector are able to improve the quality of their service because, with AIT, more comprehensive information is more readily available than with traditional methods. Consider, for example, a fitness center that uses a computer to store information about client exercise programs, changes in levels of cardiovascular fitness, weight changes, and so on—all of this information can be available at the push of a button, and so the fitness consultant is able to provide a more informed assessment of a client's future needs.

Increased Control and Integration

Control and integration are important aspects of the management process and as a result "management will therefore look to new technology to assist in meeting these requirements in ways that are more effective and less costly" (Child, 1984, p. 251). Computer-integrated manufacturing increases managerial control by allowing managers to monitor the workflow process of the sequenced jobs. The central computer controlling the manufacturing process becomes the source of information for managers whereas, when traditional manufacturing methods are used, information about the process would have to be obtained from the supervisors of the different parts of the process. Integration is enhanced because, by definition, CIM integrates the different aspects of the manufacturing process.

Information technologies improve control because they provide readily available information, which is more easily monitored and less subject to error than information supplied using traditional methods. Integration is also improved because AIT brings information from several people or units together into one place. It is also possible to link people in different places, through teleconferencing or computer networks. The Minnesota Twins baseball club, for example, uses a computer system to merge its own scouting reports with statistics supplied by the Howe News Bureau and other sources (Darrow, 1990). They also hope to equip their scouts with laptops so they can enter their own reports rather than sending them in written form, which then have to be keyed into the system.

Impact of Microelectronic Technologies on Organizational Structure

Interest in the relationship between technology and organizational structure is not just restricted to a concern with traditional technologies. With the increased use of microelectronic technologies researchers have started to examine the impact of new forms of technology on organizational structure. Table 8.4 compares the kind of structural attributes typically found in a mass-production technology organization with those found in an organization that uses CIM.

As can be seen, organizations with a CIM system are more organic than the traditional mass-production company, with a narrower span of control and a smaller number of vertical levels in their hierarchy. The work to be carried out requires a higher level of skill than needed when

Table 8.4   A Comparison of the Structural Characteristics of Sport Organizations Using Mass-Production Technology and Those Using Computer-Integrated Manufacturing (CIM)

STRUCTURAL CHARACTERISTICS	ORGANIZATIONS USING MASS-PRODUCTION TECHNOLOGY	ORGANIZATIONS USING CIM TECHNOLOGY
Span of control	Wide	Narrow
Number of vertical levels	High	Low
Tasks	Routine/repetitive	Responsive/craft-like
Specialization	High	Low
Decision making	Centralized	Decentralized
Information flow	Vertical	Horizontal
Basis of power	Position	Knowledge
Overall design type	Machine bureaucracy	Adhocracy

Based on information in Nemetz, P.L. and Fry, L.W. (1988). Flexible manufacturing organizations: Implications for strategy formulation and organization design. *Academy of Management Review, 13*, pp. 627-638.

mass-production technology is used. Employees often work in teams that are required to be innovative in their work processes; hence, decision making is decentralized. This type of team approach requires an emphasis on horizontal rather than vertical communication, so managers need the skills to integrate work groups. As Skinner (1983, p. 112) notes about these managers:

> Their skills feature the abilities to form up and lead effective teams for problem solving, systems design, and experimental manufacturing systems. . . . They seem to thrive on change, uncertainty, and ambiguity and indeed become easily bored with routine production. They delegate easily and in fact rather loosely, relying more on trust and less on formal controls and reports.

Mintzberg's (1979) adhocracy is the type of organizational structure most suitable for a company using a CIM system.

Impact of Microelectronic Technology on Job Design

When a sport organization introduces a new form of technology into its operations, the nature of the jobs within the organization will be affected. Certainly, one of the first questions is, will jobs be lost? There is no doubt that many sport organizations adopt new forms of technology to cut labor costs and this can result in a loss of jobs; however, as Child (1984) points out, the situation is not this simple. If we look at it in a broader context we find that, while

jobs may be lost in the organization adopting the technology, they may be increased in the organization where technology is produced. For example, a faculty of kinesiology might lay off secretarial support staff because faculty members use personal computers—contributing to job losses—but there will also be a need for computer support staff and programmers. In addition, the increased demand for computers means more people will be hired in the computer industry.

The adoption of a new technology also raises questions about whether the adoption will make jobs more enriching for workers or more mundane. Some arguments suggest that new technologies are a substitute for certain types of skills; with the introduction of these technologies the workers who possess these skills are relegated to lower-level mundane tasks. On the other hand, some see new technologies as providing an opportunity to develop and practice new, more cognitively-based skills (cf. Adler, 1986). In actuality, as Wilkinson (1982, p. 40) notes, "there is *no* inherent logic in microelectronics which demands that tasks become even more mundane; nor does technology *demand* that skills be increased and work become more interesting and fulfilling" (emphasis in original). The impact of technology on job design is determined by managers and their policies toward their labor force. Susman and Chase (1986) have identified a number of benefits and risks to employing a downgrading strategy (as opposed to an upgrading strategy) to skills when new technology is introduced into an organization. The benefits of downgrading, they suggest, are that, because the workers' skill level is of less value, they can be paid less, their tasks are programmable, and turnover is more affordable. The risks involve low-skilled workers not being able to deal with variances in the production process before they become major problems, overhead costs rising because of the necessity to supervise lower-skilled workers, and low-skilled workers severing "the learning loop . . . formed between workers who recognize symptoms and the diagnosis and problem-solving that can occur among them and management and support personnel" (p. 267). The upgrading strategy is merely the reverse of the downgrading strategy; the benefits of downgrading become the risks of upgrading and the risks of downgrading become the benefits of upgrading.

When new technology is introduced, we can generally expect changes in two areas: the training of shop-floor operators and the level of interdependence among personnel (cf. Adler, 1986; Susman & Chase, 1986). As was shown in table 8.4, when a sport organization adopts a technology like CIM it operates with more flexibility. The tasks of the organization change from being routine and repetitive to being craftlike; the resulting flexibility requires operators to be more accountable for keeping equipment running to maintain production levels. The operators become highly interdependent on each other, exchanging information to avoid problems and maintain output. The sequential interdependence found in traditional manufacturing is replaced by a new type of reciprocal interdependence. Adler (1986, p. 19) describes this new type of interdependence.

[It] allows for no easy decomposition of tasks, but on the contrary, demands ongoing and flexible integration of the hitherto distinct functions of operations, systems design, and training. The reciprocal nature of this interdependence in operations is exemplified in the reliance on common databases. Users thereby become dependent on other users' data input accuracy. On another level, "social skills" allowing for effective teamwork become more important. [Reciprocal] interdependence also encompasses the ongoing cooperation of system users —operations— and system designers: This cooperation has become critical to operations efficiency. New application programs to deal with new products are constantly being generated. This increased subsystem flexibility can only realize its potential if there is active cooperation between operations and support staffs to assure that the new procedures cover all contingencies and that they are rapidly debugged.

As a consequence of the increased interdependence that comes with the introduction of systems like CIM, increased training for operators becomes important. Because tasks are no longer routine and repetitive, operators have to be responsive to a variety of different possible problem situations. This responsiveness requires a commitment to continuous training (cf. Adler, 1988; Nemetz & Fry, 1988). This training is important because, as Meredith (1987) suggests, one of the main reasons for the failure of systems like CIM is a lack of in-house expertise.

Relationship Between Technology and Organizational Structure

While the debate over whether or not technology determines the structure of an organization has produced conflicting results, some important points can be made about the relationship between technology and the different elements of structure. In this section we briefly review some findings on the relationship of technology to complexity, formalization, and centralization.

Technology and Complexity

Findings about the relationship between technology and complexity yield a mixed message. Technologies such as Woodward's mass-production technology, Perrow's routine technology, and Thompson's long-linked technology are generally associated with bureaucratic structures. Therefore, we can expect this type of technology to be related to relatively high levels of task specialization and vertical differentiation. However, specialization as measured by the amount of professional training of the workforce is likely to be low (cf. Hage & Aiken, 1969). When technology is nonroutine, as in Perrow's classification or Woodward's unit production technology, we are likely to find a more organic structure. Here task specialization and the number of vertical levels in the organization will be low, but complexity as measured by the amount of professional training of staff is likely to be high. These mixed results should not be construed as a product of weak or inadequate research. Rather, they serve to underscore a point made by Hrebiniak (1974, p. 408), that both structure and technology are multidimensional concepts and "that when dealing only with general categories of either concept [such as the notion of complexity] it might be unreasonable to assume clear relationships or empirical trends."

Technology and Formalization

Notwithstanding Hrebiniak's caution about the problems of trying to relate technology to broadly based concepts of organizational structure, we do find, at least at one level, a clearer pattern in regard to technology and formalization. Gerwin (1979) reviewed five studies (Blau & Schoenherr, 1971; Child & Mansfield, 1972; Hickson, Pugh, & Pheysey, 1969; Hinings & Lee, 1971; Khandwalla, 1974) that showed technology to be positively related to formalization. However, when he controlled for size the relationship disappeared. What Gerwin's review suggests is that the smaller the organization, the greater the impact of technology on formalization. Although not controlling for size, Hage and Aiken's (1969) work supports the general trend found in Gerwin's review; they found statistically significant relationships between technology and the presence of rules and job descriptions, and between technology and the degree of specificity of job descriptions.

Technology and Centralization

While there are exceptions (cf. Hinings & Lee, 1971) the majority of studies (cf. Blau & Schoenherr, 1971; Child & Mansfield, 1972; Hage & Aiken, 1969; Hickson, Pugh, & Pheysey, 1969; Khandwalla, 1974) have shown a relationship, albeit often small and not statistically significant, between the level of technology within an organization and the extent to which decision making is decentralized. Generally speaking, organizations that employ routine technology will be more centralized; those with nonroutine technology will be more likely to be decentralized.

Summary and Conclusions

The relationship between technology and organizational structure is one of the most controversial and hotly debated issues in the study of organizations. In this chapter we looked first at what we mean when we talk about technology. At the general level technology is the process by which an organization turns inputs into outputs. However,

as we noted later in the chapter, researchers have used many different definitions of technology, and in part this may be the cause of some of the conflicting results coming from studies examining the relationship of technology to organizational structure.

Much of the work conducted on technology has been based on the studies of Woodward, Perrow, or Thompson. We looked at the principle arguments put forward in these studies and how the major concepts outlined in each related to sport organizations. We also looked at some of the critiques and extensions of this work and we raised questions as to whether or not there is a technological imperative, that is, whether technology determines structure. It was suggested that there was stronger support for the technological imperative where studies had been conducted at the work-group/department level. Studies conducted at the organizational level have produced mixed results. The issue of organizational level versus work-group/department level studies raised the issue of organizational size; through the chapter we saw evidence that size may influence the technology-structure relationship. We briefly touched on the issue of how the industry or niche within an industry in which a sport organization operates may influence its technology and we highlighted the differences between manufacturing and service technologies.

After considering traditional technologies and the debates conducted about their relationship to organizational structure, we moved on to consider microelectronic technologies, and suggested that CIM and AIT have had and will continue to have a significant impact on sport organizations. We looked at some of the benefits of these technologies for sport organizations, and the impact they could have on organizational structure and job design. In the final part of the chapter we looked at some general relationships between technology and the structural elements of complexity, formalization, and centralization. We conclude that, regardless of some of the mixed findings that research studies have produced, technology is an important variable in the study of sport organizations.

Yet, as we have seen, little theoretical or empirical work within the field of sport management has looked at the influence of technology on any type of sport organization. We need to begin to address this important omission from the sport management literature, given the rapid changes occurring in technology and the impact these changes can have on sport organizations.

Key Concepts

Organizational technology	Individual technology
Work-group/department technology	Technological complexity
Mass /large-batch production	Unit/small-batch production
Continuous-process production	Task variability
Problem analyzability	Routine technology
Craft technology	Engineering technology
Nonroutine technology	Pooled interdependence
Mediating technology	Sequential interdependence
Long-linked technology	Reciprocal interdependence
Advanced information technology	Intensive technology
Computer-integrated manufacturing	Workflow integration
Computer-aided manufacturing	Computer-assisted design

Review Questions

1. Explain the different ways in which technology has been defined and why it is difficult to arrive at a single definition.

2. What type of organizational structure would you expect to find associated with Woodward's unit and mass-production technologies? Relate them to sport organizations with which you are familiar.

3. What kinds of sport organizations would you expect to find using the types of technology proposed by Perrow?

4. Within a single sport organization could you find an example of a department that uses routine technology and one that uses nonroutine technology? How would their structures differ?

5. What commonalties can you find among the classifications of technology proposed by Woodward, Perrow, and Thompson?

6. In the Time Out that focused on Mark McCormack it was implied that his work was very unpredictable and that it was hard to analyze the type of situations in which he was going to be working. If this is the case, what can sport management professors teach students who want to be player's agents?

7. Explain the different types of sport organizations you would expect to find using long-linked, mediating, and intensive technology.

8. What is the difference between organizational-level and work-group-level technology? At what level does technology have the greatest impact on structure?

9. From what you have read, discuss what you think is the best way to explain the technology/size/structure relationship.

10. What are the differences between manufacturing and service technologies?

11. Could a sport organization use both manufacturing and service technologies?

12. What type of structural changes can a sport organization expect to undergo if it moves from a mass-production technology to one that uses CIM?

13. Why do sport organizations adopt technologies like CAD and CAM?

14. Think of a sport organization with which you are familiar. How does it use AIT?

15. If a sport organization adopts CIM, what impact will it have on the jobs within the organization?

Suggestions for Further Reading

Students who want to understand more about the technology-structure relationship should begin by looking at the original work by Woodward, Perrow, and Thompson. It would also be useful to look at the work by scholars who have sought to critique and extend these original studies; a number of these are mentioned in this chapter. Excellent overviews of studies on the technology-structure relationship and details of some of the important issues to be considered in work of this nature can be found in Fry's (1982) article "Technology-structure research: Three critical issues" in the *Academy of Management Journal*; Reimann and Inzerilli's (1979) "A comparative analysis of empirical research on technology and structure" in the *Journal of Management*; and

Rousseau's chapter "Technology in organizations: A constructive review and analytic framework" which is in Seashore et al.'s (1983) book, *Assessing organizational change*.

The only work which focuses on sport is Keidel's (1984) "Baseball, football and basketball: Models for business" in *Organizational Dynamics* (see Time Out in this chapter) and his extension of the ideas (1987) contained in "Team sports models as a generic organizational framework," in *Human Relations*. Students may, however, gain some ideas about the impact of technology on sport organizations, by looking for articles about companies such as Nike, Reebok, and Huffy which sometimes appear in business periodicals such as *Forbes*, *Fortune*, and *Business Week*.

Case for Analysis

Technology Zaps the Freeloaders

Television networks are getting ready for a crackdown on advertising freeloaders. In recent years, advertisers have discovered that buying commercial time on a televised sporting event might not be the most effective way to deliver their messages. Research has shown that a well-placed sign along the boards of a hockey rink or on an outfield wall can provide more brand recognition than a 60-second commercial, and can do so at a fraction of the price. The result has been a proliferation of signs. At least three American League baseball teams have sold advertising space on the wall behind home plate. For the past two seasons, the National Hockey League has allowed teams to sell space on the ice surface.

The rush to maximize advertising revenues also resulted in some creative ideas. In 1993 Marcel Aubut, the owner of the then NHL team the Quebec Nordiques, enhanced his reputation as a sharp businessman when he sold advertising space on the steps of the arena, a move which, it is claimed, resulted in the Quebec Colisée having more advertising signs than any other sporting venue in North America. This type of advertising is a boon to professional teams, but it doesn't provide any revenue for the television networks delivering the messages.

Until now, the networks had little choice but to carry these messages.

But modern technology has stepped in to provide TV with an alternative. A firm in Princeton, New Jersey has developed a system that allows TV to superimpose its own billboard on the top of an existing one. The technology was used for the first time in summer 1994 on local telecasts of Baltimore Orioles games. The inventors of the system say it can be used to replace existing signs or to project messages on blank surfaces such as a playing field or a wall. The messages would be seen only by TV viewers and could be projected on an area such as a centerfield wall in a baseball park, an area where an actual sign is prohibited because it would interfere with a batter's line of vision. The current application of the new technology is limited to static surfaces, but the inventors say there is no reason why it can't be adapted to moving objects.

Adapted, by permission, from P. Hickey, April 29, 1994, "Zapping freeloaders," *Edmonton Journal TV Times* (Toronto: *Edmonton Journal TV Times*), 6.

Questions

1. What impact is this new technology likely to have on the structure and operations of organizations that own sport facilities?

2. What impact will it have on the television companies that produce and sell sports programs?

3. How could this type of technology change the business of those companies involved in selling sport sponsorship?

4. If you were the manager of a sport facility like the Quebec Colisée, how would you deal with this new technology?

9

Power and Politics in Sport Organizations

You should be able to

1. explain what we mean when we talk about strategic choice,

2. distinguish between power and authority,

3. explain the sources of power that individuals within a sport organization can use,

4. explain how subunits come to acquire power in a sport organization, and

5. describe the types of political activity that we might find taking place in a sport organization.

Power and Politics in the United States Cycling Federation

When David Prouty became the first executive director of the United States Cycling Federation (USCF) he entered an organization where power plays and politics were commonplace. Here, he recalls his first day:

People wanted changes in the USCF, and they wanted them yesterday. I had no sooner begun my new job than the telephone started ringing. A board member implored me to fire so-and-so who worked in the office. A race promoter wanted me to personally approve his request for a race permit. Some of the cycling press wanted to know how soon major structural changes would start happening. I couldn't claim that these callers represented the desires of the majority of the federation's constituents. On the other hand, no one called to say, "We really like things in the USCF the way they are. Don't change anything."

Generally speaking, change within organizations can occur in one of two forms: revolutionary or evolutionary. There were many within the bicycling industry and media who were pushing for revolutionary change for the USCF. In their minds, the new executive director should cut everywhere and cut deeply. He should replace the current staff and reduce the size of the board of directors from the current 25 to a more manageable 10 or 12. The money being spent on the national team should be redistributed to produce growth at the grassroots level. In about three days, 63 years of history would be erased or reversed and the USCF would be humming. Everyone would live happily ever after. It was all so simple.

With those well-intentioned sentiments conveyed to me and a rash of white-knight editorials in the cycling press, I began my tenure as the first executive director of the USCF on February 1. My first task that day was somewhat more mundane than taking a chainsaw to the staff: I had to buy myself a desk and chair.

Nine tons of reality weighed against the possibility of revolutionary change within the USCF. First I came to realize, those who controlled the power didn't want such change. There were some on the board of directors who didn't even want an executive director. They realized that the power and perks they enjoyed would gradually flow to that office.

Second, I had no political power base among the board members. I had been hired by a group outside the organization because the organization couldn't do the job itself. Before the board meeting in January I had met only one board member. While there were many advantages in not owing allegiance to any segment of the board, there was the corresponding disadvantage of having no power base.

Third, there was no atmosphere of crisis that could be used to bring about radical change. The performance of American cyclists had been steadily improving over the previous five years. The number of competitors and racing events had been increasing. And the organization had hired an executive director. The USCF had problems to be sure. However, they were structural in nature, lacked widespread visibility, and were difficult to understand. Most importantly, it wasn't in the interest of those who held power to make the very changes which were needed.

Reprinted, by permission, from D.F. Prouty, 1988, *In spite of us*. (Brattleboro, VT: Vitesse Press), 33-34.

The vignette about David Prouty and the United States Cycling Federation introduces us to the concepts of power and politics. In chapters 6 to 8 we looked at how size, environment, and technology influenced the structure of a sport organization. Although each one of these imperatives (or contingencies, as they are sometimes called) can help us explain how a sport organization should be structured, none provides a total explanation. For each imperative there are questions about its explanatory power. Ford and Slocum (1977) suggested that more explanatory power might be obtained by combining variables. They noted (1977, p. 571) that few studies of organizational structure "have considered two of the three contingency variables together, other than size and technology, and still fewer have considered some form of all three simultaneously." However, Child (1972b) suggests that even if this approach is employed it can still leave up to 40 percent of the structural variance in an organization unaccounted for.

Because of these concerns some researchers have questioned the rational approach to understanding organizations that is the basis of contingency theory. Rather, they suggest that a focus on power and politics in organizations may be a better approach and one which would help us understand much of the unexplained variance in organizational structure. Essentially, the argument made by those who subscribe to a political model of organization is that those who hold the power in the organization will choose a set of structural arrangements that will maintain or increase their power: They will engage in politically motivated behavior. Followers of this school of thought see organizations differently from those who view them as rational entities. In the rational model, organizations are seen as entities in which members share common goals, make decisions in an orderly and logical manner, and see conflict as dysfunctional to their central purpose. In the political model it is accepted that people and groups within organizations have different goals, make decisions in their own best interests, and engage in conflictual behavior.

In this chapter we look at the issues of organizational power and politics. We look first at the concept of strategic choice. This "typically includes not only the establishment of structural forms but also the manipulation of environmental features and the choice of relevant performance standards" (Child, 1972b, p. 1). We then look at the issue of power and how it differs from another common concept in the study of organizations, authority. We examine how power is obtained, and we look at both individual and organizational sources of power. Next, we look at political activity in sport organizations and the types of political tactics that can be employed to acquire, develop, and use power.

Strategic Choice

The notion of strategic choice was first put forward by John Child in 1972 as an argument against the emphasis that was being placed on structural imperatives. Essentially, what Child suggested was that although imperatives such as environment and technology constrain managers in the decisions they make, these people still have the power to exercise choice in regard to these contingency factors and consequently they have the power to determine the type of organizational structure they adopt. For example, Child argued that the decision makers in an organization had far more power to choose their environment, technology, and size than was commonly inferred by those who argued for the importance of these imperatives in explaining organizational structure.

In terms of environment, he suggested (1972b, p. 4) that "organizational decision makers may have certain opportunities to select the type of environment in which they will operate." For example, the senior managers at Nike exercised their power of choice in 1979, when they decided to enter the sports apparel market; so, too, did managers at Brunswick when they sold off their medical division to concentrate on sporting goods. So, too, would the chair of a sport management department who chose to direct her department's efforts toward teaching and executive development rather than toward research. In deciding to enter a particular environmental domain, the senior managers of a sport organization are at the same time deciding the types of organizations with which they will have to interact, the type of regulations to which they will be subject, and who their competitors will be. These decisions in turn will influence their choice of structure. In short, senior managers influence structure by the choices they make about environmental domain, rather than the environment itself.

Like environmental domain, Child (1972b, p. 6) also maintains that technology and its relationship to structure should be "viewed as a derivative of decisions made by those in control of the organization regarding the tasks to be carried out in relation to the resources available to perform them." So, for example, when Bill Holland chose to make custom-bike frames in his small workshop in Spring Valley, California with a group of five or six employees, he was at the same time selecting to use a craft technology. It would have been very difficult for him to enter into mass production. Managers, therefore, dictate structure by their choice of domain, which in turn influences the choice of technology.

Powerplay: The Firing of Madame Monique Berlioux

Monique Berlioux's first connection with the Olympic Games movement was in 1948 when she represented France in swimming. Nearly 20 years later she was employed by the IOC to take charge of press relations; in 1968 when IOC secretary Johan Westerhoff resigned, it was Berlioux who assumed his duties. During her time with the IOC the organization changed considerably. When she first joined the IOC staff, the organization hardly had the money to pay her salary. The increased revenue from television contracts changed the IOC's financial position and, as the organization became more powerful, so, too, did Berlioux. She is described as an authoritarian figure who kept tight control of her staff at the IOC headquarters in the Chateau de Vidy in Lausanne.

Like Avery Brundage and Lord Killanin, the first two presidents she served, Berlioux was strongly committed to amateurism and opposed to any commercialization of the Games. Both Brundage and Killanin conducted their duties of IOC president from their homes and the day-to-day operation of the organization was left in Berlioux's hands.

However, in 1980 Juan Antonio Samaranch took over the presidency of the IOC from Lord Killanin. Shortly after his appointment Samaranch moved into residence in Lausanne. His staff quickly grew to rival that of Berlioux's and the two groups became suspicious of each other. It is rumored that Berlioux even told Samaranch she didn't think there was room in the city for both of them; prophetically, she was right.

Samaranch was firmly committed to the commercialization of the Games. In the early 1980s he talked to Horst Dassler of Adidas who, along with Patrick Nally, had formed International Sport and Leisure (ISL). ISL had experience marketing the rights of the Federation Internationale de Football Associations (FIFA) and the World Cup of Soccer. Dassler offered ISL's services to the IOC and in 1983 a report was presented to the IOC's Commission for New Sources of Finance. Although Berlioux was not opposed in principle to using ISL to increase the standing and influence of the IOC, her critics believed that she was concerned that their involvement would reduce her own power and prestige. As a result, she was reluctant to sanction ISL as anything more than consultants to the IOC. It soon became clear that Madame Berlioux's ideas of ISL's role and the future structure of the IOC were different from that of President Samaranch. Consequently, at the IOC's 1985 session in East Berlin, Samaranch asked Canadian IOC member Dick Pound to inform Madame Berlioux that she was "to resign." Her 17-year "reign" (as many saw her time at the IOC) was over.

Based on information in Killanin, Lord. (1983). *My Olympic years*. London: Secker & Warburg; Wilson, N. (1988). *The sports business*. London: Piatkus; Hill, C.R. (1992). *Olympic politics*. Manchester: University of Manchester Press.

Size, too, is subject to the choices made by managers. Although "the need to cope administratively with a large number of organizational members and their activities may well impose constraints upon certain structural choices . . . important avenues of choice remain open" (Child, 1972b, p. 7). For example, managers may choose to break down large units into smaller ones that can act independently; alternatively, they may choose to limit the size to which a unit can grow. We saw this in chapter 6 in the vignette outlining Bill Gore's decision to restrict the number of his plants to 150 associates. Berrett, Burton, and Slack (1993) also describe how some

entrepreneurs within the sport industry made a choice to limit the size of their business in order to maintain centralized control.

In addition to making choices about their organization's environment, technology, and size, Child (1972b, p. 4) suggests that in some cases managers "may command sufficient power to influence the conditions prevailing within environments where they are already operating." Organizations are not always influenced by their environment; some can "enact" it (Weick, 1969). In large companies in particular, managers can create a demand for a product and/or take steps to limit the amount of competition within their environment. The Canadian Football League's lobbying of Canada's federal government to prevent the World Football League from placing a franchise in Toronto, and the 1979 merger of the National Hockey League with the World Hockey Association, are both examples of the ways managers of sport organizations (in this case the CFL and the NHL) have worked to enact their environment by limiting competition.

A third argument that Child (1972b) makes for strategic choice concerns the difference between the actual environment of an organization and the way it is perceived by its managers. As we saw in chapter 7 managers make choices based on the way they perceive their environment to be, not necessarily the way it actually is. As such it is managerial choice rather than the actual nature of a sport organization's environment that is most likely to influence structural design. For example, a sportswear manufacturer may see Eastern Europe as a dynamic, growing environment with new market opportunities. To meet this demand new product lines may be developed, staff increased, and new manufacturing facilities acquired. Eastern Europe may or may not be a dynamic environment, but it is managerial perception and the choices managers make based on this perception that lead to structural change, not the actual nature of the environment.

A final area where Child (1972b) suggests the influence of strategic choice can be felt is in the area of organizational effectiveness. Most studies of organizational effectiveness treat performance as a dependent variable. Child (1972b, p. 11) suggests that, in contrast, a theory concerned with organizational structure should "posit structural variables as depending on decisions which were made with reference to some standard of performance." Structure is therefore the dependent variable. Managers do not always make decisions to utilize a structure that will produce the highest level of performance, because this decision may reduce their power or destabilize the organization. Rather, they select a structure that will achieve an optimal level of performance, allowing the decision group "to adopt structural arrangements which accord the better with their own preferences . . ." (Child, 1972b, p. 11), which in turn allows them to increase or maintain their level of power and autonomy. An example of this type of situation is once again found in Berrett, Burton, and Slack's (1993) study of entrepreneurs in the sport and leisure industry. One of the entrepreneurs was quite willing to forego the increased profits (one of the most common measures of effectiveness) that could be achieved by expansion, in order to retain the type of structural arrangements that allowed him to maintain control of his operation.

Power and Authority

Power is one of the most widespread yet more problematic concepts in the organizational theory literature. While some scholars have suggested that there is an overabundance of writing on power (Clark, 1967), others have indicated that the concept has not received much attention (Kotter, 1977). Martin (1971, p. 240) suggested that "theorizing about power has often been confusing, obscurantist, and banal"; he adds, "it is not surprising that March (1966) concluded that 'on the whole power is a disappointing concept'."

Power is not something we can see within a sport organization, but its effects can be clearly felt. While there are numerous definitions within the organizational literature (cf. Astley & Sachdeva, 1984; Pfeffer, 1992), the most commonly accepted conceptualization suggests that power is the ability to get someone to do something they would not have otherwise done or "the probability that one actor in a social relationship will be in a position to carry out his own will despite resistance, regardless of the basis on which this probability rests" (Weber, 1947, p. 152).

Notwithstanding the widespread use of this definition, these kinds of explanations of the concept of power are not without problems. Martin (1971, p. 243), for example, suggests that this type of definition implies that power involves conflict or antagonism and ignores "the possibility that power relations may be relations of mutual convenience: [and] power may be a resource facilitating the achievement of the goals of both A and B." Martin also saw as problematic the fact that the Weberian definition of power (and others like it) "transposes a property of interactions or interrelations, into a property of actors." That is, power in this type of definition is seen as being personalized, not a product of the social relationships between actors. In this regard Emerson (1962, p. 32) points out that these types of relationships are not one-sided and "commonly entail ties of mutual dependence between parties."

Also important to note about the use of the term "power" is that some writers use it interchangeably with, or to encompass, concepts such as coercion, influence, manipulation, and authority (cf. Bachrach & Baratz, 1962; Styskal, 1980). Authority is in fact one form of power; it is the power that is formally sanctioned by a sport organization, the power that accrues to a person because of his or her role within the organization (cf. Weber, 1947). Authority is only legitimate within the sport organization that grants the authority. The power by which managers exercise strategic choice is, in essence, authority—the power they derive from the position they hold in the organization. This is not to say that people who don't have authority can't influence these choices. Authority must be accepted by the role holder's subordinates, and it is exercised down the organizational hierarchy. In contrast, power can be exer-

cised vertically up or down the organizational hierarchy, and horizontally. The examples in table 9.1 illustrate acts that involve authority and those that entail the use of other forms of power.

Sources of Power

While we often think of *people* as being powerful, the way a sport organization is structured can lead to some *subunits* becoming powerful, regardless of the people within them. In this section we look first at the ways individuals acquire power. We then focus on organizational sources of power.

Table 9.1 Actions Based on Authority and Other Forms of Power

ACTIONS BASED ON AUTHORITY	ACTIONS BASED ON OTHER FORMS OF POWER
• A quarterback calling the plays in a football game • A sport management professor giving a student an extension to complete a term paper • The chief executive officer of a sporting goods company signing a contract to sponsor a sports event • The president of a university suspending a coach for recruiting violations	• The president of a national sport organization calling a friend who holds a government position to enlist help in securing grant funding • An athletic director having the university's athletic therapist treat her 14-year-old son's sprained ankle • The president of a sport consulting company asking his secretary to buy a birthday gift for his wife • A college basketball coach hiring a high school player to work at the college's summer basketball camp in order to encourage her to attend the college

TIME OUT

The Power of Mr. Fixit

Andy Norman spent much of his life as a policeman in the south of England. But in the 1970s he also emerged as one of the most powerful people in international athletics. Known in British track-and-field circles as Mr. Fixit, Norman recruited athletes for meet promoters. His power came from his encyclopedic knowledge of track and field and his wide network of contacts with European meet promoters. American athletes coming to Europe for the summer would contact Norman to arrange their competition schedule. "He knew everybody," says Stephen Aris, "their likes and dislikes, their strengths and weaknesses." Through his wide range of contacts Norman was able to exert a powerful influence over the track-and-field world. Athletes were careful not to offend him because, as Aris notes, "a word in the right direction from Andy Norman could make or break an athlete's career."

Based on information in Aris, S. (1990). *Sportsbiz: Inside the sports business*. London: Hutchinson.

Sources of Individual Power

One of the most widely cited accounts of the sources of individual power is French and Raven's (1959) five-part typology: legitimate power, reward power, coercive power, referent power, and expert power. A description of each of these types is presented below. It is important to note that the types of power cited are not discrete and in fact may overlap. Shetty (1978, p. 177) notes, for example, that the "possession of one type of power can affect the extent and effectiveness of other types. The judicious use of reward power and coercive power can increase the effectiveness of legitimate power; inappropriate use, however, will decrease legitimate power. . . ."

Legitimate Power

Legitimate power is the same as authority. People acquire it by virtue of their position within a sport organization. Managers, athletic directors, deans, members of the board of directors of a voluntary sport organization, and coaches are all examples of people who, because of the positions they hold in their respective sport organizations, can expect compliance from their subordinates when they request that things be done. They have legitimate power. This type of power comes from a person's position and not because of any other special qualities she or he may possess. This does not mean, however, that people who occupy the same position will use the power of their office in the same way. Hill (1992), for example, describes the differing ways in which Lord Killanin and his successor Juan Antonio Samaranch utilized the power of the IOC presidency. Killanin left much of the day-to-day running of the IOC to his staff, Samaranch, in contrast, is a "hands-on" president who is seen as less consultative in the way he operates.

Reward Power

The power that comes from one person's control of another person's rewards is termed reward power. The larger the reward and the greater the importance of the reward to the recipient, the more power the person who gives the reward is able to exercise. The owner of a professional sport team may offer rewards to players who perform well. Coaches can give rewards in the form of more playing time or a starting position. The volunteer president of a national sport organization can reward other volunteers by lobbying for them to be appointed to international committees or by giving them perks like naming them to honorary positions with teams traveling to major sport festivals.

Coercive Power

Coercive power is the power derived from the ability that one person has to punish another. The fear of punishment can be a strong motivator and in some ways coercive power can be seen as the counterpart of reward power. Although many people see coercive power as dysfunctional because it alienates people and builds up resentment, it is not uncommon to see this type of power used in sport organizations. For example, coaches will often bench players for not playing well or not working hard in practice and sport management professors may penalize students who hand in late assignments.

Referent Power

Referent power is based on an individual's charisma and another person's identification with this quality. In many ways referent power is very much like the Weberian notion of charismatic authority. Referent power can occur when the members of a sport organization identify very strongly with the values espoused by their leader. Coaches like Dean Smith from the University of North Carolina and Bobby Knight from Indiana are strong personalities, seen by many people as charismatic; as such they have referent power. People with referent power are often used to promote sport teams, events, and equipment.

Expert Power

Expert power accrues to a person because of the special knowledge or skill she possesses. A person does not need to be particularly high up the sport organization's hierarchy to have expert power. For example, a computer technician in a sport organization that uses computer-aided design may wield considerable power if she is the only person in the company who knows how to operate the computer. Coaches, product designers, and player's agents may all be seen to have expert power because of their credibility in their specialized area. One of the ways individuals can acquire expert power is through the information they possess.

Organizational Sources of Power

As we saw in the last section, some sources of individual power are a result of holding positions of

TIME OUT

Marketing Charisma

To the corporate mind, sporting success is only one ingredient in the marketing mix. Far more important is the star's image and personality. As Ion Tiriac, Boris Becker's manager, says:

> The sponsor is not buying a product. He is buying a relationship with a human being. More and more companies don't just buy results, they want the personality as well. That's why the charisma of the athlete is as important as his results. It's not the fact that the guy wins Wimbledon. It's the fact of how he wins and the nature of the communication between him and the consumer.

It is a subject on which Tiriac is something of an authority. In 1985, a few months before 17-year-old Boris won Wimbledon for the first time, he signed a deal with Puma, the West German sports equipment and clothing manufacturer, worth a reputed $24 million. The results were spectacular. In two years, sales of Puma racquets rose from 15,000 to 300,000 to become number one in Germany and one of the most popular brands in Europe. Shoe sales rocketed, reaching a peak of three million pairs in a single year. What Puma was selling was nothing as mundane as shoes and tennis racquets, but the magic of the Becker name. Tiriac says he sells Becker to his clients not so much as a player but as a personality.

Based on information in Aris, S. (1990). *Sportsbiz: Inside the sports business.* London: Hutchinson.

authority in a sport organization; others reflect personal qualities that are unrelated to the organization. In this section we look at the power that accrues to organizational subunits as a result of the way in which the sport organization is designed. We focus specifically on five organization-based sources of power: the acquisition and control of resources, the ability to cope with uncertainty, centrality, non-substitutability, and control over the decision making process.

Acquisition and Control of Resources

One of the primary ways a subunit within a sport organization can obtain power is through its ability to acquire and control resources. As Pfeffer (1981, p. 101) points out, because organizations require a continuous supply of resources those subunits within the organization "that can provide the most critical and difficult-to-obtain resources come to have power in the organization." The important point to draw from Pfeffer's statement is that it is not just the ability to acquire and control resources that gives an organizational subunit power, but the fact that it can secure resources critical to the organization's operations and difficult to obtain. Resources may come in a variety of forms and can include money, people, information, and legitimacy.

Money is a particularly important resource to any organization because it can be used to acquire other resources and "it can be stored and is relatively divisible in terms of its use" (Pfeffer, 1981, p. 101). In universities, those departments that are able to generate large amounts of external funding are often regarded as powerful. On many U.S. campuses the athletic department, which is often able to generate funds through its sports programs, is seen as a powerful subunit. People are also a valuable resource; nowhere is this more apparent than in the competition among professional and collegiate sport teams for highly skilled players. The teams that are able to secure the most talented group of players become the most powerful subunit within their respective league.

The Ability to Cope With Uncertainty

Sport organizations of all types are constantly coping with uncertainty, arising out of changes in the task environment of the sport organization—suppliers, competitors, fans, regulatory agencies, and the like. Uncertainty can also arise as a result of the technological interdependence we discussed in chapter 8. Because uncertainty creates problems for an organization, those subunits that can reduce or control uncertainty gain increased power

(Hinings, Hickson, Pennings, & Schneck, 1974). Hickson, Hinings, Lee, Schneck, and Pennings (1971) suggest three methods by which organizations cope with uncertainty. The first is by acquiring information about future trends. Market research units within sport organizations are designed exactly for this purpose. If they are successful in predicting trends such as product demand they can become a very powerful entity within the organization. Studies of fan attendance at various sporting events (cf. Gauthier & Hansen, 1993; Hansen & Gauthier, 1989; Schofield, 1983) are in essence designed to identify those factors that affect attendance. Subunits that can utilize this information to maintain or increase attendance can help reduce uncertainty and thus are able to increase their own power within the organization.

The second method of coping with uncertainty is absorption. Absorption involves taking action after an event has occurred (Hickson et al., 1971). For example, if a sports equipment store that encounters a sharp drop in sales can counter with some novel selling methods, it has coped via absorption. Exercycle, for instance, is one of the oldest manufacturers of exercise bicycles. In 1959 the company sold 10,000 Exercycles, a company record. However, since fitness and lifestyle products have become more popular, the company's fortunes have declined. In the mid-1980s the company was selling only 2,000 to 3,000 machines per year in what was a $2 billion-per-year fitness industry. In 1987 President Richard Baird started to take steps to turn this situation around. Using a new marketing strategy the company targeted its marketing efforts on three groups, "aging consumers who want the ease of home use; executives who don't have time for racquetball or other physical activities; and the medical therapy community" (Bottorff, 1987, p. 54).

Acquiring information and absorption are methods used to cope with uncertainty after it occurs. It is also possible to cope with uncertainty by preventing its occurrence, the third method suggested by Hickson et al. (1971). For example, in 1975 the running boom had taken off in America and Nike (or Blue Ribbon Sports, as it was then called) was a rapidly growing company. However, sales manager Jim Moodhe and his staff could see that Blue Ribbon was going to have problems meeting the demand for its product. Its credit lines were stretched and it didn't have the money to produce the shoes that were going to be needed. To solve this problem and prevent the potential uncertainty of not being able to meet the demand for the product, Moodhe developed a program he called "Futures." "The idea

behind Futures was to offer major customers . . . an opportunity to place large orders six months in advance and have them commit to that noncancellable order in writing. In exchange, customers would get a 5 to 7 percent discount and guaranteed delivery on 90 percent of their order within a two-week window of time" (Strasser & Becklund, 1991, p. 200). The plan was a success; Moodhe and his sales department were able to cope with the uncertainty facing Blue Ribbon Sports by preventing it from happening.

Centrality

A subunit's position in the work or information flow of a sport organization helps determine the amount of power that the subunit possesses. Subunits that are more central to the work or information flow will be more powerful than those on the periphery. In large part, centrality is determined by the sport organization's strategy and the problems it is facing at a particular time. Slack, Berrett, and Mistry (1994) show how the strategic emphasis on high-performance sport adopted by a Canadian national sport organization increased the power of a group of coaches employed by the organization. In an organization strategically oriented to the market place, for example, a sport equipment manufacturer, the marketing department is likely to be one of the most important functional units. If a sport organization adopts a strategy of increased efficiency and fiscal control, the finance department is likely to gain increased power merely because its activities are central to the strategic approach adopted by the organization.

Financial people are also likely to become more powerful if the sport organization faces a financial crisis. Similarly, when sales fall, the marketing and sales departments become a primary focus for the sport organization and thus their power increases. It has even been suggested that in some organizations, subunits central to the organization's operations may sometimes create problems that they have to solve. In this way the members of the subunit are able to remind others in the organization of their importance (cf. Pfeffer, 1977b).

Non-Substitutability

Being irreplaceable is an important means of gaining power for both subunits and individuals. In their strategic contingencies theory of power, Hickson and his colleagues (1971, p. 221) suggest that "the lower the substitutability of the activities of a subunit, the greater its power within the organization."

However, to retain their power base subunits and individuals have to ensure that the particular knowledge or skills they possess are not easily replaced. As Pfeffer (1981, p. 113) points out, "if others can obtain access to the expert's information" then their power base is quickly destroyed. Consequently, those with power will use strategies to maintain their status. These strategies may include "using specialized language and symbols that make the[ir] expertise look even more arcane and difficult to comprehend" (Pfeffer, 1981, p. 114), or preventing individuals with a similar expertise from being a part of the organization. In sport organizations coaches often use specialized language. Swimming coaches, for example, talk about tapering, shaving down, and bilateral breathing. This use of language elevates their specialized knowledge to a level above that which many people involved in swimming (particularly the parents of swimmers) are able to comprehend; thus the power of the coaching subunit is maintained.

Control Over the Decision Making Process

Subunits and individual members of a sport organization can gain power by controlling the process of decision making. Power is gained not only through having input into the outcomes of the decision process, but also through control of the process itself. Those subunits and individuals who can influence *when* decisions are made, *who* is involved in the decision process, and *what alternatives* are presented, become very powerful. Macintosh and Whitson (1990) suggest that we have seen this type of control exercised in Canada's national sport organizations. The growing number of professional administrators in these organizations, because of their location in the sport organization's structure, have been able to limit volunteer involvement in the decision making process. As Macintosh and Whitson point out, participation in the decision process "is restricted to those who agree on ends and [those] who are unlikely to persist in raising issues that complicate the pursuit of those ends" (p. 131). As a result, the professional administrators within these sport organizations have become very powerful.

Organizational Politics

The study of organizational politics has not received a lot of attention within the sport management literature. Yet, like power, politics pervades all sport organizations, although it is somewhat intangible and hard to measure. Political skills are not easily taught to students or would-be managers. Politics is related to the use of power; political skills involve "the ability to use the bases of power effectively—to convince those to whom one has access; to use one's resources, information, and technical skills to their fullest in bargaining; to exercise formal power with a sensitivity to the feelings of others; to know where to concentrate one's energies; to sense what is possible; to organize the necessary alliances" (Mintzberg, 1983, p. 26).

As table 9.2 shows, a study of chief executives, staff managers, and supervisors found that organizational politics is seen to be both helpful and harmful to the individual members of an organization and to the operation of the organization itself.

Some people see politics as involving coercion, dishonesty, and manipulative behavior by individuals seeking to further their own self-interests. Others see politics as an integral feature of organizations and a way in which differences among interest groups are resolved and tasks are accomplished. A study by Gandz and Murray (1980) (see table 9.3) found that people felt politics was a common feature of organizations, that political activity occurred more frequently at the higher levels of an organization, and that to be successful in an organization one had to be good at politics. However, like the study by Madison, Allen, Porter, Renwick, and Mayes (1980), Gandz and Murray's work also found that respondents felt there were problems and drawbacks to organizational politics.

We now examine some of the different types of political tactics used in sport organizations. While we focus specifically on four activities—building coalitions, using outside experts, building a network of contacts, and controlling information—there are, as table 9.4 shows, a number of other political tactics used in organizations.

Building Coalitions

One of the main ways people in sport organizations can increase their political power is by building coalitions with others (cf. Pfeffer, 1981). Coalitions are built when people spend time communicating their views to others, establishing trust relationships, and building mutual respect. While these activities can occur within the formal confines of the sport organization, they often occur over dinner, in the bar, or on the golf course. Coalitions are only effective when they are tightly united around a particular issue. Sometimes political activity is

Table 9.2   Helpful and Harmful Features of Organizational Politics

TO THE INDIVIDUAL	PERCENT RESPONSE BY GROUP			
	COMBINED	CEO	STAFF	SUPERVISOR
Helpful				
Advance career	60.9	56.7	53.6	72.4
Recognition, status	21.8	13.3	25.0	27.6
Enhance, power, position	19.5	20.0	25.0	13.8
Accomplish personal goals	14.9	26.7	10.7	6.9
Get the job done	11.5	13.3	14.3	6.9
Sell ideas, projects, programs	10.3	10.0	7.1	13.8
Feelings (achievement, ego, control, success, etc.)	8.1	6.7	10.7	6.9
Survival	4.7	3.3	0.0	10.3
Harmful				
Loss of power, stratetic position, credibility	39.1	33.3	39.3	44.8
Loss of job, demotion, etc.	31.0	30.0	32.1	31.0
Negative feelings of others	21.8	33.3	14.3	17.2
Passive loss of promotion, transfers, etc.	19.5	6.7	32.1	20.7
Internal feelings, guilt	12.6	6.7	14.3	17.2
Promotion to level of incompetence	9.2	6.7	0.0	20.7
Job performance hampered	3.5	0.0	0.0	10.3

TO THE ORGANIZATION	PERCENT RESPONSE BY GROUP			
	COMBINED	CEO	STAFF	SUPERVISOR
Helpful				
Organization goals achieved, get job done	26.4	30.0	28.6	20.7
Organization survival, health, processes	26.4	26.7	25.0	27.6
Visibility of ideas, people, etc.	19.5	16.7	21.4	20.7
Coordination, communication	18.4	23.3	17.9	13.8
Develop teams, group functioning	11.5	16.7	7.1	10.3
Esprit de corps, channel energy	10.3	10.0	10.7	10.3
Decision making, analysis	6.9	3.3	14.3	3.5
No response (unable to mention helpful result)	14.9	10.0	10.7	24.1
Harmful				
Distract from organization goals	44.8	43.3	35.7	55.2
Misuse of resources	32.3	36.7	32.1	27.6
Divisiveness, splits, fights	21.8	20.0	21.4	24.1
Climate: tension, frustration	19.5	16.7	21.4	20.7
Incompetents advanced	14.9	3.3	21.4	20.7
Lower coordination, communication	10.3	3.3	10.7	17.2
Damage organization image, reputation	10.3	6.7	10.7	13.8
No response (no harm mentioned)	3.5	3.3	7.1	0.0

Table 9.3   Characteristics of Workplace Politics

STATEMENT	PERCENTAGE AGREEMENT
(a) The existence of workplace politics is common to most organizations.	93.2
(b) Successful executives must be good politicians.	89.0
(c) The higher you go in organizations, the more political the climate becomes.	76.2
(d) Only organizationally weak people play politics.	68.5
(e) Organizations free of politics are happier than those where there is a lot of politics.	59.1
(f) You have to be political to get ahead in organizations.	69.8
(g) Politics in organizations are detrimental to efficiency.	55.1
(h) Top management should try to get rid of politics within the organization.	48.6
(i) Politics help organizations function effectively.	42.1
(j) Powerful executives don't act politically.	15.7

Adapted, by permission, from J. Gandz and V.V. Murray, 1980, "The experience of workplace politics," *Academy of Management Journal*: 244.

Table 9.4   Managerial Perception of Organizational Politics Tactics

TACTIC	PERCENT OF RESPONDENTS THAT MENTIONED TACTIC			
	COMBINED GROUPS	CHIEF EXECUTIVE OFFICERS	STAFF MANAGERS	SUPERVISORS
Attacking or blaming others	54.0	60.0	50.0	51.7
Use of information	54.0	56.7	57.1	48.3
Image building/impression management	52.9	43.3	46.4	69.0
Support building for ideas	36.8	46.7	39.3	24.1
Praising others, ingratiation	25.3	16.7	25.0	34.5
Power coalition, strong allies	25.3	26.7	17.9	31.0
Associating with the influential	24.1	16.7	35.7	20.7
Creating obligations/reciprocity	12.6	3.3	14.3	30.7

Copyright © 1979 by The Regents of the University of California. Reprinted from the *California Management Review*, Vol. 22, No. 4. By permission of The Regents.

directed at weakening coalitions by using a "divide-and-conquer" tactic. Coalitions can occur within sport organizations; for example, the coming together of the players in an organization such as the National Hockey League Players Association (NHLPA) is a form of coalition. Coalitions can also occur among sport organizations. For example, in Canada in 1993 a large number of national sport organizations came together as a coalition for a series of "Sport Forums" designed to lobby the federal government on a number of issues relating to the funding of sport.

The Use of Outside Experts

Another common method of exercising political power used in a number of sport organizations is to hire outside experts to support or legitimize one's position. While government agencies and large companies in the sport industry often have their own in-house experts, these people often "carry baggage"; that is, they are seen to represent a particular constituency within the organization and as such favor that group's position. Hiring outside experts, perhaps a consulting company, is seen as a means of gaining an "objective view." However, despite an aura of objectivity it is often possible for those people hiring the experts to manipulate the outcome of any reports. For example, government departments such as the ones responsible for sport in Canada have often commissioned reports by outside experts to look at a number of different aspects of the sport delivery system; these reports are usually tabled with the Minister, the elected official responsible for overseeing the department. If the Minister likes the report and it fits with the department's stance, it can be made public, thus supporting and legitimizing the department's position. If the report is not to the Minister's liking and contrary to the department's position, it can be merely received as information, in which case its contents will not be released to the public by the Minister's office. Similar tactics may be used by the CEO of a large corporation within the sport industry. Reports can be commissioned but, if they are not to the CEO's liking, they are not made available to other members of the organization. It is also possible to manipulate the results of studies produced by external consultants simply by choosing carefully at the outset. Consulting companies often bid or are interviewed before they are awarded these projects; those doing the selecting are quite likely to hire someone who favors their own position.

In addition to offering support and legitimacy, outside experts can be used for other political purposes. One of the most vivid and recent examples in sport is the Canadian government's use of a commission headed by the Associate Chief Justice of the Province of Ontario to investigate the events surrounding Ben Johnson's positive drug test in the 1988 Olympic Games 100 meters. Although ostensibly set up to examine the use of performance-enhancing drugs by Canadian athletes, the Dubin Inquiry (as it was known) served a number of political purposes for the Canadian government in regard to its involvement in sport, particularly track and field. As Beauchesne (cited by Hall, Slack, Smith, & Whitson, 1991, p. 224) notes, its primary purpose was "(1) to dissociate the government or government bodies from scandal; (2) to convey the impression of taking action to remedy the problem; and (3) implicit in the trial format itself, to expose the guilty and to affirm the power of sanction as the best means to deter the situation."

Building a Network of Contacts

To be politically effective in a sport organization, it is necessary to gain the support of other people.

Creating a network of contacts may involve building links with people inside and outside of the organization. Networks are established through the formal mechanisms of the sport organization but also through informal means. Kanter (1977) suggests that within an organization three types of people are important in building a network of contacts: sponsors, peers, and subordinates.

Sponsors are those individuals at a higher level of the organization. Kanter (1977) suggests these people fulfill three important networking functions. First, they can fight for their contacts at the upper levels of the organization. Second, they can often help bypass the organizational hierarchy or at least help guide someone through it. Finally, sponsors "also provide an important signal to other people, a form of reflected power" (Kanter, 1977, p. 181). Peers are sometimes overlooked in the process of building contacts. However, acceptance by one's peers is often a necessary step in obtaining the favors and recognition required to acquire political power and build the type of coalition discussed above. Subordinates are also important contacts:

> The accumulation of power through alliances [is] not always upward oriented. For one thing differential rates of hierarchical progress could mean that juniors or peers one day could become a person's boss the next. So it would be to a person's advantage to make alliances downward in the hierarchy with people who looked like they may be on the way up (Kanter, 1977, pp. 185-186).

It is also advantageous to build alliances with subordinates because they carry out the tasks necessary to acquire political power. A lack of compliance by subordinates makes the power holder powerless.

A network of contacts can often be enhanced by hiring, promoting, transferring, or firing selected individuals. Sometimes it may even be beneficial to co-opt into one's network someone with a dissenting view. For example, an academic member of staff who feels the athletic teams are getting too much money from the university's central administration may, if appointed to the department's budget committee, see the athletic director's point of view and realize that athletic teams are not overfunded. Such co-optation brings the dissenting member into the athletic department's network.

In addition to building a network of contacts within the sport organization, it is also important to build up outside contacts. Frank King, chairman of the 1988 Olympic Games organizing committee, in his book *It's how you play the game: The inside story of the Calgary Olympics*, describes how he and his committee spent large amounts of time, both prior to getting the Games and in the time leading up to the Games, networking with IOC members, government bureaucrats, international sport personnel, and corporate officials.

Controlling Information

Controlling information is a form of political activity that can be used by sport managers to influence the outcomes of the decision making process within their organization or a decision concerning their organization. By emphasizing facts that support their position, or by hiding, limiting, or ignoring other relevant information, managers can promote their own position and/or discredit the points of view put forward by others. It has been argued that this type of tactic is frequently used by those bidding to host major sporting events like the Olympic Games (cf. Auf de Maur, 1976; Reasons, 1984). Essentially what happens is that those in favor of

---

TIME OUT

The Power of the Coach

Joe Paterno of Penn State, one of the best football coaches in North America, was voted Coach of the Year in 1968. At the Coach of the Year banquet, he and Bear Bryant, who was sitting next to him, got to discussing contracts. Bryant urged Paterno to renegotiate his contract, asking for more money, a car, and a country club membership. He also told Paterno he should have 200 season tickets. "That's going to give you the power to do whatever you want with your program and with yourself," Bryant said.

Paterno, although he understood what was being said to him, felt uneasy with the ideas. In his autobiography *Paterno: By the book*, he reflects on the power of a college coach and on the discomfort he felt with Bryant's advice:

[The discomfort] was not from a difference in scruples, only style. Maybe I didn't fully understand then a coach's potential power in a college, in a community, among alumni and financial angels, and that he's got to use that power effectively or he's not serving the program he was hired to run. But I was beginning to sense that he's got to gather that power and use it in a way that fits his personality.

If a team needs facilities as a condition of success, the coach needs the power to get them—and needs to use it. If a coach has a bad year and needs protection from those ready to chop off his head without asking questions, he's at an advantage if he's surrounded by a friendly force of important alumni. People like to be around a winning coach. Not just alumni, but politicians, journalists, influential businessmen, and, believe it or not, even some celebrity professors who swing a lot of power inside a university. The more successful a football program (or any kind of program in a university—athletic, academic, research, or anything else)—the more it needs friends and supporters to help it survive and move ahead in an environment of extreme competition for dollars, for physical space, for equipment.

To the coach who can collect some of that power by controlling a stack of hard-to-get football tickets, I say (literally) more power to him. Paul Bryant, born to an old-time Southern style of politics, had, out of his genuine generosity, a natural sense for giving favors, but then turning them into power. He could get summer jobs for his players with just a phone call because he'd established many small, flattering, accommodating relationships. What he put to work wasn't raw power, but a personal charm that made people want to do what he wanted. If he wanted a new building or a new policy on grades, people did what he wanted not because they feared him, but because they wanted to please him.

From *Paterno: By the book* by Joe Paterno with Bernard Asbell. Copyright © 1989 by Joe Paterno and Bernard Asbell. Reprinted by permission of Random House, Inc.

the Games emphasize the positive aspects of staging these events—the creation of new facilities, the infusion of tourist dollars into the community, and the creation of jobs. Games advocates choose not to discuss that the cost of the Games will be borne by local taxpayers, the facilities created are often used by privately owned professional sport teams after the games, and any long-term economic benefits to hosting major Games are relatively minimal. By controlling information, supporters of a Games bid hope to influence the decision process positively.

Summary and Conclusions

Power and politics are two of the most neglected topics of study in sport management, yet they are present in every sport organization. Much of the research conducted in the area of sport management adopts a rational view of organizations, which assumes that sport organizations have specific goals, that everyone agrees on these goals, and the organization's structure is a product of rational responses to changes in contingency variables such as size, technology, and environment. In contrast, a political perspective on organizations assumes diverse goals, individuals and groups acting in their own self-interest, and organizational structure as the product of managers and/or the organization's dominant coalition making decisions to preserve their own privileged position.

In this chapter on power and politics in sport organizations we looked first of all at Child's challenge to the rational ideas of contingency theory, expressed in his notion of strategic choice. Child argued that the structure of an organization was less dependent on determinants such as size, technology, and environment, and more a product of decisions made by managers about these areas. The reconciliation of these two viewpoints is one of the major issues in the study of organizations.

The concept of strategic choice is built upon the idea that managers and/or the members of the dominant coalition have the power to make choices about their organization's domain of operations. Consequently, we looked at the concept of power and some of the issues which surround the concept. We specifically highlighted the difference between power and authority. We then focused on the different sources of power. Using French and Raven's five-part typology, we discussed sources of individual power. We also looked at the way in which different subunits or groups within an organization could acquire power.

Power is intimately related to politics and we looked at the advantages and disadvantages of the use of political activity in a sport organization. We examined some activities that people engage in to acquire political power—building coalitions, using outside experts, building a network of contacts, and controlling information.

Key Concepts

Strategic choice	Power
Politics	Authority
Legitimate power	Reward power
Coercive power	Referent power
Expert power	Charismatic authority
Resource control	Uncertainty
Centrality	Non-substitutability
Control over decision making	Coalitions
Using experts	Networks
Information control	

Review Questions

1. Pick a sport organization with which you are familiar. Who are the powerful individuals within the organization? Why?

2. How can we reconcile the arguments made by contingency theorists with Child's arguments about strategic choice?

3. Compare and contrast the concepts of power and authority.

4. Pick a sport organization that you know well. What type of strategic choices have the managers in this organization made and how have they affected their organization's structure?

5. How does the use of reward power and the use of coercive power relate to the use of authority?

6. Could someone at a lower level of sport organization be powerful? If so, how?

7. Regrettably there are very few women who hold senior level positions in sport organizations. Given what you have read about sources of individual power, how are women constrained in moving to senior level management positions?

8. If you think about a sport organization that you know well, what subunits within this organization are powerful? Why?

9. You are a recent graduate from a sport management program and you have just got a position as a marketing assistant in a professional sport franchise. What can you do to acquire power?

10. How is the use of power likely to differ in a mechanistic, as opposed to an organic, organizational structure?

11. How does control over where decisions are made confer power on someone?

12. Has the increased use of computers in sport organizations made managers more or less powerful?

13. How does a sport organization's strategy influence the power structure of the organization?

14. How do the rational and political views of organizations differ? Relate these views to Morgan's metaphorical view of organizations outlined in chapter 1.

15. Can you think of any sport organizations that are not influenced by the political activity of its members?

Suggestions for Further Reading

The best two books on power are by Jeff Pfeffer, specifically his 1981 text *Power in organizations* and his more recent (1992) and more applied work *Managing with power*. Students are advised to read both. Henry Mintzberg's (1983) *Power in and around organizations* is also good reading and although more sociologically than managerially oriented, students could benefit from Steven Lukes (1974) classic *Power: A radical view*.

There is somewhat of a dearth of writing on power in the sport management literature. Hill's (1992) book *Olympic politics* (especially chapter 3) provides useful material on issues of power and authority in the Olympic movement. Also,

many popular-press books give an idea of the type of power wielded by some of the major figures in sport. Auf De Maur's (1976) *The billion dollar games* shows the type of power exercised by Montreal mayor Jean Drapeau in obtaining and running the 1976 Olympic Games. The power of Malcolm Edwards, the owner of Manchester United soccer team, is discussed by Crick and Smith (1989) in their book *Manchester United: The betrayal of a legend* and both Stephen Aris (1990) and Neil Wilson (1988), in their respective books *Sportsbiz* and *The sports business*, provide accounts of the power plays inherent in the sports industry.

Case for Analysis

Move It or Lose It

Jim Madge was a member of the board of directors of a small Canadian national sport organization responsible for a winter Olympic sport. Although the organization had less than 200 members it had enjoyed some relative success in international competition in the late 1970s and early 1980s. In 1983 the offices of this organization, and the only international-caliber facility, were based in Jim's home town, located in Central Canada. A new facility, however, was being constructed in Calgary in Western Canada as part of the preparations for the 1988 Olympic Games, even though virtually all of the activity around this sport was concentrated in the central Canadian city. A number of the major competitors lived and/or trained there, several of the organization's national board were residents of the city, and all international-level competitions were held at this location. A number of the local residents had put considerable time and effort into the sport to raise it to the level it was currently enjoying; as such, they controlled the operation of the national organization and the way the sport was conducted in Canada. A number of the board members who were local residents had in fact been directors of the organization for a number of years and most had held more than one position. The board had hired a part-time staff member, who had family ties to one of its members, to help with the day-to-day operation of the sport. Although there were a few other clubs involved in this sport in Canada, they had little power to bring about any changes in the national organization. As one government official noted about the small group of people from this city who ran the sport, "they were totally in control of everything. I mean the national team, the national training center, the selection of athletes, the selection of members to [the international governing body], the selection of officials to go to Games . . . the whole deal."

In late 1983 Jim received some news that could have a profound impact on his sport and the way it operated. The federal government had initiated a program called "Best Ever"; the idea was that it would provide funds to national sport organizations to help their athletes produce "Best Ever" performances at the 1988 Olympics and subsequent Games. The increased funding, which was considerable, was obviously very welcome to Jim and his colleagues on the board of directors. It would enable them to do some things they had wanted to do but were previously unable to take on because of a lack of finances—their income in the past came primarily from membership fees and some small fund-raising ventures.

The federal government funds did not come without conditions, however. First, the organization's head office had to be moved to the National Sport and Fitness Administration Centre in Ottawa, where most of Canada's national sport organizations were housed. Second, the organization had to prepare a four-year plan, one which included the expectation that professional staff would be hired. These new staff members would operate out of the Ottawa office and take over much of the day-to-day operation of the organization.

As he thought through the federal government's proposal, Jim wondered how he and the other board members should deal with the issues it raised for their involvement in the sport they had helped build.

Although the situation in this case is based on actual events the name is fictitious. More details of this case can be found in Slack, Berrett, and Mistry (1994).

Questions

1. What implications does the government's proposed "Best Ever" program have for Jim and the other board members who live in the same city as he?

2. What are the advantages of moving the organization's head offices to Ottawa? What are the disadvantages?

3. What impact would it have on the development of this sport if its head offices were moved to Ottawa?

4. What would you do if you were Jim?

10

Managing Conflict in Sport Organizations

When You Have Read This Chapter

You should be able to

1. explain the essential elements found in definitions of conflict,

2. discuss whether conflict is functional or dysfunctional to the operation of a sport organization,

3. explain why conflict should be viewed as a process and not a single incident,

4. outline the major sources of conflict in a sport organization,

5. describe the various strategies that can be used to manage conflict, and

6. identify techniques that can be used to stimulate conflict in a sport organization.

Speed Skaters at Loggerheads

As Canadian speed skaters began their final preparation for the 1994 Winter Olympics, the big question wasn't who would win medals in Lillehammer but who would win control of their association. With countries and athletes set to meet in Norway in fewer than three months, the Canadian Amateur Speed Skating Association (CASSA) was split along geographical, political, and philosophical lines. On one side of the widening gap was long-track skating, based primarily in Calgary in Western Canada and composed mostly of English-speaking athletes. On the other side was short-track, based mainly in the Province of Quebec and dominated by French-speaking athletes. The major concern among skaters was that the east-west biases were affecting which athletes were being selected for teams and competitions. The situation deteriorated to the point where skaters were choosing not to eat together and refusing room assignments. Fed up with the state of affairs, a small group of skaters and officials began investigating the possibility of splitting the two disciplines into two separate associations.

Early in 1993 the CASSA's internal struggles and backroom maneuvers had become public after a failed attempt to dismiss long-time coach Jack Walters by buying out the year left on his contract. According to Patrick Kelly, long-track speed skating's athlete representative on the CASSA who led the campaign to reinstate Walters, the CASSA gave no reason for the move other than to say Walters, who had been with the association for 21 years, wasn't working within the organization's framework. Kelly suggested the decision was based on the fact that "a couple of guys in the national office just had it in for Jack." Kelly was referring to high-performance director Peter Eriksson and CASSA president John Thorpe. News of the attempted coup so stunned Kelly that he immediately mobilized skaters and launched a well-organized campaign, taking the cause to the media. With the CASSA's annual general meeting coming up, skaters lobbied provincial associations for support. After a long, often bitter debate, supporters of Walters garnered enough backing to press the board of governors to rehire him.

Reprinted, by permission, from S. Keating, November 29, 1993, "Speed skaters at loggerheads," *Globe and Mail* (Toronto: *Globe and Mail*), A17.

Anyone who has been involved in any type of sport organization, amateur or professional, national or local, profit or nonprofit, will have experienced the conflict that can occur in these organizations. The vignette above provides an example of the frustration, bickering, and political clashes that characterize many sport organizations. A 1976 study by the American Management Association found that mid- and top-level managers reported that they spent approximately 20 percent of their time dealing with conflict (Thomas & Schmidt, 1976). There is no reason to believe things are different in sport organizations. Conflict is endemic to all types of organizations; in the same study, managers rated conflict management equally important as topics such as planning, communication, and motivation, which were being taught in American Management Association courses (Thomas & Schmidt, 1976).

In the next four chapters we explore a number of the processes that, like conflict, are common phenomena in sport organizations. In addition to conflict, the focus of this chapter, we look at the process of organizational change, the process of human resources management, and finally the process of decision making. In this chapter, we look first of all at what we mean by the term "conflict." Next we discuss horizontal and vertical forms of conflict, followed by an examination of whether or not conflict is functional or dysfunctional to the operation of a sport organization. Because conflict is more than just a single incident, we look at conflict as a process and also examine the sources of conflict in a sport organization. The final two sections look at ways of managing conflict and the seemingly contradictory notion of how to stimulate conflict.

What Is Conflict?

There are many different definitions of conflict within the organizational literature (cf. Schmidt & Kochan, 1972; Thomas, 1992). March and Simon (1958, p. 112) describe it as a "breakdown in the standard mechanisms of decision making so that an individual or group experiences difficulty in selecting an action alternative." Thompson (1960, p. 390) is more succinct: Conflict is "behavior by organization members which is expended in opposition to other members"; Morgan (1986, p. 155) is even more precise, suggesting that "conflict occurs whenever interests collide." Robbins (1974) suggests that conflict should be viewed as a continuum ranging from "no conflict" at one end to "the total annihilation and destruction of the opposing party" at the other.

Notwithstanding the variety of explanations of what constitutes conflict, some important commonalties underpin most definitions. First, and of particular importance, the parties involved must perceive a conflict to exist. If no one perceives a conflict as existing then no conflict exists. (This does not mean that all perceived conflict is real; however, perceived conflict that is not real can still result in antagonism and interference.) Second, a conflict situation must involve two or more parties in opposition. Third, one or more of the parties must be involved in preventing one or more of the other parties from achieving its goal(s) by some form of blocking behavior. Finally, this blocking behavior must result in frustration, anger, or some other form of emotional response.

Kolb and Putnam's (1992) definition of conflict essentially encompasses these points. They suggest that "conflict may be said to exist when there are real or perceived differences that arise in specific organizational circumstances and that engender emotion as a consequence" (p. 312). These writers, however, caution against an over-reliance on rigid definitions of conflict, since such explanations should always take into account the contextual circumstances in which the conflict takes place "because it is always difficult to draw a line between episodes of 'conflict' and the normal give and take of social interaction."

Horizontal and Vertical Conflict

One method of categorizing the conflicts that can occur in a sport organization is to distinguish conflicts that take place between subunits at the same level of the organization (horizontal conflict) from those that take place between different hierarchical levels (vertical conflict). Figure 10.1 shows this type of distinction as it might occur in a university athletic department.

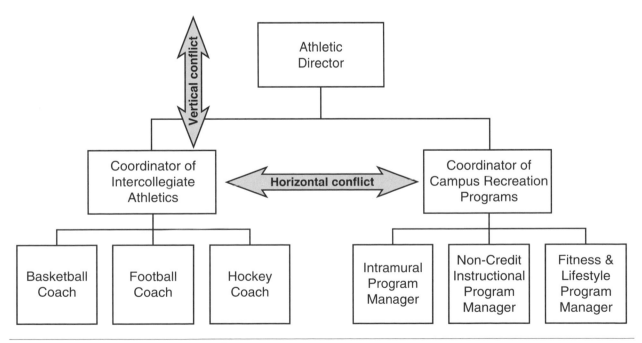

Figure 10.1 Horizontal and vertical conflict.

Horizontal Conflict

Horizontal conflict occurs between subunits, or those individuals representing subunits, that are on the same level of the organizational hierarchy. For example, as figure 10.1 shows, horizontal conflict may occur in an athletic department between those individuals within the intercollegiate athletic program and those involved in the campus recreation program. The campus recreation staff may not agree with the amount of funding given to the athletic program, or conflicts may occur over scheduling or access to facilities. The two groups, because they have different roles to play in providing sport and recreational opportunities for students, tend to develop different goals and priorities. These types of conflicts are not uncommon in athletic departments or sport organizations in general. The job of the athletic director is to resolve conflicts that do occur and prevent future flare-ups by coordinating and encouraging collaboration among the units under her direction.

Vertical Conflict

As figure 10.1 shows, vertical conflict arises between different hierarchical levels of a sport organization. Conflict between an athletic director and a coordinator of intercollegiate athletics may occur over such issues as salary, the amount of authority the coordinator is allowed to exercise, differences over the goals of the athletic department, or the way it should operate. Much of this type of conflict stems from the need for control in a sport organization and an individual's or subunit's need for autonomy. Organizational members have to balance their own needs for personal expression and fulfillment against the demands imposed by the structure of the organization, in particular its hierarchical reporting relationships and formalized procedures.

Vertical conflicts can be avoided by appropriate leadership behavior, or techniques such as management by objectives (MBO), where there is an attempt to establish some degree of congruence between individual and organizational goals. However, none of these methods will completely eliminate vertical conflicts and all generally involve a trade-off between the amount of control that can be exercised and an individual's or subunit's autonomy. A frequent form of vertical conflict involves managers (or owners) and workers. We see this type of conflict in professional sport organizations in struggles between team owners and players (see Dworkin, 1981).

Is Conflict Dysfunctional to the Operation of a Sport Organization?

For most of us, conflict is something that carries a negative connotation. We are brought up to believe

---

Owners Versus Players in the 1994-1995 Major League Baseball Strike

On August 12, 1994 major league baseball players went out on strike. Although there had been conflicts between owners and players before, this was to be the start of the longest work stoppage in the history of professional sport. At the heart of the conflict was the owners' desire to impose a salary cap that would split industry revenues 50-50 and guarantee a minimum of $1 billion (US) a year for player's salaries. The player's union opposed the cap; union head Donald Fehr suggested that owners were trying to resolve their revenue-sharing problems by making players pay for it. The owners also sought a reduction of free agent eligibility from the existing six to four years, and the elimination of arbitration. The players opposed the reduced time for free agency and fought to retain arbitration. The strike was long and acrimonious; estimates suggest that the owners lost between $400 and $700 million (US) and the World Series was canceled for the first time in 90 years. The National Labor Relations Board found that the owners had not bargained in good faith. They had threatened to lock out players and begin the 1995 season with replacement players, but an injunction in U.S. District Court brought an end to the strike on April 2, 1995. The conflict between the owners and players had lasted 234 days.

that conflict is bad, something we should avoid. Psychologist Abraham Maslow (1965, p. 185) suggested that within North America there is "a fear of conflict, of disagreement, of hostility, antagonism, enmity" and that we place "much stress on getting along with other people, even if [we] don't like them."

These ideas about conflict are reflected in our view of sport organizations. The common perception of an effective sport organization is one where everybody gets along with each other and works toward a common goal—there is an emphasis on cooperation. Members of organizations where cooperation is high are said to interact more effectively, make better progress on tasks, and strengthen their work relationships (Tjosvold, 1988). It is also claimed that employee satisfaction is higher and the managers of these organizations are held in more esteem. In contrast, conflict is seen as dysfunctional; because it hinders the achievement of organizational goals, it is something we should avoid in our organizations.

This view of conflict as dysfunctional can be found in both the classical approach to organization theory and the human relations school. In the former, with its emphasis on bureaucratic rationality, conflict is at best avoided and at worst managed through the imposition of rules and regulations (cf. Taylor, 1911). Human relations theorists (cf. Likert & Likert, 1976) also see conflict as bad. However, for these people, conflict is controlled by providing people with training sessions on how to get along, or using third-party intervention when conflict arises. Both of these perspectives are limited, because they fail to acknowledge the functional benefits of conflict to an organization.

Those who subscribe to the view that an optimal level of conflict can be beneficial to an organization's operation see it as a source of change and creativity. Pondy (1992, p. 259) even goes as far as to suggest that "if conflict isn't happening then the organization has no reason for being." Conflict, because it often arises over dissatisfaction with the way things are, prevents complacency and stimulates new ideas. Sport organizations that are totally free of conflict will have no reason to change and may ultimately flounder. This is not to say that all conflict in sport organizations is beneficial; the emphasis is on an optimal level of conflict. If conflict is too low, sport managers need to stimulate constructive conflict; we deal with ways of stimulating conflict later in this chapter. If conflict is too high, the manager's job is to reduce it. Figure 10.2 shows how levels of conflict that are too high or too low can influence an organization's level of effectiveness adversely.

The job of the sport manager is to recognize the situation within the organization and take the necessary steps to develop an optimal level of conflict. Obviously, managers need to adopt an attitude toward conflict that sees it as a source of innovation rather than a destructive force.

The Conflict Process

Often we tend to think of conflict situations as discrete events: The conflict occurs and then is resolved by some means. However, some organizational theorists (cf. Pondy, 1967; Rahim, 1986) have suggested that a conflict situation is made up of a series of interrelated stages. By being aware of these stages, and consequently the conditions that produce conflict and the events that can trigger a conflict situation, those people responsible for the operation of a sport organization can be in a better position to manage the incident. Pondy (1967) developed the most frequently cited of the stage models of conflict. Figure 10.3 shows an adaptation of Pondy's model; each stage in the model is discussed in detail.

Pondy's Five-Stage Model of Conflict

The first stage in Pondy's model is the latent stage of conflict. Essentially what Pondy argues is that certain conditions frequently found in organizations provide the latent potential for conflict to occur. These conditions are condensed into three basic types of latent conflict. The first of these involves competition for scarce resources. For example, when two or more groups, such as the teams within an athletic department, are vying for a portion of the organization's financial resources, there is a latent potential for conflict.

The second condition that creates a latent potential for conflict is the drive for autonomy. Individuals and subunits within sport organizations frequently attempt to operate autonomously. However, this ability is limited by the structure of the organization and the existence of similar aspirations in other individuals and subunits. For example, the owner/manager of a franchised sporting goods store may wish to undertake certain marketing activities to respond to the local conditions in his area, but may be constrained by the company's corporate headquarters, which has adopted a

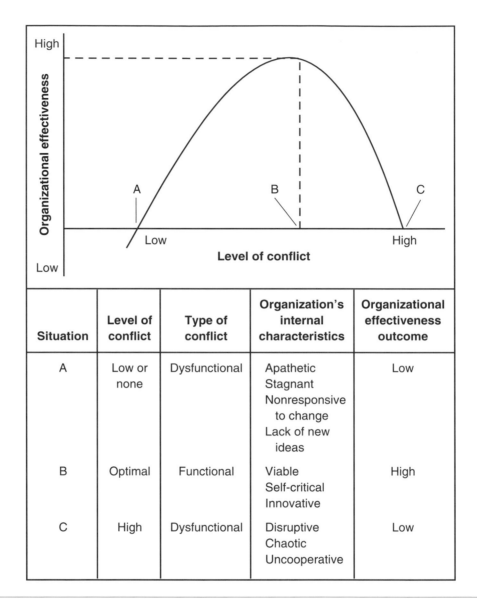

Situation	Level of conflict	Type of conflict	Organization's internal characteristics	Organizational effectiveness outcome
A	Low or none	Dysfunctional	Apathetic Stagnant Nonresponsive to change Lack of new ideas	Low
B	Optimal	Functional	Viable Self-critical Innovative	High
C	High	Dysfunctional	Disruptive Chaotic Uncooperative	Low

Figure 10.2   Conflict and organizational effectiveness.
Organization theory: Structure, design, and applications, 3/E by Robbins, © 1990. Reprinted by permission of Prentice-Hall, Inc., Upper Saddle River, NJ.

standardized approach to marketing to present a consistent image of the company. Finally, latent conflict is a product of the differing goals that subunits within an organization can have. The athletic department at a university, for example, will have different goals from the physical education department, thus creating the potential for conflict.

The second stage of Pondy's model is the perceived conflict, the stage in which one or more of the parties involved becomes aware, through some type of stimulus or information received, of the potential for a conflict. Pondy suggests that some only mildly threatening conflicts may be suppressed. Also, because organizations are often faced

with more conflicts than they can handle, only a few are dealt with, usually those "for which short-run, routine solutions are available" (Pondy, 1967, pp. 301-302).

In the third stage of Pondy's model conflict is felt. Here emotions such as anger, hostility, and frustration are encountered. The fourth stage is where the conflict becomes manifest. Here some sort of adversarial behavior is exhibited, ranging from apathy and rigid adherence to rules to violence and physical abuse, although thankfully the latter is rare in sport organizations.

The final stage of the model Pondy terms the conflict aftermath. Here the conflict is either resolved

TIME OUT

"Creative Tension": An Optimal Level of Conflict?

Managing the 1984 Los Angeles Olympic Games was a large and difficult task. Peter Ueberroth, the president of the Los Angeles Olympic Organizing Committee (LAOOC), knew it was not a normal business and didn't run in the customary way. "It was unusual," he noted. "These were not normal practices, not normal business practices. It wasn't a time for kindness, to take time to help people through problems. . . ."

"Creative tension" was the phrase some staff members used to describe the regime under which the Olympic committee was directed. Ueberroth said it was not his term. But he readily acknowledged that he intentionally created some tensions in everyday operation as a means of testing his staff. He recalled, " It was essential for Harry (Harry L. Usher, Ueberroth's executive vice president), for me, commissioners, for the leaders to set goals, create difficulties, make people perform against deadlines, against expectations, so that they were in training for some pressure that I didn't know how to measure. And if there weren't some tensions to see how people reacted, we couldn't have run the Games. . . ."

Based on information in Reich, K. (1986). *Making it happen: Peter Ueberroth and the 1984 Olympics*. Santa Barbara, CA: Capra Press.

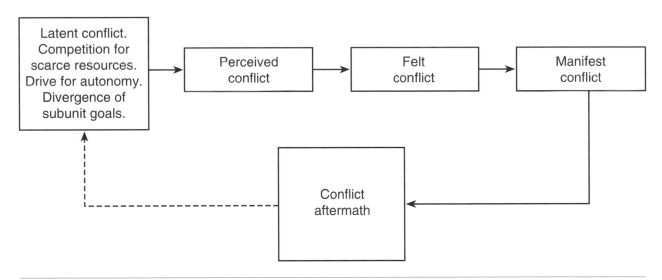

Figure 10.3 Pondy's five-stage model of conflict.

or becomes the basis for future conflicts, as indicated by the broken line in figure 10.3.

Sources of Conflict in Sport Organizations

Conflict in a sport organization can stem from a number of different sources and take a variety of different forms. Much of the work carried out on conflict in organizations has been micro in orienta-tion (Nelson, 1989), that is, it has tended to be sociopsychology-based and to focus on conflicts at the interpersonal level. In keeping with our emphasis on the structuring of sport organizations, we focus here on structurally derived conflicts, those rooted in the way a sport organization is structured. This analysis is important to our understanding of sport organizations because, as Hall (1982, pp. 151-152) points out, "conflict in organizations involves more than simple interpersonal conflict (not that interpersonal conflict is necessarily simple) . . . ; the very nature of organizations themselves contribute to conflict situations." We look specifically at those structural sources of conflict most frequently cited in the literature (cf. Corwin, 1969; Walton & Dutton, 1969; Walton, Dutton, & Cafferty, 1969) and the application of this literature to sport organizations (Amis, Slack, & Berrett, 1995).

Differentiation

In most sport organizations work is broken down and allocated to different subunits to achieve the goals of the organization more effectively. However, as we saw in chapter 7 the process of differentiation results in subunits exhibiting different goals, management philosophies, and time orientations (Lawrence & Lorsch, 1967). As Langhorn and Hinings (1987, p. 560) point out, although "organizations differentiate for technical reasons, these boundaries of task and expertise are reinforced by sociopsychological processes which result in technical boundaries becoming social and political boundaries." The more a sport organization differentiates (i.e., breaks down work and allocates it to different subunits), the greater the likelihood of conflict, because the greater the differences created between subunits. Individuals within subunits may think differently, use different work methods, have different priorities, come from different educational backgrounds, and perhaps even use a totally different set of terminology. While these differences are appropriate and necessary aspects of the operation of a sport organization, they do not engender tolerance and empathy for the problems that other subunits may confront.

Macintosh and Whitson (1990) identify how the increasing differentiation of Canadian national sport organizations, which occurred with the hiring of additional professional staff during the 1984-1988 quadrennial planning period, helped precipitate conflict in these organizations. Professional staff brought new and different goals to national sport organizations, goals which emphasized high-performance sport and new ideas about how these organizations should operate, and which led to clashes with the volunteers who had traditionally operated these organizations.

Interdependence

Where there are high levels of differentiation and subsequently considerable variations in the value orientation, mode of operation, and power of the subunits within a sport organization, the potential for conflict is high. However, as Pondy (1967) points out, this potential is latent. For conflict to become manifest, some level of interdependence between the subunits is necessary. Interdependence creates the opportunity for the interference and blocking associated with conflict.

As we saw in chapter 8, Thompson (1967) identified three types of interdependence—pooled, sequential, and reciprocal—each progressively more complex and requiring increased levels of coordination. The more complex the interdependence in a sport organization, the greater the likelihood of conflict. For example, conflict is more likely to occur in a sport and fitness center in which subunits are reciprocally interdependent, than between franchised sporting goods stores exhibiting pooled interdependence.

Low Formalization

One of the ways to manage the complexity associated with increased differentiation and reciprocal interdependence is through the use of rules, regulations, policies, and procedures. Formalization helps clarify roles, establish standard ways of operating, and reduce ambiguity. Consequently, when formalization is high, the potential for conflict in a sport organization is low; when formalization is low, the potential for conflict is high. It is important to note, however, that some writers disagree with this position and argue that rules and regulations can in fact *contribute* to conflict in organizations (cf. Corwin, 1969).

A lack of formalized regulatory mechanisms such as rules and regulations means that subunits come to rely more on political tactics and coercion to conduct their operations. As an example, a number of Canadian national sport organizations have formalized their selection criteria for national team athletes and made the criteria known well before the selection process. This formalization reduces the subjective and political nature of the selection process, helping avoid the conflicts that sometimes occur over this issue.

Competition Over Resources

When two or more subunits within a sport organization compete for a share of limited resources, they come into conflict with each other. Because sport organizations only have so much money, space, or equipment, there is conflict over who is going to get what. Also, since these resources often help subunits accomplish their goals more easily and quickly, managers often use such strategies as inflating budgets or political maneuvers to increase their share.

Conflict over resources can occur horizontally in a sport organization, for example, when the sport studies department within a university has to compete with other departments for increased funding. It can also occur vertically, particularly between owner/managers and workers. The 1993 NHL officials' strike is a good example of conflict over resources. While the NHL Officials Association accepted the league's salary offer, they also demanded a benefits package that would cost the NHL about $1.5 million per year. The league refused to meet the officials demands and a 17-day strike ensued (Deacon, 1993).

Differences in Reward Systems

The nature of the reward system used within a sport organization will help determine the extent to which subunits cooperate or are in conflict with each other (cf. Walton & Dutton, 1969). The more frequently the managers of the various departments within an organization are rewarded for achieving the overall goals of the organization, as opposed to their own departmental goals, the higher the level of cooperation within the organization (Cliff, 1987). The more rewards are based on the performance of each individual subunit, as opposed to the overall sport organization, the greater the potential for conflict. In a sport organization that produces equipment, for example, if the sales department is rewarded for increased sales volume, it will want to establish as many new accounts as possible. Some may have risky credit ratings and the accounting department, which gets rewarded for minimizing losses, will not want to take them on as new clients. These cross-purposes will lead to conflict between these two departments. In another example, Slack, Berrett, and Mistry (1994) show how, in a national sport organization, the high salary paid to coaches led to conflict with lower-paid administrators, who felt they made an equal contribution to the operation of the organization.

Power Incongruence

As we saw in chapter 9 even though subunits may be on the same level of a sport organization's hierarchy, some are able to wield more power because they are more central to the workflow or they can acquire and control needed resources. These differences in power can lead to conflict, particularly when the actual day-to-day interactions do not reflect perceived power. For example, in an athletic department the athletic director is higher up the organization hierarchy than the basketball coach. However, due to the importance attributed to the basketball program on many U.S. university campuses, the basketball coach may perceive himself and be perceived by others as having considerable power. If the coach then starts to give "orders" to the athletic director, conflict is likely to ensue.

Communication Problems

One of the most frequent causes of conflict between organizational subunits is a lack of clear and adequate communication. As information moves vertically up and down a sport organization's hierarchy, it may get distorted or misinterpreted and, as a result, conflict may ensue. Communication between subunits on the same horizontal level is also subject to misinterpretation. As we saw earlier, the personnel who staff the various subunits of a sport organization come from different backgrounds and may use a different vocabulary in order to conduct their work. For example, the terminology used in the research-and-development department of a ski manufacturing company such as Rossignol or Head will be different from that used in sales or marketing. If one of these two departments have to interact with research and development, then communication problems can occur and conflict can result.

Conflict can also occur if one subunit stops communicating with another or withholds information. Slack, Berrett, and Mistry (1994) describe one national-level sport organization that was forced to move its head offices; in the move, files were withheld, contributing to conflict between members who lived in the region where the office was located and the staff hired to run the new office. Jollimore (1992) cites accusations of a "failure to communicate with players" as an important issue in the conflict between factions of the Canadian Women's Field Hockey Association, over the firing and subsequent rehiring of national coach Marina van der Merwe.

Participative Decision Making

Although often promoted as an important means of getting people involved in an organization, "the opening up of organizational decisions to discussion and debate raises, or maintains, the level of conflict in the institution" (Zald, 1962, p. 47). By allowing more people "to have their say," participative decision making facilitates the expression of more diverse opinions; thus, the potential for conflict is heightened. The interaction that occurs between members of a sport organization, rather than breaking down barriers, can serve to reinforce differences and thus may entrench people in their position even more.

Does this mean we shouldn't use participative decision making in sport organizations? The answer is obviously no; participative decision making can be a very productive way of operating, even though it has the potential to precipitate conflict. Levels of participation in a sport organization's decision processes may range from "consultative participation," in which employees have input into the process but are not responsible for the final decision, to "employee involvement," where employees have input into how work is organized and who does what (Cotton, Vollrath, Froggatt, Lengnick-Hall, & Jennings, 1988). A number of national sport organizations in Canada and the United States have successfully adopted what is termed "representative participation"; representatives from the countries' different geographic regions, from the officials' organization, and from the ranks of the athlete are involved in the decision making process. The trade-off for the sport manager in any initiative to increase the number of different viewpoints is: Does the potential for reduced alienation and improved morale outweigh the possible conflicts that could result?

Role Conflict

People often find themselves in a conflict situation if their role responsibilities suddenly change, or if different expectations are placed on them. Changing a person's role in a sport organization, even if it is seen as a desirable move, can cause disruption and stress that can lead to conflict. If the change is viewed as a demotion, the level of stress increases and so does the potential for conflict. Roles also carry certain expectations for the person filling the role. These expectations may relate to the nature of the work, the salary, the opportunity to travel, or a new office. If these expectations are not met or if the person filling the job has different expectations from other powerful people in the organization, then they both may experience a frustration that can manifest itself in conflict. Prouty (1988), for example, describes how, when he was appointed executive director of the United States Cycling Federation, he was seen by some other organization members as

---

TIME OUT

Role Conflict:
The Problems of the Athletic Department's Academic Advisors

Many of the major U.S. university and college athletic departments employ academic advisors to tutor student athletes. Every day these people face role conflicts: How to keep players eligible for intercollegiate athletics while ensuring that they receive a college education. Coaches demand that players spend an enormous amount of hours per week training, practicing, attending team meetings, viewing game films, traveling, and playing their sports; for most athletes, this regimen precludes spending the time and effort necessary for a decent college education.

If an academic advisor is high-minded and concerned about an athlete's education, the advisor soon disputes the coach's demands on the player's time. Because ADs sympathize with their coaches, and also have the self-interest of needing winning teams, they decide most of these conflicts in favor of the coaches. Advisors who want to keep their jobs learn "to go along to get along" and to acquiesce to the coaches' commands.

The advisor's role conflict begins as soon as the athlete arrives on campus. His or her first task is to arrange the athlete's schedule of classes. Immediately, a conflict between eligibility and education arises: Should the athlete be allowed to take the same courses as other first-year students or be placed in the school's "hideaway curriculum" to ensure eligibility?

Based on information in Sperber, M. (1990). *College sports inc*. New York: Holt.

taking over some of the role responsibilities previously undertaken by board members; this perception resulted in attempts to have him fired.

Conflict Management Strategies

Because conflict has both positive and negative consequences, it has to be managed. The ideal situation for the sport manager is one where there is an optimal level of conflict within her organization. A number of strategies are outlined below that can be used to manage conflict. Conflict can be managed by either changing behavior or changing attitudes. A change in behavior is superficial and does not really get at the root of the conflict; it is a short-term solution. A change in attitude requires a greater commitment and usually takes longer to accomplish, but it is the basis for a more collaborative sport organization. We look at some strategies solely designed to change behavior, and others used to establish more long-term attitudinal changes.

Authority

One of the most common methods of managing conflict is for the senior managers of the sport organization to use their formal authority to resolve or suppress the conflict situation. While the parties involved may not always agree with the manager's decision, they will usually recognize and comply with whatever resolution is made. We see this type of resolution used in professional sport, where the commissioner has certain powers to resolve disputes. In major league baseball, for example, all parties abide to what is called the Major League Agreement and "commit themselves contractually to submit all disputes and controversies among themselves to the commissioner for arbitration, to accept the commissioner's judgment as binding, and to waive any right to recourse in the courts" (Scully, 1989, p. 15). The problem with this conflict resolution is that it is short-term, and addresses only the immediate problem, without bringing about the attitudinal changes required for long-term stability.

Avoidance

Another commonly used technique for dealing with conflict is avoidance: either directing attention away from a conflict or ignoring that it exists. If he is involved in a heated conversation with the athletic director over the resources allocated to their respective areas, the dean of a faculty of sport studies may, for example, change the subject to one less contentious. In a somewhat similar vein, an athletic director may choose to "turn a blind eye" if she sees alumnae making illegal payments to university athletes, hoping that any conflict that could ensue from such an illegal practice will be avoided. However, like the use of authority, avoidance is a short-term solution.

Separating or Merging Conflicting Units

Because conflict emanates from the interdependence between the subunits of a sport organization, one way to manage such conflict is to remove the interdependence. Where there is no need for the units to work together on organizational tasks, a manager could order the actual physical separation of the two groups, preventing any contact between them. A related but opposite way of handling this type of situation is to reduce the interdependence between two subunits by making them into one, that is, merge them. In part, notwithstanding the economic benefits, the merging of some of the major professional sports leagues has been motivated by the desire to reduce conflict. Harris (1987, p. 16), for example, notes that after the NFL/AFL merger "peace . . . descended on the football business," a stark contrast to "the war that had preceded it."

Increasing Resources

As we saw earlier, resource scarcity can precipitate conflict. It follows then that one way to manage a conflict over resources is to increase their availability. While it is not always possible to give all subunits everything they want, selected resource increases may translate into savings because wasteful conflicts are avoided. For example, in a sport management department conflict could arise between faculty and graduate students who both have to use the same photocopying machine. If use is heavy, faculty members may feel they should have priority. At the same time, graduate students who have research and teaching responsibilities feel their needs are equally as important. The simple answer to avoiding or removing any conflict over this situation is to provide each group with a photocopier. However, while it is often a very satisfactory means of resolving or preventing a conflict, all too often resources for this kind of initiative are not readily available.

Integrating Devices

Integrating devices may involve the use of a small group (a committee or a task force) or an individual. Essentially, the role of these groups or individuals is to span the boundaries between subunits. If a group is used, it usually contains representatives from the subunits that are or potentially could be in conflict. Bringing these people together is seen as an effective way of solving problems because they come to see each other's perspective (Blake & Mouton, 1984). Committees are frequently used in many sport organizations to manage or prevent conflict. For example, Cross Country Ski Canada has a high-performance committee with representatives from the coaches, athletes, and sport scientists. By having representatives from these different groups involved in decision making about high-performance sport, the incidences of conflict can be minimized. Individual sport managers themselves may sometimes fill a similar role in a committee or task force; part of every manager's job is to enhance collaboration between the subunits under managerial control. Mid-level sport managers may also act as integrators between senior managers and lower-level workers. Like those strategies that follow, the use of integrating devices is directed toward attitudinal, rather than behavioral, change.

Confrontation and Negotiation

Confrontation means that the parties involved in a conflict come together face-to-face and try to resolve their differences. Those involved recognize that conflict does exist and that it needs to be dealt with. Confrontation as a conflict resolution technique requires a certain amount of maturity; facts have to be faced, and emotions, as much as possible, have to be put aside. Although confrontations are risky, if successful they can provide a basis for continued collaboration. Negotiations occur during the confrontation process; each subunit/individual or their representative(s) work through the situation to try to come to an agreement. It is important to emphasize that in the negotiation process the focus should not solely be on points of difference but also on points of agreement. Owners and players frequently use confrontation and negotiation as a means of resolving disputes over contracts or salaries. Millson (1987) provides an account of the negotiation process that took place between Toronto Blue Jays' officials Paul Beeston and Pat Gillick, and players Ernie Whitt and Jim

Clancy. Similar accounts of this process can be seen in the many books on professional athletes and professional sport organizations.

Third-Party Interventions

If a conflict is particularly drawn out, a third-party intervention may be used to resolve the dispute. Here a person who is not associated with the conflict is brought in to try to resolve the situation. Although the person brought in will not be associated with either side in the conflict, the principals involved are often given the right to approve or disapprove of the person who will be the third party. The best example of this strategy in sport organizations is the situation where labor arbitrators resolve contract disputes between the owners of professional sport teams and their players. One of the best known arbitration decisions in sport, referred to as the Seitz decision, resulted in Jim "Catfish" Hunter of the Oakland Athletics becoming baseball's first free agent in 1974 (Scully, 1989).

Superordinate Goals

As we saw in chapter 2 the subunits within a sport organization develop their own goals. The incompatibility of these goals with those of other subunits can sometimes precipitate conflict. A strategy used to address this type of conflict is the creation of superordinate goals, higher-level goals that require subunits to work together if they are to be achieved. These goals must be seen as more important than the goals subunits possess individually. The creation of superordinate goals can enhance cooperation within an organization; attention is directed away from the individual subunit goals, the basis of the conflict, to the superordinate goals that must be achieved collaboratively.

A very powerful superordinate goal is survival. In good times, when resources are relatively plentiful, vigorous union lobbying for salary increases often leads to conflicts with owners and management. When a sport organization's survival is threatened, a situation that impacts on everyone's welfare, then groups tend to work together more, to ensure survival. Such was the case in 1975; the World Football League, in its second season, was threatened with collapse. Chris Hemmeter, the league commissioner, devised a plan which had as its goal minimizing operating expenses. Owners and players agreed to work together to try to ensure the league's survival. Owners committed to

TIME OUT

Arbitration as a Means of Resolving Conflicts in Professional Baseball

Any baseball player with three to six years experience in the major leagues who is unable to reach a salary agreement with his club can submit the dispute to arbitration. The team and player both make a final salary offer and the arbitrator is obliged to select one or the other. The "final offer selection procedure," as it is known, was insisted on by the owners. They felt that if arbitrators were allowed to mediate between the two positions players would make outrageous demands and, in their attempts at fairness, the arbitrator would go somewhere close to "splitting the difference," a decision which would have disastrous financial ramifications for the owners. The arbitrator used in a dispute is selected jointly by the Players Association and the Player Relations Committee. A number of criteria are used by an arbitrator in reaching the final salary decision, including the contribution the player made to his club in the previous season, the length of his career, the consistency of his performance, comparisons with other players' salaries, the player's past salary, any injuries he may have sustained, and the club's attendance figures. The arbitrator must not consider such factors as the player's or club's financial position, the salaries being paid in other sports, the opinion of the press, or previous offers made by either the player or the club.

Based on information in Scully, G.W. (1989). *The business of major league baseball*. Chicago: University of Chicago Press; and Dworkin, J.B. (1981). Owners versus players: Baseball and collective bargaining. Boston, MA: Auburn House.

deposit between $600,000 and $1.2 million with the league, and players agreed to work for a percentage of team gross income (Chang & Campo-Flores, 1980). Although Hemmeter's plan is a good example of the type of superordinate goal that can get the factions of a sport organization working together, the league eventually folded—some owners simply could not come up with the money.

Job Rotation

Sometimes conflict can be prevented and/or managed by engaging in job rotation. Very simply, a person from one subunit works in another subunit, usually on a temporary basis. Through this practice the person who is moved comes to understand the attitudes, issues, and problems in the subunit to which she is moved. The individual who is moved is also in a good position to relate similar information about her own department. Although it often takes considerable time, job rotation can have a significant effect on changing some of the underlying attitudes that precipitate conflict. While some types of job rotation are not feasible, for example, having the tennis coach trade places with the football coach, the concept is applicable to a variety of sport organizations, most notably those involved in the manufacturing of sports equipment.

Stimulating Conflict

Earlier in this chapter it was suggested that the effectiveness of a sport organization is influenced by the level of conflict within the organization. Because conflict can often be *below* an optimally desirable level, Robbins (1978) has suggested a number of questions (see table 10.1) to determine if the level of conflict in an organization is too low.

Robbins (1978, p. 71) notes that "while there is no definitive method for universally assessing the need for more conflict, affirmative answers to one or more of the . . . questions suggests there may be a need for more conflict stimulation." Using some of the ideas suggested by Robbins, we briefly explore how conflict could be stimulated in a sport organization.

Introducing "New Blood"

Sometimes people within a sport organization become complacent; one of the ways to "wake them up" is to introduce one or more new people into the organization, individuals who bring new and different ideas to the sport organization, people who challenge existing modes of operation, and make staff think about new ideas. Bringing "new blood" into the organization was exactly what Reebok's

Table 10.1   Is There a Need to Stimulate Conflict in Your Organization?

1. Are you surrounded by "yes people"?

2. Are subordinates afraid to admit ignorance and uncertainties to you?

3. Is there so much concentration by decision makers on reaching a compromise that they may lose sight of values, long-term objectives, or the company welfare?

4. Do managers believe that it is in their best interest to maintain the impression of peace and cooperation in their unit, regardless of the price?

5. Is there an excessive concern by decision makers in not hurting the feelings of others?

6. Do managers believe that popularity is more important for the obtaining of organizational rewards than competence and high performance?

7. Are managers unduly enamored with obtaining consensus for their decisions?

8. Do employees show unusually high resistance to change?

9. Is there a lack of new ideas forthcoming?

10. Is there an unusually low level of employee turnover?

Paul Fireman had in mind in 1987 when he hired C. Joseph LaBonté, a former CEO of Twentieth Century-Fox Film Corp., to become president and chief operating officer. Prior to LaBonté's hiring, Reebok was a one-product company. When he arrived at Reebok, LaBonté added new product lines and began a series of acquisitions designed to diversify and strengthen the company. He also cut the size of the apparel group, instituted a series of controls which created a more structured organization, and began a series of cost-cutting measures. LaBonté's initiatives created a series of conflicts: While Reebok had gained control over its internal operations, there were indications it had lost control of its external relations. Notwithstanding these problems, Reebok's profits rose 28 percent in 1989, but that same year LaBonté left the company (cf. Jereski, 1990; Van Fleet, 1991).

Manipulating Communications

Robbins (1978) suggests that manipulating communications can help managers stimulate conflict. Ambiguous or threatening information can create situations in which tensions run high. For example, information suggesting that certain intercollegiate athletic programs will be cut because of funding shortages can create the kind of conflict that can reduce complacency and improve the health of an athletic department. Leaving an individual or subunit out of the communication process can have the effect of signaling to them that they are not important. The confrontation resulting from this type of omission, however, can cause the individuals or subunits concerned to reexamine their role in the sport organization and their contribution to its strategic direction. There is, of course, an ethical question to consider when using this type of tactic.

Creating Competition

Creating competition between subunits or individuals is a third way managers can stimulate conflict. Coaches use this technique when they institute competitions between players on their teams. It is also used by sport organizations such as retail stores selling sports equipment, when they create competitions to see who can sell the most product in a particular time period. The conflict usually resulting from these ventures is rarely hostile, as invariably everybody wins in some way or other. However, if the competition results in no net gain, or if there is a duplication of effort, such as in a case when two groups of sales people in the same sporting goods company compete for a large contract, the level of conflict is likely to be higher.

Summary and Conclusions

Conflict is one of the most neglected issues in the field of sport management. There has been virtually no empirical research on the topic, and most textbooks have chosen to ignore the occurrence of conflict in sport organizations. This omission is problematic because, as the media and many popular books on sport frequently show, conflict in sport organizations is widespread. In this chapter a number of issues related to conflict in sport organizations were addressed. Definitions of conflict drawn from the literature were shown to feature a number of common elements which delineate the occurrence of a conflict situation. However, it was noted that caution should be applied when using definitions of conflict, because it is sometimes difficult to distinguish between conflict situations and the normal daily social interaction that takes place in a sport organization. Conflict was described as existing in both the horizontal and vertical levels of a sport organization. It was then shown that, contrary to what has been presented in the sport management literature, conflict can in fact be functional to the operation of a sport organization. Pondy's conflict model was used to show that conflict is not a single discrete event but rather a series of interrelated stages. The most frequent sources of structurally-based conflict in sport organizations were identified as differentiation, interdependence, low formalization, competition over resources, differences in reward systems, power incongruence, communication problems, participative decision making, and role conflict. Several strategies were presented to manage the conflict arising from these sources. A discussion of the more common ways to stimulate conflict in a sport organization if it drops below an optimally desirable level concluded the chapter.

Key Concepts

Perceptions of conflict	Blocking behavior
Horizontal conflict	Vertical conflict
Functional conflict	Dysfunctional conflict
Conflict process	Latent conflict
Perceived conflict	Felt conflict
Manifest conflict	Conflict aftermath
Sources of conflict	Conflict management
Behavioral change	Attitudinal change
Stimulation techniques	

Review Questions

1. Explain how Kolb and Putnam's definition of conflict applies to a conflict situation you have seen occur in a sport organization.

2. What did Kolb and Putnam mean when they suggested it is sometimes difficult to distinguish conflict from the normal give-and-take of social interaction?

3. Do vertical and horizontal conflicts always occur separately or could one influence the other? If you believe they do interact, provide an example.

4. How would people who subscribe to the scientific management school of thought suggest we deal with conflict? How do their ideas differ from human relations theorists?

5. Peter Ueberroth suggested that a state of "creative tension" in the LAOOC was necessary in order for him to run the 1984 Olympic Games effectively. What do you think Ueberroth meant by this remark? Explain the possible problems of this approach to management.

6. What does a sport organization gain from conflict? What does it lose?

7. Using a conflict that has occurred in a sport organization you are familiar with, identify the different stages of the conflict using Pondy's model.

8. How is structurally derived conflict different from interpersonal conflict?

9. What do Langhorn and Hinings (1987) mean when they suggest that the boundaries of task and expertise that are created in organizations become social and political boundaries?

10. Why is conflict more likely in a sport organization that exhibits reciprocal interdependence than one that exhibits pooled interdependence?

11. Although it was suggested that low levels of formalization can be a source of conflict, some people have actually argued that high levels of formalization can have just the same effect. Why would they say this?

12. Do you think that computers have added to or reduced the conflict that can occur in sport organizations as a result of poor communication?

13. Pick a situation where you have seen a sport manager use avoidance to handle a conflict situation. Discuss what other ways the conflict could have been handled.

14. You have just been hired to be the managing director of the national governing body of one of your country's major team sports. When you arrive you find that the board of directors, who are all volunteers, are in conflict with the national coach, who is a paid professional. The conflict essentially revolves around the fact that the board does not agree with the coach's selection of several of the players on the team. How will you go about resolving this conflict?

15. What do you think is the relationship between the structure of a sport organization and the incidence of conflict in that organization?

Suggestions for Further Reading

There have been a large number of books within the field of management written about conflict. One of the more comprehensive texts is Afzalur Rahim's (1989) edited book *Managing conflict: An interdisciplinary approach*. Also interesting is Dean Tjosvold's (1991) *The conflict-positive organization*. Tjosvold, unlike many writers, presents a view of conflict as a positive organizational phenomenon. Students who want more information about conflict should also look at the major organizational journals. In particular, Vol. 13, No. 3 (1992) of the *Journal of Organizational Behavior* was a special issue entitled "Conflict and negotiation in organizations: Historical and contemporary perspectives."

In terms of the sport literature, newspapers, magazines, and many popular press books contain descriptive accounts of the type of conflicts that occur in sport organizations. Students interested in

conflict in professional sport and associated issues like arbitration are referred to books such as Gerald Scully's (1989) *The business of major league baseball* and James Dworkin's (1981) *Owners versus players*, or the more popular press type books such as Jack Sands and Peter Gammons' (1993) *Coming apart at the seams*. A number of the articles cited in these books also provide useful insights into the issue of conflict in professional sport organizations. While the academic literature on conflict in other kinds of sport organizations is sparse, Slack, Berrett, and Mistry's (1994) article "Rational planning systems as a source of organizational conflict" provides some interesting ideas about how planning, an exercise normally believed to eliminate disputes from organizations, can actually precipitate conflict. Also, the article by Amis, Slack, and Berrett (1995) shows how the structural antecedents of conflict operate in voluntary sport organizations.

Case for Analysis

Bickering at the USOC

The United States Olympic Committee was designated by Congress in 1978 as the United States' principal Olympic group. The organization, which had previously had its headquarters in a small of-

fice in New York, was moved to a former Air Force base in Colorado Springs. To operate the organization, a 105-member board made up of representatives from the 38 member U.S. sport associations was established. The organization was operated by an executive director, F. Donald Miller, a former colonel in the U.S. Air Force, and well connected in the world of sport. These contacts, along with his disciplined approach to the operation of the USOC, ensured that the organization ran smoothly.

When the U.S. senior IOC member, Douglas Robey, announced he was retiring, Miller was, for many, the obvious choice to take his place. Members of the USOC were so intent on getting Miller appointed to the IOC that they offered to make a deal with its president, Juan Antonio Samaranch. If Samaranch would nominate Miller, a virtual guarantee of his appointment, the USOC would drop their opposition to TOP (the Olympic sponsorship program) and also allow Horst Dassler's ISL (the organization behind the TOP marketing program) a four-year trial operation in the United States. Samaranch needed the support of the USOC if TOP was to work, and the USOC wanted to see Miller elected. What appeared to be a mutually beneficial plan was scuttled by USOC President Robert Helmick, who went behind the backs of the USOC members who supported Miller. Helmick reportedly sold Samaranch on the idea that as president of the USOC he could be more useful to the IOC than Miller. Helmick was duly appointed.

Nine months after his appointment Helmick informed Samaranch that the IOC would be getting $7 million from the Los Angeles Olympic Games profits. There had been a dispute over the amount of money that should go to the IOC after the 1984 Games. F. Donald Miller left the USOC, replaced in 1985 by George Miller, also a former military man, who had been the deputy commander of the U.S. Strategic Air Command. Although Miller had supported Helmick when he ran for the presidency of the USOC, within months of Miller's taking over as executive director, the two began to fight. Some suggest Helmick saw Miller as a threat to his power.

George Miller's appointment to the USOC's executive director position followed on the heels of the success of the Los Angeles Olympics. As a result of the Games' profits, each athletic federation in the USOC received about $1.2 million; sponsorship opportunities were also rife. One of the consequences of this increased availability of funds was that the member federations became less dependent on the USOC, and therefore less subservient. Because of a 1985 policy decision, the remaining $85 million surplus from the Games went to a special fund created for the "long-term needs" of athletes, not to the USOC's operating budget. Consequently, when George Miller took over as executive director his

principal task was to enhance the organization's financial position. He spent much of his time, however, fighting with the member federations. An attempt to convert the regionally-based Olympic Festival Games into a national event that could generate sponsorship money failed, because most federations would not send their top athletes. A move to organize a joint marketing licensing program also received little support from the member federations. Miller was quoted as saying that trying to achieve consensus among these organizations was "nearly impossible." When he warned a number of them against competing in the 1986 Goodwill Games sponsored by Ted Turner, alleging that it would hurt the USOC, many ignored his warning and competed anyway.

Miller's relationship with Helmick also became increasingly strained. Helmick set up his own office in his hometown of Des Moines, something no other president had done. In conducting his business he ran up considerable expenses; he also alienated Miller when he legislated that all major TV and sponsorship contracts would require his signature. Previously this task was the responsibility of the executive director. Miller felt that Helmick wanted to let the member federations make all the decisions. Helmick for his part disagreed with Miller's style of operation. Helmick supporters felt Miller wanted to run the USOC like a military unit. The problems between the two came to a head in August 1987 when Helmick wanted to spend $100,000 for a Pan-American Games reception. Miller turned down the request and Helmick told him he could either resign or be fired. Miller chose the first option and negotiated a $700,000 buyout.

Despite the struggles between Miller and Helmick, the USOC did make progress. Sponsorships were obtained, which along with a commemorative coin program were expected to generate revenues of up to $200 million for the organization by 1992. This money and more, however, was needed for 8 to 10 new training centers, because only 3 existed. The plan was to locate these centers closer to the inner city, where a lot of the best athletes lived. There was also a need to get more young athletes into Olympic competition and to provide increased financial support for them.

To help with these tasks Harvey W. Schiller was appointed as the next executive director of the USOC. Schiller's plan was to create a leaner and meaner organization, something he received support for from both the membership and Helmick. However, when he took up his position at the USOC, he found he was immediately swamped with complaints and demands from the member federations. On January 15, 1988, just a few weeks prior to the Calgary Olympics, Schiller addressed a group of coaches, administrators, and other federation officials and told them of his love for the U.S. Olympic movement. Schiller spoke with passion and the crowd loved his speech. Three days later he resigned, saying he couldn't stand the infighting at the USOC. He had held the position of executive director for 19 days.

Some felt the infighting that had been going on in the organization spilled over to the competition site; the United States won only six medals in Calgary. Many blamed the weak showing on poor management and lack of support from the USOC. One sports marketing consultant described the USOC as "a national embarrassment." To address the criticism, a task force was established prior to the end of the Calgary Games. George Steinbrenner, owner of the New York Yankees, was to head the group, which was to review all the USOC's programs.

Based on information in If there were a gold medal for bickering the U.S. would win. (1988, March 21). *Business Week*, pp. 106, 108; and Simpson, V., & Jennings, A. (1992). *The lords of the rings*. Toronto: Stoddart.

Questions

1. If you were Steinbrenner, what types of issues would you see the task force addressing?

2. What types of recommendations do you think the task force would be likely to make?

3. How do the concepts of differentiation and interdependence help you understand the conflict that arose in the USOC?

4. What does this case tell you about the relationship between the professional staff and volunteers of an amateur sport organization?

11

Change in Sport Organizations

When You Have Read This Chapter

You should be able to

1. understand what we mean when we talk about organizational change and explain why change is seen as paradoxical,

2. explain the major perspectives that are used to understand change,

3. discuss the factors that cause change,

4. explain the sources of resistance to change and how this resistance can be managed,

5. describe the stages of the change process and the concept of tracks, and

6. explain why sport organizations need to be innovative.

Changes in the Structure and Operations
of the National Collegiate Athletic Association

In 1906, 38 U.S. schools formed the first national governing body of college and university athletics. The Intercollegiate Athletic Association (IAA), as the organization was then known, was established as a result of public concern over the rampant violence in intercollegiate football. The members of the organization worked together to counter this concern. They established a standard set of rules and introduced the forward pass, which opened up play and thus made the game of football safer. In 1910 the IAA changed its name to the National Collegiate Athletic Association (NCAA) and expanded the scope of its mandate to encompass all unethical conduct in college sport. In its early years the NCAA was a loosely structured group of colleges and universities operated by seven representatives of the member institutions. Although the original intent of the organization was to regulate and control intercollegiate sport through the establishment of a set of stringent rules and strict enforcement codes, this idea was dropped in favor of accomplishing its purposes through educational means. The actual control of intercollegiate sport was placed in the hands of each individual member institution. As such, the NCAA had no power to sanction; its primary role was an advisory one to its membership.

The NCAA grew rapidly. The size of its executive board increased to nine in 1921 and was further expanded in 1928. The first NCAA national championship was held in 1921 in track and field; swimming followed in 1924, wrestling in 1928, and boxing in 1937. The first NCAA basketball championship was held in 1939. Membership size increased from the initial 38 schools to 148 in 1926; by 1951 there were 368 member schools and 24 conferences. The organization hired its first full-time staff director in 1949.

Despite its considerable growth it was not until 1952 that the NCAA was granted any type of regulatory power over its member institutions. Public disclosures about unethical recruiting, the illegal payment of student athletes, point-shaving in college basketball, and tampering with student transcripts resulted in mounting pressure to do something about intercollegiate athletics. As a result a group of college and university presidents met as members of the American Council on Education to recommend that athletics be deemphasized as a part of the college and university curriculum. Faced with the threat of someone from outside intervening in their affairs, the NCAA moved quickly to develop a system under which sanctions against member institutions could be invoked. The organization's role changed, from being a passive observer and consultant on issues related to intercollegiate sport, to exercising the power to penalize member institutions that violated its rules.

Since 1952 the NCAA's power and the scope of its operations have continued to grow. It now controls virtually all aspects of big-time college and university sport in the United States, including the regulation of national championships, the eligibility of student athletes, the administering of financial aid, and the length of the playing and practice seasons. The organization has a budget of $163 million and a membership of just over 900 four-year colleges and universities. It operates 79 national championships in 21 sports and regulates a number of college football bowl games. Its headquarters are centralized in Overland Park, Kansas and it has a paid staff of 254. Along with a 44-person executive council, over 75 other committees run the affairs of the organization. Its operating policies and procedures are outlined in a manual just under 500 pages in length.

Based on information contained in the following sources: G.H. Sage's (1982) The intercollegiate sport cartel and its consequences for athletes, in J. Frey (Ed.), (1982) *The governance of intercollegiate athletics* (pp. 131-143). West Point, NY: Leisure Press; R.N. Stern (1979). The development of an interorganizational control network: The case of intercollegiate athletics. *Administrative Science Quarterly*, *24*, pp. 242-266; L. Garrison (1992, December). The centennial celebration: Intersectional play. *Athletic Administration*, pp. 10-13; and the 1991-1992 *NCAA Manual*.

Change, such as that exhibited by the NCAA, is one of the most visible features of all sport organizations. As discussed in chapters 5 through 8, to survive and grow, a sport organization must be able to adapt to changes in strategy, size, environment, and technology. As it grew larger the NCAA required a different operating structure from that used in its early years. As the scope of its mandate changed, so did its mode of operation. In the vignette at the start of chapter 1 we saw Nike undergo a similar type of transformation as it evolved from a company operating out of the trunk of Philip Knight's car to one of the biggest athletic footwear manufacturers in the world.

The purpose of this chapter is to explore the multifaceted nature of change in sport organizations. We begin by looking at the concept of change and what we mean when we talk about organizational change; we then explore the paradoxical nature of change. Next, seven major theoretical approaches to understanding change are briefly outlined. We then look at what causes the need for change in sport organizations, what are the barriers to change, and how change is managed. Some theorists have suggested that change can be conceptualized as a series of stages; we look briefly at this approach, but then argue that the concept of "tracks" provides a better and more realistic understanding of the change process. Finally, we look at the notion of innovation and why sport organizations need to be innovative.

The Concept of Change

Sport organizations are in a constant state of change; new people enter the organization, some leave, parts

of the organization's physical layout are re-organized, and new programs or product lines are developed. In this chapter our focus is not on the day-to-day fluctuations evident in all sport organizations but on planned change, change that a sport organization systematically develops and implements to retain a competitive advantage in whatever market it targets. The pressures for such change may be generated externally in the sport organization's environment or they may originate from within the organization itself. Over the past decade external pressures—the changing economic situation in North America and Western Europe, technological advances in the manufacturing of sports equipment, and increased societal interest in sport and leisure—have all contributed to changes in organizations within the sport industry. Internal factors such as an emphasis on service quality, a move to self-managed teams, and the demand for flexible operating procedures have also produced pressures for change.

As figure 11.1 shows change can occur in four different areas of a sport organization: its technology, its products and services, its structures and systems, and its people (cf. McCann, 1991).

Technological change refers to the changes that occur in an organization's production process, the skills and methods it uses to deliver its services, or its knowledge base. Huffy underwent considerable technological change when it moved to a computer-integrated manufacturing plant (Slakter, 1988). A change in the products or services of a sport organization may involve the addition, deletion, or modification of other areas. For example, in the mid-1980s when Herman's World of Sporting Goods

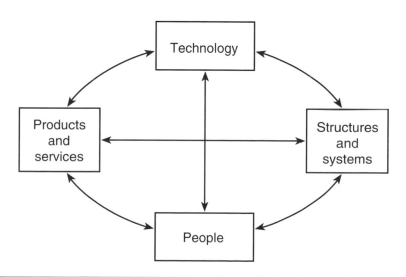

Figure 11.1   Potential areas of change in a sport organization.

expanded its line of water sport products because of increased interest in this type of activity, the change was accompanied by an increase in the amount of store space allocated to these products, and in the amount of advertising about the availability of the product (Adams, 1987). Structural and systemic changes involve modifications to areas of a sport organization such as its division of labor, its authority structure, or its control systems. Such changes occurred when the NCAA increased the size of its Council and added committees and professional staff. People change involves modifications to the way people think and act and the way they relate to each other. This type of change is often brought about through techniques such as sensitivity training, team-building exercises, and group planning. While we focus primarily on structural change in this chapter, these four areas are interrelated; a change in one area will often require a change in one or more of the others.

Change as Paradox

The paradoxical nature of change stems from the fact that a sport organization must change if it wishes to remain competitive (Peters, 1990). However, as we saw earlier, management prefers stability and predictability. A sport organization's output, costs, and workforce must remain relatively fixed if it is going to be successful. At the same time, sport managers need to look for new markets, new technology, and innovative means for service delivery. The sport organization, therefore, must find a balance between change and stability. If a sport organization fails to change it may follow what Miller (1990) refers to as a "trajectory of decline." On the other hand, if it changes too rapidly or just for the sake of change, its operations will be disrupted. If incorrectly managed, the success of previous change can become a sport organization's downfall. As Miller (1990, pp. 3-4) notes, "productive attention to detail, for instance, turns into an obsession with minutia; rewarding innovation escalates into gratuitous invention; and measured growth becomes unbridled expansion."

Achieving a balance between stability and change is not an easy task. The sport manager must recognize the need for change and understand how it can be successfully implemented and managed. Changes in environment and technology will impact the amount of change a sport organization will require. Those organizations that operate in stable environments with routine technologies will require less change than those facing dynamic environments with nonroutine technology.

Perspectives on Organizational Change

For many years the dominant models of change were what Chin and Benne (1985) describe as "normative re-educative." Essentially, change was seen as a linear process consisting of a series of steps that involved diagnosing problems in organizations, developing solutions to these problems, identifying resistance to the changes that would be needed to implement these solutions, formulating and implementing a change strategy, and monitoring and reviewing the change process. Particular emphasis was placed on the role of change agents, individuals who used a variety of organizational development techniques to guide the change process. In the last 10 to 15 years the political and economic fluctuations that have characterized North American and Western European societies have drawn increased attention to the process and management of change. As a result we have seen new theoretical developments in this area, and hence new ways of looking at change. In this section we briefly examine the most popular of these perspectives. Although these perspectives are dealt with separately, they are not necessarily discrete. Some, such as resource-dependence and institutional theory, may overlap, in that they are both variants of contingency theory. They are, however, sufficiently different from each other and from mainstream contingency theory to warrant individual consideration. Others, such as institutional theory and population ecology, have been seen as converging with each other (cf. Carroll & Hannan, 1989; Zucker, 1989) and some, for example, population ecology and the contextualist approach are considerably different in their intellectual underpinnings and their method.

Population Ecology

As we saw in chapter 7 the population ecology approach to understanding organizations developed out of the biological literature and particularly the Darwinian notion of survival of the fittest. The focus here is not on change in single organizations but on a population of like organizations in a particular geographic area or niche, for example, all sporting

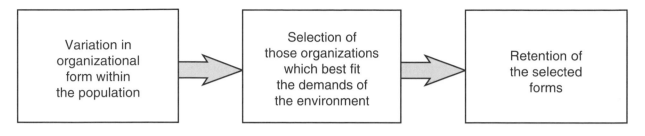

Figure 11.2   Stages of the change process: the population ecology approach.

goods stores in the state of New York (cf. Carroll & Hannan, 1989; Delacroix & Carroll, 1983). Population ecologists conceptualize organizational change as a three-stage process (see figure 11.2).

In the first stage of the process, considerable variation in the organizational form is found in a particular population of organizations. This variation occurs because entrepreneurs set up organizations to fill a gap in the market, or as a result of a perceived need. For example, in the last 15 to 20 years the number of sporting goods stores in North America increased as consumers demanded a variety of sport and recreational equipment. The stores created to fill this need show variation in their structural form, the products they sell, and the way they service their customers. Some of these variants will be better equipped to meet the demands of their environment. Some will be unable to exploit this environment to obtain the resources necessary to operate or there may be an insufficient demand for their product and/or services. Those that fail to meet the demands of the environment will be "selected out," that is, they will fail. Those that are positively selected survive and are retained within the market niche. Over time the demands of the environment will change. For instance, in our example of sport stores, over the last few years there has been a greater demand for products such as in-line skates and licensed apparel. Sport organizations have to change their structure, products, and services to meet these types of environmental demands. Those that do will be retained; those that don't will flounder and cease to exist.

Resource Dependence

The essential premise of resource-dependence theory, as we saw earlier, is that organizations are unable to generate internally the different types of resources they need to operate; consequently, they come to depend on their environment for resources critical to their survival. However, as Pfeffer and Salancik (1978, p. 3) point out, "environments can

change, new organizations enter and exit, and the supply of resources becomes more or less scarce." Because organizations depend on resources for their operation, this potential for a reduction of resources creates uncertainty for managers. Managers can reduce this uncertainty by changing their activities in response to these environmental factors. Slack and Hinings (1992), for example, show how Canadian national sport organizations, which were dependent on the federal government for much of their funding, changed aspects of their structure to meet requirements established by the government agency Sport Canada. Managers can also act to change the nature of their organization's resource environment. The techniques used include mergers, diversification, and joint ventures. Mergers between two competing organizations help reduce uncertainty by eliminating some of the competition for resources. Diversification can be used to stabilize a sport organization's dependence on its environment by reducing the uncertainty that may result from trends in individual market areas and economic fluctuations. Joint ventures reduce uncertainty by pooling resources such as capital and expertise. All of these initiatives result in changes to an organization's structure and operations; more details of such changes can be found in chapters 5 and 7.

The Life Cycle Approach

Like population ecology, the life cycle approach is based on the idea that biology "provides certain concepts and models that . . . appear to have some relevance for understanding organizational cycles" (Kimberly, 1980, p. 6). Unlike population ecology, however, the life cycle approach is concerned with single organizations or small groups of organizations, rather than entire populations. Essentially, the central theme of the life cycle approach is that organizations, like animals or people, change as they go through different life stages. These stages are described variously: creation, transformation, and decline (Kimberly, 1980); birth, growth, maturity, old age, and death (Adizes, 1979); the entrepreneurial stage, the collectivity stage, the formalization and control stage, the elaboration of structure stage, and the decline stage (Cameron & Whetten, 1983a). These stages are sequential, not random, and as such they are predictable. However, the length of time that individual organizations spend in each stage may vary considerably, and every organization will not necessarily go through every stage. Some, for example, may go straight from the entrepreneurial stage to decline. Each stage has different managerial requirements. Change is seen as a developmental progression through these stages.

Certain key events in the various stages can significantly influence future changes. For example, Kimberly (1980) argues that organizations, like people, are very much influenced by the conditions of their birth. Also, like people, an organization's history will strongly influence any future changes it may make. Although it does not specifically employ the life cycle approach, Slack's (1985) study of the Alberta Section of the Canadian Amateur Swimming Association provides some indication of the stages that a sport organization may pass through. Also, many popular press accounts of the growth of sport organizations (cf. Kogan, 1985 [Brunswick]; Geiger, 1987 [The Broadmoor]; Strasser & Becklund, 1991 [Nike]) provide implicit indications of their various life cycle stages.

Although criticized as overly deterministic, the life cycle approach is intuitively appealing as a means of understanding change. In some ways it has also been the forerunner of more recent work by John Kimberly, one of the original proponents of the life cycle approach, in which he adopts what he terms a "biographical" approach to understanding organizational change (cf. Kimberly, 1987; Kimberly & Rottman, 1987).

Institutional Theory

Institutional theorists (DiMaggio & Powell, 1983; Meyer & Rowan, 1977; Meyer & Scott, 1983; Oliver, 1991; Zucker, 1983, 1987) suggest that organizations change their formal structure to conform with expectations within their institutional environment about appropriate organizational design. Usually exerted by regulatory agencies such as the state, professions, or interest groups, these institutional expectations come to define the appropriate and necessary ways to organize. As Slack and Hinings (1992, p. 123) note, "components of the structural design of an organization become widely accepted

as both appropriate and necessary. In simple terms *a* way to organize becomes *the* way to organize." Organizations change and conform to the expectations of their institutional environment because by doing so they help increase their legitimacy and thus help ensure the continued flow of resources necessary for their operation (Hinings and Greenwood, 1988).

We saw change occurring in Canadian national sport organizations in the period 1984-1988 when the Canadian government agency Sport Canada created institutional pressures for these organizations to adopt a more professional and bureaucratic structure (cf. Macintosh & Whitson, 1990; Slack & Hinings, 1992). Ideas about the appropriateness of this particular organizational form were reinforced through government publications, by pressure from Sport Canada consultants, through the rewards and kudos given to conforming organizations, and through the increased employment of professional staff in national sport organizations (Slack & Hinings, 1994). Slack and Hinings (1992) show how, as a result of these pressures, these organizations changed, increasing the number of professional staff they employed and systematizing their operating procedures.

Contingency Theory

Contingency theory views of organizational structure and change (Burns & Stalker, 1961; Hellriegel & Slocum, 1978; Lawrence & Lorsch, 1967) are widely accepted in the literature. Essentially, contingency theorists argue that organizational structures have to be matched to such imperatives or contextual demands as size, technology, and environment. A change in these features will require an associated change in an organization's structural arrangements. Organizations successful in changing their structure to meet contextual demands will be more effective. More specific explanations of the nature of contingency relationships and their application to sport organizations can be found earlier in this book, in chapters 6, 7, and 8.

Evolution/Revolution

The evolution/revolution approach to organizational change is best exemplified by the work of Greenwood and Hinings (1988); Miller and Friesen (1980a, 1980b); Nadler and Tushman (1989a); Tushman, Newman, and Romanelli (1986); and Tushman and Romanelli (1985). These authors suggest that organizations resist change. Even when faced with the possibility of failure, organizations will often continue to do what they have been doing in the past and not make the necessary adjustments to ensure their survival. This resistance to change stems from a variety of factors, including

- the reluctance to deviate from existing programs,
- the inability of organizations to accurately appraise their performance,
- sunk costs in facilities or equipment,
- the culture of the organization, and
- the fear by some managers that change will reduce their power.

As a result of this resistance to change the dominant organizational condition is what Miller and Friesen (1980b) refer to as momentum. Momentum is merely the tendency of an organization to stay within its existing structural design (e.g., a simple structure). Evolutionary change occurs as organizations make incremental adjustments in their strategy, structure, and/or processes, while still remaining within this particular design. In contrast, revolutionary change takes place in response to a major upheaval or crisis in an organization's environment requiring a "simultaneous and sharp shift in strategy, power, structure, and controls" (Tushman, Newman, & Romanelli, 1986, p. 31). Organizations that make a change from one design type to another, that is, a move from a simple structure to a professional bureaucracy, exhibit revolutionary change. Slack and Hinings (1992) saw this type of change occurring in many of Canada's national sport organizations during the 1984-1988 period, and Kikulis, Slack, and Hinings (1992) provide a framework for understanding this type of change.

Contextualist Approach

The contextualist approach to understanding organizational change emanates from the work of Andrew Pettigrew and the staff of the Centre for Corporate Strategy and Change at the University of Warwick, Business School. Pettigrew (1985a, p. 15) criticizes much of the existing work on organizational change as being "ahistorical, aprocessual, and acontextual." Much of this work, he claims, focuses on a single change event or a discrete episode of change. There are, he notes, "remarkably few studies of change that actually allow the change process to reveal itself in any kind of substantially

temporal or contextual manner" (Pettigrew, 1987, p. 655). Research studies are therefore concerned "with the intricacies of narrow *changes* rather than the holistic and dynamic analysis of *changing*" (emphasis in original).

To address this concern, Pettigrew suggests a multilevel analysis of change over long periods of time (Pettigrew, 1985b, 1987). This work calls for examination of three areas related to change: context (divided into inner and outer context), content, and process. Pettigrew (1987) graphically portrays an interaction among these three by placing them at the corners of a triangle (see figure 11.3). The outer context "refers to the social, economic, political, and competitive environment in which the [organization] operates" (Pettigrew, 1987, p. 657). The inner context is made up of those organizational elements that influence the change process, such as the organization's structure, culture, and political makeup. Content refers to the aspects of an organization that are being changed, and may include technology, people, products, and services. The term process "refers to the actions, reactions, and interactions from the varied interested parties as they seek to move the [organization] from its present to its future state" (Pettigrew, 1987, pp. 657-658).

This approach to change, unlike several of the others examined here—population ecology, institutional theory, and contingency theory—does not focus solely on environmental pressures as a source of change. Rather, the work of Pettigrew and his colleagues emphasizes the interrelated role *over time* of environment (context), structure, and human agents, in shaping the change process (Pettigrew, 1985a; Pettigrew & Whipp, 1991). Unlike many studies of change, Pettigrew's methods draw heavily on the detailed construction and analysis of case studies.

Unfortunately, no studies within sport management have used this approach. The richness of data which the contextualist approach can yield makes it a very viable method for enhancing our understanding of sport organizations. Studies on

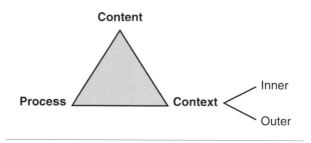

Figure 11.3 Contextualist approach to change.

organizations within our field could also be used to extend the theory.

What Causes Organizational Change?

The impetus for change may arise externally in the environment of a sport organization or from inside the organization itself. As we have seen, many theorists, for example, contingency theorists and population ecologists, focus on external sources of change, while others—resource-dependence theorists and those who adopt the contextualist approach—stress the interaction of external and internal factors. Externally a wide variety of factors can cause the need for change in a sport organization. The recession of 1982 saw Huffy sell only 7.6 million bikes when it was expecting to sell 20 million. The company changed by closing two of its three plants and consolidating its operations in Celina, Ohio. The acquisition of new equipment and technology can also cause changes in the way a sport organization operates. For example, scanners and bar codes have changed the way many retail sporting goods stores do business. Inventory and warehousing is easier to control, hence ordering can be standardized, pricing changes are easily made, and sales figures can be quickly retrieved from an in-store computer.

Changes in government legislation may also initiate changes in the way sport organizations are structured and operated. Title IX, for example, has had a significant effect on many U.S. college and university athletic programs. These organizations are also affected by legislation that deals with such issues as "unrelated business" income tax. Craig and Weisman (1994) have described how certain revenues raised by colleges and university athletic programs may be subject to this tax, a factor that may subsequently cause a change in the way they operate.

Internally, change is often initiated by "change agents," people whose job it is to ensure that a sport organization makes the necessary changes to maintain or increase its effectiveness. Chief executives, vice presidents, coaches, human resources development staff, union representatives, and external consultants can all act as change agents. It is important to realize that the changes these people recommend usually reflect their own interests and values. For example, the changes the Player Relations Committee may want to make to the collective bargaining agreement of major league baseball will likely be quite different from changes the Players Association would like to see. The types of changes senior managers want to see are different from those of the union representatives. What may be an acceptable change to some members of a sport organization will not be acceptable to others. As we noted earlier, change is a political process that may not only require changes to the structure of a sport organization but also to the dominant values expressed by its members.

One of the ways people in a sport organization try to bring some objectivity to the change process is to bring in an outside consultant. As Pfeffer (1981, p. 142) points out, these people "can serve to legitimate the decision reached and to provide an aura

---

TIME OUT

Fitness-Oriented Baby Boomers Change the Demand for Golf Carts

At one time golf was considered an old man's game. But in 1989 golf industry statistics showed that about 11 million golfers in the United States were men and women in the 20-to-40 age range, an increase of 3 million from 1985. Unlike their older counterparts these younger fitness conscious baby boomers were not interested in using motorized golf carts; they much preferred walking between holes. Sensing this change Kangaroo Products, which started with motorized carts in 1972, began selling a battery-powered caddie that could travel on its own. By merely flipping a switch the caddie could be used to transport golf bags to the next hole while the golfers themselves were free to walk. This change in product proved tremendously successful for Kangaroo; their revenue increased by over 20 percent from the previous year.

Based on information in Cole, W. (1989, July). Tee time for baby boomers. *Venture*, pp. 69-73.

of rationality to the decision process." They are purportedly hired to look impartially at the problems and issues that confront the sport organization and make suggestions for change. However, as we saw in chapter 9, it is possible for management or those doing the hiring to manipulate the results that come from this type of process, through hiring the "right" consultant and often through a consultant's realization that, even though he has been hired to be impartial, future business from those who hired him may be contingent on his coming up with the "correct recommendation" (cf. Pfeffer, 1981).

Resistance to Change

Although change is a pervasive and constant feature of sport organizations, so, too, is resistance to change. This resistance may come from within the organization itself or from external constituents. Sport managers, if they are to deal effectively with resistance to change, must understand the reasons for this opposition, and realize that resistance is not always dysfunctional. Resistance can force sport managers to reevaluate the appropriateness of their proposed actions. The opposition to change that comes from interest groups inside or outside the organization can bring forward important issues management may not have considered. Resistance is a means of identifying possible problems before they arise and taking action to prevent them. What follows is a brief discussion of four of the major sources of resistance to change.

Self-Interest

As we saw in chapter 9, subunits within a sport organization often act to maximize their own vested self-interests and help them achieve their own goals. In any change process, some groups will benefit and others may lose. As a result, individuals or groups tend to consider proposed changes in terms of their own self-interest. For example, Patti (1974) suggests that if goals relating to power, money, prestige, convenience, job security, or professional competence are threatened as a result of any potential change, the change will be resisted, even in situations where the proposed changes are beneficial to the organization as a whole. For example, in 1986 when financial problems threatened the very existence of the Canadian Football League, the CFL Players Association strongly opposed a salary cap and threatened to strike if such a program were put into place.

Lack of Trust and Understanding About the Implications of Change

Change produces a degree of uncertainty for the members of a sport organization. Employees and groups within the organization are unsure of the impact it will have on them, especially where there is a lack of trust between those initiating the change and those it will impact. This lack of trust may produce rumor, innuendo, and distorted information about the nature and consequences of a change, leading to defensive behavior on the part of those affected. To minimize this resistance, management should explain in advance to the members of a sport organization why a change is being made and what impact it will have on them.

Differing Assessments of Consequences of Change

Change will be resisted when the members of a sport organization or other significant stakeholders have differing opinions of the costs and benefits of the proposed change. This situation frequently occurs when the people affected by the change have inadequate information about the change or when they exhibit fundamentally different values in regard to the proposed change.

The Cost of Change

Some groups or individuals may resist change because it is costly in terms of time, effort, and money, particularly in the short run. They do not see the benefits of changes as being greater than the costs involved. Changes involving a significant financial investment for new facilities, technology, or machinery are often opposed on the basis of cost. For example, a sport equipment manufacturing company may wish to change to some type of computer-aided manufacturing system, but shareholders may oppose the move because of the large capital costs involved in such a change and the subsequent impact (albeit short-term) on profits.

Dealing With Resistance and Implementing Change

In the previous section we identified four of the major sources of resistance to change. Here we discuss how sport managers can deal with resistance

Environmentalists Resist Changes to Ski Area

In 1987 a long-range plan was developed to expand Sunshine Village Ski Resort in Banff National Park. The plan called for 1,100 new parking spaces, a 50-room hotel expansion, and a high-speed chair lift. However, the plan was put on hold for several years while various groups assessed its environmental impact. Despite the fact that the Canadian Parks Service Western Region found no reason for the project not to go ahead, the Canadian Parks Service (CPS) announced in March 1989 that it still had concerns about the proposed development. As a result a modified plan was put forward that addressed the concerns of the CPS; it was approved in 1992 by the environment minister, subject to a review by an environmental assessment panel. In March 1993 the CPS assessment panel approved the plan, but in June decided that potentially adverse environmental aspects of the plan were unacceptable to them. A number of lawsuits subsequently followed the dispute, between the Sunshine Village officials who felt the changes to the operation of their organization would benefit the tourist industry in Banff, and the environmentalists who wanted to keep the park free of further commercial development.

Based on information in Fuller, P. (1994, February 14). No ray of light for Sunshine Village. *Alberta Report*, p. 22.

and implement change. The approaches outlined are not independent; frequently they are used in combination to influence those who oppose change. The first six techniques identified are based on Kotter and Schlesinger's (1979) work.

Education and Communication

As we saw in the previous section, resistance to change can stem from a lack of information or inaccurate perceptions about the consequences of the change process. Sport managers responsible for initiating change often have information about the process that is not available to all members of their organization. Educating these people about the necessity for change, and using communication techniques to keep them informed of how the change is progressing—group meetings, workshops, memos, and direct discussions between those initiating the change and those affected by it—can go some way to reducing resistance. This method of dealing with resistance and implementing change works best when the different groups have relatively similar goals and when the resistance to change is based on misinformation or a lack of communication. It requires a high degree of trust between the parties involved if it is to be successful.

Participation and Involvement

One of the most effective ways to deal with resistance to change and aid the implementation pro-

cess is to involve those groups and individuals most likely to exhibit resistance to the planning and implementation process. The idea is that this involvement creates a commitment to the process, and hence reduces opposition. By involving potential opponents to the change process, it is possible to deal with problems before they escalate and also use the skills, knowledge, and political contacts these people possess to help smooth implementation. The downside of this approach is that it is time-consuming and, as we saw in chapter 10, participative decision making can actually heighten conflict, thus hindering the change process. The government of Alberta, for example, held a series of public meetings in the early 1980s when it was involved in developing a new sport policy affecting the way sport was delivered in the province. The meetings, attended by members of the sport community, were designed to obtain input from those who were likely to be affected by the new policy and the subsequent changes. A problem with these particular meetings (and this process in general) was that, despite the fact that input was obtained, there was no guarantee that the organization making the change (in this case the provincial government) would actually take heed of what was said.

Establishing Change Teams

One of the ways to get the support and cooperation that change requires is to establish change teams.

As Kanter (1983, p. 242) points out, energizing people about change "through participation in team problem-solving has indeed produced significant results for many companies." Task forces, new venture groups, and interdepartmental committees are all excellent ways to manage resistance and implement change. These groups can undertake responsibility for training, counseling, and communicating the need for change.

Idea Champions

Daft (1992, p. 273) suggests that "one of the most effective weapons in the battle for change is the idea champion." Idea champions are intensely interested and committed to the proposed changes (Chakrabarti & Hauschildt, 1989; Maidique, 1980). They play a dominant role in getting other people involved in the change process and in reducing opposition. Chakrabati (1974) suggests that, to be successful, an idea champion must have technical competence, knowledge about the company, drive, aggressiveness, knowledge of the market, and political astuteness. Wolfe, Slack, and Rose-Hearn (1993), in their study of employee fitness programs, stressed the important role that idea champions played in getting these programs implemented in a number of major corporations.

Facilitation and Support

Some resistance to change arises from the fear and anxiety that the uncertainty of the process creates. Providing a supportive atmosphere for those affected by the change can help reduce this resistance. As Zander (1950, p. 9) points out, "resistance will be prevented to the degree that the changer helps the changees to develop their own understanding of the need for change, and an explicit awareness of how they feel about it, and what can be done about those feelings." The facilitation and support provided may take the form of career counseling, job training, and therapy. This method of dealing with resistance and implementing change is particularly useful where the change can create personal problems for members of the sport organization. The biggest disadvantages of this approach are that it is time-consuming, expensive, and not accompanied by a guarantee of success. For example, employees of a large sport equipment manufacturing company that is forced to restructure its operations will be concerned that the restructuring may cost them their jobs. Consequently, some type of support during the change process, while it may not totally remove the employee's fears, may help to reduce them and thus smooth the changes that occur as a result of the restructuring.

Negotiation

Negotiation or bargaining is used when one or more powerful groups involved in a proposed change are offered some sort of incentive to comply. Negotiation is a reflection of the political reality of sport organizations. However, in many ways it is a short-term answer to suppressing resistance. If one group is given concessions then other groups may adjust their positions and begin to negotiate to get similar considerations. Such interactions are costly in both time and money and can detract from the actual change process. This type of negotiation process took place in 1994 when the owners of the Calgary Flames Hockey club threatened to move their team from Calgary. To prevent the change in location the city of Calgary contributed $16 million to the Flames organization. The Calgary Cannons AAA baseball club tried to negotiate a similar concession to upgrade their ballpark, but was unsuccessful.

Manipulation

Manipulation, although considered unethical, is frequently used as a means of bypassing potential resistance to change. Manipulation can involve such practices as distorting information or disseminating false information, splitting groups that may resist change, and influencing power brokers. Zimbalist (1992, p. 139) for example, suggests that although the Civic Center Redevelopment Corporation owned by the City of St. Louis was valued at between $75 and $90 million, August Busch, owner of the St. Louis Cardinals, was able "to manipulate behind the scenes to eliminate a competitive bidder" and buy the corporation that owned what is now called Busch Stadium for $53 million.

Co-Optation

Co-optation, as we saw in chapter 7, involves absorbing key resisters or influential individuals in a sport organization's decision making structure. King (1991), for example, describes how, as the driving force behind Calgary's bid for the 1988 Winter Olympics, he secured the support of influential individuals from the City of Calgary and the Province of Alberta before officially placing the bid.

These people were absorbed into the organization because of their ability to influence key organizations in the bid committee's environment and as such help counter potential opposition to the bid.

Coercion

Coercion is frequently used to deal with resistance and implement change when all other methods fail. It may involve the threat of dismissal, demotion, the loss of a promotion opportunity, and transfer. Coercion is most likely to be used when a crisis situation is being faced and decisions have to be made quickly. It is problematic, in that it can result in alienation and create problems in any future change attempts.

Stages of the Change Process

A number of writers have suggested that change can be conceptualized as a series of stages (Robbins, 1990; Greiner, 1967). In this section we look at one of the best known and most widely accepted of these models. We then look at the concept of "tracks," a different approach to understanding the way in which organizations change.

Greiner's Patterns of Organizational Change

Greiner (1967), surveying the change literature in an attempt to distinguish successful from unsuccessful change, found that successful change processes were characterized by six stages, each involving a stimulus and a reaction. Figure 11.4 presents a diagrammatic representation of these stages; each is explained in more detail below.

Stage 1: Pressure and Arousal

In this initial stage of the change process, strong pressures are placed on an organization's senior management. These pressures may arise from external environmental factors, such as low sales or an innovative breakthrough by a competitor, but they can also arise internally as a result of events such as a strike or interdepartmental conflict. The pressures for change increase when internal and external forces act simultaneously. These pressures arouse top management to take action.

Stage 2: Intervention and Reorientation

Although strong pressures may arouse top management and cause them to take action, they will not necessarily make the proper responses. Management tends to rationalize the problems they face by blaming another group. For example, in a professional sport team the blame for low attendance may be placed on apathetic fans. Consequently, for a change to be successful, it requires the intervention of an outsider such as a new senior manager or a consultant. This person enters the organization and is able to bring some degree of objectivity to the problems it faces. The newcomer is able to encourage managers to reevaluate their past practices and current problems; they then undergo a form of reorientation to address the real problems they face.

Stage 3: Diagnosis and Recognition

In this stage different groups within the organization join together to locate the cause of problem issues. There is a sharing of power among the members of the organization; groups from different hierarchical levels meet to diagnose and recognize problems. Greiner (1967, p. 128) describes this as an important stage because it signals that "(a) top management is willing to change, (b) important problems are being acknowledged and faced up to, (c) ideas from lower levels are being valued by upper levels." Less successful change processes did not include this step, because senior managers felt they knew what the problems were and did not need the help of other members of the organization in correcting them.

Stage 4: Invention and Commitment

Once problems have been identified, new and unique solutions have to be invented and a commitment has to be made to a course of action. Creative solutions must be developed; the newcomer plays a role in this stage by encouraging new and creative practices. Shared power is an important feature in the development of these solutions and in securing commitment to them. Members from the lower levels of the organization show a greater commitment to solutions they have helped to develop.

Stage 5: Experimentation and Search

Once the solutions to problems have been decided on, they are tested. The testing takes the form of a number of small-scale decisions made at different

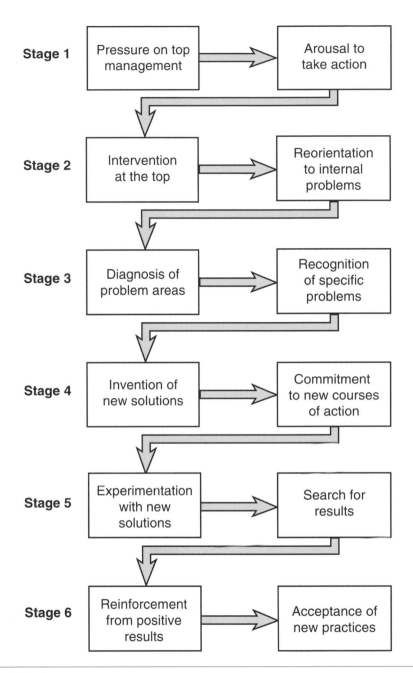

Figure 11.4 Stages of the change process.

levels of the organization. This type of experimentation serves as a credibility check before the change is introduced on an organization-wide basis.

Stage 6: Reinforcement and Acceptance

In the final stage of the change process, the positive results obtained in stage 5 start to be reinforced and expanded to all parts of the organization. Over time they become accepted as new practice. There is also an acceptance of the use of shared power as a means of introducing and implementing change.

Tracks and the Dynamics of Change

While models such as those proposed by Greiner (1967) and others are intuitively appealing as a means of explaining the change process, they do have a number of shortcomings. For example, change is conceptualized as a linear process in which organizations clearly move from one phase to the next. As such, there is no provision in these models to capture the temporal dynamic of change, or to address the fact that change is rarely a smooth or sequential process. Also, no account is taken within these models for the possibility of incomplete change or change that is only partially completed and then abandoned. An alternative and somewhat more realistic method of explaining change can be found in Greenwood and Hinings (1988) concept of "tracks."

The Greenwood and Hinings approach has its roots in the evolution/revolution theory of change. As such, it is best suited for explaining the dynamics of large-scale revolutionary change. These authors suggest that central to understanding the dynamics of the change process are the two concepts: archetypes and tracks. The concept of archetypes is related to Mintzberg's notion of configuration which was addressed in chapter 4. However, it extends Mintzberg's ideas to include not only a set of structural arrangements (which is the basis of Mintzberg's work) but also the underlying values and beliefs that hold these structures in place. As Hinings and Greenwood (1988, p. 18) note, design archetypes are to be identified by isolating the distinctive ideas, values, and meanings pervasively reflected in and reproduced by clusters of structures and systems. An organizational archetype in this sense is a particular composition of ideas, beliefs, and values connected with structural and systemic attributes.

In their work on Canadian national sport organizations, Kikulis, Slack, and Hinings (1992) identified three archetypes as being present in this particular institutional sphere. The structure of these archetypes and their associated underlying values are shown in figure 11.5. The kitchen table archetype is somewhat akin to Mintzberg's simple structure and the executive office archetype parallels many of the characteristics of the professional bureaucracy. Similar archetypes to these could probably be found in national sport organizations in other countries. Also, different institutional spheres of sport organizations may contain different archetypes.

	Kitchen table	Boardroom	Executive office
Organizational values			
Orientation	Private, volunteer, nonprofit (membership & fund raising)	Private, volunteer, nonprofit (public & private funds)	Private, volunteer, nonprofit (government & corporate funds)
Domain	Broad: mass-high performance sport	Competitive sport opportunities	Narrow: high performance sport
Principles of organizing	Minimal coordination; decision making by volunteer executives	Volunteer hierarchy; professionally assisted	Formal planning; professionally led and volunteer assisted
Criteria of effectiveness	Membership preferences; quality service	Administrative efficiency & effectiveness	International success
Organizational structure			
Specialization	Roles based on interest & loyalty	Specialized roles & committees	Professional, technical, & administrative expertise
Standardization	Few rules; little planning	Formal roles, rules, & programs	Formal roles, rules, & programs
Centralization	Decisions made by a few volunteers	Decisions made by the volunteer board	Decisions decentralized to the professional staff

Figure 11.5 Institutionally specific design archetypes for national sport organizations.
Reprinted, by permission, from L. Kikulis, T. Slack, and C.R. Hinings, 1992, "Institutionally specific design archetypes: A framework for understanding change in national sport organizations," *International Review for the Sociology of Sport* 27: 343-370.

Tracks help map and explain the incidence and nature of change and the absence of change between archetypes (Greenwood & Hinings, 1988). These researchers suggest that if an organization makes a revolutionary change from one archetype (A) to another archetype (B) there is the potential for three intermediate positions. These positions, however, should be considered indicative rather than definitive, since it is difficult if not impossible to establish empirically the discrete boundaries between positions. These three positions, along with two archetypal positions, are shown at the top of figure 11.6. Archetype coherence reflects a situation where an organization's structure and the underlying values held by members are consistent. For example, any of the three situations described by Kikulis et al. (1992) would reflect such coherence. Embryonic archetype coherence is a situation in which the structure of an organization nearly reflects the values of the members, but some items are discordant, for example, a kitchen-table organization which has started to hire professional staff. In a schizoid state the structure of an organization reflects the tensions between two sets of values. For example, the organization has competing groups, some of whom value the informal operating procedures and volunteer control of a kitchen-table archetype, and others who value the systematization and professional control of the executive office. Structure in these organizations will reflect the competing values: Certain elements will be like those found in the kitchen-table archetype and others will be more characteristic of the executive office. These design arrangements are incompatible.

The three positions can be used to establish the tracks that organizations follow when they make revolutionary change or when they attempt such a change but fail to complete it. As shown in figure 11.6, Greenwood and Hinings (1988) identify four possible tracks. An inertial track reflects evolutionary change, the type of change that occurs when an organization is in an archetype and the changes it makes are small, reinforcing the archetype. An aborted excursion occurs when an organization starts to change by moving away from its existing archetype, but for some reason returns to its original position. A reorientation track can take the form of a linear progression, an oscillation, or a delay; all represent successful change from one archetype to another. The linear progression is the normal sequential type of change process; the oscillation reflects the fluctuations that can occur as an organization changes; the term delayed is used to describe the situation when an organization resists change

for some time and then makes a rapid transition to a new archetype. In an unresolved excursion an organization sets off on a change but fails to complete the change. Kikulis, Slack, and Hinings (1995b), in their work on Canadian national sport organizations, have empirically verified the existence of these tracks in a change process in which these organizations were involved.

Innovation in Sport Organizations

One of the major challenges confronting all sport organizations is the need to be innovative. Rapid changes in market conditions demand more frequent innovations in product and service delivery, and in administrative processes and technologies, if organizational effectiveness is going to be maintained or increased. The term innovation refers to "the implementation of an idea—whether pertaining to a device, system, policy, program, or service—that is new to the organization at the time of adoption" (Damanpour, 1987, p. 676). Innovation involves the introduction of something new into the organization; as such it requires change. However, change does not necessarily involve innovation.

Three types of innovation can occur in a sport organization:

- Administrative innovation
- Technological innovation
- Product or service innovation

Administrative innovations involve changes to a sport organization's structure or administrative processes. For example, the introduction of a computer-based accounting system into a municipal sport and recreation department is an administrative innovation. A technological innovation involves the development and/or use of new tools, knowledge, techniques, or systems. Hillerich and Bradsby's move to use tracer lathes in the manufacture of baseball bats is an example of a technological innovation. A product or service innovation involves the development of a new product or service. Dupliskate's 1986 development of the first electronically powered skate sharpener is an example of a product innovation ("On the edge with Dupliskate," 1993).

A sport organization's structure influences its ability to innovate. Because of the emphasis on rigidity and control, bureaucratic organizations are seen as inhibiting innovation. In contrast, organic organizations, which are less structured, are seen

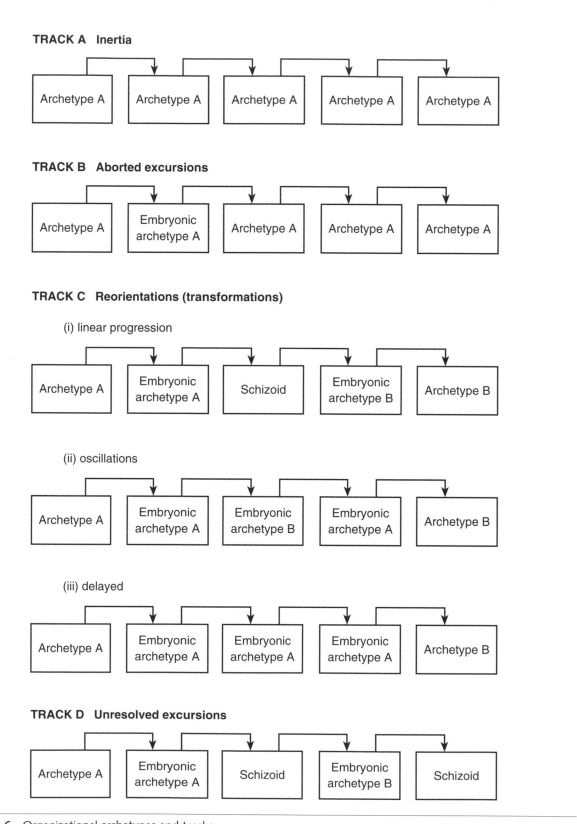

Figure 11.6   Organizational archetypes and tracks.

Reprinted, by permission, from R. Greenwood and C.R. Hinings, 1988, "Organizational design types, tracks and dynamics with strategic change," *Organization Studies* 9: 305.

as facilitating innovation. This view, however, oversimplifies the situation. Many big companies like IBM, although highly structured, are also innovative; they foster innovation through the use of such techniques as venture teams, small groups of people who are given a free hand to experiment and develop new ideas.

Summary and Conclusions

Change is an inevitable feature of all sport organizations. It can occur in an organization's products and services, its technology, its structures and systems, and its people. Managers prefer stability but the demands of a changing environment require that sport organizations change if they are to remain competitive. The last 10 to 15 years have seen considerable environmental uncertainty for organizations and consequently the need to change. As a result of the transformations occurring in organizations, change has become a major area of research in organizational theory. Consequently, a number of new and different approaches to studying change have been developed. Some, such as population ecology, focus on the environment as a major factor influencing change; others, such as the contextualist approach, focus more on the interaction of structure, environment, and agency.

These different foci demand different samples and methods. For example, population ecologists study large groups of organizations and usually use quantitative methods. Contextualists study much smaller groups of organizations, sometimes even a single organization, and rely on detailed case studies. The theoretical diversity in the change literature offers considerable potential for the study of sport organizations.

The pressures for sport organizations to change can come from a number of different sources either internal or external to the organization. Sometimes sport organizations use consultants to help initiate change. Along with pressure for change comes resistance to change—from the self-interest of those affected by the change, from a lack of trust and understanding about the change, from differing perceptions of the consequences of the change, and from the costs associated with change. We identified a number of techniques that sport managers can use to deal with resistance as they implement changes.

A number of researchers have posited different stages in the change process. One of the most common of these models, Greiner's, was outlined. However, the concept of tracks was presented as a more realistic means of explaining patterns of change. In the final section of the chapter we looked at the concept of innovation and how and why sport organizations need to be innovative.

Key Concepts

Technological change	Product/service change
Structural and systemic change	People change
Change as paradox	Population ecology
Resource dependence	Life cycle approach
Institutional theory	Contingency theory
Evolutionary change	Revolutionary change
Resistance to change	Idea champions
Archetypes	Tracks
Administrative innovation	Technological innovation
Product/service innovation	

Review Questions

1. Describe the four areas of a sport organization in which change can occur and explain how a change in one area can lead to change in the other areas.

2. Explain how sport organizations manage the dilemma of requiring both stability and change in order to be successful.

3. Why must sport organizations change if they are to remain competitive?

4. How would population ecologists see change occurring in sport organizations?

5. What are the similarities and differences between the population ecology and the resource-dependence approach to understanding change?

6. Explain what problems you see with the life cycle approach to understanding organizational change.

7. Explain how institutional theorists view change.

8. Discuss the evolution/revolution approach to change and use it to explain how change has occurred in a sport organization with which you are familiar.

9. What external factors could lead to change in a university athletic department?

10. Do population ecologists and institutional theorists see the stimulus for change arising from inside or outside the sport organization? What does this tell you about the shortcomings of these theoretical approaches?

11. What are the major sources of resistance to change? Can you think of other reasons why the members of a sport organization would resist change?

12. Select a sport organization with which you are familiar and which has recently undergone change. What were the sources of resistance to this change and how were these managed?

13. Describe the archetypes that you might find in a sample of retail stores selling sporting goods.

14. Discuss the relative merits of Greiner's model of change as compared to the notion of archetypes and tracks.

15. How do large bureaucratically structured companies promote innovation?

Suggestions for Further Reading

There is a large body of literature on organizational change and students interested in this area should consult the major organizational journals. In addition, for those interested in population ecology, Hannan and Freeman's (1989) book *Organizational ecology* and Singh's (1990) *Organizational evolution* provide what is probably the most comprehensive account of work in this area. The principal work on resource-dependence theory is Pfeffer and Salancik's (1978) *The external control of organizations: A resource-dependence view*. Those interested in the life cycle approach should see Kimberly and Miles' (1980) book *The organizational life cycle*. Institutional theory is best represented by Zucker's (1988) *Institutional patterns and organizations* and Powell and DiMaggio's (1991) *The new institutionalism in organizational analysis*. However, anyone interested in this area should also read the articles by DiMaggio and Powell (1983), Meyer and Rowan (1977), Oliver (1991), and Zucker (1983, 1987, 1988, 1989), which

can be found in the bibliography. Details of the evolution/revolution approach can be found in Miller and Friesen's (1984) difficult but valuable *Organizations: A quantum view*. Also useful and more readable is Hinings and Greenwood's (1988) *The dynamics of strategic change*. Pettigrew is the main proponent of the contextualist approach and his (1985a) book *The awakening giant* is a good example of this type of work. Also useful is Pettigrew and Whipp's (1991) book, *Managing change for competitive success*.

In the sport literature the primary work on change comes from the University of Alberta. Kikulis, Slack, and Hinings' (1992) article, "Institutionally specific design archetypes: A framework for understanding change in national sport organizations," provides a useful account of how the concept of archetype can be applied to our field. An extension of this work can be found in the article by these authors in the *Journal of Management Studies* (1995b), where they empirically explore the notion of tracks. Slack and Hinings' *Journal of Sport Management* (1992) article is a good example of how certain theoretical perspectives of change can be integrated to give a more complete picture of the process. In addition the *Organization Studies* article by Slack and Hinings (1994) shows how institutional theory can be applied to organizations in our field.

Case for Analysis

Cannondale's Ride to Success

Joe Montgomery grew up on an Ohio fruit farm. He attended three colleges but never received a degree. After trying college Joe spent some time in the Caribbean working on charter sailboats, then returned to the United States to work on Wall Street as an investment banker, working with a number of small companies. In the early 1970s Montgomery decided he would like to start his own business. Joe had an interest in camping and cycling and he noticed people making adjustments to the equipment they owned in order to meet their personal needs. He felt the bike industry was lethargic and that there was a niche for anyone with a good idea. There was also an increased interest in fitness and outdoor activities, which he felt would help a business in this area.

In 1972 Joe came up with an idea for a mini-trailer that cycling and camping enthusiasts could use to tow their equipment. Using as collateral an order from a California distributor to buy 2,000 units, he secured a $60,000 loan. Montgomery's first offices were over a pickle factory in Wilton, Connecticut. The story is that employees had to keep the windows open to get rid of the smell of pickles. The office was across the street from Cannondale railway station, so Joe called his company Cannondale. After nine months the company moved to Stanford, where they built Buggers (as the mini-trailers were called). Initial sales were slow but the Arab oil embargo of 1973 helped bike sales and Montgomery expanded his product line to include parkas, backpacks, and tents. In 1975 a recession hit and many bike stores went out of business, but Joe Montgomery had developed a sound business plan that appealed to his creditors and, with their help, he survived.

Although he had attained sales of about $8 million per year by the end of the 1970s and early 1980s, and his camping equipment was doing well, Joe wanted to build a bike. In 1982 he received a letter from an engineer named David Graham. Graham was fed up with his job at a boat facility and wrote telling Montgomery he wanted to build an aluminum bike. Montgomery hired Graham at half the salary he was making at the boat facility and they went to work. Their first aluminum bike came out in 1983. It used a large diameter aluminum tubing. The light weight of the aluminum made it possible to use the larger tubes, translating into extra "stiffness" in the bike without extra weight. The stiffness meant less of the rider's energy was dissipated and more went into propelling the bike. Although initial sales were slow, in 1984 Cannondale secured a contract with L.L. Bean to make private-label bikes. They expanded their line from one model to 15 and between 1983 and 1985 sales grew at a 30 percent annual rate.

The increasing market demand for Cannondale bikes, which retail from about $600 to $3,500, helped expand the number of North American and European dealers stocking its product. The company headquarters also expanded; in 1990, 80 people were employed in the Georgetown, Connecticut headquarters and about 175 in a Bedford, Pennsylvania production plant. The company was selling about 40,000 bikes a year and, although Montgomery wouldn't disclose financial data, in 1990 industry analysts put sales at about $30 million. By 1993 this figure had risen to $95 million. Over 30 percent of Cannondale's bikes (which unlike many other bikes are manufactured in the United States) were being sold to Europe and Japan. A wide array of designers, accountants, and engineers do the jobs that Joe Montgomery used to do, a fact he laments somewhat, as he now sees his role as "a glorified personnel manager" who spends his time shuffling papers.

Based on information in A freewheeler on firm ground. (1989, March 22). *New England Business*, pp. 34-39, 80-81; Charm, R.E. (1986, November 3). Like the company's sales, aluminum bikes of Cannondale stand out from the pack. *New England Business*, pp. 41-43; and Joe Montgomery's wild ride. (1993, April 19). *Business Week*, pp. 50, 52.

Questions

1. What changes do you think have occurred in the structure of Cannondale as it has moved from a small business over the pickle factory to the type of sport organization it is today?

2. What factors have caused the changes at Cannondale? Did they originate in the environment or were they the result of strategic decisions made by Joe Montgomery?

3. How would you explain the changes at Cannondale using the contextualist and life cycle approaches to understanding change?

4. What role has innovation played in Cannondale's success?

Managing Human Resources in Sport Organizations

When You Have Read This Chapter

You should be able to

1. describe what is involved in the process of human resources management,

2. explain what is involved in planning the human resource needs of a sport organization,

3. discuss how the recruitment and personnel selection process is conducted in a sport organization,

4. explain the various employee training methods that can be used in a sport organization,

5. list the relative merits of the different methods of appraising an employee's performance, and

6. discuss some of the new issues in human resource management confronting sport managers.

Paying Attention to Human Resources Keeps L.L. Bean Successful

The L.L. Bean company of Freeport, Maine is probably the world's biggest mail order supplier of outdoor sporting goods. The company's 120,000-square-foot retail store is open 24 hours a day and is Maine's second biggest tourist attraction (after the Atlantic Ocean). The company was started in 1912 by Leon Leonwood Bean, an avid outdoor sportsman, who built an all-weather boot and started to sell it to his friends. Although the original boot fell apart, Bean was not perturbed. He borrowed enough money to refund the purchase price to all those who had bought the boots and set about trying to improve the design. The new boot became the foundation of what is today a $1 billion-plus mail order company with major interests in the outdoor recreation industry. Much of Bean's early success came about as a result of their "down home, folksy" approach to doing business. Founder L.L. Bean was a no-nonsense sort of manager who sold good quality products at a fair price. Even today a customer can return any product that does not meet his or her satisfaction, and get a full refund or replacement.

However, the values on which Bean's early success was built also created problems. When Leon Gorman, the current CEO and L.L.'s grandson, started working in the company in the early 1960s, he found he was the only college graduate on the company's management staff. He also found lapses in product quality, an unmotivated workforce, and erratic service. The average age of the workforce was over 60, as founder L.L. Bean was a humane employer who never fired anyone. He was also described as a tightfisted "State of Mainer" whose wage policy was "minimum wage plus a nickel." He believed pension plans were an unnecessary expense, so no one retired. Gorman saw this situation as problematic, and when he took over the company in 1967 he set about revitalizing its operation.

Product lines were revamped, manufacturing and distribution centers were expanded, the mailing lists and order-entry system were brought into the computer age, and the advertising budget was increased. But the area where Gorman put the most emphasis was on the company's human resources. Salaries were increased to more competitive levels, a retirement policy was put into place, an equitable job-rating system was developed, and a performance bonus scheme was introduced. The company changed its hiring policy and started to bring in people from outside rather than just promoting from within. Training programs were introduced, and in 1988 Bean was spending nearly $1 million on training and development. For example, customer-service employees are expected to undergo eight days of training and four days of practice. For part of this time they sit at telephone consoles answering the kinds of questions they are likely to get on Bean's 24 hour toll-free customer-service line. An "after-hours program" of free personal-growth courses is also available for employees to take, on their own time but at company expense. In addition, there is a resource lending library and a tuition reimbursement program. Employees are encouraged to learn about the products they sell; they are able to borrow products from a resource pool free of charge. Each unit in Bean's operation has a team of human resources representatives who work as liaisons, resources, and problem-solvers for employees. Bean's emphasis on human resources has translated into increased profits and a workforce that is frequently commended for its customer service.

Based on information in Geber, B., (1988, October). Training at L. L. Bean. *Training*, pp. 85-89; and Skow, J., (1985, December 2). Using the old Bean. *Sports Illustrated*, pp. 84-88, 91-96.

One of the reasons L.L. Bean employees treat their customers with care and consideration is that they are treated this way by their company. When Leon Gorman took over as Bean's CEO he realized, as many other managers in the different areas of the sport industry have, that his organization's greatest asset was not its large retail outlet or its quality products, but its human resources, the people who make up the company.

The effectiveness of a sport organization is heavily influenced by how well it uses its human resources. As Kanter (1983, p. 19) points out about companies in general, those "with reputations for progressive human resources practices [are] significantly higher in long-term profitability and financial growth than their counterparts" who are not as progressive.

In this chapter we look at the issue of human resources management. We first explain what the term "human resources management" encompasses and why it is important to sport organizations. We then look at how we plan for the effective use of human resources. Next we focus on a number of the procedures involved in the management of human resources; specifically, we examine the topics of recruitment, selection, orientation, training, and performance appraisal. Finally we look at some of the more current issues facing the human resource staff of a sport organization.

The Nature of Human Resources Management

Human resources management, sometimes referred to as personnel management, since the early 1970s has become an increasingly important factor in organizational success (Mills, 1975). Changes in the economic climate, the growth of foreign competition, social legislation, an increased emphasis on collective bargaining, greater levels of automation, and the demand for more specialist personnel are all factors contributing to this concern. The term human resources management essentially refers to practices that employers use to recruit, develop, reward, maintain, retain, assess, and manage individual workers and groups of workers. It also includes the development, design, implementation, and management of systems for staffing, training and development, evaluating performance, compensating employees, ensuring they are satisfied in their job, and maintaining harmonious relations with labor groups. The central purpose of the human resources management function is to provide a sport organization with an effective and satisfied work force.

In a sport organization the human resources function may range from simply maintaining employee records to designing complex personnel training and development systems, negotiating compensation, and filing grievances. In small sport organizations the responsibility for managing human resources may fall upon the owner/manager of the company; sometimes a personnel administrator will report to a middle manager. In larger sport organizations a separate personnel or human resources department may emerge. The head of this department is often given the title Vice President of Human Resources and will report directly to the CEO. In this arrangement the Human Resources Department looks after the personnel needs of all departments in the organization. Large companies in the sport industry, such as Reebok and the Outboard Marine Corporation, operate with this type of

TIME OUT

Are Sport Management Graduates Satisfied With Their Jobs?

Parks and Parra (1994) examined the level of job satisfaction of the graduates of an undergraduate sport management program. They were interested in determining if there was any difference in the levels of satisfaction of graduates employed in positions related to sport and those employed in other fields. Using two job satisfaction instruments, they obtained responses from 118 graduates, just over 70 percent of whom held positions related to sport. The only area where the two groups differed was in the satisfaction with their present salary. The nonsport group had higher average salaries and were understandably more satisfied. The two groups showed no significant differences in several other areas related to the human resources function, including promotion opportunities, type of supervision received, and relationships with coworkers.

Based on information in Parks, J.B., & Parra, L.F. (1994). Job satisfaction of sport management alumnae/i. *Journal of Sport Management, 8,* 49-56.

arrangement, as do a number of public-sector organizations involved with sport. In some cases the human resources function may be combined with another area. As figure 12.1 shows, in the City of Winnipeg's Parks and Recreation Department, staff services, a human resources function, is combined with financial services.

Human Resources Planning

The purpose of human resources planning is to systematically forecast the future supply of and demand for employees (Milkovich & Mahoney, 1979). It is the method by which "management ensures that it has the right number and kinds of people at the right places, and at the right times, who are capable of effectively and efficiently completing those tasks that help the organization achieve its overall objectives" (Robbins & Stuart-Kotze, 1990, p. 628). While it is more common in large sport organizations, human resources planning can help small sport organizations if the time and costs involved do not become prohibitive. Planning is the first step in the process of managing human resources. By estimating the number and type of employees it will need over a particular period of time, a sport organization is better able to deal with issues such as personnel recruitment and selection, the demand for training and development programs, and career planning. The human resources planning process consists of four steps: devising a situational audit, performing job analyses, projecting the supply of and demand for human resources, and matching supply with demand.

Situational Audit

A sport organization's human resources plan is a component of its overall strategic plan. To accurately plan for the effective use of human resources the individual(s) responsible for this area must take into account those situational factors likely to influence future human resource needs and the availability of suitable personnel. A situational audit can help provide this type of information, and periodic updates to the audit can help sport managers and the professionals in charge of human resources develop and modify their personnel plans. Two components usually make up a situational audit: an environmental analysis and an organizational analysis.

Environmental Analysis

As we saw in chapter 7 several factors constitute the environment of a sport organization—legislative changes, technological advances, the economic climate, the presence of competitors, the actions of regulatory agencies, and the like. Changes in the environment can affect the human resource practices of a sport organization. Consider, for example, changes such as the Equal Employment Opportunity Act in the United States, or the Canadian Human Rights Act, both of which prohibit discriminatory employment practices. Or think of the technological advances we have seen in sport organizations, which can lead to the need for a reduced labor force. Understanding the impact of these factors on a sport organization can help human resources professionals and sport managers predict the type of personnel requirements they will need to meet their company's objectives. Those in charge

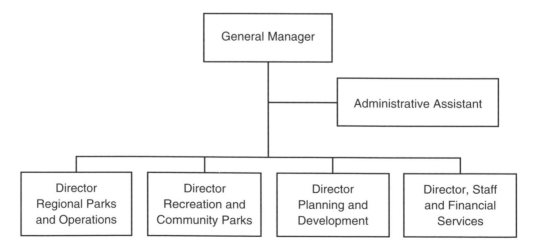

Figure 12.1   Human resource function in the city parks and recreation department.
Based on information in the City of Winnipeg's Parks and Recreation Department Policy Manual, 1990.

TIME OUT

Environmental Factors Influence Human Resource Practices at Nike

In 1971 civil rights leader Jesse Jackson founded "Operation Push" (People United to Serve Humanity), an organization designed to ensure that economic issues were included on the civil rights agenda. Jackson's plan was to target national and multinational enterprises to pressure them into hiring more minorities and utilizing the resources of the minority community. Push's premise was that corporations rely heavily on minority participation in purchasing goods; consequently, these same corporations should have a social responsibility to recognize minorities as more than consumers. On July 25, 1990, Push announced its intention to target the athletic shoe industry for greater contribution to minorities. Push invited Nike to a meeting. Speaking for Push, Jesse Jackson said "We are the margin of profit for the athletic shoe industry and we want our fair share of the jobs and investments in banks."

On July 31, 1990, Reverend Tyrone Crider, then executive director of Push, and Nike president Richard Donahue met behind closed doors in Chicago. After the meeting Donahue said he didn't rule out the possibility of working with and hiring more minorities, but that Nike was proud that 14.4 percent of its 3,500 workers were minorities and 75 percent of its philanthropic dollars were directed to minority programs. Crider replied that most of the Nike minority jobs were low paying. He felt that Nike was insensitive coming to the meeting with no precise information on the number of minorities in their management. Donahue, Crider said, did not even know the highest company post held by a minority. A follow-up meeting scheduled for August 14 never took place. Instead, on August 8, Nike canceled the meeting and charged Push with accepting a donation from its arch-competitor Reebok.

On August 11, Push called for a nationwide boycott of Nike. Two days later, Nike announced it would accelerate its hiring and promotion of minorities. CEO Phil Knight said his company had a goal of naming a member of a minority group to the board of directors within a year and another as vice president within two years. He also said the number of minorities heading departments would increase 10 percent within a year. On August 19 Crider called Nike's response inadequate, stating that "it didn't take 24 months to find Bo Jackson, it didn't take 24 months to find Michael Jordan." Over the next two months Push increased the pressure on Nike, picketing Foot Locker stores, one of the largest retailers of Nike shoes, and demonstrating at the annual Nike shareholder's meeting. Finally on October 23 Nike announced it had hired a 38-year-old African American to head its employment department. Nike also said that it had appointed a five-member internal minority advisory board to review the company's recruitment and training programs. On January 31, 1991 Nike created an outside five-member minority board to advise on minority employment goals and other minority issues.

Adapted, by permission, from J.E. Jackson and W.T. Schantz, January/February 1993, "Crisis management lessons: When push shoved Nike," *Business Horizons*: 27-35.

of human resources must take into account dozens of changes—legislation that calls for the hiring of more minority employees, affirmative action in the hiring of women, and technological changes that necessitate specialized workers—and focus their personnel planning accordingly.

Organizational Analysis

An organizational analysis is required because the human resource needs of different sport organizations will vary. Take, for example, the different needs of a bike company like Trek, a TV company such as

TSN (The Sports Network), the Dunes Golf and Beach Club at Myrtle Beach, and a sport medicine clinic. Trek will require designers and a manufacturing staff; TSN will require camera crews, announcers, and producers; the Dunes will require service staff and groundskeepers; and the sport medicine clinic will require doctors, X-ray technicians, and therapists. An organizational analysis takes into account how a sport organization's characteristics influence its personnel needs. The organizational factors usually considered are goals, resource availability, psychological climate, and structure.

Goals are important because they are an indication of what a sport organization does. One of L.L. Bean's goals is to provide excellent customer service, hence its human resources staff must ensure the company has an adequate number of well-trained customer-service personnel. A company like W.L. Gore, which is heavily involved in research and development, requires creative scientists. Resource availability, particularly financial resources, influences issues such as compensation and salary negotiations, which in turn influence a sport organization's ability to attract qualified personnel. The psychological climate of a sport organization, for example, whether it operates in a free-flowing, organic manner or in a hierarchical way, will influence the type of people who join the organization. Coaches involved with professional hockey or basketball, for example, are often heard to say they have signed a player because "he will fit with our organization" or "he complements our style of play." Essentially, what they are saying is the player fits with the psychological climate of the organization. Finally, structure is important because sport organizations differ in such areas as the extent to which they want professionally trained specialists, people with experience, or people who will happily follow rules. The presence of a union is also a structural feature which can affect human resource practices.

Job Analysis

Once the environmental analysis is completed, the next stage of the human resources planning process is the job analysis. Job analysis is simply "the process of obtaining information about jobs" (McCormick, 1979, p. 20). A job analysis involves the creation of a job description (an account of the duties to be performed), the job specifications (the education, training, and skills required to do the job), and performance standards (the expected level of performance and the criteria used to evaluate the performance).

This information is important in the recruiting and selection of appropriate human resources. It also communicates the requirements of a job to the persons filling the position and their managers, and provides details of the extent and limitations of their responsibilities. A job analysis can aid in salary negotiations and union/management issues. The means of analyzing jobs should be dynamic; for example, if the nature of a job changes due to technological advances, the job description, specifications, and performance standards should change accordingly.

Projecting the Supply of and Demand for Human Resources

Armed with details of the environmental and organizational forces affecting a sport organization's human resource requirements and an analysis of the jobs in the organization, the sport manager and human resource professional can then move to projecting the supply and demand for personnel over the short, medium, and long term. Will the sport organization need more salespeople, more marketing staff, a greater number of concession workers? Is there a need to increase the number of women or members of minority groups employed in the sport organization? Over what time period are these changes needed? These are all questions the human resources staff have to address in forecasting the demand for employees to operate the sport organization effectively and efficiently. Forecasting supply involves predicting the availability of suitably qualified employees.

There are a variety of techniques, varying in their level of sophistication, for forecasting the supply and demand of employees. The manager may use judgmental techniques, which merely involve employing informed intuition as a means of estimating the required personnel needed; or use complex mathematical models that predict supply and demand (see Bartholomew, 1978; Bryant, Maggard, & Taylor, 1973).

Matching Supply With Demand

When the supply of and demand for human resources have been estimated sport managers and human resource professionals can make adjustments to their personnel needs. If a sport organization has an excess of workers, a hiring freeze may be implemented: As people leave the organization, no new hiring takes place, and existing staff are assigned to fill the positions of those who left. Attrition, the process by which people voluntarily leave the organization, may also be used to reduce the surplus. If the excess of workers cannot be reduced through either of these means, then layoffs, the temporary removal of employment to workers, may be introduced. Another possible way of reducing staff is through offering a voluntary early retirement package. Should there still be a need to reduce the workforce after these methods have been employed, the sport organization may have to release staff. Sometimes the impact of this action can be reduced if the organization works with employees to help them seek new positions, possibly with competitors or with related companies such as suppliers or distributors.

If a sport organization does not have enough workers to meet their staff requirements, then a staff shortage exists. In this situation human resource planners have to recruit new staff or ask existing staff to expand their job responsibilities. If the latter action is taken, there may be a need to introduce staff training programs.

Recruitment

Recruitment refers to "the process of locating, identifying, and attracting applicants capable of and interested in filling job vacancies" (Bergmann & Taylor, 1984, p. 34). The process begins with the situational audit. An environmental analysis provides parameters to determine how recruitment will take place. For example, it will help establish the availability of suitable personnel and how wide-ranging the search process will need to be. Similarly, an organizational analysis will help establish such things as whether suitable internal candidates are available, and who should be involved in the recruitment process. A job analysis must also be a part of the situational audit. If a recent situational audit and job analysis have been carried out by the human resource planners, the information will already be in place; if not, a new audit and analysis must be conducted for the position(s) available.

Once this step is completed the recruitment channels to be used, that is, the ways of finding recruits, must be decided upon. If the sport organization is small the situational audit and job analysis will be carried out relatively informally by the owner/manger and maybe a mid-level manager. The number of recruitment channels used is likely to be small. In a big sport organization the situational audit and job analysis will be more formal and comprehensive. The channels of recruitment used will reflect this formality, and be more wide-ranging. The type of employee being recruited will, of course, influence the recruitment channels used. Sport organizations do not usually use a "head hunting" company to recruit lower-level workers, but they may be used if the company is looking for a vice president of marketing. Sport managers and human resource professionals can use a number of different methods to recruit potential job candidates from either internal or external sources.

Table 12.1 lists a number of possible ways of obtaining recruits for a job, and some of the advantages and disadvantages of each. The recruitment method(s) used by a sport organization will vary depending on the position to be filled, the resources available for recruiting, and the timelines for filling the job. Recruiting by visiting the graduating class of a sport management program (college/university recruiting) is useful for filling entry-level positions but is unlikely to be used to fill senior executive posts. Advertising in major newspapers is a good method of filling a senior position, but the cost can prove expensive. Professional journals may often be cheaper but may only be published every quarter, so are of little use if a job needs to be filled quickly.

Selection

Once a sport organization has recruited a group of appropriate applicants, it needs some means of screening these people to make sure that the most suitable candidate is offered the job. The screening method is referred to as the selection process; its purpose is to predict which of the applicants will perform the requirements of the job the most effectively and efficiently. In selecting a marketing manager, for example, a sport equipment manufacturer will use the selection process to predict which person will be able to produce the most successful campaign. A sporting goods store hiring a salesperson will want someone who is personable, has a good rapport with customers, and is likely to be able to sell the product. To assist them in the selection process, the managers of sport organizations often use a number of instruments or techniques to evaluate how well applicants meet the criteria identified as relevant to the job.

Table 12.1   The Advantages and Disadvantages of Recruitment Techniques

TECHNIQUE	ADVANTAGES	DISADVANTAGES
Internal search	Relatively inexpensive. Good for employee morale. Candidates familiar with organization.	Limited scope of recruitment. May result in in-fighting and jealousies between candidates.
College/university visitations	Able to deal with large group at one visit.	Usually limited to lower-level positions. Can be costly and time-consuming.
Public employment agency	Usually free, readily available.	Limited use by people looking for higher-level positions.
Private employment agencies, "headhunting" firms	Have wide network of contacts, brings credibility.	Expensive, limited to looking for senior-level positions.
Newspaper ads	Wide distribution, possible to target groups, immediately available.	Can be costly.
Ads in professional journals	Goes to target group.	Cost, may require lengthy lead time to place ad.
Job fairs	Attracts large group of potential candidates.	Not selective.

Before we turn our attention to selection devices, however, it is important to mention some of the factors that will influence the selection device we choose to use. Basically, in selecting a particular instrument or technique, a sport manager must consider its validity and reliability, the cost of using the particular approach, and how easily it is administered (Arvey, 1979).

A selection device is considered to be valid if there is a relationship between the particular device and some criteria relevant to the job. For example, some sort of typing test may be a valid means of selecting someone whose work will involve a lot of time at a computer terminal, but it is not much use in the selection of a golf pro. In fact, it may be illegal to use any sort of test unless it can be established that the test is a valid indicator of performance in the job.

As well as being valid, it is self-evident that selection instruments or techniques must be reliable. That is, the device must give a consistent score when administered to the same person in a short time span. No sport manager wants to evaluate potential employees with an instrument that gives a high score one day and a low score for the same person the next day.

Cost must also be considered. While there are a number of valid and highly reliable means of helping select an individual for a job, many are costly to use; some may also require trained specialists to administer, limiting their usefulness for many com-

panies. The different instruments and techniques described below vary considerably in their validity, reliability, cost, and the ease of administration; their strengths and weaknesses are also discussed.

Application Forms

Virtually all sport organizations require individuals seeking employment to fill out an application form. Cheap and relatively easy to administer, the forms vary in their level of sophistication; some require only basic information such as name, address, and phone number; others require detailed and comprehensive accounts of education, employment history, and so on. Some of the biographical data obtained from application forms has been shown to be a valid measure for predicting job performance (Hunter & Hunter, 1984; Owns, 1976). The type of information available on these forms also has the advantage of being verifiable—it is relatively easy to determine, for example, if someone has a master's degree in sport management or has held a supervisory position with another sport organization.

When using application forms it is important to remember that there are certain types of information, for example, religion, marital status, or sexual preference, that are illegal to ask about. Since these requirements often vary from country to country, it is wise for the human resources staff to check the legislation that applies to their organization.

TIME OUT

Hiring Concerns in the Sport Industry

There has been a considerable increase in employment-related litigation over the past two decades. Miller, Fielding, and Pitts (1993) suggest that the two principal areas prompting legal action are discrimination against people with disabilities and negligent hiring.

While most employers know it is illegal to base the selection of employees on such factors as race, color, sex, country of origin, or age, Title 1 of the Americans with Disabilities Act prohibits discrimination against people with disabilities. The legislation, which originally applied to businesses with 25 or more employees, was changed on July 26, 1994 to cover businesses with 15 or more employees. Miller et al. (1993) identify several areas related to this legislation that they suggest may create confusion for those in the sport industry. Included are selection criteria related to hiring people with disabilities, making applications accessible to these individuals, interview (and application) inquiries that can be made about disabilities, the use of medical exams and related inquiries, and creating reasonable accommodations for people with disabilities. In their article Miller et al. discuss each of these issues and present advice for sport managers involved in employee selection.

Negligent hiring, the second area Miller et al. suggest has contributed to employment-related litigation, is about the liability an employer may incur for the negligent actions of an employee. Employers may be found liable if they hire employees who are involved in practices such as assaulting fellow employees, sexual misconduct, child molestation, burglary, theft, or embezzlement. Miller et al. suggest that employers must be alert to the possibility of potential employees with criminal backgrounds and they suggest a number of factors to consider in deciding whether or not to hire an ex-criminal, including the degree of contact the employee will have with the public, the nature of the crime committed, the nature of the employment in which the person will be involved, the time lapsed since the person was released from prison, statutory legislation about access to information on criminals, and federal legislation regarding hiring practices.

Based on information in Miller, L.K., Fielding, L.W., & Pitts, B.G. (1993). Hiring concerns for the sport practitioner. *Journal of Legal Aspects of Sport*, 3, 3-15.

Tests

Standardized tests such as the Minnesota Clerical Test or the California Psychological Inventory (Agarwal et al., 1983) may be used by some sport organizations as a means of selecting personnel. A number of such tests are commercially available and have good levels of reliability and validity. Some are fairly easy to administer but others may require someone with specialist training. They offer a means of comparing candidates, but the problem is that they often do not assess the intangible factors so important for many jobs. They can also be costly to purchase because of the amount of time involved in their development. Standardized tests are most frequently used for shop-floor jobs that require limited skills. The complexity of managerial and professional jobs make them difficult to test with any degree of validity and reliability.

Interviews

Virtually all sport organizations use interviews as a means of selecting managers and staff. Companies report they have a greater level of confidence in the interview as a selection device than in any other type of information (Bureau of National Affairs, 1976). The purpose of an interview is twofold, first to determine if a candidate can fulfill the requirements of the job and second to see how she/he compares to the other candidates. Popular because they are flexible, interviews can be structured or unstructured, or can contain a mix of structured and unstructured questions. They not only allow interviewers to ask questions but the interviewee also can request information from those doing the hiring. They allow the interviewers to see how candidates perform in a variety of situations, both job-related and unrelated.

Despite their popularity, interviews are not particularly valid or reliable. Reliability, usually measured by comparing the perceptions of the interviewers, can be improved if standardized questions are used and if the interviewers systematically record responses (Andler, 1976). Validity tests, that is, tests that compare work performance with interview results, are rarely conducted.

Reference Checks

Usually as a part of their job application potential employees are asked to provide the names of people (usually three) who will act as a reference for them. However, research suggests that reference checks provide little in the way of additional valid information to the interviewers. Beason and Belt (1976) noted that less than 22 percent of reference checks look for negative information, 48 percent merely verify information that has already been acquired, and only 30 percent are used to acquire new information.

Orientation

When a new employee starts work they are often required to go through an orientation. The level of sophistication of these programs can vary—from those limited to giving the employee a tour of the worksite, telling them where the washrooms are and who to talk with if they have problems, to a comprehensive program covering all facets of the sport organization's operation and taking several weeks to complete. The nature of the orientation may also vary with the level of the job; managerial jobs usually have more extensive orientation requirements than lower-level jobs.

The purposes of the orientation are to reduce the level of anxiety for a new person entering the sport organization, socialize them into the organization's culture, and provide them with the information necessary to help them best perform their job. It also extends the information provided at the job interview. Although orientation programs can be costly in terms of time and financial resources, they pay off by reducing the likelihood of employees performing poorly and helping ensure the new employee remains with the sport organization for a longer period of time.

Depending on the nature of the sport organization, two levels of orientation may be provided. For example, a new university swimming coach may be given an orientation to the way the university is structured and operates and an orientation to the athletic department. Sometimes the orientation may involve the use of worksite tours, company films, and written material such as policy handbooks, key telephone contacts, and company goals and objectives. Figure 12.2 provides examples of the types of items that may be covered in an orientation.

Training

Even after a comprehensive orientation program, employees will, at certain times in their career, require training programs to help them perform their job more efficiently and effectively. Training refers to activities designed to improve an employee's skill level, knowledge base, or experience, or to change their attitude about aspects of their work situation. The need for training can come about for a variety of reasons. New technology or equipment can require a sport organization's staff to demonstrate new and different skills from those they have been using. Consider, for example, a fitness center that purchases computer-linked weight training equipment, or a sport medicine clinic that acquires a new ultrasound machine. In each case, staff will need to be trained in how to use this equipment.

The need for training can also be influenced by a sport organization's strategy. A sporting goods dealer seeking to grow and expand will see training as a means of achieving these goals and staying competitive in the marketplace. The structure of a sport organization is another factor that can affect the need for training. A sport organization that pushes decision making down its hierarchy is, for example, more likely to emphasize staff training than one where decisions are centralized. Likewise, in an organization that promotes from within, training is seen as a way of preparing future managers.

Before the human resources staff of a sport organization can plan and administer appropriate training programs, they must ascertain the need for training in their organization. Training can occur at three levels: the organizational level, the job level, and the individual level. At the organizational level a new strategy, market, or type of technology may

Overview of the organization	Key policies and procedures review
Traditions, customs, norms, and standards Structure of the organization Diversity of activities Community relations expectations and activities	Details of major areas covered by policies and procedures
Compensation	**Fringe benefits**
Pay scales Overtime Manner in which pay is received Holiday pay	Health care Insurance Holidays Training programs Recreational and social events
Safety and accident prevention	**Employee and union relations**
First aid stations Safety precautions Use of alcohol and drugs Reporting accidents	Terms of employment Employee rights and responsibilities Discipline Evaluation of performance
Physical facilities	**Economic issues**
Tour of facilities Parking spaces Cafeteria services Washrooms	Profit margins Equipment costs Impact of absenteeism, lateness, and accidents

Figure 12.2 Examples of items that may be covered in a sport organization's orientation program.
Adapted from Walter D. St. John (1980, May). "The complete employee orientation program," *Personnel Journal*, pp. 373-378. All rights reserved.

necessitate that employees acquire new and different skills. For example, a chain of sporting goods stores that computerizes its ordering and inventory control system will require most of its staff to become familiar with the capabilities of the computer system and the way it works. At the job level, a specific task may change and, as a result, employees will have to be trained in the appropriate skills to handle the job. For example, a change in the type of automation being used on an assembly line producing sports equipment may change the nature of the production worker's job and hence the skills she

needs to perform her work. At the individual level, managers and staff may need certain types of skills to perform their job adequately or to help them move up the career ladder. While technical skills may be part of an individual's training requirements, there is also often a need for skills such as conflict management, building interpersonal relationships, and supervisory training.

Three types of skills can be developed through training programs. While technical skills, probably the most frequent focus of training programs, may be more common for lower-level employees, senior sport managers may also require training in certain technical skills. Interpersonal skills are important because most people in sport organizations work in some type of group or work unit; success is often a product of the ability of the people in the group to work together. While many employees will possess excellent interpersonal skills, others can improve through training. Listening skills, communication techniques, and understanding group dynamics, are all examples of the type of interpersonal skills that training can improve. In sport organizations that involve work of a nonroutine nature, for example, a sport facilities architectural design company such as CRSS Inc. of Houston, problem-solving skills are frequently required and training programs are often directed at improving this area. Training activities to enhance the problem-solving ability of employees often involve improving logic and reasoning skills, working to define problems and what causes them, and developing and analyzing courses of action for dealing with problems.

Several different training programs are available to develop the types of skills outlined above. Some of the more frequently used techniques are briefly outlined here.

On-the-Job Training

On-the-job training takes place when a supervisor, trainer, or coworker teaches an employee about the required skills and knowledge as they actually perform their job. This type of training is most frequently used for individuals doing routine work. For example, a staff member who books racquetball courts, fitness appraisals, and so on, at a recreational facility may be taught the job by a coworker who has previously had this responsibility.

Job Rotation

Job rotation is a form of training that involves employees moving through a *series* of jobs carried out within the sport organization. The whole training program is relatively time-consuming and may take up to two years to complete. Job rotation is often used as a means of preparing individuals for managerial positions. For example, someone in an athletic footwear company may rotate through jobs in sales, manufacturing, marketing, research and development, and international operations. This experience provides them with a good overview of the way the organization operates.

Lectures

Lectures are used to provide large groups of employees with information in a relatively economical manner. They may often be accompanied by films and other audiovisual aids. The problem with lectures as a form of training is that communication is usually one-way. To improve this situation adequate time should be allocated for discussion.

Case Studies

Case studies are frequently used to train students in sport management programs, and are equally useful as a means of training employees in a sport organization. Case studies present the employees with a real or hypothetical situation that has occurred in a sport organization; the participants discuss the case and explain how they would handle the situation. Case studies are a particularly good training tool for improving problem-solving skills (Newstrom, 1980).

Role Playing

Role playing is somewhat similar to case studies: The people undergoing the training are presented with a real or hypothetical situation to deal with. Unlike case studies, the participants assume the identity of the people involved in the incident being examined, and act out the situation. This type of training is useful for building empathy and tolerance for other individuals. It is also a useful means of improving problem-solving skills and interpersonal skills.

Performance Appraisal

Once employees are established in their jobs the sport organization's management will usually want to evaluate their performance. Performance appraisals determine the extent to which the individual employee and/or his work group are contributing to the overall purpose of the sport organization. More specifically, appraisals contribute to enhancing the effectiveness and efficiency of sport organizations by guiding management in making decisions about promotion, compensation, and the allocation of other forms of reward. They are also a means of identifying employees who are not performing up to the required standard and either removing them from the organization, disciplining

TIME OUT

Training Sport Facility Staff to Deal With the Employee-Customer Interface

In many areas of the sport industry customers or clients come into frequent contact with employees. Martin (1990), for example, suggests that it is not unusual for a customer at a sport facility to come into contact with one or more of the facility's employees at least a half-dozen times during the course of a visit. The nature of each of these contacts has an impact on how satisfied the customers are with their visit to the facility, which in turn impacts on whether or not they return to the facility. Positive contact experiences at a sport facility will keep customers coming back; a negative contact will have the opposite effect, and will obviously reflect in profits.

Despite the importance of establishing a positive relationship in the employee/customer interface, Martin, in a study of 62 bowling centers, found that 16 specific customer-relations behaviors that consumers identified as being important were exhibited only during 42 percent of the audits carried out in his study. Frequently, customers did not receive a sincere welcome, were not invited to return to the center, were not given an apology for malfunctioning equipment, did not receive proactive comments or suggestions unless they asked for them, were not given complimentary comments about their game, and did not receive invitations to bowl in a league or a specific event.

One of the ways Martin suggests to rectify these deficiencies is to train customer-contact employees. He recommends the development of a four-step training process. First, he suggests the development of a customer-relations manual for employees, covering a wide range of "people" topics. Second, Martin believes that staff should be encouraged to conduct "mystery audits" of other service establishments to see how they are treated. Third, he proposes periodic meetings with employees to go over the contents of the manual, discuss complaints and compliments, encourage employees to role-play customer contact techniques, and signal management's commitment to improving the employee-customer interface. Finally, he recommends on-the-job training for new employees. In this situation the new staff work with experienced staff who show them how to develop good customer-service skills.

Based on information in Martin, C.L. (1990). The employee/customer interface: An empirical investigation of employee behaviors and customer perceptions. *Journal of Sport Management*, 4, 1-20.

them, or providing training to rectify their deficiencies. Performance appraisals are, in short, the key input into an organization's reward-and-punishment system. They also provide feedback to employees to assist them in career decisions. A third benefit from appraisals is that they help identify the type of training programs needed in the sport organization. Finally, performance appraisals can help managers validate the selection criteria they used in the initial hiring process.

Despite their utility, performance appraisals can exhibit a number of problems (DeVries, Morrison, Shullman, & Gerlach, 1981). To ensure they are of benefit to both the employee and the sport organization, appraisals should first and foremost be relevant. That is, there should be a link between what is expected in the job and the criteria used to evaluate the individual doing the job. For example, if a basketball coach is hired to win games and raise money for the program, then these are the main criteria that should be used in her evaluation. Performance appraisals should also, like selection devices, be reliable. Reliability here essentially means that whatever method is used, different raters evaluating the same person should arrive at a somewhat similar conclusion. Finally, the effectiveness of a performance appraisal system is enhanced if it has the support of all the members of the organization. Managers must create a context within their organizations that supports the use of accurate and timely feedback. Frequently, the senior staff of an organization do not put the commitment and resources into an appraisal system that is required to make it beneficial for the organization and its employees (Hall, 1983; Henderson, 1980; Kelly, 1984).

Some of the most frequently used and generally accepted methods of conducting performance appraisals are briefly outlined here.

Written Feedback

Written feedback is probably the simplest way of appraising an employee's performance. The person conducting the appraisal documents, usually in fairly general terms, the employee's strengths, weaknesses, and possible areas for improvement. The effectiveness of this type of appraisal depends very much on the evaluator's writing ability. Good written evaluations can provide very detailed feedback to employees about their level of performance. However, because it is detailed and focuses only on one particular individual's performance, written feedback makes it difficult to compare and rank employees. The cost and difficulty of administering written appraisals create barriers to their use (Cascio, 1978).

Critical Incidents

In this method of performance appraisal, the sport organization's manager documents notable or critical incidents (e.g., dealing with a difficult customer; handing an interpersonal conflict with a colleague) and their attendant behaviors that characterize the employee's performance. The behaviors recorded should be specifically cited. The person conducting the evaluation should record events and behaviors that indicate positive, negative, and typical reactions. The list of incidents is provided to the employee to indicate desirable and undesirable behaviors. The critical incident method of performance appraisal is limited because it is quite time-consuming and labor-intensive, and because only selected incidents and behaviors are recorded—there is the possibility that they may not be an accurate representation of an employee's overall behavior.

Rating Scales

Rating scales are frequently used as a form of performance appraisal in a variety of work settings. They require that the individual doing the appraisal rate the employee's score on a number of items related to her work. An example of a rating scale designed to evaluate the performance of a person working as an instructor at a fitness club is provided in figure 12.3. The rating scale is usually completed by the employee's immediate supervisor. The number of possible scores that can be recorded may vary from 3 all the way up to 10. Usually an odd number is used, to provide the evaluator with some type of middle ground. Responses can be tabulated and employee's scores compared. While

	1 Poor	2 Fair	3 Acceptable	4 Good	5 Excellent
1. Relationship with customers					
2. Appearance					
3. Knowledge of facility					
4. Ability to provide fitness counselling					
5. Cooperation with other employees					
6. Punctuality					
7. Knowledge of new fitness trends					
8. Work productivity					

Figure 12.3 Example of rating scale questions for a fitness club employee appraisal.

rating scales are a quick and easy way to conduct a performance appraisal, they are very subjective and often reflect the biases of the person administering them. Also, if questions are asked that are unique to a particular employee, any comparisons are compromised.

Behaviorally Anchored Rating Scales (BARS)

Behaviorally anchored rating scales are designed to reduce the bias and subjectivity often found in other types of rating scales (Schneier & Beatty, 1979). They combine elements of the critical incident approach and the rating scale method of appraisal. To develop BARS, the appraiser first identifies clearly observable and objective job-related behaviors. These behaviors may be obtained from the person doing the job, her peers, or her supervisor, or they may come from the job description. The behaviors obtained should be indicative of both positive and negative job performance. Depending on its complexity, BARS may be developed for different dimensions of the job. For a relatively simple job only one rating scale may be required; the behaviors identified are described in short written form and then numerically scaled, usually from 1 to 7, to reflect varying degrees of performance. An example of a BARS designed for a salesperson in a sporting goods store is shown in figure 12.4.

Since BARS deal with comparing specific job-related behaviors, arguably they provide a more objective measure of performance than some other appraisal methods. BARS can require considerable input of time and effort if they are to be properly developed (Bernardin & Smith, 1981).

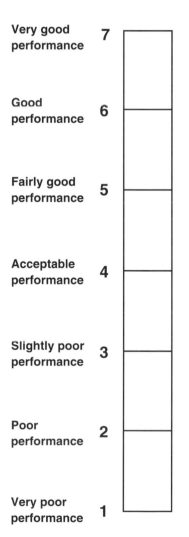

Figure 12.4 Example of a behaviorally anchored rating scale (BARS) for a salesperson in a sporting goods store.

Paired Comparisons

In the paired comparison method of performance appraisal, each employee is compared to every other employee in the work group. Usually the basis for comparison is overall work performance. An example of a paired comparison is shown in figure 12.5.

In comparing each pair of employees, the rater merely selects the best employee. The number of times each employee is rated as superior is then counted and a ranking of employees can be obtained. For example, in figure 12.5 Delgado is the top employee, rated superior to everyone; Bates is rated as the second-best employee. This method of performance appraisal is relatively simple to administer but may be easily biased by the personal opinions of the evaluator. It is also subject to what is termed the recency effect, that is, recent positive or negative behavior by an employee may affect her ranking more strongly than behavior from some time past. Also, since comparisons are made on an overall basis, not on specific job skills or work functions, this method may be subject to legal challenge (Cascio & Bernardin, 1981).

Who Should Administer Performance Appraisals and How Frequently?

Appraisals are usually conducted by an employee's immediate superior, usually the individual most familiar with the employee's performance level and the one best able to assess her performance in terms of its contribution to the sport organization's objectives. In some sport organizations, peers may perform the appraisal because they are in a better position to observe their colleagues' behaviors and evaluate their output than the immediate superior. For example, in most universities the sport management faculty will be evaluated for rewards, such as promotion and tenure, by their colleagues in the professorate.

Subordinates can also provide useful input into the appraisal process and may sometimes be called upon to offer their opinion. They are often the people in the sport organization who know firsthand how well their supervisor is doing his job. Students in a university sport management program, for example, are often asked to give their opinion on a professor's teaching performance; in

Employee	2	3	4	5	6	7	8
1. Garcia	1	3	1	5	6	1	8
2. Jordan		3	4	5	6	7	8
3. Bates			3	3	6	3	3
4. Richards				5	6	4	4
5. McTeer					6	5	5
6. Delgado						6	6
7. Mintz							7
8. Schultz							

Instructions to appraiser: Compare each employee's overall contribution to our organization with every other employee. Write the number of the employee who you feel is making the greatest contribution in the appropriate box. Employees will be ranked according to the number of times they are selected as superior.

Figure 12.5 Paired comparison of the employees of a sport organization.

a similar vein, the players on an athletic team may be asked to help in the performance appraisal of their coach. There have also been arguments for and against the use of self-evaluation as a component of a performance appraisal (Meyer, 1980; Thornton, 1980).

Performance appraisals are traditionally performed once a year, and at most twice a year. Research tends to indicate that more frequent appraisals are a better means of assessing performance (Meyer, Kay, & French, 1965). Some sport organizations conduct appraisals upon completion of each project, not a suitable method, obviously, if work is not project-based. One way to obtain frequent appraisals but avoid some of the time and costs involved is to conduct more frequent but less formal evaluations throughout the year and a more thorough and intense appraisal every year or every six months.

Current Issues in Human Resource Management

While traditionally work in human resource management has focused on activities such as the recruitment, selection, and evaluation of employees, recent societal changes have brought other issues onto the human resource management agenda. Such concerns as employee stress, drug and alcohol abuse, equal opportunities, and sexual harassment take up a great deal of the sport manager's time. We look briefly at each of these issues.

Employee Stress

In recent years employee stress has become an increasingly important concern for many organizations (Ivancevich & Matteson, 1980; Quick & Quick, 1984). Stress occurs when an individual is subject to unusual pressures, demands, or expectations. While stress does have positive qualities it is more frequently associated with negative outcomes. Stress is created by "events in the environment [stressors] that require greater than usual adaptive responses from the body" (Cohen, 1978, p. 617). Stressors may include irate customers, colleagues who don't pull their weight, a constantly ringing phone, an unsympathetic spouse, work overload, and role ambiguity. Some employees are more vulnerable to stress than others.

Although totally eliminating stress is neither possible nor desirable, sport managers and the human resource staff must understand the causes and consequences of stress in order to eliminate its negative consequences. A number of things can be done in sport organizations to help prevent employee stress, including such structural interventions as job redesign, clarifying employee workloads, and the establishment of career counseling programs. However, if excess levels of stress are already being

---

TIME OUT

Causes of Stress in Physical Education Faculty Members

In a study on stress, Danylchuk (1993) identified environmental factors that contributed to the level of stress experienced by university physical education faculty. Ivancevich and Matteson's Stress Diagnostic Survey, a multidimensional self-report inventory designed to measure employee perceptions of stress, was completed by 254 full-time physical education faculty members of Canadian universities. The results show that quantitative overload (having too much to do in too little time), time pressures, and unfair rewards caused the greatest amount of stress for the faculty members. Qualitative overload (overly complex duties that exceed ability levels), role ambiguity, and role conflict caused the least amount of stress. Women perceived significantly more stress than men from gender discrimination, quantitative overload, and time pressures. Danylchuk concluded that the administrators of sport and physical education programs need to carefully assess the workload of their staff and also examine reward systems in their organizations to ensure that performance is the basis for rewards.

Based on information in Danylchuk, K.E., (1993). Occupational stressors in physical education faculties. *Journal of Sport Management, 7*, 7-24.

experienced by some employees, stress management courses, time management programs (cf. Schuler, 1979), and the provision of recreational opportunities (cf. Braus, 1989) can all be used to help lower stress levels.

Drug and Alcohol Abuse

One of the consequences of high stress in the workplace is that some individuals have turned to drugs as a means of helping them handle their job. An increasing number of sport organizations, particularly those involved with elite athletes, require some form of periodic drug testing. For example, in the 1988-1989 season the NCAA tested 3,700 athletes (Davenport, 1994), and in the same year in Canada the government agency Sport Canada had 1,163 of its international-level athletes tested (Dubin, 1990). Drug problems, however, are not limited to elite athletes. The high level of stress in many organizations has caused an increasing number of managers to turn to drugs (Flax, 1985). As a result some organizations have established programs to help human resources staff identify drug abuse, and some support employees through rehabilitation programs.

Alcohol is one of the most common workplace drugs. Estimates suggest it affects approximately 10 percent of managers (Flax, 1985). Research shows that employees who abuse alcohol are two to four times more likely to suffer workplace accidents than those who don't, and that alcoholic employees cost three times that of nonalcoholics in terms of sickness and accident benefits (Kadan, 1977). The managers and human resources staff of sport organizations must be educated about the problems of alcoholism and about the way it must be treated.

Equal Employment Opportunities

Over the past 20 to 25 years governments have passed a variety of legislative acts, such as the 1972 Equal Opportunity Act in the United States and the federal Human Rights Act in Canada, which make it illegal to deny someone employment because of sex, race, religion, country of origin, or physical disability. Despite this legislation, job discrimination is still widespread in sport. A study by Carpenter and Acosta (1990) into the employment of women in sport surveyed 180 NCAA member institutions. The results showed that 85 percent of respondents agreed that discrimination existed, 79 percent agreed that qualified women were not selected for positions, 93 percent agreed that the "old boys"

network was a negative factor in hiring practices, and 75 percent stated that stereotypes exist about women managers (Davis, 1994). In professional sport Lapchick (1986) found that when he looked at who held coaching and administrative positions in these organizations only 6.5 percent of positions in the NFL, 5.3 percent in the NBA, and 7.4 percent in major league baseball were held by minorities; these percentages were considerably lower than the percentage of minorities playing these sports at the professional level.

In hiring employees in any sport organization it is likely that some individual(s) will not be selected. This exclusion is legitimate, provided it is based on job-related criteria. To ensure that sport organizations do not discriminate in job hirings, managers and human resource staff must provide all potential candidates the same opportunity, by ensuring that all potentially interested candidates are aware of the availability of the job, that the selection process is based on criteria related to success in the job, and that, once employed, employees are not discriminated against. If these steps are carefully followed we will see the elimination of the discriminatory situations just described.

Sexual Harassment

While there is no universally accepted definition of sexual harassment, it may include "continual or repeated abuse of a sexual nature including but not limited to, graphic commentaries on the victim's body, sexually suggestive objects or pictures in the workplace, sexually degrading words used to describe the victim, or propositions of a sexual nature. Sexual harassment also includes the threat or insinuation that lack of sexual submission will adversely affect the victim's employment, wages, advancement, assigned duties or shifts, academic standing, or other conditions that affect the victim's 'livelihood'" (Cascio, 1986, p. 83). Sexual harassment is illegal and it has become a significant issue in many organizations, including a number of those in the sport industry.

While it is unlikely that such behavior will ever be totally eliminated from the workplace sport managers and human resource staff can take steps to reduce its incidence. These steps include establishing a policy on sexual harassment, developing a set of procedures to be followed when handling complaints about sexual harassment, ensuring these policies and procedures are based on the appropriate legislation, training employees to be aware of the nature and problems of sexual harassment, and

TIME OUT

Positive Human Resource Practices at Stride Rite

One of the positive consequences of equal employment opportunity legislation is that an increasing number of women have been able to enter the workforce. However, traditionally women have also had to assume primary responsibility for child care. This situation has sometimes presented difficulties for families where both the mother and father wished to work and raise a family. One company that has adopted a very progressive human resources policy to help deal with this problem is Stride Rite, the parent company of Keds, the athletic shoe manufacturer.

For many years Stride Rite has been recognized as one of the best employers in the United States. At its centers in Cambridge and Roxbury, Massachusetts, it provides child-care facilities for 110 children from ages 15 months to six years. The child-care facility has made a big difference, particularly for female employees; they can place their children in the center where they work and see them periodically throughout the day. As one parent pointed out in describing the center, "It has taken so much stress out of our lives, because I can bring him [her son] in to work with me and the hours match my schedule" (Morgan & Tucker, 1991, p. 187).

In addition to its child-care center, Stride Rite also has an "elder care" facility in its Cambridge center. The facility provides a place where employees can get care for older relatives for whom they have responsibility. Other progressive human resource practices at Stride Rite include paid leaves for childbirth and flexible work options. These types of practices have considerably enhanced Stride Rite's relationship with its employees and they certainly have not hurt business. Between 1985 and 1991 net sales more than doubled to $574 million.

Based on information in Morgan, H. & Tucker, K. (1991). *Companies that care*. New York: Simon and Schuster; and Stone, N. (1992). Building corporate character: An interview with Stride Rite chairman Arnold Hiatt. *Harvard Business Review, 70,* 95-104.

including discussions of sexual harassment at management and staff meetings and at company orientation sessions.

Summary and Conclusions

Human resource management has emerged in recent years as one of the key factors in organizational success. Despite the fact that this topic has received little attention in the sport management literature, human resource practices are important issues for the sport manager. In this chapter we began by describing what we mean when we talk about human resources (or personnel) management. We looked at the process of planning for human resources. Four steps—the situational audit, job analysis, projecting the supply of and demand for human resources, and matching supply and demand—were identified as being important in the planning process.

Once planning for human resources is completed the sport manager will need to recruit appropriate and qualified staff. The recruitment process and the different recruitment channels that can be used by a sport organization were identified. Once appropriate personnel have been recruited the selection process begins. We looked at the need for validity and reliability in this process and discussed the strengths and weaknesses of the various tools and techniques used in selecting staff for a sport organization.

Once staff are hired into a sport organization, they usually undergo some form of orientation. We briefly discussed the orientation process and identified possible topics to be covered in an orientation. We also discussed the training of existing staff. Given the rapidly changing nature of many sport organizations, training is becoming an increasingly important means of gaining and retaining a competitive advantage. The different training techniques used in a sport organization were briefly discussed.

In addition to planning, recruitment, selection, orientation, and training, conducting performance appraisals is also an important part of human resource management. Several methods of conducting performance appraisals were identified and the relative merits of each were discussed. In the final section of the chapter, four of the more current issues in human resource management—employee stress, drug and alcohol abuse, equal employment opportunities, and sexual harassment—were addressed.

The field of human resource management is an important one for sport management. The dearth of information on human resource practices in sport organizations is regrettable and must be addressed if these organizations are going to be operated as effectively and efficiently as possible.

Key Concepts

Human resources/personnel management
Job analysis
Supply of human resources
Organizational analysis
Job specifications
Recruitment channels
Application forms
Interviews
Orientation
On-the-job training
Case studies
Performance appraisals
BARS
Employee stress
Equal employment opportunity
Situational audit

Environmental analysis
Demand for human resources
Job description
Performance standards
Selection
Standardized tests
Reference checks
Training
Job rotation
Lectures
Role playing
Critical incidents
Rating scales
Paired comparisons
Drug and alcohol abuse
Sexual harassment

Review Questions

1. Describe what is involved in the process of human resources planning.

2. In what way has social legislation such as the Equal Employment Opportunity Act in the United States or the Canadian Human Rights Act influenced human resource practices in sport organizations?

3. Pick a sport organization you are familiar with and describe the different dimensions of its human resources management activities.

4. How will human resource management practices differ in small sport organizations as compared to large sport organizations?

5. If you conducted a situational audit of your university's athletic department, what factors would you find that influence its human resource management practices?

6. Discuss what should be in a job description for the position of manager of a fitness club.

7. If a sport organization has an excess number of employees for its current needs, what methods can be used to reduce the size of the existing work force? What are the pros and cons of the various methods that can be used to reduce staff?

8. How will the recruitment process vary depending on the type of position a sport organization is seeking to fill?

9. What are the advantages and disadvantages of college recruiting?

10. What do the terms "validity" and "reliability" mean when used to describe the techniques used to select job applicants?

11. What type of skills should human resources staff be trying to develop through company training programs? Explain your answer as it might relate to a professional basketball organization.

12. What are the strengths and weaknesses of rating scales and paired comparisons as means of evaluating employee performance?

13. What factors might cause employee stress for the employees of a sporting goods store?

14. Do you agree with Carpenter and Acosta's findings suggesting that the "old boys" network and stereotypical views of women managers are limiting factors in increasing the number of women in sport management?

15. If you were the manager of a sports arena and one of your staff reported that she had been sexually harassed by a fellow employee, how would you handle the situation?

Suggestions for Further Reading

Students interested in finding out more about the topic of human resources management should probably start off by looking at one of the many textbooks dealing specifically with this topic; Cascio's (1986) book *Managing human resources* is probably one of the better texts. Students should not rely solely on textbooks, however; many good articles relating to human resource practices can be found in journals such as the *Journal of Applied Psychology, Personnel Journal*, and *Personnel Psychology*. There are also several journals that deal specifically with human resource issues, including *Human Resources Management* and *HR Magazine*.

Within the sport management literature, little has specifically focused on human resource practices in sport organizations, but articles like Miller, Fielding, and Pitts' (1993) "Hiring concerns for the sport practitioner" have relevance for human resources management. In addition, as has been the case with several topics we have looked at in this book, some ideas of the human resource issues faced by sport organizations can be gained from articles about sport organizations found in popular press publications such as *Business Week* and *Fortune*.

Case for Analysis

Nike: Just Doing It in Indonesia

While Nike is an American company, much of its production takes place in Southeast Asia. Shoes are made in countries such as South Korea, China, and Indonesia. Nike's "offshore" manufacturing facilities have been a constant source of media criticism since 1991 when the *Economist* reported that " a pair of Nike sport shoes that sells for $150 in the United States is made by an Indonesian woman paid the equivalent of 58 cents a day." Nike's human resource practices in Southeast Asia were further highlighted on July 2, 1993 when CBS Television's program "Street Stories" ran a feature on a Nike shoe manufacturing factory in Indonesia.

The story opened with pictures of Nike's millionaire athletes Michael Jordan and Andre Agassi. It quickly moved to an Indonesian shoe factory in

which women, some as young as 14, worked 8 to 10 and sometimes12 hours a day making the shoes that Jordan and Agassi made millions endorsing. The reward these young girls received for their part in the production process, the story said, was 19 cents an hour or the equivalent of about $1.30 (US) per day, 55 cents below the poverty level in Indonesia. An American union activist, Jeff Ballinger, who had conducted a wage survey of Indonesian factories, told the Street Stories reporter that most of the factories making Nikes were paying some of their workers less than the legal minimum wage. Nike defended its wage policy by pointing out that Indonesian labor policy allowed a 90-day training period and during this time workers were paid less than the minimum wage. Dusty

Kidd, Nike's PR manager, suggested that the people in their factories had good jobs and "this is as good as it gets."

The Indonesian women who talked to the Street Stories reporter told her the money they were paid was not enough to live on. While they were provided with free barrack-type housing with running water, electricity, and toilets, certainly conditions better than those found in most Indonesian villages, it came at a price: The women were not allowed to leave the factory compound except on Sunday, and then only with a signed pass. A manager at the factory suggested that most of the workers employed by Nike were young women because they were easier to control than men.

In another factory in Indonesia 6,000 Nike workers had actually gone out on strike for a minimum wage of $1.30 per day. Management eventually gave in to their demands but 22 of the strike leaders were suspended. One young female worker told a reporter for the *Far Eastern Economic Review* that "they yell at us when we don't make our production quotas and if we talk back they cut our wages."

Nike defended its activities in Indonesia. Although he refused to be interviewed by CBS, Nike CEO Philip Knight did write to them saying that they did not understand the parental role of the Indonesian factory. PR man Dusty Kidd told the reporter, "This represents the best standard a worker can attain at this point in Indonesia." He pointed out that, as Nike didn't own the factories, they didn't set the wage levels. The minimum wage, it was suggested, was below the poverty level because if the government insisted on higher wages the shoe companies would leave Indonesia and go elsewhere.

However, the story did reveal that the Bata Shoe Company, which has a factory in Indonesia, paid its lowest workers the equivalent of $3.90 (US) per day. Also, as Jeff Ballinger pointed out, it would only take 1 percent of Nike's $180 million advertising budget to put 15,000 Indonesian workers over the poverty line.

Based on information contained in the CBS program Street Stories which was shown on July 2nd, 1993 and information in Katz, D. (1994). *Just do it: The Nike spirit in the corporate world.* New York: Random House.

Questions

1. Do you think Nike's human resource practices in Indonesia are appropriate?

2. When it operates in a country like Indonesia do you think the human resources practices of a company like Nike should be based on accepted standards in the United States or those of the host country?

3. What issues does this case raise about the topic of gender discrimination?

4. Apart from increasing wage levels, what other steps could Nike take to enhance the image of its human resource practices?

13

Decision Making in Sport Organizations

When You Have Read This Chapter

You should be able to

1. explain the concept of decision making,

2. discuss the conditions under which decisions are made,

3. understand the difference between the rational approach to decision making and the concept of bounded rationality, and

4. describe the major models of organizational decision making.

Deciding on New Products at Canstar Sports Inc.

Canstar Sports Inc. sells about 1.3 million pairs of skates a year, more than any other equipment manufacturer. Over 70 percent of NHL players wear their skates. As a result, at Canstar any decision to add a new product or modify an existing one is very carefully weighed. CEO Gerald Wasserman says Canstar knows how important decisions about products are, and "commits a great deal of time and money to examining new ideas." The decision making process about product additions or modifications usually begins in October of each year. Senior marketing personnel, sales staff, and designers get together for a day-long meeting to discuss new product ideas and possible improvements on existing products. Following the meeting, any ideas considered viable are sent to the designers, who conduct a cost analysis, decide how the product will be made, or determine how an existing product will be modified. They look at what manufacturing techniques they will have to use, what materials they will need for manufacturing, and how much design and production time will be required, all to determine if the product idea is worth pursuing. "Before we start we calculate the cost and the ultimate payback," says Blaine Hoshizaki, a former biomechanics professor at McGill University and now Canstar's vice president of research and development.

In February the design team gives its report to the senior executives involved with R & D, sales, marketing, and to the CEO, although Wasserman does not get involved in the process until financial decisions have to be made. The designers show the senior management team two or three options for each project. They outline how products will be made or modified and what they will cost. The senior executives look at the costs of manufacturing and compare them to potential sales. "We know at this stage if we can make money from a project," says Hoshizaki. "For instance, we know how many Bauer Supreme skates we sell each year. If a change in the design will cost 3 percent or 4 percent of the retail price, we determine if we can raise the price of the skate or if we have to take it from our margin as a cost of doing business."

If the senior managers give a positive response to the product, the designers go back to their drawing boards and develop plans for the different models, sizes, and variations of each product. By about July the product is ready for manufacturing to start in the fall. The new or modified product is put on display in February at the annual Canadian Sporting Goods Association show.

Based on information in McDougall, B. (1991, January). Driven by design. *Canadian Business*, pp. 48-53.

Not all decisions made in sport organizations are as long and involved as the product adoption process at Canstar. At any one time, however, the members of a sport organization may be involved in identifying solutions and implementing alternatives for dozens of different decisions. Mintzberg (1973a), in his book *The nature of managerial work*, found decision making to be one of the major tasks in which managers were involved; some people see decision making as the single most important process in an organization. The decisions made in a sport organization may range from deciding on the color and style of the company's letterhead to orchestrating a multimillion-dollar takeover bid. Some decisions prove to be successful, such as the one made by Peter Ueberroth when he decided to seek private support for the Los Angeles Olympic Games, or Petro Canada's decision to sponsor the 1988 Olympic Torch Relay. Others, such as Nike's decision to use its name to get into the casual shoe market, have been less than successful (Willigan, 1992).

In this chapter we look first at the term "decision making" and what it means. We then identify the conditions under which decisions are made. Next we examine the different approaches to decision making, focusing first on individual decision making and then examining models of organizational decision making.

Defining Decision Making

In his book *The effective executive* Peter Drucker (1966, p. 143) suggests that "a decision is a judgment . . . a choice between alternatives." Sport managers use their judgment to make decisions about whether to hire or fire employees, to add new programs, to sell off a division that is losing money, or to trade a player. Simon (1960) suggests that the decisions a manager makes can be categorized into two types: programmed and nonprogrammed.

Programmed Decisions

Programmed decisions are repetitive and routine. They are made on the basis of clearly defined policies and procedures and/or a manager's past experiences. The types of problems that can be solved using programmed decision making are usually well structured, have adequate information available, and present clear alternatives whose viability is relatively easy to assess. Examples of programmed decisions in a sport organization include the decision by the manager of a sporting goods store to exchange a purchase that is returned, the decision by a pool manager to increase the number of lifeguards on duty when the number of people in the pool rises, and the decision a university's sports information director makes about what to include in a media information kit. If faced with a choice managers prefer programmed to nonprogrammed decisions.

Nonprogrammed Decisions

Nonprogrammed decisions are new and unique. There are no established guidelines or procedures to direct the way this type of decision should be handled. Often the sport organization has never faced decisions before about this exact situation. There are no clear alternatives from which to select. Decisions such as those made by the board of governors of the NHL to grant franchises to new cities could be considered nonprogrammed; so, too, could the decision by Benoit de Chassey, director of information systems for the Albertville Olympics, to build a client/server information system using "Foundation for Cooperative Processing," an untested computer-aided software engineering

(CASE) tool to provide information to officials and media at the 1992 Games (Ricciuti, 1991).

Programmed decisions, because they are well structured, are generally made by the sport organization's lower-level managers and operators. Nonprogrammable decisions, because of their novel characteristics, are more likely to be handled by senior managers or highly trained professional staff. Whenever possible, sport managers attempt to program the decision making, because these choices can be handled by less qualified, cheaper staff.

Conditions Under Which Decisions Are Made

Because sport organizations and the environments in which they exist change constantly, sport managers can never be exactly sure of the consequences of any decision they make. It is generally accepted that decisions are made under three types of conditions, each based on the extent to which the outcome of a decision alternative is predictable. These three conditions are discussed below.

Certainty

A decision is made under a condition of certainty when the manager making the decision knows exactly what the available alternatives are, and the costs and benefits of each alternative. In other words, the manager understands completely the available alternatives and the outcomes of each, with 100 percent certainty. One example often used to illustrate decision making under certainty conditions is an investment in a bond or some other security with a guaranteed rate of return. For example, a voluntary sport group that finds itself with surplus cash on hand may choose to invest it in government bonds or treasury bills. The bonds may pay 6 percent but require a minimum investment time of five years; the treasury bills may only pay 4 percent but have a minimum investment time of one year. Here the decision maker knows the alternatives and the benefits of each. It is simply a matter of making the most appropriate choice.

Risk

Unfortunately, very few decisions in sport organizations are made under conditions of certainty. Under a condition of risk (a far more common condition for decision making in sport organizations), a decision maker has a basic understanding of the available alternatives, but the potential cost and benefits associated with each are uncertain. For example, a professional sport franchise owner wants to relocate her team. Three cities have offered their facilities, all fairly similar. One will charge a rental fee of $2 million per year, give the owner the rights to concessions and parking, and guarantee no change to this arrangement for the next 10 years. Another city wants only $1 million per year, will also grant the rights to concessions and parking, but will only give a 5-year guarantee. The third city will rent at a nominal $1 per year, will guarantee this rent for 5 years, but wants to retain all revenues from parking and concessions. In this situation the owner must assign probabilities to outcomes and work out the best decision, a process sometimes done objectively with available data, but often a subjective process based on past experiences.

Uncertainty

Under conditions of uncertainty the decision alternatives and their potential outcomes are both relatively unknown. Here there is no historical data or past experience on which to base a decision. These decisions are the most difficult to make, the kind that can "make or break" a manager's career. The manager of a sporting goods equipment manufacturing company entering the Eastern European market would face conditions of uncertainty; while this part of the world holds considerable potential for sporting goods, the political and economic situation is very uncertain.

Approaches to Understanding Decision Making

A large number of different models of the decision making process can be found in the management literature, some are more applicable to the decisions made by individual sport managers, others pertain more to organizational-level decisions. In this section we look at both individual and organizational decision making.

Individual Decision Making

The two basic models of individual decision making are discussed here. The first is the rational model; the second, the administrative model, is sometimes referred to as the bounded-rationality model.

TIME OUT

Phil Knight on Risky Decisions About Advertising

In a 1992 interview with a *Harvard Business Review* writer, Nike CEO Phil Knight explained one of the strategies his company uses to maintain its preeminent position in the athletic footwear industry is innovative advertising. However, Knight also pointed out that the decision to run innovative commercials was a risky one. He cited the Hare Jordan/Air Jordan commercial that was shown during the 1992 Super Bowl. The commercial, which cost millions of dollars to produce, featured Chicago Bulls star Michael Jordan on the basketball court with cartoon character Bugs Bunny. Knight felt there was considerable risk in showing a basketball superstar, Nike's key advertising resource, with a cartoon character. Knight was afraid people would think the commercial was silly. However, it was well received and *USA Today* rated it as the best Super Bowl commercial.

Knight also found out humorous commercials can be risky. Citing a 1987 campaign directed toward females, he noted that what he and his advertising team found funny, some women saw as insulting. As a result Nike received numerous complaints and spent more than three years meeting with women to find out their views on sport and fitness.

Based on information from Willigan, G.E. (1992, July-August). High performance marketing: An interview with Nike's Phil Knight. *Harvard Business Review, 70*, 91-101.

The Rational Model

The rational model of decision making is more a description of how decisions *should* be made than an account of how they actually *are* made. This approach focuses on a linear step-by-step analysis of the problem situation and the identification of solutions. Managers define problems and then systematically look for solutions to them; each alternative is carefully weighed as to its outcomes and the single best alternative is selected. The basic premise of this approach is that managers act in an economically rational way. In addition managers are assumed to have the relevant information about each of the decision alternatives, and to act in a nonpolitical, nonemotional manner. The rational model of decision making is usually depicted as a series of steps (see Archer, 1980; Blai, 1986). Figure 13.1 depicts these steps and each is explained below.

Monitor the decision environment: In the first stage of the decision making process a manager scans the sport organization's internal and external environment to determine deviations from expected norms. The technique includes such activities as analyzing financial statements and/or sales figures, observing competitors, or talking to employees. For example, a manager of a retail sporting goods store who wants to remain competitive must monitor other stores, check what items are popular, keep up with new product availability, and so forth.

Define the problem about which a decision has to be made: If a manager detects a deviation from the expected norms, then a problem exists: a discrepancy between the existing state of affairs and the desired

state. In our example of the sporting goods retail store, the manager may define her problem as "low profits."

Diagnose the problem: Here the manager must get at the root cause of the problem so that appropriate action can be developed. In this stage it may be necessary to gather additional data. The sporting goods store may survey a number of competitors, for example, and determine that they seem to be doing a better trade because they offer a wider range of products.

Identify decision alternatives: Here all the possible solutions to the problem are identified. The manager may sometimes seek the advice of others at this stage of the decision process. For the sporting goods store manager, one decision alternative may be to increase the amount of stock she carries; another may be to focus on a narrower area; another may be to cut margins on existing stock to make it more saleable.

Analyze alternatives: When the possible alternatives have been identified the manager has to analyze each one critically, based on statistical data or on personal preference and past experiences. The merits of each alternative and its possible outcomes are assessed; for example, our sporting goods store manager will have to consider the costs of increasing her available stock and the probability that this decision will increase trade. This alternative has to be weighed against a choice such as focusing on a narrower market niche, which could be strongly influenced by fluctuations in this particular market.

Select the best alternative(s): Here the manager picks the best alternative from all of the possibilities not

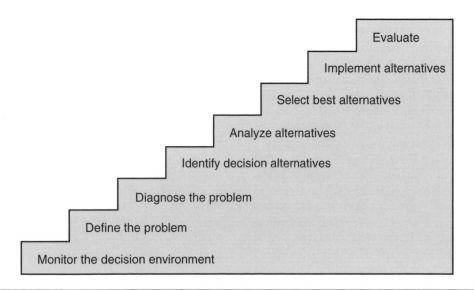

Figure 13.1   Steps in the decision making process.

eliminated in the analysis phase. Sometimes it is impossible to select just one solution. At other times two or three possible "best alternatives" may emerge from the analysis and more data will need to be collected before a choice can be made. In some sport organizations it may even be possible to implement more than one of the alternatives, to see which performs the best.

Implement the alternative: The chosen alternative must then be implemented. Sometimes this may be easy to do; in other cases the manager will have to use her administrative skills, coercion, authority, and so forth, to get the decision implemented. The implementation process may be long and involved. In our example, if the manager chooses to increase stock she may need to secure a line of credit with a bank, contact suppliers, refurbish displays, and advertise her new products. All of these can present barriers to the actual implementation of a decision.

Evaluate the decision: The final step in the rational decision making process, a step that some sport managers often neglect, is to evaluate the outcome of the decision to see if the original problem has been rectified. In our sporting goods store example, the manager will have to monitor sales and cashflow to see if increasing stock is actually helping raise profits. Managers sometimes neglect this step because they don't like to find out they made a wrong decision.

The Administrative Model (Bounded Rationality)

Despite the inherent logic of the systematic approach outlined in the rational model, managers are rarely this thorough or precise in their decision making. The limitations of the rational model were first identified by Nobel laureate Herbert Simon in his (1945) book *Administrative behavior*. Simon drew a distinction between economic reality and what happens in everyday life. Rather than being a completely rational process, he suggested, organizational decisions were *bounded*, by the emotions of the managers involved, by their limited cognitive ability to process information, and by factors such as time constraints and imperfect information. Hence, managers operate with what is referred to as bounded rationality: In any decision situation a manager has only a limited perception; he cannot possibly understand all of the available alternatives, and even if he did the limits of the human mind would not allow all of that information to be processed. In addition, any attempt at rationality is constrained by the manager's emotions and experience.

As a result of these limitations, Simon argued, decision makers construct simplified models of complex decision processes. The models contain only that information which the manager feels she is best able to handle; consequently, only a limited number of decision alternatives and outcomes are considered. This means that managers satisfice rather than strive for the optimum solution to a decision. When this solution is found the search for other potentially better solutions stops; not all decision alternatives are considered.

An example of satisficing that is often used and can be applied to our field concerns a student who has recently graduated from a sport management program and is looking for a job. To make a rational decision this person would have to look at all the available jobs everywhere. This is obviously impossible; as a result he takes the first acceptable position, rather than continuing to look for one that pays more or may lead to better career opportunities.

Table 13.1 summarizes and compares the basic premises of the rational and administrative models.

Organizational Decision Making

While individual managers may make decisions using both the rational and administrative models, most decisions in organizations are made by groups. The information, resources, and authority needed to make most of the decisions in complex organizations are rarely the domain of a single individual. Some decisions will not only require the participation of different managers but sometimes representatives of different divisions, perhaps even different organizations. Studies of organizational decision making have identified five major approaches: the management science approach, the Carnegie model, the structuring of unstructured processes approach, the garbage can model, and the Bradford studies.

Management Science

The management science approach to decision making, which involves the use of complex mathematics and statistics to develop a solution to a problem (Markland, 1983), was developed during World War II to solve military problems (Leavitt, Dill, & Eyring, 1973). If, for example, allied planes wanted to fire on enemy warships, they had to make decisions based on information about trajectories, the distance between the plane and its target, the speed at which the plane was traveling, wind speed, the

Table 13.1   A Comparison of the Rational and Administrative Models of Decision Making

RATIONAL MODEL	ADMINISTRATIVE MODEL
The decision maker is a rational person who knows and understands all decision alternatives and their outcomes. This individual is unaffected by time constraints, emotions, etc.	The decision makers are limited by their mental capacity to evaluate all alternatives and their outcomes, and must respond to time constraints, emotions, etc.
All criteria affecting a decision are considered and evaluated according to the sport organization's goals.	A limited number of criteria are identified and these form a simple model to evaluate the problem being faced.
All possible decision alternatives are considered.	A limited number of decision alternatives which reflect the decision maker's personal preference are identified.
After careful analysis of all alternatives, the most economically viable alternative is selected.	Alternatives are considered until one that is suitable is found.

altitude of the plane, and so forth. Each of these variables was modeled using mathematical equations to provide details of the best conditions under which to attack.

After the war the principles of management science were applied to industry, where they have been further improved. Military people such as Robert McNamara, who would later become the U.S. Secretary of Defense, joined companies like Ford and began using management science techniques to improve the quality of decision making. Today a number of companies use these techniques; their popularity and utility being enhanced by the advent of computers.

Linear programming, queuing theory, Monte Carlo techniques, and decision trees are all examples of management science techniques that can be used to make decisions about a problem. The management science approach is best where data relevant to the decision are easily identified and quantifiable, and where problems are structured and logical. The shortcoming of management science is that it does not consider the more qualitative aspects of decision making, such as the political climate or ethical issues.

A considerable number of management science studies have looked at decisions in sport organizations (Andreu & Corominas, 1989; Farina, Kochenberger, & Obremski, 1989). Topics include such diverse issues as scheduling major league baseball games, determining batting orders, deciding whether or not to go for the two-point conversion, assigning swimming order in a relay race, simulating road race finishes, and deciding when to pull the goalie in hockey.

The Carnegie Model

Richard Cyert and James March were both associated with what is now Carnegie-Mellon University and their approach to decision making is often referred to as the Carnegie model. Their ideas are best illustrated in their 1963 book *A behavioral theory of the firm*. Cyert and March's approach to decision making, which in some ways extends Simon's ideas of bounded rationality (Simon was also at Carnegie-Mellon), challenges the notion that an organization makes decisions rationally as a single entity. Rather, what Cyert and March show is that organizations are made up of a number of subunits, each with diverse interests. Decision making has to allow for this diversity.

Organizational-level decisions are made by coalitions of managers, who do not all have the time or cognitive ability to deal with all aspects of a problem. Consequently, decisions are split into subproblems. For example, in a sport equipment manufacturing company the R & D department deals with design problems, the production department handles manufacturing, and so forth. This process of splitting problems leads to coalition building, where managers try to find out other managers' points of view and enlist their support for a particular decision. There is a continuous process of bargaining among the various groups in the organization, each trying to influence the decision outcome. As a result, Cyert and March suggest, managers spend more time on "managing coalitions" than they do on managing the problems confronting the organization itself.

TIME OUT

Using a Computer Simulation Model to Make Decisions About Golf Course Queuing Problems

In order to maximize profits, golf course managers have to make decisions to ensure that their playing facility is used to capacity. The ability of the golfers who play the course, the speed at which they play, the need to use the course for play while still performing maintenance, the dawn-to-dusk playing hours, and the seasonal nature of the game are all factors that influence these decisions. Frequently, golfers experience queues (times when players have to wait for the party ahead of them) at certain points on the course. These delays in continuous play are a problem for golf course managers because they limit capacity: They increase the number of players on the course at any one time (and hence the number of expensive electric golf carts the club must buy), they decrease the number of players who can play the course in any day, they frustrate players so they may not return to the course, and (some studies show) golfers unhappy about queuing are less likely to use clubhouse food and beverage services. All of these factors affect profits.

In order to make decisions about start-time intervals that can reduce queuing and maximize capacity, Haywood-Farmer, Sharman, and Weinbrecht (1988) suggest the use of a simple simulation model using the Lotus 1-2-3 microcomputer spreadsheet program. Essentially, in this model each hole was broken down into segments, one for par-3s, two for par-4s, and three for par-5s. Using a standard time of nine minutes between tee-off intervals, and calculating variables that measured the different times that players were involved in waiting for, starting, and finishing each segment, Haywood-Farmer and his colleagues constructed a model of the way a group moves around the course. The model was able to predict cumulative waits on certain tees. By adjusting the time between tee-offs the model could be used to estimate how queues at various points could be affected and the influence the queues would have on capacity. With this knowledge the manager of the golf course could then make a decision about the appropriate interval between start times.

Based on information contained in Haywood-Farmer, J., Sharman, T., & Weinbrecht, M.S. (1988). Using simple simulation models to manage sports services. *Journal of Sport Management, 2,* 118-128.

Managers need to resolve the internal conflicts that result from coalition building. While they may agree with each other on organizational goals, there is often little consensus on how to achieve these goals. Decisions are therefore broken down into subproblems and allocated to subunits. But the danger is that these subunits address and solve these problems based on their own rationality and their own interests, not on what is best for the organization as a whole. Also, managers become concerned with short-term solutions rather than long-term strategies. They may involve themselves in what are called problemistic searches: When a problem occurs managers quickly search around for a way to handle or resolve it; as soon as *one* is found, the search stops. Managers tend to rely more on past experiences and procedures when problems are somewhat familiar than when they are unfamiliar, because relying on the past requires less time spent on politics and bargaining.

Cyert and March's work tells us that decision makers need to build coalitions because decision making is a political process. One of the great coalition builders in sport was Horst Dassler, the late head of Adidas. Dassler employed key figures in the world of sport on every continent, who kept him in touch with what was happening in sport in their respective areas. In this way Dassler was able to make decisions that worked in the best interest of his company.

We see the principles of the Carnegie model in action if we look at the way in which the decision is made about the host city for the Olympic Games. Ostensibly the IOC has as its goal to award the bid to the city that will stage the best Games. However, what happens in actuality is that various individuals within the IOC form coalitions. Committee members visit the bid sites to evaluate facilities, financing, security, and so forth Each individual forms his or her preference as to what would be the best site. Coalitions are formed based on what the individuals have seen or on geopolitical lines, and these groups engage in lobbying in an effort to try to make sure the committee makes the decision most favorable to them. King (1991), for example, describes how Canadian IOC member Dick Pound traveled to a number of places with the Calgary Games organizers to lobby other IOC delegates to support the Calgary bid.

The Structuring of Unstructured Processes

In their research on decision making Mintzberg, Raisinghani, and Théorêt (1976) focus on decisions made at the senior levels of an organization. They argue that much of the management science approach to decision making has focused on routine operating decisions, but it is really at the top levels where an organization must make better decisions. In contrast to the concern with political factors evident in Cyert and March's (1963) work, Mintzberg et al. (1976) focus on identifying a structure to describe the unstructured process of strategic decision making. Data were obtained on 25 decision processes that were tracked from the initial identification of a problem to the acceptance of a decision solution. Over two thirds of the decision processes took longer than a year to complete; the majority of the decisions were nonprogrammed, that is, unique.

Essentially, Mintzberg et al. (1976) suggest that major decisions in an organization are broken down into smaller decisions that collectively contribute to the major decision. Their research identified three major phases to the decision process. Each phase contained different "routines," seven in total. The decision process is also characterized by what are called interrupts, events that result in a change in the pace or direction of the decision process. Interrupts cause delays because they force an organization to go back and modify its solution, find another one, or engage in political activity to remove an obstacle. Each of these three phases, the routines they contain, and the notion of interrupts are explained more fully in the section that follows.

The first phase in the decision process is the identification phase. There are two routines involved in this phase. The decision recognition routine occurs when a manager recognizes a problem about which a decision must be made. A decision is required when there is "a difference between information on some actual situation and some expected standard" (Mintzberg et al., 1976, p. 253). Stimuli that signal the beginning of the need for a decision may originate both within and outside the organization. After the decision recognition routine comes the diagnosis routine; here issues around the problem are clarified and defined. Diagnosis can be explicit and formal or informal and implicit. The more crisis-like the problem to be addressed, the less likely there is to be formal diagnosis.

Following the identification phase is the development phase. Mintzberg et al. (1976, p. 255) describe this phase as "the heart of the decision making process . . . the set of activities that leads to one or more solutions to a problem. . . ." There are two routines within this phase. First, in the search routine, managers look for solutions to the problem situation. Initial searches are carried out by considering past experiences. If these searches fail, a more active search is carried out, involving looking in "more remote and less familiar areas."

If this search procedure is not successful, a custom-made solution is developed in the design routine. Mintzberg et al. (1976, p. 256) point out that this "is a complex, iterative procedure; . . . designers grope along building their solution brick by brick without really knowing what it will look like until it is completed."

The final phase of the decision process is the selection phase. Here, a choice is made about a solution. The first routine in the selection phase is the screening routine, used when there are too many ready-made alternatives and a custom design is not required. During screening, certain alternatives are rejected so that a usable number can be handled. The second routine is the evaluation-choice routine. Evaluation and choice can be determined either by judgment, bargaining, or analysis: "In judgment, one individual makes a choice in his own mind with procedures that he does not, perhaps cannot explain; in bargaining, selection is made by a group of decision makers with conflicting goal systems, each exercising judgment; and in analysis . . . factual evaluation is carried out, generally by technocrats, followed by managerial choice by judgment or by bargaining" (Mintzberg et al., 1976, p. 258).

The authorization routine is the final routine in the decision making process. Authorization occurs when the person or group making the decision does not have the necessary power to commit the organization to the particular solution. Consequently, the decision is passed up the hierarchy; in some cases it may even have to receive the support of external bodies who could block the decision solution. Sometimes decisions are rejected when passed up to higher levels.

Figure 13.2 shows the stages of Mintzberg et al.'s (1976) decision process and the various routines. The figure also shows the most common interrupts. At the identification phase there may be internal interrupts or political interrupts because organizational members can't agree about the need for a strategic decision. New option interrupts occur late in the development phase or in the evaluation-choice routine, and may result in going back to the design routine, to changes in the new option, or simply to evaluation and choice, where the new option is accepted or rejected. External interrupts occur in the final phase and involve attempts by external agents to block the solution. The zigzag lines in the figure signal the possible delays from scheduling, timing, and feedback that occur at each stage of the decision process.

Although there have been no analyses using the approach outlined by Mintzberg et al. (1976) of the major decisions made in sport organizations, it is quite applicable to situations in our field. Decisions such as Canstar's move into the Canadian in-line skate market, the NBA's decision to hold annual tournaments against foreign teams and broadcast games in Europe, and the Canadian Football League's decision to establish franchises in the United States, could all be analyzed using the "structuring of unstructured processes" approach.

The Garbage Can Model

Much of the work on decision making assumes that the various activities making up the process can be ordered into some logical sequence. Cohen, March, and Olsen (1972) suggest that in reality the situation is much more confusing (see also Cohen & March, 1974; March & Olsen, 1976); in the decision process of an organization many different things are going on at one time. "Technologies are changing and poorly understood; alliances, preferences, and perceptions are changing; problems, solutions, opportunities, ideas, people, and outcomes are mixed together in a way that makes their interpretation uncertain and their connections unclear" (March, 1982, p. 36). Cohen, March, and Olsen refer to this situation as organized anarchy. It is found in organizations that are highly organic in their structure and are required to change rapidly. Decision making in these organizations is an outcome of four independent streams of events.

- *A stream of problems*. Problems result from dissatisfaction with current performance. Examples include not winning enough games, declining sales, low graduation rates, or a lack of adequately trained staff.

- *A stream of choice opportunities*. This refers to the occasions when a decision is usually made in an organization. Included could be when someone is hired or fired, a budget is finalized, a new service is added, or a team is selected.

- *A stream of participants*. These are the people who make choices in an organization. They come and go as a result of hirings, firings, transfers, retirements, and so forth. Participants come from different backgrounds and have different ideas about problems and solutions.

- *A stream of solutions*. Many participants have ideas to which they are deeply committed; as a result they may try to sell their ideas to the other members of the organization. In some organizations, people such as planners and systems analysts are actually hired to come up with solutions for situations where problems do not exist. Solutions can then exist without problems being present.

The existence of these four streams means that the process of decision making is somewhat random. The organization is described as a garbage can into which problems, choices, participants, and solutions are all placed. Managers have to act with the resultant disorder; as a result decisions are rarely systematic and logical. Choices are made when problems come together with the right participants and solutions. As a consequence, some problems are never solved, solutions are put forward even when a problem has yet to be identified, and choices are made before problems are understood.

The strength of the garbage can model is that it draws our attention to the role that chance and timing play in the decision making process. Also, unlike other approaches, which tend to focus on single decisions, the garbage can approach is concerned with multiple decisions.

Bradford Studies

The Bradford studies, so named because they were conducted by Professor David Hickson and his research team at the University of Bradford in England, were carried out over approximately 15 years from the early 1970s to the mid-1980s (see Butler, Astley, Hickson, Mallory, & Wilson, 1979/1980;

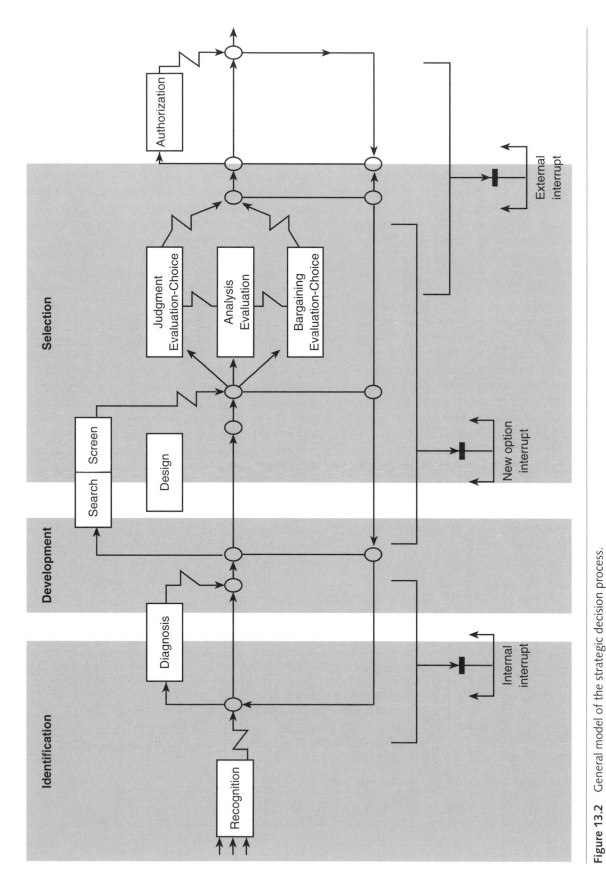

Figure 13.2 General model of the strategic decision process.
Reprinted from "The structure of 'unstructured' decision processes" by H. Mintzberg, D. Raisinghani, and A. Théorêt published in *Administrative Science Quarterly* vol. 21, no. 2 by permission of *Administrative Science Quarterly*.

Cray, Mallory, Butler, Hickson, & Wilson, 1988, 1991; Hickson, Butler, Cray, Mallory, & Wilson, 1985, 1986; Mallory, Butler, Cray, Hickson, & Wilson, 1983; Wilson, Butler, Cray, Hickson, & Mallory, 1986). Using data from 150 decisions, Hickson et al. (1985) focus on the process of decision making as opposed to the outcome and implementation of a decision. His research team identified five dimensions of process, encompassing 12 variables.

The first of these dimensions, scrutiny, concerns the information sources available to the decision maker(s). Four variables were identified as making up this particular dimension. Expertise, the first variable, was assessed by the number of internal and external sources from which information about the decision was obtained. Disparity refers to the extent to which the decision makers had confidence in the different sources from which information was obtained. Externality was "measured as the ratio of the confidence in external information to that placed in all information" (Cray et al., 1988). Effort refers to the way in which the information was acquired—was it merely the result of recalling personal experiences or did it involve the use of working groups or other similar mechanisms to generate and analyze information?

The second dimension, interaction, was comprised of three variables. Informal interaction was a measure of the extent to which the decision to be made was discussed informally, such as in hallways or over coffee. Formal interaction concerns the extent to which the decision process was structured through meetings, work groups, and so forth. Scope of negotiation, the final variable, assessed the extent to which the decision was made by one individual or was subject to negotiation before a choice was made.

The third dimension, flow, relates to the delays, reconsiderations, and disruptions found in the decision process. Two variables made up this dimension. Disruptions, the first variable, concerned the length and occurrence of disruptions that took place in the decision process. Impedance concerned the extent to which the cause of delays could be controlled.

The fourth dimension, duration, was made up of two variables. Gestation time was the length of the period from the initial mention of the decision issue until specific action was taken toward making a decision. Process time was the time from the start of the specific action to when the decision was authorized. Finally, the last dimension, authority, was a single measure of the level in the organization at which the decision was authorized.

Compiling data on each of these variables, Hickson and his colleagues analyzed 136 of the decisions they studied, using cluster analysis. There were incomplete data on 14 of the decisions, so they could not be used in the cluster program. Three distinct ways of making decisions were identified: sporadic processes, fluid processes, and constricted processes. The characteristics of these decisions are shown in figure 13.3 and explained in more detail in the following discussion.

Sporadic decision processes are made in a manner characterized by disruption and delay. Short periods of activity are followed by delays, during which information is gathered and the various constituents in the process argue over the relative merits of what has been uncovered. The scope of negotiation

Sporadic process	**Fluid process**	**Constricted process**
Higher level of disruption impedance expertise confidence disparity informal interaction process time	Higher level of formal interaction	Higher level of expertise
	Lower level of disruption impedance expertise confidence disparity process time	Lower level of authorization negotiation scope informal interaction effort
Some negotiation scope		
Higher level of authorization	Some negotiation scope	
	High level of authorization	

Figure 13.3 Characteristics of three types of strategic decision making.
Based on information in Cray, D., Mallory, G.R., Butler, R.J., Hickson, D.J., & Wilson, D.C. (1988). Sporadic, fluid, and constricted processes: Three types of strategic decision making in organizations. *Journal of Management Studies*, 25, p. 29.

is fairly wide, indicating the number of individuals and groups involved in the process but, because much of the negotiation takes place in informal settings, decision making takes longer than average. There is some tendency for the decision process to require authorization by the most senior level of the organization. In short, the actual process of decision making is fairly wide-ranging and uneven, but ultimately the decision must be approved through the organization's highest level.

In contrast to sporadic decisions, fluid decision processes have fewer and less serious interruptions; fewer experts are involved and the whole process is quicker. The information base used to make the decision is more homogeneous and much of the interaction during the actual making of the decision takes place in a formal setting. The search for a decision, while encompassing considerable scope for negotiation, is narrowed quickly and ultimately approved at the highest level of the organization.

Constricted decision processes are made with the use of expert information but there is little effort to seek data not readily obtainable. Most of the interaction around this type of decision process is informal, because the relatively few people involved are in frequent contact. There is little scope for negotiation here; decisions emanate from the lower levels of senior management and will probably be ratified by the CEO (unlike sporadic and fluid decisions, which usually require board approval). Much of this process is focused on a single decision maker, in most cases the organization's CEO.

As with Mintzberg et al. (1976), no work within the sport management literature has attempted to use the Bradford approach to understand the decision making process in sport organizations. However, the considerable number of published works emanating from this research project is one measure of its acceptance in the general field of management. The dimensions and variables identified by Hickson et al. are quite applicable to a variety of sport organizations. Replications and extensions of this work using sport organizations could not only enhance our understanding of the decision making process in the organizations in our field, but also extend existing theory on this topic and thus contribute to management studies in general.

Summary and Conclusions

All sport managers make decisions, and an understanding of how the decision process works can increase the effectiveness and efficiency of these decisions. In this chapter we began by explaining the concept of decision making, distinguishing between programmed and nonprogrammed decisions. We noted that managers prefer programmed decisions because they are more predictable and, because of their predictability, are most frequently found at the lower levels of a sport organization. Nonprogrammed decisions are found at the higher levels. We looked at the three conditions under which decisions can be made: certainty, risk, and uncertainty. Most decisions in sport organizations are made under conditions of risk and uncertainty.

In the biggest section of this chapter we looked at the major theoretical approaches to understanding decision making. We focused on individual decision making—the rational approach and the more realistic notion of bounded rationality—and compared and contrasted the two approaches. We then examined organizational decision making. Five major approaches to organizational decision making were identified: the management science approach, the Carnegie model, the structuring of unstructured processes, the garbage can approach, and the Bradford studies. We noted that no work in the sport management literature had made use of any of these approaches. Examples were provided of the type of sport organizations' decisions that these theoretical models could be used to understand. By understanding the decision process and hence the factors that influence decision making, sport managers can make better decisions and become better managers.

Key Concepts

Programmed decisions	Nonprogrammed decisions
Certainty	Risk
Uncertainty	Rational decision making
Bounded rationality	Management science

Coalitions	Problemistic search
Routines	Interrupts
Garbage can model	Organized anarchy
Sporadic decisions	Fluid decisions
Constricted decisions	

Review Questions

1. What type of programmed decisions would you expect to find being made in a university athletic department?

2. In what type of sport organization would you expect to find a large number of non-programmed decisions?

3. Think of a sport organization with which you are familiar; under what type of conditions are most of the decisions made in this organization?

4. In what way do athletic directors try to eliminate the risk involved in hiring a new basketball coach?

5. What criticism would you make about the rational approach to decision making?

6. What techniques would you use to evaluate the effectiveness of the decisions made in a sport organization?

7. What factors did Simon see as limiting the ability of managers to make rational decisions?

8. How do sport managers satisfice when they make decisions? Give examples.

9. What are the strengths and weaknesses of the management science approach to decision making?

10. How would you use the Carnegie approach to explain the decision making that takes place about an athletic department's budget?

11. What similarities can you see in Simon's idea of bounded rationality and Cyert and March's Carnegie model?

12. Select a major decision that you have seen made in a sport organization and analyze it using Mintzberg, Raisinghani, and Théorêt's approach.

13. "Managers don't make large decisions; they only make small ones." Do you agree or disagree with this statement?

14. Explain the four streams of events proposed in the garbage can model. How do they occur independently?

15. Using the variables employed in the Bradford studies, how would you describe Canstar's decision process (outlined at the start of this chapter) regarding product additions and modifications?

Suggestions for Further Reading

As we have noted at several places in this chapter, little research in the sport management literature has looked at the process of decision making in sport organizations. While some accounts of the problems confronted by decision makers can be found in the popular press, they contain little in the way of any scholarly analysis. Students looking for more information on this topic are advised to consult the general organizational literature. For work on bounded rationality, begin with Simon's (1945) text *Administrative behavior*. While this is quite an old book it does form the basis for much of the future work conducted on this concept. Examples of work that build on Simon's ideas can be found in all of the major organizational journals. For example, see Simon's (1987) article "Making management decisions: The role of intuition and emotion" in *Academy of Management Executive*; Lyles' (1987) article "Defining strategic problems: Subjective criteria of executives" in *Organization Studies*; and Jackson and Dutton's (1988) "Discerning threats and opportunities" in *Administrative Science Quarterly*.

For those students interested in the management science approach to decision making, we recommend the journal *Interfaces*, which sometimes contains research on sport organizations. In terms of the Carnegie model, students are advised (as with work on bounded rationality) to read the original research and then see the major management journals for extensions of this approach. Stevenson, Pearce, and Porter's (1985) "The concept of 'coalition' in organization theory and research," in the *Academy of Management Review*, is one example of how Cyert and March's original ideas can be extended. In terms of the unstructured processes approach, the garbage can model, and the Bradford approach, students are likewise advised to read the references cited in the chapter and look through the management/organizational journals for extensions of this work. All of these approaches have good potential for being applied to sport organizations.

Case for Analysis

The Decision to Close Swimming Pools in Saskatoon

In February 1994 Saskatoon City Council made a decision that Mayfair pool in Caswell Hill, an inner-city community, should be closed. The pool was in poor repair and in need of upgrading. The decision for closure was made by a task force of six city councilors who examined 199 city-supported programs. The decision was financially motivated; it was estimated that closing Mayfair and one other pool would save the city council about $185,000. The decision "leaves the community no option when it comes to summer recreation," said Joyce Doran, president of the Caswell Hill Community Association. A trip to the nearest other pool would mean a long bus ride, and children would have to cross two dangerous busy streets. Mayfair pool was described by people who wanted it kept open as a family-oriented pool where people can have a picnic. This wasn't the case in the indoor and competitive pools that the city operated. "The community is set to fight," said Doran. Just after the decision to close the pool was announced, a petition was circulated and 1,500 signatures obtained. People were also encouraged to write to the city council and express their views.

At a city council meeting held shortly after the decision to close the pool, a nine-year-old Caswell Hill resident presented the councilors at the meeting with a bag of money. "I know you are thinking of closing the pool because you ran out of money. . . . I have collected some money to keep the pool open," he said. "No one in Caswell Hill has a backyard pool, few have cottages, and the other city pools are too far for the children to get there on their bikes," he told the council.

Two weeks after the council meeting, residents of Caswell Hill participated in a rally in front of City Hall as a reminder to council that its decision to close the pool had not been forgotten. Bill Rafoss, one of the rally organizers, said he felt the city council was picking on lower middle-class residents. "We have indoor leisure facilities in the suburban areas. They are not in jeopardy," he was quoted as saying. Another demonstrator said the mayor and the four councilors who supported the decision didn't understand the social cost of their actions. Councilor Bev Dyck, who voted to keep the pool open, said she felt that the vitality and character of the neighborhood would be eroded by the loss of the pool; she planned to introduce a motion to reverse the decision.

Several people argued that the older neighborhoods in the city were being made to suffer unduly, leading to decay in these areas. A suggestion to have volunteers operate the pool was rejected because it could cause a problem with the unions. Councilor Glen Penner also took exception to the inequity of volunteers taking over facilities in a poorer area while the city continued to operate those in richer ones.

At a special budget meeting on March 5, a decision was made to keep the Mayfair open and increase admission fees at some of the other city pools. The budget committee suggested that Mayfair should be provided as a basic service where people could swim for free. Council accepted their recommendations, with the exception of free swimming at Mayfair; some members of council expressed concerns that the policy would just attract children from all over the city.

Based on information in articles in the *Saskatoon Star Phoenix* on February 15, 16, 28, and March 1, 7, 1994.

Questions

1. Describe the conditions under which the Saskatoon City Council made the decision to close Mayfair pool.

2. How would you use Cyert and March's work (the Carnegie model) to understand the decision process outlined in this case?

3. Do you think the city council acted rationally in the decision to close Mayfair pool?

4. Using Mintzberg, Raisinghani, and Théorêt's approach to understanding decision making, identify the different "routines" and "interrupts" that apply to this situation.

Recreational Equipment Inc., *indoor climbing structure at REI's factory store near Seattle, WA*

14

Managing the Culture of a Sport Organization

When You Have Read This Chapter

You should be able to

1. explain what we mean by the term "organizational culture,"

2. describe the manifestations of a sport organization's culture,

3. explain the difference between a thick and a thin culture,

4. explain why some sport organizations can have more than one culture,

5. describe the relationship of culture to organizational effectiveness, and

6. discuss how a sport organization's culture is created, managed, and changed.

Organizational Culture at Recreational Equipment, Inc.

Recreational Equipment, Inc. (REI) is a Seattle-based consumer cooperative that retails equipment and clothing for a wide range of outdoor sports. As the nation's largest consumer cooperative, REI returns a large portion of its profits to its members in the form of a patronage dividend. That is, the amount of dividend returned to a member is based on the member's total purchases. REI prides itself on being a caring employer committed to leadership in environmental giving and community citizenship. A tour of the company's headquarters in Kent, Washington, and a look at the type of company activities REI is involved in, confirm this commitment. The company's cafeteria is stocked with healthy food that can be purchased for breakfast, lunch, or snacks. Located a half hour's drive out of Seattle, the scenic company grounds, while not fully developed, provide the setting for lunchtime hikes and bike rides.

When asked to identify his aspirations for the company, president Wally Smith placed "being a good employer" at the top of his list. He proudly shows the 1985 bestseller *The 100 best companies to work for in America*, in which REI is listed. Smith also emphasizes that at REI employees are provided with encouragement, time, and sometimes money, to pursue their interest in outdoor sports. Many of the company's middle and senior employees have been with REI for many years, some of them starting as part-timers in high school. Executive vice president Dennis Madsen, typical of the type of employee REI likes to hire, is an avid skier, backpacker, and cyclist and at one time was a committed climber. He is heavily involved in REI Adventure's trips to the former Soviet Union. Smith is passionately committed to saving trails and rivers. During his presidency, REI has committed more than $1 million to various environmental groups such as the National Trails Coalition, the REI Wilderness Campaign, and the REI River Campaign. Funding for these projects is determined by the company's environmental committee.

In addition, REI will help support individual organizations as well as education, social, and arts programs committed to the environment. The emphasis on the environment is also carried on at local stores, which raise money for conservation projects. Staff at these stores are responsible for maintaining ties with local groups involved in conservation. They also organize "service" projects on an annual or semiannual basis. An example of one project in which the San Diego store was involved was a cleanup of the Tijuana estuary. REI contributed $8,000 and the San Diego store organized volunteers to help build trails.

Based on information in The corporate culture. (1989, August). *Outside Business*, pp. 33, 70-71.

The description of REI and the activities the company and its employees are involved in tell us about the culture of the organization. Culture, as we will see, is concerned with characteristics such as the type of values and beliefs found in an organization and the accepted modes of operation. At REI the important values about protecting the environment have become a central part of the organization's culture. Helping with national and local environmental projects is an accepted part of the mode of operation of the company. Everybody at REI is expected to work to this end. Staff are hired because they believe in and will work to promote this ideal. The culture of the company is reflected and reinforced by the fact that employees are encouraged to pursue outdoor activities. The company even provides trails for outdoor activities at its company headquarters.

In the final chapters of the book we explore two of the topics seen as crucial in bringing an organization together as an integrated whole: organizational culture and leadership. First we examine the concept of organizational culture. To begin we look at what we mean when we talk about the culture of an organization. We then look at how culture manifests itself in sport organizations. We discuss the idea of thick and thin cultures, examine whether or not a sport organization has just one culture, and explore the relationship of culture to effectiveness in sport organizations. Finally, we look at how cultures are created, managed, and changed in sport organizations.

What Is Organizational Culture?

Organizational culture is one of the most recent introductions into the field of organization theory. In part, the concern with culture has grown out of the success of Japanese industry, which began in the 1970s. Increasingly, organizational theorists began to see that Japanese organizations operated in a different way from most North American and Western European organizations. While obviously Japanese culture was different from the culture of countries in these geographic areas, it was not so much the cultural context in which Japanese organizations existed that caught and held the attention of organization theorists, but something that has been termed their "corporate culture." Japanese organizations operated using different values and beliefs, different norms of interaction, and a different set of understandings from their counterparts in North America and Western Europe.

The increased interest in organizational (or what is sometimes referred to as corporate) culture led several organizational theorists to attempt to define what the concept actually means. While no definition can do complete justice to the meaning of any term, looking at some of the more common definitions can give us a good understanding of what these people are talking about when they refer to organizational culture.

Pettigrew (1979, p. 572), for example, describes organizational culture as an "amalgam of beliefs, ideology, language, ritual, and myth." Schein (1985, p. 9) sees it as "a pattern of basic assumptions—invented, discovered, or developed by a given group as it learns to cope with its problems of external adaptation and internal integration—that has worked well enough to be considered valid and therefore, to be taught to new members as the correct way to perceive, think, and feel in relation to those problems." For Sathe (1983, p. 6) culture is "the set of important understandings (often unstated) that members of a community share in common." For Wilkins (1983a, p. 25) it is "most usefully thought of as the taken-for-granted and shared meanings that people assign to their social surroundings."

There are some general themes within these different definitions, including a concern with the

values, beliefs, basic assumptions, shared understandings, and taken-for-granted meanings on which a set of individuals base the construction of their organization, group, or subgroup. These characteristics, commonly accepted as forming the basis for an organization's culture, provide stability to an organization and convey to new members the understanding that enables them to make sense of organizational activities.

The increased popularity of the concept of culture among managers and organizational theorists, Robey (1986, pp. 426-427) insightfully suggested, can be attributed to two main qualities found in this approach: "First, for many macro organization theorists, culture provides a way to bring *people* back into their analyses without using psychological models of human behavior. . . . Second, culture is widely accepted by managers, because the concept describes organizational realities that are hard to define but very relevant to running an organization" (emphasis in original).

These are important points to consider as we think about organizational culture. While they are relevant to all types of organizations they are particularly important to the study of sport organizations. Work in sport management had traditionally employed sociopsychological approaches to explain the qualities and actions of sport managers. A focus on organizational culture provides a different approach to understanding patterns of action in sport organizations. This approach, if combined with traditional macro organizational theory, could provide for richer insights into the organizations we study. An approach that focuses on organizational culture should also have considerable appeal to those of us interested in sport, because the organizations in our field are rife with such characteristics as stories, myths, symbols, and rituals. These characteristics are some of the principle manifestations of an organization's culture, as we will see in the next section of this chapter. A focus on these characteristics would help shed new light on the way sport organizations operate.

Manifestations of a Sport Organization's Culture

Because an organization's culture is based on values, beliefs, accepted patterns of meaning, and so on, and because these features are hard to pin down, researchers who study culture have tended to focus on the way it manifests itself in organizations. To fully focus they often find it necessary to immerse themselves in the organizations they are studying. Consequently, studies of organizational culture have tended to be qualitative in nature—it is difficult to develop an understanding of an organization's culture using questionnaire-based studies. Trice and Beyer (1984) suggest a number of cultural manifestations that researchers can observe (see table 14.1). In this section of the chapter we look at some of the most important of these manifestations.

Stories and Myths

Stories are narratives recounted among employees and told to new employees. Myths are stories, often about the origins and transformations of a company, that are not supported by fact (Trice & Beyer, 1984). Both stories and myths convey a number of important messages about a sport organization. First, they present a sense of its history. As Pettigrew (1979, p. 576) notes about myths, they "anchor the present in the past, offer explanations and, therefore legitimacy for social practices, and contain levels of meaning that deal simultaneously with the socially and psychologically significant in any culture." Stories and myths, because they help establish the organization as an enduring entity, can reduce uncertainty for employees (cf. Martin, Feldman, Hatch, & Sitkin, 1983). If the stories are about hard times, as they sometimes are, the employees sense the ability of the organization to overcome problems. Stories also help transmit messages about organizational goals and the way employees should act. They are, as Wilkins (1983b, p. 82) notes, "important indicators of the values participants share, the social prescriptions concerning how things are done, and the consequences of compliance or deviance. The stories may also indicate the social categories and statuses which are legitimate in the organization and thus are important guides for what kinds of people can do what." Wilkins goes on to suggest

that this information is important for the successful participation of people in the organization.

At Nike, for example, a story is told about the company's early days when, during a particularly heated meeting in which sales reps were criticizing corporate officials for their supply mechanisms, a rep from Minnesota stood up and said to his colleagues, "Listen, these guys are at least 51 percent right so far in everything they're doing. And that's enough. You only have to be right 51 percent of the time." As Strasser and Becklund (1991) point out, long after the person making the comment was forgotten, this story became a part of Nike's culture; it was seen as an indication of what reps should and shouldn't do. The idea was "don't be afraid to make mistakes. If you take a fall, it's because you're learning and that's better than playing it safe; the name of the game is not to be right all the time . . . the name of the game is to win; there's a difference" (Strasser & Becklund, 1991, p. 195).

Symbols

Symbols are used to convey meaning about a sport organization to its members and to the public at large. The symbol of the falcon, for example, was chosen for the Atlanta-based NFL team because "the falcon is proud and dignified with great courage and fight; it never drops its prey; it is deadly and has a great sporting tradition" (Falcons, 1989, p. 13). Nike's "swoosh" conveys speed; it is also no coincidence that Nike is the Greek goddess of victory. Other examples of symbols that serve to convey meaning about sport organizations can be found in corporate documents like organizational charts. The ski resort Nakiska has inverted its organizational chart so that the employees in direct contact with customers are at the top of the chart and the General Manager, President, and Board of Directors are at the bottom. The organization thus conveys to its first-level staff their importance to the company's

---

TIME OUT

John Wooden and the Pyramid of Success

John Wooden is one of the most successful basketball coaches ever. While at UCLA his teams won numerous conference and NCAA titles. Wooden built his program around his Pyramid of Success (see figure 14.1). The pyramid outlines those values and beliefs that Wooden saw as important to a successful team. Although he never used the term, the values and beliefs outlined in the pyramid were the basis for the organizational culture of the UCLA basketball teams.

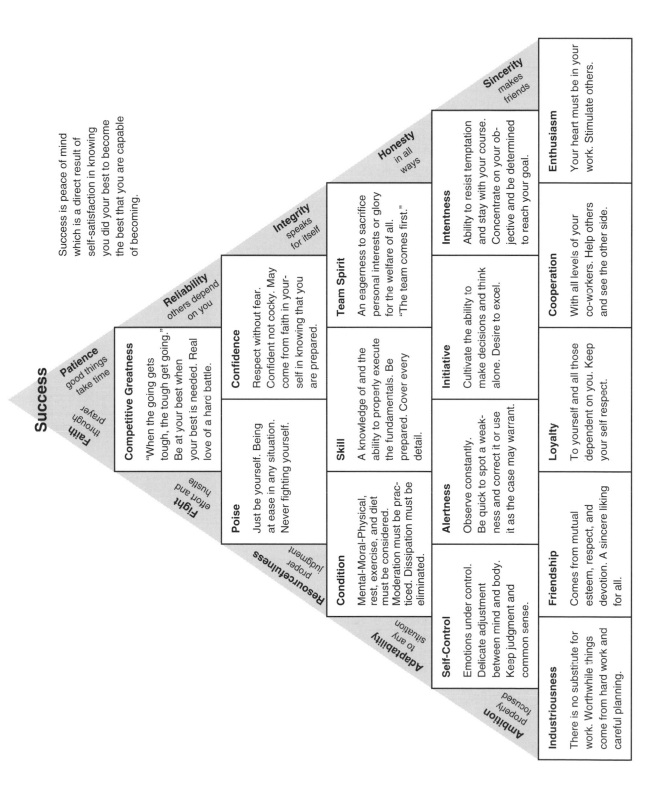

Figure 14.1 Pyramid of Success.
From Wooden, J., *They call me coach*, New York: Bantam Books, 1973.

Table 14.1   Manifestations of Organizational Culture

Rite	Relatively elaborate, dramatic, planned sets of activities that consolidate various forms of cultural expressions into one event, which is carried out through social interactions, usually for the benefit of an audience.
Ceremony	A system of several rites connected with a single occasion or event.
Ritual	A standardized, detailed set of techniques and behaviors that manage anxieties, but seldom produce intended, technical consequences of practical importance.
Myth	A dramatic narrative of imagined events, usually used to explain origins or transformations of something; also, an unquestioned belief about the practical benefits of certain techniques and behaviors that is not supported by demonstrated facts.
Saga	An historical narrative describing the unique accomplishments of a group and its leaders—usually in heroic terms.
Legend	A handed-down narrative of some wonderful event that is based in history but has been embellished with fictional details.
Story	A narrative based on true events—often a combination of truth and fiction.
Folktale	A completely fictional narrative.
Symbol	Any object, act, event, quality, or relation that serves as a vehicle for conveying meaning, usually by representing another thing.
Language	A particular form or manner in which members of a group use vocal sounds and written signs to convey meanings to each other.
Gesture	Movements of parts of the body used to express meanings.
Physical setting	Those things that surround people physically and provide them with immediate sensory stimuli as they carry out culturally expressive activities.
Artifact	Material objects manufactured by people to facilitate culturally expressive activities.

Reprinted, by permission, from H.M. Trice and J.M. Beyer, 1984, "Studying organizational cultures through rites and ceremonies," *Academy of Management Review*: 655.

success. Symbolism can also be found in something as seemingly mundane as letterhead. The Broadmoor Golf Resort uses gold-embossed letterhead, a symbolic representation of the type of luxury it provides.

Closely allied to the use of symbols is the use of slogans. Well-known clichés such as "When the going gets tough, the tough get going" and "No pain, no gain" are frequently used by athletic coaches to convey expectations about appropriate modes of behavior in their organizations. In a somewhat similar vein, Nike's "There is no finish line" and "Just do it" slogans have taken on particular significance for the company; they convey meaning about success in sport *and* about success in the Nike organization.

It has also become somewhat fashionable for company owners or chief executive officers to develop sayings or sets of sayings that convey the organization's culture to employees. Joe Montgomery at Cannondale has an 11-point corporate philosophy that contains such items as "We care about each other, our customers, and our vendors" and "We commit ourselves to quality in all we do" ("A

Freewheeler," 1989, p. 36). At W.L. Gore, Bill Gore was frequently heard to ask employees "Have you had fun today? Did you make any money?" (Blank, 1986, p. 23).

Language

Different sport organizations develop their own specialized language or jargon to communicate with each other. Through language, members "acquire the structured 'ways' of [the] group, and along with the language, the value implications of those ways" (Pettigrew, 1979, p. 575). Basketball coaches and players talk about their 2-1-2 full court press, working the ball into the paint, or screening away from the ball. While to most people these terms mean little, to the coaches and players on the team they are part of everyday communication, and as such represent one aspect of the team's culture. They serve to strengthen the team as an organization by providing commonality, and to separate the team from others who do not communicate in this way. They highlight boundaries as to who is and who isn't part of the organization (Wilkins, 1983b).

Ceremonies or Rites

All sport organizations, in fact all organizations, develop certain types of behavior that we usually refer to as ceremonies or rites. Rookie initiations, team award nights, pregame meals, an annual Christmas party, and a pep rally are all examples of the types of ceremonies we find in sport organizations. In each, certain shared values within the organization are reinforced. These events also provide evidence of what the organization values; they are symbolic representations of the type of beliefs and activities important in the organization. Trice and Beyer (1984) identify different types of rites. A rite of passage marks a change in the role and status of the person or persons involved. For example, rookie night ceremonies are designed to initiate new members and make them part of the team. A rite of degradation dissolves the social identity and associated power of the person involved by pointing out problems with his or her work performance. The firing of coaches and general managers, a common occurrence in professional sport organizations, is a rite of degradation.

Physical Setting

The physical setting in which a sport organization operates can convey meaning about the nature of its culture. Davis (1984) suggests three important parts of the physical setting useful in understanding an organization's culture: the physical structure, physical stimuli, and symbolic artifacts.

Physical Structure

According to Davis (1984, p. 272), physical structure can be defined as "the architect's design and physical placement of furnishings in a building that influence or regulate social interaction." Several aspects of the physical structure in which a sport organization operates can be used as indicators of the culture of the organization. Open offices as opposed to closed door offices, round tables instead of rectangular ones in meeting rooms, and simply the physical location of a facility can all convey messages about a sport organization. For example, in April 1985 shortly after Doug Mitchell took over as commissioner of the Canadian Football League,

---

TIME OUT

A Huffy Rep Cycles to Glory

Soft light filters down from multicolored windows as the crowd far below eagerly awaits the awards ceremony. Then a hush falls as a spotlight sweeps across the ornate old movie palace and comes to rest on a distinguished executive in a tuxedo on stage. Nearby, the trophy gleams as the speaker lists the accomplishments of the person to be honored, gradually building the suspense.

Finally, he mentions the winner's name and amid thunderous applause, the winner rises from his seat and walks toward the stage grinning. The spotlight follows him as the crowd, now standing, continues the ovation, their faces displaying a mixture of admiration, envy, and joy. It is almost like the Academy Awards. Every detail is painstakingly arranged to create and build the excitement for Steve Magers, Huffy Bicycle's Sales Representative of the Year.

The Sales Representative of the Year award is presented at Huffy's annual sales meeting in August. In attendance are the 70 salespeople from the five independent rep firms that represent the company nationwide, plus Huffy's staff and top management. The purpose of the award is to set the rep of the year up as an example to new reps. "We are in essence saying this is the person we think, particularly this year, put all the pieces together and ran their business as Huffy would like it to be run," said Steve Goubeaux, Huffy Bicycle's national sales manager and administrator of the recognition program. "Young people in the organization model themselves after what appears to be a winning style, and that is what we are trying to set up."

Reprinted, by permission, from H. Waldrop, 1986, "A Huffy rep cycles to glory," *Sales and Marketing Management*, June 1986, 116-122.

he moved the league's headquarters from cramped surroundings in downtown Toronto to plush offices in the center of the city's trendy Bloor Street shopping district, an "indication he want[ed] to upgrade the league's crusty image" (Barr, 1985, p. 1). In a similar vein, the chief executive officer of the Canadian Sport and Fitness Administration Centre, Wilf Wedmann, moved his offices from the top floor of the Centre to the ground floor, because being at the top of the building gave the wrong impression about the role of the Centre's administration.

Physical Stimuli

Physical stimuli include such activities as coffee breaks and mail delivery. These events can become rituals. They often determine who talks to whom and when. They establish patterns of interaction in a sport organization and, as such, how information is channelled.

Symbolic Artifacts

Symbolic artifacts are aspects of a sport organization that individually or collectively provide clues about its culture. Banners in hockey or basketball arenas, trophies and pictures of past teams and successful individual players, and the like are artifacts that convey a message about the team as a successful organization. The bats that were used by famous players, now found at Hillerich and Bradsby's "Slugger Park," convey messages about the company's long association with major league baseball.

Thick and Thin Cultures

The strength of a sport organization's culture will vary from one company to another. Peters and Waterman (1982, p. 75) suggest that in the organizations they studied "the dominance and coherence of culture proved to be an essential quality of the excellent companies." Schein (1984), however, points out that equally as important as the strength of a company's culture is its content, the values it reflects. Most sport organizations strive to develop strong, or what are usually referred to as thick, cultures. A thick culture is one where the members of the sport organization agree about the importance of certain values and employ them in their daily routines. A thick culture helps hold an organization together, by making frequent use of stories, rituals, slogans, and so on. Also, employees will be recruited into the organization because they are seen to fit with the culture that exists. This "fit" is further developed through the use of indoctrination ceremonies, training programs, and orientations in which new employees are expected to be involved.

Joe Montgomery built a thick culture at Cannondale with his 11-point corporate philosophy as a base. But Cannondale's culture, like any thick culture, is more than just words on paper—the words

---

TIME OUT

Designing a Corporate Identity

The design of a corporate building has a unique ability to reflect the values and culture of an organization. "I think [design] is extremely important," says Art Gensler, president of Gensler and Associates Architects, an international architectural and interior design firm. "There's no right or wrong [design]; it should reflect the company's style." "Some companies will put more of a premium on the exterior expression, and that has a lot to do with the personality of the particular corporation," adds Carol Nott, an architect with Boston-based Tsoi/Kobus and Associates. Nike Inc. serves as an excellent example of a company that successfully revealed its corporate culture through corporate design. Set on 74 sprawling acres amid the pine groves of Beaverton, Oregon, the Nike World Campus exudes the energy, youth, and vitality that have become synonymous with Nike's products. The campus is almost a monument to Nike's corporate values: the production of quality goods and, of course, fitness. Included in the seven-building campus is an athletic club with a track, weight rooms, aerobic studios, tennis, racquetball and squash courts, and a basketball court.

Based on information in Capowski, G.S. (1993, June). Designing a corporate identity. *Management Review*, pp. 37-40.

Sport as a Component of Organizational Culture

While our focus in this chapter is on the way sport organizations build culture, there are some organizations where sport forms an integral part of the corporate culture. At Microsoft Corporation "its an intense play-hard, work-hard atmosphere, " says Jon Staenberg, a marketing manager. "A lot of business is done in the fields." Employees with common interests form groups and send out information and schedules of athletic events over electronic mail. Microsoft people participate in car rallies, sailing, rock-climbing, flag football, and paragliding.

Corporate fitness centers at such companies as PepsiCo and Reebok International can be great places for all levels of employees to meet on common ground. Robert Teufel, president of Rodale Press, sweats with employees in a morning circuit class (combining aerobic exercise and weightlifting) three days a week at the company's headquarters in Emmaus, Pennsylvania. "Those people who choose to participate get a chance to communicate with him directly," says Budd Coates, director of Rodale's gym called the Energy Center.

Based on information in Bongiorno, L., & Hof, R.D. (1993, July 12). Swinging and sweating with the boss. *Business Week*, p. 126.

are put into practice. The company practices its credo about caring for employees by promoting from within. Liz Miller joined the company as a stitcher in 1977; by 1989 she was the plant manager. Ted Kutrumbos started at Cannondale loading trucks; he rose through the ranks, and became company president. Cannondale also demonstrates its concern for employees by sharing profits with them. Flexibility in working conditions is encouraged by having no formal job descriptions and moving people to jobs they enjoy ("A Freewheeler," 1989).

In a thin culture we don't see common values or the type of activities that Cannondale uses to build its culture. While thin cultures can be found in all types of sport organizations, one example could be a university faculty that encompasses both a department of sport studies and an athletic department. The dominant values among the staff involved in the athletic program will be ones concerned with producing the best teams, recruiting "blue chip" players, and catering to alumni. The sport studies staff will be more concerned with publishing and generating research grants. While these values are not mutually exclusive, their very presence can serve to produce a thin culture. A thin culture will also be found in sport organizations where the membership is constantly changing or has only been a part of the organization for a short period of time (cf. Schein, 1984).

Scholz (1987) has produced a simple set of questions to help determine how strong (thick) or how weak (thin) an organization's culture is (see table 14.2). If the answers to the questions are mainly toward the "no" end of the continuum the organization's culture can be considered thin. More "yes" answers indicate a thick culture.

One or More Cultures

Implicit in our discussion so far has been the idea that sport organizations have one single culture. This notion is implied in many of the definitions of organizational culture when they talk about shared understandings and common values. It is, however, somewhat idealistic to suggest that all members of a sport organization will think alike. The reality, that different people in different parts of the organization actually have different values and employ different norms of behavior, does not deny the possibility of "an organizational culture"; rather, it highlights the fact that sport organizations actually have a *dominant* culture, which reflects the core values of the *majority* of people in the organization (or at worst those with the most power), and a series of *subcultures*. Gregory (1983), for example, argues that organizations should be seen as multicultural. Meyerson and Martin (1987, p. 630) extend this line of thought to suggest that, because "organizations reflect broader societal cultures and contain elements of occupational, hierarchical, class, racial,

Table 14.2   Assessing the Strength of Corporate Culture

	NO				YES
1. Existence of specific slogans?	O	O	O	O	O
2. Existence of some dominating stories in the company?	O	O	O	O	O
3. Existence of well-known heroes in or at least for the company?	O	O	O	O	O
4. Existence of symbolic actions or symbols?	O	O	O	O	O
5. Overlapping social rituals and social norms?	O	O	O	O	O
6. Existence of a specific language in the firm?	O	O	O	O	O
7. Does the company have a history which is considered long?	O	O	O	O	O
8. Does membership last for many years?	O	O	O	O	O
9. Lack of acceptable cultural alternatives for members of the company?	O	O	O	O	O

Reprinted from *Long Range Planning*, volume 20, C. Scholz, Corporate culture and strategy: The problem of strategic fit, page 82, Copyright 1987, with kind permission from Elsevier Science Ltd, The Boulevard, Langford Lane, Kidlington OX5 1GB, UK.

TIME OUT

Club Corporation of America: Building a Thick Culture

Club Corporation of America (CCA) is the leading North American company in the golf and country-club business. One of the keys to CCA's success has been its commitment to building a culture that emphasizes servicing its members. CCA has developed a slogan to install a service mentality among staff members: It's an acronym for PRIDE—Personal Recognition Is Desirable Every Day. The same slogan applies to the special attention and treatment the CCA affords its staff.

CCA's hiring philosophy emphasizes attitude more than aptitude. The formal screening process includes a battery of psychological tests. "We want people who really feel that it is noble to turn someone else on, " says Bob Dedman, chairman of the board of CCA. Every employee is continually involved in some aspect of the company's extensive training program, the Educational Series for Club Operations, or ESCO. New employees recruited from hospitality programs or other segments of the industry are taught (or "brainwashed" as Dedman puts it) the CCA way, and seasoned employees attend seminars regularly to broaden and update their skills. In addition, the company has several hundred people in their management training program. CCA likes to promote from within and its management classes are filled with a mix of MBAs and maître d's. Typically, trainees spend a year or two as assistant managers in a club near the corporate headquarters before an appropriate manager's job opens up.

The success of the training program is measured continuously. In addition to frequent tests on such subjects as etiquette, wine regions, and labor law, the clubs are scrutinized closely by the regional office. Each club uses a standardized bookkeeping system and club managers get a call from regional managers if the numbers show any significant deviation from the established norms. There is also a formal—and often unannounced— inspection of every club at least once a year.

In keeping with CCA's priorities, however, the ultimate evaluators are the members. CCA has a set of quality standards but it is up to each club manager to go beyond those standards, depending on the needs of that club's membership. The company hires independent research firms to do annual in-depth surveys of every club's membership and staff, and to compare the results to a substantial data base.

Adapted, by permission, from D. Tobin, March 1989, "Selling by serving," *Club Industry*.

ethnic, and gender-based identifications [they] . . . create overlapping, nested subcultures." Slack and Hining's (1992) work on change in Canadian national sport organizations showed how a culture built around values for volunteer control and governance clashed with a new developing culture based on more professionally and bureaucratically oriented values. Subcultures may also develop in different departments of a sport organization. For example, the research-and-development department of a company producing sports equipment will most likely exhibit a somewhat different culture from the sales department. While sport managers should strive to develop unified values in the organizations they manage, it is also important for them to realize that such a goal is unlikely to be fully achieved. In actuality, as Meyerson and Martin (1987, p. 631) point out, organizations are composed of a "diverse set of subcultures that share some integrating elements of a dominant culture." It is this diversity and these common elements of culture that have to be managed.

Organizational Culture and Effectiveness

Many of the popular writers on organizational culture have stressed the links between a strong (thick) culture and an effective organization (cf. Deal & Kennedy, 1982; Peters & Waterman, 1982). Arogyaswamy and Byles (1987, p. 648) suggest, however, that it is erroneous to infer from these popular works "that there is one best culture, which if established in firms would lead to success." Rather, they suggest that certain types of cultural characteristics are appropriate in certain types of organizations. To understand culture and its relationship to performance in sport organizations, it is necessary to look at the various contingencies that influence the organization. To be effective there must be a fit between such variables as strategy, environment, technology, and culture.

Porter (1980), for example, emphasized that to be successful an organization that adopts a cost-leadership strategy (see chapter 5) will be required to develop a culture that emphasizes financial efficiency and close attention to reducing costs. When Jack Reichart of Brunswick sold off company jets and closed the executive dining room, he acknowledged that the dining room closing didn't save the company much money but it symbolized the efforts to implement a cost-cutting strategy and, as such, strengthened this aspect of Brunswick's culture (cf.

"Brunswick's dramatic turnaround," 1988). In a somewhat similar vein, a company like W.L. Gore, which follows what Miles and Snow (1978) refer to as a prospector strategy, requires a culture that emphasizes creativity, high levels of horizontal communication, and some degree of risk taking.

Sport organizations that operate in stable environments should seek to develop thick cultures. However, if its environment is rapidly changing, a thick culture may actually be detrimental to the performance of a sport organization. Thick cultures by their very nature are hard to change, but dynamic environments demand that if organizations are to be successful they must change as their environment changes.

The use of different technologies also requires a different culture. In a company like Victoriaville or Sherwood-Drolet, which mass-produce hockey sticks, we would expect to find a culture where little emphasis is placed on individual initiative but where control and conformity to hierarchical communications are emphasized. In contrast, in a company like Heery, which designs custom sport facilities, we would expect to find a culture that supports creativity, group work, and a high level of horizontal communication.

The central point here is that while culture is an important variable in determining the effectiveness of an organization, it is not (as many popular writers have implied) the only variable. A sport organization's culture must fit with contingency variables such as strategy, environment, and technology.

Creating, Managing, and Changing a Sport Organization's Culture

A sport organization's culture doesn't just happen; it is created and developed over a period of time. Some sport managers will work hard to maintain an existing culture if they feel it is benefiting their organization. Others will want to change their organization's culture. Here, we look at the tasks of creating, maintaining, and changing a sport organization's culture, important issues for the people who manage these organizations.

Creating a Culture Within a Sport Organization

While there are several differing opinions about how culture is created within an organization (cf.

Louis, 1985; Scholz, 1987), most researchers agree that the founders of an organization have a fairly significant impact on establishing its culture. There is also general agreement that the original ideas of the founder will continue to influence the organization for a long time, sometimes even after the founder is no longer with the organization (cf. Schein, 1983). Strasser and Becklund's (1991) book shows, for example, how the informal operating codes and freewheeling atmosphere created by Philip Knight and the University of Oregon track colleagues who joined him in Nike's early years continued to influence the organization, well after it was established as a major company in the athletic footwear industry. Peters and Waterman (1982) describe two important ways of developing culture for those who lead organizations. The first method, they suggest, operates at a high level of abstraction and involves the setting of a vision. The founder or leader of a sport organization must generate excitement and enthusiasm about the fundamental values and purpose of the organization. For Philip Knight the purpose of Nike was clear: to produce good quality shoes at a reasonable price for U.S. athletes and to push Adidas into the number two spot in the industry. For Sheri Poe, head of Ryka Inc., a small but rapidly growing athletic footwear company, her vision is to produce aerobic shoes designed especially for women and to work on behalf of women.

The second of Peters and Waterman's (1982, p. 287) suggestions is that founders/leaders can help develop culture by their attention to detail. They are to directly instill "values through deeds rather than words: No opportunity is too small." We saw earlier how Jack Reichart cut the executive dining room at Brunswick, saving very little money for the company but yielding considerable benefit in terms of building a culture of cost effectiveness. Sheri Poe has attempted to instill as part of Ryka's culture a belief that the organization should work on behalf of women. To this end, Poe has done more than just establish this belief as a part of the company's mission; she enforces it by putting 7 percent of her company's profits into a fund called Ryka ROSE (Regaining One's Self-Esteem Foundation), employing a predominantly female workforce (70 percent), and speaking out on women's issues (Stodghill, 1993).

Managing a Sport Organization's Culture

Once a sport organization's culture has developed, it has to be managed. Assuming the culture is one that the company wishes to maintain, the manager of a sport organization can do a number of things to sustain and reinforce the organization's culture.

Schein (1985, pp. 224-225) suggests five primary mechanisms:

1. What leaders pay attention to, measure, and control
2. Leader reaction to critical incidents and organizational crises
3. Deliberate role modeling, teaching, and coaching by leaders
4. Criteria for allocation of rewards and status
5. Criteria for recruitment, selection, promotion, retirement, and excommunication

We look briefly at these mechanisms now. It should be noted that Schein uses the term "leaders" instead of "managers." While there is some debate about whether or not the terms can be used synonymously in this book, we follow Yukl's (1989) suggestion that the two are interchangeable. For consistency the term "managers" is used in the subheadings.

What Managers Pay Attention to, Measure, and Control

Managers can reinforce the important aspects of a sport organization's culture by paying particular attention to these areas. As Schein (1985, p. 225) notes, paying attention may mean "anything from what is noticed and commented on, to what is measured, controlled, rewarded, and in other ways systematically dealt with." A basketball coach, for example, who wishes to develop a team that places a high value on defensive skills will try to build a culture that supports this approach. One way is to highlight good defensive plays, to keep statistics on such things as steals, forced turnovers, and defensive rebounds, and to ensure that players with good defensive skills are rewarded with playing time.

At L.L. Bean, the outdoor equipment supplier, great stress is placed on building a culture that emphasizes customer service, a culture reinforced when Bean's own employees are treated well by their managers. Van Fleet (1991, p. 352) points out this practice:

Employees are paid reasonable wages, are treated with dignity, and have ample opportunity for advancement. They are also given considerable freedom in how they do their job—as long as they do it well. Employees know that they can always put the needs and opinions of customers first, without fear of reprisal or rebuke from a supervisor who worries too much about the cost of something.

This attention to employee feelings and the dignity they are afforded by supervisors communicate to them what the company believes in and how in turn they should treat customers.

Manager's Reaction to Critical Incidents and Organizational Crises

If a sport organization faces a crisis or critical incident, the way the senior managers deal with the crisis can help reinforce an organization's culture. Schein (1985, p. 230) suggests that crises aid the transmission of culture because "the heightened emotional involvement during such periods increases the intensity of learning [and] if people share intense emotional experiences . . . they are more likely to remember what they have learned." Such learning may occur, for example, in an athletic department that has built a culture based on values of fair play and an ethical approach to running an intercollegiate program. If the athletic director dismisses a coach for violating some minor recruiting regulations, it may create a crisis situation for the organization, but it provides a signal to remaining coaches that this type of behavior is inappropriate to this organization and thus serves to reinforce the culture with which they operate. Likewise, if a sports equipment manufacturer faces declining sales, the way this crisis is dealt with may strengthen its culture. For instance, if the company had previously tried to develop a culture stressing the importance of each and every employee to the organization and all staff, including senior managers, take a salary cut, instead of just laying off production staff, the fairness of the gesture serves to heighten this cultural dimension. Often after these crises we hear managers say things like "we are all better for what happened" or "we are stronger because of it." The implication is that organizational learning has taken place and certain values that underpin the sport organization's culture have been reinforced.

Deliberate Role Modeling, Teaching, and Coaching

Managers can stress the type of culture they are seeking to build in a sport organization through their own actions and by directly teaching and coaching staff. Bill Gore, who has been referred to several times in this book, is an excellent example of someone who used this approach to build the culture of his company. Gore would frequently wander through his production plants meeting, talking to, and helping associates (as employees are called). He stressed that experienced associates should sponsor new associates and teach them the ways of the organization; ultimately these associates would become sponsors. In that way, the traditions and habits of cooperation and working together are managed and maintained, the essence of W.L. Gore's culture.

Criteria for Allocation of Rewards and Status

The members of a sport organization learn about the organization's culture by looking at what is rewarded, and likewise what is punished or not rewarded, in their organization. As Schein (1985, p. 234) points out, "an organization's leaders can quickly get across their own priorities, values, and assumptions by consistently linking rewards and punishments to the behavior they are concerned with." For example, the chair of a department of sport management with a culture supporting research and scholarly writing can strengthen this culture by rewarding those faculty members who engage in this type of work. A sports equipment store trying to develop a culture based on customer service would reward sales clerks on the quality of service they provide, not on sales volume.

Criteria for Recruitment, Selection, Promotion, Retirement, and Excommunication

Schein (1985) suggests that one of the most subtle yet potent ways of reinforcing an organization's culture is through the selection of new members (cf. Schneider, 1987). These selection decisions, when coupled with the criteria used to promote, pressure into retirement, or fire, are a very powerful means of strengthening and maintaining a sport organization's culture. There is, however, a problematic dimension to this type of approach, in that "organizations tend to find attractive those candidates who resemble present members in style, assumptions, values, and beliefs" (Schein, 1985, p. 235). Hall, Cullen, and Slack (1989) suggest it is one of the major reasons for the virtual exclusion of women from senior management positions in Canadian national sport organizations. Consequently, while a homogeneous group of people may strengthen a sport organization's culture (and certainly decisions about employee selection, promotion, etc. can reinforce a culture), managers must be sensitive to the fact that what Kanter (1977) calls "the homosocial reproduction of managers" can exclude certain groups from the upper levels of management.

Changing a Sport Organization's Culture

Change can involve increasing or decreasing the number of employees in a sport organization, expanding markets or product lines, and other kinds of structural modifications. However, "in a more subtle but equally important way [it also] requires a basic rethinking of the beliefs by which the company defines and carries out its business" (Lorsch, 1986, p. 97). Kanter (1984) calls this rethinking "culture change." Changing the culture of a sport organization is a long and often difficult process, because it involves changing values and beliefs that have been established over a period of years.

Changes in staff behavior do not necessarily signal that cultural change has taken place. The staff of a sport organization may comply with and exhibit the newly prescribed behavioral expectations while at the same time clinging to the values and beliefs that underpinned the organization's previous structure and mode of operations. Where this superficial compliance occurs, change is likely to be short-lived, and the sport organization involved is quite likely to revert to its former situation (cf. Kikulis, Slack, & Hinings, 1995b).

Lorsch (1986) suggests that when faced with the need for change, managers will first attempt to fix the problem with minor modifications. At times these incremental changes may be successful; however, the basic nature of the organization's culture remains the same. When environmental pressures are more severe, more substantive change is needed, calling for change in the culture of an organization. Lorsch goes on to suggest that there are four basic stages to this change. The first of these stages he labels awareness. Top management gradually becomes aware that in order to ensure its survival, substantive change is needed in their organization, necessitating changes in the underlying pattern of values and beliefs within the organization. This awareness is followed by a period of confusion. Here, managers agree that existing beliefs are not working but cannot agree about the new direction. This confusion often results in the appointment of a new leader to guide the organization. When appointed, the new manager starts to develop a strategic vision for the organization and tries to commit other top managers to this vision. The vision that is created, while it involves fundamentally new ideas, is also meshed with aspects of the company's old culture. This interlocking is one way of helping minimize resistance to this type of change.

The final stage of the change process Lorsch (1986) labeled experimentation. Here, companies experi-

ment with new products, new markets, and new people until they arrive at a suitable situation. If in this stage the managers come to realize that their vision is not realistic, they may reformulate their strategic direction.

Slack and Hinings (1992) describe a similar process to that laid out by Lorsch (1986), occurring in Canadian national sport organizations (NSO's). Throughout much of the 1970s these organizations, faced with pressures from their major funding source (the Canadian government) to establish more businesslike operations, made incremental changes to their structure and operations. In the 1983-1984 period, when increased amounts of government funding escalated these pressures, national sport organization members became confused. Should they continue to operate with the volunteer-based culture that had guided their operation for many years, or should they adopt the more professional bureaucratic and implicitly businesslike culture being advocated by government officials? As Slack and Hinings (1992, p. 127) note, to deal with these pressures for cultural change, "some NSO's made fairly radical changes in their management structure." In several cases they appointed a new chief executive officer, and often the first task of these people, the initial step in the transformation of the culture of these organizations, was to create a vision for the organization.

To determine if, in fact, change is occurring in the culture of an organization, Sathe (1985) suggests three tests. First, there should be evidence of intrinsically motivated behavior—are employees engaging in the expected behaviors without expectation of material gain? Second, is there evidence that employees "automatically do what seems to be appropriate in light of the desired culture without waiting for directions from the organization's leadership or prodding from the organization's systems?" (Sathe, 1985, p. 400). Finally, do people operate in a way that is counter to the old culture norms but in line with the new expectations? While Sathe (1985) notes that these tests are not foolproof, they can provide a reasonable indication of cultural change.

Summary and Conclusions

Culture, one of the newest concepts in the study of organizations, has great potential to enhance our understanding of the structure and processes of sport organizations. A focus on organizational culture forces us to question some of the rational notions of the contingency perspective and start to consider sport organizations as complex patterns of human interaction. By studying a sport organization's culture, we are forced to pay attention to the somewhat intangible, but no less important, aspects of organizational life, such as the values and beliefs, the accepted modes of operation, and the shared assumptions that guide behavior within an organization. Culture is in fact often defined using these terms. Because it is somewhat difficult to see, researchers often study culture by looking at the stories, myths, symbols, language, ceremonies, and rites that are integral to life in an organization. The physical setting in which an organization exists, including its physical structure, physical stimuli, and the symbolic artifacts it exhibits, are also important indicators of its culture.

Some sport organizations will try to develop strong or thick cultures because they can enhance behavioral consistency. However, if change is required this type of culture can be constraining. In contrast, thin cultures are easily changed.

While culture is often presented as a unitary entity, most sport organizations have a dominant culture and one or more subcultures. These competing cultures can lead to organizational conflict if they are not managed. Culture can contribute considerably to the effectiveness of a sport organization but it must align with the organization's strategy, technology, and environment.

The creation of a sport organization's culture is considerably influenced by the organization's founder. Culture can nevertheless be managed and, if necessary, changed; we outlined a number of ways that change can be managed.

Key Concepts

Organizational culture	Values
Beliefs	Basic assumptions
Shared understandings	Stories
Myths	Symbols
Slogans	Language
Ceremonies	Rites
Physical setting	Physical structure
Physical stimuli	Symbolic artifacts
Thick culture	Thin culture
Multicultural	

Review Questions

1. What factors have contributed to the recent emergence of culture as a key variable in understanding organizational structure and processes?

2. What are the key characteristics used to define organizational culture?

3. How does the cultural context in which a sport organization operates vary from its corporate culture?

4. Select a sport organization with which you are familiar. Describe its culture.

5. What type of symbols do we find in a professional sport organization and how do they relate to the culture of the organization?

6. What role do stories and ceremonies play in developing and maintaining a sport organization's culture?

7. Some organizational theorists have suggested that a strong organizational culture is a substitute for high levels of formalization. Why would they suggest this connection?

8. When would it be beneficial for a sport organization to have a thick culture? When would a thin culture be beneficial?

9. Some researchers have argued that organizations are multicultural. Can you think of sport organizations that have competing cultures?

10. How would you expect the culture of a sport organization with a routine technology to vary from one that uses a nonroutine technology?

11. What type of culture do you think would fit best with each of the four strategic types proposed by Miles and Snow?

12. How does the founder of a sport organization influence its culture?

13. If you were the athletic director at a small junior college, what type of action could you take to strengthen the culture of the athletic department?

14. How could the manager of a sport organization go about implementing a change in the organization's culture?

15. Under what conditions is changing a sport organization's culture most likely to be accepted?

Suggestions for Further Reading

A number of popular management texts deal to differing degrees with the issue of organizational culture. The most notable is Peters and Waterman's (1982) *In search of excellence*. However, despite the popularity of these books their academic content is limited. Better coverage of the major issues related to organizational culture can be found in Schein's (1985) *Organizational culture and leadership*; Deal and Kennedy's (1982) *Corporate cultures: The rites and rituals of corporate life*; and Sathe's (1985) *Culture and related corporate realities*. Also useful, albeit somewhat more challenging, material can be found in two collections of essays on organizational culture. The first of these, *Organizational culture,* edited by Frost, Moore, Louis, Lundberg, and Martin (1985), contains work by some of the leading writers on culture who address such issues as "Can organizational culture be managed?"; "How should organizational culture be studied?"; and "How are culture and the wider cultural context linked?" The second collec-

tion, edited by Pondy, Frost, Morgan, and Dandridge (1982), is entitled *Organizational symbolism*. It focuses on the symbolic capacity of organizations and its relationship to organizational culture. Essays are presented on "Managing organizational symbols," "Making sense of organizational symbols," and "Shaping organizational reality through language." Paul Bate's (1995) book *Strategies for cultural change* presents a somewhat different and more critical view of organizational culture. In addition to these texts, the editors of *Administrative Science Quarterly* produced a special issue on the topic of organizational culture (Vol. 28, No. 3, 1983) and the editors of *Organization Studies* produced a special issue on organizational symbolism (Vol. 7, No. 2, 1986). Despite the great potential that sport organizations offer for the study of organizational culture, there has been very little scholarly writing in this area of sport management. Weese's (1995a, 1995b) work is the exception.

Case for Analysis

Developing Organizational Culture in the Los Angeles Olympic Organizing Committee

Like all organizing committees for major sporting events, the Los Angeles Olympic Organizing Committee (LAOOC) had a fixed life span. Founded on March 26, 1979, the organization ceased to exist shortly after the Games ended on August 12, 1984. Originally staffed by only a handful of employees, the LAOOC mushroomed to 2,500 in early 1984 and

by the time the Games began there were some 20,000 paid employees along with 50,000 volunteers. One of the problems faced by the LAOOC, like any group founded very quickly and lasting only for a short time, was to get everyone to feel "a part of the organization." Specific plans were made to help people fit in, to remind them of the importance of the Games, and to make them feel like they were a part of history.

The orientation program was fairly brief; there wasn't much time to train staff. The orientation meetings were held in the LAOOC headquarters. A drab building that had once been a helicopter plant, it had the wide-open floorplan typical of a manufacturing facility. The interior had been decorated with brightly colored banners and mobiles. Large colorful pillars had been added to the building and the scaffolding that was to be used to decorate the competition sites was used to brighten up the place. The presence of these colorful decorations was a constant reminder to employees of the nature of the spectacle in which they were involved. Even getting into the headquarters was an exercise designed to reinforce the nature of the Games. Security was a major concern to the organizers and each visitor to the headquarters had to pass through four security checks, ranging from verbal questioning to X-ray machines and frisking.

The actual orientation session itself was conducted by senior staff members who talked about the organization's purpose and philosophy. They stressed that the athlete was the center of the Games. They also underscored the financial conditions under which the Games operated: Taxpayers were not to be burdened and new building was to be kept to a minimum. These were the "Spartan" Games; there would be no excess costs. Stress was also placed on the long-term benefits to the community and the decentralization of services, some contracted out to private operators.

At the orientation each new staff member was provided with a policies and procedures manual. Four policies became frequent topics of conversation among staff: the dress code, the number of signatures needed on any transaction, the "Peter" [Ueberroth] tests, and the allocation of parking passes. The dress code was a conservative one. Women had to wear dresses (not shorts), stockings, and "proper undergarments." Men were expected to wear ties and were not allowed beards. Some employees were offended by the code, although no one could ever remember anybody being fired for breaking the rules. One story was told of a woman wearing long shorts one day (because she was going to be moving boxes) being reprimanded by an older woman in "a gross polyester floral muu-muu." The requirement of numerous signatures on any transaction was a reminder of the tight fiscal constraints under which the Games were being run.

To develop an understanding of the Games, several "Peter" tests were developed. One allegedly involved each new staff member being assigned a participating country. They were told that at any time the president of the LAOOC could call them into his office and quiz them about this country. The idea was that if a delegation from this country showed up, there was a source of current information available. It also helped the staff feel they held an important role in the operations, by being one of the few experts in this area. Another "Peter" test apparently involved staff being required to take a test on the history of the Olympics, details of the local community, and the LAOOC. A number of horror stories rapidly spread about the tests and although no one was known to have been fired as a result, Peter Ueberroth was said to have personally come down to acknowledge the only person ever to receive a perfect score.

The fourth policy area frequently discussed was parking. The limited spaces at the headquarters were allocated by department heads, by rank within the department, by seniority, or by favoritism. Who had passes and who had to park in the additional spots (20 minutes away) and catch the shuttle was a hot hallway topic.

Stories also grew up around other activities at the LAOOC. One concerned a staff member who was fired for not walking fast enough. Many of these stories were exchanged in the "Cafe du Coubertin" where staff were encouraged to eat by offering them a $2.00 subsidy per day. The idea was to reduce downtime and to build camaraderie. A "Days to Go" calendar was updated, showing the progress of the Olympic torch relay. Inspirational Olympic news was shown at lunch, uniforms were modeled, and sports were demonstrated. All served to build excitement toward the Games.

Jokes developed about official suppliers. There were questions about who was the "official toilet paper" supplier. Staff were required to use IBM computers, Xerox copiers, and Brothers typewriters. They were given free M & Ms, Snickers, Coca-Cola, and Perrier. Delivery people not from official suppliers had to turn their company shirts inside out when they visited the headquarters. Distinguished guests were a frequent occurrence, each stressing the magnitude of the Games and the important role the staff played in their success.

Based on information in McDonald, P. (1991). The Los Angeles Olympic Organizing Committee: Developing organizational culture in the short run. In P. J. Frost, L.F. Moore, M.R. Louis, C.C. Lundberg, and J. Martin (Eds.), *Reframing organizational culture* (pp. 26-38). Thousand Oaks, CA: Sage.

Questions

1. What were the problems of building culture in an organization like the LAOOC, which was only in existence for a relatively short while?

2. How was culture built at the LAOOC?

3. What manifestations of culture can you see in this case? What others do you think there might have been?

4. What purpose did culture serve for this sport organization?

Dr. Donna Lopiano, *sport management leader*

Leadership and Sport Organizations

When You Have Read This Chapter

You should be able to

1. explain the basic principles of the trait approach to understanding leadership and the types of studies emanating from this research,

2. explain the principles of the behavioral theories of leadership and the way this approach has been used in sport management studies,

3. explain the major research studies that have used the contingency approach to understanding leader effectiveness,

4. discuss the basic concepts that underpin theories of charismatic and transformational leadership, and

5. describe the types of leadership studies that could be conducted in the field of sport management.

Leaders in the Field of Sport Management

Sheri Poe

In 1972 Sheri Poe, a first-year student at Southern Illinois University, was raped at gunpoint. Although she reported the crime to the authorities, Poe got little support because police, doctors, and even a therapist placed much of the blame for the attack on the fact that she was hitchhiking. Emotionally scarred by the rape, Poe dropped out of school and went through several years of psychological trauma, medical difficulties, and financial problems. She eventually moved to California where she met and married Martin Birrittella, a marketing executive for a giftware company. As her recovery progressed, Poe began a walking program and then got into aerobics. When she suffered back pains from her exercise regime, Poe began looking at the design of aerobics shoes and noticed that they did little to accommodate the higher arch and narrower heel that most women have. With husband Birrittella, Poe managed to scrape up enough money to start a small company to produce a workout shoe specifically designed for women. The company, called Ryka, Inc., was founded in 1987; with the help of a banker who was also an aerobics fanatic, the company went public in 1988. In 1993 Ryka had revenues of about $15 million. Poe has promoted the company as the only manufacturer of women's athletic shoes that is actually run by women; 70 percent of its workforce are female. She has also developed the Ryka ROSE (Regaining One's Self Esteem) Foundation as a part of her company. Ryka channels 7 percent of pre-tax profits to the foundation. Along with moneys raised through fund-raising ventures and special events, the profits are used to help women who have been the victims of violent crimes.

Dr. Earle F. Zeigler

Earle Zeigler is in many ways the founding father of the academic field of sport management. Educated at Yale, Dr. Zeigler taught in a number of Canadian and American universities. His numerous books and articles, many of which were written well before the founding of the North American Society for Sport Management, were among the first academic works in the area. His ideas have influenced many people in the field and his former graduate students have gone on to become leaders in the North American Society for Sport Management and other areas of physical education and sport studies. Dr. Zeigler has received many awards for his contributions to our field. Each year members of NASSM select an individual to give the Earle F. Zeigler lecture at a banquet held at the organization's annual conference. The award is given in honor of Dr. Zeigler's work as a leader in the field of sport management.

Dr. Donna Lopiano

Dr. Donna Lopiano graduated from Southern Connecticut State College in 1968. She holds an MA degree and a PhD from the University of Southern California. Dr. Lopiano coached both men's and women's college volleyball and women's college basketball, field hockey, and softball. She was an outstanding athlete, participating in 26 national championships in four different sports. She was a nine-time All-American at four different positions in softball. Between 1975 and 1992 Dr. Lopiano served as the director of Intercollegiate Athletics for Women at the University of Texas in Austin. She is a highly respected leader in athletic administration, having served as the president of the Association of Intercollegiate Athletics for Women (1981); she was a member of the United States Olympic Development Committee (1984-1988), and chair of the NCAA Legislative Review Committee. Since 1992 she has been executive director of the Women's Sport Foundation, an organization committed to improving opportunities for women's involvement in sport. Dr. Lopiano was a keynote speaker at the 1993 conference of the North American Society for Sport Management.

Information on Sheri Poe was obtained from Commentary. (July/August 1993). *Sports Business*, p. 98; and Stodghill, R. (1993, June 14). What makes Ryka run? Sheri Poe and her story. *Business Week*, pp. 82, 84.

Few people would argue that Sheri Poe, Earle Zeigler, and Donna Lopiano are leaders in the field of sport management. But what is it that makes them leaders? They all come from different backgrounds, they have all had different accomplishments, and each works in a different sector of the field of sport management. Leadership is in many ways one of the great mysteries in the field of management. While *Bass and Stogdill's Handbook of leadership* (Bass, 1990a) contains over 7,500 citations (Weese, 1994), Bennis and Nanus (1985, p. 4) commented on the state of leadership research that "never have so many labored so long to say so little."

The popularity of leadership research in the broader field of management is also reflected in the sport management literature. Paton (1987), after a thorough review of research in the field, concluded that leadership was the topic most frequently studied by sport management scholars. However, despite the proliferation of leadership studies in sport management, most of the work has been descriptive and atheoretical, rarely employing in any meaningful or substantive way the leadership literature that exists in the broader field of management (work by Chelladurai and his colleagues [1978, 1980, 1983, 1987b] and research by Weese [1995a, 1995b] are the exceptions to this general trend). There has also been little attempt to tie this work on leadership to other organizational phenomena. As such it has contributed little to our understanding of the structure and processes of sport organizations.

In this chapter we look at the topic of leadership, although any comprehensive review of all the literature in this area is beyond the scope of a textbook. We look at the major theoretical approaches to the study of leadership, specifically the trait approach, the style (or behavioral) approach, and the contingency (or situational) approach (Bryman, 1992). In addition, we look at the currently popular notions of charismatic and transformational leadership. After reviewing the theoretical literature and the way it has been used in the field of sport management, we examine some of the problems with work on leadership, and make some suggestions regarding the type of leadership research that should be undertaken in our field.

Trait Approach

The trait approach was one of the earliest approaches to leadership research. Its basic premise is that good leaders are born, not made. That is, leaders possess certain personal qualities that dis-

tinguish them from other members of an organization. Early researchers used psychological tests to try to identify these traits, but within this research little attention was paid to how effective these leaders were. The type of traits most frequently examined by researchers can be classified into three categories: the individual's physical characteristics (height, physical appearance, age, etc.); intellectual qualities such as intelligence, speaking ability, and insight; and such personality features as emotional stability, dominance, and sensitivity.

In a comprehensive review of 124 studies based on the trait approach carried out between 1904 and 1948, Stogdill (1948) found some support for a difference in the traits exhibited by leaders and those exhibited by nonleaders. Despite this supportive evidence, Stogdill's results showed considerable variance from one situation to the next, causing him to conclude that "the qualities, characteristics, and skills required in a leader are determined to a large extent by the demands of the situation in which he is to function as a leader" (Bass, 1981, p. 65).

What the early trait studies showed was that while some characteristics were found to be common to leaders as compared to nonleaders, simple possession of these traits was no guarantee of a person being a successful leader. A leader who exhibited certain types of traits may be effective in one situation but less than effective in another. Gibb (1947), conducting a review of research on leadership traits and arriving at a similar conclusion to Stogdill's, noted (p. 27) that "the particular set of social circumstances existing at the moment determines which attributes of personality will confer leadership status and consequently determines which members of the group will assume the leadership role."

While some suggested that Stogdill's 1948 review had brought an end to trait research, he conducted another review of such research in 1974 and uncovered that 163 studies of this type were conducted between 1949 and 1970. Table 15.1 shows some of the leadership traits identified by Stogdill in his 1974 review. The studies included in the 1974 review were more methodologically sophisticated than the earlier research studies, leading, arguably, to more consistent results than those found in the 1948 review (Yukl, 1989). Following the 1974 review Stogdill retreated somewhat from his earlier position and suggested that this work and similar reviews by others had placed too much emphasis on situational factors and downplayed the universal traits that certain leaders seemed to possess. He concluded: "The leader is characterized by a strong drive for responsibility and task completion, vigor and persistence in the pursuit of goals, venture-someness and originality in problem-solving, drive to exercise initiative in social situations, self-confidence and a sense of personal identity, willingness to accept the consequences of his or her decisions and actions, readiness to absorb interpersonal stress, willingness to tolerate frustration and delay, ability to influence other people's behavior, and the capacity to structure social interaction systems to the purpose at hand" (Bass, 1990a, p. 87).

Stogdill's position should not be accepted as some sort of claim for the absoluteness of trait research. Rather, it reflects a belief that the possession of certain traits can increase the chances of a leader being successful in certain situations.

Research on leadership traits has given rise to other more substantive lines of inquiry. However, even as recently as 1991 Kirkpatrick and Locke suggested that traits such as drive, the desire to lead, honesty/integrity, self-confidence, cognitive ability, and knowledge of business were important leadership qualities. The popular press also still continues to describe the leadership abilities of such individuals as coaches and team managers in terms of the traits they exhibit.

One of the research themes to develop from earlier work on leadership traits has been concerned with the processes of managerial selection and recruitment. Commonly referred to as the assessment center approach, the focus of this research is to use various tests, some of which are job-related, to identify traits that can predict management potential and the ability to progress to the higher levels of an organization (Gaugler, Rosenthal, Thornton, & Bentson, 1987). The assessment center approach uses projective and situational tests; such as the in-basket exercise, a hypothetical situation in which a candidate has a certain amount of time to take action on letters, memos, and so on, that have accu-mulated in the in-basket, to determine if the person taking the test has management traits and skills. These tests may often be accompanied by exercises to assess such skills as writing and oral communication. Many organizations, including some in the sport industry, use these kinds of tests to improve their managerial selection and promotion processes. The traits that best predict advancement can include such qualities as resistance to stress, the tolerance of uncertainty, and the candidate's level of activity (Bray, Campbell, & Grant, 1974). The assessment center approach, and much of the other work that has emanated from trait research, has one major limitation for our understanding of leadership: While it has been designed to identify those traits that predict managerial effectiveness or advancement, it does not necessarily follow that these are useful predictors of good leadership, although as Bryman (1986, p. 34) notes, "writers such as Yukl (1981) and Bass (1981) appear, at least by inference, to take assessment center studies . . . to be relevant to the study of leadership." The assessment center approach has also been criticized because results may be influenced by the gender of the assessor and the assessee (Walsh, Weinberg, & Fairfield, 1987).

Other extensions of the trait approach include McCall and Lombardo's (1983) work on company managers who were successful and those who "derailed." These researchers found that managers who derailed were emotionally less stable and more defensive, and had weak interpersonal skills and limited technical expertise. If their technical skills were good, they became overconfident about their abilities. Trait research has also led to work on managerial motivations. Miner (1978, 1985) identified motivations such as a desire to compete with peers, to exercise power, and to exhibit a positive attitude toward authority figures, as correlating with managerial success. McClelland (1985) found that

Table 15.1   Leadership Traits

Active and energetic	Being above average height
High socioeconomic background	Well educated
Superior judgment	Speaks well
Aggressive and assertive	Independent
Objective	Resourceful
Enthusiastic	High personal integrity
Self confident	High achiever
Responsible	Interacts easily
Cooperative	Good interpersonal skills

Based on Stogdill's 1974 review and taken from Bass, B.M. (1981). *Stogdill's Handbook of Leadership*. New York: The Free Press.

TIME OUT

Basketball and Business: The Traits of Success

Pat Riley and John Thompson are leaders in the sport of basketball and in business. Riley, while coach of the Los Angeles Lakers, won four NBA championships in nine seasons and is one of only five coaches to win the NBA Coach of the Year Award twice. Riley has transferred the leadership qualities he showed in basketball to the business world. With the publication of his book *The winner within: A life plan for team players* Riley now speaks to Fortune 500 companies on how to inject enthusiasm and teamwork into their managers. He is seen as an engaging and articulate speaker who embodies the concepts of dedication and teamwork. Writers describe Riley as tough but someone who shows compassion and deals with the truth.

John Thompson was a college basketball star who went on to win an NBA championship with the Boston Celtics. But it is as coach of the Georgetown University Hoyas that he is best known. However, Thompson is not just a leader in basketball; Nike CEO Phil Knight thought so much of Thompson's abilities that he appointed him to the board of directors of his company. Thompson, an imposing figure at 6 feet 10 inches, was described in *Success* magazine as a balanced individual with "a competitive fury restrained by conscience, a hunger to win matched by a refusal to let heated emotion take over, a seething perfectionism tempered by sharp intuition, and a deep understanding of human frailty."

Based on information in Rottenberger-Murtha, K. (September 1993). How to play above the rim. *Sales & Marketing Management*, pp. 28-29; The winner within. (1993, September). *Success*, pp. 34-39; Aronson, M. (1993, June). He creates winners. *Success*, pp. 34-38.

in different situations the need for power, for achievement, and for affiliation were motivations that could influence managerial success.

A final area of research emanating from the trait studies of leadership seeks to identify managerial skills or competencies. Several researchers in our field have attempted to utilize this approach to determine the competencies required by sport mangers. Zeigler and Bowie (1983), for example, argued that sport managers need the types of skills identified by Katz (1955): technical skills (knowledge about the manner in which certain specialized activities are carried out and the expertise to use the equipment related to that activity), human skills (knowledge about interpersonal relationships, the ability to communicate effectively and establish working relationships), and conceptual skills (the ability to think logically about one's work situation, to formulate complex ideas, and solve problems). Zeigler and Bowie (1983) add that sport managers should also have personal skills (the ability to improve in areas such as perception, assertiveness, and negotiation) and conjoined skills (the ability to balance technical, human, and conceptual skills and employ them in combination to achieve a goal). More recently Jamieson (1987) also argued for a competency-based approach to sport management.

She suggested that sport managers need competence in such areas as business procedures, resource management, personnel management, planning and evaluation, and programming techniques. Unfortunately, most studies on competencies are often seriously flawed; they are often either too general, and produce patently obvious findings (e.g., sport managers need good decision making skills), or they fail to recognize that different competencies are required, to a greater or lesser extent, in the various sectors of the sport industry. For example, the skills needed by the CEO of a professional basketball franchise will be quite different from those required by the volunteer president of a community sport club. McLennan (1967) has shown that the skill requirements of managers vary depending on such factors as the nature of the organization, its size, and the extent to which decisions are centralized or decentralized. The impact of such contingencies has not been addressed in the sport management literature.

Style or Behavioral Approach

As Stogdill's (1974) review showed, trait research was alive and well through much of the 1950s and

1960s. Leadership research during this time, however, moved increasingly toward what are called studies of leadership style or leadership behavior. The focus of this research is to identify the style of leadership or leader behaviors most likely to increase the effectiveness of subordinates. This concern with how leaders/managers treat employees paralleled the growth of the Human Relations school of management. Conducted primarily by psychologists, the two research programs that best exemplify the style approach are what are referred to as the Ohio State Studies and the Michigan Studies. We look briefly at the major concepts employed in both these approaches and, where possible, the work conducted in sport management using the ideas they contain.

The Ohio State Studies

The Ohio State researchers (Fleishman & Harris, 1962; Fleishman, Harris, & Burtt, 1955; Halpin, 1957; Halpin & Winer, 1957; Hemphill & Coons, 1957) used questionnaires to identify the types of behaviors in which leaders engaged,that is, their leadership style. From a list of about 1,800 possible leader behaviors these researchers developed a list of 130 questions. The instrument, known as the Leader Behavior Description Questionnaire (LBDQ), was administered to 300 individuals, mainly people involved in the military. The resulting factor analysis of the completed questionnaires showed that subordinates conceptualized their leader's behavior as occurring primarily along two dimensions: the extent to which the leaders exhibit consideration, and what is referred to as initiating structure. Consideration is "the extent to which leaders promote camaraderie, mutual trust, liking, and respect in the relationship between themselves and their subordinates" (Bryman, 1992, p. 5). The term initiating structure concerns the degree to which leaders structure their own work and that of their subordinates to obtain the organization's goals. Examples of actions under initiating structure include creating job descriptions, establishing performance standards, ensuring subordinates work to maximum performance levels, and establishing deadlines.

The initial conception of these two dimensions was that one was in some ways the antithesis of the other. That is, leaders who scored high on consideration were likely to score low on initiating structure and vice versa, with initiating structure being the primary correlate of effective performance. Research by Halpin (1957), however, showed that leaders who scored high on both dimensions were seen as effective by their superiors, while at the same time having subordinates who were satisfied in their jobs.

Over the years the LBDQ has been modified (the latest version is termed the LBDQ-Form XII) and has been used in some capacity in many leadership studies (cf. Katerberg & Hom, 1981; Larson, Hunt, & Osborn, 1976; Schriesheim, 1980). Bryman (1992), nevertheless, suggests that despite its popularity, the Ohio research and much of the other research characteristics of the style approach are open to a number of criticisms. First, the findings from LBDQ studies have produced inconsistent and, in some cases, statistically insignificant results (cf. Fisher & Edwards, 1988). Second, the studies using this approach rarely take into account situational factors; where they have, most notably in the path-goal approach (House, 1971; House & Mitchell, 1974), there has been "a tendency for atheoretical investigations of particular moderating variables" (Bryman, 1992, p. 7). A third problem Bryman (1992) identifies is that, because most LBDQ-type studies are cross-sectional, the direction of causality is rarely established; hence, it is wrong to conclude that leadership style influences factors such as group performance or satisfaction—quite possibly group performance and job satisfaction could influence leadership style. A fourth concern is the tendency of studies in the Ohio State tradition to focus on group-level or averaged responses, a situation by which the leader's relationship to individual organization members is masked. This tendency is problematic because we know leaders treat individual subordinates differently. There is also a failure in LBDQ studies to address the question of informal leadership, a relevant practice in many organizations. Finally, there are concerns about the validity of LBDQ measures (cf. Rush, Thomas, & Lord, 1977).

Despite these shortcomings LBDQ-type studies have been used by researchers in the sport management field. Olafson and Hastings (1988) used the LBDQ-Form XII to assess administrative behavior, relating it to what they term personal style. Their results suggest that personal style is important in understanding a leader's decision making behavior. Snyder (1990) used the LBDQ to examine the effect of leader behavior on intercollegiate coaches' job satisfaction. His work showed that the degree of consideration exhibited by leaders (athletic directors) was significantly correlated with coaches' satisfaction with their work and their supervision. Initiating structure did not correlate with either work satisfaction or supervision. In another study using the LBDQ, Branch (1990) looked specifically at athletic directors and the effect of their behavior on the effectiveness of intercollegiate athletic organizations. Using athletic directors' self-perceptions of their level of consideration and initiating structure, Branch concluded that "effective athletic organizations have leaders who are more predisposed to goal and task accomplishment than to developing good interpersonal relationships with their subordinates" (p. 161). The seemingly contradictory findings of Snyder's (1990) and Branch's (1990) research draws attention to the theoretical and methodological problems of work that has used the LBDQ in sport management. Both these two pieces of work exhibit many of the problems identified by Bryman (1986).

The Michigan Studies

At approximately the same time as the Ohio State research was being conducted researchers at the University of Michigan were also involved in an extensive program of leadership studies. The first group of these studies (Katz, Maccoby, Gurin, & Floor, 1951; Katz, Maccoby, & Morse, 1950) were directed toward determining the behaviors of effective leaders. Results show that leaders in high-performing organizational units were more likely to

- clearly differentiate their role by spending less time doing the things that subordinates did and more time in planning and supervision,
- be oriented toward their work group by being "employee-centered" as opposed to "production-centered,"
- not engage in close supervision of their subordinates and thus allow them more latitude in what they did,
- develop a sense of cohesiveness within their work group, and
- receive general rather than close supervision from their supervisors.

The results from the Michigan studies, along with information from the Ohio State research, were summarized by Bowers and Seashore (1966). These two researchers identified four dimensions of leadership emerging from the two sets of studies:

- Support
- Interaction Facilitation
- Goal Emphasis
- Work Facilitation

The first two concepts focus on relationship-oriented behaviors, the second two on task-orientated behaviors. Bowers and Seashore (1966) argued that the practices they identified could be carried out by formal leaders or members of the

particular work group. Hence they coined the terms managerial leadership and peer leadership. Taylor and Bowers (1972) developed a set of questions to assess the role played by peer and managerial leadership in contributing to the four dimensions identified by Bowers and Seashore (1966). The identification of the concept "peer leadership" drew attention to the role of informal leaders, something that had not been addressed in earlier leadership studies. It also laid the foundation for a whole series of subsequent studies that have looked at participative leadership (Miller & Monge, 1986; Strauss, 1977; Vroom & Yetton, 1973).

Summary of Behavioral Approaches to Leadership

The Ohio State and Michigan studies have a number of similarities. Both focus on the behavior of leaders or their style, not the personal qualities leaders possess. Both identify two dimensions of style, one focusing on organizational tasks and the other on employee relations. Much of the leadership research conducted in the 1970s and 1980s has its basis in the concepts that emanated from these two research programs (cf. Lord, Binning, Rush, & Thomas, 1978; Misumi & Peterson, 1985; Schriesheim, 1980; Stinson & Johnson, 1975). The Ohio State and Michigan studies are not without problems, and many of the criticisms of the Ohio State studies identified above also apply to the Michigan studies.

Researchers in sport management (Branch, 1990; Olafson & Hastings, 1988; Snyder, 1990) have used the LBDQ developed by the Ohio researchers to conduct work on sport organizations. However, rarely if ever have any of the concerns identified about this approach been addressed in the sport management literature. In addition, although not specifically dealt with here, several studies have used the LBDQ to assess the leadership qualities of coaches as opposed to managers (Case, 1987; Chelladurai & Carron, 1983; Danielson, Zelhart, & Drake, 1975). Where managers have been used they are invariably athletic directors (Branch, 1990; Snyder, 1990); only Olafson and Hastings (1988) studied managers in other sectors of the sport industry.

Contingency or Situational Approach

One of the shortcomings of the Ohio State and Michigan studies, and indeed much of the work in this tradition, is its failure to take account of how contingency or situational variables moderate the relationship between the behavior of a leader and different outcomes. While it is an intuitively appealing notion that different types of leader behavior will be more appropriate than others in particular situations, not until the 1970s did we see the emergence of a significant body of research focusing in any systematic way on the impact of contingency variables—task structure, the characteristics of the environment, or subordinate's characteristics—on leadership effectiveness. Contingency theories of leadership "draw attention to the notion that there are no universally appropriate styles of leadership, [but that] particular styles have an impact on various outcomes in some situations but not in others" (Bryman, 1992, p. 11). In this section we focus on those theories of leadership that have placed contingency factors as the central focus of their analysis. We look specifically at three of the best-known contingency approaches: the path-goal theory of leadership, Hersey and Blanchard's situational theory, and Fiedler's LPC approach. The main ideas behind each of these approaches are outlined and where it exists, work in the field of sport management that has utilized these approaches is discussed.

The Path-Goal Theory of Leadership

Developed primarily by House (1971) and his colleagues (House & Dessler, 1974; House & Mitchell, 1974) the path-goal theory of leadership is concerned with understanding how a leader's behavior influences the satisfaction and efforts of subordinates. Essentially the theory proposes that the influence of the leader's behavior on subordinate satisfaction and effort is contingent on situational variables such as the nature of the task being under-

taken and the characteristics of the subordinates. These contingency variables "determine both the potential for increased subordinate motivation and the manner in which the leader must act to improve motivation" (Yukl, 1989, p. 100). They also influence the preferences that subordinates have for a particular type of leader behavior. House and Mitchell (1974) and Filley, House, & Kerr (1976) identify four types of leader behavior, shown in table 15.2.

The path-goal model seeks to explain what effect different types of leader behavior will have under various situational conditions. When work is stressful, frustrating, tedious, or low in autonomy, supportive leadership will increase the satisfaction and effort of subordinates (House, 1971; House & Dessler, 1974; Schuler, 1976; Stinson & Johnson, 1975). This style of leadership is seen to enhance the intrinsic value of the task and, by increasing subordinate self-confidence and lowering anxiety, it raises the expectancy level that tasks will be successfully completed. When tasks are not stressful, frustrating, tedious, or dissatisfying supportive leadership does not have a major impact on the satisfaction level of subordinates or the amount of effort they put into their work. When tasks are unstructured and complex in nature, when subordinates have little experience in doing the tasks and no formalized procedures to help them complete their work, instrumental leadership (sometimes called directive leadership) will enhance the satisfaction and effort of subordinates. Indik (1986; cited by Yukl, 1989), in a meta-analysis, provided general support for the impact of instrumental leadership on employee satisfaction and motivation under conditions of low task structure.

While ideas about participative leadership are not as well developed as those about supportive or instrumental leadership, it is hypothesized that participation increases subordinate satisfaction and

Table 15.2 Four Types of Leader Behavior

Supportive leadership. The leader exhibits concern about the welfare of subordinates, considers their needs, and attempts to create a work environment that is pleasant and caring.

Instrumental (or directive) leadership. The leader places a great deal of emphasis on planning, coordinating, directing, and controlling the activities of subordinates.

Participative leadership. Leaders treat subordinates almost as equals. Subordinates are encouraged to let their views be known; there is a sharing of power with subordinates.

Achievement leadership. Leaders have confidence in their subordinates. Subordinates are set challenging goals and expected to assume responsibility for meeting these goals.

Based on information in Filley, A.C., House, R.J., & Kerr, S. (1976). *Managerial process and organizational behavior* (2nd ed.). Glenview, IL: Scott, Foresman and Company, p. 253.

effort under conditions where tasks are relatively unstructured. Participative leadership, it is felt, can increase subordinates' understanding of the relationship between their efforts and goal attainment; it helps them select goals in which they are personally interested and hence toward which they are more likely to be motivated. It can also increase subordinates' control over their own work, thus increasing satisfaction. Indik's (1986) meta-analysis found support for the fact that participative leadership can in fact increase employee satisfaction when tasks are relatively unstructured.

Like participative leadership, work on achievement leadership has not been extensively developed. It is generally felt that achievement leadership "will cause subordinates to strive for higher standards of performance and to have more confidence in their ability to meet challenging goals" (House & Mitchell, 1974, p. 91) when tasks are unstructured. When tasks are straightforward, achievement leadership has little effect.

While there are questions about the conceptual underpinnings of the path-goal theory of leadership (Schriesheim & Kerr, 1977) and concerns over the direction of causality in some of the findings attributed to this approach (Greene, 1979), it has made a significant contribution to leadership research by helping researchers identify relevant situational variables. It has also given rise to a substantial body of research.

In the field of sport management Chelladurai and Saleh's (1978) work has its basis in the path-goal model. Building on House's (1971) ideas, Chelladurai and Saleh (1978) identify five types of leader behavior in the sport setting: training behavior, autocratic behavior, democratic behavior, social support, and rewarding behavior. It was shown that athletes in interdependent sports (essentially team sports) preferred coaches to emphasize training behavior (actions akin to the Ohio State concept of initiating structure) more than did athletes in independent sports (individual sports). Athletes in what are termed "closed" sports (sports where there is low task variability, such as golf or swimming) preferred coaches to emphasize more training behavior than did those in what are termed "open" sports. Male athletes preferred more autocratic behavior and social support than females. Unfortunately, Chelladurai and Saleh's (1978) work focused only on athletes and coaches, not managers. No published work in sport management has used the path-goal approach to look at the contingencies influencing the leadership behaviors of sport managers.

Hersey and Blanchard's Situational Leadership Theory

Hersey and Blanchard's (1984) approach to understanding leadership is based on two types of leader behavior. Task behavior, very similar to the Ohio State concept of initiating structure, involves the leader in structuring how work is to be done. Relationship behavior, similar to the concept of consideration, involves providing support to employees and openly communicating with them. The mediating situational variable between task or relationship behavior and leader effectiveness is called subordinate maturity. Two dimensions make up this concept. The term job maturity describes the subordinate's technical ability; psychological maturity is the level of self-confidence and self-respect they bring to the task. Subordinates with high levels of maturity score high on both job maturity and psychological maturity. They possess the skills to do the task, will assume responsibility, and establish high aims for themselves. Subordinates with low maturity have little ability and low self-confidence. Although maturity is actually a continuum, Hersey and Blanchard divide the continuum up into four segments (see figure 15.1).

When subordinates show low levels of maturity in regard to the tasks to be performed, leaders who exhibit high task behavior are most effective; the

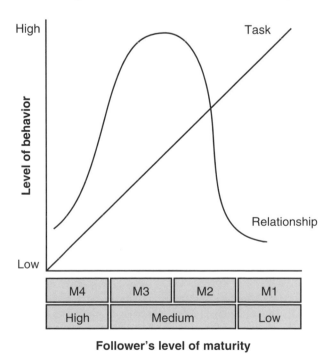

Figure 15.1 Relationship between subordinate maturity and task-oriented behavior.

leader provides direction by establishing clear ways of operating and standards of task accomplishment. At the medium levels of maturity (quadrants 2 and 3) leaders need to focus more on relationship behavior and gradually reduce the amount of direction they provide the subordinates as they exhibit more maturity relative to the task. At the highest level of maturity the leader offers little direction and allows the subordinate to make decisions about how tasks are carried out.

A leader can influence the maturity level of a subordinate by using what are termed developmental interventions, which may involve techniques such as reducing the amount of direction given a subordinate and allowing them to take responsibility for a task. If the subordinate does well, praise and support are used to strengthen the behavior. A more complex intervention, termed contingency contracting, involves negotiating the subordinate's tasks and responsibilities. The length of time may vary to "mature" to do the task well, depending on the nature of the task.

Hersey and Blanchard's work draws attention to the need for leaders to treat different subordinates in different ways as they progress in their work. It also draws attention to ways leaders can work with subordinates to build up their abilities and confidence level. There have been very few attempts, however, to empirically test the concepts and relationships outlined in Hersey and Blanchard's work, even in the general field of management and organization studies. No published work in the field of sport management has used this approach.

Fiedler's LPC Approach

Fiedler's (1967) approach is the oldest of the contingency theories of leadership. Unlike the path-goal approach and Hersey and Blanchard's work, both of which focus on leader behavior, Fiedler focuses on how situational variables moderate the relationship between leader traits and organizational effectiveness. The cornerstone of Fiedler's work is a measure called the Least Preferred Coworker (LPC) score. This score, an indicator of a leader's motivational traits, is developed using an instrument which asks leaders to think of the person with whom they can work least well, and to assess that person on a series of bipolar descriptors. The 16 pairs of descriptors include adjectives such as pleasant-unpleasant, helpful-frustrating, cold-warm, supportive-

hostile, and gloomy-cheerful. A leader who obtains a low LPC score is motivated by task accomplishment and will only be concerned with relationships with subordinates if the work unit is seen to be performing well. A leader who gets a high LPC score will, in contrast, be motivated to develop close interpersonal relations with subordinates; task-directed behavior is of a lesser concern, only becoming important when sound interpersonal relations have been established with subordinates and peers.

Mediating the relationship between the leader's motivational traits and group performance is a situation variable called situational favorability. Favorability is made up of three situational components:

1. *Leader-member relations*: the leader's personal relationship with the other members who make up the work group
2. *Position power of the leader*: the degree of formal authority the leader obtains from his or her position
3. *Task structure*: the extent to which the tasks the group have been assigned to perform are structured.

The three components of situational favorability can give eight possible conditions (see table 15.3). Fiedler suggests that task-oriented leader behavior (i.e., a low LPC leader) is most effective in situations of high situational favorability (conditions 1, 2, or 3) or unfavorable situations (condition 8). In situations that are moderately favorable or moderately unfavorable (conditions 4-7) someone who is more attentive to subordinate relations (a high LPC leader) will be more effective.

There have been a number of criticisms of Fiedler's model (Kennedy, 1982; Schriesheim & Kerr, 1977) and it has fallen out of favor within the general field of management and organizational studies. However, reviews of the large number of studies conducted using this approach (Peters, Hartke, & Pohlmann, 1985; Strube & Garcia, 1981) provide general support for the model.

Within the field of sport management, a number of doctoral dissertations have used the LPC instrument to examine leadership (cf. Soucie, 1994). However, in terms of published work there is very little research. Bagley (1975) used Fiedler's work to look at graduate departments of physical education. She found little support for Fiedler's model and suggested that these types of organizational subunits require relationship-oriented leaders.

Table 15.3   Fiedler's Situational Favorability Factors and Leadership Effectiveness

| CONDITION | SITUATIONAL FAVORABILITY | | | EFFECTIVE LEADERSHIP |
	LEADER-MEMBER RELATIONS	TASK STRUCTURE	POSITION POWER	
1	Good	High	Strong	Low LPC
2	Good	High	Weak	Low LPC
3	Good	Weak	Strong	Low LPC
4	Good	Weak	Weak	High LPC
5	Poor	High	Strong	High LPC
6	Poor	High	Weak	High LPC
7	Poor	Weak	Strong	High LPC
8	Poor	Weak	Weak	Low LPC

Adapted, by permission, from F.E. Fiedler, 1967, *A theory of leadership effectiveness* (New York: McGraw-Hill), 34.

TIME OUT

Effects of Culture as a Situational Variable Influencing Leadership Effectiveness

Chelladurai, Malloy, Imamura, and Yamaguchi (1987) suggested that one of the situational variables that could influence leadership effectiveness is culture. They defined culture as the attitudes, beliefs, and values of a society. Using a sample of 106 male Japanese students and 156 male Canadian students, Chelladurai et al. used an instrument they had developed some years earlier with Saleh (Chelladurai & Saleh, 1980), the Leadership Scale for Sports, to assess the preferred leadership of the two samples. Their results showed that Japanese students preferred more supportive leadership than Canadian students. It was also found that Japanese students in modern sports (track and field, rugby, volleyball, etc.) preferred a more participative leadership structure than Canadian students. Japanese students in traditional sports (judo, kendo, and kyuto) preferred a more authoritarian (i.e., directive) style of leadership. The researchers concluded that both the cultural background of subordinates (athletes) and the type of sport in which they were involved were situational variables that could influence leadership effectiveness.

Based on information in Chelladurai, P., Malloy, D., Imamura, H., & Yamaguchi, Y. (1987). A cross-cultural study of preferred leadership in sports. *Canadian Journal of Sport Sciences, 12,* 106-110.

Charismatic and Transformational Leadership

In the last 15 years or so leadership researchers have become increasingly interested in charismatic and transformational leadership. As Yukl (1989, p. 204) points out, the terms transformational leadership and charismatic leadership refer to the process of "influencing major change in the attitudes and assumptions of organization members and building commitment for the organization's mission or objectives. Transformational leadership is usually defined more broadly than charismatic leadership but there is considerable overlap between the two conceptions." This overlap is compounded by research that uses related terms such as "visionary leadership" (Sashkin, 1986, 1988; Westley & Mintzberg,

1989), "magic leadership" (Nadler & Tushman, 1989b), and "transferential leadership" (Pauchant, 1991). Bryman (1992, pp. 104-113) provides a good overview of the difference between transformational and charismatic leadership. In this section we first look at some of the major writings on charismatic leadership and then work at examining transformational leadership.

Charismatic Leadership

The notion of charisma has been around for a long time but it is Weber, in his book *Economy and society* (1968), who is most often credited with first using the term to describe leadership in an organizational setting. Focusing primarily on religious groups and primitive tribes Weber saw leaders as gaining authority from their charisma. Charisma for Weber was "a certain quality of an individual personality by virtue of which he is considered extraordinary and treated as endowed with supernatural, superhuman, or at least specifically exceptional powers or qualities. These are such as not to be accessible to the ordinary person, but are regarded as of divine origin or as exemplary and on the basis of them the individual concerned is treated as a leader" (1968, p. 241).

Despite Weber's early writings on charisma and its links to leadership it was not until the late 1970s and early 1980s that organizational/management researchers started to embrace the concept and examine it in any systematic way (Etzioni, 1961 and Oberg, 1972 are two notable exceptions).

House's Research on Charismatic Leadership

House's (1977) work represents one of the first and in many ways most substantive attempts to understand charismatic leadership. His theory seeks to explain the characteristics of charismatic leaders and their behaviors. It is suggested that charismatic leaders can be distinguished from other leaders in that they are able to establish "follower trust in the correctness of the leader's beliefs, similarity of follower's beliefs to those of the leader, unquestioning acceptance of the leader, affection for the leader, willing obedience to the leader, identification with and emulation of the leader, emotional involvement of the follower in the mission, heightened goals of the follower, and the feeling on the part of followers that they will be able to accomplish, or contribute to the accomplishment of, the mission" (p. 191). House also stresses that charismatic leaders are likely to have self-confidence, a strong conviction

about their own ideals and beliefs, and a desire for the power to be able to influence others.

A charismatic leader acts as a role model for followers, so that they will identify with the leader's values and beliefs. Leaders also engage in image-building to look competent and successful in the eyes of their followers. They present ideological goals which represent the types of values and beliefs they would like followers to share. There are high expectations set for followers to aspire to and charismatic leaders support and show confidence in their followers. Finally, charismatic leaders try to arouse motives relevant to the group's mission—the need to overcome a common foe, the need for excellence, affiliation, power, and the like. Phil Knight's desire to overcome Adidas and push it into second place in the athletic footwear market is an example of this type of motive.

Conger's Theory of Charismatic Leadership

Conger's initial work on charismatic leadership was conducted with Kanungo (Conger & Kanungo, 1987; 1988). Their approach is based on the idea that charisma is an attributional phenomenon. Leaders are attributed certain charismatic qualities by their followers. The focus of their research was to identify the types of leader behavior that result in these attributions.

Central to the attributional process is the creation, by the leader, of an "idealized goal" or vision that deviates sufficiently from the existing condition of the organization. Leaders are also seen as charismatic if they involve themselves in activities that call for self-sacrifice and high personal risk to achieve the vision they have created. They use unconventional means to achieve their vision and are able to assess environmental opportunities and threats realistically. Using this information they have to time the strategies they employ appropriately to help realize their vision. This type of leader is most likely to come to the fore when an organization is in a crisis, although crisis is not necessarily a precondition for their emergence. These people are confident in their ability to lead; they make great use of their personal power, for example, their expert knowledge, rather than their positional power, to commit others to their vision.

The concepts put forward by Conger and Kanungo (1987, 1988) were extended by Conger in his 1989 book *The charismatic leader: Behind the mystique of exceptional leadership*. Conger essentially viewed the process of attribution that resulted in some individuals becoming seen as charismatic leaders as a series of stages. In the first stage, the leader senses opportunity and formulates a vision. The vision is designed to bring people in the organization together; it may be a result of a dissatisfaction with the existing situation and can be a vehicle by which to challenge the status quo. The second stage involves the leader in articulating the vision. The third stage requires the charismatic leader to build trust in the vision; he or she must be seen as having the ability to lead the organization toward achieving the vision. An emphasis on previous accomplishments and shared values with subordinates can help in building this trust. The final stage involves achieving the vision. Subordinates are empowered so that they feel they can help achieve the lofty goals that have been set. Achieving success along the way is an important factor at this stage.

Transformational Leadership

In part research on charismatic leadership in organizations has been a result of the growing interest in transformational leadership. In this section we look at the work of three of the best-known writers on transformational leadership.

Burns

The central focus of Burns' work is to contrast transformational leadership with what he refers to as transactional leadership. Transactional leadership involves the leader in some form of transaction with subordinates. Appealing to their self-interest, transactional leaders exchange pay or prestige for a subordinate's compliance with their orders. However, there is no enduring bond between either of the two parties. A relationship exists between leader and followers, but it does not unite the "leaders and followers together in a mutual and continuing pursuit of a higher purpose" (Burns, 1978, p. 20).

In contrast, transformational leadership involves "leaders and followers rais[ing] one another to higher levels of motivation and morality" (Burns, 1978, p. 20). Transformational leaders work by appealing to the ideals and values of subordinates They seek to unite subordinates as they work toward a common purpose. Transformational leaders pay attention to and are sensitive to the needs of their subordinates as well as their own needs. They must appeal to the whole person and their total range of higher-level needs such as justice and equality. Lower-level emotions such as fear and greed have no place in transformational leadership.

The bulk of the early work on leadership focused on transactional leaders.

Bass

Much of the research conducted on Burns' notion of transformational leadership has been carried out by Bass and his associates (Avolio & Gibbons, 1988; Avolio & Yammarino, 1990; Bass, 1985, 1990b; Bass & Avolio, 1989, 1990a, 1990b, 1990c; Hater & Bass, 1988; Yammarino & Bass, 1990). Unlike Burns, who saw transformational and transactional leadership as being ends of a continuum, Bass sees them as separate; a leader can be both transformational and transactional (Bryman, 1992). Bass would classify leaders like Adolph Hitler and David Koresh as transformational, whereas for Burns these people, because they relied heavily on emotions such as fear, are not transformational.

Bass suggests that transformational leaders enhance their subordinates' confidence and increase awareness of selected goals and how they may be obtained. They also inspire subordinates to look beyond their own self-interests and seek to satisfy such higher-level needs as self-actualization. For Bass, transformational leaders may be charismatic; they provide personal attention to the needs of subordinates, they seek to empower them, and they provide them with a constant flow of new ideas about ways to operate.

To determine the extent to which leaders exhibit the characteristics of transformational and transactional leadership, Bass and his associates developed the Multifactor Leadership Questionnaire (MLQ). The most common version of this instrument contains 70 items asking respondents to describe the behavior of a leader in seven areas of leadership (Bass & Avolio, 1990b):

- *Charismatic leadership*: the degree to which the leader is seen as charismatic
- *Inspirational leadership*: the extent to which a leader inspires subordinates
- *Individual consideration*: how much a leader gives personal attention to subordinates
- *Intellectual stimulation*: the way in which the leader promotes new ideas and challenges old ways of operating
- *Contingent rewards*: the way in which a leader rewards subordinates for following specific directions
- *Management by expectation*: how leaders take action when irregularities occur
- *Laissez-faire*: the extent to which the leader abdicates his leadership role

The first four of these measurements assess transformational leadership behaviors, contingent rewards and management by exception assess transactional leadership, and laissez-faire is a type of non-leadership assessment. The scores from the MLQ are related to organizational outcome measures such as leader effectiveness, subordinate satisfaction, and subordinate motivation. The four transformational qualities, along with contingent rewards, are more likely to be associated with positive outcomes than management by expectation and laissez-faire.

Tichy and Devanna

In their 1986 book *The transformational leader*, Tichy and Devanna carried out a study of 12 chief executive officers. The focus of the study was to try to determine how those leaders went about transforming their organizations to meet the demands of a changing marketplace. With one exception, data were collected through interviews with the CEO and sometimes other members of the organization. Based on these interviews, Tichy and Devanna identified a three-stage process that takes place when leaders transform organizations.

First, the transformational leader must recognize a need to revitalize and change the organization. This recognition can be difficult, particularly when environmental changes are occurring gradually. The leader needs to convince other important people in the organization of the need for change. Tichy and Devanna suggest a number of strategies to help key organizational members recognize the need for change: encouraging people to look objectively at the organization and challenge the status quo, encouraging people from the organization to visit other organizations to see how they are managed and operated, evaluating organizational performance against that of competitors (not indicators from previous years), and creating an external network of contacts who can provide an objective assessment of the organization's performance. Once people recognize the need for change, the leader needs to establish what changes are necessary, and manage the transition process. Members of the organization will have to let go of existing values and beliefs and accept new ones, and there may be a change in the authority structure of the organization. The leader's job is to help people feel positive and confident about the transition.

One way of helping people feel better about the future is to create a vision of the way they want things to be. Vision is Tichy and Devanna's second stage. The vision cannot be one individual's ideas but must be the product of a diverse group of organization members. It must paint a picture of the organization sufficiently attractive to make people comfortable with the change process. The vision must provide a central purpose and a source of self-esteem for organizational members. The central component of the vision is the mission statement, which provides direction for organization members and reflects the values found in the vision. Following the establishment of a vision and a mission statement, more specific decisions have to be made, about the allocation of rewards, the authority structure of the organization, and how senior members of the organization will be selected. Members of the organization must be informed about the benefits the vision will have for them and they must be made to feel a part of the implementation process.

The final stage of the transformational process involves what Tichy and Devanna refer to as institutionalizing the vision. A new group of people committed to the vision may be brought on board, and new structures, strategies, and policies put in place. These changes can be facilitated through such activities as planning workshops, conducting team-building exercises, establishing new positions, changing the reward structure of the organization, and redesigning appraisal systems.

In looking at each of the three phases, Tichy and Devanna (1986) identified a number of characteristics that distinguish transformational leaders from transactional leaders. Transformational leaders are visionaries who see themselves as change agents; they take risks, they believe in the people in the organizations, they articulate the core values that direct the organization, they learn from experience, and they handle the complexity and uncertainty that change brings.

Ulrich (1987b) extends Tichy and Devanna's (1986) work and applies it to the field of sport management. He suggests a six-stage process that sport managers need to adopt if they are to function as transformational leaders: creating and communicating the need for change, overcoming resistance to change, making personal commitment and sacrifices for change, articulating a vision, generating commitment to the vision, and institutionalizing the vision. Ulrich makes a number of suggestions as to how sport managers can operationalize these functions.

The Critique of Leadership and Some Suggestions for Leadership Research in Sport Management

As noted at the beginning of this chapter, it is impossible to conduct a comprehensive review of all the literature on the subject of leadership in a textbook of this nature. However, in the final section, a brief overview of some of the strengths and weaknesses of leadership research is presented. Some suggestions are then made about the direction future leadership studies in the field of sport management could take.

The Critique of Leadership

As Pettigrew (1987) points out, for those scholars interested in the study of leadership, reviews of the field conducted throughout the past 20 years do not make comfortable reading. Stogdill (1974, p. vii) noted that "the endless accumulation of empirical data has not produced an integrated understanding of leadership." Miner (1975) even suggested that the concept of leadership should be abandoned, and Bass (1985) bemoaned the narrow and repetitive focus of leadership research focusing on such limited concepts as directive versus participative leadership and initiation versus consideration. Bryman (1986) describes past research as disappointing and suggests that future leadership researchers may be "clutching at straws." More recently Leavy and Wilson (1994) have criticized leadership research for being overly voluntaristic, that is, focusing too much on the actions of a single individual, and failing to consider the contextual pressures that shape leaders' actions. However, it is perhaps Kets de Vries (1994, p. 73) who sums up these concerns the best: "When we plunge into the organizational literature on leadership we quickly become lost in a labyrinth: There are endless definitions, countless articles, and never-ending polemics. As far as leadership studies go, it seems that more and more has been studied about less and less, to end up ironically with a group of researchers studying everything about nothing."

What, then, are the problems with leadership research and what types of studies should we in sport management be undertaking? One of the first problems is the failure of leadership research to produce conclusive findings; many of the complaints just cited refer to this shortcoming. While to a certain extent researchers have been able to describe the traits and behaviors that leaders possess, rarely have they been able to explain where these qualities come from, how they are developed, and why some leaders are successful when others fail. The literature has made no attempt to explain why leaders are described as effective at certain times and ineffective at others—a situation that could obviously be applied to the myriad of coaches and general managers who are "visionaries" when they win and buffoons when they lose!

Writing about leadership and organizational performance, Pfeffer (1977a) has suggested that leadership has become a repository for much of the unexplained variance. Lieberson and O'Conner (1972) found little support for the ability of leaders to influence performance; to be sure, studies of executive succession, many of which have been conducted on sport organizations, have produced inconclusive results.

Another major critique of leadership research is its failure to study leaders actually doing their jobs. Pettigrew (1987, p. 652) suggests some improvements:

> Approaches to leadership should be less short-range and atomistic—less reductionist. Leaders should be studied in natural settings using observational and other qualitative methodologies. Leadership should be examined through the holistic study of actual behavior rather than breaking down the activities of leaders and the responses of followers into categories of independent and dependent variables.

Certainly much of the leadership research in the field of sport management has been bivariate in nature. There has been no systematic attempt to study what it is leaders in sport organizations actually do and how they operate.

Leadership research should also become less reductionist in nature. Both Leavy and Wilson (1994) and Whittington (1993a) have criticized the leadership literature for focusing too much on individuals and not paying enough attention to the history and context of the organizations in which leaders operate. Similarly, Lieberson and O'Conner (1972, p. 29) suggest that "in emphasizing the effect of leadership [on organizational performance] we may be overlooking far more powerful environmental influences." Tied to this criticism is the tendency, particularly in the more recent work on charismatic and transformational leadership, to view leaders as men, (and as Whittington, 1993b, p. 45 notes "men they almost always are") heroes who ride in on white horses to rescue the organization in distress.

Bennis and Nanus's (1985, p. 218) effusive statement exemplifies this deification of leaders:

> Leadership is "causative," meaning that leadership can invent and create institutions that can empower employees to satisfy their needs. Leadership is morally purposeful and elevating, which means, if nothing else, that leaders can, through deploying their talents, choose purposes and visions that are based on the key values of the work force and create the social architecture that supports them. Finally, leadership can move followers to higher degrees of consciousness, such as liberty, freedom, justice, and self-actualization.

As Pettigrew (1987, p. 653) cryptically notes, this view is "hard to take"! Such attributions of godlike qualities are found in much of the research on this type of leadership.

A final critique of the writing on leadership is the inherent gender bias in this type of research. Women are rarely used as examples of great leaders, either in the general management literature or the sport management literature. This issue is addressed more fully in the suggestions for future research outlined below.

Some Suggestions for Leadership Research in Sport Management

While there is considerable potential for many types of different research on leaders in the field of sport management, here we look briefly at four possible areas of study: leadership and organizational change, leadership and strategy, leadership and gender, and leadership and organizational culture.

Leadership and Organizational Change

Linking leadership and organizational change is in many ways an obvious area for study. Leaders, after all, are supposed to direct and manage change in organizations. They mediate between the internal forces that promote stability and the external pressures that demand change if the organization is going to remain competitive. Despite these obvious linkages there has been little attempt to look at the relationship between leadership and change within the broader field of organization studies, and even less in the field of sport management. The exception is the work of Tushman and his colleagues (Nadler & Tushman, 1990; Tushman & Romanelli, 1985; Tushman, Virany, & Romanelli, 1986). In their 1985 and 1986 articles Tushman and his colleagues argue that organizations change by going through convergent periods or by experiencing what are called strategic reorientations or recreations. Convergent periods are times when the organization exhibits incremental change, or what Miller and Friesen (1984) call evolutionary change. During these relatively long periods, organizations elaborate on their strategic focus. In contrast, strategic reorientations, or recreations, may involve changes in strategy, power, and structure, and are triggered by contextual pressures (Tushman & Romanelli, 1985). Different types of leadership are required in convergent periods from those required in recreations: "During convergent periods executive leadership emphasizes symbolic activities and incremental change, while during recreations, executive leadership engages in major substantive as well as symbolic activities. Beyond these substantive and symbolic behaviors, executive leadership must also choose to initiate recreations" (Tushman & Romanelli, 1985, p. 214). The paradox for leaders, as Tushman and Romanelli go on to argue is to "encourage inertial forces during convergent periods" and, when necessary, to "initiate and implement reorientations" (p. 214).

In their later work Nadler and Tushman (1990) extend these ideas to deal with the notion of charismatic leadership. They suggest that in large-scale changes, leaders in the senior management team must drive the change process. While charismatic leadership is important in these kinds of changes, it is not enough on its own. "Charismatic leadership must be bolstered by instrumental leadership; [leaders must] build strong teams, systems, and management processes to leverage and add substance to [their] vision and energy" (Nadler & Tushman, 1990, p. 94). They must also work to institutionalize change at all levels of the management system.

In the field of sport management, Slack and Hinings (1992) and Macintosh and Whitson (1990) have stressed the importance of transformational leaders in the change process in national-level sport organizations. As Slack and Hinings (1992, p. 128) point out, "As well as creating a vision, transformational leaders must mobilize commitment to change. The creation of management teams, the setting of goals, and volunteer involvement through committees . . . were all indications of steps transformational leaders were taking in [national sport organizations] to generate commitment to change." If carried out across different sectors of the sport industry, further research extending some of these ideas about the intersection of leadership and change would help broaden our knowledge about leadership and the important roles leaders play in the change process.

Leadership and Strategy

While strategy and leadership are two central topics in the study of organizations, little consideration has been given to how these concepts are related. For some, leadership is merely the personification of an organization's strategy. However, as Leavy and Wilson (1994, p. 2) note, "the leader is just one important element in . . . strategy formulation. History and context are the other two." The interactions of these three factors in shaping an organization's strategy and growth are important considerations to pursue in sport management; researchers in our field have never empirically examined those interactions when trying to understand sport organizations. Detailed case studies that examined sport managers as leaders would help show how contextual features have helped shape their actions. In addition to helping bring social, political, and economic factors into an understanding of leadership choices, work of this nature would also help us understand the symbolic nature of leadership, because it would direct our attention to whether the role of the leader is in fact substantive or merely symbolic. Finally, as Leavy and Wilson (1994, p. 186) point out, research that incorporated history and context with the study of leadership would help us "avoid the danger of developing an overly heroic and somewhat mythological view of these rare and important individuals."

The actions of sport leaders like Peter Ueberroth, Marvin Miller, Sylvia Rempel, and David Stern could all be studied by linking their actions to the historical conditions of their respective organizations and the contexts in which they operate. This type of research would help show how strategy formulation is at times shaped by the autonomous choices made by individual leaders, but in other instances is more a product of opportunities and threats in an organization's context. Such studies would also help demonstrate how leaders respond to contextual pressures and, as such, why sometimes they may be effective and at other times they fail.

Leadership and Gender

Czarniawska-Joerges and Wolff (1991) suggest that the concept of leader has become culturally defined as an inherently masculine role. Calas and Smircich

(1991, p. 567) suggest the leadership literature "functions as a seductive game" and is overtly sexual. Both sets of researchers draw attention to the gender biases that exist in much of the research and writing about leadership. Studies of leadership have in fact shown that men emerge as leaders more frequently than women (Carbonell, 1984). This is certainly true in the field of sport management where women are very much underrepresented in leadership positions (Bryson, 1987; Fasting, 1987; Hall, Cullen, & Slack, 1989; White & Brackenridge, 1985). Women's underrepresentation in leadership positions has been attributed in the general field of organizational studies to the internal and external barriers that women face in progressing to the senior levels of an organization (Cockburn, 1991; Powell, 1993; Terborg, 1977; Wentworth & Anderson, 1984). Hall, Cullen, and Slack (1989) have identified the presence of similar barriers in sport organizations.

Despite the obvious lack of women in leadership positions in sport organizations, there has been little attempt within our field to look at the gendered nature of leadership in sport. Studies that have taken account of gender are restricted to examining the competencies and characteristics of female leaders, usually coaches (Klonsky, 1991; Weiss, Barber, Sisley, & Ebbeck, 1991), or looking at the relative distribution of male and female coaches (Lovett & Lowry, 1988). There is considerable potential for work relating gender to leadership in sport management.

Qualitative studies of the careers of women who are leaders in sport organizations could help shed light on the barriers these people have faced as they have risen to the senior levels of their organizations. Although research (Brenner, Tomkiewicz, & Schein, 1989) shows that the barriers to the emergence of female leaders are gradually being lowered, women who aspire to these positions still experience considerable constraints (Alimo-Metcalfe, 1994). Studies helping to identify these barriers would provide a basis for the removal of these limitations on women's career progress in our field. Useful and interesting work could also be carried out on the comparative leadership styles of women and men. While some studies have shown there are few if any differences between the sexes (Bartol, 1978; Ferber, Huber, & Spitze, 1979; Reif, Newstrom, & Monczka, 1975), others (Denmark, 1977; Muldrow & Bayton, 1979) have found differences. There has been no work within sport management that has looked at this issue.

Another possible area for work on gender and leadership in sport organizations is suggested by Hall, Cullen, and Slack (1989), who point out that in order to understand the gender structuring of sport organizations we need to look at issues of power and sexuality. Sexuality has, in recent years, become an increased focus of attention for organizational researchers. Given Calas and Smircich's (1991) assertion that the leadership literature is overtly sexual, studies of sexuality and leadership in sport organizations could produce useful insights into an area that is under-researched in our field.

Leadership and Organizational Culture

As we saw in chapter 14, over the past 15 years, the concept of organizational culture has received increased attention from organizational theorists. Leaders play an important role in creating and transmitting an organization's culture. Founders, as leaders, are important in shaping culture because, as Schein (1992, p. 211) points out, they "not only choose the basic mission and the environmental context in which the new group will operate, but they choose the group members and bias the original responses that the group makes in its efforts to succeed in its environment and to integrate itself."

Leaders also play a role in embedding and transmitting the culture of an organization. As we saw in chapter 14, what leaders pay attention to, measure, and control; how they react to critical incidents and crises; how they allocate resources; how they distribute rewards; and the criteria they use for recruitment and promotion are all actions that serve to communicate an organization's culture to its employees.

At different stages of an organization's life cycle, the leader's role in managing culture takes on different forms. In its early years culture is a force for growth; it needs to be developed and clearly articulated. Later on, as diverse subcultures form within an organization, the leader is faced with managing these subcultures by using the techniques outlined previously. When an organization reaches maturity, its culture can keep it operating smoothly, but if it is not appropriate for the situation in which the organization finds itself, it can become dysfunctional. As such, a major internal upheaval or external crisis may be needed to change the culture to a more appropriate one. The leader plays an important role in managing this process.

The significant links between organizational culture and leadership, as can be seen, present considerable potential for work in this area. However, even within the general field of management there has been relatively little research in this area. In the field of sport management only Weese's (1995a) study

has examined this interrelationship. Using a sample made up of managers from Big Ten and Mid-American athletic conference campus recreation programs, Weese's work showed that managers who scored high as transformational leaders directed programs with stronger organizational cultures and were more involved in culture-building activities. Other studies could be conducted that look at how leaders construct organizational culture, how the roles of leadership and culture change over time, and how leaders help transmit culture to new members of an organization.

Summary and Conclusions

Some researchers have suggested that leadership is a major factor in producing an effective organization (Peters & Waterman, 1982); others have been less optimistic (Pfeffer, 1977a). While there has certainly been extensive study of the topic of leadership within the organizational literature, the question remains, does it tell us anything? McCall and Lombardo (1978, p. 3) suggest about the leadership literature that "the number of unintegrated models, theories, prescriptions, and conceptual schemes . . . is mind boggling [but] much of [it] is fragmentary, trivial, unrealistic, or dull."

In many ways the same could be said of the leadership literature in sport management. While Paton (1987) was probably correct in his assessment of the area—that it is the most researched topic in our field—the majority of these studies have been doctoral dissertations or master's theses. Only a few have ever been published and many of those have used coaches, not managers, as their sample. There is very little work on the leadership of sport managers.

In this final chapter we have reviewed the major theoretical perspectives on leadership. Where possible, examples from sport management have been used to show the type of studies conducted in our field. Some of the criticisms of leadership research were also examined and four potentially fruitful areas for future research were briefly outlined. While not the only areas for possible study, work on the topics suggested would help link leadership to other organizational phenomena and, given the often "abstracted" nature of leadership studies, would be a welcome addition to the literature. Also, studies of the type outlined would challenge the highly voluntaristic and overly rational conceptions of leadership that pervade the field. While we should retain a healthy skepticism about the ability of leaders as sole creators of an organization's structure and processes, we cannot ignore the role that these senior members of an organization play in integrating and directing a sport organization.

Key Concepts

Leadership traits	Assessment center approach
Managerial competencies	Style (behavioral) approach
LBDQ	Consideration
Initiating structure	Employee-centered
Production-centered	Managerial leadership
Peer leadership	Contingency (situational) approach
Path-goal theory	Supportive leadership
Instrumental leadership	Participative leadership
Achievement leadership	Situational leadership theory
Task behavior	Relationship behavior
Subordinate maturity	Developmental interventions
Least preferred coworker	Charismatic leadership
Transformational leadership	Transactional leadership

Review Questions

1. Think of the leaders of some sport organizations that you know. Can you identify traits they possess that distinguish them from nonleaders?

2. Discuss how useful you think tests such as those used in the assessment center approach are for identifying the leadership abilities of managers.

3. Do you think it is possible for leaders who score high on consideration to also score high on initiating structure?

4. How could factors such as group performance and employee satisfaction influence a manager's leadership style?

5. How would situational variables influence leadership practices in a sport medicine clinic? In a sports equipment production company?

6. Pick a situation from a sport organization where you think work would be tedious and low in autonomy. How would supportive leadership influence subordinates?

7. Discuss how subordinate maturity would influence the amount of task behavior and relationship behavior a leader would have to exhibit.

8. What are the similarities and differences between the path-goal approach to leadership, Hersey and Blanchard's situational leadership theory, and Fiedler's work?

9. What are the major differences between charismatic and transformational leadership?

10. Some researchers have talked about "the dark side of charisma." What do you think this is and how is this notion relevant to studies of leadership?

11. Those who subscribe to the charismatic and transformational theories of leadership put great emphasis on the creation of a vision as a means of focusing organizational members on a common goal. However, the process of creating and implementing a vision can actually bring members into conflict. Discuss how you think this occurs.

12. Discuss the criticisms that have been made about leadership research. Do you think these criticisms are valid?

13. What types of studies could you design to examine the role that leadership plays in the process of organizational change?

14. What steps could be taken in a sport organization to place more women in leadership positions?

15. Leaders are often attributed as being a major factor in creating an organization's culture. Given what you have read about culture do you think this is an accurate statement?

Suggestions for Further Reading

Students interested in furthering their knowledge in the area of leadership are advised to look at the original writings of the key theorists whose works are outlined in this chapter. However, of these, Burn's (1978) book *Leadership*, and Bryman's two texts *Leadership and organizations* (1986) and *Charisma and leadership in organizations* (1992) offer the most substantive analysis of the subject. McCall and Lombardo's (1978) *Leadership: Where else can we go?* is a collection of essays by leading organizational theorists, people who have not necessarily focused on the topic of leadership, who attempt to answer the question in the book's title.

For more about the suggested research areas outlined at the end of the chapter, Leavy and Wilson's (1994) *Strategy and leadership* is a good start for the first topic area. In terms of work on leadership and change, Pettigrew's (1987) *Journal of Management Studies* article, "Context and action in the transformation of the firm," would be helpful. So, too,

would Hendry and Johnson's (1993) book *Strategic thinking: Leadership and the management of change*. In terms of leadership and gender, Calas and Smircich's (1991) article "Voicing seduction to silence leadership" is a difficult but interesting read. Alimo-Metcalfe's (1994) strangely titled "Waiting for fish to grow feet!" is also helpful, as is Rosener's (1990) more practical *Harvard Business Review* article, "Ways women lead." For those interested in culture and leadership Schein's (1985) *Organizational culture and leadership* is a must. Also interesting is Bass and Avolio's (1990b) article "Transformational leadership and organizational culture." The most substantive body of work on leadership in the field of sport management has been produced by Chelladurai and his colleagues (Chelladurai & Carron, 1983; Chelladurai & Saleh, 1978, 1980; Chelladurai et al., 1987b). However, much of this work focuses on coaches, not people in managerial positions in sport organizations.

Case for Analysis

Owner Mannie Jackson Is Set to Lead Globetrotters to Their Former Glory

As the lights dim at Madison Square Garden, silence settles over the audience. Suddenly the finger-popping melody of *Sweet Georgia Brown* fills the air—and the crowd erupts. Through a curtain of smoke and lasers, the Harlem Globetrotters jog onto the court, zipping basketballs to each other. But as the team warms up, one man is eyeing their entrance with the intensity of an over-budget Hollywood director.

Dressed in a dark double-breasted suit, Globetrotter owner Mannie Jackson strides out and takes a seat on the bench. While the crowd roars approval of the team's "Magic Circle," a dazzling display of ball-handling, Jackson scribbles notes on a pad.

Occasionally he whispers to his assistant or beckons a player for some last-minute strategizing. At one point, he shakes his head at center "Sweet Lou" Dunbar, who has missed several of his patented pregame hook shots from half-court. "I've told him that if he misses three straight, he should just walk away," Jackson says.

Three decades ago, that might well have been Jackson out there. In the 1960s, he was a Globetrotter point guard known for his poetic passes and radar-accurate jumpers. But in 1968, he traded in his high-tops and joined Minneapolis-based Honeywell Inc., where he is currently senior vice president heading the company's $2.3 billion International and Home

Building Control division. Last year, Jackson bought the Globetrotters from Minneapolis-based International Broadcasting Corp., which went into Chapter 11 in 1991. Nostalgia? Maybe a touch. But Jackson is a hard-nosed businessman who sees himself as leading the team to its former glory. His vision is to improve the team's image, fix the infrastructure, and drive value.

Years of languishing under a string of owners have left the 68-year-old Los Angeles-based Globetrotters as outdated as an underhand free throw. While Jackson declines to discuss revenues, he maintains that the team has been profitable over the years, its biggest strength being strong name recognition in the 80 U.S. and 50 foreign cities it hits each year. However, its various owners treated the team as a cash cow rather than a business to invest in. Until now, that is. When International Broadcasting operated under Chapter 11, the Globetrotters' tour schedule was cut in half. With just one of its two squads on the road, attendance fell off by two-thirds in 1991 and 1992. "While the Globetrotters is a great name, the product had become shopworn and frayed," says Dirck Post, a senior vice president at secured creditor National Westminster Bank USA (NatWest), and a member of the Globetrotters board. "It needed someone to juice it up."

In June 1993, NatWest sold 80 percent of the Globetrotters to Jackson and his partner, Dennis Mathisen, a Minneapolis-based businessman, for $6 million. Jackson and Mathisen plan to buy NatWest's remaining 20-percent stake in three or four years. Jackson says revenues have doubled over the past year under his leadership, and that operating profits, which are currently 10 percent of revenues, are expected to increase to 25 percent in two years. The team will upgrade its roster and its show in an effort to forge new marketing agreements, which Jackson wants to account for 50 percent of revenues instead of the current 20 percent. Says Jackson: "The Globetrotters don't need a makeover. . . . All we need is a face-lift."

So Jackson is nipping and tucking the Los Angeles staff he inherited, mostly by phone and fax from Minneapolis. Honeywell still comes first. The Globetrotters are a labor of love—and lots of work to boot. Training camp this year was more rigorous than ever. Jackson cut 30 percent of the old roster and brought in a bunch of college grads. The cagers also had a week of media training. "I want a team of players who are comfortable with kids or giving presentations in boardrooms," says Jackson.

Born in Edwardsville, Illinois, Jackson was an honor student and star athlete at the University of Illinois. One day Globetrotter founder Abe Saperstein came-a courtin' and signed up the 6 foot-2 inch Jackson. He played from 1962 to 1964, then moved to the National Industrial Basketball League. In 1966, he rejoined the Globetrotters. After a year, he tried out for a couple of NBA teams—but didn't make the cut. In 1968, he took a job with Honeywell as an equity employment officer.

The question now is whether Jackson can impose a business discipline on the Globetrotters. At the Garden, three seconds remain on the clock in the game with the full-time rival Washington Generals. "Sweet Lou" dribbles to half-court and prepares for one last hook. Jackson grimaces, but Dunbar is determined and launches the shot just before the buzzer. The ball seems to hang in the air forever. When it comes down, the crowd is on its feet. Nothin' but net.

Adapted, by permission, from R. Stodghill, March 28, 1994, Putting the Globetrotters back on the map: Owner and alumnus Mannie Jackson is out to restore the magic, *Business Week*, 178-179.

Questions

1. How could the different theoretical approaches outlined in this chapter help you understand Mannie Jackson as a leader?

2. What would you do if you were the one trying to lead the Globetrotters back to their former glory?

3. What contextual factors will influence the type of leadership that Jackson employs with the Globetrotters?

Bibliography

Abrams, B. (1986, January 23). Sports boss: adidas makes friends, then strikes deals that move sneakers. *Wall Street Journal*, pp. 1, 15.

Adams, M.J. (1987, July). A welcome wave hits. *Stores*, pp. 27-35.

Adizes, I. (1979). Organizational passages: Diagnosing and treating life cycle problems of organizations. *Organizational Dynamics, 8*, 3-25.

Adler, P. (1986). New technologies, new skills. *California Management Review, 29*, 9-28.

Adler, P. (1988). Managing flexible automation. *California Management Review, 30*, 234-250.

Agarwal, N.C., Alon, A., Bullock, K.M., Dimick, D.E., Jain, H.C., McPherson, D.L., Murray, V.V., Robertson, D.M., Saunders, G.S., Wallace, J.T., & Wheeler, D.J. (Eds.) (1983). *Human resources in Canada*. Scarborough, ON: Prentice Hall Canada.

Aldrich, H.E. (1972a). Reply to Hilton: Seduced and abandoned. *Administrative Science Quarterly, 17*, 55-57.

Aldrich, H.E. (1972b). Technology and organization structure: A re-examination of the findings of the Aston group. *Administrative Science Quarterly, 17*, 26-43.

Aldrich, H.E. (1975). Reaction to Donaldson's note. *Administrative Science Quarterly, 20*, 457-460.

Aldrich, H.E. (1979). *Organizations and environments*. Englewood Cliffs, NJ: Prentice Hall.

Aldrich, H.E., & Herker, D. (1977). Boundary spanning roles and organization structure. *Academy of Management Review, 2*, 217-230.

Aldrich, H.E., McKelvey, B., & Ulrich, D. (1984). Design strategy from the population perspective. *Journal of Management, 10*, 67-86.

Alimo-Metcalfe, B. (1994). Waiting for fish to grow feet!: Removing organizational barriers to women's entry into leadership positions. In M. Tanton (Ed.), *Women in Management* (pp. 27-45). London: Routledge & Kegan Paul.

Allen, M.P., Panian, S.K., & Lotz, R.E. (1979). Managerial succession and organizational performance: A recalcitrant problem revisited. *Administrative Science Quarterly, 24*, 167-180.

Allen, R.W., Madison, D.L., Porter, L.W., Renwick, P.A., & Mayes, B.T. (1979). Organizational politics: Tactics and characteristics of its actors. *California Management Review, 22*, 77-83.

Amis, J., Slack, T., & Berrett, T. (1995). The structural antecedents of conflict in national sport organizations. *Leisure Studies, 14*, 1-16.

Andler, E.C. (1976, January). Preplanned question areas for efficient interviewing. *Personnel Journal, 55*, 8-10.

Andreu, R., & Corominas, A. (1989). SUCCCES92: A DSS for scheduling the Olympic Games. *Interfaces, 19*, 1-12.

Archer, E.A. (1980). How to make a business decision: An analysis of theory and practice. *Management Review, 69*, 54-61.

Argyris, C. (1964). *Integrating the individual and the organization*. New York: Wiley.

Argyris, C. (1972). *The applicability of organizational sociology*. London: Cambridge University Press.

Aris, S. (1990). *Sportsbiz: Inside the sports business*. London: Hutchinson.

Arogyaswamy, B., & Byles, C.M. (1987). Organizational culture: Internal and external fits. *Journal of Management, 13*, 647-659.

Aronson, M. (1993, June). He creates winners. *Success*, pp. 34-38.

Arthur, C. (1989, October). Soccer cards' scheme. *Business*, pp. 200-202.

Arvey, R.D. (1979) *Fairness in selecting employees*. Reading, MA: Addison-Wesley.

Astley, W.G., & Sachdeva, P.S. (1984). Structural sources of interorganizational power: A theoretical synthesis. *Academy of Management Review, 9*, 104-113.

Auf de Maur, N. (1976). *The billion-dollar game*. Toronto: James Lorimer.

Avolio, B.J., & Gibbons, T.C. (1988). Developing transformational leaders: A life span approach. In J.A. Conger & R.N. Kanungo (Eds.), *Charismatic leadership: The elusive factor in organizational effectiveness* (pp. 276-308). San Francisco: Jossey-Bass.

Avolio, B.J., & Yammarino, F.J. (1990). Operationalizing charismatic leadership using a levels of analysis framework. *Leadership Quarterly, 1*, 193-208.

Ayoubi, Z.M. (1981). Technology, size, and organization structure in a developing country:

Jordan. In D.J. Hickson & C.J. McMillan (Eds.), *Organization and nation: The Aston program* (pp. 95-114). Westmead, Hampshire: Gower.

Azumi, K., & McMillan, C.J. (1981). Management strategy and organization structure: A Japanese comparative study. In D.J. Hickson & C.J. McMillan (Eds.), *Organization and nation: The Aston program* (pp. 155-172). Westmead, Hampshire: Gower.

Bachrach, P., & Baratz, M.S. (1962). The two faces of power. *American Political Science Review, 56*, 947-952.

Badran, M., & Hinings, C.R. (1981). Strategies of administrative control and contextual constraints in a less developed country: The case of Egyptian public enterprise. *Organization Studies, 2*, 3-21.

Bagley, M. (1975). Leadership effectiveness contingency model: Implications. In E.F. Zeigler & M.J. Spaeth (Eds.), *Administrative Theory and Practice in Physical Education and Athletics* (pp. 98-112). Englewood Cliffs, NJ: Prentice Hall.

Ballard, S. (1989, February 20). A show that has all the goods. *Sports Illustrated*, pp. 37-40.

Ballinger, J. (1993). The new free-trade heel: Nike jumps on the backs of Asian workers. In R.M. Jackson (Ed.), *Global Issues 93/94* (9th ed.) (pp. 130-131). Guilford, CT: Dushkin.

Barnes, J. (1988). *Sport and the law in Canada*. Toronto: Butterworth.

Barr, G. (1985, July 1). The daunting challenge of selling the CFL. *Financial Times*, pp. 1, 18.

Bartholomew, D.J. (1978). Statistics in human resource planning. *Human Resource Planning, 1*, 67-77.

Bartol, K.M. (1978). The sex structuring of organizations: A search for possible causes. *Academy of Management Review, 3*, 805-815.

Bass, B.M. (1981). *Stogdill's handbook of leadership*. New York: Free Press.

Bass, B.M. (1985). *Leadership and performance beyond expectations*. New York: Free Press.

Bass, B.M. (1990a). *Bass and Stogdill's handbook of leadership: Theory, research, and managerial applications*. (3rd. ed.). New York: Free Press.

Bass, B.M. (1990b). From transactional to transformational leadership: Learning to share the vision. *Organizational Dynamics, 18*, 19-31.

Bass, B.M., & Avolio, B.J. (1989). Potential biases in leadership measures: How prototypes, leniency, and general satisfaction relate to ratings and rankings of transformational and transactional leadership constructs. *Educational and Psychological Measurements, 49*, 509-527.

Bass, B.M., & Avolio, B.J. (1990a). Developing transformational leadership: 1992 and beyond. *Journal of European Industrial Training, 14*, 21-27.

Bass, B.M., & Avolio, B.J. (1990b). The implications of transactional and transformational leadership, team, and organizational development. *Research in Organizational Change and Development, 4*, 231-272.

Bass, B.M., & Avolio, B.J. (1990c). Transformational leadership and organizational culture. *International Journal of Public Administration, 17*, 541-554.

Bate, P. (1995). *Strategies for cultural change*. Oxford, England: Butterworth.

Bates, D.L., & Eldredge, D.L. (1984). *Strategy and policy: Analysis, formulation, and implementation* (2nd ed.). Dubuque, IA: Brown.

Beamish, R. (1985). Sport executives and voluntary associations: A review of the literature and introduction to some theoretical issues. *Sociology of Sport Journal, 2*, 218-232.

Beason, G.M., & Belt, J.A. (1976, July). Verifying applicant's backgrounds. *Personnel Journal, 55*, 345-348.

Beaulieu, R. (1990). *New Brunswick: Tourism, recreation and heritage*. Fredericton, New Brunswick: Department of Tourism, Recreation and Heritage.

Bedeian, A.G., & Zammuto, R.F. (1991). *Organizations: Theory and design*. Chicago: Dryden Press.

Bennis, W.G., & Nanus, B. (1985). *Leaders: The strategies for taking charge*. New York: Harper & Row.

Benoit, E. (1988, September 20). Reebok's lost youth. *Financial World*, pp. 28-31.

Benson, J.K. (1977). Innovation and crisis in organizational analysis. *Sociological Quarterly, 18*, 3-16.

Bergmann, T.J., & Taylor, M.S. (1984). College recruitment: What attracts students to organizations. *Personnel, 61*, 34-46.

Bernardin, H.J., & Smith, P.C. (1981). A clarification of some issues regarding the development and use of Behaviorally Anchored Rating Scales (BARS). *Journal of Applied Psychology, 66*, 458-463.

Berrett, T., Burton, T.L., & Slack, T. (1993). Quality products, quality service: Factors leading to entrepreneurial success in the sport and leisure industry. *Leisure Studies, 12*, 93-106.

Better customer service justifies new center. (1989, March). *Modern Material Handling*, pp. 14-15.

Bettner, J. (1988, September 12). Bowling for dollars. *Forbes*, 138.

Birnbaum, P.H., & Wong, G.Y.Y. (1985). Organizational structure of multi-national banks in Hong Kong from a culture free perspective. *Administrative Science Quarterly, 30*, 262-277.

Blai, B. (1986, January). Eight steps to successful problem solving. *Supervisory Management*, pp. 7-9.

Blair, Wm. & Company (1988). *Johnson Worldwide Associates, Inc.* (Basic Report 88-018). Chicago.

Blake, R.B., & Mouton, J.S. (1984). Overcoming group warfare. *Harvard Business Review, 62*, 98-108.

Blank, S. (1986). The future workplace. *Management Review, 75*, 22-25.

Blau, P.M., Falbe, C.M., McKinley, W., & Tracy, D.K. (1976). Technology and organization in manufacturing. *Administrative Science Quarterly, 21*, 20-40.

Blau, P.M., & Schoenherr, R.A. (1971). *The structure of organizations*. New York: Basic Books.

Blau, P.M., & Scott, W.R. (1962). *Formal organizations*. San Francisco: Chandler.

Bongiorno, L., & Hof, R.D. (1993, July 12). Swinging and sweating with the boss. *Business Week*, p. 126.

Bottorff, D. (1987, June 15). Exercycle takes detour in hot pursuit of buyers who can pay steep prices. *New England Business*, pp. 54-55.

Boulton, W.R., Franklin, S.G., Lindsay, W.M., & Rue, L.W. (1982). How are companies planning now?: A survey. *Long Range Planning, 15*, 82-86.

Bourgeois, L.J., and Astley, W.G. (1979). A strategic model of organizational conduct and performance. *International Studies of Management and Organization, 6*, 40-66.

Bowen, D.E., Siehl, C., & Schneider, B. (1989). A framework for analyzing customer service orientations in manufacturing. *Academy of Management Review, 14*, 75-95.

Bowers, D.G., & Seashore, S.E. (1966). Predicting organizational effectiveness with a four-factor theory of leadership. *Administrative Science Quarterly, 11*, 238-263.

Branch, D. (1990). Athletic director leader behavior as a predictor of intercollegiate athletic organizational effectiveness. *Journal of Sport Management, 4*, 161-173.

Braus, P. (1989, October). A workout for the bottom line. *American Demographics*, pp. 34-37.

Braverman, H. (1974). *Labor and monopoly capital*. New York: Monthly Review Press.

Bray, D.W., Campbell, R.J., & Grant, D.L. (1974). *Formative years in business: A long-term AT&T study of managerial lives*. New York: Wiley.

Brenner, O.C., Tomkiewicz, J., & Schein, V. (1989). The relationship between sex-role stereotypes and requisite management characteristics revisited. *Academy of Management Journal, 32*, 662-669.

Brooke, M.Z. (1984). *Centralization and autonomy*. London: Holt, Rinehart & Winston.

Brown, M.C. (1982). Administrative succession and organizational performance: The succession effect. *Administrative Science Quarterly, 27*, 1-16.

Brown, R.J. (1990). The management of human resources in the leisure industry. In I.P. Henry (Ed.), *Management & planning in the leisure industries* (pp. 70-96). Basingstoke, Hants, UK: MacMillan Educational.

Bruce, P. (1985, October 14). Two Barvarian companies battle for citizens soles. *The Toronto Globe and Mail*, p. B4.

Brunswick's dramatic turnaround. (1988, January/February). *Journal of Business Strategy, 9*, 4-7.

Bryant, D.R., Maggard, J., & Taylor, R.P. (1973, April). Manpower planning models and techniques. *Business Horizons*, pp. 69-73.

Bryman, A. (1986). *Leadership and organizations*. London: Routledge & Kegan Paul.

Bryman, A. (1992). *Charisma and leadership in organizations*. London: Sage.

Bryman, A., Beardsworth, A.D., Keil, E.T., & Ford, J. (1983) Research note: Organizational size and specialization. *Organization Studies, 4*, 271-277.

Bryson, L. (1987). Sport and the maintenance of masculine hegemony. *Women's Studies International Forum, 10*, 349-360.

Bullaro, J.J. (1987, February). Recreation and leisure services: Entrepreneurial opportunities and strategies. *JOPERD, 58*, 71-73.

Bureau of National Affairs (1976). *Personnel Policies Forum*. (Survey No. 114). Washington, D.C.

Burgelman, R.A. (1983). A model of the interaction of strategic behaviour, corporate context, and the concept of strategy. *Academy of Management Review, 8*, 61-70.

Burns, J.M. (1978). *Leadership*. New York: Harper & Row.

Burns, T., & Stalker, G.M. (1961). *The management of innovation*. London: Tavistock.

Burrell, G. (1984). Sex and organizational analysis. *Organization Studies, 5*, 97-118.

Butler, R.J., Astley, W.G., Hickson, D.J., Mallory, G.R., & Wilson, D.C. (1979/80). Strategic decision making: Concepts of content and process. *International Studies of Management and Organization, 9*, 5-36.

Calas, M.B., & Smircich, L. (1991). Voicing seduction to silence leadership. *Organization Studies, 12*, 567-602.

Cameron, K.S. (1980). Critical questions in assessing organizational effectiveness. *Organizational Dynamics, 9*, 66-80.

Cameron, K.S. (1984). The effectiveness of ineffectiveness. In B.M. Staw and L.L. Cummings (Eds.), *Research in organizational behaviour* (Vol. 6) (pp. 235-285). Greenwich, CT: JAI Press.

Cameron, K.S. (1986). Effectiveness as paradox: Consensus and conflict in conceptions of organizational effectiveness. *Management Science, 32*, 539-553.

Cameron, K.S., Sutton, R.I., & Whetten, D.A. (1988). Issues in organizational decline. In K.S. Cameron, R.I. Sutton, & D.A. Whetten (Eds.), *Readings in organizational decline* (pp. 3-19). Cambridge, MA: Ballinger.

Cameron, K.S., & Whetten, D.A. (1981). Perceptions of organizational effectiveness over organizational life cycles. *Administrative Science Quarterly, 26*, 525-544.

Cameron, K.S., & Whetten, D.A. (1983a). Models of the organizational life cycle: Application to higher education. *Review of Higher Education, 6*, 269-299.

Cameron, K.S., & Whetten, D.A. (1983b). *Organizational effectiveness: A comparison of multiple models.* New York: Academic Press.

Campbell, J.P. (1977). On the nature of organizational effectiveness. In P.S. Goodman, J.M. Pennings, and Associates (Eds.), *New Perspectives on Organizational Effectiveness* (pp. 36-41). San Francisco: Jossey-Bass.

Can Nike just do it? (1994, April 18). *Business Week,* pp. 86-90.

Canadian Canoe Association. (1988). *National team program for excellence.* Ottawa, Ontario: Canadian Canoe Association.

Canadian Figure Skating Association. (1994). *National championship program.* Edmonton, Alberta.

Capowski, G.S. (1993, June). Designing a corporate identity. *Management Review, 82*, 32-40.

Carbonell, J.L. (1984). Sex roles and leadership revisited. *Journal of Applied Psychology, 69*, 44-49.

Carlisle, H.M. (1974). A contingency approach to decentralization. *S.A.M. Advanced Management Journal, 39*, 9-18.

Carpenter, L., & Acosta, V. (1990). *Women in intercollegiate sport.* Brooklyn, NY: Brooklyn College.

Carper, W.B., & Snizek, W.E. (1980). The nature and types of organizational taxonomies: An overview. *Academy of Management Review, 5*, 65-75.

Carroll, G.R., & Hannan, M.T. (1989). Density dependence in the evolution of populations of newspaper organizations. *American Sociological Review, 54*, 524-541.

Cascio, W. (1978). *Applied psychology in personnel management.* Reston, VA: Reston.

Cascio, W. (1986). *Managing human resources.* New York: McGraw-Hill.

Cascio, W., & Bernardin, H.J. (1981). Implications of performance appraisal litigation for personnel decisions. *Personnel Psychology, 34*, 211-226.

Case, B. (1987). Leadership behavior in sport: A field test of the situational leadership theory. *International Journal of Sport Psychology, 18*, 256-268.

Cashmore, E. (1990). *Making sense of sport.* London: Routledge & Kegan Paul.

Castaing, M. (1970, March 7). *Le Monde,* n.p. Cited by Brohm, J. (1978) *Sport: A prison of measured time.* London: Inks Links.

Chakrabarti, A.K. (1974). The role of champion in product innovation. *California Management Review, 17*, 58-62.

Chakrabarti, A.K., & Hauschildt, J. (1989). The division of labour in innovation management. *R & D Management (UK), 19*, 161-171.

Chandler, A.D. Jr. (1962). *Strategy and structure: Chapters in the history of the industrial enterprise.* Cambridge, MA: MIT Press.

Chang, Y.N., & Campo-Flores, F. (1980). *Business policy and strategy.* Santa Monica, CA: Goodyear.

Channon, D. (1973). *Strategy and structure in British enterprise.* Boston: Harvard Graduate School of Business Administration.

Charm, R.E. (1986, November 3). Like the company's sales, aluminum bikes of Cannondale stand out from the pack. *New England Business,* pp. 41-43.

Chelladurai, P. (1985). *Sport management: Macro perspectives.* London, Ontario: Sports Dynamics.

Chelladurai, P. (1987). Multidimensionality and multiple perspectives of organizational effectiveness. *Journal of Sport Management, 1*, 37-47.

Chelladurai, P. (1992). A classification of sport and physical activity services: Implications for sport management. *Journal of Sport Management, 6*, 38-51.

Chelladurai, P., & Carron, A.V. (1983). Athletic maturity and preferred leadership. *Journal of Sports Psychology, 5*, 371-380.

Chelladurai, P., & Danylchuk, K.E. (1984). Operative goals of intercollegiate athletics: Perceptions of athletic administrators. *Canadian Journal of Applied Sport Sciences, 9*, 33-41.

Chelladurai, P., & Haggerty, T.R. (1991). Measures of organizational effectiveness in Canadian national sport organizations. *Canadian Journal of Sport Science, 16*, 126-133.

Chelladurai, P., Haggerty, T.R., Cambell, L., & Wall, S. (1981). A factor analytic study of effectiveness criteria in intercollegiate athletics. *Canadian Journal of Applied Sport Science, 6*, 81-86.

Chelladurai, P. , Malloy, D., Imamura, H., & Yamaguchi, Y. (1987). A cross-cultural study of preferred leadership in sports. *Canadian Journal of Sport Sciences, 12*, 106-110.

Chelladurai, P., & Saleh, S.D. (1978). Preferred leadership in sports. *Canadian Journal of Applied Sport Sciences, 3*, 85-92.

Chelladurai, P., & Saleh, S.D. (1980). Dimensions of leader behavior in sports: Development of a leadership scale. *Journal of Sport Psychology, 2,* 43-45.

Chelladurai, P., Szyszlo, M., & Haggerty, T.R. (1987). Systems-based dimensions of effectiveness: The case of national sport organizations. *Canadian Journal of Sport Science, 12,* 111-119.

Child, J. (1972a). Organization structure and strategies of control: A replication of the Aston study. *Administrative Science Quarterly, 17,* 163-177.

Child, J. (1972b). Organizational structure, environment and performance: The role of strategic choice. *Sociology, 6,* 1-22.

Child, J. (1973a). Parkinson's progress: Accounting for the number of specialists in organizations. *Administrative Science Quarterly, 18,* 328-348.

Child, J. (1973b). Predicting and understanding organization structure. *Administrative Science Quarterly, 18,* 168-185.

Child, J. (1975a). Comments on Donaldson's note. *Administrative Science Quarterly, 20,* 456.

Child, J. (1975b). Managerial and organizational factors associated with company performance (Part II): A contingency analysis. *Journal of Management Studies, 12,* 12-27.

Child, J. (1984). *Organization: A guide to problems and practice* (2nd ed.). London: Chapman.

Child, J., & Kieser, A. (1979). Organizational and managerial roles in British and West German companies: An examination of the culture free thesis. In C.J. Lammers & D.J. Hickson (Eds.), *Organizations alike and unlike* (pp. 251-271). London: Routledge & Kegan Paul.

Child, J., & Mansfield, R. (1972). Technology, size, and organization structure. *Sociology, 6,* 369-393.

Chin, R., & Benne, K.D. (1985). General strategies for effecting change in human systems. In W.G. Bennis, K.D. Benne, & R. Chin (Eds.), *The planning of change* (pp. 22-45). New York: Holt, Rinehart & Winston.

City of Winnipeg. (1990). *Sports services policy.* Winnipeg, Manitoba: Author.

Clark, T.N. (1967). The concept of power: Some overemphasized and underrecognized dimensions. *The Southwestern Social Science Quarterly, 48,* 271-286.

Clegg, S. (1989). *Frameworks of power.* London: Sage.

Clegg, S., & Dunkerley, D. (1980). *Organization, class, and control.* London: Routledge & Kegan Paul.

Cliff, G. (1987, May). Managing organizational conflict. *Management Review, 76,* 51-53.

Clifford, M. (1992, November 5). The China connection: Nike is making the most of all that cheap labour. *Far Eastern Economic Review,* p. 60.

Cockburn, C. (1991). *In the way of women: Men's resistance to sex equality in organizations.* Houndmills, England: Macmillan.

Cohen, J.B. (1978). Healthcare, coping, and the counselor. *Personnel and Guidance Journal, 56,* 616-620.

Cohen, M.D., & March, J.G. (1974). *Leadership and ambiguity: The American college president.* New York: McGraw-Hill.

Cohen, M.D., March, J.G., & Olsen, J.P. (1972). A garbage can model of organizational choice. *Administrative Science Quarterly, 17,* 1-25.

Cole, W. (1989, July). Tee time for baby boomers. *Venture,* pp. 69-73.

Coleman, S., & Jones, L.M. (1976). *The Coleman story.* New York: Newcomen Society in North America.

Collins, M., & Randolph, L. (1991, July). *Business or hobby? Small firms in sport and recreation.* Paper presented at the World Leisure and Recreation Association Congress, Sydney, Australia.

Commentary. (July/August 1993). *Sports Business,* p. 98.

Comte, E. (1992, October 12) Blade runner. *Forbes,* pp. 114-115, 117.

Comte, E., & Stogel, C. (1990, January). Sports: A $63.1 billion industry. *The Sporting News,* pp. 60-61.

Conaty, J., Mahmoudi, H., & Miller, G.A. (1983). Social structure and bureaucracy: A comparison of organizations in the United States and pre-revolutionary Iran. *Organization Studies, 4,* 105-128.

Conger, J.A. (1989). *The charismatic leader: Beyond the mystique of exceptional leadership.* San Francisco: Jossey-Bass.

Conger, J.A., & Kanungo, R.N. (1987). Towards a behavioral theory of charismatic leadership in organizational settings. *Academy of Management Review, 12,* 637-647.

Conger, J.A., & Kanungo, R.N. (1988). Behavioral dimensions of charismatic leadership. In J.A. Conger & R.N. Kanungo (Eds.), *Charismatic leadership: The elusive factor in organizational effectiveness* (pp. 78-97). San Francisco: Jossey-Bass.

Connolly, T., Conlon, E.M., & Deutsch, S.J. (1980). Organizational effectiveness: A multiple constituency approach. *Academy of Management Review, 5,* 211-218.

Cooper 'natural fit' for Canstar. (1990, March 13). *Globe and Mail,* p. B15.

The corporate culture. (1989, August). *Outside Business,* pp. 33, 70-71.

Corwin, R. (1969). Patterns of organizational conflict. *Administrative Science Quarterly, 14,* 507-520.

Cotton, J.L., Vollrath, D.A., Froggatt, K.L., Lengnick-Hall, M.L., & Jennings, K.R. (1988). Employee participation: Diverse forms and different outcomes. *Academy of Management Review, 13,* 8-22.

Craig, C.K., & Weisman, K. (1994). Collegiate athletics and unrelated business income tax. *Journal of Sport Management, 8,* 36-48.

Cray, D., Mallory, G.R., Butler, R.J., Hickson, D.J., & Wilson, D.C. (1988). Sporadic, constricted, and fluid processes: Three types of strategic decision making in organizations. *Journal of Management Studies, 25,* 13-39.

Cray, D., Mallory, G.R., Butler, R.J., Hickson, D.J., & Wilson, D.C. (1991). Explaining decision processes. *Journal of Management Studies, 28,* 227-251.

Creamer, R.W. (1973, April 16). Scorecard: More basketball business. *Sports Illustrated,* p. 21.

Crick, M., & Smith, D. (1989). *Manchester United: The betrayal of a legend.* London: Pan Books.

Crocker, O., Chiu, J., & Charney, C. (1984). *Quality circles.* New York: Metheun.

Crossley, J., & Ellis, T. (1988, October). Systematic innovation. *JOPERD, 59,* 35-38.

Cummings, L.L., & Berger, C.J. (1976). Organization structure: How does it influence attitudes and performance? *Organizational Dynamics, 5,* 34-49.

Cyert, R.M., & March, J.G. (1963). *A behavioral theory of the firm.* Englewood Cliffs, NJ: Prentice Hall.

Czarniawska-Joerges, B., & Wolff, R. (1991). Leaders, managers, entrepreneurs on and off the organizational stage. *Organization Studies, 12,* 529-546.

Daft, R.L. (1989). *Organization theory and design* (3rd ed.). St. Paul: West.

Daft, R.L. (1992). *Organization theory and design* (4th ed.). St. Paul: West.

Damanpour, F. (1987). The adoption of technological, administrative, and ancillary innovations: Impact of organizational factors. *Journal of Management, 13,* 675-688.

Danielson, R.R., Zelhart, P.F., & Drake, C.J. (1975). Multidimensional scaling and factor analysis of coaching behavior as perceived by high school hockey players. *Research Quarterly, 46,* 323-334.

Danylchuk, K.E. (1993). Occupational stressors in physical education faculties. *Journal of Sport Management, 7,* 7-24.

Darrow, B. (1990, April 2). PCs break into the lineup. *Infoworld,* pp. 42-43.

Das, H. (1990). *Organization theory with Canadian applications.* Toronto: Gage Educational.

Davenport, J. (1994). A double-edge sword: Drugs in sport. In P.J. Graham (Ed.), *Sport Business: Operational and Theoretical Aspects* (pp. 212-222). Madison, WI: Brown & Benchmark.

Davies, P. (1990, May). Hot shoes. *Report on Business Magazine,* pp. 91-95.

Davis, K.A. (1994). *Sport management: Successful private sector business strategies.* Madison, WI: Brown & Benchmark.

Davis, T.R.V. (1984). The influence of the physical environment in offices. *Academy of Management Review, 9,* 271-283.

Deacon, J. (1993, December 6) Blowing the whistle. *Maclean's,* p. 55.

Deal, T.E., & Kennedy, A.A. (1982). *Corporate cultures: The rites and rituals of corporate life.* Reading, MA: Addison-Wesley.

Delacroix, J., & Carroll, G.R. (1983). Organizational foundings: An ecological study of the newspaper industries in Argentina and Ireland. *Administrative Science Quarterly, 28,* 274-291.

Denmark, F.L. (1977). Styles of leadership. *Psychology of Women Quarterly, 2,* 99-113.

Dess, G.G., & Beard, D.W. (1984). Dimensions of organizational task environments. *Administrative Science Quarterly, 29,* 52-73.

DeVries, D.L., Morrison, A.M., Shullman, S.L., & Gerlach, M.L. (1981). *Performance appraisal on the line.* New York: Wiley.

Digital scores with the NFL. (1986, March 22). *Financial Post,* p. C16.

DiMaggio, P.J., & Powell, W.W. (1983). The iron cage revisited: Institutional isomorphism and collective rationality in organizational field. *American Sociological Review, 35,* 147-160.

Dodds, L.S. (1985, August 21). Heading back on the fast track. *Financial World,* pp. 90-91.

Donaldson, L. (1975). Organizational status and the measurement of centralization. *Administrative Science Quarterly, 20,* 453-456.

Donaldson, L., & Warner, M. (1974). Structure of organizations in occupational interest associations. *Human Relations, 27,* 721-738.

Drucker, P. (1954). *The practice of management.* New York: Harper & Row.

Drucker, P. (1966). *The effective executive.* New York: Harper & Row.

Dubin, C.L. (1990). *Commission of inquiry into the use of drugs and banned practices intended to increase athletic performance.* Ottawa: Canadian Government Publishing Centre.

Duncan, R.B. (1972). Characteristics of perceived environments and perceived environmental uncertainty. *Administrative Science Quarterly, 17,* 313-327.

Durkheim, E. (1933). *The division of labor in society* (G. Simpson, Trans.). London: Free Press. (Original work published in 1893)

Dworkin, J.B. (1981). *Owners versus players: Baseball and collective bargaining.* Boston, MA: Auburn House.

Eales, R. (1986). Is Nike a long distance runner? *Multinational Business, 1,* 9-14.

Economic Intelligence Unit. (1990). *The sports market overview.* (Research Rep. No. 384). London: Author.

Ehrlich, E. (1985, August 12). Behind the AMF takeover: From highflier to sitting duck. *Business Week,* pp. 50-51.

Eitzen, S.D., & Yetman, N.R. (1972). Managerial change, longevity, and organizational effectiveness. *Administrative Science Quarterly, 17,* 110-116.

Elvin, I. (1990). *Sport and Physical Recreation.* Harlow, Essex, UK: Longman.

Emerson, R.E. (1962). Power-dependence relations. *American Sociological Review, 27,* 31-41.

The entertainment economy. (1994, March 14). *Business Week,* pp. 58-62.

Equipment handbook is student manager's bible. (1988, October). *Athletic Business,* pp. 30, 32, 34, 36, 38.

Etzioni, A. (1961). *A comparative analysis of complex organizations.* New York: Free Press.

Evan, W.M. (1976). Organizational theory and organizational effectiveness: An exploratory analysis. In S.L. Spray (Ed.), *Organizational Effectiveness: Theory, Research, Utilization* (pp. 15-28). Kent, OH: Kent State University Press.

Fahey, L. (1981). On strategic management decision processes. *Strategic Management Journal, 2,* 43-60.

Falcons (1989). Atlanta: Southeastern Color.

Farina, R., Kochenberger, G.A., & Obremski, T. (1989). The computer runs the Bolder Boulder: A simulation of a major running race. *Interfaces, 19,* 48-55.

Fasting, K. (1987). Sport and women's culture. *Women's Studies International Forum, 10,* 361-368.

Feinstein, J. (1986). *A season on the brink.* New York: Macmillan.

Ferber, M., Huber, J., & Spitze, G. (1979). Preferences for men as bosses and professionals. *Social Forces, 58,* 466-476.

Ferguson, A. (1988, August). Wide tyre boys. *Management Today,* pp. 58-60.

Fiedler, F.E. (1967). *A theory of leadership effectiveness.* New York: McGraw-Hill.

Filley, A.C., House, R.J., & Kerr, S. (1976). *Managerial process and organizational behavior* (2nd ed.). Glenview, IL: Scott Foresman.

Fine, G.A. (1987). *With the boys: Little league baseball and preadolescent culture.* Chicago: University of Chicago Press.

Fisher, B.M., & Edwards, J.E. (1988). Consideration and initiating structure and their relationships with leaders effectiveness: A meta-analysis. Best Paper Proceedings, Academy of Management.

Anaheim, CA: Academy of Management. (Cited by Bass, 1990a)

Flax, S. (1985, June 24). The executive addict. *Fortune,* pp. 24-31.

Fleishman, E.A., & Harris, E.F. (1962). Patterns of leader behavior related to employee grievances and turnover. *Personnel Psychology, 15,* 43-56.

Fleishman, E.A., Harris, E.F., & Burtt, H.E. (1955). *Leadership and supervision in industry.* Columbus: Ohio State University, Bureau of Educational Research.

Ford, J.D., & Slocum, J.W., Jr. (1977). Size, technology, and environment and the structure of organizations. *Academy of Management Review, 2,* 561-575.

Fredreckson, J.W. (1986). The strategic decision process and organizational structure. *Academy of Management Journal, 11,* 280-297.

Freedman, W. (1987). *Professional sports and antitrust.* New York: Quorum Books.

Freeman, J.H., & Hannan, M.T. (1975). Growth and decline processes in organizations. *American Sociological Review, 40,* 215-228.

Freeman, J.H. (1973). Environment, technology, and the administrative intensity of manufacturing organizations. *American Sociological Review, 38,* 750-763.

A Freewheeler on firm ground. (1989, March 22). *New England Business,* pp. 34-39, 80-81.

French, J.R.P., Jr., & Raven, B. (1959). The bases of social power. In D. Cartwright (Ed.), *Studies in social power* (pp. 150-167). Ann Arbor: University of Michigan Press.

Friend, J. (1991). Personnel Issues. In B.L. Parkhouse (Ed.), *The Management of Sport:Its Foundation and Application* (pp. 292-310). St. Louis: Mosby Year Book.

Frisby, W. (1985). A conceptual framework for measuring the organizational structure and context of voluntary leisure service organizations. *Society and Leisure, 8,* 605-613.

Frisby, W. (1986a). Measuring the organizational effectiveness of national sport governing bodies. *Canadian Journal of Applied Sport Science, 11,* 94-99.

Frisby, W. (1986b). The organizational structure and effectiveness of voluntary organizations: The case of Canadian national sport governing bodies. *Journal of Park and Recreation Administration, 4,* 61-74.

Frost, P.J., Moore, L.F., Louis, M.R., Lundberg, C.C., & Martin, J.(Eds.) (1985). *Organizational culture.* Beverly Hills, CA: Sage.

Frost, P.J., Moore, L.F., Louis, M.R., Lundberg, C.C., & Martin, J. (Eds.) (1991). *Reframing organizational culture.* Thousand Oaks, CA: Sage.

Fry, L.W. (1982). Technology-structure research: Three critical issues. *Academy of Management Journal, 25,* 532-552.

Fuller, P. (1994, February 14). No ray of light for Sunshine Village. *Alberta Report,* p. 22.

Galbraith, J.R. (1974). Organization design: An information processing view. *Interfaces, 4,* 28-36.

Galbraith, J.R. (1977). *Organization design.* Reading, MA: Addison-Wesley.

Gamson, W.A. (1966). Reputation and resources in community politics. *American Journal of Sociology, 72,* 121-131.

Gamson, W.A., & Scotch, N.A. (1964). Scapegoating in baseball. *American Journal of Sociology, 70,* 69-72.

Gandz, J., & Murray, V.V. (1980). The experience of workplace politics. *Academy of Management Journal, 23,* 237-251.

Garrison, L. (1992, December). The centennial celebration: Intersectional play. *Athletic Administration,* pp. 10-13.

Gatorade is starting to pant. (1994, April 18). *Business Week,* p. 98.

Gaugler, B.B., Rosenthal, D.B., Thornton, G.C., & Bentson, C. (1987). Meta-analysis of assessment center validity. *Journal of Applied Psychology, 72,* 493-511.

Gauthier, R., & Hansen, H. (1993). Female spectators: Marketing implications for professional golf events. *Sport Marketing Quarterly, 2,* 21-28.

Geber, B. (1988, October). Training at L.L. Bean. *Training,* pp. 85-89.

Geehern, C. (1991, August 8). Balls. *New England Business,* pp. 40-45, 63.

Geeraerts, G. (1984). The effect of ownership on the organization structure in small firms. *Administrative Science Quarterly, 29,* 232-237.

Geiger, H.M. (1987). *The Broadmoor story* (rev. ed.). Denver, CO: Hirschfeld Press.

Gerth, H.H., & Mills, C.W. (1946). *From Max Weber.* New York: Oxford University Press.

Gerwin, D. (1979). Relationships between structure and technology at the organizational and job levels. *Journal of Management, 16,* 70-79.

Gibb, C.A. (1947). The principles and traits of leadership. *Journal of Abnormal and Social Psychology, 42,* 267-284.

Gill, P. (1987, July). Winning pace for footwear. *Stores,* pp. 36-38, 40, 44-49.

Give them stormy weather. (1986, March 24). *Forbes,* p. 174.

Going for gold. (1988, October). *Target Marketing,* pp. 72, 74.

Goodman, P.S., Atkin, R.S., & Schoorman, F.D. (1983). On the demise of organizational effec-

tiveness studies. In K.S. Cameron & D.A. Whetten (Eds.), *Organizational effectiveness: A comparison of multiple models* (pp. 163-183). New York: Academic Press.

Goodman, P.S., & Pennings, J.M. (1977). Perspectives and issues: An introduction. In P.S. Goodman, J.M. Pennings, and Associates (Eds.), *New perspectives on organizational effectiveness* (pp. 1-12). San Francisco: Jossey-Bass.

Goodman, P.S., Pennings, J.M., and Associates (Eds.) (1977). *New perspectives on organizational effectiveness.* San Francisco: Jossey-Bass.

Gordon, W.C., & Babchuk, N. (1959). A typology of voluntary organizations. *American Sociological Review, 24,* 22-29.

Gore, W.L. (n.d.). The lattice organization: A philosophy of enterprise. W.L. Gore & Associates. Newark, DE.

Goronzy, F. (1969). A numerical taxonomy of business enterprises. In A.J. Cole (Ed.), *Numerical taxonomy* (pp. 42-52). London: Academic Press.

Gould, A. (1989). *The new entrepreneurs.* Toronto: Seal Books.

Gouldner, A.W. (1954). *Patterns of industrial bureaucracy.* New York: Free Press.

Graham, J. (1988, July 18). Reebok scores with "Boss." *Advertising Age,* p. 22.

Graham, P. (1983). Strategic planning management concepts applied to team sports. In *Proceedings of the International Congress: Teaching Team Sports* (pp. 17-182). Rome: CONI-Scuola dello Sport.

Greene, C.N. (1979). Questions of causality in the path-goal theory of leadership. *Academy of Management Journal, 22,* 22-41.

Greenwood, R., & Hinings, C.R. (1976). Centralization revisited. *Administrative Science Quarterly, 21,* 151-155.

Greenwood, R., & Hinings, C.R. (1988). Organizational design types, tracks, and the dynamics of strategic change. *Organization Studies, 9,* 293-316.

Gregory, K.L. (1983). Native-view paradigms: Multiple cultures and culture conflicts in organizations. *Administrative Science Quarterly, 28,* 359-376.

Greiner, L.E. (1967). Patterns of organizational change. *Harvard Business Review, 45,* 119-130.

Gresov, C. (1989). Exploring fit and misfit with multiple contingencies. *Administrative Science Quarterly, 34,* 431-453.

Grimes, A.J., & Klein, S.M. (1973). The technological imperative: The relative impact of task unit, modal technology, and hierarchy on structure. *Academy of Management Journal, 16,* 583-597.

Grinyer, P.H., & Yasai-Ardekani, M. (1980). Dimensions of organizational structure: A critical replication. *Academy of Management Journal, 23,* 405-421.

Gruneau, R. (1983). *Class, sports and social development.* Amherst: University of Massachusetts Press.

Grusky, O. (1963). Managerial succession and organizational effectiveness. *American Journal of Sociology, 69,* 21-31.

Guttmann, A. (1978). *From ritual to record.* New York: Columbia University Press.

Haas, J.E., Hall, R.H., & Johnson, N.J. (1966). Towards an empirically derived taxonomy of organizations. In R.V. Bowers (Ed.), *Studies on behavior in organizations* (pp. 157-180) Athens: University of Georgia Press.

Hage, J. (1965). An axiomatic theory of organizations. *Administrative Science Quarterly, 10,* 289-320.

Hage, J. (1980). *Theories of organizations.* New York: Wiley.

Hage, J., & Aiken, M. (1967a). Program change and organizational properties a comparative analysis. *American Journal of Sociology, 72,* 503-519.

Hage, J., & Aiken, M. (1967b) Relationship of centralization to other structural properties. *Administrative Science Quarterly, 12,* 72-91.

Hage, J., & Aiken, M. (1969). Routine technology, social structure, and organizational goals. *Administrative Science Quarterly, 14,* 366-376.

Hage, J., & Aiken, M. (1970). *Social change in complex organizations.* New York: Random House.

Haggerty, T.R. (1988). Designing control and information systems in sport organizations: A cybernetic perspective. *Journal of Sport Management, 2,* 53-63.

Hall, D.T. (1983). The effect of the inividual on an organization's structure, style and process. In F. Landy, S. Zedeck, & J. Clevland (Eds.), *Performance Measurement and Theory* (pp. 11-30). Hillsdale, NJ: Lawrence Erlbaum Associates.

Hall, M.A., Cullen, D., & Slack, T. (1989). Organizational elites recreating themselves: The gender structure of national sport organizations. *Quest, 41,* 28-45.

Hall, M.A., Slack, T., Smith, G., & Whitson, D. (1991). *Sport in Canadian Society.* Toronto: McClelland & Stewart.

Hall, R.H. (1963). The concept of bureaucracy. *American Sociological Review, 69,* 32-40.

Hall, R.H. (1968). Professionalization and bureaucratization. *American Sociological Review, 33,* 92-104.

Hall, R.H. (1982). *Organizations: Structure and process* (3rd. ed.). Englewood Cliffs, NJ: Prentice Hall.

Hall, R.H., & Clark, J.P. (1980). An ineffective effectiveness study and some suggestions for future research. *Sociological Quarterly, 21,* 119-134.

Hall, R.H., Haas, J.E., & Johnson, N.J. (1967). Organizational size, complexity, and formalization. *American Sociological Review, 32,* 903-912.

Hall, R.H., & Tittle, C.R. (1966). Bureaucracy and its correlates. *American Journal of Sociology, 72,* 267-272.

Halpin, A.W. (1957). The observed behavior and ideal leaders behavior of aircraft commanders and school superintendents. In R.M. Stogdill & A.E. Coons (Eds.), *Leader behaviors: Its description and measurement* (pp. 65-68). Columbus: Ohio State University, Bureau of Business Research.

Halpin, A.W., & Winer, B.J. (1957). A factorial study of the leader behavior descriptions. In R.M. Stogdill & A.E. Coons (Eds.), *Leader behaviors: Its description and measurement* (pp. 39-51). Columbus: Ohio State University, Bureau of Business Research.

Hampton, J. (1984, October). Q. and A. One-on-one with H. R. "Bum" Bright. *Dallas Magazine,* pp. 23-25, 86.

Hannan, M.T., & Freeman, J. (1977a). Obstacles to comparative studies. In P.S. Goodman & J.M. Pennings, and Associates (Eds.), *New perspectives on organizational effectiveness* (pp. 106-131). San Francisco: Jossey-Bass.

Hannan, M.T., & Freeman, J. (1977b). The population ecology of organizations. *American Journal of Sociology, 82,* 929-964.

Hannan, M.T., & Freeman, J. (1988). Density dependence in the growth of organizational populations. In G.R. Carroll (Ed.), *Ecological Models of Organizations* (pp. 7-32). Cambridge, MA: Ballinger.

Hannan, M.T., & Freeman, J. (1989). *Organizational ecology.* Cambridge, MA: Harvard University Press.

Hansen, H., & Gauthier, R. (1989). Factors affecting attendance at professional sport events. *Journal of Sport Management, 3,* 15-32.

Harrigan, K.R., & Porter, M. (1983). End-game strategies for declining industries. *Harvard Business Review, 61,* 111-120.

Harris, D. (1987). *The league, the rise and decline of the NFL.* Toronto: Bantam Books.

Hartley, R.F. (1983). *Management mistakes.* Columbus, OH: Grid Publishing.

Hartley, R.F. (1989). *Marketing mistakes* (4th. ed.). New York: Wiley.

Harvard Business School. (1984). Nike (B). (Case No. 9-385-027). Boston: HBS Case Services.

Harvey, J., & Proulx, R. (1988). Sport and the state in Canada. In J. Harvey & H. Cantelon (Eds.), *Not just a game: Essays in Canadian sport sociology* (pp. 93-119). Ottawa: University of Ottawa Press.

Hater, J.J., & Bass, B.M. (1988). Superiors' evaluations and subordinates' perceptions of transformational and transactional leadership. *Journal of Applied Psychology, 73,* 695-702.

Hawley, A.H. (1981). Human ecology: Persistence and change. *American Behavioral Scientist, 24,* 423-444.

Haywood-Farmer, J., Sharman, T., & Weinbrecht, M.S. (1988). Using simple simulation models to manage sports services. *Journal of Sport Management, 2,* 118-128.

Hearn, J., & Parkin, P.W. (1983). Gender and organizations: A selective review and a critique of a neglected area. *Organization Studies, 4,* 219-242.

Hearn, J., & Parkin, P.W. (1987). *'Sex' at work: The power and paradox of organisational sexuality.* Brighton, UK: Wheatsheaf.

Hearn, J., Sheppard, D.L., Tancred-Sheriff, P., & Burrell, G. (1989). *The Sexuality of organization.* London: Sage.

Heise, D.R. (1972). How do I know my data? Let me count the ways. *Administrative Science Quarterly, 17,* 58-61.

Hellriegel, D., & Slocum, J.W. (1978). *Management: Contingency approaches.* Reading, MA: Addison-Wesley.

Helm, S. (1986, October). The turnaround pro. *Venture,* pp. 26-28, 30.

Hemphill, J.K., & Coons, A.E. (1957). Development of the leaders behavior description questionnaire. In R.M. Stogdill & A.E. Coons (Eds.), *Leader behaviors: Its description and measurement* (pp. 6-38). Columbus: Ohio State University, Bureau of Business Research.

Hendershott, G.E., & James, T.F. (1972). Size and growth as determinants of administrative-production ratios in organizations. *American Sociological Review, 37,* 149-153.

Henderson, R. (1980). *Performance appraisal: Theory to practice.* Reston, VA: Reston.

Hendry, J., and Johnson, G. with Newton, J. (1993) (Eds.), *Strategic thinking: Leadership and the management of change .* Chichester, UK: Wiley.

Hersey, P., & Blanchard, K.H. (1984). *Management of organizational behavior* (4th ed.). Englewood Cliffs, NJ: Prentice Hall.

Herzberg, F., Mausner, B., & Snyderman, B. (1959). *The motivation to work.* New York: Wiley.

Hickey, P. (1994, April 29). Zapping freeloaders. *Edmonton Journal (TV Times),* p. 6.

Hickson, D.J., Butler, R.J., Cray, D., Mallory, G.R., & Wilson, D.C. (1985). Comparing one hundred fifty decision processes. In J.M. Pennings (Ed.), *Organizational strategy and change* (pp. 114-142). San Francisco: Jossey-Bass.

Hickson, D.J., Butler, R.J., Cray, D., Mallory, G.R., & Wilson, D.C. (1986). *Top decisions: Strategic decision making in organizations.* San Francisco: Jossey-Bass.

Hickson, D.J., Hinings, C.R., Lee, C.A., Schneck, R.E., & Pennings, J.M. (1971). A 'strategic' contingencies theory of interorganizational power. *Administrative Science Quarterly, 14,* 378-397.

Hickson, D.J., Hinings, C.R., McMillan, C.J., & Schwetter, J.P. (1974). The culture free context of organization structure: A tri-national comparison. *Sociology, 8,* 59-80.

Hickson, D.J., Pugh, D.S., & Pheysey, D.C. (1969). Operations, technology and organization structure: An empirical reappraisal. *Administrative Science Quarterly, 14,* 378-397.

Hill, C.R. (1992). *Olympic politics.* Manchester, England: Manchester University Press.

Hill, C.W.L., & Jones, G.R. (1989). *Strategic management: An integrated approach.* Boston: Houghton Mifflin.

Hilton, G. (1972). Causal inference analysis: A seductive process. *Administrative Science Quarterly, 17,* 44-54.

Hinings, C.R. (1979). Continuities in the study of organizations: Churches and local government. In C.J. Lammers & D.J. Hickson (Eds.), *Organizations alike and unlike* (pp. 137-148). London: Routledge & Kegan Paul.

Hinings, C.R., & Greenwood, R. (1988). *The dynamics of strategic change.* Oxford: Basil Blackwell.

Hinings, C.R., Hickson, D.J., Pennings, J.M., & Schneck, R.E. (1974). Structural conditions of interorganizational power. *Administrative Science Quarterly, 17,* 22-44.

Hinings, C.R., & Lee, G.L. (1971). Dimensions of organization structure and their context: A replication. *Sociology, 5,* 83-93.

Hinings, C.R., & Slack, T. (1987). The dynamics of quadrennial plan implementation in national sport organizations. In T. Slack & C.R. Hinings, (Eds.), *The organization and administration of sport.* London, ON: Sport Dynamics.

Hisrich, R.D., & Peters, M.P. (1992). *Entrepreneurship.* Homewood, IL: Irwin.

Hodge, B.J., & Anthony, W.P. (1991). *Organization theory: A strategic approach.* Boston: Allyn & Bacon.

Holdaway, E.A., & Blowers, T.A. (1971). Administrative ratios and organization size: A longitudinal examination. *American Sociological Review, 36,* 278-286.

Holdaway, E.A., Newberry, J.F., Hickson, D.J., & Heron, R.P. (1975). Dimensions of organizations in complex societies: The educational sector. *Administrative Science Quarterly, 20,* 37-58.

Horine, L. (1985). *Administration of physical education and sport programs*. Philadelphia: Saunders.

Horvath, D., McMillan, C.J., Azumi, K., & Hickson, D.J. (1976). The cultural context of organizations: An international comparison. *International Studies of Management and Organization, 6*, 60-80.

Horwich, A. (1989, August). REI: Where good citizenship makes good business sense. *Outside Business*, pp. 30-35, 68-69.

Hot growth companies. (1994, May 23). *Business Week*, pp. 101-103.

Houlihan, B. (1991). *The government and politics of sport*. London: Routledge & Kegan Paul.

House, R.J. (1971). A path-goal theory of leader effectiveness. *Administrative Science Quarterly, 16*, 321-339.

House, R.J. (1977). A 1976 theory of charismatic leadership. In J.G. Hunt and L.L. Larson (Eds.), *Leadership: The cutting edge* (pp. 189-207). Carbondale: Southern Illinois University Press.

House, R.J., & Dessler, G. (1974). The path-goal theory of leadership: Some post hoc and a priori tests. In J. Hunt and L. Larson (Eds.), *Contingency approaches to leadership* (pp. 29-55). Carbondale: Southern Illinois Press.

House, R.J., & Mitchell, T.R. (1974). Path-goal theory of leadership. *Contemporary Business, 3*, 81-98.

Hrebiniak, L.G. (1974). Job technology, supervision, and work group structure. *Administrative Science Quarterly, 19*, 395-410.

Hrebiniak, L.G., & Joyce, W.F. (1985). Organizational adaptation: Strategic choice and environmental determinism. *Administrative Science Quarterly, 30*, 336-349.

Huffy Corporation (1989). *Annual Report*. Dayton, Ohio.

Huizenga, R. (1994). *You're OK. It's just a bruise*. New York: St. Martin's Press.

Hult, J.S. (1989). Women's struggle for governance in U.S. amateur athletics. *International Review for the Sociology of Sport, 24*, 249-263.

Hunnicutt, D. (1988). Integrating quality circles into college athletic departments. *Journal of Sport Management, 2*, 140-145.

Hunter, J.E., & Hunter, R.F. (1984). Validity and utility of alternative predictors of job performance. *Psychological Bulletin, 96*, 72-98.

I was brought up for work. (1987, December 28). *Maclean's*, pp. 24-25.

If there were a gold medal for bickering the U.S. would win. (1988, March 21). *Business Week*, pp. 106, 108.

Improving your marketing game. (1987, November). *Athletic Business*, p. 16.

Indik, B.P. (1964). The relationship between organization size and supervision ratio, *Administrative Science Quarterly, 9*, 301-312.

Indik, J. (1986). Path-goal theory of leadership: A meta-analysis. Best Paper Proceedings, Academy of Management. Anaheim, CA: Academy of Management. (Cited by Yukl, 1989)

Ivancevich, J.M., & Matteson, M.T. (1980). *Stress and work: A managerial perspective*. Glenview, IL: Scott Foresman.

Jackson, J.E., & Schantz, W.T. (1993, January/February). Crisis management lessons: When Push shoved Nike. *Business Horizons*, pp. 227-235.

Jackson, S.E., & Dutton, J.E. (1988). Discerning threats and opportunities. *Administrative Science Quarterly, 33*, 370-387.

Jacoby, A. (1965). Some correlates of instrumental and expressive orientations to associational membership. *Sociological Inquiry, 35*, 163-175.

Jamieson, L.J. (1987). Competency-based approaches to sport management. *Journal of Sport Management, 1*, 48-56.

Jamieson, L.M. (1988, October). Commitment beyond profit. *JOPERD, 59*, 42-43.

Jemison, D.B. (1984). The importance of boundary spanning roles in strategic decision making. *Journal of Management Studies, 21*, 131-152.

Jensen, C.R. (1983). *Administrative management of physical education and athletic programs*. Philadelphia: Lea & Febiger.

Jereski, L. (1990, June 18). Can Paul Fireman put the bounce back in Reebok? *Business Week*, pp. 181-182.

Joe Montgomery's wild ride. (1993, April 19). *Business Week*, pp. 50, 52.

Johnson, R. (1986, November 4). Brunswick Corp. agrees to buy Bayliner Marine. *Wall Street Journal*, p. 10.

Johnson, T.J. (1972). *Professions and power*. Basingstoke, UK: MacMillan Education.

Johnson Worldwide Associates, Inc. (1989). *Annual Report*. Racine, WI.

Joint ventures: Creating opportunities in the fitness business. (1986, January). *Athletic Business*, pp. 26, 28, 30, 32.

Jollimore, M. (1992, June 27). Women show hockey might in Canada. *Globe and Mail*, p. A20.

Kadan, S.E. (1977, July). Compassion or coverup: The alcoholic employee. *Personnel Journal*, p. 357.

Kanter, R.M. (1977). *Men and women of the corporation*. New York: Basic Books.

Kanter, R.M. (1983). *The change masters*. New York: Simon & Schuster.

Kanter, R.M. (1984). Managing transitions in organizational culture: The case of participative management at Honeywell. In J.R. Kimberly & R.E. Quinn (Eds.), *Managing Organizational Transitions* (pp. 195-217). Homewood, IL: Irwin.

Kanter, R.M., & Brinkerhoff, D. (1981). Organizational performance: Recent developments in measurement. In R.H. Turner & J.F. Short (Eds.), *Annual review of sociology* (Vol. 7) (pp. 321-349). Palo Alto, CA: Annual Reviews.

Katerberg, R., & Hom, P.W. (1981). Effects of within-group and between-groups variations in leadership. *Journal of Applied Psychology, 66*, 218-222.

Katz, D. (1994). *Just do it: The Nike spirit in the corporate world.* New York: Random House.

Katz, D., & Kahn, R.L. (1978). *The social psychology of organizations* (rev. ed). New York: Wiley.

Katz, D., Maccoby, N., Gurin, G., & Floor, L. (1951). *Productivity, supervision, and morale among railroad workers.* Ann Arbor: Survey Research Center, University of Michigan.

Katz, D., Maccoby, N., & Morse, N. (1950). *Productivity, supervision, and morale in an office situation.* Ann Arbor: Institute for Social Research, University of Michigan.

Katz, R.L. (1955). Skills of an effective administrator. *Harvard Business Review, 33,* 33-42.

Keating, S. (1993, November 29). Speed skaters at loggerheads. *Globe and Mail,* p. A17.

Keeley, M. (1978). A social-justice approach to organizational evaluation. *Administrative Science Quarterly, 23,* 272-292.

Keidel, R.W. (1984). Baseball, football, and basketball: Models for business. *Organizational Dynamics, 12,* 5-18.

Keidel, R.W. (1987). Team sports models as a generic organizational framework. *Human Relations, 40,* 591-612.

Kelly, C.M. (1984). Reasonable performance appraisals. *Training and Development Journal, 38,* 79-82.

Kelly, T.W. (1991). Performance evaluation. In R.L. Boucher & W.J. Weese (Eds.), *Management of recreational sports in higher education* (pp. 153-165). Carmel, IN: Benchmark Press.

Kelowna golf club going women-only. (1994, April 14). *Saskatoon Star Phoenix,* p. C1.

Kennedy, J.K. (1982). Middle LPC leaders and the contingency model of leadership effectiveness. *Organizational Behavior and Human Performance, 30,* 1-14.

Kets de Vries, M.F.R. (1994). The leadership mystique. *Academy of Management Executive, 8* (3), 73-89.

Khandwalla, P.N. (1974). Mass output orientation of operations technology and oranizational structure. *Administrative Science Quarterly, 19,* 74-97.

Khandwalla, P.N. (1977). *The design of organizations.* New York: Harcourt Brace Jovanovich.

Kidd, B. (1988). The elite athlete. In J. Harvey & H. Cantelon (Eds.), *Not just a game: Essays in Canadian sport sociology* (pp. 287-307). Ottawa: University of Ottawa Press.

Kikulis, L., Slack, T., & Hinings, C.R. (1992). Institutionally specific design archetypes: A framework for understanding change in national sport organizations. *International Review for the Sociology of Sport, 27,* 343-370.

Kikulis, L., Slack, T., & Hinings, C.R. (1995a). Does decision making make a difference: Patterns of change within Canadian national sport organizations. *Journal of Sport Management, 9,* 273-299.

Kikulis, L., Slack, T., & Hinings, C.R. (1995b). Sector specific patterns of organizational design change. *Journal of Management Studies, 32,* 67-100.

Kikulis, L., Slack, T., Hinings, C.R., & Zimmermann, A. (1989). A structural taxonomy of amateur sport organizations. *Journal of Sport Management, 3,* 129-150.

Killanin, Lord. (1983). *My Olympic years.* London: Secker & Warburg.

Kimberly, J.R. (1976). Organizational size and the structuralist perspective: A review critique, and proposal. *Administrative Science Quarterly, 21,* 571-597.

Kimberly, J.R. (1980). The life cycle analogy and the study of organizations: Introduction. In J.R. Kimberly, & R.H. Miles (Eds.), *The organizational life cycle* (pp. 1-14). San Fransisco: Jossey-Bass.

Kimberly, J.R. (1987). The study of organizations: Toward a biographical perspective. In J.W. Lorsch (Ed.), *Handbook of organizational behavior* (pp. 223-237). Englewood Cliffs, NJ: Prentice Hall.

Kimberly, J.R., & Miles, R.H. (1980). *The organizational life cycle.* San Fransisco: Jossey-Bass.

Kimberly, J.R., & Rottman, D.B. (1987) Environment, organization and effectiveness: A biographical approach. *Journal of Mangement Studies, 24,* 595-622.

King, F.W. (1991). *It's how you play the game: The Inside story of the Calgary Olympics.* Calgary: Writers' Group.

Kirkpatrick, S.A., & Locke, E.A. (1991). Leadership: Do traits matter? *Academy of Management Executive, 5,* 48-60.

Klonsky, B.G. (1991). Leader's characteristics in same-sex sport groups: A study of interscholastic baseball and softball teams. *Perceptual and Motor Skills, 72,* 943-964.

Kmetz, J.L. (1977/78). A critique of the Aston studies and results with a new measure of technology. *Organization and Administrative Sciences, 8(4),* 123-144.

Kogan, R. (1985). *Brunswick: The story of an American company from 1845 to 1985.* Skokie, IL: Brunswick Corporation.

Kolb, D.M., & Putnam, L.L. (1992). The multiple faces of conflict in organizations. *Journal of Organizational Behavior, 13,* 311-324.

Kotter, J.P. (1977). Power, dependence and effective management. *Harvard Business Review, 55,* 125-136.

Kotter, J.P., & Schlesinger, L.A. (1979). Choosing strategies for change. *Harvard Business Review, 57,* 106-124.

Kuc, B., Hickson, D.J., & McMilan, C.J. (1980). Centrally planned developments: A comparison of Polish factories with equivilants in Britain, Japan, and Sweden. *Organization Studies, 1,* 253-270.

L.A. Gear: Valley-girl cheek. (1988, November 29). *Financial World,* pp. 14, 16.

Langhorn, K., & Hinings, C.R. (1987). Integrated planning and organizational conflict. *Canadian Public Administration, 30,* 550-565.

Lapchick, R. (1986). The promised land. In R. Lapchick (Ed.), *Fractured Focus* (pp. 111-135). Lexington, MA: Lexington Books.

Larson, L.L., Hunt, J.G., & Osborn, R.N. (1976). The great hi-hi leader behavior myth: A lesson from Occam's razor. *Academy of Management Journal, 19,* 628-641.

Larson, M. (1977). *The rise of professionalism: A sociological analysis.* Berkeley: University of California Press.

Latham, D.R., & Stewart, D.W. (1981). Organizational objectives and winning: An examination of the NFL. *Academy of Management Journal, 24,* 403-408.

Lawler, E., & Mohrman, S. (1985). Quality circles: After the fad. *Harvard Business Review, 63,* 64-71.

Lawrence, P.R., and Lorsch, J. (1967). *Organization and environment.* Boston: Harvard Graduate School of Business Administration.

Lawson, H.A. (1984). *Invitation to physical education.* Champaign, IL: Human Kinetics.

Leavitt, H.J., Dill, W.R., & Eyring, H.B. (1973). *The organizational world.* New York: Harcourt Brace Jovanovich.

Leavy, B., & Wilson, D.C. (1994). *Strategy and leadership.* London: Routledge & Kegan Paul.

Lebow, F. (1984). *Inside the world of big-time marathoning.* New York: Rawson Associates.

Leifer, R., & Huber, G.P. (1977). Relations among perceived environmental uncertainty, organizational structure, and boundary spanning behavior. *Administrative Science Quarterly, 22,* 235-247.

Lenz, R.T., & Engledow, J.L. (1986). Environmental Analysis Units and strategic decision making: A field study of selected "leading edge" corporations. *Strategic Management Journal, 7,* 69-89.

Lesly, E. (1992, November 30). What next, Raider's deodorant? *Business Week,* pp. 65.

Lesly, E. (1993, August 23). A burst bubble at Topps. *Business Week,* p. 74.

Lieberson, S., & O'Conner, J.F. (1972). Leadership and organizational performance: A study of large corporations. *American Sociological Review, 37,* 117-130.

Likert, R. (1961). *New patterns of management.* New York: McGraw-Hill.

Likert, R. (1967). *The human organization.* New York: McGraw-Hill.

Likert, R., & Likert, J.G. (1976). *New ways of managing conflict.* New York: McGraw-Hill.

Lincoln, J., Olson, J., & Hanada, M. (1978). Cultural effects on organizational structure: The case of Japanese firms in the United States. *American Sociological Review, 43,* 829-847.

Lincoln, J., & Zeitz, G. (1980). Organizational properties from aggregate data. *American Sociological Review, 45,* 391-405.

Lindblom, C.E. (1959). The science of muddling through. *Public Administration Review, 19,* 79-88.

Litterer, J.A. (1973). *The Analysis of Organizations* (2nd ed.). New York: Wiley.

Lord, R.G., Binning, J.F., Rush, M.C., & Thomas, J.C. (1978). The effects of performance cues and leader behavior on questionnaire rating of leader behavior. *Organizational Behavior and Human Performance, 21,* 27-39.

Lorsch, J. (1986). Managing culture: The invisible barrier to strategic change. *California Management Review, 28,* 95-109.

Louis, M.R. (1985). An investigator's guide to workplace culture. In P.J. Frost, L.F. Moore, M.R. Louis, C.C. Lundberg, & J. Martin (Eds.), *Organizational Culture* (pp. 73-93). Beverly Hills, CA: Sage.

Lovett, D.J., & Lowry, C.D. (1988). The role of gender in leadership positions in female sport programs in Texas colleges. *Journal of Sport Management, 2,* 106-117.

Lovett, D.J., & Lowry, C.D. (1994). "Good old boys" and "good old girls" clubs: Myth or reality. *Journal of Sport Management, 8,* 27-35.

Lukes, S. (1974). *Power: A radical view.* London: Macmillan.

Lyles, M. (1987). Defining strategic problems: Subjective criteria of executives. *Organization Studies, 8*, 263-280.

Macintosh, D., Bedecki, T., & Franks, C.E.S. (1987). *Sport and politics in Canada*. Kingston, Ontario: McGill-Queen's University Press.

Macintosh, D., & Whitson, D.J. (1990). *The game planners: Transforming Canada's sport system*. Montreal & Kingston: McGill-Queen's University Press.

MacMillan, I.C. (1983). Competitive strategies for non-profit agencies. In R.B. Lamb (Ed.), *Advances in Strategic Management* (Vol. 1) (pp. 61-82). Greenwich, CT: JAI Press.

Macnow, G. (1985, July 17). Eastern Michigan's plan to tie coaches' pay to performance derided on other campuses. *Chronicle of Higher Education*, pp. 27-28.

Madison, D.L., Allen, R.W., Porter, L.W., Renwick, P.A., & Mayes, B.T. (1980). Organizational politics: An exploration of managers' perceptions. *Human Relations, 33*, 79-100.

Magnet, M. (1982, November 1). Nike starts on the second mile. *Fortune*, pp. 159-162.

Mahoney, T.A., & Frost, P.J. (1974). The role of technology in models of organizational effectiveness. *Organizational Behavior and Human Performance, 11*, 122-138.

Maidique, M. A. (1980). Entrepreneurs, champions, and technological innovation. *Sloan Management Review, 21*, 59-76.

Major, C. S. (1990, November). On course with Jack Nicklaus. *CFO, 6*, pp. 71-72.

Mallory, G.R., Butler, R.J., Cray, D., Hickson, D.J., & Wilson, D.C. (1983). Implanted decision making: American owned firms in Britain. *Journal of Management Studies, 20*, 192-211.

Manley, D., & Friend, T. (1992). *Educating Dexter*. Nashville, TN: Rutledge Hill Press.

Mansfield, R. (1973). Bureaucracy and centralization: An examination of organizational structure. *Administrative Science Quarterly, 18*, 77-88.

March, J.G., & Simon, H. (1958). *Organizations*. New York: Wiley.

March, J.G. (1966). *The power of power*. In D. Easton (Ed.) Varieties of political theory. pp. 39-70. Englewood Cliffs, NJ: Prentice Hall.

March, J.G. (1982). Theories of choice and making decisions. *Society, 20*, 29-39.

March, J.G., & Olsen, J.P. (Eds.). (1976). *Ambiguity and choice in organizations*. Bergen, Norway: Universitetsforlaget.

Markland, R.E. (1983). *Topics in management science* (1st ed.). New York: Wiley.

Markland, R.E. (1989). *Topics in management science* (3rd ed.). New York: Wiley.

Marsh, R.N., & Mannari, H. (1981). Technology and size as detrminants of organizational structure of Japanese factories. *Administrative Science Quarterly, 26*, 33-57.

Martin, C.L. (1990). The employee/customer interface: An empirical investigation of employee behaviors and customer perceptions. *Journal of Sport Management, 4*, 1-20.

Martin, J., Feldman, M.S., Hatch, M.J., & Sitkin, S.B. (1983). The uniqueness paradox in organizational stories. *Administrative Science Quarterly, 28*, 438-453.

Martin, R. (1971). The concept of power: A critical defense. *British Journal of Sociology, 22*, 240-256.

Martindell, J. (1962). *The scientific appraisal of management*. New York: Harper & Row.

Maslow, A.H. (1943). A human theory of motivation. *Psychological Review, 50*, 370-396.

Maslow, A.H. (1965). *Eupsychian management*. Homewood, IL: Irwin.

McCall, M.W., Jr., & Lombardo, M.M. (1978). *Leadership: Where else can we go?* Durham, NC: Duke University Press.

McCall, M.W., Jr., & Lombardo, M.M. (1983). *Off the track: Why and how successful executives get derailed* (Technical Report No. 21). Greenboro, NC: Center For Creative Leadership.

McCann, J.E. (1991). Design principles for an innovating company. *Academy of Management Executive, 5*, 76-93.

McCarthy, M.J. (1987, October 19). Bally plans sale of health clubs for $500 million. *Wall Street Journal*, p. 34.

McClelland, D.C., (1985). *Human motivation*. Glenview, IL: Scott Foresman.

McCormack, M.H. (1984). *What they don't teach you at Harvard Business School*. Glasgow, Scotland: Fontana.

McCormick, E.J. (1979). *Job analysis*. New York: AMACOM.

McDonald, P. (1991). The Los Angeles Olympic Organizing Committee: Developing organizational culture in the short run. In P.J. Frost, L.F. Moore, M.L. Reis, C.C. Lundberg, and J. Martin (Eds.), *Reframing organizational culture* (pp. 26-38). Newbury Park, CA: Sage.

McDougall, B. (1991, January). Driven by design. *Canadian Business*, pp. 48-53.

McGregor, D. (1960). *The human side of enterprise*. New York: Van Nostrand.

McKelvey, B. (1975). Guidelines for the empirical classification of organizations. *Administrative Science Quarterly, 20*, 509-525.

McKelvey, B. (1978). Organizational systematics: Taxonomic lessons from biology. *Management Science, 24*, 1428-1440.

McKelvey, B. (1982). *Organizational systematics.* Los Angeles: University of California Press.

McLennan, K. (1967). The manager and his job skills. *Academy of Management Journal, 3*, 235-245.

McMillan, J. (1989). *The Dunlop story.* London: Weidenfeld and Nicolson.

Medcalf, L. (1991, July 1). Rolling in dough. *Marketing*, pp. 1, 3.

Meredith, J.R. (1987). The strategic advantage of the factory of the future. *California Management Review, 29*, 27-41.

Merton, R.K. (1957). *Social theory and social structure.* London: Free Press of Glencoe.

Metcalfe, A. (1983). 1937: The demise of amateurism in Canada. In S. Kereliuk (Ed.), *Proceedings of the FISU Conference-Universiade '83 in association with the Xth HISPA Congress* (pp. 308-315). Edmonton: Universiade '83 Corporation.

Meyer, H.H. (1980). Self appraisal of job performance. *Personnel Psychology, 33*, 291-295.

Meyer, H.H., Kay, E., & French, J.R.P., Jr. (1965). Split roles in performance appraisal. *Harvard Business Review, 43*, 123-129.

Meyer, J.W., & Rowan, B. (1977). Institutionalized organizations: Formal structure as myth and ceremony. *American Journal of Sociology, 83*, 340-363.

Meyer, J.W., & Scott, R. (1983) *Organizational environments: Rituals and rationality.* Beverly Hills, CA: Sage.

Meyer, M. (1972). Size and the structure of organizations: A causal analysis. *American Sociological Review, 37*, 434-440.

Meyer, M.W., & Zucker, L.G. (1989). *Permanently failing organizations.* Newbury Park, CA: Sage.

Meyerson, D., & Martin, J. (1987). Cultural change: An integration of three different views. *Journal of Management Studies, 24*, 623-647.

Michael, D.N. (1973). *On learning to plan—and planning to learn.* San Francisco: Jossey-Bass.

Miles, R.E., & Snow, C.C. (1978). *Organizational strategy, structure, and process.* New York: McGraw-Hill.

Miles, R.E., Snow, C.C., Meyer, A.D., & Coleman, H.J. (1978). Organizational strategy, structure and process. *Academy of Management Review, 3*, 546-562.

Milkovich, G.T., & Mahoney, T.A. (1979). Human resource planning models: A perspective. In J.W. Walker (Ed.), *The challenge of human resource planning: Selected readings* (pp. 75-86). New York: Human Resource Planning Society.

Miller, D. (1981). Toward a new contingency approach: The search for organizational gestalts. *Journal of Management Studies, 18*, 1-26.

Miller, D. (1986). Configurations of strategy and structure: Towards a synthesis. *Strategic Management Journal, 7*, 217-231.

Miller, D. (1987a). Strategy making and structure: Analysis and implications for performance. *Academy of Management Journal, 30*, 7-32.

Miller, D. (1987b). The structural and environmental correlates of business strategy. *Strategic Management Journal, 8*, 55-76.

Miller, D. (1988). Relating Porter's business strategies to environment and structure: Analysis and performance implications. *Academy of Management Journal, 31*, 280-308.

Miller, D. (1990). *The Icarus paradox: How exceptional companies bring about their own downfall.* New York: HarperCollins.

Miller, D., & Droge, C. (1986). Psychological and traditional determinants of structure. *Administrative Science Quarterly, 31*, 539-560.

Miller, D., & Friesen, P. (1980a). Archetypes of organizational transition. *Administrative Science Quarterly, 25*, 268-292.

Miller, D., & Friesen, P. (1980b). Momentum and revolution in organizational adaptation. *Academy of Management Journal, 23*, 591-614.

Miller, D., & Friesen, P. (1984). *Organizations: A quantum view.* Englewood Cliffs, NJ: Prentice Hall.

Miller, G.A. (1987). Meta-analysis and the culture free hypothesis. *Organization Studies, 4*, 309-325.

Miller, K.I., & Monge, P.R. (1986). Participation, satisfaction, and productivity: A meta-analytic review. *Academy of Management Journal, 29*, 727-753.

Miller, L.K., Fielding, L.W., & Pitts, B.G. (1993). Hiring concerns for the sport practitioner. *Journal of Legal Aspects of Sport, 3*, 3-15.

Mills, A.J., & Tancred, P. (1992). *Gendering organizational analysis.* London: Sage.

Mills, D. (1991). The battle of Alberta: Entrepreneurs and the business of hockey in Edmonton and Calgary. *Alberta: Studies in the Arts and Sciences, 2*, 1-25.

Mills, P.K., & Margulies, N. (1980). Toward a core typology of service organizations. *Academy of Management Review, 5*, 255-265.

Mills, T. (1975). Human resources: Why the new concern? *Harvard Business Review, 53*, 120-134.

Millson, L. (1987). *Ballpark figures: The Blue Jays and the business of baseball.* Toronto: McClelland and Stewart.

Milne, M.J. (1985, March). The Gorey details. *Management Review, 74*, 16-17.

Miner, J.B. (1975). The uncertain future of the leadership concept: An overview. In J.G. Hunt and L.C. Larson (Eds.), *Leadership frontiers* (pp. 197-208). Kent, OH: Kent State University Press.

Miner, J.B. (1978). Twenty years of research on role motivation theory of managerial effectiveness. *Personnel Psychology, 31,* 739-760.

Miner, J.B. (1985). Sentence completion measures in personnel research: The development and validation of Miner Sentence Completion Scales. In H.J. Bernardin & D. A. Bownas (Eds.), *Personality assessment in organizations* (pp. 145-176). New York: Praeger.

Mintzberg, H. (1973a). *The nature of managerial work.* New York: Harper & Row.

Mintzberg, H. (1973b). Strategy making in three modes. *California Management Review, 16,* 44-53.

Mintzberg, H. (1978). Patterns in strategy formulation. *Management Science, 24,* 934-948.

Mintzberg, H. (1979). *The structuring of organizations.* Englewood Cliffs, NJ: Prentice Hall.

Mintzberg, H. (1980). Structure in 5's: A synthesis of research on organizational design. *Management Science, 26,* 322-341.

Mintzberg, H. (1981). Organization design: Fashion or fit? *Harvard Business Review, 59,* 103-116.

Mintzberg, H. (1982). A note on that dirty word "efficiency." *Interfaces, 12,* 101-105.

Mintzberg, H. (1983). *Power in and around organizations.* Englewood Cliffs, NJ: Prentice Hall.

Mintzberg, H. (1984). A typology of organizational structure. In D. Miller & P. Friesen, *Organizations: A quantum view* (pp. 68-86). Englewood Cliffs, NJ: Prentice Hall.

Mintzberg, H. (1990). The design school: Reconsidering the basic premises of strategic management. *Strategic Management Journal, 11,* 171-195.

Mintzberg, H., Raisinghani, D., & Théorêt, A. (1976). The structure of "unstructured" decision processes. *Administrative Science Quarterly, 21,* 246-275.

Misumi, J., & Peterson, M. (1985). The performance-maintenance (PM) theory of leadership: Review of a Japanese research program. *Administrative Science Quarterly, 30,* 198-223.

Mizruchi, M.S., & Stearns, L.B. (1988). A longitudinal study of the formation of interlocking directorates. *Administrative Science Quarterly, 33,* 194-210.

Molnar, J.J., & Rogers, D.L. (1976). Organizational effectiveness: An empirical comparison of the goal and system resource approaches. *Sociological Quarterly, 17,* 401-413.

Morgan, G. (1986). *Images of organization.* Beverly Hills, CA: Sage.

Morgan, H., & Tucker, K. (1991). *Companies that care.* New York: Simon & Schuster.

Morrow, W.W., & Chelladurai, P. (1992). The structure and processes of Synchro Canada. *Journal of Sport Management, 6,* 133-152.

Muldrow, T.W., & Bayton, J.A. (1979). Men and women executives and processes related to decision accuracy. *Journal of Applied Psychology, 64,* 99-106.

Nadler, D.A., & Tushman, M.L. (1989a). Organizational frame bending: Principles for managing reorientation. *The Academy of Management Executive, 3,* 194-204.

Nadler, D.A., & Tushman, M.L. (1989b). What makes for magic leadership? In W.E. Rosenbach & R.L. Taylor (Eds.), *Contemporary issues in leadership* (pp. 135-138). Boulder, CO: Westview.

Nadler, D.A., & Tushman, M.L. (1990). Beyond the charismatic leader: Leadership and organizational change. *California Management Review, 32,* 77-97.

National Collegiate Athletic Association. (1991). *1991-92 NCAA Manual.* Overland Park, KS: NCAA.

Nelson, R.E. (1989). The strength of strong ties: Social networks and intergroup conflict in organizations. *Academy of Management Journal, 32,* 377-401.

Nemetz, P.L., & Fry, L.W. (1988). Flexible manufacturing organizations: Implications for strategy formulation and organizational design. *Academy of Management Review, 13,* 627-638.

New York Yankees. (1990). *Information Guide.* New York City.

Newstrom, J.W. (1980, January). Evaluating the effectveness of training methods. *Personnel Administrator,* pp. 55-60.

Nord, W.R. (1983). A political-economic perspective on organizational effectiveness. In K.S. Cameron & D.A. Whetten (Eds.), *Organizational effectiveness: A comparison of multiple models* (pp. 95-131). New York: Academic Press.

Oberg, W. (1972). Charisma, commitment, and contemporary organization theory. *MSU Business Topics, 20,* 18-32.

Olafson, G.A. (1990). Research design in sport management: What's missing, what's needed? *Journal of Sport Management, 4,* 103-120.

Olafson, G.A., & Hastings, D.W. (1988). Personal style and administrative behavior in amateur sport organizations. *Journal of Sport Management, 2,* 26-39.

Oliver, C. (1988). The collective strategy framework: An application to competing predictions of isomorphism. *Administrative Science Quarterly, 33,* 543-561.

Oliver, C. (1991). Strategic responses to institutional processes. *Academy of Management Review, 16,* 145-179.

On the edge with Dupliskate. (1993, January/February). *Sports Business,* p. 44.

Oneal, M. (1988, June 6). At Wilson, it's a whole new ball game. *Business Week,* p. 82.

O' Reilly, B. (1984, November 12). Club Corp makes clubs pay. *Fortune,* pp. 58-60, 64, 68.

Owns, W.A. (1976). Background data. In M.D. Dunnette (Ed.), *Handbook of industrial and organizational psychology* (pp. 609-644). Chicago: Rand McNally.

Parkinson, C.N. (1957). *Parkinson's law.* Boston: Houghton Mifflin.

Parks, J.B., & Parra, L.F. (1994). Job satisfaction of sport management alumnae/i. *Journal of Sport Management, 8,* 49-56.

Parsley, J.D. (1987, January). Solving the facility scheduling puzzle. *Athletic Business, 11,* 72-75.

Parsons, T. (1956). Suggestions for a sociological approach to the theory of organizations. *Administrative Science Quarterly, 1,* 63-85.

Paterno, J. (1991). *Paterno: By the book.* New York: Berkley.

Paton, G. (1987). Sport management research: What progress has beeen made? *Journal of Sport Management, 1,* 25-31.

Patti, R.J. (1974). Organizational resistance and change: The view from below. *Social Service Review, 48,* 367-383.

Pauchant, T.C. (1991). Transferential leadership. Towards a more complex understanding of charisma in organizations. *Organization Studies, 12,* 507-527.

Payne, R.L., & Mansfield, R. (1973). Relationship of perceptions of organizational climate to organizational structure, context, and hierarchical position. *Administrative Science Quarterly, 18,* 515-526.

Pennings, J.M. (1973). Measures of organizational structure: A methodological note. *American Journal of Sociology, 79,* 686-704.

Pennings, J.M. (1987). Technological innovations in manufacturing. In J.M. Pennings & A. Buitendam (Eds.), *New Technology as Organizational Innovation* (pp. 197-216). Cambridge, MA: Ballinger.

Pennings, J.M., & Goodman, P.S. (1977). Toward a workable framework. In P.S. Goodman, J.M. Pennings, & Associates, (Eds.), *New perspectives on organizational effectiveness* (pp. 146-184). San Francisco: Jossey-Bass.

Perrow, C. (1961). The analysis of goals in complex organizations. *American Sociological Review, 26,* 854-866.

Perrow, C. (1967). A framework for the comparative analysis of organizations. *American Sociological Review, 32,* 194-208.

Perrow, C. (1968). The effect of technology on the structure of business firms. In B.C. Roberts (Ed.), *Industrial relations: Contemporary issues* (pp. 205-219). London: St Martin's Press.

Perrow, C. (1970). *Organizational analysis: A sociological view.* Belmont, CA: Brooks/Cole.

Perrow, C. (1972). *Complex organizations: A critical essay.* Glenview, IL: Scott Foresman.

Pestolesi, R.A. (1987, February). Opportunities in physical education: What the entrepreneur can do. *JOPERD, 58,* 68-70.

Peters, L.H., Hartke, D.D., & Pohlmann, J.T. (1985). Fiedler's contingency theory of leadership: An application of the meta-analytic procedures of Schmidt and Hunter. *Psychological Bulletin, 97,* 274-285.

Peters, T. (1990). Get innovative or get dead. *California Management Review, 33,* 9-26.

Peters, T.J., & Waterman, R.H. (1982). *In Search of excellence.* New York: Harper & Row.

Pettigrew, A.M. (1979). On studying organizational cultures. *Administrative Science Quarterly, 24,* 570-581.

Pettigrew, A.M. (1985a). *The awakening giant.* Oxford: Basil Blackwell.

Pettigrew, A.M. (1985b). Contextualist research: A natural way to link theory and practice. In E. Lawler (Ed.), *Doing research that is useful in theory and practice* (pp. 222-248). San Francisco: Jossey-Bass.

Pettigrew, A.M. (1987). Context and action in the transformation of the firm. *Journal of Management Studies, 24,* 649-670.

Pettigrew, A.M., & Whipp, R. (1991). *Managing change for competitive success.* Oxford: Basil Blackwell.

Pfeffer, J. (1977a). The ambiguity of leadership. *Academy of Management Review, 2,* 104-112.

Pfeffer, J. (1977b). Power and resource allocation in organizations. In B.M. Staw & G.R. Salancik (Eds.), *New directions in organizational behavior* (pp. 235-265). Chicago: St. Clair Press.

Pfeffer, J. (1981). *Power in organizations.* Marshfield, MA: Pitman.

Pfeffer, J. (1992). *Managing with power: Politics and influence in organizations.* Boston: Harvard Business School Press.

Pfeffer, J., & Davis-Blake, A. (1986). Administrative succession and organizational performance: How administrator experience mediates the succession effect. *Academy of Management Journal, 29,* 72-83.

Pfeffer, J., & Salancik, G. (1978). *The external control of organizations: A resource-dependence perspective.* New York: Harper & Row.

Pittsburgh Pirates. (1990). *Pittsburgh Pirates job descriptions.* Pittsburgh: Author.

Pondy, L.R. (1967). Organizational conflict: Concepts and models. *Administrative Science Quarterly, 12,* 296-320.

Pondy, L.R. (1969). Effects of size, complexity, and ownership on administrative intensity. *Administrative Science Quarterly, 14,* 47-60.

Pondy, L.R. (1992). Reflections on organizational conflict. *Journal of Organizational Behavior, 13,* 257-261.

Pondy, L.R., Frost, P.J., Morgan, G., & Dandridge, T.C. (Eds). (1982). *Organizational symbolism.* Greenwich, CT: JAI Press.

Porter, M.E. (1980). *Competitive strategies: Techniques for analyzing industries and competitors.* New York: Free Press.

Porter, M.E. (1985). *Competitive advantage: Creating and sustaining superior performance.* New York: Free Press.

Porter, M.E. (1989). *The competitive advantage of nations and their firms.* New York: Free Press.

Powell, G.N. (1993). *Women and men in management* (2nd ed.). Newbury Park, CA: Sage.

Powell, W.W., & DiMaggio, P.J. (1991). *The new institutionalism in organizational analysis.* Chicago: University of Chicago Press.

Price, J.L. (1968). *Organizational effectiveness: An inventory of propositions.* Homewood, IL: Irwin.

Price, J.L. (1972). The study of organizational effectiveness. *Sociological Quarterly, 13,* 3-15.

Prouty, D.F. (1988). *In spite of us: My education in the big and little games of amateur and Olympic sport in the U.S.* Brattleboro, VT: Vitesse Press.

Pugh, D.S., Hickson, D.J., & Hinings, C.R. (1969a). An empirical taxonomy of work organizations. *Administrative Science Quarterly, 14,* 115-126.

Pugh, D.S., Hickson, D.J., Hinings, C.R., & Turner, C. (1968). Dimensions of organizational structure. *Administrative Science Quarterly, 13,* 65-105.

Pugh, D.S., Hickson, D.J., Hinings, C.R., & Turner, C. (1969b). The context of organizational structures. *Administrative Science Quarterly, 14,* 91-114.

Pugh, P. (1989). *The Belfry: The making of a dream.* Trowbridge, Wilts, UK: Cambridge Business.

Quick, J.C., & Quick, J.D. (1984). *Organizational stress and preventive management.* New York: McGraw-Hill.

Quinn, J.B., Mintzberg, H., & James, R.M. (1988). *The strategy process: Concepts, context, and cases.* Englewood Cliffs, NJ: Prentice Hall.

Quinn, R.E. (1988). *Beyond rational management.* San Francisco: Jossey-Bass.

Quinn, R.E., & Cameron, K.S. (1983). Organizational life cycles and shifting criteria of effectiveness: Some preliminary evidence. *Management Science, 9,* 33-51.

Quinn, R.E., & Rohrbaugh, J. (1981). A competing values approach to organizational effectiveness. *Public Productivity Review, 5,* 122-140.

Quinn, R.E., & Rohrbaugh, J. (1983). A spatial model of effectiveness criteria: Towards a competing values approach to organizational analysis. *Management Science, 29,* 363-377.

Radding, A. (1989, April 10). Spalding Sports moves cautiously in pitching laptops to sales reps. *Computerworld,* pp. SR9-SR10.

Rahim, M.A. (1986). *Managing conflict in organizations.* New York: Praeger.

Rahim, M.A. (Ed.) (1989). *Managing conflict: An interdisciplinary approach.* New York: Praeger.

Reasons, C. (1984). It's just a game?: The 1988 Winter Olympics. In C. Reasons (Ed.), *Stampede city: Power and politics in the west* (pp. 122-145). Toronto: Between the Lines.

Reich, K. (1986). *Making it happen: Peter Ueberroth and the 1984 Olympics.* Santa Barbara, CA: Capra Press.

Reichert, J. (1988, January). Reichert bowls a perfect game: Keeping up with the Joneses. *Management Review, 77,* 15-17.

Reif, W.E., Newstrom, J.W., & Monczka, R.M. (1975). Exploding some myths about women managers. *California Management Review, 17,* 72-79.

Reimann, B.C. (1980). Organizational structure and technology in manufacturing: System versus workflow level perspectives. *Academy of Management Journal, 23,* 61-77.

Reimann, B.C., & Inzerilli, G. (1979). A comparative analysis of empirical research on technology and structure. *Journal of Management, 5,* 167-192.

Rhodes, L. (1982, August). The un-manager. *Inc.,* pp. 34-43.

Ricciuti, M. (1991, Sepember) A CASE for Client/Server. *Datamation,* pp. 28-30.

Richards, B. (1986, December 1). Brunswick Corp. plans to acquire Ray Industries. *Wall Street Journal,* p. 15.

Richards, M.E., & Edberg-Olson, G. (1987, August). A manual for all seasons. *Athletic Business,* pp. 38-40.

Robbins, S.P. (1974). *Managing organizational conflict: A nontraditional approach.* Englewood Cliffs, NJ: Prentice Hall.

Robbins, S.P. (1978). Conflict management and 'conflict resolution' are not synonymous terms. *California Management Review, 21,* 67-75.

Robbins, S.P. (1990). *Organization theory: Structure, design and applications.* (3rd ed.), Englewood Cliffs, NJ: Prentice Hall.

Robbins, S.P., & Stuart-Kotze, R. (1990). *Management concepts and applications* (Canadian 2nd ed.). Englewood Cliffs, NJ: Prentice Hall.

Robey, D. (1986). *Designing organizations* (2nd ed.). Homewood, IL: Irwin.

Robinson, A. (1994, April 4). Ball groups to run fields. *Saskatoon Star Phoenix,* p. A3.

Roethlisberger, F.J., & Dickson, W.J. (1939). *Management and the worker.* Cambridge, MA: Harvard University Press.

Rohrbaugh, J. (1981). Operationalizing the competing values approach. *Public Productivity Review, 2,* 141-159.

Rosener, J. (1990). Ways women lead. *Harvard Business Review, 68,* 119-125.

Ross, I. (1985, July 1). Irwin Jacobs lands a big one—finally. *Fortune,* pp. 130-136.

Roth, T. (1987, February 6). Puma hopes superstar will help end U.S. slump, narrow gap with adidas. *Wall Street Journal,* p. 24.

Rottenberger-Murtha, K. (September, 1993). How to play above the rim. *Sales & Marketing Management,* pp. 28-29.

Rousseau, D.M. (1983). Technology in organizations: A constructive review and analytic framework. In S.E. Seashore, E.E. Lawler III, P.H. Mirvis, & C. Cammann (Eds.), *Assessing organizational change* (pp. 229-255). New York: Wiley.

Rozin, P. (1995, July 24). Olympic partnership. *Sports Illustrated,* n.p.

Rumelt, R.P. (1974). *Strategy, structure, and economic performance.* Boston: Harvard Graduate School of Business Administration.

Rush, M.C., Thomas, J.C., & Lord, R.G. (1977). Implicit leadership theory: A potential threat to the internal validity of leaders behavior questionnaires. *Organizational Behavior and Human Performance, 20,* 93-110.

Rushing, W.A. (1967). The effects of industry size and division of labor on administration. *Administrative Science Quarterly, 12,* 273-295.

Rushing, W.A. (1980). Organizational size, rules and surveillance. In J.A. Litterer (Ed.). *Organizations: Structure and behavior* (3rd ed.) (pp. 396-405). New York: Wiley.

Sack, A.L., & Kidd, B. (1985). The amateur athlete as employee. In A.T. Johnson & J.H. Frey (Eds.), *Government and sport: The public policy issues* (pp. 41-61). Totowa, NJ: Rowman & Allenheld.

Sage, G.H. (1982). The intercollegiate sport cartel and its consequences for athletes. In J. Frey (Ed.), *The governance of intercollegiate athletics* (pp. 131-143). West Point, NY: Leisure Press.

Samuel, Y., & Mannheim, B.F. (1970). A multidimensional approach toward a typology of bureaucracy. *Administrative Science Quarterly, 15,* 216-228.

Sandefur, G.D. (1983). Efficiency in social service organizations. *Administration & Society, 14,* 449-468.

Sands, J., & Gammons, P. (1993). *Coming apart at the seams.* New York: Macmillan.

Sashkin, M. (1986). True vision in leadership. *Training and Development Journal, 40,* 58-61.

Sashkin, M. (1988). The visionary leader. In J.A. Conger & R.N. Kanungo (Eds.), *Charismatic leadership: The elusive factor in organizational effectiveness* (pp. 122-160). San Francisco: Jossey-Bass.

Sathe, V. (1983). Implications of a corporate culture: A manager's guide to action. *Organizational Dynamics, 12,* 5-23.

Sathe, V. (1985). *Culture and related corporate realities.* Homewood, IL: Irwin.

Sator, D. (n.d.). Huffy bikes will remain Ohio-built. *Dayton Daily News and Journal Herald.* p. 1.

Schein, E.H. (1983). The role of the founder in creating organizational culture. *Organizaional Dynamics, 12,* 13-28.

Schein, E.H. (1984). Coming to a new awareness of organizational culture. *Sloan Management Review, 25,* 3-16.

Schein, E.H. (1985). *Organizational culture and leadership.* San Francisco: Jossey-Bass.

Schein, E.H. (1992). *Organizational culture and leadership* (2nd ed). San Francisco: Jossey-Bass.

Schendel, D.G., Patton, R., & Riggs, J. (1976). Corporate turnaround strategies: A study of profit decline and recovery. *Journal of General Management, 3,* 3-11.

Schlender, B.R. (1990, August 13). Take me out to the gold mine. *Fortune,* pp. 93-94, 96, 98, 100.

Schmidt, S.M., & Kochan, T.A. (1972). Conflict: Towards conceptual clarity. *Administrative Science Quarterly, 17,* 359-370.

Schneider, B. (1987). The people make the place. *Personnel Psychology, 40,* 437-453.

Schneier, C.E., & Beatty, A.W. (1979, August). Developing behaviorally anchored rating scales (BARS). *Personnel Administrator, 24,* 59-68.

Schofield, J.A. (1983). Performance and attendance at professional team sports. *Journal of Sport Behavior, 6*, 196-206.

Scholz, C. (1987). Corporate culture and strategy: The problem of strategic fit. *Long Range Planning, 20*, 78-87.

Schriesheim, J.F., Von Glinow, M.A., & Kerr, S. (1977). Professionals in bureaucracies: A structural alternative. In P.C. Nystrom & W.H. Starbuck (Eds.), *Prescriptive models of organizations* (pp. 55-69). Amsterdam: North-Holland.

Schriesheim, J.F. (1980). The social context of leader-subordinate relations: An investigation of the effects of group cohesiveness. *Journal of Applied Psychology, 65*, 183-194.

Schriesheim, J.F., & Kerr, S. (1977). Theories and measures of leadership: A critical appraisal. In J.G. Hunt and L.L. Larson (Eds). *Leadership: The cutting edge* (pp. 9-45). Carbondale: Southern Illinois University Press.

Schuler, R.S. (1976). Participation with supervisor and subordinate authoritarianism: A path-goal reconciliation. *Administrative Science Quarterly, 21*, 320-325.

Schuler, R.S. (1979, December). Time management: A stress management technique. *Personnel Journal*, pp. 851-855.

Scott, B. (1973). The industrial state: Old myths and new realities. *Harvard Business Review, 51*, 133-148.

Scully, G.W. (1989). *The business of major league baseball.* Chicago: University of Chicago Press.

Seashore, S.E., Lawler, E.E. III, Mirvis, P.H., & Cammann, C. (Eds.). *Assessing organizational change.* New York: Wiley.

Secrets of the front office. (1991, July 9). *Financial World*, pp. 28-43.

Sedgwick, J. (1989, January). Treading on air. *Business Month*, pp. 28-34.

Seeger, J.A. (1984). Reversing the images of the BCG's growth share matrix. *Strategic Management Journal, 5*, 93-97.

Sheffield, E.A. (1988, October). Entrepreneurship and innovation in recreation and leisure services. *JOPERD, 59*, 34.

Shenoy, S. (1981). Organization structure and context: A replication of the Aston studies in India. In D.J. Hickson & C.J. McMillan (Eds.), *Organization and nation: The Aston program* (pp. 133-153). Westmead, Hampshire England: Gower.

Shetty, Y.K. (1978). Managerial power and organizational effectiveness: A contingency analysis. *Journal of Management Studies, 15*, 176-186.

Simmons, J. (1987). People managing themselves. *Journal for Quality and Participation, 10*, pp. 14-19.

Simpson, V., & Jennings, A. (1992). *The lords of the rings.* Toronto: Stoddart.

Simon, H.A. (1945). *Administrative behavior.* New York: Macmillan.

Simon, H.A. (1960). *The new science of management decision.* Englewood Cliffs, NJ: Prentice Hall.

Simon, H.A. (1987). Making management decisions: The role of intuition and emotion. *Academy of Management Executive, 1*, 57-64.

Singh, J. (Ed.). (1990). *Organizational evolution: New directions.* Beverly Hills, CA: Sage.

Skinner, W. (1983). Wanted: Managers for the factory of the future. *Annals of the American Academy of Political and Social Science, 470*, 102-114.

Skow, J. (1985, December 2). Using the old Bean. *Sports Illustrated*, pp. 84-88, 91-96.

Slack, T. (1985). The bureaucratization of a voluntary sport organization. *International Review for the Sociology of Sport, 20*, 145-166.

Slack, T. (1991a). Sport management: Some thoughts on future directions. *Journal of Sport Management, 5*, 95-99.

Slack, T. (1991b). The training of leisure managers. *Proceedings of the CESU Conference* (pp. 63-83). Sheffield, UK: FISU.

Slack, T. (1993). Morgan and the metaphors: Implication for sport management. *Journal of Sport Management, 7*, 189-193.

Slack, T., Bentz, L., & Wood, D. (1985). Planning for your organization's future. *CAHPER Journal, 51*, 13-17.

Slack, T., Berrett, T., & Mistry, K. (1994). Rational planning systems as a source of organizational conflict. *International Review for the Sociology of Sport, 29*, 317-328.

Slack, T., & Hinings, C.R.(Eds.) (1987a), *The organization and administration of sport.* London, ON: Sport Dynamics.

Slack, T., & Hinings, C.R. (1987b). Planning and organizational change: A conceptual framework for the analysis of amateur sport organizations. *Canadian Journal of Sport Sciences, 12*, 185-193.

Slack, T., & Hinings, C.R. (1992). Understanding change in national sport organizations: An integration of theoretical perspectives. *Journal of Sport Management, 6*, 114-132.

Slack, T., & Hinings, C.R. (1994). Institutional pressures and isomorphic change: An empirical test. *Organization Studies, 15*, 803-827.

Slakter, A. (1988, Winter). Productive plant puts Huffy in the lead. *Mid America Outlook*, pp. 8-9.

A slimmed-down Brunswick is proving Wall Street wrong. (1984, May 28). *Business Week*, pp. 90, 94, 98.

Smith, A. (1937). *An inquiry into the nature and causes of the wealth of nations*. New York: Modern Library. (Original work published in 1776)

Smith Barney (1989, September 15). *Consumer products research: Huffy Corporation*. (Investment report).

Smith, G.D., Arnold, D.R., & Bizzell, B.G. (1991). *Business strategy and policy*. Boston: Houghton Mifflin.

Snow Valley Ski Club. (1992). *Snow Valley Ski Club*. Edmonton, Alberta: Author.

Snyder, C.J. (1990). The effects of leader behavior and organizational climate on intercollegiate coaches' job satisfaction. *Journal of Sport Management, 4*, 59-70.

Soucie, D. (1994). Effective managerial leadership in sport organizations. *Journal of Sport Management, 8*, 1-13.

Sparks, R. (1992). "Delivering the male": Sports, Canadian television, and the making of TSN. *Canadian Journal of Communication, 17*, 319-342.

Sperber, M. (1990). *College sports inc*. New York: Holt.

Sport makes £8 billion to defeat the recession. (1992, September 16). *International Express*, p. 10.

Sport the way ahead. (1992). Ottawa: Ministry of Supply and Services.

St. John, W.D. (1980, May). The complete employee orientation program. *Personnel Journal*, pp. 373-378.

Starbuck, W.H. (1976). Organizations and their environments. In M.D. Dunnette (Ed.), *Handbook of industrial and organizational psychology* (pp. 1069-1123). Chicago: Rand McNally.

Starbuck, W.H. (1981). A trip to view the elephants and rattlesnakes in the garden of Aston. In A.H. Van de Ven & W.J. Joyce (Eds.), *Perspectives on organization design* (pp. 167-198). New York: Wiley.

Staw, B.M., & Szwajkowski, E. (1975). The scarcity-munificence component of organizational environments and the commission of illegal acts. *Administrative Science Quarterly, 20*, 345-354.

Steers, R.M. (1975). Problems in the measurement of organizational effectiveness. *Administrative Science Quarterly, 20*, 546-558.

Steers, R.M. (1977). *Organizational effectiveness: A behavioral view*. Santa Monica, CA: Goodyear.

Stern, A.L. (1987, August). Reebok in for the distance. *Business Month*, pp. 22-25.

Stern, R.N. (1979). The development of an interorganizational control network: The case of intercollegiate athletics. *Administrative Science Quarterly, 24*, 242-266.

Stevenson, W.B., Pearce, J.L., & Porter, L.W. (1985). The concept of "coalition" in organization theory and research. *Academy of Management Review, 10*, 256-268.

Stinson, J.E., & Johnson, T.W. (1975). The path goal theory of leadership: A partial test and suggested refinement. *Academy of Management Journal, 18*, 242-252.

Stodghill, R. (1993, June 14). What makes Ryka run? Sheri Poe and her story. *Business Week*, pp. 82, 84.

Stodghill, R. (1994, March 28). Putting the Globetrotters back on the map: Owner and alumnus Mannie Jackson is out to restore the magic. *Business Week*, pp. 178-179.

Stogdill, R.M. (1948). Personal factors associated with leadership: A survey of the literature. *Journal of Applied Psychology, 25*, 35-71.

Stogdill, R.M. (1974). *Handbook of leadership: A survey of theory and research*. New York: Free Press.

Stone, N. (1992). Building corporate character: An interview with Stride Rite chairman Arnold Hiatt. *Harvard Business Review, 70*, 95-104.

Strasser, J.B., & Becklund, L. (1991). *Swoosh: The unauthorized story of Nike and the men who played there*. New York: Harcourt Brace Jovanovich.

Strauss, G. (1977). Managerial practices. In J.R. Hackman and J.L. Suttle (Eds.), *Improving life at work* (pp. 279-363). Santa Monica, CA: Goodyear.

Strube, M.J., & Garcia, J.E. (1981). A meta-analytic investigation of Fiedler's contingency model of leadership effectiveness. *Psychological Bulletin, 90*, 307-321.

Stubbs, D. (1989). Swimming Canada charts a new course for the future. *Champion, 13*, 20-23.

Stuller, J. (1982, June). For Roy Eisenhardt, business is a ball. *Inc.*, pp. 31-36.

Styskal, R.A. (1980). Power and commitment in organizations: A test of the participation thesis. *Social Forces, 58*, 925-943.

Sun Ice. (1989). *Annual Report*. Calgary, Alberta Canada.

Sun Ice. (1990). *Annual Report*. Calgary, Alberta Canada.

A Survey of the sports business (1992, July 25). *Economist*. Suppl. 3-19.

Susman, G.I., & Chase, R.B. (1986). A sociotechnical analysis of the integrated factory. *Journal of Applied Behavioral Science, 22*, 257-270.

Symonds, W.G. (1989, June 19). Driving to become the IBM of golf. *Business Week*, pp. 100-101.

Taylor, F.W. (1911). *The principles of scientific management*. New York: Harper & Row.

Taylor, J., & Bowers, D.G. (1972). *The survey of organizations: A machine scored standardized questionnaire instrument*. Ann Arbor: Institute for Social Research, University of Michigan.

Teens. (1994, April 11). *Business Week*, pp. 36-39.

Telander, R. (1989). *The hundred yard lie: The corruption of college football and what we can do about it.* New York: Fireside Press.

Terborg, J.R. (1977). Women in management: A research review. *Journal of Applied Psychology, 62,* 647-664.

Terkel, S. (1972). *Working.* New York: Avon.

Terrien, F.W., & Mills, D.L. (1955). The effects of changing size upon the internal structure of organizations. *American Sociological Review, 20,* 11-14.

Thibault, L., Slack, T., & Hinings, C.R. (1991). Professionalism, structures and systems: The impact of professional staff on voluntary sport organizations. *International Review for the Sociology of Sport, 26,* 83-99.

Thibault, L., Slack, T., & Hinings, C.R. (1993). A framework for the analysis of strategy in nonprofit sport organizations. *Journal of Sport Management, 7,* 25-43.

Thibault, L., Slack, T., & Hinings, C.R. (1994). Strategic planning for nonprofit sport organizations: Empirical verification of a framework. *Journal of Sport Management, 8,* 218-233.

Thomas, K.W. (1992). Conflict and conflict management: Reflections and update. *Journal of Organizational Behavior, 13,* 265-274.

Thomas, K.W., & Schmidt, W.H. (1976). A survey of managerial interests with respect to conflict. *Academy of Management Journal, 19,* 315-318.

Thompson, J.D. (1960). Organizational management of conflict. *Administrative Science Quarterly, 4,* 389-409.

Thompson, J.D. (1967). *Organizations in action.* New York: McGraw-Hill.

Thompson, P., & McHugh, D. (1990). *Work organizations.* London: Macmillan.

Thompson, V.A. (1961). *Modern organization.* New York: Knopf.

Thornton, G.C. (1980). Psychometric properties of self appraisals of job performance. *Personnel Psychology, 33,* 263-271.

Tichy, N.M., & Devanna, M.A. (1986). *The transformational leader.* New York: Wiley.

Timelines. (mimeographed) distributed by Nike.

Tjosvold, D. (1988). Cooperative and competitive interdependence: Collaboration between departments to serve customers. *Group and Organization Studies, 13,* 274-289.

Tjosvold, D. (1991). *The conflict-positive organization.* Reading, MA: Addison-Wesley.

Tobin, D. (1989, March). Selling by serving. *Club Industry*, n.p.

Tolbert, P.S. (1985). Institutional environments and resource dependence: Sources of administrative structure in institutions of higher education. *Administrative Science Quarterly, 30,* 1-13.

Tolbert, P.S., & Zucker, L.G. (1983). Institutional sources of change in the formal structure of organizations: The diffusion of civil service reforms, 1880-1935. *Administrative Science Quarterly, 23,* 22-39.

Tracy, P., & Azumi, K. (1978). Determinants of administrative control: A test of a theory. *American Sociological Review, 43,* 80-94.

Trice, H.M., & Beyer, J.M. (1984). Studying organizational cultures through rites and ceremonials. *Academy of Management Review, 9,* 653-669.

Tsouderos, J.E. (1955). Organizational change in terms of a series of selected variables. *American Sociological Review, 20,* 206-210.

Tung, R.L. (1979). Dimensions of organizational environments: An exploratory study of their impact on organization structure. *Academy of Management Journal, 22,* 672-693.

Tushman, M.L., Newman, W.H., & Romanelli, E. (1986). Convergence and upheaval: Managing the unsteady pace of organizational evolution. *California Management Review, 29,* 29-44.

Tushman, M.L., & Romanelli, E. (1985). Organizational evolution: A metamorphosis model of convergence and reorientation. In L.L. Cummings & B.M. Staw (Eds.), *Research in organizational behavior* (Vol. 7) (pp. 171-222). Greenwich, CT: JAI Press.

Tushman, M.L., & Scanlan, T.J. (1981a). Characteristics and external orientations of boundary spanning individuals: Part I. *Academy of Management Journal, 24,* 83-98.

Tushman, M.L., & Scanlan, T.J. (1981b). Boundary spanning individuals: Their role in information transfer and their antecedents: Part II. *Academy of Management Journal, 24,* 289-305.

Tushman, M.L., Virany, B., & Romanelli, E. (1986). Executive succession, strategic reorientations, and organizational evolution: The microcomputer industry as a case in point. *Technology in Society, 7,* 297-313.

U.S. dollar decline helps cut brand-name counterfeiting. (1988, September 20). *Globe and Mail*, p. B30.

Ulrich, D.R. (1987a). The population perspective: Review, critique, and relevance. *Human Relations, 40,* 137-152.

Ulrich, D.R. (1987b). The role of transformational leaders in changing sport arenas. In T. Slack & C.R. Hinings (Eds.), *The organization and administration of sport.* London, ON: Sport Dynamics.

Ulrich, D.R., & Barney, J. (1984). Perspectives in organizations: Resource dependence, efficiency, and population. *Academy of Management Review, 3*, 471-481.

Urwick, L.F. (1938). *Scientific principles and organization.* New York: American Management Association.

Van de Ven, A.H. (1976). A framework for organizational assessment. *Academy of Management Review, 1*, 64-78.

Van de Ven, A.H., & Delbecq, A.L. (1974). A task contingent model of work unit structure. *Administrative Science Quarterly, 19*, 183-197.

Van de Ven, A.H., Delbecq, A.L., & Koenig, R. (1976). Determinants of coordination modes within organizations. *American Sociological Review, 41*, 322-338.

Van de Ven, A.H., & Ferry, D. (1980). *Measuring and assessing organizations.* New York: Wiley.

VanderZwaag, H.J. (1984). *Sport management in schools and colleges.* New York: Wiley.

Van Fleet, D.D. (1991). *Contemporary management* (2nd ed.). Boston: Houghton Mifflin.

Virtual reality. (1992, October 5). *Business Week,* pp. 96-100, 102, 104-105.

von Bertalanffy, L. (1950). The theory of open systems in physics and biology. *Science, 3*, 23-29.

von Bertalanffy, L. (1968). *General systems theory: Foundations, development, applications.* New York: Braziller.

Vroom, V.H., & Yetton, P.W. (1973). *Leadership and decision making.* Pittsburgh: University of Pittsburgh Press.

Waldrop, H. (1986, June). A Huffy rep cycles to glory. *Sales & Marketing Management,* pp. 116-122.

Walsh, J.P., Weinberg, R.M., & Fairfield, M.L. (1987). The effects of gender on assessment center evaluations. *Journal of Occupational Psychology, 60*, 305-309.

Walton, E.J. (1981). The comparison of measures of organization structure. *Academy of Management Review, 6*, pp. 155-160.

Walton, R.E., & Dutton, J.M. (1969). The management of interdepartmental conflict: A model and review. *Administrative Science Quarterly, 14*, 73-84.

Walton, R.E., Dutton, J.M., & Cafferty, T.P. (1969). Organizational context and interdepartmental conflict. *Administrative Science Quarterly, 14*, 522-542.

Walvin, J. (1975). *The people's game.* Newton Abbot, Devon England: Readers Union.

Warriner, C.K. (1965). The problems of organizational purpose. *Sociological Quarterly, 6*, 139-146.

Watman, M. (Ed.). (1979). *The ghost runner.* Kent, UK: Athletics Weekly.

Weber, M. (1947). *The theory of social and economic organizations* (T. Parsons, Trans.). New York: Free Press.

Weber, M. (1968). *Economy and society* (Vol. 1) (G. Roth & C. Wittich, Trans.). Berkeley: University of California Press. (Original work published in 1925)

Weese, J. (1994). A leadership discussion with Dr. Bernard Bass. *Journal of Sport Management, 8*, 179-189.

Weese, J. (1995a). Leadership and organizational culture: An investigation of Big-Ten and Mid-American Conference campus recreation administrators. *Journal of Sport Management, 9*, 119-134.

Weese, J. (1995b). Leadership, organizational culture, and job satisfaction in Canadian YMCA organizations. *Journal of Sport Management, 9*, 182-193.

Weick, K.E. (1969). *The social psychology of organizing.* Reading, MA: Addison-Wesley.

Weiss, M.R., Barber, H., Sisley, B.L., & Ebbeck, V. (1991). Developing competence and confidence in novice female coaches: Perceptions of ability and affective experiences following a season-long coaching internship. *Journal of Sport and Exercise Psychology, 13*, 336-363.

Wentworth, D.K., & Anderson, L.R., (1984) Emergent leadership as a function of sex and task type. *Sex Roles, 11*, 513-523.

Westley, F.R., & Mintzberg, H. (1989). Profiles of strategic vision: Levesque and Iacocca. In J.A. Conger & R.N. Kanungo (Eds.), *Charismatic leadership: The elusive factor in organizational effectiveness* (pp. 161-212). San Francisco: Jossey-Bass.

White, A., & Brackenridge, C. (1985). Who rules sport?: Gender divisions in the power structure of British sport organizations from 1960. *International Review for the Sociology of Sport, 20*, 95-107.

Whitson, D. J., & Macintosh, D. (1989). Gender and power: Explanations of gender inequalities in Canadian national sport organizations. *International Review for the Sociology of Sport, 24*, 137-150.

Whittington, R. (1993a). Social structures and strategic leadership. In J. Hendry and G. Johnson with J. Newton (Eds.), *Strategic thinking: Leadership and the management of change* (pp. 181-197). Chichester, Sussex England: Wiley.

Whittington, R. (1993b). *What is strategy and does it matter?* London: Routledge & Kegan Paul.

Wholey, D.R., & Brittain, J.W. (1986). Organizational ecology: Findings and implications. *Academy of Management Review, 11*, 513-533.

Wilkins, A.L. (1983a). The culture audit: A tool for understanding organizations. *Organizational Dynamics, 12*, 24-38.

Wilkins, A.L. (1983b). Organizational stories as symbols which control the organization. In L.R. Pondy, P.J. Frost, G. Morgan, & T.C. Dandridge (Eds), *Organizational symbolism* (pp. 81-92). Greenwich, CT: JAI Press.

Wilkinson, D. (1982, October). Managing with new technology. *Management Today*, pp. 33-34, 37, 40.

Williams, P. (1995). *Cardsharks: How Upper Deck turned a child's hobby into a high stakes, billion dollar business.* New York: Macmillan.

Williamson, R. (1993, December 6). Chairman of the boards. *Globe and Mail*, p. B6.

Willigan, G.E. (1992, July-August). High performance marketing: An interview with Nike's Phil Knight. *Harvard Business Review, 70*, 91-101.

Wilson, D.C., Butler, R. J., Cray, D., Hickson, D.J., & Mallory, G.R. (1986). Breaking the bounds of organization in strategic decision making. *Human Relations, 39*, 309-332.

Wilson, N. (1988). *The sports business.* London: Piatkus.

The Winner within. (1993, September). *Success*, pp. 34-39.

Winter, R.E. (1987, November 30). Upgrading factories replaces concept of total automation. *Wall Street Journal*, pp. 1, 8.

Withey, M., Daft, R.L., & Cooper, W.H. (1983). Measures of Perrow's work unit technology: An empirical assessment and a new scale. *Academy of Management Journal, 26*, 45-63.

Witt, C.E. (1989, March). Reebok's distribution on fast track. *Material Handling Engineering*, pp. 43-45, 48.

Wolfe, R., Slack, T., & Rose-Hearn, T. (1993). Factors influencing the adoption and maintenance of Canadian, facility based worksite health promotion programs. *American Journal of Health Promotion, 7*, 189-198.

Wooden, J. (1972). *They call me coach.* Waco, TX: Word Books.

Woodward, J. (1958). *Management and technology.* London: Her Majesty's Printing Office.

Woodward, J. (1965). *Industrial organization: Theory and practice.* London: Oxford University Press.

XV Olympic Winter Games Organizing Committee. (1988). *Official report.* Edmonton, Alberta: Jasper.

Yammarino, F.J., & Bass, B.M. (1990). Transformational leadership and multiple levels of analysis. *Human Relations, 43*, 975-995.

Yavitz, B., & Newman, W.H. (1982). *Strategy in action: The execution, politics, and payoff of business planning.* New York: Free Press.

Yuchtman, E., & Seashore, S.E. (1967). A systems resource approach to organizational effectiveness. *American Sociological Review, 32*, 891-903.

Yukl, G.A. (1981). *Leadership in organizations.* Englewood Cliffs, NJ: Prentice Hall.

Yukl, G.A. (1989). *Leadership in organizations* (2nd ed). Englewood Cliffs, NJ: Prentice Hall.

Zahary, L. (1991). *An analysis of the Running Room.* A paper submitted for the course PESS 350. University of Alberta, Edmonton.

Zald, M. (1962). Power balance and staff conflict in correctional institutions. *Administrative Science Quarterly, 7*, 22-49.

Zander, A. (1950, January). Resistance to change: Its analysis and prevention. *Advanced Management*, pp. 9-10.

Zeigler, E.F. (1987). Sport management: Past, present and future. *Journal of Sport Management, 1*, 4-24.

Zeigler, E.F. (1989). Proposed creed and code of professional ethics for the North American Society for Sport Management. *Journal of Sport Management, 3*, pp. 2-4.

Zeigler, E.F., & Bowie, G.W. (1983). *Management competency development in sport and physical education.* Philadelphia: Lea & Febiger.

Zimbalist, A. (1992). *Baseball and billions.* New York: Basic Books.

Zucker, L.G. (1983). Organizations as institutions. In S.B. Bacharach (Ed.), *Advances in organizational theory and research* (Vol. 2) (pp. 1-43). Greenwich, CT: JAI Press.

Zucker, L.G. (1987). Institutional theories of organization. *Annual Review of Sociology, 13*, Palo Alto, CA: Annual Review.

Zucker, L.G. (1988). *Institutional patterns and organizations.* Cambridge, MA: Ballinger.

Zucker, L.G. (1989). Combining institutional theory and population ecology: No legitimacy, no history. *American Sociological Review, 54*, 542-545.

Author Index

Organization Index

Subject Index

About the Author

Dr. Trevor Slack is professor and head of the School of Physical Education, Sport, and Leisure at De Montfort University in Bedford, England. Before assuming his current position, Slack was a professor and associate dean of physical education and recreation as well as adjunct professor of business, at the University of Alberta in Canada. He also has been a visiting fellow in the Centre for Corporate Strategy and Change, a research unit in Britain's premier business school at the University of Warwick in England.

Since receiving his master's degree and PhD in physical education from the University of Alberta, Dr. Slack has pursued research interests primarily in the areas of organizational change and strategy. His articles have been published in the *Journal of Sport Management*, *International Review for the Sociology of Sport*, *American Journal of Health Promotion*, *Leisure Studies*, *Organization Studies*, and *Journal of Management Studies*. Dr. Slack also has been a keynote speaker at major conferences around the world.

Editor of the *Journal of Sport Management*, Dr. Slack also is an editorial board member of the *International Review for the Sociology of Sport*, *Avante*, and the *European Journal of Sport Management*. In 1995 he won the Earle F. Zeigler award for his contributions to the North American Society for Sport Management.

Bernard J. Mullin, PhD, Stephen Hardy, PhD, and William A. Sutton, EdD

1993 • Cloth • 312 pp • Item BMUL0449
ISBN 0-87322-449-3 • $42.00 ($62.95 Canadian)

This user-friendly book covers all segments of the sport industry—from sport and recreational facilities to professional and amateur sports—and includes extensive examples and case studies from today's world of sport.

The book provides an overview of the reasons and foundations for sport marketing, important theoretical and research issues a marketer confronts early in strategy formation, and principles of control in a management system. It also includes detailed explanations and applications of the five P's of sport marketing: product, price, promotion, place, and public relations.

Neil Dougherty, EdD, David Auxter, EdD, Alan S. Goldberger, JD, and Gregg S. Heinzmann, EdM

1994 • Cloth • 328 pp • Item BDOU0512
ISBN 0-87322-512-0 • $38.00 ($56.95 Canadian)

Sport, Physical Activity, and the Law takes a practical approach, showing you how to use the law as a management tool to address day-to-day issues like the right to participate, liability for injuries, the effective assertion of legal rights, risk management, the legal status of organizations that govern sport, and statutes such as the American with Disabilities Act. The book features 68 real world cases that illustrate legal concepts as they have been applied in sport and recreation programs. And special Canadian applications, written by a Canadian attorney, address the major differences between U.S. and Canadian law.

Human Kinetics
The Information Leader in Physical Activity
http://www.humankinetics.com/
2335

Prices are subject to change.

To request more information or to place your order, U.S. customers call **TOLL-FREE 1-800-747-4457**. Customers outside the U.S. use appropriate telephone number/address shown in the front of this book.